WHEN DID INDIANS BECOME STRAIGHT?

WHEN DID INDIANS BECOME STRAIGHT?

Kinship, the History of Sexuality, and Native Sovereignty

MARK RIFKIN

OXFORD
UNIVERSITY PRESS

OXFORD
UNIVERSITY PRESS

Oxford University Press, Inc., publishes works that further
Oxford University's objective of excellence
in research, scholarship, and education.

Oxford   New York
Auckland   Cape Town   Dar es Salaam   Hong Kong   Karachi
Kuala Lumpur   Madrid   Melbourne   Mexico City   Nairobi
New Delhi   Shanghai   Taipei   Toronto

With offices in
Argentina   Austria   Brazil   Chile   Czech Republic   France   Greece
Guatemala   Hungary   Italy   Japan   Poland   Portugal   Singapore
South Korea   Switzerland   Thailand   Turkey   Ukraine   Vietnam

Published by Oxford University Press, Inc.
198 Madison Avenue, New York, New York 10016

www.oup.com

Oxford is a registered trademark of Oxford University Press.

Library of Congress Cataloging-in-Publication Data
Rifkin, Mark, 1974–
When did Indians become straight? : kinship, the history of sexuality, and native sovereignty / Mark Rifkin.
    p.   cm.
Includes bibliographical references and index.
ISBN 978-0-19-975545-5; 978-0-19-975546-2 (pbk.)
1. American literature—White authors—History and criticism. 2. American literature—Indian authors—History
and criticism. 3. Indians in literature. 4. Homosexuality in literature. 5. Heterosexuality in literature.
6. Self-determination, National, in literature. 7. Imperialism in literature. 8. Indians of North America—Kinship.
9. Indians of North America—Ethnic identity. 10. Indians of North America—Government relations. I. Title.
PS173.I6R54   2010
810.9'352997—dc22   2010011180

9 8 7 6 5 4 3 2 1

Printed in the United States of America
on acid-free paper

CONTENTS

ACKNOWLEDGMENTS

This book began as a way to avoid my dissertation. I had just completed the penultimate chapter, and I simply could not think about the project anymore. I desperately needed a break, and I decided that the best way to do that would be to focus on some other intellectual topic. While I had been interested a great deal in queer theory throughout my undergraduate studies and in graduate school, I ended up forming a dissertation project that had absolutely nothing to do with it. I think this pattern is true for a lot of people who end up doing work in queer studies. For me, it was not a strategic plan to credential myself in something before turning to queer questions and materials, but the sum total effect of it was to direct me elsewhere. In the middle of writing my dissertation, I felt the need to turn back to questions of sexuality which I had not been asking, and I decided as a thought experiment to see what a queer analysis of Zitkala-Ša's *American Indian Stories*, which I was teaching at the time, might look like. The article that eventually emerged from that process, which was an early version of what became chapter 3, served as the germ for this book.

That is all to say that this book has been longer in coming than it might initially seem, and the path to and through it has been somewhat circuitous. For that reason, I have a lot of people to thank stretching over a long period. I owe Carol Barash, Ed Cohen, Elaine Chang, and Marjorie Howes for first introducing me to queer studies while still an undergraduate. When I returned to the project, I already had taken up my first tenure-track position at Skidmore College, and I would like to thank Janet Casey, Jennifer Delton, Kristie Ford, Ross Forman, Dana Gliserman Kopans, Catherine Golden, Kate Greenspan, Regina Janes, Richard Kim, Michael Marx, Tillman Nechtman, Pushi Prasad, Mason Stokes, Daniel Swift, and Josh Woodfork for their support, guidance, feedback, and friendship during my time in Saratoga. The book was completed after I joined the faculty of the University of North Carolina at Greensboro, and I have felt warmly received there, due to the efforts of numerous friends and colleagues, including Danielle Bouchard, Liz Bucar, Sarah Cervenak, Tony Cuda, Michelle Dowd, Asa Eger, Jen Feather, Mary Ellis Gibson, Tara Green, Greg Grieve, Ellen Haskell, Jennifer

Keith, Karen Kilcup, Sarah Krive, Derek Krueger, Christian Moraru, Noelle Morrisette, Kelly Ritter, Gene Rogers, Scott Romine, Hepsie Roskelly, María Sánchez, Ali Schultheis, Amy Vines, Anne Wallace, and Karen Weyler. I owe a debt to Mishuana Goeman, Karen Kilcup, Scott Morgensen, Bethany Schneider, and Audra Simpson for reading parts of the manuscript, talking extensively with me about it, and offering feedback (although, of course, all errors and failures that remain are my own fault), and over the years, conversations with Nancy Bentley, Kevin Bruyneel, Jessica Cattelino, Eric Cheyfitz, Jean Dennison, Qwo-Li Driskill, Lisa Kahaleole Hall, Daniel Heath Justice, Mike Millner, Beth Piatote, Martha Schoolman, Andy Smith, and Craig Womack have proven invaluable in challenging, complicating, and extending my thinking on the issues I address here, and on so much more.

I also need to convey how much I have enjoyed working with Shannon McLachlan and Brendan O'Neill at Oxford University Press, who always have been wonderfully gracious and helpful (despite the fact that I quite stupidly neglected to thank them in the acknowledgments for my first book). The interlibrary loan staff at Skidmore and UNCG, the special collections staff at Vassar College, and the staff of the American Philosophical Society were of immense help in securing materials for this study.

I also owe a great deal to those who have taught and aided me in less academic ways. Thanks to Alex Avelin, Sheila Avelin, Zivia Avelin, Keith Brand, Craig Bruns, Gail Dichter, Jonathan Dichter, Justin Dichter, Kevin Dichter, Christian Hansen, Mike Hardin, Albo Jeavons, Kent Latimer, Erika Lin, JJ McArdle, Christina Nicosia, Neal Rifkin, Sharon Rifkin, Tammy Sears, Jon Van Gieson, Geoff Wall, Ali Zweben, and all the radical faeries I have known through the years for continually reminding me that intimacy and kinship take on many enduring forms and that my life is made of more than writing monographs and seeking tenure.

Earlier versions of two of the chapters were published previously: chapter 3 as "Romancing Kinship: A Queer Reading of Indian Education and Zitkala-Sa's *American Indian Stories*" in *GLQ: A Journal of Lesbian and Gay Studies* (12.1 [2006]: 27–59); and chapter 6 as "Native Nationality and the Contemporary Queer: Tradition, Sexuality, and History in *Drowning in Fire*" in *American Indian Quarterly* (32.4 [2008]: 443–470). Thanks to Duke University Press and University of Nebraska Press, respectively, for allowing me to use them here. Research for this project was supported by a New Faculty Grant from the University of North Carolina at Greensboro.

WHEN DID INDIANS BECOME STRAIGHT?

INTRODUCTION

I mean, the issue here is marriage. And to me, the building block—and I think, to most people in America, number one, it's common sense that a marriage is between a man and a woman. I mean, every civilization in the history of man has recognized a unique bond.

Why? Because—principally because of children. I mean, it's—it is the reason for marriage. It's not to affirm the love of two people. I mean, that's not what marriage is about. I mean, if that were the case, then lots of different people and lots of different combinations could be, quote, "married."

Marriage is not about affirming somebody's love for somebody else. It's about uniting together to be open to children, to further civilization in our society.

And that's unique. And that's why civilizations forever have recognized that unique role that needs to be licensed, needs [to be] held up as different than anything else because of its unique nurturing effect on children.

—Rick Santorum, appearance on *Fox News Sunday*

By kinship all Dakota people were held together in a great relationship that was theoretically all-inclusive and co-extensive with the Dakota domain. . . .

Before going further, I can safely say that the ultimate aim of Dakota life, stripped of accessories, was quite simple: One must obey kinship rules; one must be a good relative.

—Ella Deloria, *Speaking of Indians*

In articulating his critique of legal recognition for same-sex unions in the United States, then-senator Rick Santorum suggested that the failure to specify "marriage" as "between a man and a woman" constitutes an assault on "civilization" itself.[1] While I do not want to rehearse the debates for and against same-sex marriage, including the argument for the latter position made by queer folks themselves,[2] I was struck at the time, and still am, by the sheer scope of his comments. Rather than appealing to particular religious traditions or the merely personal beliefs of a large chunk of the U.S. populace, he argues that officially defining conjugality in other than hetero terms will plunge the nation into barbarity. To be more precise, though, he actually offers a more positively universalizing claim—that "every civilization in the history of man" has acknowledged the connubial tie between a single man and woman as "unique." This phrasing seems to indicate that humanity from time immemorial has had an unchanging conception of the marital "bond." Or does it? The phrase "every civilization" could be read simply as a rhetorical flourish that possesses the same content as "history of man," the one providing a grandiose gloss to the other. Yet one also can understand "civilization" as qualifying "history," as specifying which aspects of the latter count as relevant in addressing the future and fate of the United States. If "every civilization" has acknowledged the "unique bond" of heteroconjugality, what about those parts of history, and peoples, that have not been characterized as having "civilization," that have provided the *savage* counterpoint against which to define the *civilized* and that have been made the object of a mission to bring to them the saving grace of enlightenment?

The attempt here to naturalize a certain version of *marriage* as self-evidently necessary to the continuation of the species—"children" are the "reason for" it—remains haunted by the vexed history of efforts to define which kinds of persons, practices, and principles get to count as paradigmatically "human." In other words, the assertion of a necessary relation between "marriage" and reproduction is supplemented, and intriguingly also undercut, by the normative citation of "civilization" as a set of ideal relations that matrimony is supposed to embody and transfer to the next generation. If marriage "further[s] civilization in our society," as opposed to simply facilitating procreation per se, what is the content of "civilization"? If "society" and "civilization" are not coextensive, instead the one providing the context for "further[ing]" the other, what lies at the boundaries of "civilization"? Santorum suggests a possible answer, noting that if "love" were made the primary criterion, "lots of different people and lots of different combinations could be, quote, 'married.'" At the edge of "civilization" lies the possibility of uncoupling affect and intimacy, eroticism, lifelong commitment, reproduction, child care, and homemaking from each other, instead seeing "lots of different combinations" of these various elements of social life as potentially viable ways of being human. However, a "society" in which such permutations are lived, defying the obvious value of bourgeois homemaking to the health and welfare of the people, is not "civilization" but instead something else, an unnamed absence that provides the unspoken comparative referent in Santorum's intimations of impending disaster.

In addition to demonstrating the hyperbolic and largely hysterical rhetoric that accompanies discussion of the place of homoeroticism in U.S. policy, this quotation by a prominent U.S. official points toward a largely unaddressed dimension of the public and political debate over things queer, namely, its embeddedness in an imperial imaginary that provides the organizing framework in which heterosexuality signifies. More than linking same-sex pleasure and romantic partnership to degeneration into savagery, the statement indicates that forms of sociality that do not carve out a "unique" status for the reproductively directed marital unit can be treated not simply as inferior within the scope of human history but as threatening to retard, or reverse, the progress of those that do. The invocation of "civilization" appears less as a residue of an outmoded nineteenth-century language of Euro-conquest than a trace of the ongoing enmeshment of discourses of sexuality in the project of fortifying the United States against incursions by *uncivilized* formations that jeopardize the "common sense" of national life. While homosexuality may serve as the most prominent foil to the vision of depoliticized privatization Santorum embraces, his comments gesture toward a more multivalent history of heteronormativity in which alternative configurations of home, family, and political collectivity are represented as endangering the state and in which conjugal domesticity provides the condition of possibility for intelligibility within U.S. institutions.

Can Dakota sociality, as described in the epigraph from Ella Deloria, be included under the rubric of heterosexuality? While certainly potentially incorporating the sort of affective and reproductive pairing Santorum addresses, her description of "kinship" as "a great relationship that was theoretically all-inclusive and co-extensive with the Dakota domain" extends far beyond marital couplehood and seems to include the full sociospatiality of Dakota peoplehood within that "relationship," depicting what it means to be a "relative" in terms that have little to do with the nuclear family unit that provides the focal point for "civilization." In *The Invention of Heterosexuality*, Jonathan Ned Katz argues, "The intimidating notion that heterosexuality refers to everything differently sexed and gendered and eroticized is, it turns out, one of the conceptual dodges that keeps heterosexuality from becoming the focus of sustained, critical analysis" (13). Following this logic, what are heterosexuality's contours and boundaries, and where in relation to them do indigenous forms of sex, gender, kinship, household formation, and eroticism lay? Pushing the matter a bit further, can the coordinated assault on native social formations that has characterized U.S. policy since its inception, conducted in the name of "civilization," be understood as an organized effort to make heterosexuality compulsory as a key part of breaking up indigenous landholdings, "detribalizing" native peoples, and/or translating native territoriality and governance into the terms of U.S. liberalism and legal geography?[3] What would such a formulation mean for rethinking the scope and direction of queer studies? These are the questions addressed by this study, exploring the ways placing native peoples at its center would alter the history of sexuality in the United States and how doing so would allow for a reconceptualization of both the meaning of heteronormativity and understandings of the scope and shape of native sovereignties.[4]

In her immensely provocative and ground-clearing essay "Punks, Bulldaggers, and Welfare Queens," Cathy J. Cohen observes, "queer politics has often been built around a simple dichotomy between those deemed queer and those deemed heterosexual" (440), "map[ping] the power and entitlement of normative heterosexuality onto the bodies of all heterosexuals" and thereby failing to recognize that " 'nonnormative' procreation patterns and family structures of people who are labeled heterosexual have also been used to regulate and exclude *them*" (447). She further argues, "many of the roots of heteronormativity are in white supremacist ideologies which sought (and continue) to use the state and its regulation of sexuality, in particular through the institution of heterosexual marriage, to designate which individuals were truly 'fit' for full rights and privileges of citizenship" (453). This trenchant critique points to a larger problematic in the history of sexuality, suggesting that the ideological structure and regulatory force of heteronormativity cannot be grasped through versions of the homo/hetero binary.[5] In this vein, the effort to *civilize* American Indians and the attendant repudiation of indigenous traditions can be understood as significantly contributing to the institutionalization of the "heterosexual imaginary," in Chrys Ingraham's evocative phrase, helping to build a network of interlocking state-sanctioned policies and ideologies that positioned monogamous heterocouplehood and the privatized single-family household as the official national ideal by the late nineteenth century.[6] Such an analysis of the history of federal Indian policy enables discussion of the ways questions of kinship, residency, and land tenure lie at the unspoken center of the heteronorm, which itself can be understood as always-already bound up in racializing and imperial projects.

This kind of queer critique, tracing the unacknowledged genealogies and lineaments of heteronormativity, also builds on recent work in Native Studies that seeks to reconstruct traditional forms of gender diversity. In *Changing Ones: Third and Fourth Genders in Native North America*, Will Roscoe argues that the study of indigenous sex/gender configurations, particularly their development and normalization of non-procreative statuses and identities, "helps break the cycle of projection in which Western observers constantly replicate heterosexual binarism wherever they turn their gaze" (210).[7] However, while rejecting the use of Euramerican sexological vocabularies in understanding native sex/gender systems, this scholarship only minimally develops what seems to me a crucial corollary— that heterosexuality is an equally inappropriate concept through which to consider traditional native family organization, land tenure, eroticism, and divisions of labor. From this perspective, heterosexuality refers less to attraction between men and women or the conditions of reproductive intercourse per se than to a kind of social formation in which coupling, procreation, and homemaking take on a particular normative shape exemplified by the nuclear family. The heterosexual imaginary, therefore, is equally inappropriate and obfuscating when considering native marriage, family, and procreation as it is when addressing more "queer" topics such as transvestism and homoeroticism. Following this logic, what would a queer critique of U.S. imperialism against native peoples look like if divorced from the search for statuses that would signify as aberrant within Euramerican notions of normality? Moreover, how does the construction and contestation of sexual normality by non-natives provide an important institutional and ideological context for efforts to conceptualize native sovereignty?

Beyond making visible the lives of "queer" persons in native communities (historically and in the present), engaging with the forms of critique found in queer studies opens the possibility within Native Studies for a more expansive and integrated analysis of the U.S. assault on indigenous social formations.[8] Such an approach helps foreground the processes through which a particular configuration of *home* and *family* is naturalized and administratively implemented while also emphasizing the discursive and institutional connections between what might otherwise appear as distinct forms of imperial abjection (attacks on "berdaches," polygamy, and kinship-based governance, for example). The "heterosexual binarism" Roscoe cites functions not just as a conceptual block to comparative intellectual work but as a material force—imposing an alien configuration on native cultures and providing ideological cohesion for a disparate collection of detribalizing and/or regulatory initiatives in U.S. Indian policy. The effort to insert American Indians into the ideological system of heterosexuality imposes an alien social logic while also discounting the particular ways family and household formation are central to native peoples' functioning as polities. Official and popular narratives from the early Republic onward demeaned and dismissed the kinds of social relations around which native communities were structured, denying the possibility of interpreting countervailing cultural patterns as principles of geopolitical organization. While others have chronicled

U.S. efforts to reorganize native social life, understanding such initiatives as compulsory heterosexuality provides a more integrated framework for considering imperial interventions into native residency, family formation, collective decision-making, resource distribution, and land tenure. This approach also highlights the political work performed by native writers' depictions of quotidian elements of tradition, conceptualizing such descriptions as an effort to register and remember modes of governance disavowed by the United States.

In this way, *When Did Indians Become Straight?* explores the complex relationship between contested U.S. notions of sexual order and shifting forms of Native American political representation. Offering a cultural and literary history that stretches from the early nineteenth century to the early twenty-first century, it demonstrates how U.S. imperialism against native peoples over the past two centuries can be understood as an effort to make them "straight"—to insert indigenous peoples into Anglo-American conceptions of family, home, desire, and personal identity.[9] Conversely, though, a parallel tradition of non-native representations has employed native peoples as a counterhegemonic symbol of resistance to heterohomemaking, *queering* the norm by citing native customs as a more affectively expansive and communalist model for settler sociality. The positive valuation of native practices and lifeways by those resisting compulsory heterosexuality, however, does not equal support for indigenous self-determination. Both the denigration and celebration of native social structures depend on interpreting indigenous social dynamics in ways that emphasize their cultural difference from dominant Euramerican ideals *as opposed to* their role in processes of political self-definition. Native writers have responded to these intertwined modes of interpellation by affirming the specificity, legitimacy, and rightful autonomy of their peoples' forms of collectivity. Their work highlights the role performed by native "sexuality" in traditional forms of political identification and placemaking while also tracking the violence at play in U.S. attempts to translate native social life into Euramerican terms.

I show how attempts to cast native cultures as a perverse problem to be fixed or a liberating model to be emulated both rely on the erasure of indigenous political autonomy; reciprocally, the book illustrates how native writers in several different periods, in response, have insisted on the coherence and persistence of native polities by examining the ways traditions of residency and social formations that can be described as *kinship* give shape to particular modes of governance and land tenure. The book takes up these issues in its three sets of paired chapters. It examines depictions in the 1820s of native kinship as an integral part of narratives about the relation between white romance and national identity, rethinking the role of the trope of captivity (chapters 1 and 2); native writers' description of traditional kinship networks as a way of responding to major changes in federal Indian policy in the late nineteenth and early twentieth centuries (chapters 3 and 4); and the contrasting portraits of indigenous peoples offered in contemporary queer texts by native and non-native writers (chapters 5 and 6). These examples provide the anchorage points for a double-sided genealogy, exploring the work performed by representations of native peoples in (re)shaping notions of sexual normality and the role played by discourses of sexuality in the struggle over what will constitute imperially intelligible modes of native political identity. The rest of this introduction will address some of the key critical terms for the study—kinship, sovereignty, heteronormativity, and race—specifying how the queer methodology I develop depends on and enables a reconceptualization of these concepts and the relations among them in the process of developing a native-centered history of sexuality.

KINSHIP'S TRANSLATIONS

If discourses of sexuality play a central role in interpellating native peoples into Euramerican hegemonies, the trope of kinship can provide a powerful tool through which to mark and contest that process. In "Go Away Water!," Daniel Heath Justice observes, "Indigenous intellectual traditions have survived not because they've conceded to fragmenting Eurowestern priorities, but because they've *challenged* those priorities," and from this perspective, he suggests that a critical orientation predicated on kinship can provide an alternative to the prevalent pursuit of authentication in which native people(s) seek to disqualify other people's, or peoples', claims to indigeneity on the basis of the somewhat unreflexive employment of Euramerican (legal) categories (like blood quantum).[10] He argues that "kinship is best thought of as a verb, rather than a noun, because kinship, in most indigenous contexts, is something that's *done* more than something that simply *is*"; similarly, "indigenous nationhood," or "*peoplehood*," can be understood as based less on a logic of jurisdiction than "an understanding of common social interdependence within the community . . . that link[s] the People, the land, and the cosmos together in an ongoing and dynamic system of mutually affecting relationships" (150–151). This line of analysis seeks to position kinship as an active principle of peoplehood while also reorienting it away from reproductive notions of transmitted biological substance or privatized homemaking. Instead, it marks extended forms of "interdependence," which remain largely unintelligible within interlocking settler notions of politics and family. *When Did Indians Become Straight?* seeks to foreground the rhetoric of kinship, however, in order to explore the obverse of this point. How has heteronormativity played a central role in rendering the terms and aims of settler jurisdiction self-evident by transposing modes of indigenous peoplehood into discourses of sexuality (the basis for both hegemonic straightness and counterhegemonic queerness), in which they no longer signify as forms of autonomous political collectivity but as a "special"/"savage" aberration from the nuclear household?

The "straightening" and "queering" of indigenous populations occur within an ideological framework that takes the settler state, and the state form more broadly, as the axiomatic unit of political collectivity, and in this way, native sovereignty either is bracketed entirely or translated into terms consistent with state(/ist) jurisdiction. However, the concept of kinship, as it has emerged in anthropological discourses since the late nineteenth century, offers a means of disjointing the political imaginary of the settler state by refusing the distinction between governance and "sexuality," understanding the facets of social life fused to each other within the latter as actively taking part in *political* processes. Put another way, "kinship" provides a way of redefining what constitutes governance by seeing dynamics of family formation and household construction, for example, as central aspects of the kinds of collective identification, spatiality, decision-making, and resource distribution that conventionally are understood as outlining the contours of a polity. That shift potentially opens room for attending to other modes of sovereignty without translating them as an aberration or diminished alternative *within* the dominant structure of the settler state. The rhetoric of kinship, then, can enable a rethinking of the ways the component parts of "sexuality" may index forms of native political autonomy that are distinct from settler policy logics, thus thwarting efforts to represent indigenous peoples as merely domestic subjects of the state.

The portrayal of indigenous kinship systems as forms of governance, though, also runs the risk of reifying native cultural difference in ways that actually short-circuit struggles for self-determination. As Elizabeth Povinelli argues in *The Empire of Love*, "The intimate couple is a key transfer point between, on the one hand, liberal imaginaries of contractual economics, politics, and sociality and, on the other, liberal forms of power in the contemporary world": "If you want to locate the hegemonic home of liberal logics and aspirations, look to love in the settler colonies" (17). The role of "couple"-hood as symbolically central to the social logic of liberalism is captured in the imagination of romance as an "intimate event," one sealed off from public/state imperatives that gives unqualified expression to unencumbered individual freedom. This vision of personal liberty depends upon the fact that "others must be trapped in liberal intimacy's nightmare—the genealogically determined collective" (183), and "kinship and the family, tribalism, and patriarchy are obvious examples of discourses of genealogical inheritances" (199). Depicting indigeneity as wedded to structures of kinship feeds into both civilizing and multicultural liberal discourses by casting native peoples as anomalous, constrained by an unchangeable tradition imagined as needing to be either eliminated or tokenistically recognized by the settler state. Both approaches accept liberal assumptions about individual freedom, as expressed through conjugal intimacy: the equation of adulthood with independence from one's birth family and pursuit of a romantic union through which to form one's own distinct household. From this perspective, the kinship system marks indigenous specificity as oddity, positioning it either as a block to national citizenship to be eradicated or as a curiosity to be preserved so as to indicate the nation's positive inclusion of aboriginal residues. The kinds of collectivity and governance associated with kinship, then, do not get to count as fully political, in the sense that they are presented as idiosyncratic and archaic—a holdover from a past that continues to survive as a sign of continuing indigenous presence within a modernity defined by the terms of settler occupation.

Instead of simply reaffirming liberal logics, might the trope of kinship help mark the ways heteronormative ideologies of "couple"-hood provide the frame for inserting indigenous peoples into the political geography of the settler state? In other words, what happens when the rhetoric of "kinship" is taken as indexing a history of indigenous-settler struggle rather than as merely describing particular arrangements of *home* and *family*? Povinelli argues that "liberal adult love depends on instantiating its opposite, a particular kind of illiberal, tribal, customary, and ancestral love" (226), juxtaposing "the autological subject" (the participant in the liberal intimate event) with "the genealogical subject" (the kinship-entrapped indigene) in ways that suggest that the former depends on the abjection of the latter. Rather than seeing them as *opposites*, the "intimate event" can be understood as providing the frame through which native social formations are made intelligible within U.S. policy and public discourses. Other forms of home and family are measured against the standard of bourgeois homemaking, with deviations appearing as failed domesticity due to a racial propensity toward perversity; as Cathy Cohen suggests, nonwhite populations are cast as nonheteronormative regardless of object choice, presented as occupying a pathologized relation to conjugal domesticity. Populations are racialized through their insertion into a political economy shaped around a foundational distinction between public and private spheres, with the latter defined by a naturalized, nuclear ideal against which other modes of sociality appear as lack/aberrance. Within this system, native forms of collectivity ordered around "kinship" signify as local, racially defined enclaves

rather than fully sovereign governments. In other words, kinds of indigenous sociality unintelligible within a social geography shaped by privatization are represented as a *special* case within the broader framing
heteronormative logics of settler governance, cast as extralegal cultural
difference rather than as the basis for competing kinds of legality or governance. At one point, Povinelli observes that "heteronormativity" possesses
a "genealogical underbelly" that depends on the expansion of the "private"
to encompass all of the "dependencies" inconsistent with liberal political
economy (198). In this way, the rhetoric of kinship operates as a tactic
within discourses of sexuality, consigning nonliberal models of sociality to
the structural position of (failed) "family" and thereby preserving state
structures and mappings from the potential challenge they pose. Thus, the
nonnuclear social dynamics marked by the term "kinship" appear as
"genealogical" because they are inserted into a system organized around a
notion of privatized "family" and in which the apparent contradiction
between these two forms of intimacy is due to forcing one social system to
signify within the terms of another. To portray native peoples through the
trope of kinship does not so much make them the counterpoint to liberal
love and the intimate event as mark an imperial process of incorporation.
"Kinship" points toward the processes by which indigenous socialities
are domesticated—both made to fit a model centered on the bourgeois
household and represented as internal to settler sovereignty. The rhetoric
of kinship functions as a matrix of translation in which social formations
that do not fit a liberal framework are recast as deviations from heteronormative homemaking.

This interpellative dynamic, often presented as a recognition of indigenous difference, is captured perhaps most ably in David Schneider's
Critique of the Study of Kinship, in which he argues that the concept
of kinship provides anthropology with a means of narrating non-
Euro-derived social formations from within a Euro-"ethnoepistemology"
focused on biologically defined genealogy.[11] Schneider argues that the
anthropological tradition of utilizing kinship as a conceptual framework
for comparative cultural analysis unreflexively installs Euro-notions of
"family" as universal in ways that badly distort the internal dynamics of
other social systems. He asserts that "[b]etween the fieldwork and the
monograph falls the shadow of translation" (3), claiming that the use
of "genealogy or kinship . . . as a sort of grammar and syntax" for producing knowledge within anthropology ends up inserting native concepts into a structure defined by alien categories. Putting in question the
distinction between depictions that are "emic" (derived from native
self-understandings) and "etic" (derived from scholarly imperatives), he
suggests that what is taken for "emic" often "is a description formulated

in etic terms" (153), making the principles of "kinship" foundational to the intellectual enterprise regardless of the actual terms used. This rubric conventionally refers to "relations arising out of sexual reproduction," and "the structural and logical priority of genealogy is built into the premises embodied in the way in which kinship is defined" (130–131). In other words, patterns of reproductive relation and inheritance—often referred to as "a genealogy" when graphically represented in terms of parental, sibling, and conjugal connections—lie at the heart of the deployment of kinship as a concept. Its various usages within anthropology are linked by a shared presumption that the "primary meanings" of kinship terms "are the kin types closest to ego [the focal point for tracing the genealogy] which then are extended outward," a practice that either explicitly or implicitly presents kinship as radiating "out from the nuclear family" (90). Without this presumed reproductive unit at its base as the literal referent for "social" and "fictive" kinship elaborations, anthropology would run into an insurmountable comparative crisis: "If each society had a different social convention for establishing a kinship relationship . . . by what logic were these all considered to be *kinship* relations since each constituted a different relationship" (108)? This unexamined, yet paradigmatic, investment in a biologically imagined genealogy patterned after conjugal domesticity leads Schneider to describe the kinship concept as dependent on the "Doctrine of the Genealogical Unity of Mankind," which presumes that "all human cultures have a theory of human reproduction or similar beliefs about biological relatedness, or that all human societies share certain conditions which create bonds between genetrix and child and between a breeding couple" and that "these genealogically defined categories, in their primary meaning, are comparable regardless of the wider context of each culture in which each is set" (119–120). The rhetoric of kinship, then, transposes other social formations into a model organized around Euro-notions of "family." For this reason, "*social kinship* could never be completely freed of its defining feature, human sexual reproduction or the folk theory of it" (111), and anthropologists who utilize the notion of "kinship" "are simply bringing *our* biology . . . back into what is presumed to be *their* (the natives') cultural theory of reproduction" (118).[12]

However, having traced the scholarly trope of kinship back to a particular "folk theory" of reproductive genealogy, Schneider asserts the uselessness of the concept, rather than considering how the process of translation he describes functions as a vector of imperial governance by recasting the structures of bourgeois homemaking as necessarily following from the biology of human reproduction. He declares, "Robbed of its grounding in biology, kinship is nothing" (112). In considering the Euro-ethnoepistemology that gives shape to the rhetoric of kinship, he argues that "[h]uman sexual reproduction has been viewed by anthropologists as an essentially biological process, part of human nature, regardless of any cultural aspects which may be attached to it." From this point, he deduces that the second central doctrine that undergirds the use of the trope of kinship is that "Blood Is Thicker Than Water," that biology provides "kinds of bonds" that "take priority over" others and "are in principle unquestionable" (165). However, the genealogical grid that serves as the basis for mapping kinship relations is not simply an expression of "biology," or even folk theories of it, per se. Treating such a concept in isolation runs into the same problem Schneider observes of the logic of kinship, overlooking the "cultural aspects" to which "biology" attaches or its place in "the wider context" of the culture under discussion.[13] The explicit or implicit representation of the nuclear family model as simply an expression of the necessary conditions of sexual procreation itself helps legitimize a particular political economy, employing biological discourses to naturalize a specific set of heteronormative social arrangements.[14]

The invocation of biology as the means of explaining dominant, institutionalized Anglo-American ideologies of domesticity fuses a collection of potentially disparate phenomena together as an inherently integrated, interdependent, natural bundle. In *The History of Sexuality: Vol. I*, Foucault suggests that "the notion of sex made it possible to group together, in an artificial unity, anatomical elements, biological functions, conducts, sensations, and pleasures, and it enabled one to make use of this fictitious unity as a causal principle, an omnipresent meaning, a secret to be discovered everywhere" (154). In this way, an ethnoepistemology centered on biology helps in forging an "artificial unity" between, among other things, marital heteroromantic pairing, bourgeois homemaking, private propertyholding and dynamics of inheritance, legal determinations of familial relatedness, and a specific gendered division of labor—naturalizing as foundational a distinction among social spheres or domains. As Antonio Gramsci suggests, "If every State tends to create and maintain a certain type of civilisation and of citizen . . . , and to eliminate certain customs and attitudes and to disseminate others, then the Law will be its instrument for this purpose" (246). In other words, the "doctrines" that Schneider indicates shape the use of the kinship concept are animated and disseminated not just as a folk theory but by U.S. law, which implicitly mobilizes such doctrines as part of validating and maintaining a political economy of privatization enacted through various legal measures with respect to issues such as marriage, the transmission of property, home ownership, zoning, and child welfare.[15] The emphasis on anthropologists' de facto investment in "biological processes," therefore, leaves aside the ways biological rhetorics work to legitimize a legally entrenched heteronormative system whose ordering principles far exceed the terms of reproductive connections of consanguinity.[16]

If one pushes Schneider's insights further, the trope of kinship can be understood as a key technology of settler imperialism, and if read in reverse, it can function not as a positivist set of claims about other peoples but as a way of marking the dynamics of heteronormative interpellation, revealing how indigenous self-representations and forms of self-governance are recoded as a kind of collective identity exterior to the sphere of "politics" proper and thus as subject to settler jurisdiction. Such a shift also highlights the ways the political economy of privatization is legitimized by portraying it as the natural expression of "the family," illustrating the crucial role played by "kinship" in the self-imagination and self-justification of the liberal state. The rhetoric of kinship translates social formations by viewing them through a conceptual/ideological paradigm ordered around the biologically validated nuclear family, in which they can appear as perversely aberrant or a special exemption from the general form of privatization as discussed earlier.

However, narrating the dynamics of indigenous peoplehood *as kinship* also troubles the naturalized ideal of conjugal domesticity and the separation of public and private spheres, pointing to alternative kinds of sociality even while attempting to insert them into a dominant liberal framework. Schneider indicates that in much of the early (proto-)anthropological writing through which kinship is constituted as an analytical trope, "primitive" societies are described as being "kin-based," "treating the kinship group and the polity as a single body" (45), or, as Janet Carsten suggests of the persistence of this trend into the mid-twentieth century, "They saw kinship as constituting the political structure and providing the basis for social continuity in stateless societies" (10). Ethnology's fusion of the spheres of the familial and the political in describing native peoples threatens to undo the supposedly inevitable distinction between these two domains. While privileging the kinds of domesticity dominant in the liberal settler state, the trope of kinship registers the existence of social formations that do not have a privatizing distinction between social domains, even as that fact is transposed into an ideological register in which nuclear intimacy and insularity provides the standard.

If kinship has served as a matrix through which to recast indigenous polities in ways consistent with Euramerican institutions and ideological imperatives, why retain it as part of an anti-imperial critical vocabulary? One answer would be that it has come to serve as a way for native people to name their own social structures, such as in the epigraph from Ella Deloria with which I began, or in Justice's work discussed earlier, and to decry it now is less to facilitate native self-representation than for non-native scholars (such as myself), yet again, to dictate the proper ways of portraying indigeneity. Audra Simpson observes in "Paths Toward a Mohawk Nation" that "when articulating and analysing indigenous nationhood, we must account for and understand the foreignness that embeds their aspirations—the machinery of settlement that has hardened into institutions of governance" (122). In a similar vein, scholars should not ignore how settler terminologies have come to serve, in complicated and multivectored ways, as vehicles for expressing indigenous identity. Following this logic, though, one could ask about the reasons for the indigenous redeployment of the kinship concept. Beyond simply its prevalence in the history of scholarly and governmental strategies for characterizing and categorizing native peoples, it also marks fairly precisely the history of settler efforts to dismantle, reconfigure, and regulate indigenous sociality, spatiality, and self-governance. As demonstrated throughout *When Did Indians Become Straight?*, the assessment of native peoples against the standard of conjugal domesticity in official and popular, as well as scholarly, accounts has served as a consistent means of constraining possibilities for self-determination by positioning "kinship-based" native modes of governance as not really governance: defining sovereignty recognizable by the federal government on the basis of political institutions that are completely differentiated from familial relations (chapters 1 and 4); depicting modes of governance in which these *spheres* are mixed as a perverse and primitive communalism that must be abandoned in favor of entry as citizens into the settler nation, itself signified by the division of the "tribe" into privatized, propertyholding nuclear families through allotment (chapters 3 and 6); or casting such modes as a way of regenerating the settler public by opening it to forms of subjectivity not defined by heteroconjugality (chapters 2 and 5).[17]

"Kinship" operates as a threshold concept that is both inside and outside the ideological structure of privatized domesticity, interpellating other kinds of sociality while simultaneously marking their *nonidentity* with respect to the dominant system.[18] As such, "kinship" provides a way for indigenous people to indicate how their sociopolitical formations, whether officially recognized by the state or not, differ from liberal formulations; the concept also offers a means of tracing the multiple ways discourses of sexuality take part in enabling, naturalizing, and managing the ongoing project of settlement, regulating what gets to count as a polity, geopolitical identity, and proper modes of collective decision-making, land tenure, and resource distribution. Thus, in treating kinship as a matrix of translation, I less am trying to enfold various social formations into its terms—Haudenosaunee clans (chapters 1 and 5), Algonquian adoption and networks of alliance (chapter 2), Sioux tiospayes (chapters 3 and 4), Creek talwas (chapter 6)—than to use it to mark the varied and historically shifting ways these kinds of collectivity are subjected to settler assault, appropriation, and/or erasure through an enforced comparison to bourgeois domesticity that denies or diminishes the possibilities for native self-representation and sovereignty.[19]

SOVEREIGNTY AND (THE LIMITS OF) TRADITION

Like kinship, sovereignty is a translation, articulating native peoples' existence as polities through a comparison to the logics and structures of the settler state. However, as with kinship, the concept of sovereignty interpellates indigenous modes of collectivity into a liberal framework while also marking their nonidentity with respect to it. More than bearing an analogical relationship to each other, kinship and sovereignty are intertwined, the former providing a way of variously managing, containing, and/or disassembling social formations that do not readily fit the dominant ideological and institutional matrix of Anglo-American governance. This process is part of what I elsewhere have characterized as the settler state's exertion of metapolitical authority over indigenous peoples—its arrogation to itself of the right to define what constitutes political identity, intelligible land tenure, and meaningful consent.[20] In this way, sovereignty refers less to something that indigenous peoples simply have, preceding and outside of the terms of settler occupation, than to the uneven and fraught dynamics by which the settler state recognizes/disavows indigenous modes of peoplehood and indigenous peoples negotiate the shifting imperatives/contingencies of settler rule. Putting the concepts of kinship and sovereignty in dialogue emphasizes not only the ways the former can serve as a strategy in limiting and regulating native expression of the latter but the ways official articulations of peoplehood, in response, come to be shaped by heteronormative principles. The critique of heteronormativity, then, can reveal both how U.S. control over native peoples is legitimized and naturalized by reference to the self-evident superiority of bourgeois homemaking and how native intellectuals and governments have sought to validate tribal autonomy through investments in native *straightness*.

The term "sovereignty" often is used to mark the rightful autonomy of native peoples—their existence as polities that precedes and exceeds the terms of settler-state jurisdiction. Dating from the Treaty of Westphalia in 1648, the notion of "sovereignty" has been used by Europeans and Euramericans as a way of indicating the separateness of political entities, the legitimate exercise of authority by national governments over the territory claimed by them as the nation, and the noninterference in the *domestic* affairs of such nations by *foreign* powers.[21] Within the idioms of Euramerican governance, recognition of "sovereignty" is equivalent to acknowledging the presence of a polity and its legitimate rule over its territory and people. In *Uneven Ground: American Indian Sovereignty and Federal Law*, David E. Wilkins and K. Tsianina Lomawaima offer such a formulation in defending the authority of native nations against settler encroachment: "American Indian tribes are sovereign nations. Their sovereignty is inherent, pre- or extraconstitutional, and is explicitly recognized in the Constitution." However, later on the same page, they indicate that this vision must be qualified, observing, "Are tribes today unlimited sovereigns? Certainly not. The political realities of relations with the federal government, relations with state and local governments, competing jurisdictions, complicated local histories, circumscribed land bases, and overlapping citizenships all constrain their sovereignty" (5). The portrait they offer is of an "inherent" sovereignty intruded upon due to contemporary "political realities." Such "relations" appear as a pragmatic, logistical, and historically accreting set of interferences in the underlying principle of indigenous sovereignty, which itself does not derive from the U.S. Constitution. Yet this *inherent* authority is not simply exterior to U.S. governance, having been "affirmed in hundreds of ratified treaties and agreements, acknowledged in the commerce clause of the U.S. Constitution, and recognized in ample federal legislation and case law" (8–9). These various strands of U.S. legal discourse are presented as simply registering what already was there, "sovereignty" apparently referring to modes of peoplehood whose contours and content are neither defined nor inherently "constrain[ed]" by the settler regime.

When, though, did U.S. procedures for constituting the field of "political" relations create "realities" that undermined or intruded upon this preexistent "sovereignty"? Wilkins and Lomawaima's argument can be thought of as playing the early history of treaties against the developments of the late nineteenth century that set the stage for a diminished status for native self-governance, including the following: congressional declaration of an end to treaty-making in 1871; the Supreme Court's allocation of "plenary power" to Congress in 1886 (in *U.S. v. Kagama*); and the passage of the General Allotment (Dawes) Act in 1887, which sought to break up tribal lands into privately held plots.[22] This staging gestures toward the fact that native peoples cannot be reduced to a function of settler-state law due to the former's indigeneity—that their presence on the land as political entities predates the formation of the United States. At the same time, though, "sovereignty" marks that disjunction, their nonidentity with respect to U.S. jurisdiction, from within the terms of settler governance. While seeking to index the separateness of native peoples, the formulation "inherent sovereignty" also speaks to their necessary interpellation within settler discourses of "political" identity, but in its attempt to emphasize distinctness and priorness in order to create conceptual space within settler law for indigenous self-determination, this assertion of native nations' status as *sovereign* brackets that process of forced *relation*—the effects on native governance and peoplehood of needing to articulate their legitimate autonomy in ways that make it intelligible to the settler state.

Other scholars in Native Studies have sought to foreground the violence at play in the state's insistence that native peoples signify their political collectivity in ways conducive to settler logics of jurisdiction, seeing the representation of peoplehood through "sovereignty" as itself a mark of this structural subordination. In a piece titled simply "Sovereignty," Taiaiake Alfred argues that the institutionalized language of sovereignty has "limited the ways we are able to think, suggesting always a conceptual and definitional problem centered on the accommodation of indigenous peoples within a 'legitimate' framework of settler state governance," adding that "[w]hen we step outside this discourse, we confront a different problematic, that of the state's 'sovereignty' itself" (34–35).[23] Using "sovereignty" to frame the issue of native self-representation and self-determination is necessarily *limiting*, measuring indigenous collective claims and articulations against a standard set by the settler state. Engaging in this de facto process of adjudication and assessment backgrounds a fundamental set of questions about the state's authority to evaluate indigenous formations of peoplehood, its a priori assertion of the right to be the arbiter of what constitutes a viable "political" identity. Native peoples "must conform to state-derived criteria and represent ascribed or negotiated identities in order to access these legal rights" (43); in doing so, they must make arguments "within a liberal paradigm" that is "in direct opposition to the values and objectives found in most traditional indigenous philosophies" (39, 43).[24] If the notion of *inherent sovereignty* gestures toward the recognition of modes of association, inhabitance, and governance that predate and cannot be encompassed within settler constitutionalism, that concept, from Alfred's perspective, still recycles the terms of settler law and is structured by an effort to make indigenous peoplehood legible within state logics that are dedicated to eradicating traditional native forms of sociality and spatiality—the "values" at the heart of native life. The "relations" that Wilkins and Lomawaima suggest qualify an underlying, unfettered sovereignty are, for Alfred, actually central to the settler "objectives" immanently at play in the discursive and ideological matrix of sovereignty itself.

Alfred's argument points to how forms of abjection and disavowal within settler governance are coupled to forms of recognition that ostensibly seek to give voice to native peoples while implementing "state-derived criteria" for what will constitute collective native subjectivity.[25] The process of engaging with the state involves taking up "ascribed or negotiated identities," such as the treatment of peoples as aggregations of persons bearing a reproductively inherited racial Indianness (chapter 1), the extension of national citizenship as a way of redeeming the absence of *home* and *family* within tribes (chapter 3), and the acknowledgment of native governments so long as they fit a liberal separation of political and familial spheres (chapter 4). Reciprocally, this reading of recognition as interpellation draws attention to the nonliberal dimensions of native social formations that are occluded in the representation of native peoples in dominant official and popular accounts, like the role of familial terminologies and logics within international diplomacy (chapter 2), the persistence of traditional forms of local politics ordered around clans and connections among relatives despite the policies of allotment and reorganization (chapters 4 and 6), and continued attachments to homelands in the wake of dislocation/urbanization (chapter 5). Thus, following Alfred, one way *When Did Indians Becomes Straight?* addresses the issue of sovereignty is to suggest how discourses of sexuality crucially shape and legitimize the "criteria" utilized by the United States in engaging with native peoples, naturalizing settler ideologies of governance as simply what it means to be (part of) a polity and normalizing ongoing settler oversight as an effort to extend such awareness to indigenous populations.

Yet if the rhetoric of sovereignty works to insert native peoples into state jurisdiction, that dynamic also can go the other way, marking the enforced *relation* generated by state policy and also potentially stretching the terms of legal discourse to make indigenous practices of peoplehood legible as governance. While Wilkins and Lomawaima do not flag it as such, their use of the notion of "inherent sovereignty" attempts this kind of double-sided work, gesturing toward indigenous sociospatial formations that precede and exceed U.S. constitutionalism while marking those formations as properly protected within the U.S. constitutional order in ways that try to provide a means of registering intrusions on native self-determination as violations of the fundamental principles of U.S. law. However, without an explicit effort to mark the institutionalized imperial process of translation, to which the employment of the language of settler governance is a response, the assertion of native *sovereignty* can appear as a reference to a particular content— a pregiven set of principles and practices of sociospatiality–instead of as an intervention within an imposed dialectic. The danger lies in reifying the terms of native governance, such that a static version of it, largely generated by the state itself, comes to be recognized within settler law rather than opening room for indigenous self-representation.

In this vein, while foregrounding the imposition of Euramerican criteria, conceptual frameworks, and legal categories, analytical strategies that imagine a clear separation between Euramerican technologies of rule and native philosophies–between *sovereignty* and *tradition*—can overlook the ways the narration and institutionalization of the latter as a kind of content also can abet the dissemination of settler norms. What constitutes tradition? Who decides, and under what circumstances are such determinations made? Or, put another way, can the effort to locate tradition be distinguished entirely from the process of imperial interpellation, including its heteronormative dimensions?[26] How might what gets named as *tradition* be part of the "ascribed or negotiated identities" Alfred critiques, and how might such identities be dependent on ideologies of straightness?[27]

The citation of tradition does not itself guarantee that whatever is being designated remains unaffected by or exterior to settler socialities and governance; moreover, such formulations of tradition can function as a way of legitimizing native identity in ways that ultimately confirm, in Alfred's terms, liberal "values and objectives." Native feminists have explored the ways that contemporary articulations of peoplehood can rely on heteropatriarchal ideologies which are inherited from imperial policy but cast as key elements of tradition. As Jennifer Denetdale argues, "Navajo leaders, who are primarily men, reproduce Navajo nationalist ideology [in ways that] re-inscribe gender roles based on Western concepts even as they claim they operate under traditional Navajo philosophy."[28] She notes that Larry Anderson, the council member who introduced the statute banning same-sex marriage in the Navajo Nation, justified his actions by asserting, "Traditionally, Navajos have always respected the woman and man union. Family values are important."[29] As Denetdale suggests, the citation of certain practices/principles as tradition validates a heterogendered order, one that helps install a vision of "family" defined by conjugal domesticity as central to collective native "values."[30] Similarly, Joanne Barker explores the ways that the history of the legal privileging of the male-headed, nuclear-family household in Canadian Indian policy, which functioned as a strategy of assimilation, over time came to be defended as part of the "sacred rights" held by indigenous peoples, positioning women who challenged the imposed patriarchal system for determining band membership as "embodying all things not only non- but anti-Indian" (127): "The effect of such representations was that existing, exploitative relations of power between Indian women and Indian men were perpetuated as culturally authentic and integral, even traditional" (148).

If these examples might be read as indicating the problem of institutionalizing a version of *tradition* ultimately defined within the (state-directed) imperatives of *sovereignty*, Brian Joseph Gilley's work on contemporary Two-Spirit communities further suggests that the heteronormalization of tradition extends beyond acts by governmental bodies.[31] "Two-Spirit men are surrounded by tribal members who speak reverently of the traditions of the past and how realignment with the old ways would cure the ills of Indian people. At the same time they understand that the tradition of gender diversity is one that most Indians do not venerate or wish to revive. They also hear Indian people rebuke colonialism and the political-economic situation caused by European intervention in the same breath that these tribespeople apply Western value judgments on their sexuality" (57–58). This last example, in which nonheterogendered forms of sexual and gender expression are understood as perversity and outside the acceptable bounds of "tradition," suggests that the distinction between tradition and sovereignty, aligning the one with native philosophies/ontologies and the other with settler ideologies/intervention, breaks down with respect to discourses of sexuality.[32]

One way of addressing this use of the discourse of tradition would be to claim that the ideas and practices attached to it are not *really* traditional, but doing so preserves the idea of a clear boundary, retaining the image of tradition as a discrete content rather than emphasizing the ways it signifies within the forced *relation* indicated by sovereignty. Hiving off tradition as exterior to sovereignty underemphasizes the extent to which the mobilization of the former concept takes shape in the context of the imposition of shifting "state-derived criteria" designated by the latter.[33] In other words, the effort to locate a particular set of practices and/or principles as tradition takes place within a context in which there are numerous incentives toward straightness and in which adopting (aspects of) heteronormativity can serve as a means of carving out space for certain kinds of indigenous association, belief, and practice. As one of Gilley's informants (Sean) observes, "They want to pick and choose the traditions that sound good to white people and make them look good to white people" (59). Put another way, the heterosexual imaginary can be thought of as multivectored, not a single, coherent logic but an agglomeration of a range of "taxonom[ies] of perversions" working along diverse axes simultaneously (in terms of gender expression, racial identification, sexual object choice, family and household formation, marital status or ability to get married, reproductivity, etc.),[34] and parts of this artificial unity of the *normal*, itself a shifting and unstable nexus, might be activated so as to provide recognition for native peoples through the specification of certain practices as tradition. One version I explore is the effort to distinguish native *culture* from the legal matrix of *sovereignty*, preserving a sense of indigenous difference (which often includes acknowledgment of distinct kinship patterns) but disarticulating it from formal politics in ways that maintain the normative distinction between social spheres that characterizes U.S. liberalism (such as the localization of tradition within the regime instituted under the Indian Reorganization Act, addressed in chapter 4). Another variation is for marginalized persons and groups to play aspects of normality against each other as part of a counterhegemonic claim to legitimacy, distinguishing themselves from other, more stigmatized modes of deviance.[35] This dynamic, which I refer to as the "bribe of straight-ness," includes arguing for the validity of indigenous kinship systems (native family formations, homemaking, and land tenure) in ways that make them more acceptable/respectable to whites, disavowing the presence of sexual and gender practices deemed perverse within Euramerican sexology (such as Zitkala-Ša's simultaneous defense of the tiospaye and erasure of the social status of the winkte among Dakotas, discussed in chapter 3).[36] In this way, the circulation of practices and principles as tradition can engage in processes of (hetero)normalization even as it may challenge other historic erasures and current institutionalized forms of denigration.

As with the earlier discussion of Elizabeth Povinelli's distinction between "the autological subject" and "the genealogical subject," the tropes of *tradition* and *sovereignty* could be thought of less as "opposites" than as moments within a dialectic in which the forms of political representation understood as legitimate by the state provide the framework for acknowledging differ-ence while circumscribing its scope. Thus, instead of conceptualizing sover-eignty as a set of "values and objectives" that can be juxtaposed to "traditional philosophies," it can be characterized as a coercive relation in which *tradition* marks a limited sphere of exception to the dominant logics of the state, potentially signifying concrete forms of indigenous difference that can be institutionalized/tolerated as cultural recognition in ways that provide a further alibi for the continued exertion of authority by the settler state—including its ongoing regulation of what will constitute (native) politics.[37]

How might "sovereignty" be employed in ways that call attention to the ongoing history of imperial interpellation while opening up other possibil-ities for imagining and living peoplehood? The concept of sovereignty can be used in ways that draw attention to the system of translation it manages, deconstructing and engaging the legal and political discourses of the state by illustrating how they already depend on an acknowledgment of indigenous presence, in ways reminiscent of the critical redeployment of kinship discussed earlier. As Jessica Cattelino argues, "Settler states, including the United States, establish national sovereignty in part through relations of in-terdependency with indigenous peoples" (163), adding that "U.S. sovereignty does not lie outside or above the settler-indigenous relationship" (177). However, not only is the work performed by *sovereignty* like that of *kinship*, the one centrally relies on the other. The concept of kinship has been, and continues to be, crucial in representing native politics (within U.S. adminis-trative discourses, policy enacted by native nations, and popular narratives by natives and non-natives alike), and it offers a means of reimagining sov-ereignty by linking it to principles of collectivity and forms of sociospatiality displaced, disavowed, and/or disassembled by U.S. policy. Native "kinship" can index alternatives to the heteronormative ideal precisely because of their historical enmeshment: the fact that the emergence and maintenance of the heteronorm depends on sustaining the broader rubric of kinship as a kind of conceptual dumping ground for anything that does not fit the dominant model of privatized *home* and *family*. This dialectical relation is why native socialities have been so attractive to non-natives as an imaginative resource to be taken up in challenging the naturalization of heteronuclearity (chapters 2 and 5). Although such counterhegemonic projects largely have reinforced rather than challenged state jurisdiction, the citation of native kinship systems has the potential to rework the framework of settler authority when articulated with sovereignty.

In her study of contemporary Seminole self-representations, Cattelino observes that many Seminoles understand the power for greater control over their own governance afforded them by the profits of gaming, which they name as *sovereignty*, as enabling them to return to clan-based principles assaulted by the United States in its mid-twentieth-century effort to train them in conjugal domesticity (in ways that resemble the allotment policy earlier implemented elsewhere). In fact, the general counsel for the Seminoles, Jim Shore, presents his work in terms of what can be characterized as kinship; as Cattelino describes his position, "Law is at the service of . . . an indigenous system of legal rule: the 'dos and don'ts' of matrilineal clans" (185). The effort to make visible and redress the imposition of nuclear homemaking helps reshape the meaning of *sovereignty*, drawing on the legal tropes of settler rule while opening them up to signify forms of native self-understanding not acknowledged by the United States as constitutive of political collectivity. Moreover, this way of articulating sovereignty can be read as drawing attention to the legacy of U.S. intervention into Seminole social life, staging the current performance of Seminole political identity in ways that refuse to bracket that history and that actually foreground it as a basis for formulating peoplehood in the present. Reciprocally, while the clan system functions as *tradition*, it does not appear as outside the history of settlement (a position that, as suggested earlier, can lead to an unacknowledged reification of settler ideals—like heteropatriarchy—as if they always-already were present). Instead, the citation of the clans indexes the specific ways Seminole peoplehood has been assaulted, creating a kind of continuity that is not outside of sovereignty but that inhabits that category in ways that highlight those elements tagged and targeted as deviant in processes of imperial interpellation.

Similarly, I less am seeking to offer *kinship* systems as a privileged model of contemporary *sovereignty* than trying to mark how the insertion of native peoples into Euramerican discourses of sexuality provides a central matrix through which the sphere of politics is defined. A kind of queer analysis that extends beyond discussion of the policing of homoeroticism and gender expression, then, can aid in developing an immanent critique of the dimensions and effects of imperial superintendence, foregrounding the role of discourses of sexuality in U.S. regulation of what will count as native governance, as well as the related self-censuring that can guide native representations of *tradition* and *sovereignty*. Additionally, linking kinship to sovereignty within the critique of heteronormativity can help mark how efforts by non-natives to appropriate indigenous social formations fail to interrogate ongoing processes of settlement and the (limited) possibilities for political subjectivity they generate. Furthermore, conjoining discussion of kinship with sovereignty, or self-determination more broadly, helps mark and seeks to undo the work of the rhetoric of kinship, and associated tropes of cultural difference, in segregating nonliberal forms of indigenous sociality from the geopolitics of jurisdiction. Instead, *When Did Indians Become Straight?* insists that the interpellation of indigenous sociality as kinship through an enforced (if implicit) comparison to heterohomemaking works as part of the broader, ongoing process in which indigenous governance is managed through its translation into the terms of the reigning settler model of what can constitute political identity.

QUEER KINSHIP?

Retaining the concept of kinship and foregrounding it helps highlight both the ways native sociopolitical formations cut across the liberal division between social domains and the ways discourses of sexuality insert native peoples into a settler framework, which provides the terms for dominant and counterhegemonic articulations. Heteronormativity legitimizes the liberal settler state by presenting the political economy of privatization as simply an expression of the natural conditions for human intimacy, reproduction, and resource distribution; thus, the critique of heteronormativity offers a potent means for challenging the ideological process by which settler governance comes to appear (or at least to narrate itself as) self-evident. Much of the critique of heteronormativity as it has emerged within queer studies, however, focuses on how various kinds of populations are denied access to social resources based on their supposed failure to embody an idealized vision of conjugal domesticity, reciprocally attending to how that mapping of deviance does not simply position existing groups with respect to the norm but actually produces them as populations. Much of the work in queer studies focused on the United States, including that which takes up the notion of *kinship*, continues to accept citizenship as the implicit horizon of political possibility, addressing the effects of heteronormativity in terms of exclusion from full participation in or recognition by the national polity. While implicitly drawing on the anthropological discourses through which the concept of kinship has emerged, this queer scholarship by and large does not acknowledge its connection to that intellectual history or the political struggles (including between settler governance and indigenous peoples) in which that intellectual tradition has been enmeshed. In this way, queer analyses of kinship and the use of kinship in defining and critiquing heteronormativity have failed not only to challenge the ways discourses of "kinship" work to incorporate indigenous peoples into settler frameworks but also to observe queer scholarship's own imbrications in ongoing projects of settlement. A queer methodology organized around kinship that places native peoples at its center, however, does not take the (settler)state as its de facto frame, instead attending to forms of place-based political collectivity abjected or rendered unintelligible within U.S. governance. From this perspective, heteronormativity is not an internal set of distinctions within citizenship or among national subjects but a system that emerges in relation to the ongoing imperial project of (re)producing the settler state as against competing indigenous formations.

When engaging directly with the concept of "kinship," queer studies scholars have tended to treat it as the central matrix of (hetero)normalization, exclusion from which constitutes queers as such. As Kath Weston suggests in *Families We Choose*, "By shifting without signal between reproduction's meaning of physical procreation and its sense as the perpetuation of society as a whole, the characterization of lesbians and gay men as nonproductive beings links their supposed attacks on 'the family' to attacks on society in the broadest sense" (25), situating them "in an inherently antagonistic relation to kinship solely on the basis of their nonprocreative sexualities" (27). Queer subjects are those cut loose from genealogical imaginings, categorized as exterior to dominant formulations of *home* and *family*, in which heteroconjugality serves as the precondition for procreation itself. The disarticulation of queers from reproduction leaves them without a place in "society." If queers largely are alienated from a national hegemony legitimized by references to the naturalness of nuclear modes of "kinship," what political strategies are available to them? Put in very schematic terms, the answers largely have taken one of two paths: repudiate the features of normality, rejecting participation in dominant discourses; or seek to disjoint the terms of normality, creating a counterhegemony through the scrambling and selective recombination of its central features.

One of the most forceful, and widely cited, examples of the former strategy is Lauren Berlant and Michael Warner's essay "Sex in Public."[38] They argue for the importance of forms of "queer culture building" that "unsettle . . . the hierarchies of property and propriety that [can be] describe[d] as heteronormative" (548). Such a challenge to the system of "national heterosexuality" contests the privatization of intimacy, or perhaps more precisely refuses the equation of intimacy with (marital) privacy that helps validate the dislocation of certain (perverse) persons and activities from public space and the displacement of issues of sexual freedom from public discourse.[39] As against this insulating fantasy—with its depoliticized, limited, and unevenly accessible promise of privatized fulfillment in relative isolation—queer sociality engages in a "world-making project" that engenders "modes of feeling that can be learned rather than experienced as a birthright," creating an open-ended potential for association in which sexual connections are understood neither as exclusive to a particular kind of relationship nor as the privileged basis for residency or lifelong commitment (558). They add, "Queer culture . . . has almost no institutional matrix for its counterintimacies," creating *counterpublics* that "support forms of affective, erotic and personal living that are . . . accessible, available to memory, and sustained through collective activity" while remaining unallied to the logics and apparatus of the state (562). In this way, they envision oppositional cultural formations that may exist within the nation but are not *national*.

While this formulation of "queer culture" can be subjected to Cohen's critique of an implicit queer/straight binary, and the attendant presumption of a symmetrical lack of privilege among all queers, what seems more striking to me is how it conceptualizes opposition to heteronormativity as the purging of those aspects of social life fused to each other within compulsory heterosexuality. If queers are abjected as such through their exile from kinship, the argument goes, they simply can do without it, have, and are the better for it. In addressing the problems generated by privatization, Berlant and Warner observe, "Community is imagined through scenes of intimacy, coupling, and kinship; a historical relation to futurity is restricted to generational narrative and reproduction" (554). This summary locates rather precisely the kinds of equivalence forged by institutionalized heteronormative ideologies. However, more than noting that these dimensions of social experience are conjoined in a particular normative configuration, in which each element comes to serve as a metonym for every other and for the whole, the article seems to accept this assemblage and to present "queer" as what exists outside or beyond it. The authors observe, "Making a queer world has required the development of kinds of intimacy that bear no necessary relation to domestic space, to kinship, to the couple form, to property, or to the nation," suggesting that queer "world-making" takes place in a space beyond the chain of equivalence they cite. Defining that project as lacking any institutional infrastructure and as being "*unrealizable* as community or identity" casts it not simply as having no "necessary relation" to the assemblage, or *artificial unity*, of heteronormativity but as having no relation to any of its constituent elements that would indicate belonging of one kind or another (to a kinship group, a household, a community). The effort to inhabit these forms in ways that disaggregate or reconstellate the terms of compulsory heterosexuality appears always-already doomed to failure, simply recapitulating normative (and national) structures: "Same-sex couples have sometimes been able to invent versions of such practices. But they have done so only by betrothing themselves to the couple form and its language of personal significance, leaving untransformed the material and ideological conditions that divide intimacy from history, politics, and publics" (562).[40] Although earlier indicating that "national heterosexuality" is not a "monoculture" due to the fact that "hegemonies" are "elastic alliances" (553), the article offers little sense that there is any elasticity within dominant strategies of normalization or that queers might stage counterhegemonic challenges so as to realign the "system of forces in unstable equilibrium" which comprises the state.[41] This approach does not envision a process of hegemony-making, both that queers might utilize to alternate ends and in which queers might be implicated, instead portraying queer counterpublics as exterior to normativity—defining them as the inversion of its guiding principles and seeming to accept as axiomatic the notion that queerness necessarily exists outside of dynamics that could be understood as *kinship*.

The other prominent approach to that relationship has been to imagine the concept of kinship as something that might be *queered*, brought into a critical/oppositional relation to its dominant formulation so as to shift the terms of public debate and engagement. In *Families We Choose*, Weston argues that gay and lesbian efforts in the United States to create new forms of what they name as "family" require that the latter be thought of less "as an institution" than "as a contested concept" (3); she later indicates that her study "treat[s] gay kinship ideologies as historical *transformations* rather than derivatives of other sorts of kinship relations" (106), indicating the possibility of shifting the current "equilibrium" in ways that would "undercut procreation's status as a master term imagined to provide the template for all possible kinship relations" (213).[42] From this perspective, the trope of kinship can be seen both as a key technology of heteronormativity and as registering the unevenness of its interpellations, opening the possibility of using a version of the kinship concept to make visible and legible social formations that contest the self-evidence of privatized (hetero)conjugality. In this vein, Elizabeth Freeman in *The Wedding Complex* emphasizes the potential discontinuity between weddings and marriage, the former serving as a site for imagining and remembering an extensive matrix of associations, affections, and identifications seemingly foreclosed in the dominant, institutionalized ideal of companionate couplehood. She suggests, "The ordinary wedding seems to provide neither psychic nor narrative closure, but rather an array of detachable narrative parts—characters, genres, story lines—that can be recombined into 'proto-narratives of possible lives'" (xiii). The texts she addresses employ what she terms a "kin-aesthetic" as a way of "formalizing the very relationships that do not count as lawful kinship" (98), engaging in "queer" acts of imagination that have less to do with creating room for subjectivities predicated on same-sex eroticism than generating "fantasized, acted-out, and lived transformations of historically specific public symbolic fields" (51). While not discounting or subordinating the kinds of queer intimacy and sociality Berlant and Warner address, these other queer ways of narrating kinship emphasize a more elastic relationship to that concept as well as the political possibilities opened by seeing the aggregation of elements within the heteronorm as the result of an ongoing (set of) process(es), into which marginalized subjects can intervene.[43] The contours of "lawful kinship" may be *transformed*, or at least other possible configurations of residency, enduring solidarity, intimacy, eroticism, dependence, reproduction, child care, and resource distribution can be articulated through the prism of *kinship* in ways that contest the naturalized metonymic unity produced by heteronormative discourses.

If kinship can provide a vehicle for contesting modes of normalization, what are the limits of such counterhegemonic intervention? Or, more to the point, what are its conditions of possibility? To what extent is such a politics dependent on a (largely disowned) commitment to membership in the (settler) state? As noted earlier, Berlant and Warner present queer culture as something other than "national" even as their analysis remains very much specific to the United States and offers no alternative mode of political collectivity that could take the place of the state, thus implicitly framing their argument within the contours of citizenship. However, Freeman also seeks to present the queer(ing) imaginings she chronicles as separate from the regime administered by the state. Her call for an effort "to genuinely socialize the distribution of public resources by decoupling this system from marriage" is itself coupled to the idea of not "looking to the state for 'recognition'" (216–217). Assuming that the state continues to serve as the mechanism for regulating the distribution of public resources, how is a call for alternative formations of resource allocation not about recognition by the state? The mode of that recognition may no longer be conjugal couplehood, including same-sex pairings, but does that make such a new configuration of entitlements and legal possibilities separate from the state? This formulation of "recognition" seems to conceptualize the state in fairly monolithic ways that are at odds with the vision of "detachable" parts in the discussion of weddings and kinship, and that totalization appears to be in the service of locating queer aspirations as distinct from incorporation into the logics of the "state." What is at stake in positing this distance/difference? Gramsci suggests that when groups cannot gain significant traction or representation within a given political system, "political questions are disguised as cultural ones" (149), situating themselves as outside a flawed political structure while advocating for political change in a register different than avowedly govern-mental discourses. Such a tactic can be understood as a maneuver within broader processes of hegemony-making, but presenting *queer* "cultural" projects in this light leaves aside the ways that the terrain of ideological struggle on which such projects are moving is delimited by the nation-state—taking place within its boundaries, dialectically affected by shifting legal and administrative formations, addressed in de facto ways to a national public, and articulating forms of belonging contingent on citizenship (or legal residency).⁴⁴ The difference between the interpretive strategies I have been discussing seems to be whether kinship is viewed as irredeemably bound up in state-managed norms or whether it can be seen as (part of) a wider set of possibilities that can be recombined in ways at odds with the heteronorma-tive imperatives of the state.

Placing queer politics in a purely negative relation to the state in these ways, however, frames heteronormativity as an exclusion of queer subjectiv-ities and modes of sociality, instead of exploring how these queer maneuvers with respect to (dominant and oppositional formulations of) kinship remain embedded within a sociopolitical geography shaped by state policy. In *Anti-gone's Claim*, Judith Butler explores the ways the rhetoric of kinship cannot be severed from the work it performs in defining the proper subjects, objects, and contours of state authority. She argues that Antigone's choice to bury her brother in defiance of the edict of the king has been interpreted in ways that portray "*kinship as the sphere that conditions the possibility of politics without ever entering into it*" (2 – emphasis in original), and in this way, "a certain idealized notion of kinship" is imagined as serving as the basis for "cultural intelligibility" (3). Raising the issue of hegemony, but in a different critical register, she asks, "What happens when the perverse or the impossible emerges in the language of the law and makes its claim precisely in the sphere of legitimate kinship that depends on its exclusion or pathologiza-tion" (68)? If Butler foregrounds how discourses of kinship shape what will be recognized as a legitimate political claim (or claim about what will count as "politics"), she also does not acknowledge the anthropological tradition and its use of kinship to name/interpellate native social formations.⁴⁵ Butler describes the kinds of possibility she envisions through Antigone as what happens when "an inhabitant of the form . . . brings the form to crisis" (71), obliquely echoing a Gramscian vision of counterhegemony. However, can native peoples be described in simple terms as "inhabitant[s]" of the "form" of the settler state? What kind of "crisis" for the state's legal and polit-ical discourses is generated when the speaker already is understood as *inhabiting* a space defined by the state's mapping of its own territoriality and jurisdiction? To what extent does the "crisis" thus created itself depend on presuming the geopolitical identity and integrity of the state even as the precise relation between (the spheres of) kinship and politics is being contested and renegotiated? If, as Janet Jakobsen suggests, "the incoherence within the network can be played differently so as to shift the relations that make up the network itself" ("Queer Is," 526), what are the terms of participating in the "network" in the first place? If the "network" is the settler state, to what extent does "shift[ing] the relations" within it in order to achieve different policy outcomes depend on accepting the givenness of settlement? To what extent does such acceptance foreclose possibilities for indigenous self-representation and self-determination? What are the limits, or at least costs, of engaging in a process of (counter)hegemony-making largely structured around settler institutions and publics?

Taking the anthropological tradition and its imbrication in settler imperialism as a starting point shifts critical focus from the ways legal discourses promote "an idealized notion of kinship" for those already seen as *inhabitants* of the state, instead directing attention toward how the trope of kinship functions as a means of presenting indigenous peoples as domestic—as *inhabiting* land over which the U.S. government exercises legitimate authority. If heteronormativity shapes the terms of political subjectivity by contradistinguishing "kinship" from "politics," modes of collectivity that challenge U.S. claims to governance can be characterized as kinship, set in comparison (as failure/deviation) to the paradigmatic model of conjugal domesticity in ways that disallow them from signifying as governance. Narrating native social formations as kinship casts them as under "the law" of the state that encloses them, suggesting that indigenous efforts to "make [a] claim . . . in the sphere of legitimate kinship" still occur within the "language" of the settler regime—subordinating indigenous sovereignties to the presumed coherence of U.S. nation-statehood.

How do some renegotiations of the relation between "kinship" and "politics" depend on foreclosing or disavowing others? To what extent are queer critics' efforts to imagine themselves, and their *world-making* and *kin-aesthetics*, as separate from state projects dependent on disowning the ways their status as U.S. subjects implicates them in the ongoing dynamics and imperatives of settlement?[46] How might such counterhegemonic strategies rely on treating the jurisdictional field of the state as stable? In this vein, chapters 2 and 5 explore how non-natives have positioned native sociality as an imaginative resource for challenging the self-evidence of nuclear homemaking and organizing more inclusive oppositional movements, drawing on ostensibly more capacious and less reproductively oriented native notions of community while displacing the issues of sovereignty and the legal status of indigenous geopolitical formations. Conversely, chapters 5 and 6 address how contemporary formulations of queer native identity (specifically Mohawk and Creek) and responses to it can be situated within the history of the U.S. assault on indigenous modes of peoplehood, exploring how native writers contextualize queer people within native *kinship* systems and thus connect homophobia to the process by which the settler state manages what kinds of indigenous self-representations will count as *politics*.

PERVERSITIES OF COLOR

Another way of placing native peoples within queer studies would be to address how their status as people of color positions them within the history of sexuality, applying the insights of queer of color critique.[47] Such scholarship foregrounds the role of compulsory heterosexuality in processes of racialization and the (re)production of white privilege, understanding racial differentiation and hierarchy as key components of heteronormativity. As Cathy Cohen has argued in ways discussed earlier, the term "queer" often is positioned as the binary opposite of straightness in ways that fail to acknowledge how putatively straight people of color continue to be characterized as sexually aberrant, a charge used to justify increased surveillance and state management and decreased access to social resources. Recent scholarship has developed this line of analysis, illustrating how discourses of sexuality, in Foucault's sense, are implicated from the outset in projects of racial formation.[48] The creation of "homosexuality" as a distinct category, for example, cannot be separated from contemporaneous rhetorics of racial perversion and imperial progress. In "Beyond the Closet as Raceless Paradigm," Marlon Ross explores the ways that the invention of terminologies to designate nonnormative sexual identity in the late nineteenth century indicated not simply the fabrication of a new way of talking about "the body" but the eruption of a crisis within whiteness. He observes, "While the perceived racial difference of an African or Asian male could be used to explain any putatively observed sexual deviance, racial sameness became ground zero for the observed split between heterosexual and homosexual Anglo-Saxon men," "such that racial difference necessarily overdetermines the capacity for sexual deviance as a bodily affair." Moreover, if racial identity already is coded as a capacity for sexual normality, largely defined in terms of conjugal domesticity, the appearance of perverse deviance signifies in racial terms, positioning homosexuality in whites as a kind of *racial retardation* (168). The distinction between those who are straight and not, then, remains always-already complicated by the ways the differentiation of persons based on object choice is predicated on being seen as racially capable of conforming to standards of healthful, disciplined, civilized sexual order in the first place; to be the subject of sexological designations like "homosexual" is already to be understood as potentially a competent participant in modernity, which nonwhites by definition were not.[49]

Viewing the legacy of sexology, and its construction of sexual identity, in light of the copresence of ideologies of white supremacy suggests that heteronormativity entails not only the marginalization/pathologization of queer subjects but the simultaneous linkage of normality to unmarked whiteness in ways that consign people of color to an undifferentiated sexual savagery outside of the hetero/homo binary.[50] Attending to processes of racialization, therefore, helps indicate a significant distinction between heterosexuality and heteronormativity, in which even those persons whose object choice can be deemed "straight" are still seen as perverse due to the racial meanings attached to their performance of desire, homemaking, and family. As Roderick Ferguson argues in *Aberrations in Black*, communities of color in the United States historically "rearticulated normative familial arrangements and thereby violated a racialized ideal of heteropatriarchal nuclearity" (13). In this way, *kinship* can mark social formations that are deemed racially deficient and threatening to the nation due to their failure to conform to the nuclear model of conjugal domesticity: "African American familial forms and gender relations were regarded as perversions of the American family ideal . . . reproductive rather than *productive*, heterosexual but never *heteronormative*" (86–87). Populations of color, then, have their own "taxonomy of perversions" (78), or one might say the process by which nonwhite populations are defined as such involves representing them as perversely deviating from the bourgeois sexuality attributed to normative whiteness. In light of these histories of sexualized racialization, the specific discourses of perversion and familial pathology used to diagnose "the erotics of African American" social formations cannot be reduced to a variation on the sexological categories developed to describe Europeans and Euramericans; "we must reconsider explanations of sexuality that presume our emergence out of the same epistemological traditions, . . . and our production through the same methodologies" (78). The distinction between heterosexual and homosexual cannot capture the ways African Americans, and following the implications of Ferguson's argument other populations of color as well, are cast as *abnormal*, as lacking *respectability*, due to their innate inability to conform to the model of national health illustrated by white nuclearity. Such a process "locates African American sexuality as wild, unstable, and undomesticated, . . . and therefore outside the bounds of the citizenship machinery" (87), further explaining the ways they are excluded "as consequences of their own nonheteronormativity" (91).

If practices in and by communities of color are assessed through an enforced comparison to the *artificial unity* of (white) conjugal homemaking, the trope of kinship may be useful in marking that process of interpellation. Put another way, if racial difference partially is produced through that very (invidious) comparison—defining the meaning and contours of nonwhiteness by reference to the (potentially discrepant) ways various populations supposedly fail to meet the standard of bourgeois normality— then race can be understood as itself generated within the matrix of kinship. Using kinship in this way as a lens through which to trace the dimensions and effects of heteronormativity allows for an expansion of queer critique beyond analysis of the creation, dissemination, and management of the various forms of sexual identification that emerge from sexology. Instead, attention is directed toward the ways interwoven ideologies of household and family formation, privacy and private property, marital eroticism and intimacy produce a racializing "taxonomy of perversions" that is not defined by object choice and cannot be comprehended within a politics of visibility centered on the closet. To the extent that "queer" serves as an encompassing synonym for LBGT, the use of the concept of kinship to point to the multifaceted ways different populations are racialized as deviant indexes forms of subjectivity, sociality, and spatiality that are not *queer* but also are not heteronormative. Rather than foregrounding queer "culture" or "world-making," or even a queer "kin-aesthetic," queer of color critique points toward the ways the elements of *kinship*—such as residency, reproduction, and romance—provide a range of, in Freeman's terms, "detachable narrative parts" that both serve as the basis for modes of racialization and potentially provide sites for oppositional organizing and collective subjectivity.

Like the oppression of African Americans, the dispossession of native peoples also has been justified by portraying them as primitively perverse, as needing to be trained in the ostensibly natural kinds of privatized intimacy organizing bourgeois family life, but unlike the emphasis on exclusion from citizenship that tends to predominate in discussions of other racialized populations *within* U.S. national space, Native Studies confronts the status of native peoples as separate polities, raising a series of questions about the relationship between discourses of sexuality and the recognition of tribes as political entities. In ways reminiscent of the strategy discussed in the previous section of separating queer cultural projects and formations from the state, queer critique focused on processes of racialization also tends to link heteronormativity with nationalism per se, seeking to displace statist structures but without envisioning an alternative mode of collectivity. For example, Ferguson argues that "revolutionary and cultural nationalisms" have "measured the authenticity of subjects of color and defined the reality of minority cultures in terms of heteropatriarchy," "suppress[ing] the critical gender and sexual heterogeneity of minority communities"; placing "black and Chicano nationalism" within this pattern, he suggests the need to "discard the myth of nationalism's coherence and viability for understanding agency, culture, and subjectivity" (140–141).[51] What space, both literally and figuratively, is there for indigenous peoplehood within this formulation? If "nationalism" is inherently (hetero)normalizing, what ways are available for naming and registering native collectivities within queer critical mappings, or is positing such "coherence" itself also seen as reinforcing oppressive *nationalist* logics?[52]

Part of the difficulty here may lie in viewing all "subjects of color" as members of "minority cultures," in the sense that doing so reinstalls the nation-state as the sole way of framing geopolitical identity rather than acknowledging the existence of competing forms of sovereignty and self-determination (especially that of native peoples) on lands claimed by the United States.[53] While the exertion of authority over native peoples certainly has relied on racialization, and the deployment of discourses of authenticity (especially with respect to "tradition") also can have (hetero) normalizing effects,[54] the fact that the existence of indigenous polities precedes and exceeds the terms of settler governance raises the question of how to think about racialization in relation to native modes of governance. More specifically, are there possibilities for political collectivity—for native *nationalisms*—that do not reproduce existing state procedures for authenticating and adjudicating Indianness, that can acknowledge "gender and sexual heterogeneity" by refusing to measure social formations against a heteronormative standard? What role, historically and currently, do racial discourses play in interpellating such formations into the dominant heteronormative ideologies and institutional structures?

If racial identification and discourses of sexuality are intimately, inextricably interwoven, how are liberal social mappings—of what constitutes family, the distinction between public and private, the relation of reproduction to personal identity and inheritance—embedded in the understanding of native peoples as belonging to a *race*, their categorization as *Indians*?[55] As discussed earlier, the kinship concept emerges out of the ethnological narration of non-European peoples, particularly the indigenous peoples occupying land claimed by the United States, as failing to perform proper conjugal domesticity but also as lacking true governance because political processes were too intermixed with familial relations. This strategy of representation depends on portraying homemaking based on reproductive couplehood as the inevitable atom of social life, putting alternative social imaginings in relation to this unit. In the United States, "race" as a kind of category has been understood and legally defined as a biological substance transmitted to children through procreative pairing, a key but unexamined part of the "Blood Is Thicker Than Water" doctrine Schneider addresses, and as such, discourses of race bolster the paradigmatic self-evidence of reproductive couplehood, reinforcing its centrality as the primary model for conceptualizing sociality. More than excluding populations defined as nonwhite from full access to social resources, racial discourses in the United States can be understood as circulating a grammar of reproductive union, positioning the intimate event as central to the construction of legal personhood inasmuch as racial identity emerges form the mixture that is conception and is defined in thoroughly genealogical terms.[56] As Schneider suggests, biology and genealogy are fused to each other within the dominant Euro-ethnoepistemology. Like *kinship*, no matter how much *race* is characterized as socially symbolic and not merely descriptive, it will continue to pivot around a biological imaginary, but more than that, it will continue to call forth the vision of conjugal couplehood upon which that biological imaginary relies. To clarify, as numerous scholars have noted (including Cohen and Ferguson), people of color in the United States have been denied access to legally legitimizing forms of kinship, like marriage, but my point is that, like the interpellation of non-European social formations as *kinship*, race in the United States definitionally relies on the couple-centered notion of identity/inheritance that always-already depends on the image of conjugal domesticity.[57]

The concept of race, then, reinforces the "artificial unity" produced through discourses of sexuality while enabling social formations at odds with the state-sanctioned political economy of privatization to be characterized as (perverse) tendencies in the blood rather than as alternative modes of collectivity, decision making, and resource distribution to those of liberalism. Within processes of heteronormalization, race and kinship dialectically are entwined,[58] not simply characterizing populations and practices as deviant on the basis of race but employing the logic of race to interpellate *as kinship* sociopolitical dynamics that exceed state logics—to portray them as failed nuclearity within a conceptual framework in which the centrality of reproductive pairing appears as obvious. Put another way, if native people are understood as *Indians*, a category defined by the procreative transmission of a certain kind of "blood" (a point developed further in chapter 1), they can be characterized as (primarily) a racial population, which also means the following: they are not first and foremost *political* entities whose status is irreducible to U.S. jurisdictional formulations; their forms of sociality need not be interpreted as equally legitimate modes of governance to that of the United States; and modes of social organization in which reproduction, romance, and household formation are not utterly distinct from governance, such as Iroquoian clans or Siouxian tiospayes, can be depicted as something other than full governance—as *kinship*. Thus, if racialization is a tool of U.S. nationalism, incorporating native peoples into a heteronormative system, it also is implicated in the representation of indigenous forms of peoplehood—native nationalisms—as not truly *politics*. Such an analytical approach further connects the repudiation of racializing taxonomies of perversion to the pursuit of self-determination by native peoples as peoples. In other words, rather than understanding what can be termed "native nationalism" as inherently problematic, as necessarily abetting the very kinds of normalization enacted by the state, the pursuit of queer methods with a focus on native sovereignty highlights the ways the racialization of indigenous peoples as Indians works in the service of delegitimizing modes of collectivity at odds with U.S. jurisdictional logics/claims, engaging in an antiracist project whose aim is opening additional room for self-representation by native polities.

Focusing on the matrices of native social relations that have come to be narrated as *kinship*, then, reveals, in Ferguson's terms quoted earlier, forms of collective "agency, culture, and subjectivity" which the United States has refused to engage with as sovereignty. The aim of doing so is not to note how indigenous peoples have been *excluded* from participation in the United States but to illustrate the ways heteronormativity, including its racializing procedures, is a key part of the grammar of the settler state. More than regulating social life on the basis of sexual object choice and gender expression, the most prominent legacies of sexology, compulsory heterosexuality can be conceptualized as an ensemble of imperatives that includes family formation, homemaking, private propertyholding, and the allocation of citizenship, a series of potential "detachable parts" fused to each other through discourses of sexuality. Indigeneity puts the state in crisis by raising fundamental questions about the legitimacy of its (continued) existence, and to contain this crisis, state institutions and allied nongovernmental discourses, like late-nineteenth-century and early-twentieth-century anthropology, interpellate forms of indigenous sociality, spatiality, and governance that do not fit within liberal frameworks as *kinship*, coding them as aberrant or anomalous modes of (failed) domesticity when measured against the natural and self-evident model of nuclear conjugality. In addition, indigenous peoples are interpellated as a nonwhite population, defined by the reproductive transmission of racial Indianness, and the attendant presumption of heterocouplehood as the atom of social life helps position other logics of identification, affiliation, and self-representation as ancillary to such *blood* inheritance. While they are not *queer*, per se, native social formations are translated as something other than proper politics in ways that can be foregrounded through the critique of heteronormativity developed

within queer studies, expanding the scope of heteronormativity by understanding it as naturalizing not only the privatized domestic space of the
(white) marital household but also the domestic space of settler nationalism.

The chapters of the project are organized chronologically, sketching a native-
centered history of sexuality stretching from the early nineteenth to the
early twenty-first century. They explore the role of settler politics and native
presence in the emergence of normative discourses of sexual and familial
(dis)order, and reciprocally, they trace the ways that such discourses have
served as a key matrix through which to represent and regulate native
decision-making, land tenure, and resource distribution. Chapters 1 and 2
pivot around readings of novels from the 1820s, a crucial decade both in
Indian policy and in the transition to the nuclear family ideal. Chapter 1
explores the ways the biopolitics of race supersedes the geopolitics of kinship
within U.S. public and policy discourses with respect to native peoples. This
racialization of native peoples as Indians depends on the erasure, or at least
marginalization, of modes of kin-making, and I illustrate the political effects
of imposing a heterosexualizing logic of racial "blood" on native peoples
through a reading of *A Narrative of the Life of Mrs. Mary Jemison* (1824). The
story of a white woman kidnapped during the Seven Years' War (in which
Cooper's novel is set) and made Seneca through adoption, the text highlights
the disjunction and ongoing conflict between Euramerican understandings
of native identity and Iroquoian ways of conceptualizing familial and political
belonging. More specifically, I argue that the attribution of a primary whiteness to Jemison, and the treatment of her adoption as epiphenomenal with
respect to her real identity (conceived in racial terms), indexes the creation of
kinds of legal subjectivity that disavow Seneca processes of collective decision-making and land tenure, a pattern observable in the "treaties" of 1826
and 1838.

The 1820s mark a shift in approaches to "the Indian problem" from a
late-eighteenth-century Jeffersonian view of amalgamation as ending the
transmission of Indianness to future generations, and thus making possible
assimilation into Euramerican households and the nation, to a notion of
blood Indianness as inherently unassimilable, as exemplified in James Fenimore Cooper's *Last of the Mohicans* (1826). Cooper's novel makes marital
pairing a topos for the construction of an insulated white nationality, and in
the novel's championing of an emergent vision of the conjugally centered
household as the premier site of privatized intimacy, Indians are presented
as having a racialized incapacity for sentimental affect that brands them as
lacking any true sense of home, or boundaries broadly stated. They, therefore, are bound to be displaced, providing an account of native nature that
powerfully supplements and legitimizes the political logic of removal by

translating native intransigence to displacement as a congenital inability to belong to the national household/family. This transposition of a struggle over territory and jurisdiction into a matter of procreative pairing and the inheritance of racial substance provides a broadened framework in which to understand the emergence of specific measurements and regulations with regard to "blood quantum" in the late nineteenth and early twentieth centuries (addressed in chapters 3 and 6), recontextualizing that development within a longer history of interpellating native peoples into a reproductive imaginary organized around conjugal homemaking.

Chapter 2 explores the ways the early-nineteenth-century ascendance of (white) marital privacy as a metonym for national identity was contested by non-natives and the role of discourses of Indian captivity in doing so. Catharine Maria Sedgwick's *Hope Leslie* (1827) utilizes figures of captivity (both by and of Indians) to illustrate native traditions of generosity and community. Set in the early seventeenth century, the novel juxtaposes the supposedly expansive forms of kin-making among the Pequots with the authoritarianism of the patriarchal family, itself cast as a holdover of monarchy and thus as an inappropriate ideal for American (proto)nationalism. English colonists are depicted as learning from native models of kinship which are less privatizing and couple-centered, instead offering a vision of siblinghood as the basis for expansive connections among adults that include but reach beyond the attachments of blood-relation, and I indicate the connection between this formulation and changing contemporary notions of family in the early nineteenth century. In this way, a possibility for settler-native union is posited that rejects the contemporaneous discourses of blood difference addressed in the previous chapter. However, this counterhegemonic challenge to nuclear homemaking and logics of racial identification does not translate into a more robust engagement with native modes of peoplehood. The novel's idea of a native pedagogy that can reformulate non-native publics, in particular teaching whites through examples of cross-cultural affection, ignores the ways that native kinship networks are less a form of interracial bonding than a mode of geopolitical boundary-making and diplomacy. I demonstrate this dynamic through a reading of Hendrick Aupaumut's "Short Narration of My Last Journey to the Western Country" (1792), the report of a Mahican chief who served as a U.S. envoy to tribes in the Ohio region—particularly apt given that the Mahicans only a decade earlier had lived in Stockbridge, Sedgwick's childhood home. The text provides a mapping of ongoing relations among peoples stretching from the Atlantic coast to beyond the Mississippi, suggesting a transnational system structured around kinship whose ordering principles cannot be encompassed in the logic of U.S. Indian policy. Thus, even as Sedgwick's novel can be said to queer the emergent national norm of privatized conjugality through the citation of native sociality as a counterexample, doing so relies on the displacement of indigenous sovereignty and self-determination, folding native polities into the settler regime as fellow subjects of a shared community.

In chapters 3 and 4, I turn to discussion of how native writers use representations of traditional kinship dynamics to challenge the conception of indigenous polities institutionalized in U.S. policy in the 1880s and the 1930s. While offering radically different visions of the relationship between American Indians and the U.S. government, the General Allotment Act (1887) and the Indian Reorganization Act (1934)—arguably the two most important statutes in the history of federal Indian law—both inserted native peoples into Euramerican frameworks, the one trying to "detribalize" them by breaking up indigenous territories into separate lots held privately by nuclear families and the other interpellating native polities into a form consistent with U.S. liberal ideologies. In chapter 3, I argue that allotment and the Indian boarding school program work together to enact what I describe as a "romance plot," the narration of native communities as properly divided into distinct households each organized around conjugal couplehood. Through readings of statements by officials of the Bureau of Indian Affairs (BIA) and annual reports by school principals and reservation agents, I illustrate how Indians are portrayed as lacking "home" and "family," casting systemic efforts to break up native social networks, landholding patterns, and modes of governance as an attempt to teach Indians the forms of domestic affect that will enable them to gain equality as national citizens. This representation of native social systems as a perverse threat to the nation helps legitimize an exponential increase in the U.S. government's extension of authority over indigenous peoples, discourses of sexuality providing a way of bridging both the crisis in U.S. jurisdiction generated by the continuing presence of native polities and the absence of an existing legal mechanism to allow for their wholesale dismantling. Zitkala-Ša's *American Indian Stories* (published in 1921 but composed almost entirely of turn-of-the-century pieces) responds to the heteronormative impositions of Indian policy by contextualizing marriage within complex kinship systems, which themselves are shown to be durable, extensive, emotionally rich, and central to native political life. Yet while critiquing the fragmenting force of privatized domesticity, Zitkala-Ša offers images of Dakota marriage that disavow elements of tradition that do not fit the norm of monogamous heterocoupling, displacing discussion of the presence of polygamy and homoeroticism among Sioux peoples in ways that try to make tradition more acceptable to white readers by editing out the features likely to be read as sexually deviant. I further situate her writing within both the controversy surrounding Mormon plural marriage and the prominence of

Lewis Henry Morgan's evolutionary theory of family formation as key to the achievement of civilization, examining the role played by ideas of native barbarism in dominant discourses of marriage in the late nineteenth century.

Allotment policy repeatedly was characterized as about the transformation of Indian subjectivity and affect, as an effort to shift the objects of native feeling—from clans and kinship networks to nucleated families, from collective territory to private property, from tribe to nation-state. By contrast, U.S. officials presented the Indian Reorganization Act as a vehicle for native autonomy, displacing the atomizing dynamics that had structured Indian policy for the previous half century and replacing them with a sustained commitment to promoting native "community." In chapter 4, I argue that the continuing legacy of allotment shapes the conditions of native political representation under reorganization. The kinds of native collectivity produced by reorganization implicitly depend on the heteronormative dynamics of allotment—particularly the self-evidence of the nuclear-family form and of a stable distinction between public and private spheres. Looking at significant policy statements about the Indian Reorganization Act before and after its passage, I illustrate how the conjugally centered privatization performed by allotment helps structure and provide an ordering limit for what can count as legitimate native governance, using the Pine Ridge reservation as an example. Counterposing the notion of "domestic relations" institutionalized under reorganization to Ella Deloria's representation of "kinship" in *Speaking of Indians* (1944) and *Waterlily* (completed in the late 1940s, published in 1988), I show how she locates forms of identification and interdependence that cannot be registered in an allotment imaginary and, therefore, exposes the series of assumptions about home and family that continue to undergird U.S. Indian policy in the 1930s and 1940s. Further, through a discussion of Deloria's sustained participation in Boasian anthropology and its role in reorganization policy, I indicate the ways her work reframes existing anthropological discourses in order to contest institutionalized assumptions about the character of native "culture" and "community," illustrating how such notions abet dominant ideologies of privatization by divorcing practices cast as *tradition* from family and household formation, land tenure, and collective decision-making.

The final chapters move forward to the current moment, addressing how the historical dynamics I have been tracing still animate and shape the intersection of discourses of sexuality and native self-representation at the end of the twentieth century and beginning of the twenty-first. Examining Leslie Feinberg's *Stone Butch Blues* (1993), chapter 5 traces the novel's repeated use of native people as a counterpoint to other non-natives' inability to accept the main character's form of gender expression. While developing a complex, intersectional account of identity and community and explicitly linking movements for gender and sexual justice to working-class struggles through its emphasis on the union as a model of political organizing, the novel positions native peoples as a tool for raising the consciousness of non-natives about the presence and need to include gender and sexual minorities, presenting indigenous polities as a pedagogical and imaginative resource for reconfiguring non-native publics in ways that resemble those discussed in chapter 2. Suggesting Indians possess an alternative perspective from which non-Indians can view sexuality and gender, the text further claims that traditional forms of gender diversity among native peoples are part of a history to which non-native gender and sexual minorities can lay claim. This assertion of a shared past creates an imagined queer continuity across time that seeks to compensate for the trauma of alienation from families of birth and to provide a basis for rethinking the contours and direction of contemporary non-native social movements. However, such a sense of connection or, in the text's terms, "solidarity" not only occludes native peoples' existence as autonomous political entities but the specific struggles of Iroquoian groups in the vicinity of the very places where the novel is set (Buffalo and New York City) during the period in which it occurs (the 1960s to the 1990s). In contrast to Feinberg's displacement of ongoing challenges to native sovereignty and recirculation of the conventional narrative of the liberating potential of the city for queers, the stories by Beth Brant in *Mohawk Trail* (1985) highlight the histories of displacement and multilayered heteronormative pressures that shape native urban experience. Tracing the history of her family, their ongoing connection to Tyendinaga (the Mohawk reserve from which they came), and her own experience of coming-of-age as a lesbian in Detroit, she examines the continuity of shame that links native and queer people in their disciplined deviance from dominant heterohome-making. Less a narrative of coming out or of queer-friendly embrace by her native relatives and community, her work illustrates the refusal of insulated domesticity in the performance of Mohawk identity and the persistence of links to the homeland via familial and clan networks, even while they also provide a matrix through which to remake the city as a Mohawk place. In this way, Brant addresses dynamics of dislocation produced by mid-twentieth-century processes of urbanization and termination elided in Feinberg's narrative while offering an account of native queerness that firmly links it to the project of sustaining Mohawk peoplehood.

The final chapter offers a reading of Creek scholar and novelist Craig Womack's *Drowning in Fire* (2001), investigating the ways he situates intra-tribal homophobia among the Creek people within the history of imperial intervention. Moving back and forth between the early and the late twentieth century, the text connects erotic exploration among two Creek boys/men in the 1970s and 1990s to the fight against Oklahoma statehood in the 1900s, linking "sexuality" to the struggle for self-determination. Womack presents a reconnection with traditional forms of family and community-making as predicated on a rejection of imposed norms of sexual moralism that are themselves embedded in efforts to justify continued U.S. control over native peoples. Rather than focusing on the possibility for coming out among the Creeks or seeking to represent forms of self-consciously queer native identity, the novel suggests that the critique of heterosexism in the present leads toward an archaeology of the ways it came to be part of everyday Creek consciousness. More specifically, he juxtaposes different time periods to illustrate how the kinds of assaults and restrictions on native sovereignty I address in chapters 3 and 4 are not simply in the past but continue to constrain Creek self-understandings, including conceptions of proper homemaking and family formation. Foregrounding Christian tropes of fire, water, and snakes as figures for state-endorsed ideologies, Womack recontextualizes them within Creek tradition, suggesting that longstanding forms of collectivity organized around alternative principles (particularly clan membership and town belonging) remain submerged beneath the apparent ubiquity of ideologies of straightness which validate a limiting liberal conception of politics. Making visible queerness among contemporary Creeks, then, becomes part of a project not only of revealing the presence of homoeroticism in earlier periods but of connecting resistance to the heteronorm to ongoing struggles against the U.S. management of native peoplehood.

1

REPRODUCING THE INDIAN

Racial Birth and Native Geopolitics in A Narrative of the Life
of Mrs. Mary Jemison *and* The Last of the Mohicans

The women are submitted to unjust drudgery. This I believe is the
case with every barbarous people. With such, force is law. The stronger sex therefore imposes on the weaker. . . .
The same Indian women, when married to white traders, who feed
them and their children, plentifully and regularly, who exempt them
from excessive drudgery, who keep them stationary and unexposed
to accident, produce and raise as many children as the white women.

Very possibly there may have been antiently three different stocks,
each of which multiplying in a long course of time, had separated
into so many little societies. This practice results from the circum-
stance of their having never submitted themselves to any laws, any
coercive power, any shadow of government. Their only controuls are
their manners, and that moral sense of right and wrong, which, like
the sense of tasting and feeling, in every man makes a part of his
nature.

      —Thomas Jefferson, *Notes on the State of Virginia*

Beginning in the second half of the nineteenth century, the thematics
of blood was sometimes called on to lend its entire historical weight
toward revitalizing the type of political power that was exercised
through the devices of sexuality. Racism took shape at this point
(racism in its modern, "biologizing," statist form): it was then that a
whole politics of settlement (*peuplement*), family, marriage, education, social hierarchization, and property, accompanied by a long
series of permanent interventions at the level of the body, conduct,
health, and everyday life, received their color and their justification

from the mythical concern with protecting the purity of the blood and ensuring the triumph of the race.

—Michel Foucault, *The History of Sexuality, Vol. 1*

In *Notes on the State of Virginia*, Thomas Jefferson responds to the claims of the Compte de Buffon that the climatic conditions of the Americas produce a degeneration in animal life by indicating that the distinction between native peoples in the New World and the populations of Europe has more to do with the barbarity of the former than the ecological propensities of their environment.[1] His argument seems to suggest that if Indians lived in the same social conditions as Europeans, the one would have the same intellectual, moral, and physical capacities as the other. As many scholars have suggested, this position does not assume the kind of immutable racial disparity that increasingly would characterize depictions of Euramerican-native difference in the decades following.[2] Yet even as he appears to eschew the notion that there is an immanent biological barrier which definitively blocks Indian uplift, he focuses on marital unions and reproduction as indicative of Indian character. Not only does the subjection of wives to "drudgery" synecdochically stand in for native "people"-hood, but marriage of Indian women to white men remedies the conditions that heretofore have been misinterpreted as a congenital lack of fecundity. Conjugal couplehood is envisioned as providing the key to distinguishing between Indian and white ways, such that interracial pairing breaks the cycle of Indianization and generates social—and even physiological—possibilities foreclosed in the replication of Indian family structures. While Jefferson avoids the language of blood here, he does imply that being Indian entails being the child of Indian parents rather than, say, belonging to a specific indigenous polity. In fact, he disowns the idea that native peoples have governments at all, instead possessing tendencies that are "a part of [their] nature" and are perpetuated in the process of "multiplying" through which various "stocks" extend their geographic reach over time. Representing native identity as more or less a function of certain kinds of connubial relations which produce generational effects, Jefferson seems to replace politics with reproduction, to argue that Indianness inheres in sexual-spousal "manners" rather than participation in a kind of ordered social formation that might be counted as a regime of "law."

Taking companionate marriage as the paradigm for defining Indianness depends on a kinship logic defined around conjugal pairings instead of one predicated on clan membership or extended familial networks that serve as the basis for residency and political affiliation. Jefferson understands native patterns, in Foucault's terms quoted above, of "family, marriage, education, social hierarchization, and property" as expressions of instinctual drives, and in this way the text displaces indigenous forms of social organization and self-representation that depend on kinship. Jefferson's racialization of native peoples as Indians substitutes the matrimonial-reproductive unit for broader webs of kinship as the ideological matrix in which to conceptualize the character of indigeneity. Instead of seeking to distinguish populations from each other for the purposes of segregating them, the racializing representation of native identity offered by Jefferson in the preceding passages works to translate a geopolitical problematic into biopolitical terms, defining "Indians" as a population rather than a collection of polities.[3]

Although this chapter primarily will be concerned with narratives from the 1820s, specifically James Seaver's *Narrative of the Life of Mrs. Mary Jemison* (1824) and James Fenimore Cooper's *Last of the Mohicans* (1826), I have chosen to begin with Jefferson because the role of Indian-white marital pairing in his writings shifts attention from attitudes toward Indians as a race to the work performed by interpreting native peoples through the prism of reproductive Indianness. From the perspective of the 1820s, race can appear as the central mechanism for the exertion of Euramerican power, providing the primary validation for the dispossession of native peoples.[4] As a discursive and ideological formation, though, how does "race" function as a vehicle of interpellation? What sorts of identity, territoriality, affect, and association does it presume, and what kinds of subjectivity, occupancy, and collectivity does it disavow or render unintelligible? In *Toward a Global Idea of Race*, Denise Ferreira da Silva argues that efforts to understand race as a social process rather than a biological category have "fail[ed] to demonstrate why racial difference, which is already an appropriation of the human body in scientific signification, should constitute a central dimension of social representation" (xxvi); she suggests that this lack is predicated on a "sociologic of exclusion" that envisions racialized populations as awaiting inclusion into the nation-state or the family of nations, rather than examining how "the racial" "constitutes the modern grammar" of "the nation" (11, 3).[5]

As suggested in the Introduction, processes of racialization involve coding the social formations of those deemed nonwhite as perverse deviations from the proper model of healthful (white) domesticity. The "thematics of blood" at play in late-eighteenth- and early-nineteenth-century depictions of Indianness functions as a discourse of sexuality, centralizing and naturalizing the metonymic linkage of reproduction, marital union, and conjugal homemaking. Reciprocally, the coalescence in the United States over the course of the nineteenth century of the ideal of the nuclear, sentimental family can be understood partially as an effect of the emergence of an imperial hegemony that helped legitimize the exertion of settler state authority over indigenous peoples and territory. Rethinking Foucault's genealogy of the concept of "sexuality" in light of eighteenth- and nineteenth-century

European colonialism, Ann Laura Stoler has suggested that "the nineteenth-century discourse on bourgeois sexuality may better be understood as a recuperation of a protracted discourse on race" (193). She has illustrated how calibrations of racial identity in the colonies—particularly for lower-class Europeans, non-European people educated in European institutions, and the children of unions between Europeans and non-Europeans—often depended on signs of erotic and familial order usually associated by scholars with the nineteenth century. If "an implicit racial grammar underwrote the sexual regimes of bourgeois culture" (12), it also provided the syntax for incipient European nationalisms, serving as a means of distinguishing those who were proper participants in the state from those who simply were the objects of its authority: "the question of who would be a 'subject' and who a 'citizen' converged on the sexual politics of race" (133). The "racial grammar" of bourgeois sexuality, however, not only manages the status of persons and populations in relation to imperial institutions (as domestic/citizen or alien/subject) but also effaces the significance of extended kinship networks by transposing indigenous modes of sovereignty, cohesion, alliance, diplomacy, and placemaking into discourses of sexuality in which they are unintelligible as processes of political identification and negotiation.[6] Such formations appear as ancillary (irrelevant when matched against the "blood" transmission of Indianness) or as symptomatic (expressions of an Indianness primarily imagined via procreative pairing).

In this way, racial discourse can be understood as supplementing U.S. Indian law in the early national period by providing a contextual frame in which native sociopolitical dynamics organized around kinship appear as merely racial genealogy.[7] In "Domestic Frontier Romance, or, How the Sentimental Heroine Became White," Ezra F. Tawil argues, "By describing race in terms of kinship, domestic frontier fiction used one kind of classification to produce another," adding that when such texts speak about "whiteness" they reference "a special kind of subjectivity that was in turn the product of a particular kind of household" (101). At stake in the racialization of native peoples, though, is not just their reduction to a subordinate population within the codes of citizenship (the ascendance of whiteness or, in Foucault's terms, "the triumph of the race") but the consolidation of a familial norm that elides native kinship structures which challenged the jurisdictional imaginary of the incipient settler state. This translation of the geopolitics of indigenous self-determination into the biopolitics of race extends beyond official U.S. policy statements to the larger print public sphere in the range of texts concerned with native peoples, including Seaver's *Narrative* and Cooper's novel. Contextualizing popular writings in relation to shifting currents within Indian policy not only helps reveal what is at stake in nongovernmental public discourse for native peoples but also promotes forms of interpretation attuned to the ways available discursive formations, such as race, intersect with the kinds of concerns usually grouped under the rubric of sovereignty—such as collective occupancy and decision-making. Seaver's and Cooper's texts are among the best sellers of the 1820s,[8] and as such they can be read for the ways that they participate in uneven processes of hegemony construction occurring in Indian affairs in that period, particularly through discourses of racialized sexuality. This decade is of particular consequence, as it marked a concentration in efforts to purchase native lands, a notable entrenchment of peoples east of the Mississippi against such sales, as well as a tipping point toward removal as a solution to "the Indian problem." Moreover, both *A Narrative of the Life of Mrs. Mary Jemison* and *The Last of the Mohicans* concern native peoples in New York, a state in which the push of white settlement and commercial development was particularly intense and rapid.[9]

Written by Seaver based on several days of conversation with Jemison, the *Narrative* presents itself as the (auto)biography of a Euramerican woman captured during the Seven Years' War and eventually adopted by Senecas, now living on the Genesee River on treaty-guaranteed land. In chronicling her life, the text adopts a stance of incredulity, casting as spectacle the fact that this white woman has lived and continues to live among Indians. The text insistently centers racial genealogy as the paradigm through which to conceptualize Jemison's experiences and the social geography that shapes them. Similarly, most critics have focused on the question of Jemison's identity, how to place her in relation to extant racial categories, and in this way, they largely have taken as given the frame that the text provides, viewing relative racial difference as the discursive and ideological terrain on which to locate both the text's strategies and the struggles of native peoples in the period.[10] By contrast, I will argue that the text's intimate braiding of racial identity, familial relations, and Jemison's voice needs to be understood in the context of efforts to acquire Seneca lands in the 1810s and 1820s. More specifically, envisioning Jemison's subjectivity in racial terms allows for her whiteness to be set in opposition to her Senecaness, privileging the former as more (biologically/reproductively) authentic and using that identification as a means of casting kinship networks as a secondary and minor concern in the determination not only of Jemison's legal status (and thus that of her property) but of what constitutes native collectivity, governance, and consent for the purpose of land sales. However, the *Narrative* also offers ample evidence, usually noted in passing, that kinship remains a viable, if pressured, modality of Seneca politics. I read these moments in relation to documents of U.S.-Seneca negotiations from the 1790s to the 1830s in order to suggest how the text's employment of discourses of sexuality—its conjugally conceived raciality—takes part within the broader imperial project of recoding native forms of sociospatiality in ways that facilitate dispossession.

In rather stark contrast to Jefferson's vision of Indian-white amalgamation, James Fenimore Cooper's *Last of the Mohicans* utterly disavows the possibility of interracial union. The shift in emphasis from civilization/assimilation where Indians currently live to removal of them west occurs at the same time as the emergence of the nuclear family as the normative icon of affectively saturated and privatized intimacy. Cooper's text suggests how these parallel developments are interwoven, each animating and helping give shape to the other. As other critics have suggested, the incessant repetition of the linked metaphorics of "blood" and "gifts" in the novel specifically seems designed to affirm the impossibility of crossing the color line, while simultaneously evidencing an extreme and pressing anxiety about that very likelihood.[11] What has received less attention is the way the drama of interracial association and mixture serves as a means of mapping (proto)national geography, making whiteness into not only a racial/sexual grammar but a spatial one as well. More than providing a content to whiteness and determining what populations can achieve citizenship, bourgeois kin-making and homemaking function as a topos for the boundaries of the nation-state. Other kinds of kinship systems—and the political formations and geographies they enact—are positioned as an unnatural intrusion on the national family, such as the procreatively dead-end domesticity of Chingachgook and Hawkeye's relationship. Reciprocally, this dismissal of alternative family formations helps shape the nuclear norm and imperially overdetermines its significance within public discourse. In this vein, the novel reduces the complex and changing dynamics of intertribal alliance to the urgings of the blood, and it presents articulations of nonnuclear modes of kinship as an Indian misunderstanding of the true meaning of family.

More than presenting native peoples as savage and unassimilable within Euramerican life, racial identification displaces other types of sociality, spatiality, and governance that are dependent on kinship. In reducing native identity to a supposed biological essence understood in terms of reproductive couplehood, the tropology of Indianness helps install a topology of governance from which kinship is excluded as an ordering principle. The racializing discourses of settler sexuality, then, work to naturalize a particular understanding of family that then functions as the template against which to assess, and abject, native kinship formations,[12] and, by extension, through which to establish the natural inevitability of defining "politics" as separate from the privatized sphere of "family." This fashioning of indigeneity as the transmission of "Indian" substance through procreative pairing prefigures the emergence of "blood quantum" measurement at the end of the nineteenth century, suggesting how an emergent logic of nuclear homemaking during the treaty period contributes to the insertion of native peoples into settler frameworks of governance as collections of raced individuals rather than self-determining polities—a process that reaches its apotheosis in the allotment program (which will be addressed in chapter 3). Yet while popular writings like the *Narrative* and Cooper's novel fetishize reproductive couplehood and the conjugally centered household in ways that marginalize the importance of kinship to native leadership, placemaking, and diplomacy, they also register traces of the continuing significance of such kinship systems to indigenous peoples and, by implication, the trivialization of such sociopolitical formations within the archive of U.S. governance.

CAN MARY JEMISON SPEAK?

Is Mary Jemison Indian? Is she Seneca? Are these the same question? Regardless how they characterize Jemison's identity, most discussions of the *Narrative* treat these terms as relatively synonymous, as signifying more or less the same thing for the various persons and parties involved in or reading about Jemison's life. The question is how to locate her on the spectrum from white to Indian. However, these terms suggest several different, and potentially competing, ways of conceptualizing native identity—as racial inheritance, as participation in a polity, as inclusion within a broader kinship matrix based on clan membership. Rather than being mutually exclusive, these various options intersect, overlap, and refract in U.S.-native relations in the early national period. Refusing to collapse them into each other, to cast them as all pointing to approximately the same thing, opens the possibility of analyzing the stakes of these assorted versions of nativeness as they swirl around Jemison. More specifically, how does the emphasis on her whiteness take part in the construction of forms of legal and political subjectivity for her, for the Senecas, and for other native peoples? How does conflating racial Indianness and full participation in native collectivity work as a way of disavowing the Seneca kinship system as a mode of governance and geopolitics, installing U.S. legal norms in its stead? Highlighting the multiple models of indigeneity at play in the period helps draw attention to the role racial conceptions of family play in struggles over how to represent native voice and sovereignty, and thus to the role the *Narrative* plays with respect to emergent formations in Indian policy.

Captured during the Seven Years' War by Shawnees and traded to a Seneca family that adopted her, Jemison lived among the Senecas from about the age of fifteen onward.[13] Among the Six Nations of the Iroquois Confederacy (Haudenosaunee), such a substitution of an alien for a lost kinsman was not unusual, especially given high population losses due to disease and warfare over the previous century.[14] The head of a matrilineage would decide whether to replace a deceased relative and the means for doing so; that woman would be an elder who led the family group of those living near her—her daughters and granddaughters, her younger sisters, and their daughters (who would also be known as her children).[15] Among the Haudenosaunee, kinship belonging and residency, including land ownership and use, correlated with one's mother's line, and the matrilineages were part of larger clans, of which the Senecas had eight. "The matrilineage was not only the core unit of kin relationships but also functioned as the distributor of the political roles of chief and advisor. The political networks which underlay the League of the Iroquois were essentially kinship networks."[16] The clans provided the basis for governance, with each contributing leaders to the national and Confederacy councils. These leaders were chosen by the clan mothers (the heads of the lineages) and could be broken, or replaced, by them; the clan mothers also had local councils of their own.[17] To be part of a lineage, and thus a clan, was to be part of the Seneca polity,[18] and such belonging, and attendant participation in various levels of collective decision-making, did not distinguish between birth and adoption. From this perspective, Mary Jemison was as much Seneca as her Seneca sisters; her children, then, also would be Seneca, gaining their clan membership through her, referring to her sisters as mothers, and understanding her sisters' children as their siblings.

The land on which Jemison and her family lived was set aside in the Treaty of Big Tree (1797) as the Gardeau Reservation, a twenty-eight-square-mile tract on both sides of the Genesee River and one of the eleven reservations retained by the Senecas when they ceded the rest of their remaining territory.[19] Known as the "western door" of the Confederacy, they had been under far less pressure from Euramerican settlers than their neighbors to the east, but the push for Seneca lands began to pick up speed in the late 1780s. Much of their territory had been part of a dispute between Massachusetts and New York over these states' western boundaries, both claiming a pre-emptive right to Seneca-occupied space based on conflicting royal charters. In 1786, a deal was struck in which the area was placed under the jurisdiction of New York while Massachusetts retained the exclusive authority to purchase, and sell, land to which native peoples still had claims. The speculation frenzy that had driven the acquisition of Haudenosaunee lands to the east now came to Seneca territory.[20] Preemption rights to the expanse from the Genesee River west to Lake Erie and south to the Pennsylvania border passed through several hands before coming to rest in the Ogden Land Company, founded by David Ogden in 1810. State and federal officials colluded with these various investors in order to make possible the creation of a transportation infrastructure via canals and turnpikes, which would make New York into one of the centers of trade in the new nation.[21] By the 1820s, the Ogden company had a small army of agents on its payroll, including Jasper Parrish, the subagent to the Six Nations, and the interpreter Horatio Jones.[22] This pressure to gain access to Seneca territory as part of an empire-for-commerce is the context in which Jemison's story is both set and told, the narrative itself coming on the heels of Jemison's signing of an agreement—sanctioned by Seneca chiefs—to sell almost the entirety of the Gardeau Reservation to employees of the Ogden Land Company.

Given these circumstances, the effort to represent Jemison's voice seems particularly overdetermined, caught up in the politics of acquiring native territory. However, while touching on the circumstances of the sale of the Gardeau lands, the *Narrative* largely leaves aside the mounting demands for Seneca sales in favor of telling Jemison's story as a tale of individual adversity, one in which race and subjectivity intimately are entwined. In particular, the text's staging of Jemison's individuality and the authenticity of her voice is inextricable from its characterization of her as white, helping to position her as a speaking subject whose personal identity, legal status, and decision-making are not dependent on her relations with Seneca kin. This predication of her personhood on reproductively determined whiteness helps displace the importance of kinship networks as the primary matrix for Seneca collectivity, abetting efforts to make U.S. legal norms the standard for conceptualizing Seneca sovereignty and, thereby, to simplify the process of officially managing and legitimizing land cessions.

James Seaver's introduction presents the text as a biography, thereby positioning himself as the author of someone else's life story, but the main body appears to be a first-person account, suggesting a recording of Jemison's own speech.[23] He describes the purpose of biography as "transmit[ting] to future generations the poverty, pain, wrong, hunger, wretchedness and torment, and every nameless misery that has been endured by those who have lived in obscurity," and this particular "piece of biography" "shows what changes may be affected in the animal and mental constitution of man . . . when stern necessity holds the reins, and drives the car of fate" (50). The purpose of the genre is to name the "nameless," providing a voice and historical presence for those who likely would remain silent and forgotten. In Jemison's case, this process involves chronicling the "changes" wrought by the peculiar twists and turns of her life, the way it has deviated from the normal pattern, and given that Seaver refers to her as "The White Woman," a title supposedly bestowed by her settler neighbors, the "interest and curiosity" aroused by her account have to do with her having fallen away from her presumed racial destiny (54). As Susan Walsh suggests, "readers seem initially drawn to the story because Mary Jemison *lived with the Indians,* but inevitably end up focusing . . . on her essential *whiteness*" (50). The expression, or perhaps more accurately construction, of Jemison's voice, then, is predicated on her relation to whiteness, since that is the part of her "constitution" that is under stress in ways that would make the text both interesting and educative to the reading public.

In addition to replicating the conventions of the captivity narrative, and potentially drawing on the sustained popularity of that form, Jemison's ostensibly first-person narration lends a sense of empirical authenticity to the story of racial "wretchedness" and "misery" toward which Seaver gestures, fulfilling his initial promise of delivering Jemison fully to readers and completely dispelling the cloud of "obscurity" that would otherwise hang about her.[24] While her "life history" is "mediated by the interpretive agendas of assorted white male editors," the *Narrative* and as-told-to texts like it, Walsh argues, "are not monological but rather are sites of intersection," and to treat them as fabrications "would be to dismiss the very idea of an Indian subject position, to ignore the possibility of voices, perspectives, and narrative traditions in opposition to the progressivist ideology of well-intentioned white editors" (49–51).[25] To this end, Walsh seeks to locate Jemison's voice amid Seaver's attempts to frame her experience. Rather than seeing Jemison as occupying "an Indian subject position," though, Hilary Wyss suggests in "Captivity and Conversion" that "the tensions in Jemison's story involve not only those of an editor and an oral storyteller but also the competition of narrative forms that ultimately mirrors the opposing racial identities that structure the entire narrative," such that "Jemison's ambivalent textual presence echoes her cultural position as a hybrid figure" (69, 72). Is *Indian* subjectivity equivalent to *Seneca* subjectivity, and in the same vein, is "the competition of narrative forms," of representational frameworks, in the text primarily a function of *racial* difference? If emphasizing Jemison's whiteness elides her Senecaness, as Walsh indicates, the latter identity must already be conceptualized as racial, and construing Jemison as "hybrid" does not address why the text would portray her subjectivity in terms of "opposing racial identities" in the first place. In trying to generate a subjectivity for Jemison, both approaches end up reproducing the logic of the *Narrative*, or perhaps more accurately, they skip over two related questions: what is made possible, as well as effaced, in folding Seneca identity into racial discourse; and how does endowing Jemison with a specifically racialized subjectivity position her voice, as putatively recovered by the text, in relation to the extant dynamics of Seneca politics? Put another way, in the context of U.S.-Seneca affairs in the early 1820s, what does it mean to speak as white, as Indian, as Seneca, and what role does race (defined via reproductive coupling) play in U.S. efforts to manage available forms of legal and political subjectivity?

Looking at the text's discussion of the disposal of Jemison's lands offers a way of beginning to address these questions, exploring the connections between race, voice, land, and law at play in Indian affairs. In 1817, Jemison signed two agreements ceding control of land in the Gardeau Reservation to Micah Brooks and Jellis Clute, one selling 7,000 acres and the other leasing the rest of the reservation except for a 4,000-acre plot for Jemison and a section that had been promised to Thomas Clute (Jellis's brother) for his service as Jemison's guardian. In describing this series of events, though, the text raises the issue of Mary Jemison's legal status without fully confronting the complexities surrounding it and the interests at play in adjudicating and adjusting it. The narrator says of Brooks that "he was disposed to assist me in regard to my land, by procuring a legislative act that would invest me with full power to dispose of it for my own benefit," and "he would get an act passed in the Congress of the United States, that would invest me with all the rights and immunities of a citizen, so far as it respected my property" (153–154). However, the text earlier notes that Jemison already had been authorized by the Seneca chiefs "to lease or let my lands to white people" as part of the agreement that created the Gardeau Reservation (122), so there is no need for her to be *invested* with citizenship, except in order for her to be able to *sell* her lands without consulting Seneca leaders. While presented as only a means of confirming Jemison's ownership, as consolidating an existing connection to her lands, the extension of citizenship actually changes Jemison's relation to the Seneca chiefs in order to alter the nature of her land tenure, thereby facilitating its purchase. If she is a citizen of the United States, her "property" is not subject to Seneca sovereignty and can be sold like any other piece of private land.[26] In other words, citizenship serves as a way of transmuting treaty-guaranteed Seneca lands into Jemison's property, such that her individual consent—her voice—is all that is necessary for its transfer.

This proposed transformation-by-naturalization, for the purposes of a territorial transaction, begs the question of what Jemison is *before* she can be made a citizen. While the text slides past that particular point, it provides an account of the debate over where to send the citizenship appeal that is worth quoting at length for the way it is haunted by this very problem:

> Soon after this Thomas Clute saw Esq. [Jellis] Clute, who informed him that the petition for my naturalization would be presented to the Legislature of this State, instead of being sent to Congress; and that the object would succeed to his and my satisfaction. Mr. Clute then observed to his brother, Esq. Clute, that as the sale of Indian lands, which had been reserved, belonged exclusively to the United States, an act of the Legislature of New York could have no effect in securing to me a title to my reservation, or in depriving me of my property. They finally agreed that I should sign a petition to Congress praying for my naturalization, and for the confirmation of the title of my land to me, my heirs, &c.

> Mr. Brooks came with the petition: I signed it, . . . and then returned [it]
> to Mr. Brooks, who presented it to the Legislature of this state. . . . On the
> 19th of April, 1817, an act was passed for my naturalization . . .
> Thomas Clute having examined the law, told me that it would probably
> answer[.] (154)

Since jurisdiction over Indian affairs lies entirely with the federal government, the legislature of New York State can do nothing on its own with
respect to "Indian lands." From this perspective, Jemison's claim is *as an
Indian*, one of the Seneca people and subject to Seneca sovereignty. However, making Jemison a federal citizen still would not give her private property rights over Seneca land, but the text seems to assume that an alteration
in her legal status would affect that of the territory she occupies, putting it
outside the domain of Seneca governance. The very fact that Jellis Clute and
Micah Brooks are willing to submit the naturalization petition to the New
York legislature, as well as Thomas Clute's sense that "it probably would
answer," suggests serious doubt as to whether the place in question is Indian
land.[27] Given that the Gardeau Reservation federally was recognized as
Seneca territory in the Treaty of Big Tree and that Mary Jemison, not being
a U.S. citizen, must be Seneca, how could that land not be Indian, and thus
be subject to state authority?

Unless, the person and property of Jemison as a *white* woman cannot fully
belong to, or be subject to the power of, the Senecas as an *Indian* tribe. Both of
the Clutes' propositions for "securing" Jemison's land are incoherent unless
one already presumes a preexisting disjunction between Jemison and the Senecas that the legislature (state or federal) merely *confirms*. The focus on Jemison's voice here, her individual consent to dispose of her lands, is predicated
on separating her from (the rest of) the Seneca people, and the text initiates
that process of distinction from the outset. As Seaver states in his introduction,
"Her appearance was well calculated to excite a great deal of sympathy . . .
when comparing her present situation with what it probably would have
been, had she been permitted to have remained with her friends, and to have
enjoyed the blessings of civilization" (55). Her racial status at birth, which
would have given her access to "civilization" and citizenship, clings to her,
providing a ghostly potentiality against which to measure her dislocation
from her proper "situation," but this Mary-that-could-have-been also can be
tactically realized, partially fulfilling her lost birthright in her naturalization,
which seems in the text merely to recognize what naturally was waiting there
all along.[28]

The unease with respect to how to position Jemison in relation to Seneca
sovereignty, both in the text and in the sale, however, reappears in the need
to get an official confirmation of her cession by Seneca leaders in council:

Finding their title still incomplete, on account of the United States government and Seneca Chiefs not having sanctioned my acts. . . .

In the winter of 1822–3, I agreed with them, that if they would get the
chiefs of our nation, and a United States Commissioner of Indian Lands, to
meet in council . . . and concur to my agreement, that I would sell to them all
my right and title to the Gardow reservation, with the exception of a tract for
my own benefit . . . This arrangement was agreed upon, and the council
assembled at the place appointed, on the 3d or 4th day of September, 1823.
(155)[29]

While noting the doubt lingering around the previous transaction, the text
does not dwell on the implications of referring to the Senecas as "our
nation." By what logic is she part of the Seneca nation, and if that form of
connection is politically pertinent in 1822–1823, how could it not be relevant in 1817? The insecurity over the proper process of purchase serves as
the trace of a broader anxiety over the legal meaning of Jemison's adoption
by the Senecas, an issue that affects not just the title to the Gardeau lands but
the applicability of U.S. ideologies of property and political identity to
Indian affairs. If Jemison can be fully Seneca, what does that imply about
Senecas' understandings of their own polity, and to what extent are those
conceptions of native collectivity recognized in U.S. Indian policy, including
the acquisition of territory? The text seeks to assuage, or perhaps more
accurately disavow, these concerns by emphasizing the underlying and
unbreakable continuity of Jemison's whiteness. The seeming undeniability
of her race, which serves as the foundation on which her citizenship can
rest, appears to make legally and politically moot her participation in
Seneca kinship networks.

The *Narrative*'s discussion of the sale indexes the kinds of ideological
work performed by racial discourse in (re)shaping representations of native
collectivity and sovereignty, offering a sense of the geopolitical stakes of the
text's way of formulating Indian-white difference—how such depictions
help reinforce a conception of Seneca subjectivity and governance disjointed
from clans and kinship networks. The story of the transfer of Jemison's lands
is the final chapter before a brief conclusion, and the introduction mentions
the fact that Seaver's interview with Jemison in November 1823 was
prompted by the interest of "many gentlemen of respectability" in
"preserv[ing] some historical facts" (54), which in light of the meeting of a
Seneca council to ratify this cession in June of that same year and the widespread network of respectable men in the employ of the Ogden Land Company seems hardly coincidental.[30] The *Narrative*, then, is bookended by the
project of acquiring territory and the centrality of Jemison's voice to that
process, and foregrounding race as the preeminent way of framing Jemison's

identity and the significance of her speech privileges (racial) birth over (clan) adoption as a way of reckoning belonging.

Figuring Jemison in this way not only undermines her Senecaness but turns her testimony into confirmation of the marginality of Seneca kinship formations with respect to questions of governance—such as citizenship and land tenure. The text's emphasis on Jemison's ability to represent herself, to speak directly to the reader and to consent to land sales (which as I have suggested are bound up with each other), is dependent on the representation of her in terms of, in Wyss's terms quoted earlier, "opposing racial identities."[31] Considering attempts to celebrate dominated populations' ability to speak for themselves, Gayatri Spivak has cautioned that doing so can efface the ideological conditions in which such speech occurs, treating voice as empirical, concrete, and transparent in ways that elide how its availability is dependent on the speaker inhabiting forms of subjectivity that have been normalized through their institutionalization. In offering the impression of unmediated access to the voice(s) of the oppressed, "two senses of representation are being run together: representation as 'speaking for,' as in politics, and representation as 're-presentation,' as in art or philosophy" (256). Spivak suggests that critics must keep in view "how the staging of the world in representation—its scene of writing . . . —dissimulates the choice of and need for 'heroes,' paternal proxies, agents of power" (264).[32] Following this logic, the Narrative's portrayal of Jemison's whiteness can be seen as containing within it an operative, yet unacknowledged, set of institutionalized assumptions about what makes a person or group a viable speaking subject, and reciprocally, the ability to speak in governmentally recognized ways—as a private landowner or a native polity—requires conforming to the discourses circulating within such institutions, which offer particular (intertwined) visions of what constitutes personhood, family, occupancy, and governance.

The significance of the running racialization of Jemison as white, then, lies less in the denigration of "Indians" by comparison than in the ways a discourse of racial birth works to foreclose alternative formulations of what it means to be Seneca and thus what it would mean for the Senecas to speak as a people, and Jemison's public voice is predicated on that foreclosure. Spivak suggests that analysis of how the two kinds of representation collude with each other to naturalize existing power arrangements "within state formations and systems of political economy" leads to "not only a critique of the subject as individual agent but even a critique of the subjectivity of a collective agency" (257, 260). Jemison's subjectivity and speech in the Narrative, and in the sale of the Gardeau lands, becomes intelligible in the context of a portrayal of "Indian" identity in which the biopolitics of race supplants the geopolitics of kinship. This displacement not only overdetermines

Jemison's individual agency—shaping the context in which she acts, the possibilities available to her, and how her acts will signify to the state—but dismisses the significance of the clan system and thus helps undermine Seneca political self-representation more broadly. If Jemison's speech is predicated on her racial access to citizenship, from what position do the Senecas speak? If what makes a Seneca truly Seneca is racial inheritance as an Indian, the resulting conception of Seneca collective subjectivity is predicated not so much on their status as an autonomous political entity with its own modes of social organization and governance as on their formal legal designation as belonging to a special category distinguished from whites (such as in the phrase "Indian lands" quoted earlier). From this perspective, Seneca difference from the United States—in terms of ways of reckoning membership, conceptualizing land tenure, methods of decision-making (all of which are embedded in clan-based kinship networks)—is transmuted into Indian-white racial difference, leaving the disjunction between Seneca and U.S. sociopolitical formations in an institutional and ideological limbo.[33]

Later events in the 1820s suggest the ramifications of this process of translation. In the wake of the 1823 agreement, Secretary of War John C. Calhoun described it as less a treaty than something "considered in the nature of a private contract [that] does not require the special ratification of the Government"; that perspective is confirmed by Commissioner of Indian Affairs Thomas McKenney four years later, describing the formal meeting of the chiefs attended by a federal commissioner as "a useless ceremony."[34] The *privatization* of the Gardeau lands could be seen as an isolated instance if not for the circumstances surrounding the 1826 "treaty" ceding the rest of that reservation, the other reservations on the Genesee River, and large portions of the Buffalo Creek, Tonawanda, and Cattaraugus reservations as well. Conducted under pressure from the Ogden company, overseen by a federal commissioner with financial interests in the territory in question, and found in a subsequent government-ordered report to have been negotiated under circumstances shot through with threats, bribery, and fraud, this supposed agreement was never approved by the Senate, never mind being ratified by a two-thirds majority. However, the Senate also passed a resolution stating that the vote against ratification was "not intended to express any disapprobation of the terms of the contract entered into by individuals who are parties . . . , but merely to disclaim the necessity of an interference by the Senate with the subject matter," and despite extensive Seneca protest, the cession was taken as legal.[35] By what logic can a cession of native land not be the subject of a treaty? The use of the term "individuals" here seems instructive, casting the Senecas as just another party to a contract—one without the diplomatic status of an independent government.

Moreover, characterizing U.S.-native relations as a "contract" suggests that indigenous peoples are situated within the terms and structures of liberalism, that their modes of political and economic organization and engagement match those of the United States. The 1823 agreement confirming Jemison's sale functioned as a precedent for the much larger loss of territory in 1826, including the lands she still occupied. The treatment of the earlier document as merely a "private contract" was made possible by the understanding of Jemison, due to her whiteness, as not really one of the Senecas, and from within that individualizing racial logic, the Senecas appear as a collection of Indians rather than a distinct polity, enabling the Senate to regard Seneca territoriality (and its circumscription) with greater casualness. Additionally, even if the Senecas are regarded as a collective, the individualization of native identity as a function of blood inheritance presents that collectivity as having a parallel structure to that of the United States, as operating within the same ideological framework for what constitutes governance and legitimate land tenure. The threshold for determining Seneca consent to land sales is lowered considerably inasmuch as it can be divorced from the convention of consensus among recognized chiefs that emerges out of the traditional relation between the operation of Seneca councils and the kinship system.

This problem of what constitutes representativity for the purposes of acquiring *Indian* land appears even more dramatically in events surrounding the treaty of 1838, in which the Senecas supposedly ceded their remaining reservations (Buffalo Creek, Cattaraugus, Allegany, and Tonawanda).[36] Members of the Senate and other federal officials repeatedly expressed concern that the Ogden company had engaged in irregular practices, including having random Seneca men sign as "chiefs," in order to make the agreement appear legitimate. The Senate ultimately determined that a majority of chiefs needed to sign in order for the cession to be valid, a measure passed by a bare majority of the Senate. This calculation of consent had little relation to existing Seneca processes or precedents in U.S.-Seneca negotiations, as will be discussed further in the next section, and the absence of approval by two-thirds of the Senate made the document something other than a treaty. While acknowledging that assent by some form of Seneca collectivity was necessary to make the sale legal, the Senate offered an account of native identity sundered from Seneca self-understandings, one in which Senecaness does not inhere in clan structures of belonging and governance. The assumption is that majority rule without question can serve as an appropriate modality for decision-making among an aggregate of Senecas.[37] This implicit portrayal of them as a collection of individuals whose political processes necessarily resemble those of the United States depends upon reducing the Seneca people to a group of Seneca persons. In this way, the racialization of Seneca identity as a quality of bodies rather than one of social structure abets the casualization of Indian affairs, in which a treaty appears as something akin to a "private contract" that (sometimes) needs congressional sanction rather than a diplomatic negotiation with a polity which has its own distinct system of governance.

Rather than claiming that the 1823 agreement and Jemison's actions are directly responsible for the "treaty" of 1826 or 1838, I am suggesting that the discourse surrounding the earlier document offers useful insights in interpreting the later ones. More specifically, an attention to Jemison's position, the representation of her, and the pressures exerted to produce her voice help explain how the characterization of Senate ratification as "interference" becomes thinkable. The process of constructing a voice for Mary Jemison, within both the legal record and the *Narrative*, works to render subaltern Seneca modes of political self-representation, particularly the clan system, by displacing them as a legally meaningful way of conceptualizing jurisdiction and land claims. In this way, the text's depiction of her story and speech abets the ideological (re)configuration of Seneca collective subjectivity within official U.S. discourses, which seek to bring it in line with U.S. jurisdictional principles and to facilitate the appropriation of native land. Jemison's voice is predicated on a racial imaginary in which her whiteness ultimately separates her from the Senecas, an *Indian* tribe, and this understanding of her adoption as epiphenomenal to her true identity, including in political and legal terms, delegitimizes the kinship system as a way of understanding Seneca geopolitics. The appearance of Jemison's speech in the *Narrative* occurs within this ideological formation, and critical efforts to differentiate her from Seaver end up overlooking the relation between the text's staging of Jemison's racial subjectivity and its marginalization of kinship-based governance.

WHITE WOMAN OR CLAN MOTHER?

While drawing on an ideology of racial genealogy in which Indianness is defined through reproduction, the *Narrative* offers an account of Indian-white difference at odds with the Jeffersonian vision I discussed at the beginning of the chapter. Rather than portraying conjugal homemaking as pedagogical, as training native people for assimilation where they are, including through intermarriage, the text depicts Indians as congenitally resistant to the forms of sentimental affection and privatized intimacy that increasingly served as the normative ideal of family formation in the early nineteenth century.[38] At one point in talking about the practice of torturing some of the captives turned over to those who are grieving deceased loved ones, the *Narrative* observes, "It is family, and not national, sacrifices amongst the Indians, that has given them an indelible stamp as barbarians" (78). The two kinds of identification—*familial* and *national*—appear as utterly distinct, presenting the former rather than the latter as the context in which to make sense of the treatment of captives, including Jemison, and if native peoples cannot be made amenable to progress, that fact is due to the "indelible" barbarity of their family life. If bourgeois discourses of sexuality are shaped by a *racial grammar*, in Ann Laura Stoler's terms discussed earlier, the growing dominance of the idea of the intimate private sphere intensifies the sense of racial difference, but in ways that depoliticize it. From that perspective, the deviation of native governance from U.S. norms appears as an accumulation of private (racial) failures that have overwhelmed political process rather than as an alternative political logic. In this way, the *Narrative* repeatedly works to displace kinship as a mode of political collectivity by foregrounding conjugal couplehood and reproduction as the frame through which to conceptualize Indianness. However, the text remains haunted by the kinship formations it renders subaltern, and reading the text for such traces draws attention to the moments that together offer a portrait of Jemison less as white outsider than matrilineal authority—as a clan mother. Yet, to be clear, such a reading does not hinge on an effort to differentiate Jemison's voice from Seaver's (a move that tends to recapitulate the kinds of racial and political subjectivity the text produces, in ways discussed in the previous section); instead, it attends to the ways extant Seneca sociopolitical formations and struggles leave their mark on the *Narrative* despite its best effort to erase them in its construction of Jemison's voice.[39]

The text helps abject the dynamics and significance of Seneca kinship by proliferating examples of interracial couplehood that cast familial relations as most importantly nuclear in nature and make personal identity contingent on reproductive pairing. Jemison's marriages are the most prominent example of this pattern. In describing her first husband, the text fixates on the incongruity of their union:

> Sheninjee was a noble man . . . He supported a degree of dignity far above his rank, and merited and received the confidence and friendship of all the tribes with whom he was acquainted. Yet, Sheninjee was an Indian. The idea of spending my days with him, at first seemed perfectly irreconcilable to my feelings: but his good nature, generosity, tenderness, and friendship towards me, soon gained my affection; and, strange as it may seem, I loved him! (82)

The passage seems spellbound by the crossing of the racial boundary itself, expressing a kind of bewilderment at the very idea of it. This somewhat horrified astonishment persists in the acknowledgment of the "strange[ness]" of her affection for him. The tone of incredulity here works to intensify the very difference that it seems merely to recognize, presenting her initial horror and lingering amazement as perfectly obvious in ways that make racial distinction the most prominent aspect of the relationship.[40] Despite her having lived among the Senecas for several years at this point in her story, or for almost her entire lifetime in the moment of retrospection supposedly captured by the text, what remains most salient about her is her whiteness, brought into bold relief through contrast with Sheninjee's Indianness. These identities are envisioned as immutable, and since they are acquired through reproduction, Jemison's and Sheninjee's matrimony, with its potential for procreative mixing, seems "perfectly irreconcilable" with her sense of self, both then and now. The concern over racial lineage helps center marriage as a site of identity-making, increasing the significance of conjugal coupling (as against other forms of affiliation) while indirectly defining native identity as an individually possessed trait rather than as participation in a matrix of peoplehood.

Depicting their marriage as high racial drama, however, involves extricating it from the social formations in which they lived. The fact that both Jemison and Sheninjee are residing among native peoples at the town of Wiishto on the Ohio River, taking part in the seasonal cycles of movement that were part of patterns of subsistence, appears irrelevant. The oddity of the match is highlighted further by the pressure her adopted family supposedly needs to exert on her before she agrees to wed: "Not long after the Delawares came to live with us, at Wiishto, my sisters told me that I must go and live with one of them . . . Not daring to cross them, or disobey their commands, with a great degree of reluctance I went; and Sheninjee and I were married according to Indian custom" (81). Her sisters appear to push her across the threshold, forcefully intervening in matters that implicitly are cast as properly those of only the couple themselves, and fear of defying the intrusive "commands" of her Seneca relatives predominates over affection and attraction as the basis for her marriage. The emphasis on incontrovertible racial inheritance and the spectacle of conjugally crossing the color line overwhelms any discussion of why Jemison's sisters would desire her to "go and live with" Sheninjee. Their interest in the match seems only an invasive, and somewhat unnatural, thwarting of the proper process of romantic pairing, which apparently should tend toward racial homogeneity. Within this logic, any attempt to connect marriage to broader kinship networks is itself envisioned as inherently coercive. As Elizabeth Povinelli argues in *The Empire of Love*, individual consent to marriage historically has served in liberal settler states as one of the most crucial sites for "representing modern intimacy as if it were actually other than genealogy, outside it, opposed to it" (215).

When Jemison and Sheninjee's marriage is put in the context of the complex kinship politics of the region in the late eighteenth century, however, it appears less as miscegenation than alliance-making. Western Senecas had longstanding relationships with peoples in the Ohio Valley and beyond, including through marriage and adoption, residence in each other's villages, and joint participation in political campaigns (such as the various attacks on Euramerican garrisons and settlements grouped together as "Pontiac's Uprising").[41] Given that their union occurred in the late 1750s in the middle of ongoing warfare among English, French, and native forces, its significance for Jemison's family seems to lie in its capacity to build sustainable connections with "the Delawares [who] came to live" in their village, since shared kin often provided a vehicle among native peoples for more extensive diplomatic and trade relations.[42] In seeking to limit the scope of its discussion to the couple themselves, however, the *Narrative* makes marriage into, in Povinelli's terms, an "intimate event," heightening the sense of Jemison's and Sheninjee's differences from each other by dislocating their pairing from its enmeshment in the dynamics of Seneca collectivity.[43] They each appear as the product of distinct, diachronic racial genealogies rather than co-participants in a synchronous kinship nexus—a multilayered political and spatial formation shaped around familial bonds and through familial idioms.

Although Jemison's second marriage, to Hiokatoo (a fellow Seneca), occasions far less comment, the consequences of such racial amalgamation are brought home forcefully in the text's discussion of Jemison's decision not to try to reunite with her birth family. In considering whether to return to them in the wake of the American Revolution, she is given pause by the fact "that I had got a large family of Indian children, that I must take with me; and that if I should be so fortunate as to find my relatives, they would despise them, if not myself; and treat us as enemies; or, at least with a degree of cold indifference, which I thought I could not endure" (119–120). While her birth family might have responded in this way, the passage does not so much seem to contest that perception of her children as suggest a kind of resignation to its brute facticity. Notably, they are presented as "Indian" rather than as mixed-race, indicating that any reproductive dilution of whiteness leads to its total loss, which also implies that if one is of pure white birth, as Jemison is, one never can lose that status.[44] At one point the *Narrative* directly affirms the immutability of inborn Indian identity:

I have seen in a number of instances, the effects of education upon some of our Indians, who were taken when young, from their families, and placed at school before they had had an opportunity to contract many Indian habits, and there kept till they arrived to manhood, but I have never seen one of those but what was an Indian in every respect after he returned. Indians must and will be Indians, in spite of all the means that can be used for their cultivation in the sciences and arts. (84–85)

As against a Jeffersonian vision of assimilation, here the behavioral traits of Indianness are depicted as arising from an innate drive that defies all efforts to *cultivate* other ways of being more conducive to civilization; conversely, the "habits" of native people do not constitute a kind of sociopolitical system, instead deriving from instinct. Non-Indians might reside among Indians, but they could never become one of them. In the discussion of her children, Jemison appears tied to the Seneca people less by personal choice or participation in the kinship system—connections to her *relatives* in the Turtle clan—than by her nuclear intimacy with her offspring, her implication in Indianness established through the reproductive family unit. That alienation from her family of origin cannot be remedied until her children are adults and thus, from the perspective of bourgeois homemaking, no longer dependents within her household. At that point, as the text illustrates, her natural connection to other whites legally can be recognized through the formal extension of citizenship, and despite the fact that she continues to live at Gardeau up through the time of the text's publication, her naturalization appears as a kind of symbolic reunification with her white heritage, the racial lineage to which she was born.

Even had Jemison's son Thomas wanted to live among his mother's birth family, Seneca leaders, according to the text, forbade him from doing so. When Jemison had the possibility of rejoining her birth family, the *Narrative* notes, "My son, Thomas, was anxious that I should go; and offered to go with me . . . But the Chiefs of our tribe, suspecting from his appearance, actions, and a few warlike exploits, that Thomas would be a great warrior, or a good counsellor, refused to let him leave them on any account whatever" (119). Even before observing her white family's likely rejection of her Indian children, Jemison suggests that she was tied to the Senecas by their refusal to relinquish at least one of her children. Due to the contiguity of these two moments, the chiefs' decision is cast as the mirror image of that of Jemison's birth family; the latter will not accept Thomas due to his Indianness whereas Seneca leaders desire him for precisely that reason. However, when examined, this somewhat chiastic structure is incoherent, or rather, it depends for its coherence on an ideology of reproductive raciality that cannot explain the dynamics at hand. After relating the tragic circumstances of Thomas's murder by his brother John, as retaliation for the former's persistent accusation that he was a "witch," the text reiterates its earlier claim: "[T]he Chiefs would not suffer him to leave them on the account of his courage and skill in war . . . He was a great Counsellor and a Chief when quite young; and in the last capacity went two or three times to Philadelphia to assist in making

treaties with the people of the states" (126). In fact, he is one of the signa-
tories to the Treaty of Big Tree.[45] Although from one perspective Thomas is
"Indian" due to Sheninjee's identity as a Delaware, that legacy has little relevance for making Thomas a "Counsellor and a Chief" for the Senecas, and
given their matrilineality, his father's racial, tribal, or clan identification is
not the deciding factor in positioning him among the Seneca people.[46]
Rather, what makes him Seneca is his status as the child of a woman who
belongs to one of the Seneca clans, by adoption or otherwise, so his potential
to serve as a Seneca leader comes through Jemison, not Sheninjee, contra-
vening the conclusion implied by the *Narrative*.[47] This kinship matrix, its
role in Seneca politics, and Jemison's intimate enmeshment in it, though, are
effaced by the text's presentation of Thomas's participation in Seneca governance as an Indianization that distinguishes him from Jemison.

The text's procreatively based partitioning of Indians and whites, and its
consequent pose of astonishment at examples of intermixture, is reinforced
by the additional examples of Ebenezer Allen and Cornplanter. The one is
the white father of native daughters, and the other is the native child of a
white father. Allen rates an entire chapter in the *Narrative*, an inclusion that
seems to have more to do with increasing audience interest due to his outra-
geous behavior than with illuminating Jemison's life, whereas Cornplanter, a
famous Seneca leader, appears in only one anecdote—the often-told story of
his accidental meeting with his father during the American Revolution as
part of a Seneca raid on a white settlement aligned with the rebels.[48] More
than offering something like local color, though, these stories provide a kind
of contextualizing surround for the portrayal of Jemison, echoing the terms
of racial distinction foregrounded in her story in ways that confirm the obviousness of its account of Indian-white difference. Allen had fled Pennsylvania for New York during the American Revolution, probably having gotten
into trouble with neighbors due to his Loyalist sympathies. After taking up
residence on Jemison's land, he seduced the native wife (Sally) of a local white
man, fraudulently sent a wampum belt of peace from hostile Indians to the
United States to end the fighting, illegally sold alcohol to native people, killed
a man to gain access to his daughter whom Allen married despite already
being married to Sally, and married a third woman (Morilla) without noti-
fying the previous two (109–118). Of particular interest, though, is that he
had two daughters with Sally for whom he secured a tract of Seneca land in
1791 only then to sell it afterward to Robert Morris, the primary person with
preemption rights to Seneca territory in the 1790s, and to abandon Sally and
his daughters when he moved with his two white wives to Canada.[49]

Other than increasing the text's sensational appeal,[50] this chapter suggests
the intractability of whiteness. Despite having lived among Senecas for a
number of years, intermarrying, and having Seneca children, Allen never

saw himself as one of them, exploiting their trust and resources and leaving his Seneca wife and children while retaining his white spouses. Even knowing of his various acts of duplicity, cruelty, and outright violence, Jemison continues to aid Allen for reasons that remain obscure. Absent any additional explanation, the text leaves the reader to believe that she feels some sort of connection to him in his whiteness that motivates her continuing compassion for him.[51] While Allen is situated differently than Jemison with respect to the Senecas, never having been adopted into a clan, he also is the parent of *Indian* children, and in this way, his story seems positioned as a reflection, or perhaps refraction, of Jemison's own that corroborates the innateness of racial distinction.

As Susan Walsh observes, "if Dehgewanus's [Jemison's Seneca name] mother and Cornplanter emerge as stellar exempla (Indians are noble, charitable, and faithful), Ebenezer Allen stands in dark counterpoint (whites are sneaky, rapacious, and feckless)" (61),[52] and while the anecdote of Cornplanter saving his father during a raid on white settlements clearly contrasts with the examples of Allen's deviousness and vicious cupidity, especially given that the former appears in the text immediately prior to the chapter on Allen, what is at stake in the text's staging of Indian/white difference through this particular example? What is effaced through this framing? Cornplanter is perhaps the Seneca leader most well known to whites after Red Jacket, having been one of two commanders of Seneca forces fighting for the British in the American Revolution, a central figure in the Treaty of Fort Stanwix (1784) and the Treaty of Fort Harmar (1789), the brother of the well-known Seneca prophet and leader Handsome Lake, and one of the principal representatives of the Senecas and the Haudenosaunee more broadly in negotiations with the United States from the 1780s through the 1820s.[53] In this episode in the text, he gives his father, John O'Bail, a choice:

> I am your son! I am a warrior! I was anxious to see you, and to greet you in friendship. I went to your cabin and took you by force! But your life shall be spared. Indians love their friends and their kindred, and treat them with kindness. If you choose to follow the fortune of your yellow son, . . . I will cherish your old age . . . and you shall live easy: But if it is your choice to return to your fields and live with your white children, I will send a party of my trusty young men to conduct you back in safety. (107)

O'Bail decides to remain among the settlers and, accordingly, is brought back to his home. Cornplanter's generosity is cast as consistent with "Indian" principles of "love" and "kindness,"[54] and regardless of the fact that his father is white, his birth connection to the Senecas enmeshes him in *Indianness*, even if he acknowledges that he is "yellow" rather than pure "red."

Here the text once again indicates that possession of a native romantic partner and children cannot make a person native, a status attainable only through birth. Yet even as the text's repetitious return to instances of mixed-race mating might suggest the permeability or instability of racial boundaries, the representation of these unions and births in terms of race is itself a function of the text's fixation on *the intimate event*—romantic pairing—as the context in which to assess personal identity. The focus on coupling does not undo or undermine ideologies of race but instead is the condition of possibility for such ideologies, operating in Stoler's terms quoted earlier as the *grammar* for discourses of reproductive raciality in which belonging to a native people is reduced to inheritance of physiological Indianness.

From this perspective, presenting Cornplanter as the exemplary Indian is quite notable. While perhaps an obvious choice for the *Narrative* given that he probably is the most famous Seneca with white parentage, he also was a deeply controversial figure among the Senecas themselves in the late eighteenth and early nineteenth centuries. As noted earlier, he was one of the central figures in U.S.-Seneca negotiations throughout the 1780s and 1790s. Often described in documents as the "Chief Warrior," he likely was the official spokesperson for the warriors, a position in which he both conveyed the views of others and served as a leader in his own right.[55] As a result of his participation in the cession of Haudenosaunee lands in treaties during the 1780s, though, he was ostracized and threatened by many, including having his actions disavowed repeatedly by other Seneca leaders.[56] The hostility arose out of the belief that Cornplanter not only was responsible for surrendering native lands, and he (along with several others) had received personal gifts of money and territory for doing so, but that he had claimed an authority to speak for the Seneca people which he lacked.[57] At stake in these charges was who had the ability to make decisions about territorial matters, which is to say what constituted the fundamental structure of Seneca governance. Events just prior to and during the Treaty of Canandaigua (1794) shed light on the terms of this conflict. In the lead-up to the treaty conference, which was to allay anxieties that had resulted from the rhetoric of conquest employed by the United States in the wake of the Revolution and its attendant assertion of rights to large swaths of land claimed by members of the Iroquois Confederacy, Cornplanter increasingly adopted a hostile stance, threatening to align with native peoples in the Ohio Valley who successfully had challenged U.S. policy initiatives in the region for the previous four years. While perhaps overcompensating in an effort to dispute perceptions of him as complicit with U.S. designs, Cornplanter not only tried, and failed, to override the prerogative of the women's councils to decide on questions of war in a council at Buffalo Creek prior to the meeting at Canandaigua, but at the meeting itself, he was chastised by Little Billy, one of the sachems, who "spoke roughly to him—told him he should consider who he was; that he was only a war-chief, and it did not become him to be so forward as he appeared to be—it was the business of the sachems, more than his, to conduct the treaty."[58] These examples point to the ways Cornplanter repeatedly upset, and sought to short-circuit, normative processes of Seneca decision-making; the attempt to bypass the leading women (clan mothers) as well as the sachems (who themselves would have been nominated for their positions by the clan mothers) suggests that the controversy generated by Cornplanter's actions has to do with his trying to assert forms of political authority that ignored Seneca kinship structures. The *Narrative*'s attempt to present Cornplanter as emblematically Indian erases these tensions, substituting a vision of reproductively transmitted racial Indianness for one predicated on clan belonging. Thinking in terms of Spivak's analysis discussed earlier, this shift in representation (the conception of Seneca identity) changes the dynamics of representativity (what forms of subjectivity and speech will be seen as standing for the Seneca people). In this way, the Cornplanter anecdote complements the text's construction of Jemison's voice: if he must speak as an *Indian*, she can only speak as *white*.

While Cornplanter's story reinforces the racial logic guiding the depiction of Jemison without referencing her directly, Red Jacket's presence in the *Narrative* explicitly confirms that Jemison's whiteness renders impossible an understanding of her as truly Seneca. He was a central figure within Seneca politics from the late eighteenth century through to his death in 1830, serving as one of the key spokesmen for the Senecas over that forty-year period. While also not holding one of the League titles, he was recognized as a prominent and compelling leader and served as perhaps the most visible opponent of removal in the 1810s and 1820s; he also was celebrated in the Euramerican press for his eloquence, a point to which I will return later.[59] In its depiction of the Treaty of Big Tree, which created the Gardeau reservation, the text presents Red Jacket as the principal opponent of Jemison's acquiring part of Seneca territory. This appearance seems to confirm that Indian perceptions of racial difference mirror those of whites, such that the employment of a racial imaginary within popular and administrative discourses is not a displacement of native political and cultural frameworks but a basis for mutual recognition:

> When the Council was opened, and the business afforded a proper opportunity, Farmer's Brother presented by claim, and rehearsed the request of my brother [who had asked that land be set aside for Jemison]. Red Jacket . . . opposed me or my claim with all his influence and eloquence. Farmer's Brother insisted upon the necessity, propriety and expediency of his proposition, and got the land granted. The deed was made and signed,

securing to me the title to all the land I had described; under the same restrictions and regulations that other Indian lands are subject to.

That land has ever since been known by the name of the Gardow Tract.

Red Jacket not only opposed my claim at the Council, but he withheld my money two or three years, on the account of my lands having been granted without his consent. Parrish and Jones at length convinced him that it was the white people, and not the Indians who had given me the land, and compelled him to pay over all the money which he had retained on my account. (121)

The passage initially provides no reason for Red Jacket's resistance, but given that he relents upon being told that the allocation is the work of "white people," his objection appears to be predicated on Jemison's non-Indianness. While the approval offered by Farmer's Brother could offer a countervailing perspective, in which Red Jacket's view is a minority opinion, the text observes that Farmer's Brother was responding to a direct appeal by Jemison's brother and that he was the parallel cousin (in Seneca terms, the brother) of Jemison's husband Hiokatoo (129), positioning his actions as a kind of family favor or an intrusion into the sphere of governance. The conflict, then, seems to be one of kinship versus politics, in which Farmer's Brother is swayed by a kind of sentimental appeal to which Red Jacket is immune.

Despite the fact that Farmer's Brother argues for Jemison's claim, and apparently wins the battle, the last word on her status comes from Jasper Parrish and Horatio Jones, themselves whites who served as interpreters in Haudenosaunee-U.S. relations from the 1780s through the 1830s. Given that Parrish and Jones are official participants in the treaty process, their description of the basis for Jemison's claim seems both tactical (to get Red Jacket to assent to a fait accompli) and quasi-authoritative (a statement of the legal foundation of Jemison's occupancy rights, which resonates with the text's later discussion of her naturalization). Her relation to the land is cast in the terms of property, as a "title" for which she receives a "deed" rather than a notion of possessory use, so the land *belongs* to her instead of her residing on land that belongs to the Seneca people, even as it supposedly remains within the broader category of "Indian lands." The idea that the U.S. government, notably represented metonymically here as "the white people," can assign a plot of land to Jemison does not seem to need further explanation.

Red Jacket appears immediately to grasp the logic of that transaction, in which Jemison's innate racial identity provides obvious grounds for inclusion as a U.S. subject and exclusion from being a Seneca subject. This presentation of him draws on his public persona as an outspoken proponent of Indian/white distinction. Red Jacket's speeches often were printed in various newspapers and pamphlets, and in the most widely cited examples of his oratory, some authentic and some possibly fictionalized, he decries efforts to missionize the Senecas: "The Great Spirit has made us all, but he has made a great difference between his white and red children. HE has given us different complexions and different customs. . . . . Since HE has made so great a difference between us in other things; why may we not conclude that HE has given us a different religion according to our understanding?"[60] The gap between those of different "complexions" appears absolute and unalterable, a divine dispensation with which people should not attempt to tamper. The circulation of such statements not only increases Red Jacket's notoriety as a Seneca leader but makes him into a metonym for popular native sentiment, the representative of a kind of generic Indian perspective. The *Narrative*'s depiction of Red Jacket as leading the opposition to Jemison's claim, then, bears great symbolic weight in its intertextual allusion to these other accounts of his defense of Indian difference.

The scene of Red Jacket's outrage creates the impression that Jemison's presence on Seneca land was controversial, producing a clash resolvable only through reference to the inevitable power of white law over white people, but in generating this effect, the text engages in a complex process of condensation and displacement, rescripting crucial elements of the Treaty of Big Tree and importing later developments in ways that work to distance Red Jacket from the clan system for which he actually served as a spokesperson. There was a disagreement during the treaty negotiation involving Farmer's Brother and Red Jacket, but it had nothing to do with Jemison.[61] Instead, it turned on how much land to sell to Thomas Morris, the son and proxy of Robert Morris who was the current holder of the preemption rights to Seneca territory and who was desperately in need of access to the land in order to pay back his many creditors. In bargaining with Morris, Red Jacket offered to let him buy a tract of six square miles at one dollar per acre; when Morris responded by declaring that if that was the only offer they might as well cover the council fire, thereby ending the meeting, Red Jacket got up and preceded to do so. Afterward, Farmer's Brother approached Morris and said that since Morris was the one who had lit the council fire, Red Jacket had acted inappropriately in quenching it. From that point, talks continued, eventually resulting in the creation of eleven reservations, including the Gardeau tract, and the sale of the Senecas' remaining lands in New York, but none of the accounts of the treaty mention a specific fight over whether to award land to Jemison. The *Narrative* transforms a debate over strategy in engaging with settler intervention into one on the limits of Seneca identity; questions of place (geopolitics) morph into those of race (biopolitics), substituting the issue of Jemison's belonging for the pressure exerted on the Senecas by state-sanctioned speculation.

The text's transposition of Jemison for Morris, and the resulting shift in the stakes of the disagreement between Farmer's Brother and Red Jacket, appears even more overdetermined when one considers how the Big Tree council was resolved and that conclusion is placed in the broader context of Red Jacket's career. After rekindling the council fire, Morris talks with "the chief women" to secure their consent to the deal he has proposed, and they, along with the warriors, assent.[62] From one perspective, this meeting may seem like an end run around the sachems, appealing to other sectors of Seneca society in order to generate a groundswell of support for the agreement; however, the warriors and the women had their own councils that also played prominent roles in collective decision-making. Not only had the clan mothers been present at treaties and meetings with U.S. officials throughout the 1790s and the first decade of the nineteenth century, but when they communicated their opinions in council, they often did so through Red Jacket, whose prominence in Seneca political affairs in many ways was derived from his role as the speaker for the clan mothers.[63] At the council at Tioga Point (1790), the first one in which Red Jacket appears as a significant figure in the documentary record, there was a public disagreement about the place of women in negotiations, with the U.S. commissioner, Timothy Pickering, observing that bringing so many people to the council "is not the way of the nations of white men in America . . . , they hold their treaties by a deputation of only one or of a few of their chiefs," further suggesting "the advantage of committing the management of all treaties to a deputation of a few of your . . . men." Speaking through the chief Little Billy, however, the clan mothers responded that women "are the principal support of the nation," indicating that Pickering should "know that women attend treaties."[64] In addition to indicating Pickering's loss on this point, the continuing vocal presence of women in councils over at least the next decade highlights the centrality of the clans, and thus of matrilineal leadership and principles of kinship, to Seneca governance at all levels. Given Red Jacket's intimate first-hand awareness of these dynamics and his dependence for his own authority as a spokesperson on the clan mothers, the *Narrative*'s portrayal of him as blocking the land claims of an acknowledged member of the Turtle clan seems doubtful. Additionally, in light of the clan mothers' actions later in the Big Tree council, his earlier protest seems more tactical than anything else, taking up an extreme position in order to pull Morris toward an acceptable compromise.

The *Narrative* further dissociates Red Jacket from Seneca conceptions of kinship in its presentation of him as at odds with Parrish and Jones. As discussed earlier, they appear as more or less outsiders who, as whites themselves, speak for the interests of the white woman by endorsing the overriding power of white law. Although both of them eventually would come to serve as employees of the Ogden Land Company, they previously had been valued enough by the Senecas to be granted land in 1798, not simply for their service as interpreters but as fellow Haudenosaunees. In the council meeting where the land was awarded, Farmer's Brother observed that the "whirlwind" of the American Revolution "was so directed by the Great Spirit above, as to throw into our arms two of your infant children, Jasper Parrish and Horatio Jones. We adopted them into our families, and made them our children. We loved them and nourished them. They lived with us many years"; in an 1802 council, Red Jacket also described them as "our adopted children."[65] In the late 1810s and throughout the 1820s, Red Jacket fought to have both of them removed from government service for participating in efforts to acquire Seneca land and pressuring the Senecas to accept removal,[66] but this situation postdates the Treaty of Big Tree by three decades. Inserting the later conflict into the earlier period conflates two different moments in ways that implicitly explain Red Jacket's relation to Jones and Parrish as an inevitable function of their whiteness, while also subtly attributing their later actions to the same cause (not unlike the text's portrait of Ebenezer Allen's indiscretions). What is lost in this temporal collapse is precisely the willingness of the Senecas, including Red Jacket, to accept adopted whites as Seneca, a process controlled by women that further illustrates the role they play as keepers of the clans in shaping the contours of Seneca peoplehood in all its aspects.

The text's representation of Red Jacket draws on his image among the Euramerican reading public to position him as endorsing a racialized understanding of Seneca identity, one which mirrors that structuring the text's portrayal of Jemison's history and subjectivity, but his documented support for the clan system provides an alternative prism through which to view the apparent commitment to racial discourse in his speeches. When he speaks of Indian/white difference, he often talks about the discrepancies between Euramerican and native "customs," and this observation usually is situated in discussion of the precedence of native peoples on the territory that settlers now claim. That connection to the land is registered in particular principles of social organization and diplomacy, which themselves often are cast as an inheritance. For example, during a council in 1790, he asserts, "The old rules came from this Island: they were the rules of our forefathers—Other practices came from people of y[ou]r color." In 1791, he asks, "Now you begin to get acquainted with our way of doing business. But what shall we say? Shall the way of doing business all be on one side? in one way? And we not follow any of our ancient customs?"[67] In these moments, the focus is not on the immutability of blood but on the issue of whose "rules" or "way[s] of doing business" will predominate in U.S.-Haudenosaunee affairs. While clearly concerned with the question of who ultimately will control the space currently occupied by the Senecas, Red Jacket draws attention to the ways the problem of imperial intervention concentrates around process as much as possession. He emphasizes how the ability to set the terms and dynamics of dialogue is itself a key part of shaping the negotiation and, thus, its outcome. The "business" he refers to is, in part, the necessity of conducting the Condolence ceremony at the beginning of council meetings.[68] In addition to acknowledging the death of leaders since the last council, this ritual foregrounds kinship—the importance of relatives and the role of the clan mothers in raising up those who will replace the deceased—as a central aspect of Seneca governance. Within this frame, the invocation of Seneca "forefathers" signifies more than a Euramerican sense of inheritance, rather serving as a mnemonic for the Condolence ceremony and the clan system itself. Reciprocally, whiteness in his speeches takes on the character less of a biologically transmitted set of capacities or propensities than an ensemble of "customs" that literally leave no room for native principles and social formations; at one point, he refers to "the mighty torrent of the white population" that threatens to overwhelm the "red" population completely.[69]

Red Jacket's rhetoric can be read as disjointing the reproductive imaginary in which whiteness and Indianness refer primarily to physical types and for which the conjugal unit provides the context, instead seeking to correlate these identities to differences in "practices." Doing so highlights the ways the "Indian" subjectivity produced within U.S. official and popular discourses is not merely a given or a reflection of native self-understandings but involves a strategic disavowal of indigenous "way[s] of doing business." When considered in light of this expanded vision of Red Jacket and his role in Seneca political life, disavowed in the *Narrative*'s somewhat conspicuous citation of him, Mary Jemison's whiteness becomes more of an open question. From within the logic of U.S. racial ideology, she is born into an identity from which she never can be separated, and that genealogical tie embeds her within certain sociospatial formations (like the citizenship that seems to be more of a retrospective acknowledgment of belonging than an active endowment of political membership) and forever alienates her from others (living among the Senecas but never *being* Indian). In this vein, her whiteness is presumed to create a particular relation between her and the land on which she resides, presenting her occupancy as ownership of property in ways that seek to place her and it outside the field of Seneca governance. The need for an agreement to be signed with Seneca leaders in a council attended by a U.S. commissioner in order to sell the Gardeau lands, however, suggests an ambivalence and anxiety about her status, pointing to an alternative matrix of identification and Seneca self-understanding that haunts the text's representation of (the conditions of possibility for) her voice. To what extent does Jemison's participation in Seneca "customs" and "way[s] of doing business" make her no longer white? I mean this question in two senses: she is not part of the "torrent" to which Red Jacket refers, herself having important connections to Seneca "forefathers" (or rather foremothers); and the attempt to portray her placemaking and relations to others through racial discourse obscures more than it illuminates. How is an alternative sense of subjectivity and territoriality opened by bracketing the supposed self-evidence of her whiteness?

I have suggested that various aspects of the *Narrative* when examined further invaginate into effaced kinship contexts (alliance with the Delawares, Thomas's position as a leader, the untold story of Cornplanter's diplomacy, Red Jacket's role as speaker for Seneca women), but there are moments in the text that more directly point toward Jemison's embeddedness in a clan-based conception of Seneca sovereignty. Rereading the *Narrative* through the prism of the kinship contexts it marginalizes and effaces brings into relief otherwise incongruous moments that together suggest a kind of subjectivity for Jemison—namely, that of clan mother—bracketed in the text's emphasis both on her ascension to citizenship through whiteness and on interracial coupling. As noted earlier, when she receives "title" to the Gardeau tract, it remains "under the same restrictions and regulations that other Indian lands are subject to" (121). For the purposes of landholding, Jemison functions as an "Indian," but the term "title" suggests a kind of individual ownership found within U.S. property law, one that will be presented later in the text as recognized in Jemison's naturalization. Perhaps, then, her relation to the land could be described as "Indian" only in the sense that it was given to her by Indians. However, Jemison indicates after the purchase of almost all of the Gardeau Reservation, "Whenever the land which I have reserved, shall be sold, the income of it is to be equally divided amongst the members of the Seneca nation, without any reference to tribes or families" (156). Not only does this condition indicate an enduring connection to the Senecas that belies the separation from them suggested by her U.S. citizenship, but the mention of "tribes" and "families" implies that the distinction she is making is less concerned with white inheritance norms than Seneca ones. The point seems to be that the money from the sale will not belong to a clan (for which the term "tribe" often was used) or a matrilineage, suggesting that the operative frame here is the kinship system.[70]

If so, how can one explain the apparent singularity of her control over the Gardeau lands? Why are they persistently described as belonging to her? When sold, the Gardeau tract's principal residents were dozens of Jemison's children and grandchildren, which from one angle may look like an estate but from another is a traditional residency pattern for a matrilineage with Jemison as its head. In that position, she, like other clan mothers, would be recognized as having control over the area occupied by her lineage group.

This dynamic would help explain the assent of male Seneca leaders to the retention of the Gardeau territory as a reservation in 1797 and to its sale in 1823, acknowledging Jemison's existing claim to the land on the Genesee (due to her inhabitance after the Revolutionary War and her kin's prewar claims in the vicinity of Gardeau) and her right to relinquish it when she chooses.[71] While the endorsement of the transfer of her land to whites and out of Seneca control entirely clearly was influenced by the decades-long strategy of ceding Genesee territory in the hope of maintaining the integrity of the larger reservations, particularly Buffalo Creek, the chiefs' actions, which included Red Jacket, are consistent with a respect for the expressed wish of the leader of the kinship group to dispose of the vast majority of her lineage lands. Like the presence of women at treaty councils, often speaking through Red Jacket, Jemison's agreement can be seen as less that of an individual propertyholder than that of a Seneca leader with specific authority over her family's lands. When thought of in this way, Jemison's participation in the Treaty of Big Tree takes on a different cast. The text describes her as being "sent for" by Farmer's Brother, who allowed her to "describe the bounds of a piece that would suit" her (120). However, the presence and prominence of clan mothers at that council and others in the 1790s, as discussed earlier, raises questions about this image of male power and largesse. Was Jemison summoned to be endowed with a land grant as a favor to her brother and husband, or was she there as part of the women's council who, along with the warriors and sachems, were a necessary part of collective deliberations?

Continuing in this vein, is her son Thomas chosen by Seneca leaders to be one of them, or is he chosen by Jemison, exercising the right and responsibility of a clan mother in raising up chiefs? I have found one passing reference to Jemison's Seneca mother being the sister of Big Tree, who lived on the Genesee and was a leader of great importance in the late eighteenth century and in early negotiations with the United States.[72] Big Tree died in 1792, and the *Narrative* notes that Thomas became "a Chief when quite young" and that he "went 2 or 3 times to Philadelphia [the then U.S. capital] to assist in making treaties" (120). If Big Tree was Jemison's maternal uncle, making him part of the same clan and matrilineage as she, her relatives would have chosen his successor, and if Jemison was the oldest of the remaining women, that task largely would have fallen to her.[73] Is it merely coincidence that Thomas becomes part of Seneca governance right around the time of Big Tree's demise? Furthermore, documents generated during the struggle against the fraudulent treaty of 1838 indicate that James Shongo was a recognized chief; he was the son of Jemison's youngest daughter, Polly, and was reputed to be Jemison's favorite grandchild.[74] Was Shongo a chief through Jemison's lineage? Was he chosen by Jemison?

These questions remain only suggestive, pointing toward possibilities disavowed by the text's emphasis on interracial conjugality and the immutability of racial inheritance. They also gesture toward the politics of Seneca kinship displaced in the search for Jemison's "voice." The ideological matrix of Indian/white difference that the *Narrative* both reflects and extends leaves no room for a kinship imaginary in which clans transect the supposed divide between "family" and "nation." The text's condensations and displacements help produce a popular narrative that confirms official U.S. accounts of Seneca governance which seek to simplify it and facilitate the acquisition of native lands, but these moments scattered throughout the text also index the possibility of an alternate representation of Seneca peoplehood to the reproductive vision of Indianness dominant in the text. This presence within the text registers the possibility of a kind of Seneca self-representation, a mode of *speaking for* rooted in the kinship system, increasingly marginalized by U.S. policy, and the discontinuity of that presence within the text suggests both the role of the *Narrative* in helping consolidate an image of native peoples as collections of individual Indians and the unevenness of that process of hegemony-making. The ascendance in the early to mid-nineteenth century of an ideology of privatized intimacy organized around heterohomemaking intersects with "the Indian problem," providing a grammar of racial birth that aids in translating native polities into the terms of U.S. liberalism, particularly with respect to defining what constitutes identity, politics, and consent. These dialectically entwined discourses of sentimental family and settler state nationality achieve perhaps their most pointed articulation in Cooper's *Last of the Mohicans*.

BLOOD SENTIMENT

In Red Jacket's obituary in 1830 in the *Niles Weekly Register*, he is described as the "last of the Senecas."[75] This designation suggests that in a very short time Cooper's *Last of the Mohicans* had become not simply an immensely well-known text but had taken on incredible symbolic importance as a way of imagining the current state of native peoples. The novel was published in the same year as the supposed treaty with the Senecas that ceded parts of several of their reservations, discussed earlier, indicating that the text's proclamation of Indian disappearance less describes an accomplished fact (especially given that it is set in the 1750s) than functions as an ideological intervention within extant efforts to grapple with the persistence of native presence and the growing intractability of native peoples in response to U.S. jurisdictional strategies. Theorizing struggles for control over political institutions and policy agendas as well as the broader matrix of social authority in which such struggles take place, Antonio Gramsci has distinguished between what he calls a "war of maneuver" and a "war of position": the former "subsists so long as it is a question of winning positions which are not decisive"; the latter coalesces when "only the decisive positions are at stake," creating what amounts to a kind of "siege warfare" (239). The increasing opposition of native peoples in various regions to the piecemeal cession of lands through treaty-making created a political impasse for the United States, in that it could not satisfy the clamor of citizens and states to "extinguish" Indian "title" while simultaneously presenting Indian policy as predicated on native consent (as against imperial coercion). This clash of state projects—the tensions between extension of authority over Indian lands and the production of legitimacy for the federal government—led to, in Gramsci's terms, a "crisis of hegemony" in which "legal equilibrium is recognized to be impossible" (210, 257). The question of native land tenure was becoming "decisive," allowing for far less ideological maneuvering—in the sense of the Jeffersonian stratagem of the civilization program (teach them to farm and they will take up less space) or the adoption by native peoples of modes of governance modeled on the United States (as in the ratification of the Cherokee Constitution in 1827).[76]

In this vein, *The Last of the Mohicans* can be read as part of a process of hegemony-making, negotiating the incipient crisis in Indian affairs by providing a way of narrating the emergent war of position that recodes political conflict as less the result of imperial imposition than the natural laws of family formation.[77] As I have argued, Seaver's biography of Jemison repeatedly positions race as immutably inherited at birth, focusing on the *intimate event* of conjugal coupling. Jemison's uncontested whiteness insulates her from Indianness, and reciprocally, Seneca identity appears to inhere not in matrilineal clan membership but in the procreative transmission of blood. While phobically fixated on racial mixture, *The Last of the Mohicans* does not so much contest the representation of native peoples in the *Narrative* as extend it, drawing on a metaphorics of blood to abject not only intratribal kinship systems but the work of kinship in intertribal political economy. Discourses of sexuality provide a spatial as well as a racial grammar, presenting native geopolitics as less a complex system (or systems) with which the United States needs to engage than the expression of racially distinct forms of feeling which give rise to unwieldy and unworkable kinds of inhabitance. Tropes of sentimental domesticity enter Cooper's text as a vehicle for racializing native identity, depicting indigenous sociality as predicated on inherited kinds of familial affection that are antithetical to settler nationality. Indians are intelligible as such not so much due to their participation in indigenous polities as their individual racial propensities, their blood-based "gifts" leading them toward forms of association and occupancy for which there literally is no place in the new nation. In this way, the novel suggests how the growing prominence of the ideology of nuclear homemaking in the 1820s is animated by "the Indian problem."

The removal of native peoples from areas surrounded by white settlers is not a novel policy philosophy in the 1820s, but what is new is its intensity and the extent to which it achieves dominance over other formulations and formations as a framework for Indian affairs. In this vein, the movement from Jefferson to Cooper can be characterized less as that from Indian-mixture to Indian-hating than from a vision of the nation-state as a network of sympathetic identifications among (heads of) households to one that draws on the insulating sentiment of conjugal homemaking, positioning the nuclear family ideal as a vehicle through which to represent the determinate coherence of the nation.[78] Other scholars have demonstrated the shift over the course of the eighteenth and early nineteenth centuries from an understanding of the household as a juridical and productive unit to a space of companionate care for members of a "family," a term that itself once referred to everyone living in a single dwelling or estate and that increasingly came to mean people related by blood who, for that reason, maintained durable emotional ties.[79] This process had much to do with changing patterns of labor, greater mobility, and decreased possibilities for land inheritance, as I will discuss further in chapter 2. While colonists railed against British efforts to put a brake on their westward settlement, they still could look to the imperial government to secure the juridical and territorial coherence of the colonies themselves and of colonial landholding.[80] The link between property, autonomy, and civic engagement in Jefferson, drawing on Scottish Enlightenment models,[81] occurs in the context of still extant notions of patriarchal privilege and enmeshment within a network whose dimensions are secured by the empire, even as Jefferson champions resistance to that very control. In this frame, the question is, can Indians be trained to manage proper households, or be incorporated into them, as coparticipants within a political economy whose model is still largely the British Empire.[82] Whether due to racial tendencies or situational circumstances, native kinship systems are not understood as generating households that can enter into the matrix of landholding and trade that is civilized society, but the Indianness that one inherits easily can be rerouted into more productive forms of sociality.

In the wake of the Revolution, conjugal union comes to serve as a metonym for political union in what Elizabeth Dillon has described as "marital nationalism" (183), depicting governance as rooted in consent and natural bonds of affection,[83] but the idea of the single-family home, in its affective self-sufficiency and enclosure of a sphere of intimacy, also bore the burden of signifying the territorial integrity of the nation, as against its perforation by competing claims—particularly those by native peoples "within" the states and on the "frontier." As the image of homes linked by the similarity of their composition and states of feeling gradually replaces that of patriarchal empathy among heads of households who manage a complex collection of (nonrelated) residents, Indians appear less as potential coparticipants in interhousehold relations than as outsiders who cannot enter into the metonymic chain forged by the symmetry of shared blood affection within white homes.[84] Put another way, the icon of the nuclear family can provide a "naturally" insulated model that creates a sense of boundedness for the nation, transposing the geopolitical difficulty of defining state borders and jurisdiction into an affective imaginary in which the blood of race merges with the blood of familial relation and in which the crossing of the former marks an invasion into the controlled domain of the latter. Not only are native kinship systems not a proper form of (household) governance, but they illustrate the absence of (the capacity for) the kinds of feeling that provide the basis of affective nationality. Native spatiality is coded as an unnatural, or at least unnational, expression of wrong feeling, creating a de facto *location* for the state by casting Indianness as innate kinds of sentiment and association that cannot be sustained in/by the national family. In its twinning of race, place, feeling, and family, *The Last of the Mohicans* serves a vital ideological function in disavowing native kinship as a mode of sovereignty and discursively reconstituting it as the reproductive transmission of a racial essence.

The text's linkage of racial and spatial formations through conjugal coupling appears perhaps most dramatically in the story of Cora. While many have noted the novel's ambivalence toward her, the narrative of her birth, as told by Colonel Munro, establishes a firm correlation between territorial and blood boundaries.[85] After noting that he was denied permission to marry by the father of his beloved, the owner of a large estate in his native Scotland, Munro recounts the following:

> duty called me to the islands of the West Indies. There it was my lot to form a connexion with one who in time became my wife, and the mother of Cora . . . [who was] descended, remotely from that unfortunate class, who are so basely enslaved to administer to the wants of a luxurious people! Ay, sir, that is a curse entailed on Scotland, by her unnatural union with a foreign and trading people! (159)

After his wife's death, "enriched by the marriage," he returned to Scotland and wed his first love, who became the mother of his younger daughter, Alice. The crossing of racial lines is attributed here to Scottish participation in an imperial network whose "trading" imperatives have led it to venture into "foreign" spaces in ways that distend and jeopardize Scottish identity.

The figure of "union" forges a metonymic link between cross-racial matrimony and the political economy of British imperialism in which the one expresses the "unnatural" dynamics of the other. The danger of territorial overextension is conveyed through the image of inappropriate coupling, the bond of marriage serving as an overdetermined topos for jurisdictional integrity.

Race mixing here both indexes a larger threat to the geopolitical identity of the (Scottish) nation and is itself the substance of that threat, creating a relay between biological reproduction and the spatial coherence of peoplehood. This confession of Cora's mixed-race identity emerges in a conversation in which Duncan Heyward asks Munro for permission to marry Alice. The parallel between Munro's and Heyward's appeals to the fathers of their intendeds, and the far different response received by the latter, indicates a different set of possibilities for coupling, and thus also of incipient peoplehood, in the American colonies than in Scotland. Heyward also is of Scottish descent (151, 157), positioning his and Alice's relationship as a repetition-with-a-difference in the New World in what would become America—a familiar device in historical novels of the 1820s. The protonationalist nature of Alice and Duncan's romance is further suggested by its cross-sectional quality, Heyward having come "from one of the provinces far south" while Munro's stationing at Fort William Henry in New York presents Alice as a de facto northerner (38).[86]

The potential for Indian/white mixture represents not merely a crossing of the color line but an "unnatural" transection of the territorial identity of the United States, for which white couplehood serves as a symbolic stand-in. While the relation between race and territoriality is far less explicit in the novel's representation of native peoples than in the discussion of Cora's origins, the discourse of "blood" and "gifts" that it employs with respect to settler/indigenous difference transposes the relation between kinship, political collectivity, and land tenure into a question of relative conformity to a sentimental vision of domesticity that is itself aligned with reproductive whiteness. While first introduced by David Gamut, the missionary musician who accompanies Hawkeye and the others on their various travels, the idea of inheriting particular "gifts" due to one's racial identity is taken up by Hawkeye and used throughout the novel as a way of distinguishing between white and Indian moral and physical capacities (25). In explaining his facility as a marksmen, Hawkeye notes, "all the Bumppos could shoot; for I have a natural turn with a rifle, which must have been handed down from generation to generation, as our holy commandments tell us, all good and evil gifts and bestowed" (31). What begins as a discussion of the relation between genealogy and personal abilities/ tendencies, though, quickly moves into a vision of the differences among the races; as he remarks to

Chingachgook, "you are a just man for an Indian! and as I suppose you hold their gifts, your fathers must have been brave warriors, and wise men at the council fire" (33). All Indians share similar "gifts" which are transmitted from their "fathers," suggesting that Indianness as a set of qualities, beliefs, or practices is a function of procreative transmission across generations— "bestowed" via bloodlines. Here we see an earlier version of what would become commonplace in early-twentieth-century official employments of Indian racial difference, in which social dispositions and dynamics associated with tribalism were understood as directly proportional to relative quanta of Indian "blood" (although in that case, positing a greater potential for less blooded natives to assimilate rather than arguing for the necessity of total removal).[87] Later, contemplating Chingachgook's murder of a French soldier standing guard on their approach to Fort William Henry, Hawkeye explains, " 'Twould have been a cruel and unhuman act for a white-skin; but 'tis the gift and natur of an Indian" (138), suggesting that what might be "unnatural" for whites is moral for Indians due to the discrepancies between them in their inherent "natur." Hawkeye's repeated expression of this theory of "gifts" usually is accompanied by a declaration that he has "no cross in his blood" (35), indicating that while he may seem to be like the Indians in living among them there remains an impassable boundary between them.

The novel insistently reiterates this sense of "blood" belonging, which would be disastrously confounded by race mixture, but its plot largely is driven by the threat of such crossing, namely, Magua's (the renegade Wyandot's) plan to make Cora his wife as payback for her father's whipping of him due to his drunkenness when in the employ of the British army. During their flight through the woods from Magua on their way to Fort William Henry to reunite with Colonel Munro, Duncan responds to Cora's claim "that the worst to us can be but death" that "There are evils worse than death" (80), a portentous statement whose threat is clarified shortly in Magua's declaration that he plans to take Cora to "live in his wigwam forever" as a replacement for the wife who "was given to another chief" when he was driven out by his people for being a drunkard (104). This fate, Cora declares to Alice, is "worse than a thousand deaths" (109). While Cora herself is mixed-blood, the potential for her (coercive) union with Magua remains deeply troubling to all of the novel's white protagonists. Such fear, if not terror, is perfectly understandable given the threat of rape and subjection to hostile, enemy forces, but the anxiety seems to extend beyond the use of force against Cora by Magua and those with him, encompassing a broader unease that pivots around dangers to "blood" purity. In conducting the funeral rites for Cora and Chingachgook's son Uncas (the eponymous last of the Mohicans), both of whom are murdered during the final pursuit of Magua (who himself is shot by Hawkeye), a group of Delaware women "alluded . . . to the stranger maiden, who had left the upper earth at a time so near [Uncas's] own departure, as to render the will of the Great Spirit too manifest to be disregarded" (342). Understanding their songs, and the implication of a union for the two in heaven, Hawkeye refuses to translate these sentiments for his white companions: "when they spoke of the future prospects of Cora and Uncas, he shook his head, like one who knew the error of their simple creed" (344). Such a romantic pairing is intimated early in the novel in its depiction of "Uncas act[ing] as attendant to the females, performing all the little offices within his power, with a mixture of dignity and anxious grace, that served to amuse Heyward, who well knew that it was an utter innovation on the Indian customs, which forbid their warriors to descend to any menial employment, especially in favour of their women" (56). Without providing any explanation, the novel leaves the reader to guess at the feelings that generate such uncharacteristic behavior.[88] Despite Uncas's gallantry, he too is cast as an unsuitable suitor for Cora, even in the hereafter. Marriage to an Indian who seems to act in ways against Indian nature, contrary to the promptings of blood, still is too much of a "cross" for Hawkeye's, and by implication the novel's, comfort.

Prior to the revelation of the fact that Cora is of African descent through her mother, readers perhaps are led to view her becoming Magua's "wife" as a violation of the purity of whiteness, but in the wake of Munro's admission to Heyward, the novel's continued horror at the prospect of that union remains haunted by the anxiety of mixture, as suggested in Uncas's funeral. If Cora already represents the melding of white and nonwhite "blood," why does her union with an Indian (whether Magua or Uncas) produce such dismay? The issue must be less preserving the unsullied integrity of whiteness than the threat posed by a crossing with Indianness. As suggested earlier, Uncas's "delicacy," also characterized as his "sympathy" for Cora and Alice, is presented as at odds with the usual disregard for women supposedly shown by native warriors (115). This kind of affect appears to mark a significant difference between Indian and white masculinities, further indicated by Magua's willingness to wed Cora exclusively to satisfy "revenge" against her father (313). In the novel's terms, native men lack the sentimental orientation that would lead them to treat their wives, and women more broadly, with greater respect and tenderness, recycling the image of the "squaw drudge" that littered settler accounts of native homemaking from at least the seventeenth century onward (including the epigraph from Jefferson with which this chapter began).[89] Uncas is the exception that proves the rule, itself illustrated in the extreme by Magua, and in the context of the growing prominence in the 1820s of the nuclear family model—of residency organized around couple-centered, privatized intimacy—the routine absence of such feeling indicates a fundamental disjunction between white and Indian modes of family and household formation. Since within the novel's imaginary such dispositions are passed in the blood, the possibility of marital union with an Indian man implies not only the potential ill-treatment of a non-native spouse but the loss of civilized domesticity to future generations.

This potential expansion of Indian modes of sociality at the expense of the "delicacy" and "sympathy" of non-native romance looms even larger in the novel in light of Indians' failure to recognize this frontier of feeling, their seeming inability to see the importance of maintaining the boundaries of racial bloodlines in order to preserve the "gifts" associated with sentimental domesticity.[90] As discussed previously, the Delaware women performing the mourning ritual for Uncas and Cora presume the obviousness of their union in heaven, suggesting less a distinction between what is proper to this life and to the next than the ways the latter can make possible what should have occurred in this world. While Hawkeye characterizes this lack of concern for blending of different types of "blood" as a "simple creed," the narrator also notes that the nontranslation of the women's songs preserves "the self-command of both Heyward and Munro" (344), suggesting their likely outrage not at just the prospect of an Indian wedding for Cora but at the unself-conscious ease with which the Delawares could envision such a bond. This tendency toward merger, or at least the absence of resistance to it, is presented as having significant spatial implications in the lament by Tamenund, the positively ancient sachem who leads the Delaware band(s) in the novel. Decrying expropriation of native land by settlers, he declares, "I know that the pale-faces are a proud and hungry race. I know that they claim, not only to have the earth, but that the meanest of their colour is better than the Sachems of the red man. The dogs and crows of their tribes . . . would bark and caw, before they would take a woman to their wigwams, whose blood was not of the colour of snow" (305).[91] The passage links white supremacy to the violence of expansionism, indicting settlers for justifying their consumption of territory through appeal to racial superiority but also mirroring the text's consistent positioning of conjugality as a metonym for the coherence of national geography—in many ways serving a similar function as Red Jacket in the *Narrative* by challenging white encroachment while confirming the text's ways of representing settlement and native identity. Tamenund's formulation, conversely, presents the survival of native peoples in light of the presence of whites as dependent on miscegenation; the persistence of native territoriality seems implicitly correlated with the incorporation of foreigners through intermarriage. This version of the relation between native kinship and landholding seems to position reproductive coupling—"pale-faces" "tak[ing] a woman to their wigwams"—as the primary means for non-natives to recognize native occupancy and collectivity.

The novel seems to suggest that while whites seek to preserve the whole-ness of their "blood"-lines, Indians actually desire mixture, which paradox-ically appears as a kind of racial trait, and these different attitudes toward racial blending are cast not merely as incommensurate but as threatening the integrity of national domesticity—in both its senses and in the mutually reinforcing relation between them. In light of the concerns expressed throughout the novel about the deformation of patterns of heterohomemak-ing that would result from exposure to Indian "blood," the loss of the dis-tinctness of the "gifts" of civilization, the apparent native yearning for union with non-natives, including Tamenund's presentation of color-crossing intermarriage as a condition of indigenous continuance, threatens the boundaries of (proto)national identity. Recalling the explanation of Cora's origins discussed earlier, the prospect of widespread racial amalgamation with Indians appears as an even more menacing example of "unnatural union with a foreign . . . people." This anxiety is heightened by the fact that very soon after delivering the preceding speech, itself a response to Cora's attempts to appeal to the sachem's familial feelings to convince him to return her to Munro ("is Tamenund a father?"), Tamenund assents to Magua's assertion of a right to claim Cora as his own, adding, "A great warrior takes thee to wife. Go—thy race will not end" (313). The scene also evidences the novel's displacement of native kinship systems, given that, as Barbara Alice Mann notes, the proper persons to be consulted about Cora's status are the women, since they would have been in control of what happened to captives among both the Delawares and the Wyandots (86).[92]

Within the novel's logic, in which the boundedness of domestic space is both reflected and made possible by proper homemaking organized around companionate affect and sentimental ties (as opposed to household produc-tion), native equanimity to miscegenation represents a kind of boundary-lessness, which cannot be accommodated in/ by the nascent (white) nation. This perspective is expressed most forcefully by Gamut when he declares that he will aid in the effort to recapture Cora from Magua: "your men have reminded me of the children of Jacob going out to battle against the Schech-mites, for wickedly aspiring to wedlock with a woman of a race that was favoured of the Lord" (327). While the novel most often portrays Gamut as ridiculous, wholly unsuited to just about any useful endeavor, his comments and actions tend to be offered as a caricatured version of "civilized" society, preserving the spirit if in an exaggerated form that suggests the need for greater moderation in practice. His account of the settlers as Israel, the chosen people needing to rescue one of their own from the enemies that surround them, conveys in extreme form the ideological structure of the novel, fusing the potential for invasion to the crossing of the boundaries of "race" via inappropriate kinds of "wedlock."

"STOCK" MAPPINGS

In ways both subtle and direct, echoed by various characters in different registers, the text presents geopolitical struggle in racial terms, which are themselves conceptualized through heterocoupling.[93] Assertions of control over territory, as well as differences in ways of conceptualizing territoriality, appear as competing blood tendencies. As in my reading of Jemison's narrative, what is at issue is less whether or not the text denigrates Indians as a race than the stakes of racializing native peoples as Indians. How does framing political contestation as a function of race shape the possibilities for recognizing alternative forms of governance and for envisioning the dynamics of U.S.-native affairs? If, as I have suggested, the logic of race articulated in both *A Narrative of the Life of Mrs. Mary Jemison* and *The Last of the Mohicans* is organized around reproductive couplehood, the emergent nuclear family ideal becomes the basis for comparing settler and native modes of sociality, understanding discrepancies among them as kinds of feeling that are traceable to the conjugally centered transmission of "blood."

In fact, Cooper's text at several points uses the term "treaty" to refer to pointless negotiations that can do nothing in the face of inborn predispositions. When discussing the onetime alliance between Delawares and Mohawks, Hawkeye observes, "Such a treaty was made in ages gone by, through the deviltries of the Dutchers, who wished to disarm the natives that had the best right to the country, where they had settled themselves," adding that "the Mohicans . . . never entered into the silly bargain, but kept to their manhood" (127). Later, when Munro surrenders Fort William Henry to the French, he is described as "having signed a treaty, by which the place was to be yielded to the enemy" in a peaceful cession (166), which soon becomes a massacre by the Indian allies of the French; when an Oneida warrior is discovered as Hawkeye and the others flee from the scene of the massacre in pursuit of Cora and Alice, taken by Magua, Heyward indicates that killing the Oneida "would have been an abuse of our treaties, and unworthy of your character," to which Hawkeye responds with a diatribe on Iroquoian duplicity, insisting, "a red natur is not likely to alter with every shift of policy" (196–197). These moments suggest that formal political engagement is nothing but a cheap tactic designed to manage temporarily the raging racial drives (in "blood" as well as lusting for it) that animate Indian action, one which inevitably will fail and which indicates more about white manipulation than the possibility for actual diplomatic reciprocity and geopolitical conciliation. The reproductive logic of racial identifications and predilections transmitted through conjugal union makes treaty-making into a pointless effort to use "policy" to alter "red natur," and such effort, according to the novel, further indicates a fundamental misunderstanding of Indian "manhood."

In reducing settler-indigenous political negotiation to an incommensurable clash of inherited "gifts," the novel recasts relations among native peoples as a function of promptings in the blood, radically simplifying the shifting geographies and alliances at play in the mid-eighteenth century into a static binary. Rehearsing the terms of John Heckewelder's *History, Manners, and Customs of the Indian Nations* (1818),[94] the account of a Moravian missionary who had lived among native converts for decades, Cooper suggests that there were two *stocks* that inhabited the territory that would become New England and the middle states: the Lenape, in which he includes the Delawares and the Mohicans; and the Mengwe, a term that is presented as synonymous with Maguas, Mingoes, and Iroquois (2–3). As is made more explicit in Heckewelder, all peoples speaking Algonquian languages are seen as belonging to a single group, as are all peoples speaking Iroquoian languages, whether Haudenosaunee or not (23–43, 83–99). This equation of language families with lineage leads to the conflation of separate peoples with each other (combining the Mahicans and the Mohegans in ways I will discuss further), creating the impression of shared interests and organization across widely dispersed and self-consciously distinct polities. It further presents warfare, diplomacy, land tenure, and the distribution of resources among native peoples as a function of reproductive genealogy, seeing these two *stocks* as de facto families in which enmity has been passed down as a kind of ingrained instinct.

If Heckewelder's narrative tends toward such a portrait of intertribal relationships, *The Last of the Mohicans* makes that vision explicit, using it to suggest the perverse effects of white intervention in native affairs while simultaneously presenting native geopolitical formations as a *nature* transmitted through blood like Indianness itself. About halfway through the novel, Hawkeye offers an extended discussion of the military alignments at that point in the Seven Years' War, providing the text's most condensed commentary on the political cartography in which the characters move. The centrality of this statement to the text's mappings makes it worth quoting at length:

It is true, that white cunning has managed to throw the tribes into great confusion, as respects friends and enemies; so that the Hurons and the Oneidas, who speak the same tongue, or what may be called the same, take each other's scalps, and the Delawares are divided among themselves; a few hanging about their great council fire, on their own river, and fighting on the same side with the Mingoes, while the greater part are in the Canadas, out of natural enmity to the Maguas—thus throwing every thing into disorder, and destroying all the harmony of warfare. Yet a red natur is not likely to alter with every shift of policy! so that the love atwixt a Mohican and a Mingo is much like the regard between a white man and a sarpent. (196–197)

The narrator soon adds:

The confusion of nations, and even of tribes, to which Hawk-eye alluded, existed at that period in the fullest force. The great tie of language, and, of course, of a common origin, was severed in many places; and it was one of its consequences that the Delaware and the Mingo, (as the people of the Six Nations were called,) were found fighting in the same ranks, while the latter sought the scalp of the Huron, though believed to be the root of his own stock. (197)

The war seems to have produced a hurly-burly muddle of associations and alliances in which those who seem most intimately related appear on opposite sides of the fighting. This effect, however, has more to with "white cunning" than with native peoples' shifting strategies and tactical assessments of their position within complex and malleable political topographies. The "enmity" between Alongonquian and Iroquoian populations is "natural," envisioned almost as a kind of species difference ("between a white man and a sarpent"), and the "disorder" exemplified by the crossing of these "stock[s]" is a freak occurrence that utterly defies the lineal logic of filiation to "common origin[s]." The contrast between "policy" and "red natur" lies at the heart of the novel's evaluation of native politics, the maneuverings of Europeans disrupting the proper patterns of "love"—of instinctual bonds and collective modes of feeling—that shape Indian sociality.

While the shifting alignments of native peoples on territory claimed by New York and Pennsylvania and in the Ohio region over the course of the 1750s and 1760s are far too complicated to detail here, a brief sketch of some aspects of these configurations can help highlight the kinds of relationships and identifications foreclosed by Cooper's narration, particularly those structured through extended kinship networks.[95] The novel presents "Mingo" as a synonym for "Iroquois," conflating those Haudenosaunees who had moved to the Ohio region in the early to mid-eighteenth century with the members of the Six Nations remaining in the east. While these groups were related, they operated somewhat independently, or more precisely, those labeled "Mingoes" were primarily Senecas, many of whom descended from populations who had been adopted in the wake of Haudenosaunee wars in the late seventeenth century (including numerous Wyandots, otherwise known as "Hurons"). Their relation to Seneca councils in the east and the decision-making of the Iroquois League was fraught, and they remained tied to other Senecas largely through clan connections rather than substantive political oversight by the former. Moreover, the presence of these relatives in the Ohio region, their kinship relations with peoples there and to the north and west, and their growing diplomatic and trade relations with the French helped redirect eastern Seneca sentiments and strategy away from alignment with the British. This increasing western political orientation of eastern Senecas brought them into conflict with the Mohawks remaining in New York, the most eastern of the Haudenosaunee peoples and the ones most enmeshed in British political and economic networks. The question of how to negotiate European spheres of influence in order to secure greater autonomy from them split the Iroquois Confederacy, the Oneidas and Onondagas largely, if rather ambivalently, siding with the Mohawks. Such tensions are registered in the conflict in the novel between Magua's prior allegiance to the Mohawks, who had adopted him in the wake of his exile from the Wyandots, and his renewed connection to the Wyandots in the wake of General Munro's disciplining of him. Yet the text portrays such evidence of these discrepant military affiliations as proof of the derangements of sentiment produced by white intervention, rather than as the result of a multivectored geopolitical calculus in which kinship plays a prominent role. When the novel makes statements like "Mohawks and Oneidas" "may pretend to serve the king," but "in nature they belong, among the French" (50), it does not simply offer a skewed history but rather installs a dehistoricizing vision of native diplomacy and intertribal relations in which native politics is reduced to a function of *natural* impulses that are themselves imagined as lineally passed through the reproductive transmission of blood.

As noted previously, this lumping of Iroquoian peoples works in the service of creating the impression of a clear distinction between them and the "Delawares," or Algonquian peoples, but that differentiation obscures the shifting association between various Delaware groups and members of the Iroquois League, Delaware groups' changing relations to each other, and the character of the multilayered linkages between various Delaware populations and other Algonquian peoples—particularly the Mahicans. At one point, Hawkeye declares, "it is not to be denied, that the evil has been mainly done by men with white skins. But it has ended in turning the tomahawk of brother against brother, and brought the Mingo and the Delaware to travel in the same path" (227). Here the novel reaffirms the familial imaginary in which "Delawares" are envisioned as properly bound to each other, as against association with "Mingoes" who are cast as belonging to a different "path" but for the "evil" done by whites. In this framework, the blood logic of the nuclear family, and the quasi-racial differentiation of native *stocks*, provides a de facto explanation for native action in ways that utterly efface indigenous geopolitics, which responded to white presence without simply being determined by it. The term "Delaware" emerged over the eighteenth century as a way of referring to a collection of peoples inhabiting an area roughly bordered by the Atlantic, the lower Hudson, and the Susquehanna. They did not function as a single polity nor necessarily understand themselves as possessing what may be described as a shared ethnicity, even though members of each group likely had relatives living among nearby groups and land tenure often involved overlapping spheres of use. As a result of various displacements by English settlers over the course of the late seventeenth century and early eighteenth century, these groups came to be concentrated in the vicinity of the Delaware, Schuylkill, and Susquehanna rivers in ways that facilitated the emergence of a new kind of collective identity, one whose creation was aided by the efforts of the colony of Pennsylvania to consolidate native forms of geopolitical authority so as to facilitate negotiations for land rights. Those groups who had been pushed up the Schuylkill and onto the Susquehanna over the first decades of the eighteenth century began moving into the Ohio River region, and those who had been displaced from northern New Jersey and the Forks of the Delaware, the latter as a result of the infamous Walking Purchase of 1737, largely moved up the Susquehanna, many taking up residence in the town of Wyoming where a number of Mahicans had been living in Moravian communities. Yet these two clusters of Delawares were not utterly distinct; bonds of kinship, and mutual belonging to three central clans (Turtle, Turkey, and Wolf), created extended relationships among these geographically dispersed populations. Moreover, both sets of Delawares had longstanding and shifting relations with the Iroquois League. Many of the Delawares to the west lived among or in close proximity to Seneca bands, whose own position with respect to the League council was vexed,[96] and the Delawares and Mahicans living at Wyoming, on the northern Susquehanna, largely had gone there at the request, or perhaps demand, of the League.

Cooper, however, does allude to the complex kinship dynamics just sketched, even as they are distorted in their projection through the prism of a conception of family modeled on bourgeois homemaking. Hawkeye says of Chingachgook, "The Sagamore is of the high blood of the Delawares, and is the great chief of their Tortoises!" (226–227), pointing to the role of clans in Delaware sociopolitical formations while simultaneously effacing the distinction between the "Mohicans" (Mohegans/Mahicans) and the Delawares.[97] Similarly, both Chingachgook and Uncas declare at different points that their "tribe" or "race" "is the grandfather of nations" (33, 309), alluding to the fact that other Algonquian peoples referred to the Delawares as grandfathers—a designation that increasingly becomes a prominent feature of Delaware self-representation in official English accounts in the mid-eighteenth century.[98] Notably, the novel does not note that Delawares and

Mahicans referred to the Six Nations as their "uncles," and the latter spoke of the former as their "nephews," indicating the importance of kinship as an encompassing political imaginary across the *natural* division between *stocks* at the center of the text's history.[99]

Further, the fact that the text consistently presents the Mohicans as if they were Delawares recasts "grandfather" less as a marker of a relationship among peoples structured through discourses and conceptions of kinship than a metaphorization of reproductive lineage. If the "Mohicans" occupy the status of "grandfather," the representation of Uncas remakes the term as one of diachronic inheritance rather than synchronic alliance. Not only is Uncas the "last" of this line, but Tamenund mistakes him for the long-dead leader of the same name: "[I]s Uncas before him, . . . the eldest son of the Lenape, the wisest Sagamore of the Mohicans! Tell me, ye Delawares, has Tamenund been a sleeper for a hundred winters" (310)? Uncas seems to appear out of the past, and the "Mohicans" clearly have no future in light of his singularity as the sole remaining one and his death. In this way, "grandfather" marks less a way of envisioning a geopolitics among peoples than a kind of generational succession. This elevation of lineage over alliance is reinforced by the fusion of Mahican and Mohegan. The historical Uncas to whom Tamenund refers was Mohegan, and in conflating Mohegans and Mahicans as "Mohicans," Cooper draws on the narrative of Mohegan disappearance over the course of the eighteenth century constantly propounded by the colony, and then state, of Connecticut as a justification for dispossessing living people, who also were presented as having lost their authentic status as natives through racial mixture—largely with people of African descent.[100]

The doubling of the name Uncas positions the character as, to use the term that circulated in both official and popular discourses, a "remnant" of the past rather than a figure of sustained intertribal solidarity organized through a kinship imaginary. A similar effect is generated by the substitution of Tamenund for Teedyeschung. Given the location of the fighting in the novel, the most likely candidate for a Delaware village of significant size would be Wyoming, and the recognized leader there was Teedyeschung, who did not hold a hereditary position as the head of a clan but did function as the primary spokesperson for eastern Delawares in negotiations with Pennsylvania, New York, the Iroquois League, western Delawares, and other native peoples on land claimed by Pennsylvania and in the Ohio region during and in the wake of the Seven Years' War.[101] Heckewelder's account includes a chapter comparing the two leaders (300–305), but Cooper edits out Teedyeschung entirely, instead putting the deceased Tamenund (who had become a crucial figure in colonists' and early nationals' attempts to "play Indian") at the center of his account.[102] In fact, the period covered by the novel coincides with a treaty meeting at Easton in Pennsylvania, in which Teedyeschung raised the issue of lands lost as a result of the Walking Purchase, so the figure of Tamenund not only casts Delawares as a kind of anachronistic residue but effaces the complex negotiations over land tenure among native peoples and with settlers at the center of which Teedyeshung pivoted.

Even as it seems invested with the sense of heredity, the concept of "grandfather" in the novel is not literal, instead serving as a metaphor for genealogical transmission. While Tamenund describes Uncas as an ancestor, the narrator notes that he "separated [from Uncas] with the reluctance that a parent would quit a long lost, and just recovered, child" (321), and when Cora asks Tamenund if he is "a father," he replies, "Of a nation" (305). These moments seem to gesture toward an expanded or alternative framework in which kinship terms and relations mean something different than their apparent biological referents within Anglo-American conventions. The novel, however, also consistently undercuts the possibility of representing Iroquoian and Algonquian sociality by fusing native peoples together and then dividing them along a single binary to which they belong by genealogically inherited "natur," the dynamics of which resembles that of Indian/white difference and the terror of "unnatural" marital crossings that difference engenders. Thus, the appearance of these familial terms—"father," "son," "grandfather"—suggests less a kind of social formation that differs from that of Cooper's white readers than a native deformation of the latter. Like the supposed desire of Indians for marriage to whites (or at least the lack of horror at race mixing) discussed earlier, the seemingly merely figural use of these designations indicates a native failure truly to understand the proper dynamics and boundaries of home and family, a confusion that also threatens to infect the white nation.

HOMO-SYMPATHY IN THE RUINS OF KINSHIP

The novel depicts recognition of the impossibility of a substantive rapprochement between settler and native kinds of occupancy (especially given the boundary-crossing desires of Indians for mixture) as an acceptance of Indian character, portraying authentic knowledge of native identity as an understanding of the impassable difference between types of blood-borne sentiment. In this way, the political impasse of native resistance to removal in the 1820s is transmuted into the innate dynamics of Indian/white interaction. Using reproductive coupling as a metonym for collective identity casts elements of that identity as an unchangeable function of "nature," narrating the failure of the United States to recognize native sociopolitical formations (including the role of kinship networks as a form of governance) into a practical acknowledgment of the incommensurability of racially inflected dispositions. Within this framework, the only appropriate and humane response to such irresolvable disjunction is sympathy for those whose presence has no place in geographies of settlement. Hawkeye's feelings for Chingachgook, Uncas, and the Delawares illustrate the proper pathos with which the displacement of native peoples should be approached, mourning the ways the unbridgeable gap between Indian and white "gifts" makes inevitable the former's removal.

Through Hawkeye, the novel generates a kind of subjectivity that works to resolve the war of position in U.S. Indian policy. Hawkeye's compassion for the plight of native peoples seems to suggest a critique of the displacements produced by Euro-American settlement, but as a structure of feeling it draws on the dynamics of the emergent formation of the intimate private sphere. Modifying earlier discourses of Indian birth, such as in Jeffersonian notions of civilization-through-amalgamation, the novel's representation of Hawkeye's sympathy depends on sentimental domesticity not only for the form it takes (images of couple-centered homemaking) but for its structuring disavowal of native kinship systems. More than underlining the dangers of miscegenation, Hawkeye's repeated insistence that he has "no cross in his blood" and is "a white man with no taint of Indian blood" indicates that he cannot possibly *be* Indian (35, 121). Much like the *Narrative*'s depiction of Jemison's identity, this stark distinction between white and Indian as kinds of birth inheritance militates against considering adoption as a means of *becoming* native. Abjecting this possibility discursively works to install Indian "blood" as the foundation for native collectivity in ways that efface indigenous modes of governance and geopolitics, and doing so helps provide a "solution" for the political impasses surrounding removal. If Jemison's whiteness means that she is always-already a citizen-in-potentia and that she and her land can be understood as not truly Seneca, Hawkeye's whiteness makes him a vehicle for white readers, creating possibilities for audience identification with Hawkeye and with Chingachgook and Uncas but in ways that bracket native modes of collectivity, reaffirm the coherence of national boundaries, and render problematic "older forms" of Indian policy—like treaty-making.

I am suggesting less that this sentimental structure of feeling directly replaces the negotiation of treaties, or that Cooper's novel becomes the basis for policy-making in a direct way, than that the text's account of Indianness and ethical white relation to it index and extend a process of hegemony-making through which Indian removal can be legitimized despite the absence of substantive native consent. Transposing the dynamics of native governance and land tenure into discourses of sexuality, coalesced around conjugal couplehood, allows for native peoples to be envisioned less as polities than populations. This conversion of geopolitics into biopolitics through the metaphorics of racial inheritance facilitates the increasing casualization of treaty-making, including for removal, such as the representation of these agreements as more or less "contract[s] entered into by individuals who are parties"—as the Senate described the 1826 "treaty" with the Senecas. The discursive and ideological formation that constitutes Hawkeye's sympathy does not eliminate the legal problem of securing some version of native consent, but it radically diminishes the possibilities for what will be recognized as politics and filters native dissent to displacement through the prism of the impossibility of Indians joining the national family.

The novel's articulation of settler sympathy helps constitute, in Peter Coviello's terms, an "affect-nation" through the racial and spatial grammar of an emergent intimate domesticity. While extending across the boundaries of whiteness, Hawkeye's feelings depend on reifying racial identity, understanding whiteness and Indianness as reproductive categories—in which nativeness inheres in, and is transmitted through, heterocoupling. After rescuing Alice from captivity among Magua's Hurons, Hawkeye still needs to reclaim Uncas from their grasp, and in describing the nature of this relationship, the narrator describes Uncas as "the child of his adoption." In his own effort at explanation, Hawkeye observes to Heyward, "I have heard . . . that there is a feeling in youth which binds man to woman, closer than father is tied to the son. It may be so. I have seldom been where women of my colour dwell; but such may be the gifts of natur in the settlements!" He adds, "so long as I could hear the crack of his piece in one ear, and that of the Sagamore in the other, I knew no enemy was on my back. Winters and summers, nights and days, have we roved the wilderness in company, eating of the same dish, one sleeping while the other watched" (265). This moment establishes the intensity of Hawkeye's affections for Uncas, as his "child," and for Chingachgook as well ("the Sagamore" whose gun "crack" is as familiar and comforting as Uncas's). Notably, the comparative frame for the discussion of this intimacy is the "feeling" "which binds man to woman," positioning his relation to Uncas and Chingachgook as standing in the place of what he might have had had he "been where women of my colour dwell." In Hawkeye's description, the three of them function as a distinct unit, bound together by deep emotional ties that come from their shared residency ("company, eating of the same dish"), which both directs the force of their feelings toward each other and is itself expressive of their affective connection.[103] My point is less that there is necessarily a homoerotic undercurrent than that Hawkeye uses the nuclear family model as a vehicle for conveying the relation among them. Put another way, the intimation that Hawkeye and Chingachgook's relationship is homoerotic arises out of the fact that romantic couplehood is the paradigmatic structure through which intimacy signifies here.[104]

How else might one represent a powerful emotional attachment among adult men? Ivy Schweitzer has argued that "the claims of masculine interracial friendship that motivate Hawkeye combine elements of erotic, romantic, and paternal love"; she further suggests that "critical myopia with respect to friendship themes suggests the powerful totalizing effect of heteronormativity" (143). In this formulation, "friendship" provides an alternative to couplehood. Yet rather than suspending or displacing the novel's account of reproductive racial difference, the discourse of friendship reaffirms the logic of racial bloodlines, disowning possibilities for affiliation that would undermine the novel's privileging of conjugality. To put the matter more directly, why not make Hawkeye Mohican in the same way that Jemison is Seneca, through adoption into the kinship network?[105] The novel seems to hint at this possibility in the fact that Hawkeye at one point refers to Chingachgook as "my brother," and Uncas describes Hawkeye as "his father's brother" (77, 273). Both Mohegans and Mahicans (the two peoples fused together in the novel's "Mohicans") would not have distinguished among the children of same-sex siblings (the son of my same-sex sibling is my son, rather than my nephew), so adoption of Hawkeye actually would make Uncas his son, creating a certain indeterminacy in the phrase "the child of my adoption" (Uncas adopted by Hawkeye, in the model of the nuclear family, or Hawkeye adopted into Chingachgook's lineage group).

Yet while obliquely alluding to this potential, the text forecloses it. Positioning "brother"-hood as a metaphor for friendship among nonrelated persons, it displaces the possibility of literally being made brothers through adoption, assuming that kinship must follow the heteroreproductive lines of "blood" transmission. The text presents Hawkeye's affection as significant precisely because it traverses the otherwise impassable border of white/Indian distinction. When Hawkeye tries to volunteer to be taken by Magua in Cora's place, he says to Uncas, "you have found friends among your natural kin [referring to the Delawares]," adding, "I loved both you and your father, Uncas, though our skins are not altogether of a colour, and our gifts are somewhat different. Tell the Sagamore I never lost sight of him in my greatest trouble" (315). What makes his "love" important is that it is not that of "kin"-ship, which is guided by the dictates of *nature* (including the allocation of racially specific "gifts"), but instead transects the seeming impassable lines of "colour." In this way, the novel's account of masculine "interracial friendship" does not so much offer an alternative to racializing heteronormativity as provide a key supplement to it, continuing to displace native systems of kinship and governance while mediating the violence of that erasure through a modified version of the sentimental structure of feeling.

If Hawkeye (a man "without a cross") can cathect in this way, extending sentimental affect across the boundaries of blood difference, other whites can develop a sympathetic relation to Indian suffering and displacement, which is not so much avoidable as regrettable. The most compelling example of this possibility for cross-racial identification occurs at the very end of the novel, after Uncas's death when the other whites have left and Hawkeye remains to try to comfort Chingachgook: "Deserted by all of his colour, Hawk-eye returned to the spot where his own sympathies led him, with a force that no ideal bond of union could bestow" (348). Even as the "sympathies" at play here are cast as exceeding those of the "ideal bond of union," marriage continues to provide the reference point for understanding the meaning of intense feeling among nonrelated persons. The fact that their relationship is not that of kinship is underlined in the dialogue that follows. Chingachgook declares, "My race has gone from the shores of the salt lake, and the hills of the Delawares . . . I am alone," to which Hawkeye immediately responds, "The gifts of our colours may be different, but God has so placed us as to journey in the same path. I have no kin, and I may also say, like you, no people. He was your son, and a red-skin by nature; and it may be, that your blood was nearer . . . The boy has left us for a time, but, Sagamore, you are not alone!" (349). Rather than indicating the possibility of a white-blooded person entering into native sociality, which might suggest that the latter is not merely a function of blood and has political dimensions with which the United States must engage, this bit of dialogue presents Hawkeye's and Chingachgook's affections as exceptional, as occurring in a kind of interracial limbo in which both are separated from "natural kin" and their "friendship" is a bulwark against being "alone."[106] Even if their relationship is different/greater than the "ideal bond of union," its terms here eerily resemble those of narratives of bourgeois homemaking and maturation, a separation from kin in adulthood that requires a person go in search of a companion of one form or another with whom to find intimacy. While I will discuss this dynamic further in the next chapter, I want to highlight the disparity between this vision and the normative dimensions of native kinship systems in which one remains living among relatives one's entire life and adulthood is not defined through the creation of a separated sphere of (privatized) intimacy.

Moreover, the occasion for this outpouring of homosentiment suggests something of the symbolic and ideological work it performs. Just following this exchange, the narrator observes, "Chingachgook grasped the hand that, in the warmth of feeling, the scout had stretched across the fresh earth, and in that attitude of friendship, these two sturdy and intrepid woodsmen bowed their heads together, while scalding tears fell to their feet, watering the grave of Uncas, like drops of falling rain" (349). The most powerful display of interracial affection in the novel comes over the grave of the "last of the Mohicans," suggesting the union's enmeshment in tragedy, and the linkage of interracial friendship to death also emphasizes its nonreproductive character. Their bond may be more intense than the "ideal" one of marriage, but it cannot produce the bloodlines that will serve as the basis for (bounding) the nation. Schweitzer suggests that the source for the imagery of this scene was that of the Condolence ceremonies that were part of the reaffirmation of the Iroquois Covenant Chain (139). However, as noted earlier, those are occasions in which a deceased leader is replaced with someone chosen by the head of the relevant matrilineage, making them expressions of the embeddedness of the kinship system in processes of governance. Although the grief around Uncas's death appears collective, it does not produce an affirmation of the continuance of the Mohicans as a people, actually suggesting the opposite. Moreover, while Uncas consistently is described as a "chief," we are left to presume that he inherited that status from Chingachgook, who at one point notes, "I am an unmixed man. The blood of chiefs is in my veins" (33), collapsing native governance into notions of racial purity and once again defining indigenous peoplehood as the reproductive transmission of a "blood" essence. Rather than tying the expression of settler sympathy to a recognition of native kinship systems and their importance in internal native governance, intertribal engagement, and, consequently, settler-native diplomacy, the scene folds affection back into the logic of couplehood. Given the novel's fusion of futurity to the preservation of blood lineage through conjugal copulation, this nonreproductive union indicates the ultimate sterility of interracial friendship even as it works to ameliorate the violence of native disappearance.

Within the text's imaginary, Hawkeye can be Chingachgook's "brother" only in a metaphoric sense. The portrayal of this bond as necessarily extrafamilial marks a disavowal that depends on the novel's broader twofold depoliticization of kinship: taking couple-centered homemaking as the natural norm; and making family formation a metonym for nationality that displaces discussion of processes of governance and political negotiation, including the potential role of kinship within them. As with Jemison, Hawkeye's incontrovertible whiteness means that he can never be *Indian*, a contention that rests on the reduction of native collectivity to a function not merely of biology but of reproductive pairing. The nuclear family serves as the prism through which to view personal and political identity, understanding the latter as an expression of natural bonds of intimacy that coalesce around a certain set of "gifts." To try to introduce native populations into the space of white nationality produces an "unnatural" crossing. However, the need to preserve white modes of domestic feeling, and thus to resist innate Indian desires for mixture that would result in the distension of

sentimental homemaking, does not preclude the possibility of nonreproductive affection across this difference.

When viewed from this perspective, the war of position in Indian policy
does not result from a clash among geopolitical mappings and the refusal
of the United States to engage with native modes of spatiality and self-
understanding (including the role of kinship in both) so much as it indicates
the inevitable role of boundaries of blood in the reproduction of American
peoplehood. The move from the eighteenth-century vision of the productive
household to the ideology of affectively saturated nuclear homemaking that
was gaining dominance in the 1820s marks a shift in discourses of sexuality
(of marriage, intimacy, and procreation) that, at least in part, is animated by
anxieties over how to cohere national territoriality and jurisdiction in the
face of the continued presence of indigenous peoples on land claimed by the
United States as "within" its boundaries. The racial grammar of Indian/white
difference as articulated in this period depends on a vision of native identity
that is soldered to procreative couplehood, rather than imagined in terms
of clans and other more expansive forms of kinship-based collectivity.
The installation of a conjugal imaginary works to displace the possibility of
seeing such kinds of family formation, and their articulation with other
social processes like governance, as central to native sociality rather than as
an epiphenomenal expression of a blood-borne Indianness. In Spivak's
terms, the representation (portrayal) of native peoples within an ideology
organized around reproductive couplehood disavows the possibility of
native peoples to represent (make meaningful within or to U.S. institutions)
their existing modes of sociality and governance. That marginalization
works to recast native politics as an extension of U.S. liberalism, in terms of
sharing conceptions of collective decision-making, landholding, and consent as well as at times presenting U.S.-native relations as just an extension
of U.S. domestic law (as a simple "contract" under existing property law). An
emergent heteronormativity, then, plays a crucial role in recasting the geopolitics of settler-state occupation and indigenous sovereignty as a question
of a negotiation among racial(ized) populations.

2

Adoption Nation

Catharine Maria Sedgwick, Hendrick Aupaumut,
and the Boundaries of Familial Feeling

In the previous chapter, I argued that discourses of conjugal couplehood came to serve as a way of foreclosing discussion of native kinship systems, helping create a political ecology in which the failures of U.S. policy in legitimizing the acquisition of native lands or in recognizing native sociopolitical systems on their own terms could be renarrated as an irresolvable difference among races. I suggested that the failure to acknowledge the possibility that a person born *white* could be truly Seneca or "Mohican" indicated a vision of *Indianness* as racial lineage that sundered it from native social and political formations, allowing them increasingly to be displaced from public discussion of "the Indian problem." Yet this formulation runs the risk of casting the adoption of whites as expressive of the essence of native identity. In "Captivating Eunice," Audra Simpson argues that "captivity narratives could be used to justify the domestications of space and lives upon that space" given that they offer "alchemies of white transformation (into indigeneity) in order to 'settle' foreign lands, as well as to assuage identities fractured by the moral and epistemological questions of origins presented by their own foreign-ness within a land that they had to settle *quickly*" (108). If emphasizing the potential for adoption opens up alternative possibilities for conceptualizing the relation between kinship and politics, whose interests are served by such alternatives? Or, put another way, to what extent can the potential for turning non-natives into natives serve as a metonym for indigenous sovereignty?

As against the racialized conjugality at the center of Jemison's and Cooper's narratives, one also can see in public discourse in the 1820s an attempt to undo the equation of sustained emotional connection among adults with marital union, an effort in which the possibility of native-settler family-making patterned on indigenous modes of adoption is crucial. Catharine

Maria Sedgwick's *Hope Leslie; Or, Early Times in the Massachusetts* (1827) provides a prominent counterpoint to Cooper, offering a competing narrative of the nation's becoming (this one set in Massachusetts Bay in the wake of the Pequot War of 1637) in which the promise to be fulfilled in the unfolding of American history and destiny cannot be contained in a romantic dyad like that of Heyward and Alice. Instead, the language of familial feeling provides a way of expanding the boundaries of intimate association beyond heteropairing, imagining networks of care and concern that not only breach the increasing nuclear insularity of bourgeois homemaking but create lateral bonds of brotherhood and sisterhood defined in terms other than those of literal biological relatedness.[1]

Might we describe such an effort to decenter the conjugal imaginary as a project of queering family? In *The Wedding Complex*, Elizabeth Freeman traces the ways that representations of wedding rituals seem less to confirm the privatizing tendencies of marriage than to point to the webs of relation and history abjected in the fetishization of couplehood, unleashing a "queer desire" that conjoins radically disjunctive images in "an expansive symbolics of affiliation" (49). Less making visible minoritized subject-positions than articulating an alternative vision of social connection, this "queering" involves "imagin[ing] social configurations and narrative forms that can refigure both the horizontal bonds between peers beyond couplehood and the vertical bonds between generations beyond parenthood" (65). In its insistent emphasis on the presence of chords of affection and responsibility that extend past those of husband-wife and parent-child, *Hope Leslie* offers such an alternative vision, accreting a wildly disparate set of intimacies under the shared rubric of family and its associated terminologies (especially those of siblinghood). Drawing on Freeman, we can describe this prevalent feature of Sedgwick's text as a "kin-aesthetic," providing as it does "an embodied means of formalizing those very relationships that do not count as lawful kinship" (98). The novel situates marriage within a wide field of familial feeling, positioning conjugality as only one among a range of possible processes of kin-making and thus offering a critique of emergent nineteenth-century norms of nuclearity, and understanding that alternative as in some sense *queer* helps historically open up the heteronorm, moving the concept's center of gravity away from individual gender expression and sexual object choice (and other sexological formulations that emerge in the late nineteenth and early twentieth centuries)[2] and more toward the political economy of bourgeois family formation homemaking, and propertyholding.

If marital union serves as a way of figuring the political union of the nation-state, as discussed in the previous chapter, Sedgwick's *queering* of conjugality can be seen as an effort to rethink the nature of national adhesion. The novel juxtaposes two models of statehood, elite and democratic, each of which is signified metonymically by a particular vision of kinship. Dispersing the hierarchical preservation of bloodlines (exemplified by English royalism) into a horizontal web of familial association, cast as enabling greater respect and reciprocity among citizens, the text incorporates the Pequots as models and participants in new forms of kin-making. The novel makes native peoples the medium through which to reconceptualize the relation between intimacy and collectivity. Pequot influence appears pedagogical in its introduction of the colonists to modes of feeling and interaction that can serve as a basis for democratic community-building, and in this way, Sedgwick suggests a limitless potential for emotive union between Euramericans and Indians frustrated only by the lingering trauma of prior violence.

Yet the text's effort to remap the relation between public spirit and private feeling so as to challenge the paradigmatic status of conjugal homemaking depends on dissolving the boundaries of native polities. Within this framework, the ultimate expression of native subjectivity seems to be an ability to bond with whites, a proclivity highlighted through the trope of captivity—itself presented as about intercultural "love" and adoption. As Philip Deloria has illustrated, the invocation of native people(s) by whites often serves less as an acknowledgment of their sovereignty and autonomy than as a maneuver within non-native social formations. "Indianness has, above all, represented identities that are unquestionably American. Despite the shifting nature of individual, social, and national identities, Indianness has made them seem fixed and final . . . ma[king] one a citizen, not of an impermanent government, but of the land itself" (183). *Hope Leslie* consistently presents the colonists' emotionally saturated associations with Indians as a process of Americanization, depicting exposure to, and partial embrace of, native social dynamics as a crucial part of breaking with interlocking English conceptions of home, family, and the state. The novel nationalizes its challenge to couple-centered privatization by routing it through indigeneity, citing natives as precedent in ways that give a romantic primitivist genealogy to its disjointing of bourgeois homemaking.

In referencing native kinship systems in order to explore the (queer) possibilities they offer for envisioning new kinds of family formation and community-making among non-natives, the novel makes them into a metaphor for U.S. national identity. Representing native social dynamics in this way can be understood as an effort to grapple with seemingly disparate anxieties in antebellum social life, in particular those surrounding the increasing prominence of the independent conjugal household as both practice and ideal and the ongoing state project of Indian removal.[3] The text's interweaving of discourses of marriage and Indian affairs gives shape to a structure of feeling—a configuration of "affective elements of consciousness and relationships" that "go beyond formally held and systemic beliefs," registering a "tension between the received interpretation and practical experience." That "tension is often an unease, a stress, a displacement, a latency," and it can mark "experiences to which the fixed forms do not speak at all, which indeed they do not recognize."[4] Taking aspects of native life marginalized within the official narratives of Indian policy (as discussed in the previous chapter), Sedgwick reconstellates them as an aesthetics of kinship, which then provides the framework for reimagining the possibilities of affective connection among whites. The topos of native kinship celebrates elements of native cultures often denigrated or dismissed by the U.S. government while at the same time impressing them into the project of Euramerican community-building and nationalism, at the expense of recognizing the specific functions of kinship in indigenous governance and diplomacy. In other words, the visibility of native cultural forms in Sedgwick's narrative as a positively valued counterpoint to emergent U.S. norms of home and family is premised on their recontextualization in ways that efface their role in indigenous political life.[5] This way of challenging compulsory heterosexuality uses native people(s) to give form to a counterhegemonic critique of the privatizing imaginary of marital couplehood, constructing an alternative "symbolics of affiliation" that reifies the geopolitical symbolics of the settler state. *Hope Leslie*'s circulation of nativeness depends on divorcing it from transtribal networks—geographies of occupancy, governance, and diplomacy.[6] While contesting interwoven norms of racialization and homemaking, further presenting such a shift as the fulfillment of the democratic ideals of the nation, the novel's kin-aesthetic renders subaltern the connection between native modes of kinship and their persistence as independent peoples.

This line of analysis, tracking the limits of counterhegemonic uses of native cultural difference, points to a set of discursive conventions or strategies in which culture does not simply surrogate for race.[7] To understand non-native appropriations of native modes of sociality as necessarily a form of racialization positions racial inequity as the central issue in settler-indigenous relations rather than understanding race as one among several ways that native peoples are inserted into imperial frameworks. The process of Indianization discussed in the previous chapter displaces/diminishes sovereignty by transposing the geopolitics of treaty relations into the biopolitics of racial reproduction in ways that cast U.S. legal structures and geography as self-evident. Reciprocally, portraying native kinship systems as a set of principles that can be taken up by non-natives without consideration of their role in native modes of governance and land tenure also evades the politics of indigenous-settler relations (or separates *kinship* from what gets to count as *politics*), however doing so in ways different from—and largely at odds with—the kinds of racialization at play in Jemison's narrative and Cooper's novel. In this chapter, then, I am tracing a mode of oppositional discourse that is co-present with the ideological and rhetorical maneuvers discussed in the last chapter, a kind of discourse that seeks to challenge the reproductive imaginary on which such racializing maneuvers rely, but the critique it offers nevertheless also forecloses the relation between kinship and native self-determination. As suggested in the Introduction, strategies of queer resistance do not necessarily yield a greater engagement with indigenous peoplehood, yet neither for that reason are they simply equivalent to dominant, heteronormative formulations of conjugal homemaking. Acknowledging the complexity of this intrasettler dialogue involves attending to the multiple and simultaneous avenues for managing native self-representation offered by Euramerican discourses of sexuality, a variability that can aid in explaining oscillations in Indian policy between forms of detribalization and tribal recognition while also helping to address the specific kinds of regulation and naturalization at play in these different policy formulations (which I take up more specifically in chapters 3 and 4).[8]

Hope Leslie offers an antipatriarchal vision of national belonging that depends on the citation of Indians as precedent while evacuating native tradition of its capacity to signify autonomous sovereignty. Using native customs to make legible and legitimize an alternative to the insulated intimacy of the nuclear household overlooks the role of kinship in defining and negotiating native political subjectivities. By contrast, Hendrick Aupaumut's "Short Narration of My Last Journey to the Western Country" (1792) utilizes the language of family to outline relationships among native groups. As a Mahican chief, Aupaumut had been part of the Mahicans' migration in the early 1780s from Stockbridge, Sedgwick's childhood home, to Oneida territory in western New York. The text is a report of his trip to the Ohio region as a U.S. envoy. It chronicles his attempt to advocate for peace with the United States, but it also challenges U.S. Indian policy, emphasizing forms of intertribal association that precede and seek to thwart U.S. jurisdictional pretensions. The text traces longstanding bonds of affection and alliance while also emphasizing the distinctness of the peoples involved, their processes of collective decision-making, and the complex political matrix formed by their shifting interests and identifications. In this way, Aupaumut's narrative employs a familial imaginary at odds with Sedgwick's, suggesting a very different structure of feeling than the novel's and one whose elements the novel disavows. Sedgwick's queer intervention, then, reaches its limit in appropriating (or perhaps inventing) native subjectivity in ways that implicitly deny the possibility of indigenous self-determination.

FROM PATRIARCHY TO SIBLINGHOOD, OR IMAGINING INCESTUOUS NATIONALITY

In perhaps the most well known early-nineteenth-century invocation of the Puritan past, Daniel Webster's career-making speech commemorating the bicentennial of the Pilgrims' landing at Plymouth roots American history in seventeenth-century migration, presenting the colonists' construction of a "home" in the "wilderness" as the origin of a peoplehood distinct from that of Great Britain.[9] This 1820 address provides a useful critical foil by which to elaborate the maneuvers and stakes of Sedgwick's novel, drawing attention to the centrality of figures of family in the articulation of national identity.[10] Webster describes the act of commemoration itself as "looking before and after, to hold communion at once with our ancestors and our posterity," "connect[ing] with our whole race through all time" and "binding together the past, the present, and the future" (64–65). Such broad gestures, though, increasingly are constrained by a more rigidly conceived genealogy, culminating in the claim that "the voice of acclamation and gratitude, commencing on the Rock of Plymouth, shall be transmitted through the millions of the sons of the Pilgrims, till it lose itself in the murmurs of the Pacific seas" (117). Such moments cast the nation as the sum of unbroken lines of reproduction, an ever-expanding mass of Pilgrim/Puritan progeny progressing west across the continent. American history appears as the diachronic extension of bloodlines, situating the present as a moment in a relentlessly procreative push toward the future in which identification with the past is a function of filiation to a long line of dead fathers.

Disregarding interactions among families and eschewing any notion of collectivity distinct from a linearly defined relatedness, the address's representation of space makes clear the *kind* of family through which it envisions time. In his description of the exceptionality of New England, and by implication the United States, Webster emphasizes that other forms of colonization in both the ancient and modern world did not produce "a child . . . distant, indeed, and independent of [the mother country's] control, yet speaking her language and inheriting her blood, springing forward to a competition with her own power" (80), a process in which the former child finds himself "*at home* in the colony" (82). The analogy between becoming "another people" and individuating from one's birth family in establishing one's own household is made even more explicit: "As a son, leaving the house of his father for his own, finds, by the order of nature . . . nearer and dearer objects around which his affections circle, while his attachment to the parental roof becomes moderated . . . ; so our ancestors, leaving their native land . . . found here a new circle of engagements, interests, and affections; . . . shutting out from its embraces the parent realm, [becoming] *local* to America" (89–90). The formation of national identity parallels the dynamics of this family drama, in which the residential unit is defined as a couple and minors who are their offspring. Adulthood means moving to a new "local"-ity and thereby developing a different (although equivalent) set of affections to those of one's father. Such a generational dispersion, organized around nuclear homemaking, is, paradoxically, inevitable and new, following from "nature" and innovating on the "feudal policy" dominant in Europe. In fact, Webster credits New England's elimination of primogeniture and requirement that land be partitioned among all a propertyholder's children with producing and sustaining the democratic character of the nation (100–101). Thus, the nuclear family appears as both instinct and invention, providing the *natural* building block of this account of national space-time while also signaling the world-historical transformation that makes possible a sense of American mission and destiny.

As against Webster's linkage of national continuity to that particular model of home and family, Sedgwick stages a contest among different ways of configuring kinship, exploring the implications of such struggle for how national collectivity is imagined and lived.[11] Before turning to the novel's employment of native kinship, I first want to establish its investment in an alternative model of familial feeling to the kind of conjugal insularity Webster celebrates. The novel indicates its interest in the relay between political and familial identity from the outset. It begins in England with a discussion of the nuptial prospects of William Fletcher. His uncle, who shares his name, has orchestrated a betrothal to Alice, the senior William's daughter. However, this arrangement is predicated on the young man's forgoing "all confederacy, association, or even acquaintance with the puritans" and instead swearing "unqualified obedience to the king, and adherence to the established church" (8, 10), Sir William earlier having insisted in a letter to his brother that his nephew must "be taught unquestioning and unqualified loyalty to his sovereign" (7). The younger William defies his uncle, plotting to take Alice with him in his transatlantic migration with other Puritans, but before they can board the ship, Alice is seized "by a cavalcade of armed men, in the uniform of the King's guards" (13), spirited away, and wed to another man within two weeks. This opening foregrounds several of the concerns that will shape the rest of the text. Marriage is coordinated with, and expressive of, state policy, positioning the patriarch as a monarch in microcosm but also suggesting how conjugal union is made to reinforce existing ideologies of governance, with agents of the state literally intervening to secure such compliance. Furthermore, the semi-incestuous logic of the proposed pairing, given that William and Alice are first cousins and that his name makes him a stand-in for her father, indicates a desire (although ultimately thwarted) to maintain the integrity of the Fletcher bloodline in ways that replicate the structure of royal inheritance.[12] Thus, while Webster presents the nationalization of lineage as democratic possibility, the novel's initial framing of family formation depicts such a political investment in generational succession as inherently authoritarian.

If the Puritans initially are cast as disrupting interdependent patterns of monarchical authority and matrimonial management, these upstarts do not themselves offer an altered conception of couplehood, instead also making it an extension of state power. In the case of both William Fletcher and his son Everell, marriage serves as a vehicle for consolidating Puritan sovereignty. William weds "a ward of Mr. Winthrop" (14), creating an alliance with the family of the Puritan leader that can help unite the fledgling colony of Massachusetts Bay (which William helps found), and when Everell comes of age, Winthrop, now governor, seeks to arrange a union between him and Esther Downing, Winthrop's niece: "In taking care for the spiritual growth of our young people, who are soon to stand in their father's places, we do, as we are bound, most assuredly build up the interests of our Zion" (153). Mr. Fletcher later echoes Winthrop's sentiments, observing, "We have laid the foundation of an edifice, and our children must be so coupled together, as to secure its progress and stability when the present builders are laid low" (161–162). These moments cast conjugality as a central pillar of the Puritan regime, the younger William enacting a similar politico-familial dialectic as that envisioned by the elder William.[13] This parallel is highlighted by the fact that these pronouncements are to justify pairing Everell with Esther rather than Hope Leslie, Alice's daughter who accompanied her mother to New England in the wake of her father's death and who was raised in the Fletcher household after her mother's demise upon reaching the colony. The later love plot, then, is a reprise of the earlier one but displaced in time and space, indicating the failure of the Puritans to break with the social structures organizing English tyranny. Not unlike Webster's vision of the nation as an unbroken chain of patriarchal inheritance, the serial genealogy projected by Winthrop and Fletcher—the children literally taking the place of the parents in supporting the "edifice" of the state—casts peoplehood (the construction and maintenance of "Zion") as a kind of mechanical reproduction in which each generation assumes the position and function of the previous one in an unending cycle. Everell responds to this proposition by declaring to his father, "I entreat you not to dispose of us as if we were mere machines" (162), rejecting the political matrix of procreation as dehumanizing in its use of marriage as a means of sustaining a collectivity denuded of feeling (depicted as an inanimate object—a building).

One could read the novel's critique of royalist and Puritan efforts to manage romance as an argument for the democratizing power of affective individualism, the pursuit of emotional fulfillment in a private sphere whose insulation from political interests makes possible the achievement of real and lasting intimacy.[14] Something like this liberal notion of freedom is at play in Webster's description of the salutary effects of bourgeois inheritance, the ways it frustrates accumulation of vast estates and promotes the dispersion of the population in single-family households. Yet in the novel, the separation of the home from public affairs does not yield greater possibilities for self-expression or recognition by others with whom one is bonded in love, instead enabling a different kind of patriarchal authority. Upon reaching the Americas, Mr. Fletcher becomes disheartened with the actions of Puritan authorities, "seeing power, which had been earned at so dear a rate . . . sometimes perverted to purposes of oppression and personal aggrandizement" (16), and in 1636, he retreats to the recently created settlement at Springfield, "fix[ing] his residence a mile from the village" so as to avoid "the surveillance of an inquiring neighbourhood" (17). Here, Mr. Fletcher achieves the kind of independent homemaking toward which Webster gestures, making a space around which new, local affections can form. However, rather than facilitating emotional closeness, the separateness of the household brings into relief the subordination of its residents to the will of the father.

In particular, Sedgwick highlights the ways Mrs. Fletcher's agency is constrained. Just after noting Mr. Fletcher's refusal to accept the misuse of government power, the novel observes, "Mrs. Fletcher received his decision as all wives of that age of undisputed masculine supremacy" (16), further characterizing the Fletcher home as "a patriarchal family" in which Mrs. Fletcher shows "habitual deference" to her husband (18). The proximity of these comments to the novel's decrying of political perversion suggests a continuity between the two; Mr. Fletcher's semiauthoritarian rule parallels the "oppression" enacted by Puritan officials, just as Puritan efforts to manage marriage are represented as replicating the royal logic of preserving bloodlines.[15] As the novel later observes of the colonists, "the only divine right to govern, which they acknowledged, was that vested in the husband over the wife" (144). Monarchy gives way to matrimony as a way of conceptualizing social order. Consensual couplehood supersedes the hierarchy of royalty, but in doing so, the conjugal union itself becomes the site of another kind of self-evident power, a subordination organized around, and legitimized through, naturalized gender difference. From this perspective, Webster's narrative of the displacement of a network of "feudal" obligations by the generational proliferation of single-family homes appears less as the achievement of freedom than the exchange of one reproductively regulated imaginary for a differently configured one.

At stake in Webster's and Sedgwick's narratives is the question of how to characterize the difference between England and the United States, both looking to the seventeenth century as a way of locating the origin of national peoplehood. While evoking the Pilgrim/Puritan past, these texts are embedded in the post-Revolutionary problematic of how to signify and legitimize the emergent state in the wake of formal separation from the British Empire. Marriage and family formation serve as the discursive anchor for this pro-leptic projection, providing a mode of collectivity around which to coalesce, and through which to characterize, national identity.[16] In *Public Vows*, Nancy Cott observes, "No modern nation-state can ignore marriage forms . . . The laws of marriage must play a large part in forming 'the people.' They sculpt the body politic" (5), and she later notes, "Revolutionary-era discussions of appropriate marriage partners and the usefulness of marriage in the repub-lican social order assumed that household conduct was linked to political government" (21). Predicated on individual consent, marriage provided an analogy for republican governance, including the voluntary submission of citizens to legally constituted authorities in ways imagined as parallel to the wife's accession to be ruled by her husband. The conjugal household also offered a model for how people were to be trained in the kind of sentiments needed for citizenship. If in Webster's address the seriality of reproduction provides the natural structure for historical continuity and national becoming, Sedgwick's novel presents the fetishization of conjugal couplehood and reproduction as a hallmark of a patriarchal perspective that fundamentally has failed to break with the monarchical regime from which the colonies sought independence, thereby casting the assumptions underlying Webster's historiography as un-American.

Not only is *Hope Leslie*'s portrait of the seventeenth century a displaced stand-in for ongoing debates about the proper contours of home and family and their role in national life, but it collapses a number of historically differ-entiated social dynamics into each other, creating a composite portrait of monarchical/patriarchal/authoritarian rule that it sets against an affectively saturated communitarianism. The emotionally rich vision of familial con-nection the text uses as a figure for community-making, which I will illus-trate later, (con)fuses seventeenth-century and post-Revolutionary social norms.[17] For the first century or so of English settlement, homemaking in southern New England among white settlers depended heavily on forms of barter, among households and with merchants, creating webs of interdepen-dency, and the children in adulthood tended to stay fairly close to their par-ents, moving onto family lands or nearby plots. Given that the home explicitly was understood as a space of production and that laws—enforced by extensive neighborly surveillance—regulated all manner of sexual, mar-ital, and labor relations, there was no clear distinction between public and private spheres. Such community involvement in each other's affairs, how-ever, largely was animated not by extensive bonds of affection but rather by the exigencies of a largely cashless and wageless agricultural economy as well as prominent notions of the need to promote moral discipline as a vehicle of maintaining social order, itself imagined as a series of nested, analogical hierarchies in which everyone participated. In this vein, the "family" itself was not a unit of blood and feeling but the residents of a given household, including indentured servants.

The kind of profound affect Sedgwick associates with kinship becomes a defining feature of the discourse of family only in the late eighteenth and early nineteenth centuries, partially due to transformations in the political economy of household formation that fractured the kind of community networks the novel seems to juxtapose with privatized conjugality. Over the course of the eighteenth century, diminishing agricultural resources due to the demographic explosion in New England prompted greater debt, promoted urbanization, and undermined patriarchal authority. These changes, including the lesser availability and greater cost of non-kin household labor, expanded the cash economy, which helped promote a gendered distinction between kinds of household production—that which yielded salable goods (largely men's) and that which was consumed within the household (largely women's). As work increasingly came to be associated with the cash economy (in terms of profit-generating and waged labor), mobility increased, and the household tended to have fewer if any non-kin members, the domestic sphere emerged as its own kind of social space, one in which love and intimacy among family members was thought to predominate as against the calculations, interests, and hostilities of the "public" world outside. The associated ideology of motherhood as sentimental socialization became increasingly pervasive, with women imagined as naturally suited to the promotion of such civilized/civilizing affect. The heightened feeling associated with "family" that the novel invokes in its proliferation of figures of siblinghood actually is a product of an increasingly privatized social landscape. *Hope Leslie*'s intervention into contemporary conjugality, then, works through an amalgamated history in which the embeddedness of affective dynamics in particular political and economic formations is only minimally recognized, instead offering a sentimentalized allegory of national regeneration.[18]

Rather than affirming domesticity as an autonomous space of intimacy, the text repeatedly suggests a continuity between privatization and tyranny, chronicling the protagonists' attempts to extend affection beyond the confines of the household in ways that seek to reshape existing public policy. When the novel most dramatically and emphatically mobilizes interpersonal feeling against government power, the concept of privacy is cast not merely as insufficient but as a complete misunderstanding of the nature and import of the emotional connections at play. These moments come in response to Governor Winthrop's detainment of Magawisca, the daughter of a Pequot chief captured during an English assault. She had been raised with Everell until an attack on the Fletcher home by her father that resulted in the death of Mrs. Fletcher and her infant; returning seven years later to make contact with Hope in order to allow her communication with her sister Faith, who had been kidnapped in the attack and who subsequently had married Magawisca's brother Oneco, Magawisca is captured by colonial authorities. When Everell discovers that she has been arrested and is to be held as a prisoner, he exclaims, in horror, "You a prisoner—here, Magawisca! . . . impossible; injustice, gratitude, humanity, forbid it. My father—Governor Winthrop, you will not surely suffer this outrage," to which Winthrop replies, "You will do well, young Mr. Fletcher, to bridle your zeal; private feelings must yield to the public good; . . . it is somewhat bold in you to oppose the course of justice—to intermeddle with the public welfare" (234). Later, after further pleading from both Hope and Everell, Winthrop observes:

> I know thou art ever somewhat forward to speak the dictates of thy heart, . . . but now let me caution you both, especially Everell, not to stir in this matter, any private interference will but prejudice the Pequod's cause . . . And as the old chief and his daughter are accused, and I fear justly, of kindling the enmity of the tribes against us, . . . it will be difficult to make a private benefit outweigh such a public crime. (274)

In dismissing their appeal as merely "private feelings" that must be superseded by "the public good," Winthrop rejects their bond with Magawisca as merely particularistic or idiosyncratic, an unsuitable foundation on which to predicate not simply political decision-making but collectivity itself. From the perspective of the colonial authorities, the emotional exuberance they express ("the dictates of thy heart") is "intermeddl[ing]" and "interference," an irruption of sentiment breaching its proper sphere and threatening to overwhelm the considerations that should provide the basis for good governance. Moreover, the concerns that Winthrop expresses are based on a misinterpretation of Magawisca's purpose, imagining her as coordinating an assault when she is only trying to reunite Hope with her sister, Faith. The complex bonds of kinship connecting Hope and Everell to Magawisca are supplanted by a narrative in which her Indianness necessarily signifies a threatening externality, in which a constrained concept of the "public" disavows the possibility of an emotive sociality that can incorporate her.

While in the next section I will address at length the ways Magawisca and other Indians are presented as the model for the kind of familial affect addressed in the preceding moments, exploring the attendant implications for imagining native-settler relations, I want here to highlight how the novel depicts care that exceeds the boundaries of the conjugal household as the basis for reimagining the "public." The plot of the last third of the novel is organized around various challenges to the will of Puritan officials with respect to Magawisca's imprisonment, including two efforts (the latter successful) to break her out of jail. Through the text's positive portrayal of this insistent repudiation of the decisions of colonial officials, it develops an alternative notion of collectivity built around "private" attachments. While organizing one of the attempts to free Magawisca, Everell says to a resistant Esther, "there must be a warrant, as you call it, for sometimes resisting legitimate authority, or all our friends in England would not be at open war with their king. With such a precedent, I should think the sternest conscience would permit you to obey the generous impulses of nature, rather than to render this slavish obedience to the letter of the law" (278).[19] Conceived in this way, the "feelings" animating Hope and Everell's efforts cannot be exiled from the field of politics as merely individualistic; in fact, such *natural* impulses are the stuff of popular political reformation, suppressed by an autocratic administration itself disconnected from the life of the people. More than indicating the possible validity of extralegal action, the comparison of freeing Magawisca with the English Civil War positions the former as a transformation in the social order, a reconfiguration of what constitutes legitimate political authority.[20] Furthermore, given the novel's running representation of the Puritans as the origin of U.S. national identity, the citation of the English rebels' overthrow of the monarchy implicitly alludes to the American Revolution, casting the kind of emotive union that prompts Everell's actions on behalf of Magawisca as a figure for national union. The attempt to label such adhesion as "private," and by extension categorically to distinguish "private" sentiment from "public" policy, appears as de facto support for a vision of law in which the population remains in "slavish obedience" to a government that renders their bonds of affection politically meaningless, thereby alienating them from each other.

In divorcing law from sentiment, colonial authorities, the text implies, have made the former a coercive imposition rather than a consensual expression of popular will, and in that way, the Puritan government has become no better than the monarchy from which they fled and against which their compatriots still in England are at war. By invoking "nature," Everell alludes to an alternative set of principles that could guide political process, proposing a counterhegemonic framework for conceptualizing "public"-ness. Winthrop's administration of the law is portrayed as privatizing "feelings," banishing affect to an extragovernmental realm and thereby radically circumscribing the kinds of subjectivity that will be recognized as legitimate, or significant, beyond the domestic sphere. As discussed earlier, the novel deprecates the Puritan attempt to manage marriage and family formation, to stabilize them as the "pillars" that support the "edifice" of the state; the limited definition of "public" concerns appears as the flip side of that same pattern, an ultimately undemocratic effort to constrain the possibility of forms of association that exceed, or undermine, the structure of the patriarchal household. In contrast to what he depicts as Esther's heartless submission "to the letter of the law," Everell casts himself as acting in conformity to the underlying spirit of community life. Through him, the novel presents the embrace of expansive and multivectored kinds of affect as more "generous" and *natural* than territorializing such "feelings" in a depoliticized elsewhere, thereby implicitly challenging the ideology of marital homemaking.

The sorts of emotional attachment at stake in the Magawisca plot are conveyed through the idiom of kinship, further pressuring the ideal of a domestic space that can be separated—or even substantively differentiated—from the "public welfare" Winthrop cites. On multiple occasions, Everell and Magawisca are described as siblings, a nonconjugal connection that provides a counterpoint to the reproductive couplehood invoked at the beginning of the novel by Sir William and later by Winthrop.[21] After Everell is captured in the Indian attack on the Fletchers' home and is saved by Magawisca, who loses her arm in preventing his murder by her father, "He threw his arms around her, and pressed her to his heart, as he would a sister that had redeemed his life with her own" (93), and this designation is reaffirmed in the penultimate chapter in an exchange between them:

" . . . I had worn away the days and nights in the solitudes of the forest
musing on the memory of thee, and counting the moons till the Great Spirit
shall bid us to those regions where there will be no more gulf between us,
and I may hail thee as my brother."
    "And why not now, Magawisca, regard me as your brother?" (330)

While Magawisca's demurral of the possibility of union will be addressed later, the appropriateness of siblinghood as a way of characterizing their relationship is embraced explicitly by both, further reinforcing the naturalness of their feelings by rendering them in familial terms while also positioning such familiality as an alternative framework for conceptualizing "public"-ity. Moreover, Magawisca and Hope are linked as semisiblings; at the close of their first meeting, Hope observes, "mysteriously have our destinies been interwoven. Our mothers brought from a far distance to rest together here—their children connected in indissoluble bonds" (192).[22] In light of the proliferation of sibling and sibling-like attachments throughout the novel (William-Alice, Magawisca-Everell, Hope-Faith, Everell-Hope,

Esther-Hope-Everell—the latter two to be discussed later), the "bonds" between Hope and Magawisca appear as another example of this pattern, especially in light of the description of their connection as one inherited from their mothers—which if not sisterhood proper seems to partake of a similar kinship principle. The social network mislabeled as "private" by Governor Winthrop, then, is cast as a constellation of sibling relations among adults, an affective network that provides the basis for an alternative sociality to that of the "law" and that is structured through a familial imaginary but one that cannot be reduced to the conjugal household.

Rather than charting a trajectory of maturation that culminates in a marriage in which one's affections are localized around the residents of a single-family dwelling, the novel conflates siblings and spouses in ways that situate conjugality within a wider network of feeling, rendering it relatively equivalent in importance and intensity to the range of family-like relationships also described as "friendship."[23] The persistent association of conjugality with other kinds of kinship gives a notably incestuous cast to marriage in the text, resembling much of the fiction of the early national period, which, as other critics have noted, fixates almost obsessively on this issue.[24] Unlike other authors, though, Sedgwick does not use the topos of incest to induce horror in the reader so as to indicate the presence of severe forms of social confusion/disjunction. Blurring the distinction between brother-sister and husband-wife allows Sedgwick to subsume the latter as an element within the larger set of the former, displacing the privatized marital home as the paradigmatic unit of social life in favor of a network of sustained emotional connections among households.[25]

The final chapter highlights this porous matrix of kinship, offering a vision of (national) collectivity that challenges the antidemocratic dialectic of bloodlines and anonymous publicity that characterizes state policy in the text. The epigraph with which it begins, "Quelque rare que soit le véritable amour, il l'est encore moins que la véritable amitié" (336, "However rare true love may be, it is still less rare than true friendship" [365]), signals the displacement of conjugal closure in favor of a more open-ended set of emotional attachments. In addition to conveying Esther's expression of siblinghood and her eventual union in bonds of "warm and tender friendship" with Hope and Everell (349), the novel's conclusion establishes a series of familial associations between the couple and virtually all the characters with whom they have been aligned, with the exception of Magawisca, her father Mononotto, Faith, and Oneco, who are dispatched by sending them on a "pilgrimage to the far western forests" (339). Master Cradock, Hope's ungainly and inept instructor who somewhat inadvertently aids her in her freeing of Magawisca from prison, is made "a life-member of her domestic establishment"; of Digby, a former handyman in the Fletcher household, we are told, "A friendship between him, Everell and Hope subsisted through their lives, and descended, a precious legacy, through many generations of their descendants"; and Barnaby Tuttle, the less-than-fastidious jailor who unknowingly enables Magawisca's escape, is "enabled by an annual stipend" from Hope to retire and live "comfortably with his daughter Ruth" (349). More than simply providing an update on the characters with whom readers have been called to identify, this final summary solidifies a network of compassion and caring built throughout the novel. It privileges sustained relationships among households over discussion of intimacy in the marital home, including as an intergenerational bequest ("legacy"). The final moment of the novel, in fact, focuses not on Hope and Everell's blissful union but on the richness of Esther's life without one. Rather than being exiled to a place separate from the romantic pair toward whom she has expressed sisterhood, Esther returns to the colonies and "renew[s] her intercourse with Everell and Hope" on terms of "warm and tender friendship" (349), and the novel closes with the statement: "She illustrated a truth . . . that marriage is not *essential* to the contentment, the dignity, or the happiness of woman" (350). In light of the novel's prior reference to her sibling-like ties with the couple, and their web of kinship-like relations with others, closing with a description of Esther's fulfillment as a single woman reinforces the idea that the affective fullness attributed to martial intimacy and privacy is less natural (or "essential") than conventional.[26]

In the place of the interdependent dynamics of the "patriarchal family" and "public" policy defined by the absence of extended webs of affection, the novel offers siblinghood, and the collateral concept of friendship, as a way of envisioning collectivity that fulfills the Revolutionary promise of a break from monarchical hierarchy and tyranny. Elizabeth Maddox Dillon has argued that emergent modes of liberalism in the late eighteenth and early nineteenth centuries did not so much separate public and private spheres as publicly produce privacy: "[T]he exposition of subjectivity in the literary public sphere works to produce privacy and bourgeois subjectivity and this subjectivity is the predicate for participation in the political public sphere," creating "a recursive loop between privacy and publicity in which the intimate sphere 'prequalifies' certain subjects for participation in the political public sphere" (35). In this dynamic, "marriage is precisely the site where private and public lines are seemingly drawn, yet where the creation of these lines reveals the fundamental interdependence (the sociality) of public and private spheres" (127). *Hope Leslie*, however, subordinates marriage to other nonbiological modes of kin-making, creating a kind of "sociality" that frustrates the possibility of distinguishing public from private and that, therefore, puts into question what issues, subjects, and arrangements constitute the "political public sphere." In contrast to what is presented as the authoritarian tendencies at play in the fetishization of inheritance and cou-plehood, the novel creates a proliferating web of affective relations, replacing the image of the insulated conjugal household with what is literally a new structure of feeling.

CAPTIVITY, COLLECTIVITY, AND MODEL INDIANS

> Others are not conscious (at least I believe they are not) of any dimi-nution in their affections for me—but others have taken my place naturally and of right I allow it. It is the necessity of a solitary condi-tion—an unnatural state.
>
> . . . .
>
> I have troops of friends—some devotedly attached to me—yet the result of all this very happy experience is that there is no equivalent for those blessings which Providence has placed first and ordained that they should be purchased at the dearest sacrifice . . . While I live I do not mean this shall be read and after, my individual experience may perhaps benefit some one of all my tribe.
> —Catharine Maria Sedgwick, journal entry for May 18, 1828

The discussion of Esther's singleness quite directly resonates with Sedgwick's choice not to marry, opening the novel onto the queer (or at least nonconju-gal) possibilities for homemaking and emotional attachment that she herself explored.[27] Although as suggested by Sedgwick's journal entry, written only a year after *Hope Leslie*'s publication, this alternative lifestyle was not with-out psychological and social costs.[28] She worries, as she often does, about the ways the spouses of her brothers and sisters have superseded her, occupying the "place" she once did in the "affections" of her siblings. Even though she spent the majority of her life living in her brothers' houses, she describes herself as "solitary," emphasizing that despite the social network she has assembled (the "troops of friends"), she experiences her situation as iso-lating and aberrant. From this perspective, the affective fullness of the text's matrix of siblinghood can be read as a social fantasy, an effort to imagine different configurations of kinship and residency in which her feelings would not be deviant but would instead be "natural," and the novel projects that ideal onto the seventeenth century so as to envision it as an important element in the emergence of national peoplehood and thus an integral part of the ongoing fulfillment of national promise. If so, however, why would she characterize her family, friends, and/or others in her situation as a "tribe"? In what ways is this description an attempt to reconceptualize her supposedly "unnatural state," and how might it provide a framework through which to understand the cultural work performed by *Hope Leslie*'s representation of native peoples?

"Tribe" here indexes an indeterminate collectivity, one whose boundaries are porous and defined by an unspecified principle of association. The referent is not clear. Does she mean those biologically related to her, her "troops of friends," other single adults (particularly women), or perhaps some combination thereof? The ambiguity seems purposeful, shading these various options into each other and blurring the distinctions among them. If Indians in the early to mid-nineteenth century often were depicted as lacking a proper understanding of family as well as a future, as discussed in the previous chapter, native practices were not cast as perverse or pathological in the pointed way that they would be by the late nineteenth century (as will be addressed in chapter 3).[29] While unlikely to be portrayed as equivalent to Anglo-American marriage and homemaking, native social formations in this period did not necessarily connote for the white reading public the utter absence, or inversion, of social order. In fact, persistent strains of Rousseauian romantic primitivism continued to see native peoples as closer to "Nature" and thus less likely to have fallen into the various kinds of vice, artifice, and luxury that proliferate in civilized life. In *Inventing the American Primitive*, Helen Carr observes, "since the time of Montaigne one of the elements of a European critique of their own society had been the topos of the virtuous, childlike savage whose natural goodness and good sense contrasted with the corruption and folly of courts and with the civilized abuse of power" (23–24), adding that by the eighteenth century " 'nature' was no longer the world of the sinful flesh as opposed to the redeemed spirit" and instead "had become an ethical and aesthetic norm" (31).[30] Following this post-Enlightenment logic, the "tribe" becomes a decontextualized figure through which to allegorize alternatives to contemporary life, enacting a similar dehistoricizing as that of sentimental affection. It can signal not only a flexible kind of collectivity that exceeds the limits of the conjugal household but a different version of the *natural* in which marital pairing and childbirth are not paradigmatic.

The novel persistently invokes "the natural" to signal a capacity for emotional connection that is central to the relationships and forms of subjectivity it privileges.[31] Of Hope, the novel observes, "she lived in an atmosphere of favour and indulgence, which permits the natural qualities to shoot forth in unrepressed luxuriance—an atmosphere of love, that like a tropical climate, brings forth the richest flowers and most flavorous fruits" (122), depicting "love" as giving rise to wild, "unrepressed" growth. Extending beyond the main characters, this association between desirable forms of emotional expressivity and uncultivated instinct expands to include the entire Puritan community. After hearing the testimony in Magawisca's trial, the audience is caught in "a strange contrariety of opinion and feelings. Their reason, guided by the best lights they possessed, deciding against her—the voice of nature crying out for her" (294). Here we see a similar split to that at play in Everell's argument with Esther discussed earlier—the law (or "reason") versus webs of empathy and identification. Together these examples indicate the importance of "nature," and associated metaphors, in expressing and validating the text's vision of expanded spheres of (familial) feeling.

Sedgwick further portrays Indians as an extension of nature in ways that implicitly present aspects of native life as deserving of Euramerican emulation. The novel often states rather explicitly that native residency in New England had to be supplanted by the Puritans and the national people for whom they are the origin,[32] and native peoples often appear indistinguishable from the surrounding flora and fauna: "[T]he natural gardens of the earth, where the soil is mellowed and enriched by the annual overflowing of the streams, and prepared by the unassisted processes of nature to yield to the indolent Indian his scanty supply of maize" (17). Yet at other moments, the very connection to "nature" that disqualifies indigenous inhabitance from counting as a recognizable form of occupancy makes it indispensable as a precedent for European settlement: "The first settlers followed the course of the Indians, and planted themselves on the borders of rivers—the natural gardens of the earth" (16); "the tangled foot-path expanded to the thronged high-way" (73); "the sites for future villages, already marked out for them by clusters of Indian huts" (100). Readers are offered seemingly incommensurate impressions: Indians are so different that they fall outside the domain of personhood; native ways are the necessary forerunners of American civilization and nation-building.

This contradictory fusion is crystallized in the first chapter. In the letter to his brother warning about the younger William's attachment to the Puritans, Sir William proclaims that they deserve to be exiled to New England, "where they might enjoy with the savages that primitive equality, about which they make such a pother" (8). In contrast to Sir William's royalist commitments and investment in associated forms of hierarchy, including patriarchy, the novel here endorses the perspective of "the savages." Note, though, that in aligning them with what is perhaps the master trope of national feeling in the early Republic—"equality"—the passage also declares them to be "primitive," a contention that the novel does not so much revise as revalue. To be "primitive" is to be outside the matrix of monarchical power represented by Sir William, to have access to a kind of legitimacy lacking in the royalist state and its fetishization of lineage. Indianness serves as a catalyst for New World regeneration, but only in moderation.

Native peoples are cast as prototypically democratic, as the bearers of "natural" emotions which offer a counterpoint to couple-centered privatization and thus a way of reconceptualizing "public welfare." Such a dynamic can be seen in the novel's initial depiction of Magawisca. Daughter of the Pequot chief Mononotto, she as well as her brother and mother are captured while escaping from a Pequot village destroyed by the English.[33] Magawisca's mother dies brokenhearted, and Magawisca and Oneco are sent by Governor Winthrop to be servants in the Fletcher home. Like her mother, Magawisca refuses to be converted or to adopt English dress (22), and after recounting the assault on her home and the decapitation of her other brother, Samoset, for choosing not to collaborate with the attackers, she says of the effort to civilize her, "You English tell us, Everell, that the book of your law is better than that written on our hearts, for ye say it teaches mercy, compassion, forgiveness—if ye had such a law and believed in it, would ye thus have treated a captive boy" (51)? Introducing the disjunction between "hearts" and "law" that will become crucial in the second half of the novel, this passage positions intuitive Indian affect as more just than a legal code precisely because of the latter's alienness with respect to individual consciousness and its consequent failure to produce moral behavior. Underlining the value of Magawisca's unadorned experience, the text notes that to Everell "she seemed . . . to embody nature's best gifts, and her feelings to be the inspiration of heaven" (53), suggesting not only the instinctive purity of her perspective but the ways her fundamental goodness is indicated by her emotional expressivity—"her feelings."

Magawisca's capacity for "mercy, compassion, forgiveness" is illustrated most dramatically in her ability to form new familial bonds, a quality highlighted in her response to her father's efforts to rescue his children and exact retribution for English violence. Having been informed of Mononotto's plans by Nelema, a survivor of one of the tribes allied with the Pequots who lives near the Fletcher residence, Magawisca "shrunk, as if her own life were menaced, from the blow that was to fall on her friends. She would have done or suffered any thing to avert it—any thing but betray her father" (55). The invocation of friendship here foreshadows its use later in the text to designate the web of sibling-like affection among the characters. This sense of intimate relation is amplified by the rhetorical fusion of her body with those of her ostensible captors, her claim that their deaths would result in her own. Further intensifying that connection, Magawisca pleads with her father, "take vengeance on your enemies—but spare—spare our friends— our benefactors—I bleed when they are struck" (63), reiterating the trope of friendship and linking it to blood. Describing her sympathy in these terms not only corporealizes her feelings, portraying emotional wounding as physical assault, but plays on the idea of consanguinity, that she is linked to the

Fletcher household by blood ties. This metaphor implicitly contests the differentiation of Indians and whites by reference to racial types (themselves naturalized through the trope of blood) and reverses the logic of lineage. Here we see an inversion of the notion of Indian incapacity discussed in the previous chapter, with the supposed inability to understand sentimental domesticity portrayed not as a failing due to racial inheritance but as an increased openness to less artificial bonds of affection.

Rather than emanating from the matrix of procreation, the experience of kinship, of relatedness, is generated by sustained ties of support and care. An exchange between Mrs. Fletcher and Magawisca just prior to her father's attack conveys this sense of familial connection while rendering its contours ambiguous:

> "Magawisca, you are neither a stranger, nor a servant, will you not share our joy? do you not love us?"
> "Love you!" she exclaimed, clasping her hands, "love you! I would give my life for you." (62)

Magawisca feels "love" for those she describes as her "friends," suggesting that the latter term designates something deeper and more durable than agreeable companionship, but the range of those who could fit the description "neither a stranger, nor a servant" is quite wide, depicting the sphere of "love" as potentially vast.

Magawisca illustrates a remarkable facility in forming exceptionally close relationships with those who recently were strangers. Depicting her as possessing the skill of kin making, while simultaneously de biologizing what constitutes kinship, the novel presents this emotional capaciousness and adaptability as a hallmark of her Pequot upbringing. Her refusal to adopt English dress or customs implies that her feelings are not influenced by the conventions of "civilization," that the bonds she creates with the colonists express a kind of subjectivity shaped in a native context. After she is reclaimed and Everell is captured during her father's raid on the Fletcher home, Mononotto accuses her of having forgotten her past, in particular her familial ties: "Magawisca, has thy brother vanished from thy memory? I tell thee, that as Samoset died, that boy shall die" (75).[34] Yet given the novel's repeated suggestion that Magawisca views Everell as a brother, the substitution that Mononotto presents as a kind of amnesia instead can be understood as adoption, with Everell replacing Samoset in ways consistent with widespread native processes of kin-making in the wake of the death of loved ones particularly in warfare. Such a practice would have been familiar to Sedgwick due to the adoption of her relative Eunice Williams by Kahnawake

Mohawks in the early eighteenth century, which will be addressed at greater length later. In this way, the emotional connections Magawisca makes, which themselves prefigure the later representation of Hope and the network of familial feeling that surrounds her, implicitly are attributed to native custom.[35]

The impression of continuity between Magawisca's relations with the Fletchers and prior patterns of affection learned among the Pequots is heightened by the multiple references to the care shown by Mononotto's family to the English. In recounting to Everell the events surrounding the attack on Mystic village, Magawisca notes that her "mother had shielded the captive English maidens," alluding to two girls taken from Wethersfield in early 1637, and further indicates that "the English had been so often warmed and cherished" at the "hearth-stone" of her family (48–49).[36] After the attack, those surrounding Mononotto assail him for his former kindness: "Every eye was turned with suspicion and hatred on my father. *He* had been the friend of the English; *he* had counselled peace and alliance with them; *he* had protected their traders; . . . now *his* wife and children alone were living, and they called him traitor" (50). The example provided for her, then, was to welcome strangers into one's home and to "shield" and "cherish" them as de facto family. While the other Pequots castigate Mononotto after the fact for his intimacy with the English, the novel does not suggest that they objected prior to the massacre, having continued to acknowledge him as a chief. In fact, the only Pequot described as acting directly counter to the sentiments of her mother and father is Wequash, who Magawisca reveals was the true "traitor"—aiding English forces in their assault (48). Hope later demands recognition for "the many obligations of the English to the family of Mononotto—a debt, that has been but ill paid" (274). Offering Magawisca's family as a model of ethical affection, the novel here also presents their actions as a merging of public and private concerns, the term "obligations" drawing together the language of contract and of interpersonal gratitude.[37]

Indian culture is cast as synonymous with the generous natural impulses of the human heart, providing a counterpoint to Euramerican formality, legalism, and hierarchy. While native subjectivities are envisioned by the novel as a democratizing legacy that helps shape the character of the American people, such practices and forms of identification cannot substitute for progress and civilization. In *The Cunning of Recognition*, Elizabeth Povinelli addresses how citizens of settler states draw on amorphous and elliptical notions of indigenous tradition as a way of reaffirming the tolerance and capaciousness of liberal governance:

> This referential nonspecificity is not the result of a lack of knowledge or a
> failure to report it. Rather, "ancient protocol" is experienced as maximally

symbolic at exactly the moment when it seems minimally determinate. This semiotic hinge allows readers to fantasize a maximal variety of images of the deserving indigenous subject at the very moment the description of the content of the social geography approaches zero. (58)

Povinelli here is discussing contemporary Australia, but *Hope Leslie* reveals an earlier version of this dynamic. In the novel, indigenous alterity functions as an imaginative space from which to extract forms of sociality at odds with bourgeois homemaking while containing the potential disruption of Anglo-American political economy. Equating Indianness with *nature* valorizes it as a nexus of regeneration/transformation for Euramericans by displacing the possibility of Euramerican loss—of land, of jurisdiction, of metapolitical control over the terms of native occupancy. Indigenous difference is invoked to present as extrapolitical a particular position within a struggle for hegemony over the relation between "private" and "public," a struggle from which native peoples are excluded as participants. The text, therefore, does not so much actively advocate the dispossession of native peoples, endorsing removal per se, as unevenly seek to separate Indian modes of feeling from indigenous political and land claims, decrying white violence while still in a different register insisting on the legitimacy of Euramerican occupation and the emergence of the United States.[38] Sundered from sovereignty, native family formation and affect can signify counterhegemonically, leveraging the logic of separate spheres and marital intimacy coalescing in the early nineteenth century. I should clarify, though, that I am not so much suggesting that the disavowal of sovereignty is an intentional project as that it is a necessary corollary of the particular strategic choices the novel makes about how to displace an increasingly dominant nuclear family model.[39] By presenting Indian social life as a more *natural* way of structuring the relay between public spirit and private sentiment than the isolated conjugal household, *Hope Leslie* can depict extended networks of kinship, ostensibly derived/learned from native peoples, as a preferable set of principles around which to order national identity and community.

If the trope of the noble savage allows Sedgwick simultaneously to portray native peoples as exemplary and on the way to extinction, the discourse of Indian captivity offers a useful set of narrative strategies through which to frame Indian-white interaction around familial feelings, bracketing native geopolitics.[40] The kidnapping of Euramericans by native peoples during times of military conflict had been a durable topic for a range of different kinds of writings since the 1680s. The memoirs of those taken, categorized generically as captivity narratives, were among the most salable and widely circulated texts in the colonies produced before the Revolution. While current examples of such stories were in shorter supply by the late eighteenth century, they increasingly became material for what have come to be called frontier romances, a novelistic genre whose popularity was on the rise.[41] The incredible success of *Hope Leslie* itself testifies to this pattern. While war gave rise to captivity, it enters only peripherally into such narratives. Rather than foregrounding the political context—the struggles over territory, resources, and jurisdiction that create the conditions for the detainment of noncombatants—these texts focus on the experience of the captive. In particular, they emphasize the violence of the initial Indian attack and the loss of friends and family members, the oddity of and adaptation to native customs, and the (partial and uneven) incorporation of the stranger into the captors' social routines. While many other Euramerican prisoners taken in the raid are killed, the narrator is spared, often in order to be adopted. Replacing a recently deceased kinsperson with someone who previously had been an alien to the group was a common and longstanding practice among many peoples, especially given the massive losses of native population in the seventeenth and eighteenth centuries (at times as great as 90 percent) due to European diseases. This process, however, regularly is not recognized as such by the captive, who believes himself or herself to be possessed by a "master." From one angle, the story of captivity may be summarized as the loss of one family (Euramerican) to be absorbed into another (native). In its attention to affect and eschewal of political history, this narrative structure provides Sedgwick with a way of recuperating the sociality of the Indian "tribe" for the project of contesting the ideology of conjugal privacy.

Captivity potentially could serve as a means of foregrounding the discrepancy between native peoples' self-understandings and the schemes employed in British and U.S. Indian policy, using firsthand experience (or its fictionalization) to illustrate the failure of Anglo-American formulations and procedures to acknowledge the actual dynamics of indigenous governance and collectivity. However, the rhetoric of Indian captivity, in its various narrative instantiations, is not articulated to the matrix of treaty-making; the multiform kin-aesthetics at play in texts featuring captivity operate in a different discursive register than diplomacy and formal geopolitical negotiation. Rather than attempting to make visible "experiences to which the fixed forms do not speak at all, which indeed they do not recognize,"[42] highlighting elements of native social formations ignored or disavowed in Indian policy, the narration of captivity fixates on interpersonal relations between Indians and Euramericans, especially in light of the decreasing influence of a providential interpretive framework by the mid-eighteenth century.[43] As Michelle Burnham argues, "the scene or event of Indian captivity metonymically links, with chains of feeling, the micropolitical realm of family to the macropolitical representation of America's current state and future conditions."[44] Such rhetoric registers cultural discrepancies but in the context of assessing the relative potential for communication and compassion. The question of sovereignty is bracketed in elaborating the (im)possibility of connection among individuals, as opposed to polities.

When viewed through this prism, native kinship itself loses its political dimensions. More than merely an expression of forms of homemaking and reproduction, the kinds of relations and idioms conventionally character-ized as *kinship* helped in structuring and negotiating collective identity, both intra- and intertribally. Among coastal Algonquian groups in southern New England, positions of leadership—sachemships—were allocated based on complex genealogical reckonings along both matrilineal and patrilineal lines of descent, and marriages between persons from powerful lineages served as a way of cementing political relationships, including between different peoples. Representing political authority in familial terms helped reinforce the coherence of the domain of a given sachem while also vali-dating the exertion of chiefly authority by connecting it to the kinds of reciprocity seen as the social ideal in kinship relations. Moreover, extensive intermarriage among peoples in the region created flexible networks of association and allegiance that could minimize routine conflict and be activated tactically by small groups for the purposes of mobility, trade, and land use.[45]

Casting kin-making as primarily about the mutual expression of "nat-ural" "love" among persons with no biological connection, therefore, leaves aside its crucial role in shaping native governance and as a vehicle of alliance among peoples in micrological and macrological ways. Thus, while the dynamics of sovereignty and of family were intertwined for native peoples in and around New England, which is precisely what gives them their value as metaphor/model in troubling the distinction between "public welfare" and "private feelings," the novel divorces the familial forms and connections dis-covered in captivity from the official process of recognizing native political structures and land tenure. The text uses the topos of Indian captivity to le-verage increasingly normative notions of gender and marriage, while sus-pending the questions surrounding native political identity, boundaries, and internal governance at the center of U.S. Indian policy. In Gramsci's terms, the project of achieving hegemony, or altering an existing hegemonic forma-tion, involves "a process of differentiation and change in the relative weight that the elements of the old ideologies used to possess" (195), and the kind of social reimagining the novel offers relies on the citation of Indian differ-ence to dislodge ideologies of conjugal privacy while leaving the organizing structures of U.S. jurisdiction undisturbed.

This pattern can be seen in the text's allusion to Sedgwick's family history, its embrace of the life of Eunice Williams as a basis for major elements of its plot.[46] She was captured as part of an attack by French and Indian forces on the town of Deerfield in early 1704. Although her father and several of her siblings also were taken, they were ransomed and returned to New England by 1706, whereas she was adopted by Kahnawake Mohawks, chose to remain among them, and by 1713 had married a Mohawk man named Arosen. They visited her relatives in New England several times in the early 1740s and 1760s, and two of her great-grandchildren were enrolled in a school in Longmeadow, Massachusetts, for about five years at the beginning of the nineteenth century. Sedgwick's grandparents, parents, and Sedgwick herself, then, almost certainly had repeated contact with Eunice and her Kahnawake descendants.[47] Other critics have noted the parallels between Eunice's story and that of Faith Leslie in the novel, including her marriage to an Indian man, choice not to rejoin her birth family, forgetting of the English language, and conversion to Catholicism.[48] However, the connection is even tighter than previously has been noticed. The text consistently links Mononotto to "Mohawks," indicating that they became his protectors and accomplices in the aftermath of the English massacre.[49] Not only were the Pequots and Mohawks not aligned, despite occasional rumors to the contrary, but as allies of Massachusetts Bay, Mohawks killed Pequots who had escaped the English militia, including the sachem Sassacus.[50] Moreover, the Pequots took no English captives after the destruction of Mystic village because when they came near the settlements of the colonists they were seized and either killed or enslaved.[51]

These errors suggest that Sedgwick implicitly (or strategically) merges two separate and quite different historical moments, the Pequot War and the conflicts with allied French and Indian forces in the early to mid-eighteenth century. That fusion pries captivity out of its embeddedness in identifiable struggles, creating a generic narrative that avoids reference to the practices, histories, and geopolitical claims of particular peoples. Echoing the novel's projection of sentimental family feeling back into the seventeenth century, such a stripping of specificity allows the topos of captivity to signify an amalgamated Indian culture divorced from place and metapolitical contestation over how to map jurisdiction and land tenure.

In *Hope Leslie*, the origin of Indian-Euramerican relations seems to lie not in negotiations over territory and trade but in captivity itself. When Winthrop sends Magawisca to the Fletcher home, she already knows English, "having been taught it by an English captive, who for a long time dwelt with her tribe" (21). What is most odd about this plot point is not that Magawisca learns the language but the fact that knowledge comes from a "captive." Prior to the kidnapping by Pequots of two women from Wethersfield in 1637, noted earlier, there are no known instances of English captives among native peoples in the New England region.[52] While perhaps a simple error or a necessary conceit to move the plot forward without the cumbersome intrusion of translators, this choice seems notable in light of the emphasis on kin-making elsewhere in the text. Given that the next sentence notes that Magawisca "was much noticed by the English who traded with the Pequods" due to her fluency in English (21), why not have her learn the language from them? Why trace the possibility of mutual intelligibility to this invented captive?

Describing him as having "dwelt with her tribe" for some duration implies that he is not being held by force, that at some point he has chosen to remain and been accepted into Pequot social networks. In order to learn his language, Magawisca would have to have had sustained contact with him over an extended period, suggesting a certain amount of intimacy and per-haps close proximity of residence. Such routine interaction intimates a quasi-familial relation, or at least a very close friendship. Linking literacy to this kind of figure presents Euramerican-Indian communication in quite a different light than would acquiring a language through trade. The latter suggests a limited, if peaceable, relation between separate communities, whereas captivity as introduced here gestures toward incorporation, a process of enfolding others into community life by transforming strangers into kin. The diplomatic and commercial problem of translation is resolved through a form of feeling divorced from wrangling over land and resources, also illustrating the ways Indian culture merges "public" and "private" spheres. Furthermore, how did this captive become so? In the absence of a description of a prior conflict, his captivity appears completely distinct from geopolitical contention or concerns. The novel, then, frames captivity from the outset as a native proclivity for emotional connection with aliens. Part of what Magawisca learns before meeting the Fletchers is this ostensibly Indian ability to bridge cultural difference through affective bonding. Thus, the novel envisions Indian difference as the capacity for boundary crossing. In Povinelli's terms, not only is "the social geography" of the Pequots "mini-mally determinate" but it becomes "maximally symbolic" at the moment it facilitates the intimate embrace of Euramericans.

If Magawisca's childhood experience teaches her how to make family of strangers, she conveys such instruction to Hope in the discussions sur-rounding Hope's reunion with Faith. When Magawisca informs Hope that her sister has married Oneco, Hope cries out, "God forbid! . . . My sister married to an Indian!", to which Magawisca responds by asking, "Think ye that your blood will be corrupted by mingling with this stream?", further adding that Faith "is dear to Mononotto as if his own blood ran in her veins" (188). The invocation of blood here displaces racial division in favor of an image of mixture and flow, one that reaffirms the link between Indians and nature and the consequent advisability of attending to native perspectives and practices. This description of Faith's status alludes back to Magawisca's earlier expressions of love toward the Fletchers, particularly her insistence that she "bleed[s] when they are struck" (63). Again, rather than making kinship dependent on consanguinity, blood becomes a concrete figure for alternative forms of familial feeling.[53] Although Mononotto's affection for Faith comes as the result of matrimony, it recalls his and his wife's generosity and affection toward the English, including the anonymous "captive." Faith's link to Oneco appears as merely the last in a series of native-settler bonds that extend the boundaries of who can count as family, thereby demonstrating the possibilities made available by following the "generous impulses of nature" as opposed to "the letter of the law" (278). Thus, captivity lies at the center of the novel's narration of the triumph of expansive emotional networks over state-managed privatization, making native adoption into the prism through which to reimagine the symbolics of affiliation among nonnatives. This relationship of tutelage is expressed by Hope in her eventual acceptance of Faith's marriage; taking "a more . . . natural view of the affair," she adopts "the suggestions of Magawisca," which "combin[ed] with the dictates of her own heart" (339). Not only does (a generic rendition of) Indian thought predominate, but it is imagined as merely an expression of the "natural" tendencies already existing within the hearts of Euramericans.

Prior to their eventual retreat into western "obscurity," Magawisca, Faith, and family teach Hope, and by extension the reader, how to feel in more expansive ways. The emotional dynamics of Indian life become the basis for imagining new formations of affect that can reshape the social topography of the (proto)national community. Seizing upon romantic primitivism as a way of illustrating the democratic potential that lies in less constricted notions of kinship, though, involves creating a simulacrum of native customs divorced from the matrix of indigenous occupancy, diplomacy, and trade. Blood may no longer signify race in the novel, but the text's metaphorics of friendship and siblinghood prove incapable of registering native land claims. In taking up native culture as a way of queering the conjugal imaginary, of proposing alternative formations of home and family, what is lost is not simply the sense of indigenous peoples as separate polities but the ways kinship systems are themselves deeply enmeshed in native governance. The topos of captivity offers a way of representing a web of lateral, nonbiological relations that challenges the kind of nuclear lineality envisioned by Daniel Webster, but such a fetishization of the supposed openness of native societies forecloses exploration of how discourses of kinship function as a mechanism of boundary-making, as well as overlooking the challenge they pose to the organizing principles of U.S. Indian policy. In making the Indian "tribe" a discursive vehicle for redeeming kinds of affection and collectivity deemed "unnatural," non-native counterhegemonic projects, such as Sedgwick's novel, run the risk of reifying a version of Indian identity that itself disables discussion of political difference—the distinctions between Euramerican and indigenous modes of sovereignty.[54]

REMAPPING THE FAMILY OF NATIONS

By divorcing captivity from the representation of native governance and making it a vehicle for signifying settler subjectivity, *Hope Leslie* retools kinship as a resource for reforming the American public sphere, thereby displacing its operation as a definitional nexus for indigenous publics and polities. In this way, the novel's queer structure of feeling implicitly relies on the normalization of the principles of U.S. Indian law. The novel implies that native notions of kinship could close the breach between "private feelings" and "public welfare" that the central characters often bemoan, indicating how intimate relations among non-natives can be reconceptualized in light of principles learned through Euramerican bonds with Indians. However, such borrowing genericizes native practices by dislodging them from their historical and geopolitical contexts.

Situating native kinship within one struggle for hegemony (the definition of home and family within the settler state) can erase its participation in another (the struggle over what will constitute sovereignty or the process of determining the legitimacy of political claims and forms of identity). As Dale Turner notes, "there are intellectual landscapes that have been forced on Aboriginal peoples . . . These intellectual traditions, stained by colonialism, have created discourses on property, ethics, political sovereignty, and justice that have subjugated, distorted, and marginalized Aboriginal ways of thinking" (88). Traditional social formations as they operated within and among peoples, conventionally characterized by non-natives through the rhetoric of *kinship*, militated against the strategies of U.S. Indian policy by challenging the naturalization of liberal governance, maintaining relations among peoples not managed by the United States, and refusing the nuclear family ideal promoted by the civilization program;[55] such systems, therefore, had no place in the discursive and institutional landscape of U.S. law. In deferring discussion of metapolitical authority—who will define what constitutes "politics"—while appropriating native kinship for reimagining the symbolics of the settler state, *Hope Leslie* locates its cultural maneuvering on the terrain of U.S. jurisdiction.

In Sedgwick's portrayal of the Mahicans of Stockbridge, one can see the exception that highlights this broader pattern. They enter the novel's narrative only briefly, as the space of respite for Mononotto after the English massacre to which he brings his children, Faith, and Everell in the wake of his attack on the Fletcher home.[56] The text describes the area and its inhabitants in pastoral terms: "The lower valley of the Housatonick, at the period to which our history refers, was inhabited by a peaceful, and, as far as that epithet could ever be applied to our savages, an agricultural tribe, whose territory, situate midway between the Hudson and the Connecticut, was bounded and defended on each side by mountains, then deemed impracticable to a foe" (85). The Mahicans here are pacific farmers, an image that itself strains against the depiction of Indians elsewhere in the novel as an extension of the wilderness. The passage intimates this tension in its qualification of the "epithet" "agricultural," framing Mahican land use within the implicit assertion that the territory always-already was incorporated into the "our" of (proto)national jurisdiction. The tone of confident possession, though, falters at the end, the phrase "then deemed" gesturing toward later Anglo-American occupation of the land and casting such settlement as invasion by a "foe."

The anxiety over the transfer of inhabitance appears again, intensified, on the next page: "Within the memory of the present generation the remnant of the tribe migrated to the west; and even now some of their families make a summer pilgrimage to this, their Jerusalem, and are regarded with a melancholy interest by the present occupants of the soil" (86). Reversing the Puritan equation of the English with the Israelites, Sedgwick here portrays the Mahicans as a people thrust into diaspora by the loss of their homeland. This moment breaks the proleptic relay between the seventeenth and nineteenth centuries that is central to the presentation of the Puritans as the origin of the American nation, and to the projection backward of sentimental family feeling, instead noting a "memory" at the edge of the lives of "the present generation." It also contravenes the sense of native disappearance conveyed in the final chapter in the description of the Indian characters as going on a "pilgrimage to the far western forests" in which they are lost in the "voiceless obscurity of those unknown regions" (339). On the contrary, some Mahicans, the text informs readers, regularly make a "pilgrimage" back to Stockbridge, further suggesting Sedgwick's intimate awareness of their dispossession. Note that the current residents of Stockbridge seem to engage with the Mahican "families" that return only as a "melancholy" spectacle. Utterly absent here are the expansive possibilities for kin-making that appear elsewhere, introduced early in the novel through Magawisca and her family and continued later through the network established and maintained by Hope (particularly as dramatized in the effort to rescue Magawisca).

These Stockbridge moments seem to illustrate how familial bonds between Indians and Euramericans are made impossible by the latter's failure to acknowledge native sovereignty, a refusal that generates not connection but a profound, amorphous, and pervasive unease for the current inhabitants. Here we see a brief and circumscribed portrait of another strand of Sedgwick's family history. While the novel makes Eunice Williams a decontextualized symbol for native adoption, and the capaciousness of Indian familial feeling more broadly, it almost entirely disavows the story of Ephraim Williams and his son Elijah.[57] The former was part of the first group of English families to settle in Stockbridge after it was granted township status by the Massachusetts General Court in 1736, on the heels of the founding of a mission there two years earlier.[58] By the 1730s, the Mahicans largely had coalesced in western Massachusetts, combining with remaining local groups, and in the late 1740s, they moved the council fire of their people to Stockbridge. Ephraim Williams was relentless in his efforts to acquire land from them, asserting claims to hundreds of acres above what he was allotted and maneuvering to have them secured by the General Court. After his death, his son Elijah used his positions as sheriff of the county and town selectman to facilitate Mahican land loss through debt, becoming the largest purchaser and landowner in the town. By the 1790s, he had acquired a farm of more than 1,000 acres and had bought or leased almost 1,300 acres of land from the Indians of Stockbridge. Having their lands slowly whittled away through illegal seizures, fudged and sometimes coerced agreements, interested legislative and judicial decisions, and various kinds of inflated indebtedness, the vast majority of Mahicans chose to leave Stockbridge, moving in 1783 to territory donated by the Oneidas in western New York. The descendant of Ephraim's daughter Abigail and an intermittent resident of Stockbridge for her entire life, especially during her childhood, Catharine Sedgwick would have had ample opportunity to become aware of this part of her family's past. What I want to emphasize is the ways Eunice's and Ephraim's histories are more or less isolated from each other in the novel. In fact, the latter seems to contravene, and even fracture, the organizing tropes of the former, drawing attention to a long history of ostensibly peaceful Indian-white interaction that is not emotionally unifying but instead marked by extensive and sustained forms of exploitation, manipulation, and dispossession.

If the text's brief reference to the Mahicans unsettles its broader associations and aims, sustained critical attention to Mahican self-representation can help elaborate the kinds of political projects effaced in Sedgwick's use of native kinship to queer non-native notions of home and family.[59] Specifically, Hendrick Aupaumut's account of his service as a U.S. envoy to peoples in the Ohio region, "A Short Narration of My Last Journey to the Western Country" (1792), illustrates the complex ways kinship can serve as an idiom of governance, and in so doing challenge the organizing logics of U.S. policy.[60] Born in Stockbridge in May 1757 and educated at the mission school there, Aupaumut had been raised amid, and trained in, Euramerican social life, including service in the Continental army during the Revolution in which he earned the title of "Captain." Yet he also was a hereditary sachem and in the 1780s led his people from western Massachusetts to Oneida territory to evade increasing forms of white intrusion and exploitation. His role as a U.S. negotiator began in 1791. U.S. Indian commissioner Timothy Pickering had been searching for a prominent person in the Iroquois League to serve as a liaison with western peoples, but receiving only tepid responses, he heeded an offer from Aupaumut, who likely hoped to use the position as leverage against potential interference in Mahican affairs by either their Haudenosaunee neighbors or the state of New York. From 1791 to 1793, he went on four missions of peace; "A Short Narration" is the chronicle of his third trip west.[61] His narrative contests U.S. ideologies by insisting on the centrality of native traditions in understanding and negotiating with indigenous peoples, particularly the role of kinship as a paradigmatic mode of native internationalism.[62]

The failure of the U.S. to engage with, or even acknowledge, native geo-politics immediately in the wake of the Revolution produced volatile confrontations with nations northwest of the Ohio River. In the immediate aftermath of the war, the United States attempted to treat native peoples, particularly those who had sided with the British, as conquered subjects to whom policy could be dictated. Such unilateralism involved the imposition of several treaties between 1784 and 1786, which if accepted by some chiefs were greeted by many native peoples in the region as an illegitimate intrusion on their lands. The U.S. attempt to extend its boundaries northwestward through treaty-making was an effort both to impose terms of peace on former enemies and to acquire land that could then be sold to white settlers in order to offset the extensive debt from the war. In response to these incursions, a confederacy emerged, with representatives from a range of peoples including the Six Nations of the Iroquois, Miamis, Delawares, Shawnees, and Potawatomies meeting regularly at Brownstown (south of what would become Detroit) in the late 1780s with on-again, off-again support from British officials. The coalition demanded that the United States cede all claims to lands north of the Ohio River, acknowledge that lands in the Ohio region were under the joint control of members of the confederacy, and accept that their unanimous support for sales would be necessary for any U.S. purchase to be valid. In 1789, the council fire of the confederacy was moved to Kekionga (Miami Town) on the Maumee River. In 1790 and 1791, Josiah Harmar and Arthur St. Clair, respectively, led disastrous assaults on the village, the latter resulting in the death of 600 U.S. soldiers and an additional 800 casualties. As a result of these defeats, Major General Anthony Wayne was appointed commander of U.S. forces in the west in 1792. In 1794, he led a campaign against the remaining forces of the confederacy, which had dwindled over the previous year, and on August 20, in what has come to be known as the Battle of Fallen Timbers, he pushed them back to the gates of Fort Miami, at which point the British refused to give them protection, thereby effectively ending the armed conflict. The Treaty of Greenville was signed in August 1795, reaffirming the terms of the previous treaties.[63]

U.S. unwillingness to comprehend native sociospatiality had produced an incredibly expensive and horribly bloody conflict that threatened the security and solvency of the new nation. In his orders to Aupaumut, Pickering indicates that he should "convince them of the moderation, justice, and desire of the United States for peace," further emphasizing that "the business on which you are employed is of high importance to the United States."[64] A central part of Aupaumut's mission was to find a basis for rapprochement through which the United States and the peoples of the Ohio could engage in meaningful dialogue. As he makes clear at the beginning of his account, the political matrix into which the United States seeks to enter is shaped first and foremost by relations of kinship. He observes, "Before I proceed in the business I am upon, I think it would be necessary to give a short sketch what friendship and connections, our forefathers, and we, have had with the western tribes" (76). He then proceeds to detail the web of relations in which the Mahicans, Iroquois League, and the peoples with whom he was sent to negotiate are enmeshed: the Delawares are the Mahicans' grandfathers; the Shawnees are the younger brothers; the Miamis, grandchildren; the Wyandots, uncles; the Ottawas and Chippewas, grandchildren; and the Six Nations of the Iroquois, uncles (76–79). These familial connections are not simply individual links between the Mahicans and other peoples but also express the relative positions of the latter with respect to each other. All these peoples belong to a shared system in which kinship terms encode the dynamics of their past (for "near 200 years" [77]) and shape their ongoing interactions. Aupaumut intimates that the struggles of the present cannot be resolved without knowledge of the sociopolitical framework inherited from "our forefathers," implicitly insisting that the United States can enter into this internationalist network only by appreciating and accepting its organizing structures.

This initial conceit works to place the United States within a native-centered history and geography, and the text uses the recounting of diplomatic exchanges to indicate the coherence of these peoples as peoples. Rather than using letters and documents, native nations transmit messages through speeches in council.[65] Within each one, the speaker names his audience by invoking the kinship relation that obtains between their peoples. For example, "the Chief of Shawanese" begins his address to Aupaumut with the following:

Elder brother Muhheuconneew–

    We now speak in one voice to you—we all rejoice that you have come to us—you have taken great pains to come on the long and tedious journey. Our ancestors have long ago fixed our feelings which we ever maintain—and it is so ordered by the Great Good Spirit that we this day see each other after a great length of time, and that we now set together. (90)

Similarly, in a later address to a council of Delawares, Aupaumut observes:

Grandfather–

    We the poor remnant of our ancestors are met together. Our good fathers have left good customs, and path to go by, so that in all occasions we are to put each other in remembrance of the ancient Customs of our fathers as well as the friendship. (99)

These moments illustrate that the familial idiom is less an expression of individual feelings and relationships than of enduring bonds among collectivities. The Shawnee chief and Aupaumut speak as part of a "we" who have a longstanding connection with the Mahicans and Delawares, respectively, both invoking a "friendship" that subsists not between villages or enclaves but between peoples. From this perspective, each people has a unity, a cohesive identity as a sociopolitical entity, that enables it to be personified as a relative; conversely, the language of kinship reinforces such collective subjectivity as a vital feature of interactions within, and negotiations among, indigenous communities.

The presentation of intertribal ties as an inheritance from "ancestors" suggests more than simply their duration, further expressing something of their form and content. Unlike a contract, a mutually agreed upon set of conditions and responsibilities between two or more parties, the double-sided invocation of kinship—as an intratribal familial legacy and an intertribal familial connection—casts diplomacy as ongoing participation in a network of intimate relationships that depends on periodic renewal. In a speech to the Delawares, Aupaumut observes:

It is a happy thing that we should maintain a Union. But to us it is not a new thing. For our good Ancestors (who used to have compassion to each other,) many, many years ago, have agreed to this. And we, who are of their descendance, should not hisitate, or, as it were, ask one another whether we should like it. But we must always remind each other how our ancestors did agree on this Subject, that we may never forgo that. (101)

The ongoing expression of "compassion" and care is crucial to sustaining the "friendship" among people. Moreover, the familial idiom marks a sense of interdependence and reciprocal responsibility that is not reducible to the notion of contingent national self-interest that shapes Euramerican policy decisions. The language of kinship, then, suggests that each people functions as an autonomous entity while at the same time indicating that such identity gains its meaning within an intertribal matrix that provides the geohistorical context for native national formation and identification.

These relationships are replicated on a smaller scale as well. Once he has reached the Maumee River, Aupaumut encounters a fellow Mahican who lives in the area. Named Pohquonnoppeet, he is "one of the chiefs" and "has been with these nations ever since he was a boy." However, his residence has not cut him off from other Mahicans; rather, he "has long[ed] to see us" and "has been strengthen[ing] our message these several years" (87). This seemingly isolated figure is situated within a broader geography of alliance in which peoples continually renew the bonds established in generations past. Pohqunnoppet's local connections are presented as an extension of broader patterns of intertribal affection and alliance, his relationships of kinship with those around him mirroring, renewing, and helping concretize bonds among peoples. Such residence can be understood as a local instance that helps cohere and sustain the larger network of "friendship." In this way, kinship provides a flexible framework for native geopolitics, avoiding a rigid territoriality in which overlap and mixture necessarily would mean the abandonment or dissolution of prior identities.[66]

Aupaumut's detailed account of both Mahican kinship relations with other peoples and the active rehearsal and renewal of those connections as a central feature of their present engagement with each other subtly contests the norms of U.S. Indian policy. His report's foregrounding of the role of native tradition as an indispensable part of diplomatic routine implicitly indicates that U.S. preemption claims and modes of treaty-making have no place in the Ohio country. The assumption that the peoples with whom Aupaumut has been sent to negotiate reside on U.S. territory and that they can be approached individually for cessions of territory simply makes no sense in his narrative. In fact, claims by non-natives to superintend intertribal relations appear not merely presumptuous but preposterous. During a conference with Aupaumut, the Delaware sachem Big Cat recounts an exchange he had with Captain Matthew Elliot, a British agent in the region. After Elliot asks "where these Indians come from, and what is their business," Big Cat responds, "how came you to ask such questions? . . . Can you watch, and look all around the earth to see who come to us? or is what their Business? Do you not know that we are upon our own Business? and that we have longed to see these our friends, who now come to us, and for which we rejoice" (103)? The inclusion of this dialogue can be seen as an effort to put U.S. officials on notice that meddling in native international affairs, and especially insisting on the right unilaterally to set the terms of U.S.-Indian relations, will not be tolerated. Aupaumut here, via Big Cat, challenges the imperial arrogation of metapolitical authority to determine the proper contours of political identity. The narrative sketches, in Dale Turner's terms, an *intellectual landscape* in which native peoples do not remain insulated from each other on isolated reserves mapped and managed by non-native governments. In this vein, not only does kinship offer a different understanding of the social topography of native life than that of European and Euramerican regimes, but through this optic, the attempt to use the legal structure of the settler state to mediate the relation between peoples, to cast that structure as a neutral vehicle for registering native geopolitics, appears as itself an intrusion on native sovereignty and self-determination.

The self-interested nature of U.S. policy, and the wary stance of the Mahicans toward it, is made clear in one of Aupaumut's addresses to a mixed council of Shawnees and Delawares. He states:

> I will acquaint you some things of our situation, lest you may have wrong appr[e]hension. Since the British and Americans lay down their hatchets, then my nation was forgotten. We never have had invitation to set in Council with the white people—not as the [Iroquois] Nations and you are greatly regarded by the white people—but last winter was the first time I had invitation from the great man of the United States to attend Council in Philadelphia. (92)

Beyond simply providing background on his status as an envoy, Aupaumut here offers critical commentary on the guiding principles of U.S. Indian affairs. In contrast to the rituals of renewed kinship that mark ongoing intertribal memories of ancestral affections, relationships with the United States are shaped by a capricious forgetfulness in which governmental "regard" waxes and wanes depending on perceived national need. The "invitation" to Aupaumut to meet in council with U.S. officials appears here as a fickle gesture, unlike the sustained relations of "friendship" among native peoples. Even though he speaks on behalf of the U.S. government, Aupaumut distances the Mahicans from it, implying that the idea of an intimate alliance between them would be a "wrong appr[e]hension" and raising questions about the ability of the United States to engage in good-faith diplomacy.

Including this speech in his report serves as a way of chastising U.S. officials for previously ignoring Mahican presence and interests while also suggesting that substantive engagement with native political networks will require a reformed attitude toward such relations. In this way, the text not only provides a kinship-centered mapping of native geopolitics, which increases U.S. intelligence on peoples in the Ohio region, but intimates that the failure of the United States to adhere to indigenous political norms will result in diplomatic disaster and further bloodshed. Toward the end of the narrative, Aupaumut observes that he has omitted some quite damning details in his talks with western peoples:

> I have as it were oblige to say nothing with regard to the conduct of Yorkers, how they cheat my fathers, how they taken our lands Unjustly, and how my fathers were groaning as it were to their graves, in loseing their lands for nothing, although they were faithful friends to the Whites; and how the white people artfully got their Deeds confirm in their Laws, &c. I say had I mention these things to the Indians, it would agravate their prejudices against all white people, &c. (128)

Referencing current pressures on the Oneidas' territory and New Stock-bridge as well as struggles earlier in the century over extensive tracts of land in the vicinity of Albany, this passage denounces the seizure of native lands as a violation of the "faithful friend"-ship between the Mahicans and whites.[67] In light of the report's repeated use of "friendship" to represent intertribal kinship, the term's appearance here portrays Anglo-American modes of land acquisition as having failed to uphold native notions of right conduct, as a wholesale inability to be a good relative and to offer appropriate forms of respect and reciprocity. By indicating that such actions if revealed to western peoples "would agravate their prejudices," Aupaumut seeks to leverage more just treatment for the Mahicans and to signal the nonviability of the usual Euramerican documentary and bureaucratic sleights of hand in negotiations with native nations. Legalistic "artfull"-ness must be replaced with a "compassion" predicated on a sense of sustained connection among autonomous peoples.[68]

While challenging the United States to change its modus operandi in order to bring itself in line with indigenous internationalism, the narrative does not imply that the relationships among the peoples it discusses are untroubled and free of conflict. Rather, the report carefully chronicles disagreements and captures some incredibly pointed accusations leveled by various groups against others. When confronted with the Wyandot delegation's desire to wait for more representatives to arrive before setting up a meeting with U.S. officials, Puckonchehluh, the head warrior of the Delawares, asserts,

> You gave me the tomahawk—You laid the foundation of our ruin—now you are setting still, as soon as you hear me speaking of peace you are displeased. Why—because you live in a safe place—yonder. You use me as your front door, now let us exchange our seats, let me live or set yonder, and you set

here as my fronter door see whether you would not rejoice to hear the offers
of peace. (111)

Similarly, Shawnee, Miami, and Cherokee delegates charge the Haudenosaunees (here referred to as the "Five Nations" rather than six) with pushing
them into war: "[T]he English and the Five Nations did lay a foundation for
our ruin. They gave us the tomahawk, and the English are at the bottom of
this war ever since . . . Let the English and Five Nations lose their lands"
(115). A little more than a week later, the Shawnees say to the delegates from
the Iroquois League, "Now you may return home, and tell your white people
all what you have heard" (121). The inclusion of this last statement seems
somewhat ironic, since it appears to function as a critique of British intervention in Indian affairs, especially the alliance with the Six Nations, but
Aupaumut in the report is in fact "tell[ing his] white people all what [he had]
heard." The difference seems to rest in the idea that the Six Nations have lied
to other native peoples in order to serve British interests, whereas, as one of
the Delaware sachems observes of the Mahicans, "we could not [find] any
instance wherein your ancestors have deceived our fathers" (130). In this
vein, the confrontations Aupaumut describes stem from the perception that
a (group of) people(s) is using the longstanding network of relationships
inappropriately, invoking the customs of kinship only to twist them for self-
ish ends. Rather than undermining the principles of native diplomacy articulated at the beginning of the narrative, the discussion of quarrels among
peoples actually confirms them.

Even as he speaks on behalf of the United States as an official envoy, Aupaumut maintains a distance from the dynamics of U.S. policy. Appealing for
peace and reconciliation, he differentiates the "Big Knives" (the white squat-
ters and assailants in native territories) from the government, insisting that
these intruders are not representative of the new nation and that the United
States has promised to deal with them (126–128);[69] he also argues that the
United States desires "to lift . . . the Indians up from the ground," gesturing
toward the incipient civilization program and distinguishing it from British
policy that seeks simply "to cover them with blanket and shirt every fall"
(127). Yet these initiatives are presented in the context of a reaffirmation of a
traditional matrix of intertribal solidarity whose structuring idiom is familial. As portrayed in the narrative, this framework does not merely use the
terminology of kinship but privileges forms of memory, intimacy, interdependence, and periodic renewal associated with intratribal kinship systems.
Moreover, the text subtly, and sometimes by proxy, refuses Euramerican preemption, intervention, and legalism, casting them as presumption, deception, and violation while indicating the integrity of native modes of diplomacy
and the necessity of respecting them if the United States seeks lasting peace.

As presented in Aupaumut's narrative, intertribal kinship systems treat peoples as coherent, separate collectivities. Boundaries are not banished but peacefully negotiated and renewed as part of an internationalist network itself predicated on native nations' simultaneous autonomy and sustained association with each other. Such a vision of familial relation as a vehicle of sovereignty and geopolitical identification is fundamentally at odds with the image of boundaryless, "natural" affection and adoption at play in *Hope Leslie*. As the text's brief references to the history of Stockbridge suggest, its effort to make captivity a trope for the possibility of intercultural kin-making, and by extension a model for non–conjugally centered community formation, founders when confronted with the dynamics of U.S. jurisdiction and property law. Putting Sedgwick's novel in dialogue with Aupaumut's narrative helps reveal the extent to which the former's employment of native modes of collectivity as a way of reimagining, or queering, the U.S. national public depends on effacing the geopolitics of native kinship. Put another way, Sedgwick's counterhegemonic reformation of home and family requires not simply overlooking the legal dynamics of native dislocation but dislodging native traditions from their role in ongoing struggles with the U.S. government over how to map the intellectual landscape of sovereignty, thereby depoliticizing and despatializing kinship.

DOMESTICATING INSURGENCY

Aupaumut's narrative helps highlight the kind of native opposition to U.S. political paradigms for which there is no place in Sedgwick's novel. However, more than appropriating native modes of kin-making to challenge the dominance of conjugal homemaking, *Hope Leslie* uses the language of family to code native actions that could be seen as a challenge to the political imaginary of the settler state as exceptional, as extreme expressions of emotion. In this way, the text's conflation of kinship with interpersonal feeling functions as a discourse of counterinsurgency, recasting native modes of governance as merely a series of temporary emotional eruptions without clear political import. In "The Prose of Counter-Insurgency," Ranajit Guha illustrates how accounts of popular uprisings in India by British colonial administrators portray such actions as isolated aberrations, akin to natural disasters in their unpredictability and disconnection from anything that could be described as political will or organization (61). Such official reports give shape to later accounts that replicate this logic, adopting "the optics of a colonialist historiography" in which "the rebel has no place in this history as the subject of rebellion" (71). When addressing native decisions about occupancy and warfare, the novel uses kinship as an optic in ways that help foreclose the issue of self-determination, depicting debates over migration and military mobilization as about excessive individual affect—mourning or anger—rather than collective subjectivity and placemaking.

If the text employs figures of family to suggest a potentially boundaryless bond between Indians and whites, its representation of native residency through that same idiom works to evacuate inhabitance of political content. Critics have noted that *Hope Leslie* portrays the displacement of Magawisca and her family to the west as their choice, by extension implicitly casting Indian removal as consensual.[70] However, these readings have not focused on the logic of Magawisca's decision. Given that she repeatedly shows a great deal of affection for Everell, Hope, and others among the colonists, and that much of the plot hinges on their reciprocation of those feelings, why would she suggest that native peoples cannot remain in the vicinity of the English settlers, that "the Indian and the white man can no more mingle, and become one, than night and day" (330)? As discussed earlier, Magawisca herself chastises Hope for being outraged at Faith and Oneco's marriage, using the image of mingling streams to challenge the horror of (supposed) miscegenation and eventually persuading Hope of the foolishness of her earlier perspective. Moreover, the text repeatedly envisions the possibility of deep, sustained emotional connection between Indians and whites, including Magawisca's relationship with the Fletcher family, her education by the unnamed English captive, and Mononotto's affection for Faith. In light of these textual dynamics, what animates Magawisca's insistence on the impossibility of mixture?

A potential answer can be found in her earlier expression of a similar sentiment. During her trial, she asserts, "Take my own word, I am your enemy; the sun-beam and the shadow cannot mingle. The white man cometh—the Indian vanisheth. Can we grasp in friendship the hand raised to strike us?" She closes her speech by saying to Governor Winthrop, "to my dying mother, thou didst promise, kindness to her children. In her name, I demand of thee death or liberty!" (292–293).[71] What makes her an "enemy" is neither unbridgeable natural difference nor political allegiance but the ongoing history of Euramerican violence—a wounding that appears most grievously as the murder of kin. The image of Magawisca's "dying mother" is offered as the ultimate expression of the horrific attack on Mystic village. The unprovoked invasion of the Pequots' territory, the systematic dispersion of them from their homeland, and the official repudiation of their continued existence as a distinct geopolitical entity are signified by the scene of her mother's death. The text seems to speak *as if* Magawisca's mourning for her mother, and the feelings of guilt she seeks to prompt in Winthrop for not fulfilling his promise, were capable of encompassing the meaning of the attempted destruction and erasure of the Pequot people. The scene seems to offer this death as sufficient explanation for why she would be an "enemy" of the English. A similar logic is at play in Mononotto's earlier accusation, "has thy brother vanished from thy memory?" (75), suggesting that Magawisca's closeness to the Fletchers, Everell in particular, is predicated on a failure to remember Samoset's murder by English soldiers. In this moment as well, the death of a family member serves as a metonymic stand-in for the broader effects of English imperial assault.

Or does it? From one angle, the emphasis on mourning for deceased kin can be seen as a way of concretizing and personalizing collective loss. From another, however, the text's representation of such grief does not so much link it to the larger struggles of the Pequot people as substitute the former for the latter; peoplehood appears as an ensemble of kinship connections, however less in the sense of a particular kind of political formation than an accumulation of affect-laden relations among individuals.[72] As against Aupaumut's depiction of kinship as a mode of political relation among peoples, here it appears as a native version of the bonds of sentimental domesticity. The decision to move away from whites appears to be due to the failure of colonial authorities to acknowledge the *private feelings* of Pequot families as part of the *public welfare*. Depicting Pequot outrage at their dispossession almost exclusively in terms of mourning for kin allows the novel to fold Indians into the broader logic of community-making it articulates, imagining them as potentially members of the (proto)national public rather than as participants in distinct indigenous publics and forms of placemaking structured around kinship.[73] Sedgwick presents the kinds of emotional bonding that she clusters around captivity as having been made unsustainable by Anglo military aggression, implying that in the absence of bereavement for murdered relatives Magawisca and other Indians could embrace the offer by right-feeling whites for them to "dwell with us" (330). This particular rendition of native familial feeling circumscribes the critique of imperialism, emphasizing physical assault and bloodshed but effacing the more diffuse modes of coercion at play in the extension of foreign jurisdiction over native territory (as in the Mahican passages). The novel's portrayal of Indian grief dissolves native publics (governance, land tenure, diplomacy, etc.) into an aggregation of interpersonal associations, sentimentalizing kinship in ways that dislodge it from sovereignty and thereby creating a simulacrum of Pequot identity with which readers might more easily identify.

The novel also privatizes relations among native peoples, casting diplomatic negotiations and conflicts as expressions of the personal proclivities of individual Indians. In the final chapter, after Magawisca and her family have relocated to "the far western forests" (339), Sedgwick explains Winthrop's reason for not trying to pursue her:

[H]e had one good, sufficient, and state reason for extenuating the offence of the young conspirators [in breaking Magawisca out of jail] . . .A messenger had that day arrived from the chief of the Narragansetts, with the information that a war had broken out between Miantunnomoh and Uncas, and an earnest solicitation that the English would not interfere with their domestic quarrels. . . .

It became, therefore, very important to avoid any act that might provoke the universal Indian sentiment against the English, and induce them to forgo their civil quarrel, and combine against the common enemy. (341)

While initially describing the intertribal struggle as a "war," the passage then personalizes and minimizes it by characterizing it as a "quarrel" between prominent individuals. This "domestic"-ation presents ongoing tensions among peoples in the region as a family squabble, overlooking not only the geopolitical stakes of Narragansett-Mohegan relations but the ways such antagonism was shaped by persistent forms of English intervention.[74] A history of intertribal kinship and of competition for allegiance and resources—enflamed by the English destabilization of regional politics—is reduced in *Hope Leslie* to the status of a family spat. Sedgwick earlier characterizes intertribal struggles as "petty rivalships" animated by "long transmitted hatred," and this trivial yet endemic contention thwarts Mononotto's efforts to "unit[e] all the tribes of New-England in one powerful combination" due to the unwillingness of Miantonomi to settle or move beyond "his private feud with Uncas" (195). The "hatred" that fuels that conflict does not seem to have a cause, instead appearing as an illogical pattern explicable only in terms of individual idiosyncrasies. Describing Mohegan-Narragansett conflict as "domestic" and "petty" demotes it in scale from international to interpersonal, recasting native geopolitics in southern New England within a framework in which they signify as "private" dynamics. In Aupaumut's account, indigenous internationalism mirrors the kinds of ongoing responsibility and reciprocity at play in intratribal kinship relations, but for Sedgwick, this connection depoliticizes diplomacy, understanding it as the sentimental expression of "private" feelings. Such a view neither recognizes the ways complex networks of kinship mediate the relations among these peoples as peoples nor acknowledges the central role played by the English in inciting the animosities the novel notes. In other words, the text disavows the presence of a political matrix separate from that of Euramerican jurisdiction by suggesting that intertribal diplomacy and warfare are shaped by the vicissitudes of individual emotion while simultaneously speaking of the absence of Indian unity as if it were like bickering within a household.

Hope Leslie's depiction of native decision-making as familial feeling (either grief or animosity) implicitly offers a counterinsurgent portrait of regional politics by denying the existence of forms of collective subjectivity that could challenge English claims. While kinship did serve as a crucial part of intra- and intertribal dynamics, Sedgwick's kin-aesthetic divorces native family formation from the questions and concerns of sovereignty, using tropes of kinship to signal relative Indian openness to bonding with whites rather than the autonomous functioning of indigenous polities. In order for Indian subjectivity to be available as a model for white emulation, it needs to be made generic, which involves evacuating it of geopolitical specificity. The novel uses figures of familial sentiment to efface the customs and claims of particular peoples, as well as to transpose their historical and ongoing inter-actions with each other into a more tractable discursive register, one in which boundaries are transected or transcended by intercultural intimacy and are maintained solely as a result of "private" trauma and hostility.

The text's queer structure of feeling employs decontextualized elements of native culture, using the penumbra of Indianness to naturalize and nationalize a remapping of Anglo-American notions of genealogy and homemaking. The novel seems to desire to open a dominant ideology of matrimonial normality to lateral relations of siblinghood defined in terms of emotional connection rather than biology, challenging the vision of serial genealogy offered by Webster and imagining community in ways that do not render people like Sedgwick herself "unnatural." Linking the patriarchal, nuclear family to the monarchical fixation on bloodlines, the text envisions native peoples as providing a different model, one with democratizing pos-sibilities. Sedgwick presents Indian interaction with whites as a pedagogical process in which the latter are trained in more affectively expansive—and less fetishistically conjugal—ways of being, in contrast to contemporaneous accounts of an innate Indian failure to understand true *home* and *family* (as discussed in chapter 1). The text foregrounds adoption and generosity as structuring elements of Indian identity. Portrayed as "natural" expressions of sentiment at odds with the unfeeling law of the father and the state, native customs serve as a "semiotic hinge."[75] Through them, *Hope Leslie* envisions and seeks to validate alternatives to the heterohousehold by locating the possibility of a new start in the New World in the intercultural education of captivity, itself cast as the paradigmatic form of Euramerican-native rela-tions. Thus, the text's counterhegemonic effort to leverage the increasingly normative structure of bourgeois homemaking depends on an appropria-tion of native traditions that disjoints them from native politics.

In comparing the dynamics of kinship in Sedgwick's novel and Aup-aumut's report, I have sought to highlight how one set of oppositional aims not only can displace but foreclose another operating in a different register.

The attempt to denaturalize the nuclear family form, to "queer" it by proposing a countervailing mode of familial attachment and association, ends up reinforcing the framework of U.S. jurisdiction. The novel imports aspects of native social formations into (proto)national life as a catalyst for transformation, but in so doing, it effaces the ways those same formations participate in a political struggle over the terms of U.S. Indian policy, over what kinds of indigenous self-representation, territoriality, and diplomacy will be recognized as legitimate. Native kinship systems are recontextualized within a framework that casts native peoples as part of a single Euramerican-dominated public rather than as occupying their own publics shaped by their own principles of association and identification. Aupaumut's narrative illustrates how native kinship produces subjectivities that are embedded in collective histories of geopolitical alliance and intertribal negotiation, and in seizing upon captivity as a means of queering conjugal homemaking, Sedgwick creates a generic form of Indian subjectivity in which sovereignty is rendered subaltern, made unintelligible as anything other than expansive, sentimentalized familial feeling. The novel illustrates how the critique of compulsory heterosexuality can depend upon stabilizing the geopolitical framework of U.S. governance, and in its failure to contest the metapolitical authority asserted by the United States in unilaterally setting the terms of engagement with native peoples, the text strategically contests marital privatization while normalizing the imperial ideologies structuring the settler state.

3

Romancing Kinship

Indian Education, the Allotment Program, and Zitkala-Ŝa's
American Indian Stories

The Monogamian Family—As finally constituted, this family assured
the paternity of children, substituted the individual ownership of real
as well as personal property for joint ownership, and an exclusive
inheritance by children in the place of agnatic inheritance. Modern
society reposes upon the monogamian family. The whole previous
experience and progress of mankind culminated and crystallized in
this pre-eminent institution.
> —Lewis Henry Morgan, *Ancient Society* (1877)

Marriage, while from its very nature a sacred obligation, is nevertheless, in most civilized nations, a civil contract, and usually regulated
by law. Upon it society may be said to be built, and out of its fruits
spring social relations and social obligations and duties, with which
government is necessarily required to deal. In fact, according as
monogamous or polygamous marriages are allowed, do we find the
principles on which the government of the people, to a greater or less
extent, rests.
> —Majority opinion, *Reynolds v. U.S.* (1879)

In *Ancient Society*, Lewis Henry Morgan lays out an intellectual framework
that will guide ethnological study for the next several decades, including
that conducted by government agencies, and he places the concept of kinship at the forefront of anthropology, where it becomes one of the discipline's organizing tropes until its eclipse in the late twentieth century.[1] At the
center of his account is the emergence of the couple-defined single-family
unit as the apex of humankind's development thusfar. Bourgeois homemaking

facilitated the individuation of propertyholding, the intensification of familial feeling, and the construction of political institutions separate from bloodlines and nonconjugal processes of kin-making. All of the major elements of liberal privatization, seen as the aim of evolutionary progress, appear as contingent on the creation and institutionalization of the nuclear family as the building block of modern social organization. While Morgan's work both expresses and provides further ideological cohesion for broad-based sentiments about the relation between family, property, and civilized nationality in the 1870s, that normative vision explicitly is endorsed and enforced by the state in the opinion for *Reynolds v. U.S.*, quoted earlier. The case turned on the constitutionality of the Morrill Act (1862), which outlawed polygamy in U.S. Territories, including Utah.[2] Depicting Mormon plural marriage as antinational, the decision presents monogamous heteromarriage, and the conjugal household, as necessary to the proper, republican functioning of U.S. governance. Alternative formations of residency and kinship not only register the perverse (abnormal and amoral) propensities of participating individuals but threaten to undo the "principles" structuring national life— the travestying of the "civil contract" of marriage leading to the traducing of the compact ("obligations and duties") that binds the American union. Nonnuclear modes of habitation, identification, and eroticism are cast as a challenge to the operation of U.S. sovereignty, and reciprocally, the exertion and extension of state power is justified on the basis of the need to protect the "social relations" that lie at the heart of civilized existence.[3]

If the Mormons are perceived as a territorial enclave whose cultural difference represents a dangerous challenge to the dominant U.S. ideals of politics and privacy, and the relation between them, how much more alarming is the presence of native peoples, and how much larger must these nonnational, aliberal polities loom in the U.S. popular and policy imagination? Morgan's tracing of the role of kinship in the rise of Anglo-American civilization and the targeting of the Mormons for federal prosecution can be understood as expressions of the ongoing ideological and legal efforts to address the tensions generated by native presence, portraying their social formations as an anachronism or sublimating those concerns in the disciplining of whites-gone-wild. The narration of the nuclear family structure as self-evidently crucial to American identity, though, marks a shift from the dynamics addressed in the previous chapters. *The Last of the Mohicans* and *Hope Leslie*, and the frontier imaginary of the 1820s more broadly, do not presume the inevitability of seeing conjugal homemaking as a synecdochic stand-in for national order, instead positioning white romance as necessary to cohere the nation against territorial and racial dissolution or as a patriarchal/tyrannical legacy from which the Republic must be liberated. In both cases, Indians appear as a counterexample, illustrating the dangers of 1) losing the capacity for sentimental affect and the attendant ability to maintain the kinds of interiority crucial to national space and subjectivity, or 2) losing the natural capacity for generating expansively imagined forms of caring community. Neither of these representational strategies takes the bourgeois household as a given, instead casting it as precariously emergent and endangered or residual and in need of reformation. Together they suggest that depictions of native peoples played a significant role in the ideological struggle over the nuclear family form—in its twining of reproductive lineality, privatized intimacy, and demarcated domestic spatiality—prior to its ascendancy in the following decades. Conversely, they also indicate the importance of interwoven notions of residency, kinship, eroticism, and affect in nongovernmental conceptualizations of Indian affairs. The complex negotiation between incorporation and removal as policy options, and more broadly as ways of envisioning the status and future of native peoples, is refracted into novelistic discourse in which the tensions surrounding the treaty system (Indians as foreign polities vs. subjects of domestic policy) are recast as a question of how to locate native peoples in relation to the national family/ the nation's families. These texts, then, bespeak an intersection between two processes of hegemony formation occurring simultaneously, and each of the novels offers its own intervention on both fronts, maneuvering within a multidimensional structure of feeling in which Indians and white romance signify in and through each other.

By the 1870s, however, the political and ideological configurations that were emergent in the 1820s had become entrenched, reconfiguring the terms, stakes, and strategies of social contestation over domesticity. As suggested by Morgan and the response to the Mormons, the possibilities for imagining and realizing alternative ideals to that of the nuclear family had been constricted greatly, the latter achieving prominence as the normative, natural standard against which to measure variations. The image of the conjugal home appears as a prominent figure in debates over the validity and necessity of government action on a range of issues, including the scope of suffrage, the kinship and housing arrangements of ex-slaves, federal superintendence of the South, the dangers of divorce, the undesirability of immigration, and the pitfalls of unionization.[4] The relations among the federal government, state governments, corporations, and private households, and the limits of their autonomy with respect to each other, were an ongoing source of popular and legal contention in which the maritally centered household repeatedly was cited as the transcendent source of legitimacy for competing arguments about the proper character and contours of U.S. political economy. In fact, one could suggest that the struggles over the shape of sovereignty—of political and legal power and its exercise—in the United States in the last decades of the nineteenth century take place quite firmly within a heterosexual imaginary in which normality, nationality, and nature all are defined by reference to bourgeois nuclearity. In this context, the articulation of the difference between civilization and barbarism on the basis of monogamous union (seen in both Morgan and *Reynolds*) seems like merely an extension of the terms of the dominant formation of the period, with native peoples functioning as just another object inserted into it.

Rather than seeing indigenous polities as being incorporated into an already hegemonic gaze, I would suggest that the centrality of conjugal homemaking to articulations of sovereignty in the late nineteenth century can be understood as partially an effect of the effort to address the continuing presence of native polities. As indicated in chapters 1 and 2, the depiction of white couplehood and family-making was enmeshed in representations of Indian/white difference, with native peoples being characterized—for good or ill—as lacking a privatized intimate sphere, and the normalization over the course of the nineteenth century of a particular vision of residency and kinship is not separate from its imbrication in ideas about the place of nativeness within the nation-state. The difficulties that indigenous peoples posed for U.S. geopolitical self-representation, federalism, and constitutionalism did not abate in the intervening decades, but in many ways were intensified. If slavery largely displaced Indian affairs as the primary figure of jurisdictional and sectional conflict in the mid-nineteenth century, the end of Reconstruction and of treaty-making put it back at the forefront. While federal-state tensions, particularly with respect to African Americans, certainly did not end in 1876, the constitutional prerogatives of the state vis-à-vis the federal union had been settled; what remained at stake was the nature of citizenship and its rights, not the scope of national sovereignty.[5] The place of native peoples within U.S. legal frameworks had always been ambiguous and contentious; they were treated like foreign nations for some purposes and domestic subjects for others. This confusion, and the competing institutional actors and interests that generated it, was mediated by the treaty system, which engaged Indians as autonomous polities while also allowing for the acquisition of native land and the translation of native governance into a form more consistent with U.S. legal logics. Due to objections by the House of Representatives to their constitutional lack of a role in treaty-making, the process was brought to an end in 1871, through a rider to an appropriations bill.[6] Existing treaties were unaffected, and the government continued to sign "agreements" of various kinds with tribes, but the displacement of treaties as the premier vehicle of Indian policy left the government with the problem of how to locate native peoples within U.S. legal geography and how to manage settlers' and states' designs on native resources. This set of political quandaries, combined with the numerous well-publicized armed conflicts between U.S. citizens and soldiers and native groups, positioned Indian affairs as a crucial site in the struggle to (re)define U.S. sovereignty in the late nineteenth century.

Figures of familial order increasingly were deployed within Indian policy as a way of indexing the aims of federal intervention and legitimizing it in the absence of existing legal or constitutional models for such extensive, direct restructuring of native lifeways. Although hearkening back to the civilization program and the promise of incorporating Indians into the states as private landholders, boarding school education and allotment were mandatory as opposed to earlier programs that at least formally were made contingent on choice. In this context, the biopolitical model of the nuclear unit (and its racializing logic of *Indian* lineage as discussed in chapter 1) was positioned as itself a quasi-legal principle, as having a kind of constitutional force that validated the measures used to realize it. While not arguing for a direct causal relation between these developments in Indian policy and the types of political familialism discussed earlier, I want to suggest that the representation of native peoples was a dense site for intersecting discourses of sexuality and sovereignty in the late nineteenth century and that this institutional and ideological formation can be seen as an important, and heretofore largely unaddressed, influence on other interarticulations of family and politics.

In *Ethnocriticsm*, Arnold Krupat argues that law "seeks to *make* history by *imposing* a story" (132), suggesting that legal discourse should be understood not merely as a set of juridical propositions or directives but as a mode of emplotment. In this vein, one can understand the vision of social order articulated in federal Indian policy as a *romance plot*—a narration organized around the ineluctable movement toward marriage as the culmination of the education/civilization process.[7] More than justifying particular legislative enactments, though, this heteronormative emplotment works to deny the possibility of registering indigenous residential and kinship formations as *political*, positioning the adoption of legally recognized, monogamous, companionate marriage and heterogendered bourgeois domesticity as the self-evident basis for American political identity.

Indian education policy, and the boarding school system in particular, served as one of the main avenues for generating and institutionalizing this imperial narrative. The discourse of Indian education presents the emotional connection and division of labor between husband and wife as the paradigmatic model for appropriate social order and interaction, and the construction of a bourgeois home predicated on legally recognized matrimony continually is cited as the goal of boarding school training in ways that link the acquisition of a proper understanding of family life to the splintering of tribal territory into single-family households. In this way, the abandonment of indigenous kinship networks, patterns of residence, and forms of communal identification appears as a self-evidently desirable exchange of "degraded" traditional sociality for the marital bliss and private homeownership portrayed as constitutive of civilized life.

The writings of Zitkala-Ša (Gertrude Simmons Bonnin), a self-identified Dakota born on the Yankton Reservation in 1876, provide an excellent starting place for an examination of how native writers opposed this institutionalized representation of tradition as degenerate, instead foregrounding indigenous family formations and their positive role in sustaining tribal communities.[8] A former pupil at White's Manual Institute and instructor at Carlisle Institute, the first and most famous of the off-reservation boarding schools, Zitkala-Ša was an adamant and well-known native critic of Indian education, publishing a number of essays and stories focusing on the horrors of the boarding school system and the pitfalls of assimilation.[9] *American Indian Stories* (1921) reprints many of these turn-of-the-century pieces. Though not directly concerned with education policy, "The Trial Path" and "A Warrior's Daughter" are the only tales that involve love stories. In these stories, romance does not mark an isolating passion between individuals, rather highlighting the ways couples remain intimately entwined within the larger web of social relations and responsibilities organized through kinship networks. Yet unlike non-native celebrations of such nonnuclear modes of interdependence, such as Sedgwick's, the texts in *American Indian Stories* emphasize the relation between native *family* and *politics*, the existence of Dakota peoples as autonomous polities. In this way, Zitkala-Ša offers a counternarrative to administrative efforts to impose a detribalizing teleology justified as the achievement of real and stable love, home, and family, instead connecting romance to the maintenance of indigenous collective identity and forms of self-determination.[10]

Elaborating how federal policy functions as a romance plot indicates the ways the representation of heterosexual desire within U.S. discourses is imbricated within a larger set of assumptions and associations hostile to native traditions and extended kinship formations, and elucidating Zitkala-Ša's rejection of this vision of privatized couplehood illustrates the ways alternative figurations of "home" and "family" within native writing contest the political economy of imperial domesticity. Yet *American Indian Stories* also disavows Sioux social identities and practices that might be taken by white readers as specifically *sexually* nonnormative. Zitkala-Ša studiously avoids discussion of polygamy and portrays Sioux gender in ways that cast homoeroticism as unimaginable, erasing extant practices and statuses so as to straighten custom. Thus, the text's effort to contest the privileging of conjugal domesticity as the national, natural norm, and thereby make room for recognizing tradition and its role in native political dynamics, also illustrates the layered quality of the heterosexual imaginary and the ways the "bribe of straightness" can serve as a lure for native peoples to disown the elements of their communities deemed most perverse by the white power structure.

KILLING THE INDIAN, SAVING THE HETEROSEXUAL HOMESTEADER

> They must stand or fall as men and women, not as Indians.
> —Commissioner of Indian Affairs Thomas J. Morgan,
> "Supplemental Report on Indian Education" (1889)

By the early 1890s, Indian education had transformed from a primarily missionary-led affair on treaty-guaranteed land to a federally sponsored bureaucratic infrastructure with more than 1,000 employees and almost 10,000 students enrolled in boarding schools located on- and off-reservation.[11] As part of a reoriented formulation of "the Indian problem," education would play a key role by providing the mechanism for breaking native children's connection to backward traditions and teaching them how to be individuals, while simultaneously clearing millions of acres of supposedly "surplus" land for settlement and development. The drive toward the creation of a formal Indian education program begins in the late 1870s with both the founding of a number of Indian reform associations in the east and the enrollment of native students at Hampton Institute and creation of the Carlisle Institute by Colonel Richard Henry Pratt.[12] Pratt's education program was based on two major organizational principles: mandating that classroom activity and manual training, strictly differentiated by gender, each take up half of the school day; and creating what came to be known as the "outing" system, which Pratt described as "by far the most important feature of our work," in which students would be placed with white families over school breaks in order to "receive an adequate idea of civilized home-life."[13]

Scholars have tended to focus on the language of "individualism" and its centrality to education discourse and the broader assault on indigenous governance and land tenure, contrasting such an atomized notion of selfhood with traditional communal conceptions of identity among native peoples. However, this line of critique tends to overlook or minimize the ways that monogamous marriage, the nuclear family, and privatized homemaking are necessary conditions for the ideological and material (re)production of this generic individual. In *Individuality Incorporated*, Joel Pfister argues, "Those who sought to 'individualize' Indians ... developed strategies of subjectivity and emotion production that aimed to prescribe how an 'individual' should properly pursue happiness, meaningfulness, and work" (12–13). While recognizing that the normalization of "sentimental American life" organized around lifelong heterocoupling was an important aspect of the education process, Pfister's argument treats notions of "home" and "family" as a "stage" "for the performance of productive individuality" rather than reading the individual subject as an (after)effect of a primary restructuring of kinship and household formations (59–63). Interpreting "individualization" as the goal of Indian policy performs an intellectual inversion, subordinating discussion of the contours and significance of the material conditions that enable and sustain such subjectivity. "Productive individuality" presupposes the installation of a political economy in which land tenure, subsistence, and residency have been reorganized in ways that break down extended social networks and break up shared territory and in which affective ties have been rerouted from various larger communal formations to the nuclear family. In other words, individualism is inseparable from the larger process of privatization, which is naturalized through the representation of monogamous marriage and the single-family dwelling as the self-evident basis for true intimacy and human reproduction. We therefore need to examine the ways that reference to the generic "individual" in the discourse of Indian policy condenses a larger heteronormative matrix that is the horizon for the imperial restructuring of native social relations. As David Wallace Adams notes, "In the eyes of reformers no sphere of Indian life was more reprehensible than the relations between the sexes" (173).

The writings of Thomas J. Morgan provide an excellent index of the de facto consensus held by officials and reformers and the policy goals of Indian education in the late nineteenth century.[14] Commissioner of Indian Affairs from 1887 to 1892, he was one of the major forces in the expansion and standardization of the boarding system, including campaigning to make such schooling compulsory and drafting the first official curriculum for federally funded Indian schools (1890).[15] As the chief figure in federal Indian policy at a time when the scope of the government's civilization program was increased exponentially, he was well positioned to exert an immense amount of influence on the shape it took. Morgan's ideas about Indian education, shared by most reformers and officials connected to the boarding system, are presented perhaps most succinctly and forcefully in his "Supplemental Report on Indian Education," which was included in his annual report to Congress in 1889.[16] The text persistently invokes *home* and *family* as key figures for what Indians lack and what must be inculcated through education; in this way, his formulations echo the Jeffersonian perspective discussed in chapter 1, positing the possibility of training those who were genealogically *Indian* in civilized/civilizing modes of sentimental domesticity. Here, though, there is no hint of interracial coupling, preserving the reproductively constituted color line while arguing for a malleability in Indian character (as against the notion of immutable racial "gifts"), and the earlier invocation of the need for native consent is abandoned entirely, using the supposed absence of an Indian understanding of *real* domesticity to justify the broader imperial program of total detribalization.

According to Morgan, tribal identity must be eradicated utterly. He offers some sense of how this goal will be achieved in his description of the primary aims of the education program:

> That which is fundamental in all this is the recognition of the complete
> manhood of the Indians, their individuality . . . They should be free to make
> for themselves homes wherever they will. The reservation system is an
> anachronism which has no place in our modern civilization. The Indian
> youth should be instructed in their rights, privileges, and duties as American
> citizens; . . . should be imbued with a genuine patriotism, and made to feel
> that the United States, and not some paltry reservationis their home. (95–96)

Sketching a correlation between the literal building of houses and a patriotic investment in national identity, the passage indicates that Indian conceptions of "home" perpetuate affective bonds to reservations. In order to gain "individuality," Indians must shift the horizon of their thinking and, more importantly, their feeling, connecting "home" not to specific tribal territories but to the great expanse of the entire United States. Broadening the Indian's perspective in this way trades a vision of "home" based on sustained connections within native communities for an abstract and metonymic relation between privatized households and the nation. Moreover, he asserts, "Owing to the peculiar surroundings of the mass of Indian children, they are homeless and are ignorant of those simplest arts that make home possible" (99), reducing native kinship and residency to the status of "peculiar" deviation.

The larger project of reordering native affect, "arous[ing] the feeling that they are Americans" (102), is to be accomplished through fostering a sense of self-reliance that is inextricably tied to the performance of heterogender, itself presented as alien to native peoples. "No pains should be spared to teach them that their future must depend chiefly on their own exertions, character, and endeavors. They will be entitled to what they earn . . . They must stand or fall as men and women, not as Indians" (102). Most notably, Morgan presents "Indians" as something apart from "men and women," tying contradistinguished gender identity to particular forms of production and social organization that native societies apparently lack. The (re)gendering of native students further is linked to the creation of appropriate states of feeling, with romance as the paradigm: "Co-education of the sexes is the surest and perhaps only way in which Indian women can be lifted out of that position of servility and degradation which most of them now occupy, on to a plane where their husbands and the men generally will treat them with the same gallantry and respect which is accorded to their more favored white sisters" (96). Morgan's vision of "the sexes" seeks to channel affect toward companionate marriage, casting the current division of labor among native peoples as virtual slavery and presenting native relationships as lacking affection by comparison. Note how the central relation between "men and women" is that of husband and wife, all other interactions between the sexes to be modeled on this one, which is understood as emblematic rather than contextualized as one in the vast network of relationships that constitute a given community. Morgan encapsulates the connection between right feeling, marriage, and property in his discussion of the goals of Indian grammar schools: "It is during this period particularly that it will be possible to inculcate in the minds of pupils of both sexes that mutual respect that lies at the base of a happy home life, and of social purity" (101). Teaching "Indians" to be "men and women" involves developing in them a sense of "respect" that reaches its apogee in marriage, which itself regulates gender expression, promotes seclusion through a clearly demarcated and privatized "home," and ties the latter to individualistic self-provision disconnected from one's tribe, validating such training as merely imparting the self-evident truths of intimate life in the nation and also making monogamous bourgeois marriage the framework through which to imagine relations to place.[17] Clearly, there is no room here for non-native efforts to reimagine national bonds in other than conjugal terms, repudiating the kind of settler investment in native kinship systems as (decontextualized and depoliticized) examples for altered white communal life discussed in the previous chapter.

The boarding school must also regulate social interaction between the sexes. They are to be kept entirely apart (classes and meals excepted), but "at stated times, under suitable supervision, they may enjoy each other's society": "such occasions should be used to teach them to show each other due respect and consideration ... and to acquire habits of politeness, refinement, and self-possession."[18] In essence, the schools are to orchestrate and manage the process of courting, forbidding virtually all communication unless superintended by teachers and matrons,[19] and there is little to no concern about relations among boys and among girls, positioning moments of hetero-association as the primal scene of socialization and implicitly casting cross-sex connections with non-kin as the center of one's social world.

In addition to working to make Indian children's perception of normal social relations conform to a vision of "gallantry" hostile to indigenous tradition, school policy reinforces the federal program of allotment. Passed in 1887, the General Allotment Act (otherwise known as the Dawes Act) sought to divide native territory into privately owned plots that, after this division, would cease to be under tribal control of any kind.[20] One of the chief mechanisms for doing so was the institutional erasure of native forms of kinship and the collective geographies established and maintained through these webs of attachment/obligation. Not only were allotments parceled out to each "head of a family," thereby soldering occupancy to a particular vision of what constitutes a family unit, but the act mandated that "the law of descent and partition in force in the State or Territory where such lands are situate shall apply thereto,"[21] creating a barrier to native efforts to merge land claims through extended chains of familial belonging or to maintain ties of tribal identification through the transfer of land along alternate lines of descent/affiliation.

Indian education directly participates in this attack on native kinship and on associated forms of collective mapping and self-representation by extending the terminologies employed in allotment.[22] In addition to interrupting the transmission of traditional knowledge and social logics to native children, the education program adopts the system of naming used to remake Indians as Americans. Morgan observes:

> When Indians become citizens of the United States, under the allotment act, the inheritance of property will be governed by the laws of the respective States, and it will cause needless confusion and, doubtless, considerable ultimate loss to the Indians if no attempt is made to have the different members of a family known by the same family name on the records and by general reputation. (clx)

The act of naming functions as a way of reconstellating "family" while simultaneously speaking as if it merely acknowledges the simple fact of relatedness—members of the same family should be known by the same name. The implicit structure of this normative model of kinship which despite its supposed self-evidence needs to be imposed institutionally by way of Morgan's order—is made clear a bit later: "[I]f agents and school superintendents will systematically endeavor, so far as practicable, to have children and wives known by the names of the fathers and husbands, very great improvement in this respect will be brought about within a few years" (clx). This imagined family unit, then, is defined by the connection between a husband and wife and their offspring. Beyond completely disavowing the matrilineal bonds that regulate belonging and social position in many tribes (including the Haudenosaunee discussed in chapter 1), this insistence on the name of the father/husband makes marriage and biological parenthood the core of personal and social identity in ways that both atomize tribes into aggregations of heteropairings and proscribe other, more collective, forms of subjectivity articulated within familial idioms (such as the modes of intertribal diplomacy discussed in the previous chapter). Morgan goes on to note the broader significance of naming as part of the project of dismantling native polities, arguing that "[t]he matter is important . . . because it will tend strongly toward the breaking up of the Indian tribal system which is perpetuated and ever kept in mind by the Indian's own system of names" (clxi).[23] Indian education policy plays a crucial part in this process of heteronaming, literally extending the bureaucratic mandates of allotment while training students to see these institutionalized terminologies as expressive of normal, natural, and healthful forms of sentiment and civilized social order.

ROMANCE (COUNTER) PLOTS

The potential for Native Americans to circulate radical counternarratives of home and family was greatly curtailed by the institutionalization of the romance plot organizing federal Indian policy, which in depicting traditional social life as "degraded" denied its legitimacy as a subject position from which to critique capitalist heterohomemaking and the program of detribalization. Native writers publishing during the heyday of the Indian education program, however, did offer positive descriptions of traditional practices and community dynamics. Such loving accounts, though, were presented as scenes of bygone days, either prior to the narrator's own entry into white-run schooling or set in a period before substantial contact with whites. These textual moments can appear coded as nostalgia for childhood, childish naïveté, ethnography, or as a quasi–fairy tale separated by an unbridgeable gap from the writer/reader's contemporary life. Thus, in response to the official depiction of traditional kinship as a savage anachronism, native writers cast their own favorable representation of such networks as a relation to the past.

One can see this dynamic at work in Zitkala-Ša's writing. The pieces of hers that have received the most critical attention are three autobiographical sketches describing her life before and decision to attend boarding school, her time as a student, and her stint as a teacher at Carlisle.[24] These three pieces along with six others were collected and reprinted in 1921 as *American Indian Stories*. As Susan Bernardin notes, there is an "omission of romance and marriage plots" in the three autobiographical selections.[25] This absence of "romance," however, does not characterize the collection as a whole. In fact, two of the pieces, "The Trial Path" and "A Warrior's Daughter," are structured around love plots. What also marks these two as different from the rest is that they are set before the advent of the reservation system. In a letter in March 1901 to her then fiancé Carlos Montezuma, Zitkala-Ša justifies her choice of setting: "Already I've heard that at Carlisle my story ["The Soft-Hearted Sioux"] is pronounced 'trash' and I–'worse than Pagan'. . . . . Last week Harper's accepted another story of mine—'The Trial Path'—that is purely Ancient history and won't bear hard on anyone's pet co[nc]erns."[26] In response to the harsh criticism of her previous piece's endorsement of Dakota spirituality and condemnation of overzealous and missionizing Christian converts, she declares her intent to sidestep the "pet concerns" of those involved in Indian education and reform by reaching back to "Ancient history."[27] Rather than denoting a disengagement from U.S.-Indian politics or the tale's actual location in the remote past, however, this phrase suggests a particular strategy for circumventing white "concerns."[28] In other words, "Ancient history" is less a straightforward description of when the story takes place than an ironic comment on the kinds of temporal disjunction necessary in order to depict elements of traditional Dakota life while avoiding censure by white officials, reformers, and publishers.

The fact that the stories that supposedly take place in the distant past (or rather simply before the routine appearance of whites among the Yankton) are also the only ones that contain romance plots, then, is no coincidence. This alignment suggests the ways that narrative projections into the past allow a bracketing of the civilizing imperatives of white readers and their attendant assumptions about the nature of home and family so as to tell a different story about the possibilities of and for Dakota life. Moreover, focusing on the writings of hers that neither involve white characters nor directly reference U.S. policy requires a greater awareness of and attention to tradition as an enduring force in Dakota life.[29] While appearing less explicitly oppositional than the other pieces in the collection, "The Trial Path" and "A Warrior's Daughter" implicitly challenge the pathologization of native kinship networks within U.S. legal and political discourse. The texts emphasize the disparity between U.S. ideologies of sexuality/domesticity and traditional Dakota social organization, foregrounding the latter's sustaining sense of community and thereby seeking to render it publicly intelligible as something other than the degraded absence of civilized normality.

While the plot of "The Trial Path" is organized around the story of a man who kills his best friend because the latter is his rival for the woman he loves, the text repeatedly displaces discussion of the romance that inspires this crime of passion in favor of making the murder and its aftermath the occasion for an explanation of the workings of kinship. The story opens with a late-night conversation between a woman and her twenty-year-old granddaughter, and in response to the younger woman's description of one of the stars as "my dear old grandfather" (127), the older woman recalls the tragic events of her youth. She says:

Listen! I am young again. It is the day of your grandfather's death. The elder one, I mean, for there were two of them. They were like twins, though they were not brothers. They were friends inseparable! All things, good and bad, they shared together, save one, which made them mad. In that heated frenzy the younger man slew his most intimate friend. He killed his elder brother, for long had their affection made them kin. (128)

Although the killing is characterized as motivated by jealousy, the emphasis here is not on the overwhelming romantic fervor that leads to violence but on the nature and strength of the bond severed in the name of love—or, rather, that one profound love gains expression only through the destruction of another. The deep "affection" between the men and the ways that mutual feeling has made them "kin" seems to be given far more weight in the grandmother's account than her love toward either of them. In fact, readers are given no background on the romantic relationship that inspires the act of murderous rage at the center of the story. Moreover, the grandmother's claim that her granddaughter has two grandfathers seems to reaffirm the persistence of the men's bond even in death. In some sense, the text introduces the love story only to subordinate it to an elaboration of the creation of kinship bonds, particularly the process of adopting people into familial networks in ways that make them socially virtually indistinguishable from blood relations. Rather than highlighting the construction of a new family unit through companionate marriage, the incipient romance plot is detoured into a commentary on the capaciousness of Dakota family to absorb new members along lines dissociated from procreation and heterogendered pairing.[30]

As the grandmother's initial description implies, her narrative will focus not on the emotional exchange between her and the man who killed to get her but on the potentially destructive impact of this rash act on the community and the social mechanisms of adoption through which it is resolved. The means of communal resolution is the trial path of the title. The father of the murdered man is given control of the life of the murderer, and he decides that the killer must ride a horse from the home of the murdered man's family to the outer ring of the camp circle. If he falls, he dies, but if he completes the ride, his life will be spared. Although the pony races and bucks and the rider is thrown forward and almost loses his grip, he successfully completes the challenge. At this point, the father of the murdered man rises, goes to the murderer, and "he cries, with compassionate voice, 'My son!'" (133), thereby incorporating the killer into his family in the place of his dead child. While the story is set in motion by an expression of individual passion as part of what may appear as heteroromance, its dramatic arc is constituted by the struggle over how and whether this person can be reintegrated into Dakota life, the title reinforcing the sense that the love plot functions as a background against which to stage the resiliency of Yankton tradition—its structuring by a kinship system flexible enough to respond to change and durable enough to maintain social cohesion.

Rather than merely surprising white readers in a kind of generic bait-and-switch where they are presented with the beginnings of a love story only to find themselves veering into another sort of tale entirely, Zitkala-Ŝa circulates and capitalizes on the markers of heteroromantic feeling in order to help make potentially alien forms of sociality affectively intelligible—using sentiment in this way as a kind of teaching tool. After readers are told of the murder, we are given some insight into the grandmother's emotional state. When a messenger arrives with the news about the murder, she notes, "How fast, how loud my heart beats," adding, "I longed to ask what doom awaited the young murderer, but dared not to open my lips, lest I burst forth into screams instead" and that "My temples throbbed like a pair of hearts!" (130). Later, during the trial, she thinks, "Do not fall! Choose life and me!", holding her "thick blanket" over her lips (132). These moments when readers are given access to her consciousness suggest an interior life whose terms seem to conform to a certain set of romantic conventions: the repeated figures of "hearts"; an all-consuming desire that leaves her speechless; the depiction of her feelings as inhabiting a purely private realm separate from, and in conflict with, public life; and the imagination of coupling as the ultimate horizon of personal fulfillment. These gestures draw readers into the story by implicitly affirming marriage as the goal of the emotional trajectory the text seems to chart. Yet the focus of the story pivots away from the question of whether or not the killer will survive to be paired with his lover and toward whether or not he will be accepted by the family of his victim. The lover's fear and passion slide into the emotional response of the women in the murdered man's family to the prospect of accepting the murderer as one of them. The mother addresses him as "My son!," but "on the second word her voice shook, and she turned away in sobs" (132). The sister of the dead man, after having been instructed by her father to embrace her brother's killer, "cries, with twitching lips, 'My brother!,'" upon which we are told, "The trial ends" (134). The "trial" is not merely the successful riding of the horse but the resolution of a social crisis produced by passion through the processes of kin-making, and the lover/grandmother's romantic feelings for the murderer are eclipsed by the drama of familial (re)formation. The mother and sister's simultaneous show of pain and act of forgiveness suggest as powerful an emotional investment as that of the lover/storyteller and illustrate a negotiation between personal emotion and collective well-being in which kinship is the mediator. In other words, rather than affectively saturating the love plot as the greatest expression of sentiment, the story juxtaposes romantic feeling with that of kinship distinct from companionate coupling, privileging such nonmatrimonial kin-making as a site of reconciliation and somewhat noble self-sacrifice for communal harmony.

The story, however, does not end here. After noting in passing "the fifteen winters of our wedded life," the grandmother moves to a discussion of how Ohiyesa, the horse on which her lover rode, "was a constant member of our family" (134). Describing her narration of the horse's burial with her husband as "sacred knowledge,"[31] the grandmother observes that her grand-daughter has fallen asleep, although she had been awake for the end of the tale of the trial itself. The grandmother bemoans her lapse in attention, saying, "I did wish the girl would plant in her head this sacred tale" (135), implying that the extension of kinship to the horse—and the attendant sense of kinship as the central social form and force of Dakota life—is the primary "knowledge" that she sought to convey.[32] In this sense, the girl serves as a figure for the reader who is only or primarily interested in the romance plot—the tale of her grandparents' love—chastising her for having missed the point and thereby further framing the story as an intergenerational lesson in ways that implicitly critique the paradigms at work in federal Indian education. While the effort to teach non-native readers a lesson about the possibility of having more flexible notions of *family* may be reminiscent of the kind of teaching native characters perform in texts like *Hope Leslie*, the fact that there are no whites in the tales most concerned with extended kinship networks suggests less the offering of a Dakota example for settler emulation than the insistence that it functions as its own coherent system of social order. Invoking and then displacing romance while staging the act of storytelling as a pedagogical effort within the family to instill the value of kinship, the text serves as a challenge and corrective to U.S. policy in its effort to interpellate native youth into heteronormative affect.

In addition to contesting the heterosexual imaginary of the boarding school system, Zitkala-Ša's stories respond to changing conditions on the Yankton reservation. Looking at the annual reports from the agent to the Yanktons, one can see how the official weave between education, allotment, and bourgeois marriage and homemaking in federal Indian discourse was brought to the reservation.[33] Moreover, an attention to these documents acknowledges Zitkala-Ša's presence on the Yankton reservation during much of her childhood.[34] One of the primary aims of the agent was to supplant the chiefs, a project in which the dispersion of the Yanktons on privately owned plots was considered crucial. The allotment of reservation territory into family farms appears as a mechanism through which to attenuate such loyalty. "One of the prime objects of the Government in the management of Indians, and to make them self-supporting, is to break up the old tribal relations and effectually destroy tribal authority over them," and the "division of land separates the people from the chiefs."[35] More importantly, though, the members of the tribe needed to be separated from each other: "Successful farming requires isolation, and their habits and disposition lead them into gangs. They want to be together."³⁶ Of course this dissolution of social ties is cast as liberating: "Farming a home, the accumulation of property, a higher social and political status, a feeling manhood, a consciousness that they have the capacity to do and act for themselves, freed from tribal dictation, will wean them from these old customs."³⁷ The reason behind this repudiation of cooperative farming, though, is that such "gangs" are the backbone of native identity. More than allegiance to the chiefs themselves, the framework of traditional life and governance is sustained through webs of intimate affiliation that provide an alternative to the abstract individualism of U.S. citizenship. As the agent notes, "the fraternal feelings existing between the Yankton was [sic] much stronger than the obligations imposed by official duty; nor is this strange when it is understood that by marriage and blood the Yankton are nearly all connected."³⁸ Given the linkage of traditional affective bonds to extensive networks created "by marriage and blood," the reordering of Yankton land tenure must be accompanied by a reconfiguration of kinship. The attempt to replace native geopolitics by superimposing a political economy based on isolated (bourgeois) households and centralized governance is conducted through a coordinated attack on the material conditions that sustain kinship, including restricting travel to visit relatives both on and off their reservation.³⁹

If the shattering of kinship bonds is structurally necessary in the imperial transformation of Yankton political identification and land tenure, the depiction of plural marriage and native gatherings as depraved and unnatural works to legitimize such intervention by presenting traditional erotic and familial formations as perverse. Dances are characterized as "weekly orgies." "Here in feathers and paint, with the jingling of bells and beating of drums, the men dance, recounting their deeds of valor in speech and song. At last, carried away by frenzied excitement, they at times give away their property, occasionally their wives," and such events are "entirely at variance with progressive industry and civilization."⁴⁰ These "carnivals of vice" also were charged with "corrupting" women and "the young."⁴¹ Through the depiction of native social events as sites of orgiastic excess, promiscuity, and the defilement of the innocent, the reports try to present Yankton sociality itself as promoting rampant immortality, defining tradition not just by the lack of "civilization" but as its active antithesis. More broadly, beyond their incitement of "depraved lusts," dances were seen as a structural impediment to the implementation of the privatizing imaginary ("the blessings of home and family") discussed earlier, the agent instead seeking to interest "the Indians in farming to such an extent as should wean them from the dance."⁴² Dances, like communal labor, helped promote and concretize a feeling of collectivity that militated against the material reorganization of production, homemaking, and land tenure—and the euphemization of this process as the acquisition of a sense of individual identity—promoted by the agents.

Often these events are listed with other practices that contribute to "the utter unsanctity of the martial relations," the chief of which is polygamy. "While Indians are . . . born and reared to abhor manual labor, in morals, they come into the world with the polygamous taint attached to them," suggesting that plural marriage is less a particular kind of sociosexual system than a form of congenital stigma.[43] Polygamy functions here as a kind of stand-in for original sin, connecting moral bankruptcy to heredity and casting monogamy as salvational in its ability to cleanse native children of their (racial) "taint." The practice of having multiple wives is offered as a hyperbolic example of what is presented as the overarching insecurity of "the family relations between husband and wife."[44] The campaign against polygamy, then, is the most visible part of the broader project of reconstructing Yankton "family relations" in ways that sever them from traditional practices and formations in order to subject them to the ostensibly sacralizing and stabilizing force of U.S. (marriage) law. Such transformation is in the interest of privileging the companionate couple over the more diffuse webs of "fraternal feeling" organizing residence and labor as well as discursively soldering the remapping of Yankton economies and land tenure to the promotion of marital and moral purity, thereby reaffirming a capitalist vision of isolated nuclear families as necessary in order to stave off the chaos of a surrender to degeneracy.[45] The reports of the agent, though, also reveal that the Yankton people did not simply adopt "civilized" ways. They largely continued their traditions—including collective labor, dances, visiting, and polygamy—except when directly punished by the agent, thereby implicitly illustrating the persistence of the kinship networks at stake in all these practices despite the government's insistence on the nuclear logic of detribalization.

In response to such imperial efforts to reorganize Dakota social life, Zitkala-Ša further emphasizes the importance of extended family relations to virtually all aspects of Dakota life. "The Warrior's Daughter" contextualizes the love story at its center within kinship connections that prove crucial to the plot in several ways, providing the conditions of possibility for the romance. In this way, the text opens up the heteropairing at its heart by illustrating how its consummation relies on a broader affective and affiliative network, suggesting that the social bonds constitutive of Dakota tradition are crucial to the maintenance of home and family rather than, in Commissioner Morgan's terms, acting as "peculiar" impediments to them. The text begins by introducing the reader to "a warrior father" sitting with his wife and his eight-year-old daughter in the camp circle. The young girl, Tusee, "is taking her first dancing lesson" in preparation for participation in the ceremony taking place that evening. We also are told that the father "was the chieftain's bravest warrior" but that a good deal of his status in the community comes from being "one of the most generous gift givers to the toothless old people" (137), immediately situating his individual bravery and this vision of familial comfort within a larger framework of social responsibility and interdependence and suggesting that the text will work to complicate the image of the Dakota household with which it opens.

Into this seemingly complete domestic scene the text inserts another figure—"an elderly man" who rides up to the tepee and speaks "with a stranger's accent" (138–139). His history is as follows: "From an enemy's camp he was taken captive long years ago by Tusee's father. But the unusual qualities of the slave had won the Sioux warrior's heart, and for the last three winters the man had had his freedom. He was made [a] real man again. His hair was allowed to grow. However, he himself had chosen to stay in the warrior's family" (139). Not only does "family" appear as a flexible concept here, defined in ways that are not routed exclusively through marriage and procreation, it serves as a mechanism through which Dakotas negotiate relations with outsiders. In addition to allowing for intraband realignments of feeling and responsibility, as in "The Trial Path," articulations of kinship provide a means for crossing the gulf marked by war, thereby positioning kinship as a mode of political identification.[46] Emphasizing the primacy of familial relation to Dakota identity, the discussion of the unnamed character's incorporation into the tiospaye indicates a unity between Dakota band or tribal belonging and the matrix of kinship—one is either kin or a captive. To be Dakota, to be accepted as a full member of the band (indexed here by the right to be a "real man" and to grow his hair), is dependent on being accepted as part of a Dakota family. Kinship appears here as the immanent nexus of native sociality, encompassing yet exceeding romantic pairings.[47]

More than merely a marginal character who tangentially illustrates the elasticity of kinship and its role in defining Dakota identity, the former slave and his inclusion within the warrior's family as Tusee's "uncle" is the linchpin to the romance plot. After the reader is introduced to Tusee and her family, the text abruptly skips an indeterminate number of years, picking up again after Tusee has aged enough to have acquired her own tepee. However, she "is not alone in her dwelling. Near the entranceway a young brave is half reclining on a mat" (141–142). Described as "her lover," he explains that he has had a confrontation with Tusee's father, who tells the young man he must first get "an enemy's scalp-lock, plucked fresh with your own hand," before he can make her his "wife" (143). Early the next morning, the warriors set out en masse to attack their enemies, traveling "southward" to their territory (144). While quite elliptical about whom precisely they are fighting, this mention of direction recalls the description of Tusee's uncle as having "features . . . of the Southern type" (139), implying that the warriors (including Tusee's father and lover) are going off to do battle with the former people of this slave-cum-kinsman. A number of women, including Tusee, go along on the campaign, waiting hidden in a nearby ravine while the men attack.[48] Two Dakotas are killed and one captured—Tusee's lover. As the others pack up and begin the journey homeward, she resolves to stay and save him. Blending into the crowd at the enemies' victory celebration, she discerns the man responsible for capturing her lover. After flirting with him over the course of the evening, she lures him "out into the night" by "speak[ing] to him in his own tongue" (149); once they are far enough away from the camp, she leaps toward him, "like a panther for its prey," revealing her identity to him ("I am a Dakota woman!") just before stabbing him to death (150–151). Disguised as an old woman, she sneaks back into the enemy's camp while everyone is asleep, cuts her lover free, and carries him off toward home.

The relationship between Tusee and the young (would-be) warrior is the backbone of the story, acting as the driving force behind the dramatic action, and their reunion is where it closes, implying a somewhat conventional happily-ever-after coupledom, albeit one in which she saves him rather than the reverse. Yet if the romance is the point, the story's opening seems rather incongruous given its focus on Tusee's childhood and her relationship with her uncle, the former captive. Additionally, as I have suggested, the love plot references elements of the opening scene—the implication that the enemy is the uncle's former tribe and that Tusee's ability to speak to the warrior she kills "in his own tongue" is due to her having learned the language from her uncle (earlier having spoken to him "[i]n the man's own tongue" (141)—note the parallel phrasing).[49] Moreover, the initial scene with the former slave is recalled later in the fact that the uncle is described as having been a "captive" (134), the same term used for Tusee's lover, and that the uncle proves his affection for Tusee by his willingness to go out to capture one of her father's ponies so that she can have the necessary gift to bring to participate in her "first dance" (140)—a dance being the context in which she later uses his language and rescues her lover.[50]

What do these repetitions/resonances mean? The text does not make these connections explicit in the sense of offering commentary on them. Instead, they appear as echoes of the story's preface, suggesting the ways the romance plot is built out of the set of relationships and dynamics described at the outset. The subtlety of these traces may itself point toward the obviousness of kinship as the foundation of Dakota social life—its presence is everywhere and unremarked on because so self-evident. If in "The Trial Path" the reader implicitly is compared to the young woman who falls asleep at the end of the love story, thereby missing the "sacred" lesson about kinship, here the reader is called on to remember the framework of kinship that precedes and makes possible the romance. Otherwise, the tale's climax— the luring of the enemy warrior in his own language—would be inexplicable. The story at the text's heart, then, is constructed out of reassembled elements of what can be described as the kinship plot with which it opens. Rather than serving as a process of breaking away from her family and tribe to create an independent household, as in the romance plot of federal policy, Tusee's reunion with her lover reaffirms her identity as Dakota and the fact that expansive notions of family suffuse all Dakota relationships, providing a shared conceptual and political basis for individual and collective action.

In light of the efforts in education and reservation policy to inculcate proper forms of affect, by associating interpersonal intimacy and self-sufficiency with bourgeois marriage and homemaking, the link in Zitkala-Ša's stories between evoking romantic feeling and illustrating its embeddedness in the webs of Dakota kinship works to open room within U.S. public discourse for valuing otherwise abjected native subjectivity(/ies). Through the strategy of combining love stories with temporal displacement, these tales are able to cannibalize and reconstellate the central elements of official narratives (marriage, home, and family) in ways that affirm tradition and disjoint the heteronormative logics organizing policy but do so without explicitly condemning government initiatives per se. Adopting a less immediately oppositional framework allows for a tacit denunciation of the program of detribalization and affirmation of the political economy of Dakota kinship without appearing to engage in what could be dismissed as a perverse repudiation of civilized homemaking. In other words, Zitkala-Ša's writing can be seen as trying to make traditional native social formations and modes of self-representation intelligible to white readers by avoiding an outright rejection of compulsory heterosexuality.

MORMONS, MORGAN, AND PLURAL MARRIAGE

While the tales I have examined resist the official forms of romantic emplotment that help cohere and validate the federal assault on native sovereignty, they also have couples at their center. Actually, they have couples at the periphery as well, leaving readers with the impression of monogamous male-female pairings as the exclusive form of romantic association among the Dakotas. The use of romance to highlight traditional kinship networks can be seen as part of an effort to shift the perceptions of Zitkala-Ša's predominantly white readership and to open some room for representing non–conjugally focused native subjectivity(/ies). Yet one must also ask about how in the process she strategically simplifies Yankton gender and sexuality, making tradition more palatable while effacing elements that might be objectionable to a white audience. In the title of one of her pieces, she proudly proclaims herself to be a "pagan," offering a principled argument against conversion to Christianity,[51] but in the texts collected in *American Indian Stories*, she makes no reference to the other p-word with which natives were connected—polygamy. The coordinated legal and military attacks on the Mormons in the latter half of the nineteenth century, including several U.S. Supreme Court decisions that speak of monogamous marriage as central to civilized social order, certainly would have given anyone pause in discussing familial and residential arrangements in which someone has multiple sexual partners.[52] However, the possession of several spouses by Yankton men was neither unusual nor condemned,[53] and the absence of any mention of such relationships in Zitkala-Ša's stories, especially those set before sustained contact with whites such as "The Trial Path" and "A Warrior's Daughter," suggests an effort to make Yankton practices fit certain white Christian notions of respectability.

This process of self-editing is a response to what can be described as the "bribe of straightness."[54] As I have been arguing, native peoples were represented in the late nineteenth century as lacking "home" and "family," and thus as having no access to the sentimental bonds of affection that characterized civilized life as exemplified in conjugal homemaking. Simultaneously, a notion of sexual order was developing in which normality was defined as against deviant desires, a proclivity for acts deemed unnatural that increasingly was seen as testifying to innate tendencies. This period at the end of the nineteenth century is when Foucault and others have located the shift from *acts* to *identities*, from a criminalization of certain kinds of conduct to a medicalization of certain kinds of persons. In that transition, the nuclear family remained the dominant paradigm, providing the vehicle for connecting the incipient proliferation of sexual types to the existing gendered division of labor by casting marital reproductivity as the apotheosis of healthful sexual expression.[55] Yet the differentiation of civilization from barbarism on the basis of the presence of proper domesticity did not simply vanish with the advent of the ideology of sexual identity; rather, the supposed backwardness of non-European peoples was evidenced by reference to the inconsequence of marital union among them as illustrated by non-couple-centered forms of kinship and residency and the performance of depraved sexual practices.[56] Normative sexuality, as that bundle of discourses and statuses emerged in the late nineteenth century, then, had multiple facets, opening the possibility of playing them against each other. Put another way, aspects of the dominant ideal could be cited in order to make a claim for normality, to characterize a people or practice as nonpathological due to conformity to (enough of) the conditions of civilization. Thus, even while critiquing the privatizing dynamics of federal detribalizing initiatives, Zitkala-Ša emphasizes romantic couplehood in ways that direct reader attention away from extant practices that would signify as *perverse*.[57]

Polygamy most certainly belonged to that category. If those who practice polygamy are *tainted*, in the words of the Yankton agent quoted earlier, avoiding reference to such unions can allow for a portrayal of native kinship networks, and associated dynamics of land tenure and governance, as unblemished by sexual deviance. The balance was to represent native practices as different but not *deviant*, which would feed into discourses of inborn racial degeneracy that succeeded the notion of Indians as innately incapable of understanding sentimental domesticity discussed in chapter 1. Plural marriage sits at the intersection of the two kinds of nonnormativity sketched above, seen as signaling both the absence of conjugal intimacy and the presence of unnatural desire. One can see why, in light of this ideological crossover, it would become such a site of public panic in the middle to late nineteenth century. That crisis coalesces around the Mormons, including the prominent inclusion of denunciations of polygamy in the Republican Party platforms of 1856 and 1860 (as, along with slavery, a "relic of barbarism") and the passage of a series of increasingly harsh statutes targeted at the territory of Utah the aim of which was not just to root out the practice of polygamy but to punish the Mormon Church through a legal assault on its members, holdings, and political power.[58] If lingering anti-Mormonism provides an important context for Zitkala-Ša's turn-of-the-century writing, attitudes toward Mormons can be seen as racial rage against whites perceived as having gone Indian, expressing a deep anxiety about the coherence of the nation that derives less from the threat ostensibly posed by Mormons to U.S. legal and moral order than from the ongoing challenge to official narratives of settler sovereignty posed by the persistence of native peoples on their traditional lands. As I have discussed in the preceding chapters, U.S. narratives that domesticated native peoples relied on topoi of familial and household formation that validated, and in many ways naturalized, geopolitical and jurisdictional assertions of authority over indigenous territory. The narrative of Mormonism as posing a danger to the nation is part of this legacy.

In this vein, the two Supreme Court cases that bookend the federal assault on Mormon polygamy—*Reynolds v. U.S.* (1879) and *Late Corporation v. U.S.* (1890)—can be understood as haunted by a native presence they disown. The first was an appeal of the conviction of George Reynolds, a Mormon with two wives, under the Morrill Act (1862), which outlawed polygamy in the Territories;[59] the second was over the constitutionality of the Edmunds-Tucker Act (1887), which revoked the corporate license of the Mormon Church and enabled the federal seizure of all its property and assets.[60] The opinions in these cases make no explicit mention of native peoples, but they are obsessed with depicting polygamy as a foreign institution that will corrupt U.S. culture and governance and, reciprocally, with asserting the absolute authority of the federal government over areas under, in *Reynolds's* terms, its "exclusive control" (166). The *Reynolds* decision declares, "Polygamy has always been odious among the northern and western nations of Europe, and . . . was almost exclusively a feature of the life of Asiatic and African people" (164), and it adds, "according as monogamous or polygamous marriages are allowed, do we find the principles on which the people . . . rests" (165–166). Not only does marital life appear as the distinguishing feature of European lineage and globalized racial difference, but it is imagined as marking a geopolitical boundary, delimiting the sphere of Euro-American "principles" and "people"-hood. The problem of Mormonism, then, is that it has introduced a disruptive alienness into the (white) nation.[61]

What is puzzling about this claim is that the racialized foreignness represented by plural marriage was always-already part of domestic space; native polygamy had been noted since the earliest texts of Euro-contact. Since it is doubtful that the justices simply had never heard of such relationships, why are they not mentioned? More to the point, how would doing so undermine the equation of civilization, monogamy, and uncontested U.S. sovereignty at the heart of the decisions' logic? A clue can be found in *Kobogum v. Jackson Iron Company* (1889), a case decided by the Supreme Court of Michigan. Although the case was focused on the claims of a deceased Ojibwe man to profits promised him by a corporation, one of the points to be adjudicated was whether both his wives and all his children with them could be recognized as proper inheritors and plaintiffs, and thus whether his polygamous unions could be validated in a U.S. court. The court finds that they may:

> We must either hold that there can be no valid Indian marriage, or we must hold that all marriages are valid which by Indian usage are so regarded. There is no middle ground which can be taken, so long as our own laws are not binding on the tribes. They did not occupy their territory by our grace and permission, but by a right beyond our control . . . , and we had no more right to control their domestic usages than those of Turkey and India. (508)

The judgment turns not on the relative merits of polygamy or marital freedom but on the question of jurisdiction. As autonomous polities, Indian tribes can have whatever "domestic" forms they want, and the United States has no authority to pick and choose which Indian marriages it will acknowledge. The status of native "usages" in U.S. law correlates directly with the degree to which native peoples are not bound by U.S. laws due to their indigeneity ("not . . . by our grace or permission"). Polygamy here becomes a metonym for sovereignty, suggesting a de facto foreignness with respect to U.S. legal control not unlike that of other countries.[62] While this decision appears after *Reynolds*, it suggests that the global imagery of the Mormon decisions signals a fear less of, in the terms of *Late Corporation*, a generic "blot on our civilization" than the presence of a government on territory claimed by the United States that is not operating under federal control (49). As the *Kobogum* decision indicates, an alienness like that of "Turkey and India" had already been established in national space through indigenous occupancy.

In this way, the Mormon problem can be seen as signifying in the context of the Indian problem, the virulence of approaches to the former being animated by the profound and unsettled implications of the latter.[63] *Reynolds* alludes to this parallel by describing the Mormons as "an exceptional colony of polygamists" (166); *Late Corporation* refers to "their defiance of the government authorities" and "their attempt to establish an independent community," also noting that Mormon practice "is contrary to . . . the civilization which Christianity has produced in the Western world," marking "a return of barbarism" (49). The Mormons appear as an *imperium in imperii*, replicating in many ways extant characterizations of native sovereignty as undermining U.S. jurisdiction. While the Supreme Court's Mormon decisions present a barbarous *there* as having made its way to a civilized *here*, the image of a "return" seems to signal a lurking insecurity about the extent to which the federal government's "principles" can be rooted in the soil of "the Western world," a concern about the efficacy of U.S. law over the entirety of the territory claimed by/as the nation. *Late Corporation* insists on the "general and plenary" power of Congress over the Territories, declaring that "the power to acquire territory . . . is derived from the treaty-making power" and that "the incidents of these powers are those of national sovereignty, and belong to all independent governments": "The territory of Louisiana, when acquired from France, and the territories west of the Rocky Mountains, when acquired from Mexico, became the absolute property and domain of the United States" (42). To some extent, these statements merely provide jurisdictional justification for the Edmunds-Tucker Act in legislating for the Territory of Utah, but they notably edit out native peoples in their insistence on the "plenary" authority of Congress, an issue very much at stake in Indian affairs throughout the 1870s and 1880s and judicially settled only in 1886 in the case of *U.S. v. Kagama*.[64] Moreover, the Edmunds-Tucker Act was passed in the same session as the General Allotment Act, suggesting the contemporaneity of concerns about the political and familial dynamics of Mormons and native peoples.[65]

Even when foregrounding the "treaty-making power," the decision effaces the existence of indigenous occupancy, and this profound oversight strikes me as indicative less of a simple lapse in memory or lack of knowledge than an overdetermined elision. The very anxiety about the status of native land and polities raised by the treaty system is channeled here into an assertion of "absolute" power understood as necessarily following from existence as an independent state. Such insecurity was heightened by the ending of treaty-making in 1871. While leaving existing treaties in force, the elimination of treaties as the paradigmatic mode of Indian affairs placed native peoples in more of a political limbo than they had occupied previously, creating even greater confusion about their jurisdictional status and what constituted a legitimate legal means of engaging with them. In light of this change, the invocation of "civilization" crucially comes to supplement "sovereignty," the former providing a means of rhetorically shoring up the coherence and supremacy of the latter when it cannot be sustained fully in legal or consti-tutional terms. The spectacle of whites who seem to have seceded from the "Western world," then, bears a dialectical relation to Indian affairs: deriving its symbolic power by substituting for the ongoing difficulties native sover-eignty poses for federal jurisdiction and national self-representation; and enabling a resolution of that conflict by positing the syllogistic equivalence of conjugal couplehood, whiteness, and national territoriality.

More than decrying supposed immorality, the decisions' use of the con-cept of "barbarism" conflates racial and geopolitical boundaries, signifying that overdetermined line of difference through the trope (or perhaps topos) of polygamy. The normality of marriage serves as a flexible figure for the cohesion of the nation-state, condensing multiple forms of foreignness and displacing them as an unnatural intrusion by contrast with the self-evidently Western, democratizing, and affectively more fulfilling "principles" of monogamy. The normative ideology of matrimony, and of bourgeois home-making, takes on a quasi-constitutional status in the sense that it functions in the decisions as an uncontestable ideal, seen as a fundamental basis of American "people"-hood and thus as underwriting the extension by the fed-eral government of various kinds of legal authority over "domestic" popula-tions. The boarding school program and allotment policy can be understood as following a similar logic, the inherent desirability of the nuclear family serving as validation for heretofore legally implausible forms of U.S. inter-vention into native affairs. In presenting Indian policy as a kind of romance plot, federal officials draw on the supposed obviousness of nuclear home-making in order to supplement federal jurisdiction given the absence of a workable theory of its exercise in the wake of the end of treaty-making.

As I have argued, Zitkala-Ša's writings contest this sentimentalization of federal authority and the attendant legitimization of congressional "plenary" power, particularly as enacted through education and allotment. However, in light of the social dynamics addressed earlier, how can we read her avoidance of polygamy? Rather than seeing it as expressive of shame about the practice, or a tacit denunciation, it can be understood as a tactical maneuver. As I suggested earlier, she chooses to set some of her pieces in what she describes as "Ancient history" to avoid stepping on the "pet concerns" of some white readers. Doing so does not necessarily mark a retreat from involvement in political commentary (or, more explicitly, commentary on the limits of what the United States will recognize as native politics). Instead, the displacement in time avoids a confrontational engagement with readers who support Indian education, missionization, and allotment in favor of an exploration of the existence and value of traditional patterns of kinship, residency, and collective identification. Similarly, while sidestepping polygamy can be interpreted as an effort to make Sioux sociality appear straight, that gesture itself may be to avoid the appearance of confronting U.S. jurisdiction head-on, given the ways polygamy came to signify as a sign of "barbarous" inheritance (a limit case for national sovereignty) and the sign of the "absolute" authority of the federal government over domestic space. Avoiding discussion of polygamy allows Zitkala-Ša's stories to gesture toward a kind of Dakota normality, bypassing the supposed sexual and racial excesses of plural marriage and thereby muting the apparent threat native peoples pose to the geopolitics and genealogy of the nation-state.

This vision of Mormon plural marriage as a white reversion to barbarism—a condition for which Indians were the implicit model—appears not only in the court decisions but also in ethnological discourses, particularly the work of Lewis Henry Morgan. At one point in *Ancient Society*, his most famous and arguably most influential book, he describes the Mormons as "relics of the old savagism not yet eradicated from the human brain . . . They are explainable as a species of mental atavism" (59).[66] This description emerges out of a theory of kinship in which "the monogamian family" is envisioned as perhaps the greatest achievement of mankind's evolutionary development thusfar, as the marker of the entry into "civilization." Morgan is quite explicit about the fact that the indigenous peoples of the Americas occupy a lower stage on the ladder of man's progress as a species, as evidenced by their family structures—in particular the presence of clans (or, in Morgan's terms, "gens"), which indicate a "social organization" structured around "relations [which] were purely personal" rather than a "political organization" in which "relations were purely territorial" (61). Of the "Dakotas or Sioux," Morgan observes that they "have allowed the gentile [adjectival form of "gens"] organization to fall into decadence" (158), suggesting that they possess a degraded version of the generic structure of kinship-centered native sociality. The text positions American Indians in what Anne McClintock has characterized as "anachronistic space," in which the geographic separation of contemporaneous populations is envisioned as a temporal rift such that one can be understood as existing in an earlier evolutionary period.[67] In doing so, Morgan resolves the jurisdictional conundrum of an alien invasion/eruption, for which polygamy serves as the metonym, by casting the sociospatial dynamics of barbarity as a residual survival of an earlier period, suggesting that they necessarily will give way to the obviously superior arrangements of Euro-American liberalism. Moreover, making the distinction between the "personal" and the "political" the primary marker of civilizational advancement consigns Indians to a sovereignty-less status, their non-nuclear family formations indicating not a competing set of geopolitical logics/claims but instead the absence of a determinate territoriality.

Within this frame, Zitkala-Ša's recourse to "Ancient history" threatens to confirm Morgan's developmentalist logic, with the kinship systems of native peoples appearing as a kind of relic soon to be supplanted by the innovations of a conjugally conceived modernity in which the "political" scope of national space is self-evident. Morgan distinguishes between "descriptive" and "classificatory" terminologies, the former referring to a nuclear logic of genealogy and the latter to systems where relatives in ostensibly different genealogical positions have the same designation (e.g., referring to my "father" and his "brother" by the same term). He further links "classificatory" structures to social systems in which membership and collective decision-making depend on belonging to extended groups of relatives (such as "gens," or clans), thus treating these formations as a deviation from a "descriptive" standard that is given logical priority, and he stages the relation between "classificatory" and "descriptive" modes as developmental, the shift to the latter signaling progress toward bourgeois homemaking, private propertyholding, and representative government, which are the apex of man's evolution thusfar. For Morgan, nuclear homemaking is a central feature of the entry into modernity, a stage of human development marked by statehood, and "a state must rest upon territory and not upon persons, upon the township as the unit of a political system, and not upon the gens which is the unit of a social system" (123). From this perspective, however, the historical setting of "The Trial Path" and "A Warrior's Daughter" also may open room for imagining a kind of collectivity that is not a state, one to which the geopolitical logics of the United States do not apply. Within ethnological discourse, such a formation appears inferior to nation-statehood, but given that under allotment entry into the civilized present of U.S. citizenship is conditioned on the fracturing of kinship-centered modes of governance and land tenure, these stories can be seen as drawing on ethnology as a way of providing a framework through which to reconceptualize the dynamics of native sociality, not as the absence of "home" and "family" as indicated in official narratives but as the presence of an alternative structure. As Thomas R. Trautmann suggests, "It is the peculiar property of the social evolutionism of Morgan and those in his camp that it both validates modern Euroamerican institutions, as the vanguard of the sequence of forms, and undermines their authority by showing that they have not always been and will not always be" (251). Morgan presents as a fallacy the notion that the monogamian family is the transhistorical default setting of humankind;[68] doing so allows non–conjugally centered systems to be understood as something other than a perverse deviation from the natural order of things. Additionally, Morgan's ethnology places some distance between a people's position in humankind's developmental trajectory and the idea of their having a distinctive racial status.[69] Unlike Cooper's concept of "gifts," Morgan's social stages cannot be reduced to physiological properties, opening the possibility of emphasizing kinship as a sign of cultural difference rather than biological deficiency, and thus as marking a qualitatively distinct geopolitics instead of just the absence of Anglo-American property.

Might Zitkala-Ŝa be seen as selectively employing ethnological premises in order to disjoint the romance plot of forced education and detribalization, to scramble its terms in ways that seek to validate traditional modes of Dakota sociospatiality? Morgan's work is less a recapitulation or reflection of federal law than a contemporaneous cultural production in a complex dialogue with governmental Indian affairs. In Gramscian terms, it formed part of the ideological terrain on which U.S. policy was moving, part of a *historical bloc* in which ethnological discourse helped provide broader forms of legitimation for institutional action. As Gramsci argues, though, " 'popular beliefs' and similar ideas are themselves material forces," and such ideas do not necessarily translate into only one set of institutional arrangements or policy imperatives. They may be used as a vehicle for critiquing an existing "ideological complex," and "this criticism makes possible a process of differentiation and change in the relative weight that the elements of the old ideologies used to possess. What was previously secondary and subordinate, and even incidental, is now taken to be primary—becomes the nucleus of a new ideological and theoretical complex."[70]

The correlation of emotion and civilization in Morgan's logic serves as such a point of leverage for Zitkala-Ŝa. Outlining the threshold over which peoples must pass on their way to civilization, Morgan emphasizes certain kinds of affect as symptomatic of its achievement. In earlier stages, "men did not seek wives as they are sought in civilized society, from affection, from the passion of love, which required a higher development than they had attained, was unknown among them. Marriage, therefore, was not founded upon sentiment but upon convenience and necessity" (463); "the passion of love was unknown among the barbarians. They are below the sentiment, which is the offspring of civilization and superadded refinement" (484). In a fairly literal sense, civilization for Morgan is a particular structure of feeling.

Given the emphasis on familial feeling in Zitkala-Ša's stories, folding romantic "passion" into broader networks of kinship in ways discussed earlier, they
can be read as drawing on aspects of the "ideological complex" of ethnology
in order both to translate Dakota lifeways for white readers and to invoke
dominant ideas about family—as an affective/intimate structure—so as to
make them "primary" in a reconfigured understanding of native sociality. In
other words, Zitkala-Ša utilizes emotion as a way of gaining traction for a
counterhegemonic staging of native kinship formations as a valid type of
sociopolitical structure. Playing the terms of ethnology against its aims, her
stories challenge the official image of Indian life as lacking in affect, seeking
to open ideological room for recognizing native forms of collectivity as more
than the residue of a vanishing barbarism.

The choice of genre further illustrates the ways Zitkala-Ša simultaneously
mobilizes the discourse of sentiment to register cultural distinctions while
dislodging them from Morgan's teleological narrative. As discussed in chapter 2, Elizabeth Freeman's notion of a "kin-aesthetic" refers to "an embodied
means of formalizing those very relationships that do not count as lawful
kinship" (98), but the phrase also can indicate the ways aesthetic choices
help facilitate the legitimation of kinship structures. Rather than retreating
from the realities of native life, the decision to write fiction may be seen as
eschewing ethnography in favor of a kind of writing less likely to be interpreted as inserting native peoples into a developmental hierarchy. Through
fiction, aspects of the ethnological imagination can be reconstellated to
validate divergence from dominant Euramerican norms, in particular
emphasizing emotional relationships in ways that provide a bridge between
readers' assumptions about "home" and "family" and the dynamics of
Dakota kinship.[71]

If the pieces in *American Indian Stories* seek to reorient the ethnological
emphasis on conjugal "passion" toward more capacious forms of familial
affect in order to legitimize nonliberal modes of social organization, Zitkala-
Ša's silence on polygamy is crucial to that goal. Polygamy not only operates
in the period as an overdetermined figure for jurisdictional crisis, such as in
the Mormon cases, but functions as a privileged signifier of perversity in all
its senses. In the words of the Yankton agent quoted earlier, polygamy is the
catchword for invoking the range of "depraved lusts" that characterize
Dakota life. Or, rather, polygamy serves as a way of recoding the sociopoli-
tics of native kinship as "depraved," as "tainted" by immorality and sexual
excess and thus antithetical to the wholesome sentiments of civilized domesticity.[72] To the extent that the stories aim to alter "popular beliefs" about the
Dakotas, that tactic depends on foregrounding the ways native peoples are
sociopolitically different while avoiding the impression that they are eroti-
cally deviant (in a way that also signifies racial incapacity) or a survival from

a (soon to be) bygone age. In this period, polygamy is a discursive site at which undisciplined "lust," domestic chaos, unnatural sexual drives, evolutionary (dis)order, and geopolitical confusion are condensed and signify each other; it sits at the crossroads of jurisdiction, race, ethnology, and sexology, operating as a dense transfer point among them in which their tensions and contradictions resolve around the image of a violated nuclear norm. Staying clear of that particular ideological minefield allows Zitkala-Ša to cast the kin formations of the Dakotas, and native peoples more broadly, as an alternative to statist structures rather than an inferior anachronism or a failure to adhere to dominant family relations. The absence of references to polygamy in Zitkala-Ša's stories, then, serves as a trace of the dialectic addressed earlier: native sovereignty continued to disrupt U.S. national self-representations; monogamous, conjugally centered homemaking came to serve as a metonym for the identity and integrity of the nation, supplementing the absence of legal principles by which to cohere U.S. jurisdiction; and ethnological discourse reinforced that familializing of the nation by casting other kinship formations as lingering remnants of an uncivilized past. In light of this particular ideological complex, effacing polygamy can be seen as a maneuver, representing Dakota collectivity in ways that contest the kinds of romantic emplotment at play in federal policy while avoiding a direct confrontation. Yet even as this choice is part of a negotiation over hegemony, an effort to open room for validating native modes of sociality and governance, it also to some extent works to straighten tradition by editing out forms of eroticism, matrimony, and residency that would trigger certain assumptions and anxieties on the part of white readers. In seeking to navigate shifting discourses of normality and to avoid charges of perversity, Zitkala-Ša ends up foreclosing discussion of relationships that would signify as specifically *queer*, as sexually aberrant; accepting some of the premises of the heterosexual imaginary may be the cost of her oppositional effort to validate native social formations.

ERASING THE WINKTE, OR THE NAUGHTY BITS OF TRADITION

While registering native challenges to the imperially imposed heteronorm, queer critique should also track where such accounts engage in a process of straightening, editing indigenous histories and cultures as a response to U.S. pressures or attendant internalized moral strictures. The issue in the case of Zitkala-Ša is less a failure to mention everything than a series of choices that suggests a systemic elision—a consistent effort to avoid discussing particular beliefs, practices, and/or identities. What is the boundary of acceptability?

How do Zitkala-Ša's writings represent tradition in ways that push against readers' assumptions while also implicitly drawing a line that she refuses to cross, creating a dialectic of anti-imperial critique and self-censorship? In *American Indian Stories*, one axis of distinction seems to be forms of gender expressivity and desire that point toward the regularity of homoeroticism. Zitkala-Ša sometimes rigidifies Dakota masculinity in ways that play to white assumptions about sex and gender in order to gain reader sympathy while erasing forms of male identity and practice that involved same-sex eroticism—specifically those surrounding the winkte.

The term denotes someone who is classified as male who occupies a nonmasculine gender status, which is associated with, among other things, a vision calling the person to this other role, specific kinds of clothing, and specialized roles in religious ritual and child care. Winktes traditionally were recognized and respected members of Sioux communities.[73] While the category was not based on sexual object choice per se, winktes most often would engage in romantic relationships with non-winkte men—whose own social identities were not affected by this sexual activity. In fact, winktes often were married to non-winkte men, having similar relationships to them as their wives.[74] "Homosexuality" as a concept, then, simply does not apply to this cultural arrangement, since the relevant distinction was not based on object choice but what can be termed "gender identity," such that two men could have a relationship with each other but not two non-winkte men. As Will Roscoe argues in *Changing Ones*, "Europeans, having no comparable roles, had no appropriate terms to describe their particular combination of gender, sexual, economic, and religious traits. Unable to name the gestalt, they labeled those parts of multiple gender roles that could be correlated to European experience" (120); he adds, "Western categories like 'gay' and 'homosexual,' which lack native equivalents, create confusion and tend to encourage informants to comment on Western practices rather than their own" (122).[75] Roscoe suggests that "gender" is a more appropriate rubric for this kind of social status than "sexuality," given that the former tends to address divisions of labor and role within broader social structures more so than the latter. Perhaps more to point, though, is that feelings and behaviors conceptualized as deviant with respect to normative gender were understood by Euramericans as also signaling the presence of homoerotic desire. The appearance of polarized gender identities within some of Zitkala-Ša's stories, and the attendant erasure of forms of identity that do not fit a binarized correlation of social role with sexed embodiment, might be read as indicating an awareness on her part of emergent notions of sexual perversity, so that the emphasis on gender dualism and elision of the winkte may signal an effort to straighten Dakota sociality. By offering a portrait of Dakota masculinity that effaces the existence of winktes,

Zitkala-Ša not only strategically circumscribes the representation of Dakota gender permutations to conform to white expectations but edits out the nonstigmatized participation of non-winkte men in forms of same-sex eroticism with winktes, thereby ignoring the ways such sexual activity and romance (including marriage) were an acceptable part of normal Dakota masculinity.

In the late nineteenth century, "gender inversion" was linked to erotic aberrance in ways that made discussion of third and fourth genders more treacherous for native writers, particularly given the ethnological assumptions about populations of color—especially indigenous peoples of the Americas—that pervaded sexological narratives.[76] The emergence of the category of the "invert" marked a shift from the earlier designation "hermaphrodite" in that the former indicates a congenital predilection toward forms of sensation and behavior that violate heteronormative ideals, as against the notion that the person with homoerotic desires possesses a different kind of corporeality—belongs to a *third sex*.[77] As Roscoe demonstrates, the presence of concepts of thirdness in native ways of labeling bodies but also in understandings of the relation between embodiment and social roles had a significant impact on incipient Euro-American discourses of sexuality: "[A]ccounts of North American gender diversity were cited in ongoing discourses on gender and sexual difference. These discourses eventually gave rise to the modern conception of homosexuals as a category of persons" (170); "the construction of the medical model of inversion (and, later, homosexuality) *required* historical and cross-cultural examples. If sexual variations were indeed diseases, natural not cultural phenomena, then cases of them surely occurred in other societies" (182). Sexological studies often cited earlier reports of homoeroticism and what was described as cross-dressing among American Indian groups, using them to justify the idea that such practices represent a transhistorical and transcultural permutation in which some persons do not fit the category of "man" or "woman" but are of, in Edward Carpenter's terms, an "intermediate type." Prior to the equation of homosexuality with object choice, which gained prominence over the course of the twentieth century,[78] homoerotic inclinations largely were conceived of as part of a continuum of gender difference, whether seen as primarily due to psychological or physiological causes. Representations of divergence from dominant gender dynamics, therefore, potentially could function as a metonym for the broader phenomenon of inversion, including its sexual dimensions, and reciprocally, an emphasis on the maintenance of gender boundaries implicitly could serve to indicate the absence of specifically sexual disorder.

Moreover, while sexology posited the universality of inversion, its continual reliance on non-European examples, often featuring native peoples of the Americas, tended to associate divergence, or deviancy, from Euro-American sexual norms with populations of color. As Marlon Ross argues, "While the perceived racial difference of an African or Asian male could be used to explain any putatively observed sexual deviance, racial sameness becomes ground zero for the observed split between heterosexual and homosexual Anglo-Saxon men" (168), and the appearance of a distinct homosexual type was perceived as indicating the presence of a more *developed* sex/gender system. In addition to casting native peoples as a counterpoint through which to make visible the appearance of sexual variation across widely different populations, sexology asserts their difference from Euro-Americans by foregrounding their failure to demonize homoerotic desires. In *Sexual Inversion*, the second volume of his *Studies in the Psychology of Sex*, the renowned British sexologist Havelock Ellis remarks, "If we turn to the New World, we find that among the American Indians, from the Eskimo of Alaska downward to Brazil and still farther south, homosexual customs have been very frequently observed. Sometimes they are regarded by the tribe with honor, sometimes with indifference, sometimes with contempt, but they appear to be always tolerated" (30). This description of prevalent native attitudes, however, is given a more pejorative cast a bit later: "[T]he evidence shows that among lower races homosexual practices are regarded with considerable indifference, and the real invert, if he exists among them, as doubtless he does exist, generally passes unperceived or joins some sacred caste which sanctifies his exclusively homosexual inclinations" (34). The absence of outrage at "homosexual practices" among indigenous peoples of the Americas marks them as "lower" (not unlike the failure to care about miscegenation discussed in chapter 1). The fact that "the real invert" can pass among them, is not suitably and sufficiently distinguished from the rest of the population, appears here as scientific "evidence" of a lack of development.[79] From this perspective, domestic and sexual arrangements that highlight the oddity of persons with congenitally inverted inclinations, that emphasize the abnormality of such preferences, are crucial to the emergence of civilization. The ability to demarcate perversity as such, then, signifies entry into modernity. Not only are native peoples perceived as lacking proper familial and residential arrangements, as demonstrated by their reticence toward (or outright refusal of) conjugal homemaking, but these social dynamics are seen as camouflaging sexual deviance, providing a cultural ecology in which it can flourish.

In trying to valorize Dakota kinship formations, then, Zitkala-Ša bears the implicit burden of defending them from the charge of perpetuating unnatural desires. As with the elision of polygamy, the erasure of homoeroticism works to legitimize traditional native sociality by dispelling its equation with depravity, effacing those elements of Dakota life most likely to be conceptualized as sexually nonnormative—as queer—and to be taken as evidence of the lack of civilization.[80] The portrayal of Dakotas as properly heterogendered can be conceptualized as part of an effort to normalize native difference, to cast it as divergence rather than deviance. This process of gender accommodation is most evident in "The Soft-Hearted Sioux." The story follows a Dakota man from when he is a sixteen-year-old boy living with his parents and grandmother to his return to the reservation as a missionary after nine years spent in Indian schools, noting the community's hostility toward him (including the moving of the camp circle away from him and his family) and his inability to provide food for his sick father and elderly mother. The drama of the text rests on the unnamed title character's failure to fulfill what are presented as the gender ideals of Dakota manhood. Beginning with him and his family clustered around the fire in their tepee, the story's first bit of dialogue is his grandmother inquiring, "when are you going to bring home a handsome woman?" (110). She continues in this vein, despite her grandson's protestations ("Not yet!"), and his parents join in, his father noting that "learn[ing] to provide much buffalo meat" is a necessary precursor to "bring[ing] home a wife" (111). Impending adulthood is connected to finding a female partner and becoming an adequate provider, the latter serving as a signal of maturation toward matrimony. The main character, who narrates the story in the first person, observes, "my heart was too much troubled by their words, and [I was] sorely troubled with a fear lest I should disappoint them" (111). His expression of "fear" is tied to his concern about his ability to fulfill this social role, although not clarifying whether his trepidation is about his relationship to women, buffalo, or both.

Here the narrative breaks off, skipping "[n]ine winters' snows" in which he "hunted for the soft heart of Christ" (112). Returning to preach Christianity to his people, he exhibits signs of anxiety, including "nervous fingers" and sweating before speaking (113, 116), and he is continually described as "soft-hearted." While explicitly marking his lack of hunting skills, the multiple references to his "soft"-ness by members of the reservation community and his family also implicitly suggest a broader failure to live up to the terms of Dakota manhood, casting his Christianization as an unacceptable feminization and taking it as evidence that he is a "traitor to his people" (117). The failure properly to perform masculinity is represented as the sign of his abandonment of Dakota ways, reciprocally implying that the role of husband/provider lies at the core of native male identity.

More than bemoaning how Indian schooling works to disrupt the transmission of tradition or condemning the misguided effort of such converts to eradicate native beliefs and customs, the story fuses this twofold critique to a representation of the resulting deracination as an unnatural gender inversion. Opposition to Indian policy here works through a form of gender baiting that appeals not only to white stereotypes of native mascu-linity but to dominant notions of dimorphic gender identity and its in-herent fulfillment in the heterocoupling of marriage.[81] The main character's later "fears" about killing allude back to his earlier concerns about both hunting and courting (118), so that readers are encouraged to see his dis-tancing of himself from his tribe as a sort of perversion. The text creates an equivalency between his inability to do the following: connect with his people; support himself and his family (his father starving to death because he cannot find food in time); and "bring home a wife." This chain of associ-ation, however, depends on the assumption that in order to become/remain an accepted member of traditional Dakota society a boy must follow one particular (hetero)gendered path whose trajectory is toward (monoga-mous) marriage. Such a proposition simply makes no sense in light of the conventionality of the winkte as an acknowledged and valued social option for boys. In addition, the emotional force and logic of the story require merging Dakota manhood with heteroromance so as, implicitly yet power-fully, to pathologize the "soft-hearted" convert, but as I indicate earlier, normative masculinity did not preclude having sex with or even marrying people of the same sex.

While not claiming that the central character is a winkte, I am suggesting that the story's efforts to generate white feeling against U.S. policy relies on the erasure of winktes as part of Dakota communities and a consequent straightening of Dakota sex/gender, especially for men, so as to cast the civ-ilization program, rather than tradition, as perverse.[82] While rejecting the image of the isolated household and the notion of the married couple as an independent family unit, *American Indian Stories* does not displace hetero-romance as a lens through which to represent Dakota tradition, in some cases fetishizing it so as to heighten reader sympathy for resistance to white intrusion. In the effort to oppose the pathologization of native kinship, resi-dency, and collective identity, Zitkala-Ša offers a truncated representation of Dakota gender identities that screens out forms of eroticism and romantic attachment that might trouble white readers, but that also might signal the kinds of *inversion* and laissez-faire attitudes toward the presence of perver-sity that were thought to mark nonwhite savagery.

Rather than suggesting that *American Indian Stories* constructs some-thing like a queer subjectivity, I have argued that Zitkala-Ša's use of romance seeks to preserve and transmit embattled tradition in response to a sus-tained imperial assault. Yet in rejecting the broader privatizing imaginary and nuclear political economy of normality, she also effaces what could be (mis)taken by whites as the most perverse/queer elements of Dakota cul-ture. This complex dialectic between championing and censoring tradition reflects the layered quality of compulsory heterosexuality and suggests the need for multipronged forms of queer analysis that are not focused exclusively on sexual identity/diversity but that do not overlook its suppression either. Focusing on the ideological structure of Indian policy—its organization as a romance plot—and the attendant political implications of native representations of kinship works to provide greater leverage in defining and dislocating the force of heteronormativity while also marking how straight privilege functions as a bribe within imperial efforts to get native peoples to disidentify from tradition.

4

ALLOTMENT SUBJECTIVITIES AND THE ADMINISTRATION OF "CULTURE"

Ella Deloria, Pine Ridge, and the Indian Reorganization Act

There was a time when it was the policy of the United States Government to crush Indian life and even to crush the family life of Indians and during that time laws were passed and those laws are still the laws, though it is no longer the policy of the Government to rob you or to crush you, but they are the laws and by them we must work and you must live.

This Bill does not set up any one system of self-government. It does not seek to impose on the Indians a system of self-government of any kind. It sets up permission to the Indians to work out self-government which is appropriate to the traditions, to their history and to their social organization.

> —John Collier, Commissioner of Indian Affairs,
> *Minutes of the Plains Congress* (1934)

By kinship all Dakota people were held together in a great relationship that was theoretically all-inclusive and co-extensive with the Dakota domain . . .

Before going further, I can safely say that the ultimate aim of Dakota life, stripped of accessories, was quite simple: One must obey kinship rules; one must be a good relative.

> —Ella Deloria, *Speaking of Indians* (1944)

If the goal of allotment was the transformation of Indian subjectivity and affect, the aim of the Indian Reorganization Act (1934) was the creation of self-directed tribal political economies.[1] Allotment policy repeatedly was characterized as an effort to shift the objects of native feeling—from clans and communities to nucleated families, from collective territory to private property, from the tribe to the nation-state—so as to create proper, individuated citizens out of primitive masses. While the imposition of this naturalized vision of kinship, residency, and personhood clearly operated as part of a systemic program of *detribalization* whose goal was to dismantle native governance and expropriate native lands, in ways discussed in the previous chapter, it was not portrayed as a means to that particular end. In other words, the allotment program tended to be articulated and legitimized in ways that portrayed the brutal and sustained assault on indigenous geopolitical formations, subsistence and trade systems, and knowledges as merely a side-effect of the benevolent effort to modernize Indians, to liberate them from the shackles of tradition. By contrast, U.S. officials presented the Indian Reorganization Act (IRA) as a vehicle for native autonomy, displacing the atomizing dynamics that had structured Indian policy for the previous half century and replacing them with a sustained commitment to promoting native "culture" and "community."[2] As indicated in John Collier's comments quoted above, "it is no longer the policy of the Government to rob you or to crush you"; instead, it "sets up permission to the Indians to work out self-government which is appropriate to the[ir] traditions."[3] The project of producing (hetero)normative patriotic subjects appears to give way to official recognition for forms of indigenous collectivity.

However, if allotment and its associated ideologies were no longer to be the guiding principles of Indian policy, what happened to the subjectivities generated by this regime? How does the continuing legacy of allotment, and the various kinds of identities and practices engendered by it, shape the conditions of native political formations and representations under reorganization?[4] How is the "self" of "self-government" in the IRA present haunted by the persistent dynamics of the allotment-saturated past?[5] In casting allotment policy primarily as a repressive force, as an effort to "crush" various aspects of "Indian life," Collier, who was Commissioner of Indian Affairs, overlooks its fashioning of individual and collective forms of subjectivity, production of codes of intelligibility, and enforcement of them against native peoples. Rather than simply negating existing native kinship networks, political structures, and forms of land tenure, allotment reorders the field of possibility for the articulation and experience of native sociality, giving rise to new modes of representation and association that in various ways follow, mediate, and oppose the terms of the law. When measured against Collier's characterization of the statute as a restoration of what had been lost or buried over the previous half century, the continued operation of allotment-era strategies of administration can be described as a contradiction. In *Organizing the Lakota*, Thomas Biolosi argues, "The Indian New

Deal was about Indian *self-government*, and the technologies of power deployed by the OIA which disempowered the tribal councils clashed glaringly with the official discourse" (150). Yet the relation between the IRA's expressed intent to consolidate native political economy and the continued support for allotment subjectivities on-reservation is not simply an inconsistency but instead itself is generative, purposively regulating the kinds of native "self"-hood that will be seen as viable by the U.S. government.

In other words, the absence of discussions of subjectivity and affect from the official discourse of reorganization is not happenstance but indicates that the allotment imaginary helps structure and provide an ordering limit for what will count as legitimate native governance—what kinds of "traditions," "social organization," and "history" will be federally recognized as suitable bases/vehicles for native political identity. In this way, the representation of native peoples under reorganization is in some sense the inverse of that discussed in chapter 2. *Hope Leslie* depicts native peoples as teaching whites how the affective ties of adoption and siblinghood can provide a way of reconceptualizing the relation between "private feelings" and "public good," generating bonds of transhousehold cohesion that frustrate the isolating domesticity and tyrannical patriarchy that shape the nuclear family model, but this lesson in community caring leaves little room for acknowledging native peoples as sovereign entities. By contrast, reorganization foregrounds the existence of tribes as polities but in ways that presume allotment-era ideologies with respect to kinship and residency, resulting in the displacement of existing tribal councils (which tended to retain more of preallotment "traditions" than the "system of self-government" that superseded them).[6] The kinds of native collectivity produced by reorganization implicitly depend on the heteronormative subjectivities and domesticating affective economies of allotment as a way of defining the horizon of possibility for native political self-representation, a process I will explore through discussion of several key policy statements about the IRA and analysis of the ways it was implemented among a specific people—the Oglala Sioux on Pine Ridge.[7] Under reorganization, the sorts of privatization at play in the previous policy help define the boundaries of federally acknowledged tribal identity, naturalizing conjugal homemaking and using the supposedly self-evident distinction between domesticity and governance to normalize liberal assumptions about citizenship, property, and the work of political institutions that then are cast as the foundation for native politics.

In this vein, Ella Deloria's insistence on a "kinship" that is "all-inclusive" can be seen as a challenge to the organizing political logics/schematics of reorganization, locating forms of identification and interdependence that cannot be registered in an allotment imaginary and conceptualizing them as central to the very kinds of "social organization" and "history" Collier claims to champion. In *Speaking of Indians* (1944), she offers a subtle yet powerful counterpoint to, and critique of, reorganization, most particularly its operation on the Teton reservations with which she was familiar (including Pine Ridge, where she was residing with her brother during the debate over whether or not to adopt the terms of the IRA). Deloria uses kinship to generate a framework for investigating the complex legacy of allotment, its uneven effects on Dakota people(s), and the ways the new regime draws on while apparently disowning the old one.[8] Developing what can be described as a *transectional* analysis, she illustrates how the practical and normative dimensions of "be[ing] a good relative" necessarily cross the boundaries of the segregated spheres employed by reorganization in its mapping of native sociality on reservation, thereby contesting the reifying categories through which "Dakota life" is divided up under—and thus made more amenable to—U.S. policy.[9] Deloria suggests that the very kinds of interpersonal affect and quotidian subjectivity that reorganization seems to overlook in fact provide the infrastructural support for the broader political and economic dynamics it seeks to target, using the prism of kinship to reveal the ongoing paternalistic management of native "self"-hood and the kinds of regulation enacted through the (limited) institutionalization of "culture."

Official expressions of support for native "culture" and "community" function as a way of legitimizing the new policy regime as more democratic than its predecessor, but these tropes of "tradition" end up dividing up native sociality into units that fit Euramerican categories. Illustrating how social relations conventionally characterized as kinship provided the primary nexus for meaningful individual and collective association, Deloria's work disorients the assumptions animating reorganization, refusing the segmentation of native life into distinct spheres (i.e., the domestic, religion, governance) and showing how supposedly primitive residential arrangements that distended the nuclear family unit were saturated with the kind of sentimental affect usually reserved for descriptions of the conjugal household. In this way, Deloria employs the concept of kinship to contest the effort under reorganization to sustain allotment's privatization of "family" and to cast U.S. policy as facilitating the restoration of native forms of "social organization." Her novel *Waterlily*, set among the Teton Sioux in the pre-reservation period, indicates how such networks sustained a range of social statuses for which there is no place in the de facto conjugal imaginary of postallotment policy; the text uses the principles of individual and collective connection it gathers under the rubric of "kinship" as a way of linking the range of practices and associations that had been outlawed as "Indian offenses"—including the Sun Dance, polygamy, redistribution or destruction of the belongings of the deceased, and regular travel to visit relatives (only the first one of which comes to be recognized as a legitimate expression of "culture" under Collier).[10] In this way, the novel provides a historically located account of Teton sociality that demonstrates the limits of Indian policy's multicultural fetishization of a particular version of "culture." Ella Deloria's work, in both *Speaking of Indians* and *Waterlily*, then, helps reveal the kinds of social mappings that implicitly define and constrain "self-government" under reorganization. In doing so, these texts help point toward the ways post-IRA political discourses rely on heteronormative subjectivities in fashioning modes of sovereignty that will be recognized as legitimate by the U.S. government.

COMPETING CONFIGURATIONS OF "COMMUNITY"

Reorganization does not so much eliminate the administrative apparatus, subjectivities, or effects of the allotment program as selectively deploy them within a framework in which the goal has shifted from detribalization to self-government.[11] That change in the aims of federal policy has vast implications for the status of native governance and land tenure, but it does not mark an utter negation of the technologies, discourses, and ideologies of privatization put in play under allotment. Rather, in changing the dominant scale and topoi of policy from the nuclear family home to the reservation "community," reorganization in one key pushes for forms of political, territorial, and economic integration that appear antithetical to the previous policy while in another key continuing to draw on the imaginary of allotment in formulating what should occur at the level of kinship and residency. In this way, the IRA replaces and extends the prior regime simultaneously, but in different registers. Those patterns are not in fact fully separable, however, in that the logic by which political and familial formations can be divided into distinct domains/spheres is itself reliant on a distinction between public policy and domesticity that is a legacy of allotment. Thus, reorganization remains complexly inflected by allotment even as the one embraces the idea of native collectivity targeted for erasure by the other. The nexus of "private" personhood, intimacy, and propertyholding operative under allotment comes to be treated as an incontestable given under reorganization, providing the kernel around which native "communities" would be formed.[12]

   In an effort to gain native support for the bill while it was still under discussion in the House and Senate committees, Collier arranged a series of what were described as "congresses" in which Indian leaders within a given geographic area were gathered together to discuss the terms of the new legislation at length. The elaboration of the IRA's provisions and its implications in these meetings provides an important index of what "self-government" under reorganization would mean, since the proposed legislation already had been drafted and the audience present at these meetings would lead officials to put the best face on the possibilities for native peoples' authority over themselves under the new law. The Plains Congress, attended by representatives from the Sioux reservations, among others, was the first of these meetings, and in Collier's efforts to explain the workings and significance of the bill, one can see the tensions that animate the entire project of reorganization, particularly the ways the choices available to native peoples are conditioned by the mandated retention (and, in some ways, the naturalization) of allotment modes of land tenure and homemaking.

Collier describes the new legislation as an effort to redress the catastrophic effects of existing policy, to alleviate the bureaucratic caprice under which Indians currently are forced to live, and to replace the current assault on native sociality with an acknowledgment of collective native agency. Describing native peoples as "at the mercy of the Indian Bureau,"[13] Collier highlights the absence of any meaningful structural constraint on its authority in the management of Indian affairs, further observing that "the guardianship maintained by the United States is carried out under a body of laws which are wicked and stupid" (7–8). Under the new law, however, dictatorial domination will be replaced by consultation and consent: "We intend to act in partnership with the Indians and we are not going to act unless the Indians are willing to go with us" (4–5). That "partnership" includes generating a legally guaranteed "plan according to which Indian tribes or groups may develop the kind of self-government that they want, that is fitted to them, and may take on more power or less power as they prefer" (27).[14] Yet "partnership" does not mean eliminating U.S. superintendence. As Collier argues, "The cure for the evils done by the Government is not to abolish but to reform it and make it do good things instead of evil things, and that is true of the guardianship over Indians" (6), and at several points he indicates that under the proposed law "the guardianship of the Government . . . is made permanent."[15] While the concept of "guardianship" may simply be taken as marking the end of allotment, asserting that the process of fee patenting through which millions of acres had been lost will be discontinued and that native lands will be held in trust in perpetuity,[16] it is accompanied by the claim that Indians remain "ward[s] of the government," thereby legitimizing ongoing U.S. intervention in native affairs; at several points, Collier offers versions of the sentiment that "if the tribe made a mess of its undertaking, then Congress would have the power to take it back and put it in the hands of the Indian Bureau to straighten out" (33). Thus, if the proposed legislation indicates a desire on the part of officials "to build on the old Indian traditions" in ways that make sense with respect to the "social organization" of native communities (29), the United States still maintains the authority to adjudicate what "traditions" are suitable for institutionalization as part of resurgent collective native "self"-hood.

More than simply managing the emergence of postallotment modes of native governance, fashioning them to fit an implicit image of what constitutes a proper policy "partner," reorganization as described by officials necessarily entails the preservation of the subjectivities, spatiality, and scale structure of allotment, making the heterosexual imaginary at the heart of the prior policy into the de facto normative architecture for the new one. In explaining the relationship between the new law and the existing legal status of native persons and land, Collier notes, "allotment has created individual valid property rights in individuals [*sic*]. That fact is there and has to be dealt with." He goes on to observe:

> [A]s a result of allotment, thousands of Indians live on or are the holders of parcels of land. They own that land. . . . It is their right, not only to continue to own what they own but they have the right to transmit what they own to their children, to their heirs. This right is theirs, fundamentally under the Constitution of the United States and could not be taken away from them no matter what Congress did. So that, in addition to stopping the loss of land and getting more land, any change of laws, must protect these individual property rights in living allottees and their heirs. (9–10)[17]

The minutes record that this last statement was greeted with applause. Such a response is not surprising in light of the profound anxiety expressed by native allottees who had been able to retain their land that under the new policy it might be seized in whole or in part in order to provide for those who had become landless due to economic hardships in the wake of fee patenting.[18] However, just as the implications of "guardianship" extend beyond simply discontinuing fee patenting, the matrix of "property rights" that Collier pledges to defend shapes the contours of native political identity and action under the IRA in ways that far exceed shielding allottees from displacement. The "right" to the land allottees' "own" appears sacrosanct, as an inviolable set of claims whose "protect"-ion lies at the very heart of U.S. law. This incontrovertible and indissolvable "fact" is taken to mean that any change in Indian policy, including through legislation enacted by Congress, must recognize and retain the matrix of "individual"-ity produced under allotment.

However, what makes this particular structure of land tenure more legally inviolable than prior indigenous modes of placemaking? Forms of native sociospatiality that preceded the passage of the Dawes Act, whose dimensions and dynamics were acknowledged in treaties (albeit unevenly) for more than a century, could be disregarded by the federal government in its initiation of the program of detribalization, and if Congress had the authority to alter the terms of native inhabitance and political status previously, why does it lack such power now? While at points Collier seems to suggest that the retention of the privatizing geographies of allotment is a tactic ("if Legislation is passed which over-rides property rights . . . the Courts will prevent the Legislation from being put into effect" [10]),[19] he more consistently describes "individual property rights" as beyond the scope of federal adjustment, as constitutionally beyond the scope of congressional control. Why is this type of landholding legally privileged in ways preallotment tribal occupancy rights are not?

More precisely, if the new statute's purpose is to end the "wicked and stupid" regime of allotment, why are many of its key components to be maintained? The mention of "children"/"heirs" provides an implicit answer. As discussed in the previous chapter, the central unit of allotment was the nuclear family, made paradigmatic in both the assignment of plots of land and the laws governing inheritance. This nexus of kinship and residency provides the context for the generic "individual" cited in allotment-era discourses, and therefore by Collier in his discussion of the need to retain such arrangements under reorganization. More than providing an ordering principle of territoriality, though, the nuclear imaginary helps naturalize a particular kind of household formation, as well as a definitional distinction between the familial and the governmental. Within Anglo-American common-law traditions, the conjugally centered home not only has been cast as the fundamental building block of social life but has been envisioned as itself prior to and outside the sphere of law and policy, appearing as that which government was created to defend as well as that which must be defended from governmental intrusion.[20] In short, bourgeois homemaking, with its production of properly civilized individuality and insulation of privatized intimacy, counts as a claim to "property" in ways that collective native processes for determining land use and distributing resources do not.[21]

Conversely, the rejuvenation of native "traditions" and "social organization" promised by Collier necessarily must conform to the heteronormative imperatives that serve as both the ends and limits of governance. In explaining the kind of jurisdiction that will be available to native peoples under the IRA, Collier notes the impossibility of doing anything to remove landowning whites from reservations; the federal government "does not have power over land that it does not own or control, where white people are living, and we can't give that power to the Government and the Government can not give it to an Indian community" (82). White homemaking and propertyholding define what constitutes political "power," serving as that which necessarily is protected by law and what lies beyond its "control." In this way, native sovereignty is narrated here not only as a gift from the federal government but as one whose appeal is the possibility that native communities might be able to approximate the autonomy of the white household despite ongoing federal superintendence.

Treating this domestic formation as a "right" that transcends any given administrative program further normalizes the insertion of native governments into the scale structure of federalism.[22] In speaking of "property" as if it were an immutable aspect of contemporary native life, a legacy of allotment from which there is no possibility of retreat, Collier obfuscates the issue of precisely which laws are applicable in outlining the contours of landholding and inheritance and the significance of such importations/impositions for conceptualizing the meaning of "self-government." For example, invoking "heirs" begs the question of how they will be determined, and although Collier equates this concept with "children" in ways that assume the nuclear family model, the General Allotment Act indicates that "the law of descent and partition in force in the State or Territory where such lands are situate" shall guide inheritance.[23] Thus, state laws with respect to the definition of family and transmission of land implicitly provide the social infrastructure for reorganization, suggesting that native governance will mold itself around those statutes.

In this vein, Collier repeatedly refers to the jurisdiction made available to native peoples under the IRA as "local,"[24] a designation that positions indigenous governments not just as operating over a smaller geographic expanse than state law but as of a lesser legal stature, as a feature of U.S. law but one lacking a recognized constitutional status of its own. Indicating that governments recognized under the IRA would be "clothed with the authority of the Federal Government," an image itself redolent with the history of the civilization program, he observes that "the organized bodies of Indians will become Agencies of the Federal Government, instrumentalities or, if you like, branches of the Federal Government" (11). He later adds, "the community [as the prospective unit of governance under the IRA was called] is an instrumentality of the Federal Government and by agreement between the Community and the Secretary of the Interior the Secretary could delegate to the community his own regulative powers over allotments in severalty" (112). The "powers" of government, and attendant assumptions about the character of governance itself, remain constant while they are transferred from one "agency" to another. Political "self"-hood for native peoples, then, inheres in their becoming the "instrument" for maintaining an unchangeable core of allotment-orchestrated relations, and political collectivity as acknowledged under the IRA will take shape around the privatizing structures of the prior policy. No longer seeking to dissipate native communities,

federal policy will now utilize them as the vehicle for forms of "local" regulation whose dynamics largely depend on state law—not simply retaining
the compulsory heterosexuality of allotment but making its terms the neutral register of the fact that Indians are "rights"-bearing members of the
United States.

In *The Cunning of Recognition*, as part of a discussion of the effects of
liberal multiculturalism on indigenous policy in Australia, Elizabeth Povinelli explores how "the discourse and affect of shame play" a significant role
"in making an expansion of legal discriminatory devises seem the advent of
the law of recognition or a rupture of older models of monocultural nationalism and the grounds for national optimism, renewal, and rebirth" (155).
The rhetoric of officials during the Plains Congress repeatedly comes back to
the assaultive dynamics of prior U.S. Indian policy, its efforts to "crush" native peoples, assuring participants that the new law will mark a break from
that program of intervention and dispossession and instead will enable them
to have a substantive say over what happens on-reservation. Yet this performance of what in Povinelli's terms can be called national "shame"—the
denunciation of prior administrative perspectives as, in Collier's words
noted earlier, "wicked and stupid"—actually does not undo the forms of interpellation through which native peoples are subjected to U.S. jurisdiction
or, more to the point, through which they are made *subjects of it*. At one
point, Collier observes, "This new system will give to the Indians and to the
employees of the Indian Bureau a chance to work on a footing of friendly
equality. It gives to the Indians a chance to become real citizens in the American
community" (31). Characterizing the IRA as enabling full Indian belonging
in the "American community" does not displace allotment-era aims, especially insofar as such membership is predicated on embodying a certain
kind of individuality. In addressing the Indian Court provisions of the draft
bill, Collier notes, "wherever there is a provision which seems as if it might
work an injustice on an Indian, that Indian will have the right to come before
this court and insist, first, on his constitutional rights as a citizen of the
United States, and, second, on his special rights as are given him by the charter of his community" (39). Casting "constitutional rights as a citizen" as
foundational in thinking about the status of native peoples under U.S. law,
Collier positions citizenship as the underlying basis for all native political
claims, implying that the possessive individualism that emerges out of the
heterosexual imaginary of allotment will provide the normative ground on
which reorganization will build. The trope of citizenship is the form of "recognition" through which native peoples will achieve "equality" and on top of
which their "special rights" can be perched. Thus, more than indicating that
native governments must preserve the private sphere of propertyholding
created by prior policy, Collier's comments suggest that the regime instituted

by the IRA will make political "community" contingent on the acceptance of the principles of liberal individualism at play in allotment's attack on prior native networks of kinship and residency.

If citizenship and individual propertyholding are central in efforts to outline the contours of native governance under the IRA, the questions posed by participants during the Plains Congress point to the persistence of form(ul)ations of native identity that exceed this official mapping of native politics. Inquiries by native attendees allude to the ongoing presence of an alternative normative framework, namely that of treaty-making, and to the complex ways native peoples had accommodated the legal imperatives of allotment while still preserving kinship-based forms of political collectivity. Members of the Sioux delegations in particular keep calling on Collier to clarify the relation between the proposed provisions of the IRA and treaty-based obligations and ongoing controversies over land claims. At one point, George White Bull, one of the delegates from the Standing Rock reservation, observes, "I believe that something is not very clear in our minds and that is this, that the passage of the new Bill would in turn jeopardize our interests in some of the allotment and treaties that are known by the year '68, '78, and '89. Treaties that are known by the years would be jeopardized and that part of those will be relinquished if we accept the new proposed Bill" (67–68). He adds an immensely compelling analysis of the situation, worth quoting in full:

> I have some claims and suits against the U.S. Government. We are looking forward to the day when a judgment shall be reached in connection with our claims that we may realize some compensation on behalf of the claims. How does it happen there are no monies to settle our claims and reach judgment on our claims or pay the amount of those claims, but when a time comes for the transfer of our allotments into another system then we are told that a large amount of money—millions—would be appropriated for this purpose? I believe that it would be an easy matter for us to reach an early decision in this matter had the Government been anxious to settle our claims and pay up our claims in full than if a new proposition were presented. I believe we would have been just as anxious to answer just as readily and go into it whole heartedly. Also, because by the settlement of our just claims we know our rights and we would have no fear towards any other matter that they may present. (68–69)

In response to these points, Collier argues that placing the provisions of the IRA and grievances related to treaties and agreements with the federal government in "one bill . . . that would bring all these claims to judgment" would be "a big mouthful" that "will choke us to death," citing the sheer expense of settling native claims ("It will cost the Government so much that Mr. Douglas, Director of the Budget, would faint") (70–71). Considered in light of his earlier insistence when addressing the issue of treaty-based annuities that "first, this loss of land by the Indians must be sharply stopped" (52), Collier's presentation of claims growing out of the history of treaty-making as a secondary matter, as of less immediate importance than forging a "partnership" between native peoples and BIA,[25] suggests that he views the identities and principles at stake in such claims to be only marginally relevant to the kind of native political subjectivity envisioned as the aim of reorganization.

The position articulated by White Bull, however, suggests not only the continuing existence of forms of Sioux collectivity that precede allotment but that "self-government" as imagined by the IRA implicitly disavows the persistence of such older modes of governance. White Bull links consent to the new legislation ("an easy matter for us to reach an early decision") to federal acknowledgment of existing obligations ("settle our claims"), a recognition that would illustrate acceptance of Sioux self-understandings ("our just claims" and "our rights"). In addition, he indicates that the government is making a choice about where to place its resources, deciding not only to ignore the payment of outstanding claims but to create "another system" that bears little relationship to the treaty system and the *traditions* that had accumulated around it through which Sioux peoples had come to conceptualize their own *social organization* and their relation with the U.S. government.

Collier's discussion of reorganization tends to efface the existence of tribal councils among native peoples, even as his efforts to generate native support for the bill to some extent presume them. For this reason, attendees' attempts to draw attention to treaties and related agreements with the government also can be seen as pointing to the tribal councils to which the treaties gave rise, a framework that predates and persists in modified forms alongside allotment. The growing need in the late nineteenth century to speak in semi-unified ways as supra-band entities in negotiations and ongoing engagements with the United States led many native groups to create governing bodies that could function as intermediaries with federal institutions and agents. While Teton Sioux peoples had signed several earlier agreements with the United States, including the treaties of 1851 and 1868 (which established the "Great Sioux Reserve") and the agreement of 1877 (by which the Black Hills were ceded, later found by the Supreme Court in 1980 to be an illegal taking), this process of centralization was particularly intense in the lead-up to and wake of the Sioux Act of 1889, which divided Teton territory into six distinct reservations and opened 11 million acres of "surplus" lands to white settlement.[26] These emergent forms of governance largely drew on the traditional leaders of the tiospayes, the kinship-based residential units around which Teton sociality was organized (discussed in chapter 3).[27]

In the late 1880s, the people of Pine Ridge created the Oglala Omniciye (or Oglala Council), which "marked a departure from pre-reservation Oglala political organization, in that it met regularly on behalf of all Oglala bands. It sought to integrate those bands, which had been autonomous."[28] Composed of chiefs and headmen from the tiospayes, it advocated around the treaties and agreements with the federal government, including with respect to land rights and guaranteed rations and annuities; the Omniciye also organized popular opposition to the implementation of allotment on Pine Ridge, challenged the terms of government land-leasing programs (which largely gave white ranchers access to reservation lands at well below the market price or at no cost) and served as a means of helping coordinate the activities and decision making of local councils (themselves representing groups of tiospayes but organized around the farm districts instituted by the BIA): "[M]embers of any central council in this model were more on the order of delegates than elected officials or public administrators."[29] In 1916, the Oglalas adopted a constitution that gave each local council ten representatives in the Omniciye, the document noting that the "making of new chiefs and the making of new bands will be managed by the chiefs at their camps at home, and not to be handled within the Council."[30] Over the course of the 1920s, the agent worked to reduce the number of people on the Council and to divorce it, except in the most nominal ways, from the local councils, a move explicitly rejected by the Oglala public in votes taken in 1931. They were in the process of drafting a new constitution that reflected the principles of the Omniciye when the IRA was introduced in Congress.[31] In neither version of the IRA, Collier's original nor the bill eventually passed by Congress, was there any mechanism for simply accepting as legitimate such existing structures of native governance.[32]

As suggested by this brief history of Pine Ridge politics, references to treaties in the Plains Congress can be understood as recalling a conception of Indian policy quite at odds with the vision of native governments as a semimunicipal stand-in for the current non-native bureaucracy. Invoking the history of the treaty system implicitly displaces the allotment-derived conceptual prism through which U.S. citizenship and individual property rights appear as the inevitable building blocks for native politics. Rather than serving as an *instrumentality* of federal policy, reproducing its foundational split between the familial and the governmental, pre-IRA Teton tribal councils largely were ordered around tiospaye-based constituencies and their traditional forms of leadership, with kinship serving as a crucial modality of Teton politics. By contrast, to be recognized under the IRA is to be made "real citizens," naturalizing the features of regular U.S. jurisdiction by presenting their imposition as a renewed commitment to individual and property "rights" in which the distinction between public policy and the

intimacy of the domestic sphere is taken as obvious. Within this heterosexual imaginary, the tiospaye-centered councils cannot serve as legitimate
vehicles of political decision-making. Yet Teton delegates subtly disjoint this
logic. They repeatedly assert that they "are here with the sole purpose of
listening and we are not here to pass on questions," "and whatever we learn
we will take back with us to our own people" (2). Such insistence defers the
legitimizing moment of collective consent Collier seeks while also implicitly
alluding to the presence of mechanisms of popular decision-making, a for-
mat for "pass[ing] on questions," not acknowledged by the congress itself—
namely, the existing tiospaye-based tribal councils. The comments of native
participants in the congress indicate not only hesitancy in becoming a "partner" of the BIA but, despite Collier's assurances of "equality," a fundamental
unease about the entailments of accepting a position within another
U.S.-orchestrated policy framework.[33]

This tension persists in the wake of the adoption of the IRA and its implementation on Sioux reservations. The critique of reorganization governments often takes shape around the idea that they have left aside the treaty
system and its unresolved claims against the government. Appearing before
the House Committee on Indian Affairs in 1937, representatives from several of the Teton reservations spoke of their discontent with the governments instituted under the IRA in terms of the failure of the latter to press
forward on pursing remedies for past and continuing violations of
agreements with the United States. An Oglala named Edward Stover, who
was serving as interpreter, observes, "this delegation that I am here with
represents quite a majority of the Indians of the Pine Ridge Reservation,"
and he explains that they are part of "the treaty organization," a "voluntary"
body that is "different from the tribal council as organized for the reservation."[34] Benjamin American Horse, recognized as a chief among the Oglalas,
adds:

> One reason for our confusion and hard times on the reservation is because
> of the Wheeler-Howard Act which was introduced and we are fighting on it
> amongst ourselves . . . standing about half and half. One goes under the
> name of the tribal council and the other goes under the name of the treaty
> council. This tribal council was not consented to by the treaty council . . . We
> realized that those treaties were the supreme laws of the Indians and,
> therefore, we established the treaty council[.] (11)[35]

If the treaties are presented as the source of political authority and the
"tribal council" is cast as illegitimate due to its lack of concern for them,
they also serve as a way of figuring a distinction between two different
structures of governance, one based on the model of the Omniciye and the

other on IRA principles. The "treaty council" first appears in official records in 1931 (the same year as the vote to displace the agent-engineered council, discussed earlier); it "referred to the whole pre–New Deal organization . . . involving district (local) councils in which all people—or at least men— could participate, as well as tribal councils in which representatives from the district councils conveyed the sentiments of the grassroots."[36] Thus, while reference to the treaties marks a federal policy structure seen as at odds with the procedures of reorganization, it also condenses a broader struggle over what will constitute Sioux governance, especially the relationship between reservation-level politics and district-based decision-making which previously had been through councils in which tiospayes played a prominent role.[37]

In the Plains Congress, Collier casts reorganization as the Indians' liberation from the violence of allotment under the continuing benevolent care of their federal "guardian." The gift of political recognition for native polities, however, is predicated on their interpellation into an allotment-inspired conception of "citizenship" in which native politics can be nothing more than a "local" instantiation of the principles of settler-state liberalism, themselves naturalized within a heterosexual imaginary in which generic individuals emerge into political life out of a properly privatized domestic sphere. The vision of "constitutional rights" and "self-government" offered by Collier presupposes a fusion of personal property, the nuclear family, and bourgeois homemaking that then is treated as the apolitical core around which governance revolves, ignoring the coercive process by which such a geography of social life is imposed on native peoples. Tribal authority comes to be cast as the right to embody the civilizing mandates and regulatory architecture of allotment, an *instrumentality* through which to administer existing regulations that appear as the obvious precondition for political identity and agency.

Collier not only portrays the kinds of individual and familial subjectivity formed under allotment as axiomatically shielded from the discretionary powers of native governments, but this intrusion on self-determination appears as the gift of inclusion, while displacing alternative frameworks for conceptualizing U.S.-Indian affairs. More than simply ignoring a set of issues clearly of great concern to native attendees, the IRA's deferral of treaty-related matters makes possible its simultaneous rejection of allotment's de-tribalizing aims and reification of allotment's nuclear imaginary. While the provisions of the IRA do not abrogate or adjust existing treaties, the proposed legislation does seek to replace the forms of native governance that had grown up around treaty-making with a "system" for which allotment serves as the horizon in defining what will constitute public policy, as contradistinguished from privatized homemaking. In this way, reorganization disavows the existence of kinship-based councils in ways that facilitate the insertion of native politics into the nested hierarchies of U.S. federalism.

"DOMESTIC"-ATING NATIVE SELF-HOOD

In the wake of the passage of the IRA, officials in the Indian service were left with the question of what the statute and its provisions would mean in practice. As part of an effort to clarify the principles and parameters of reorganization, Collier called on Nathan Margold, the chief solicitor of the Department of the Interior, to draft an opinion outlining the nature and premises of the "home rule" promised in the statute. Issued on October 25, 1934, and likely authored by Felix Cohen(Margold's assistant who worked extremely closely with Collier), the opinion, entitled "Powers of Indian Tribes," lays out the theory of native governance that would guide the conceptualization and implementation of reorganization.[38] Taking up the brief mention in section 16 of the IRA that acknowledges "all powers vested in any Indian tribe or tribal council by existing law,"[39] the opinion uses this seemingly throwaway reference as the legal basis for developing a broad notion of native political powers as emanating not from congressional conferral but from an indigenous sovereignty that precedes that of the United States. As Vine Deloria and Clifford Lytle observe, "Delegated powers would have made tribal government a part of the federal government; inherent powers preserved an area of political independence for the tribes across which the United States could not venture," and due to this distinction, they conclude, "Modern tribal sovereignty thus begins with this opinion" (160). Yet how is native sovereignty made intelligible within U.S. administrative discourses in the wake of the IRA's passage, particularly in the opinions of the Interior Department and the regulations issued by Collier? What kinds of subjectivity, individual and collective, are recognized as "sovereignty," and how are they envisioned in relation to allotment-era precedents?

While "Powers of Indian Tribes" is at pains to indicate that the kinds of authority it addresses do not result from a process of federal investiture, instead being derived from the autochthonous status of native peoples, its description of the legibility and character of such autonomy offers a fairly circumscribed portrait of native political identity. The opinion states, "it is the prerogative of any Indian tribe to determine its own form of governance," placing the burden of proof on the U.S. government to demonstrate that any *interference* by "administrative officials" in native affairs can be validated by reference to a specific piece of legislation directly authorizing it (445). This presumption in favor of native political license, however, is turned inside out in the opinion's effort to anatomize the areas over which tribal governments can exert control and the methodology used to provide that list: "It is possible, however, on the basis of the reported cases, the written opinions of various executive departments, and those statutes of Congress which are of general import, to define the powers which have heretofore been recognized as lawfully within the jurisdiction of an Indian tribe" (447). In setting out to catalogue "the whole body of tribal powers which courts and Congress alike have recognized as properly wielded by Indian tribes" (447), the text inverts the logic of inherent sovereignty, shifting from searching for negative limits (what has been disallowed by Congress) to identifying positive content (tribal authority already "recognized" by the U.S. government).[40] This reversal suggests that forms of native political subjectivity, in order to be acknowledged as legitimate by the United States, need to be constructed around the citation of federal precedent. Thus, sovereignty becomes sovereignty-as-already-narrated within U.S. institutions; reciprocally the term "inherent" does not so much refer to a domain that precedes or is separate from U.S. administration as assert a claim of priorness/exteriority within a regime of regulation. As a topos, "inherent" allows for U.S. officials to manage what constitutes authentically governmental matters while presenting this ongoing process of intrusion in ways that make, in Povinelli's terms quoted earlier, an "expansion of legal discriminatory devises seem the advent of the law of recognition."

Such translation conducted under the sign of autonomy can be seen in the opinion's expansion of the legal norms to which native governments are seen as always-already having committed themselves in order to be understood as governments. While initially presenting "original sovereignty" as only "curtailed by restrictive legislation" (447), the text later notes "that those provisions of the Federal Constitution which are completely general in scope . . . apply to the members of Indian tribes as well as to all other inhabitants of the nation" (451). Mobilizing the topology of citizenship discussed earlier, this caveat imagines the jurisdiction of native governments as extending over "inhabitants" whose status as political subjects is shaped first and foremost by their belonging to "the nation," meaning the United States, enfolding native peoples within a somewhat nebulous set of constitutional imperatives taken to be the "general" background against which sovereignty can signify.[41] The opinion further observes that "the tribe has all the rights and powers of a property owner with respect to tribal property" and that "the powers of an Indian tribe over tribal property are no less absolute than the powers of any landowner" (467–468). While declaring the authority of native governance over tribal property to be "absolute," the character of that power is envisioned as like existing Anglo-American principles of land-holding, making it into an expression of generic "landowner" rights already laid out in U.S. law. Thus, beyond bracketing land covered by the laws of allotment (463), this portrayal of indigenous jurisdiction envisions it as definitionally committed to the kind of political economy in which Indians were to be trained through allotment, and in analogizing native polities to bourgeois property owners, it further emphasizes the "local" nature of their control—a point noted numerous times in the opinion.[42] From this perspective, the IRA "afford[s] statutory recognition of these powers of local self-government and administrative assistance in developing adequate mechanisms for such government" (454), again positioning the act as making possible an acknowledgment of what came before while creating a political infrastructure organized around a municipalization of native governments—their rendition as miniaturized models of existing "mechanisms" within U.S. law.

If conceptions of what constitutes "adequate" governance at play in prior Indian policy are redeployed as the basis for new forms of official political recognition, that process takes shape around, and draws on, a naturalized vision of native homemaking. In its opening moments, the opinion states as one of its chief tenets, "The domestic relations of members of an Indian tribe are subject to the customs, laws, and jurisdiction of the tribe" (445), presenting such issues as free from state and federal interference.[43] Although immediately qualifying this premise by noting that tribes' "inheritance laws and customs" do not apply "with respect to allotted lands" (445), the text seems to suggest that questions of landholding and family life not controlled by allotment law will serve as a site at which "customs" previously prohibited by U.S. officials formally may be legalized by native governments. In fact, the opinion notes at several points that the decisions of agents and the BIA, inasmuch as they were not mandated by Congress, cannot be construed as impairing tribal sovereignty, thereby insinuating that administrative efforts to control native marriage, eroticism, and home life no longer have any purchase on the internal dynamics of native polities.

Yet, curiously, this apparent openness to other configurations of residency and kinship is only ever discussed in terms of regulations regarding marriage. In particular, the opinion emphasizes the authority of native governments "in defining and punishing offenses against the marriage relationship" (461). The traditional role of kinship in structuring modes of native governance is overlooked, which seems particularly notable given the presence of versions of such *customs* among many peoples in the years leading up to the IRA and their potential significance in giving substance to "the prerogative of any Indian tribe to determine its own form of government" (445). Moreover, the notion of "domestic relations" is winnowed down to concern over policing "the marriage relationship." The possibility of expanding the trope of *domesticity* to signify various kinds of land tenure, forms of sustained affective and material ties, and complex dynamics of household and family formation largely is foreclosed. Instead, "domestic relations" refers only to the marital unit,[44] implying the kinds of atomized, privatized homemaking favored in allotment. Further, it positions the "domestic" not as a space in which different patterns of intimacy and interdependence can proliferate and receive legal sanction but as a set configuration from which deviations should be penalized as "offenses," a term itself resonant with the prior system for disciplining violations of the heteronormative ideals of allotment policy and the civilizing mission—the Courts of Indian Offenses, which I will discuss further later.

In a rather odd rhetorical move, the opinion actually cites the practice of matrimonial management as exemplary of the nature of native jurisdiction: "The powers of an Indian tribe in the administration of justice derive from the substantive powers of self-government which are legally recognized to fall within the domain of tribal sovereignty. If an Indian tribe has power to regulate the marriage relationships of its members, it necessarily has power to adjudicate, through tribunals established by itself controversies involving such relationships. So, too, with other fields of local government" (471). In this way, marriage serves as a metonym for native political identity, imagining not only that there necessarily is a paradigmatic form of it to which each native government is committed but that kinship is not continuous with governance. Marriage is a relationship whose terms officially can be *adjudicated* rather than only one node within a network out of which politics itself is constituted. This perspective casts as obvious a split between social spheres, which, especially since it is demarcated with respect to marriage, makes the dynamics of native governance appear as consistent with the organizing premises and structures of other intranational forms of jurisdiction—a semidistinct "local" version of a broader U.S. pattern.

More than slotting native "domestic relations" into a familiar Anglo-American framework, the presentation of marriage regulation as the archetypal example of "the administration of justice" among native peoples serves as part of a broader effort to reposition the technologies of social restructuring at play under allotment, especially the Courts of Indian Offenses, as the substance of indigenous political "self"-hood. Created by order of the Secretary of the Interior in 1883, the Courts of Indian Offenses (hereafter referred to as the Courts) were a vehicle for implementing regulations promulgated by him outlawing aspects of native life perceived as promoting continued savagery, such as the following: the performance of the Sun Dance and similar "religious ceremonies"; polygamy; the presence of "medicine men"; the destruction of property, including as part of mourning rituals; and the movement of bands among reservations.[45] While Collier publicly critiqued the Courts prior to becoming Commissioner of Indian Affairs, their use as a technology of straightness was not discontinued under the IRA.[46] Instead, they were renarrated as both a paradigmatic symbol of the inherent sovereignty of native peoples and an invaluable tool in *educating* them.

Although repeatedly insisting that regulations created by the BIA cannot constrain tribal governments, the opinions of the Interior Department solicitor reaffirm the validity of the regulations issued by the Secretary of the Interior and the Commissioner of Indian Affairs and their implementation through the Courts, whose cases overwhelmingly were concerned with violations of the conjugal domesticity promoted by the agents.[47] The solicitor finds that the Courts "derive their authority from the tribe, rather than from Washington" (476).[48] While somewhat of a side comment in the 1934 opinion I have been discussing ("Powers of Indian Tribes"), this contention is reaffirmed as the basis for a later opinion—"Secretary's Power to Regulate Conduct of Indians" issued on February 28, 1935. It argues that both Congress and the federal courts explicitly and implicitly have acknowledged the existence of the Courts of Indian Offenses and de facto have given their blessing to this administrative contrivance, despite the absence of any statute formally endowing the BIA or agents with such authority. Citing a case on another matter, the opinion observes that "the tacit approval of Congress for a number of years [in this case by providing funding for the Indian police and agent-appointed justices of the Courts] is sufficient to authorize otherwise unauthorized regulations." Beyond validating the Courts as a legitimate part of the ongoing exercise of BIA oversight over native peoples, the opinion asserts that they are "manifestations of the inherent power of the tribes to govern their own members," recasting the invasive policing of eroticism, kinship networks, homemaking, and other aspects of native life as merely an expression of the collective will of "the tribes" (535–536).

Through this discursive maneuver, the collective subject of "sovereignty" is envisioned as a macro version of the privatizing subjectivities of allotment, fabricating a communal identity out of the heteronormative ideologies and punitive mechanisms of the prior policy regime. That process becomes more apparent if one examines the parallels between federal officials' presentation of reorganization and the rhetoric of *U.S. v. Clapox* (1888), often cited as justifying the authority of the Courts.[49] In a phrase quoted in both the Interior Department solicitor opinions noted earlier, the decision describes the Courts of Indian Offenses as "mere educational and disciplinary instrumentalities, by which the government of the United States is endeavoring to improve and elevate the condition of these dependent tribes to whom it sustains the relation of guardian" (577). In other words, administrative regulations with respect to native sexuality, marriage, kinship, and homemaking have the power and validity of law because they are necessary tools of civilization by which Indians can be "improve[d] and elevate[d]."

Only by breaking them of their savagely perverse habits and training them in proper nuclear domesticity can the U.S. fulfill its moral role as their protector. Note that the terms of subjugation/subjectification utilized here—the need for institutions that serve as "instrumentalities" in the fulfillment of the United States' responsibilities as "guardian"—mirror the language used by Collier in characterizing reorganization during the Plains Congress, suggesting the extent to which the language of native choice surrounding the IRA always was shaped around a heterosexual imaginary that delimited what could/should constitute governance.

More than merely recycling a blatantly paternalistic and racist perspective in order to justify retaining the Courts, the Interior Department opinions repackage it as an affirmation of native self-representation.[50] They describe the initial creation of the Courts as a "necessary" effort by the federal government "to stimulate tribal judicial action," "to allow for enforcement by the tribal courts of the laws, customs and ethics of the tribe and for the handling of individual problems of the tribes" (536).[51] Thus, rather than imposing a repressive system that forbade crucial practices of collectivity, the BIA simply made possible the continuance of native "customs." This line of argument retools the subjectivities and domesticities of allotment as a mode of recognition under reorganization. Put another way, the persistence of BIA-instituted and enforced codes of conduct is represented as a means of giving formal shape to existing principles that already have been accepted by Indians as perfectly compatible with—in fact, as vital to—their existence as self-governing polities.

One could argue, though, that the Courts merely provide a convenient legal hook on which to hang validation of native judicial systems, but such an interpretation is undercut by the ways official accounts and ongoing policies reiterate the centrality of the civilizing imperative.[52] In the regulations issued by Collier in late 1935, he abandons the attacks on the Sun Dance and medicine men in prior regulations but retains the concern for promoting conjugal and domestic order: "[T]he tribal council shall have authority to determine whether Indian Custom Marriage and Indian Custom Divorce . . . shall be recognized in the future as lawful"; "pending any determination by the Tribal Council" they "shall continue to be recognized as heretofore."[53] Yet "illicit cohabitation" is included as among the "offenses" for which one can be tried, positioning the regulation of kinship and homemaking as a significant feature of reservation governance. While there is no outright ban on polygamy, the code does define "adultery" as "hav[ing] sexual intercourse with another person, either of such person being married to a third person" (16), indicating that marriage is a union of two people and making any erotic relationship beyond that punishable. Additionally, although formal restrictions on interreservation travel are not contained in the 1935 regulations, many reservations continued to have local subagents from whom passes were required to take such trips, a practice that further constrained and managed kinship relations by fracturing transreservation networks.[54]

Taking the Constitution and law-and-order regulations adopted at Pine Ridge as an example of how the IRA was implemented, one can see the ways that the form of sovereignty that emerges under reorganization cleaves rather tightly to the contours outlined in the administrative opinions and codes I have been discussing. [55] Prior to the IRA, Pine Ridge had been in the process of drafting a new constitution, three years earlier having repudiated the agent-instituted constitution of 1928 that radically diminished the scope of the tribal council and instead deciding to return to a system much more like the Oglala Omniciye.[56] This effort was preempted by reorganization, the terms of which did not reflect the prior struggle for the expansion of the council, greater attention to treaty issues, and a recognition of persistent modes of local governance (including tiospayes and their chiefs).[57] As against "the Interior Department's origin myth of tribal government," "tribal governing machinery based on the constitutions was designed by the OIA, not Lakota people, who had little input into these instruments"; "even the order of the enumerated powers in both constitutions [for Pine Ridge and Rosebud] largely matches the order of items in the outline" provided by the BIA.[58] In laying out the powers of the Council, the constitution makes clear that virtually all of them are "subject to review by the Secretary of the Interior," giving non-native administrators a huge amount of discretion in managing tribal affairs. Notably, one of the very few areas spared this scrutiny is the power "to regulate the domestic relations of members of the tribe," although the authority "to promulgate and enforce ordinances . . . for the maintenance of law and order" is contingent on the Secretary's approval. Again, "domestic relations" appears as a metonym for sovereignty, standing in for an autonomy belied by the stifling oversight institutionalized in the constitution.

Furthermore, the law-and-order code adopted by the Oglala Sioux Tribal Council in February 1937 bears a striking resemblance to the regulations issued by Collier.[59] In addition to referring questions "as to the meaning of any law, treaty, or regulations" to "the superintendent" (21751), the code includes a chapter titled "Domestic Relation," the longest section by far, which spells out in great detail the rules for marriage, divorce, and homemaking. Among its provisions, it disallows "Indian custom marriages and divorce," regulates the legitimacy of children, and penalizes with imprisonment failures to "comply with any of the foregoing provisions . . . with reference to domestic relations not otherwise provided" (21753–21759). Furthermore, the code defines nonallotment heirship by reference to "the rules of the State of South Dakota," outlaws adultery and "illicit cohabitation," and criminalizes "vagrancy" ("wander[ing] about in idleness, living off of others who are able to work").[60] Cumulatively, these measures suggest less an embrace of tradition or a reflection of existing practices than that the code and the judicial apparatus (which itself retains the structure of the Courts of Indian Offenses—three judges appointed by a federal official [21749]) function, in the words of *U.S. v. Clapox* quoted earlier, as "educational and disciplinary instrumentalities," constructing and enforcing a normative domestic ideal that serves as the icon of (re)organized collective "self"-hood.[61]

While the constitution and code ostensibly indigenize governance due to their adoption through the mechanisms of representative governance, the disjunction between federally recognized institutions and popular Oglala understandings is registered by the numerous complaints filed by Pine Ridge residents in the years following the passage of the IRA. These protests include a 1938 petition to Congress signed by 1,061 people to revoke the constitution and testimony before Congress on the failures of the IRA government—particularly the use of the regulations and court system as instruments of oppression. The latter charge seems particularly apt given that of the 9,000 Indians tried in various courts in 1938, 10 percent of them (909) were from Pine Ridge, 90 percent of those cases being heard in reservation courts, with a conviction rate approximating 95 percent.[62] In addition, these protests often called for, in the words of Frank Short Horn and Benjamin American Horse in their statement before Congress, a return to a system of governance "by chiefs, headsmen, and their councilmen," obliquely invoking the tiospayes and the ways that they had been displaced from Oglala governance under reorganization.[63]

Efforts to specify the scope and meaning of the IRA after its passage proclaim the existence of an "inherent" native sovereignty separate from U.S. legal norms, principles, categories, and modes of mapping. That political identity, however, is described in ways that cast it as axiomatically analogous to U.S. jurisdictional logics: its terms and contours are made present through examination of U.S. statutes and judicial decisions; its powers are qualified by "general" constitutional provisions; and its subjects are envisioned as holding a primary status as U.S. citizens. In that process of "local"-ization, "domestic relations" serves as a key conceptual hinge, distinguishing politics from familial relations and homemaking while installing a proper version of privacy whose defense is cast as the sine qua non of public policy. The official account of the political internality of tribal sovereignty and jurisdiction under reorganization, therefore, turns on the presence of a certain kind of "domestic" formation, but the maintenance of a system of nuclear intimacy/ insularity itself depends on the presence of a disciplinary apparatus. If tribal governance is an *instrumentality* of the federal government, it is predicated on the subjectivities and forms of sociality generated through the *instrumentality* of the Courts of Indian Offenses. Rather than seeing the Courts as an intrusive imposition, though, the post-IRA position described earlier treats them as a bureaucratic prosthetic that enables the preservation of tribal *customs*. Thus, the rhetoric of support for native "traditions," at play, for example, in the Plains Congress, functions as an endorsement for the recoding of BIA-imposed institutions and ideologies *as tradition* and the basis for sovereignty, making the heterosexual imaginary of allotment foundational while foreclosing traditionalist adaptations to U.S. demands such as the tiospaye-based councils that preceded reorganization.

NO MORE SEPARATE SPHERES, OR ELLA DELORIA'S TRANSECTIONAL CRITIQUE

The official representation of reorganization as a liberatory embrace of autonomous native political "self"-hood depends on the deployment of a series of dichotomies.[64] These include the IRA vs. allotment, government vs. family, federal vs. local, delegated vs. inherent, normal vs. criminal, and coercion vs. custom. Rather than functioning as analogies, these binaries work to support each other by cumulatively constructing a vision of sovereignty whose terms coalesce around the self-evidence of modes of privatization that supposedly provide continuity between tribal and U.S. structures of governance—a core around which politics as such can cohere and, simultaneously, from which it can be contradistinguished. As suggested in the previous section, though, this presumption of equivalence is generated by the translation of the enforced discipline of one regime into the supposed facilitation of native desires by the next, effacing competing frameworks to that of allotment such as the treaty system and its legacy of intra- and inter-reservation councils organized around kinship networks. In *Speaking of Indians*, Ella Deloria provides an account of Dakota sociality that cuts across these distinctions, offering an analysis that I describe as *transectional*.[65] She refuses to divide up native life in ways that fit U.S. administrative logics while also highlighting how forms of government recognition depend on a reification of particular practices that divorces them from their role within a broader web of shifting collective relationships. In contesting such fragmentation by cutting across the categories used by officials, Deloria exposes the series of assumptions about home and family that continue to undergird U.S. Indian policy in the 1930s and 1940s, thereby offering a de facto critique of the ways the apparent acknowledgment of native sovereignty continues to rely on compulsory heterosexuality as a framework through which to make native peoples into suitable political subjects.

While Deloria was present on various reservations (especially Pine Ridge) during the period in which the IRA votes were held and the resulting new governments were put into effect, and thus was witness to the various and complex struggles generated by this policy change, scholars have not read her work in relation to reorganization.[66] Born on the Yankton reservation in 1888, she was the daughter of the Reverend Philip Deloria, who served as an Episcopal missionary to residents of the Standing Rock reservation; her mother, Mary, had been married previously and had children living on the Rosebud reservation. Moreover, Deloria's brother Vine became a minister at Pine Ridge, and she lived with him for extended periods. Thus, she had sustained connections with people at several Teton reservations. She graduated from Teachers College at Columbia University in 1915, where she had studied with Franz Boas, and while teaching at Haskell Indian School in 1927, she was contacted by Boas, beginning a correspondence and complicated process of collaboration that would last until his death in 1942.[67] Deloria has been seen by scholars as employing the conceptual tools and professional contacts of anthropology as part of an effort to preserve what she had learned in her time living among Sioux peoples as both a child and an adult, using her books as a pedagogical tool through which to convey Dakota stories, language, philosophies, practices, and ethics to younger generations who may not have had the benefit of the on-reservation education she received on these topics. In addition to the vital work of transmitting tradition, sustaining what had been taught to her by elders and passing that knowledge on to future generations, her work can be understood as contesting the dominant representations of native identity at play in U.S. policy in the period in which she was writing. More than a project of survivance, her work is engaged in a counterhegemonic effort to shift the terms of public discourse, tracking the disruptive effects of reorganization and the entrenched assumptions animating it but doing so through an expansive account of Dakota sociality that draws on while reshaping the official and popular interest in native "culture."

While addressing a wide array of issues, including native histories, current anthropological approaches, and various aspects of contemporary native life, *Speaking of Indians* keeps returning to the contention that an awareness of and engagement with the matrix of kinship is central to any substantive effort to understand Dakota people(s). More than indicating a particular set of blood and marital connections, a distinct domain of relatives, kinship refers to an array of active processes of interdependence that provide the shape and substance for collective identity. In an intriguingly layered description, Deloria observes, "By kinship all Dakota people were held together in a great relationship that was theoretically all-inclusive and co-extensive with the Dakota domain" (29). Exceeding Anglo-American notions of "family," kinship appears here as an encompassing, binding force, one that has explicitly geopolitical dimensions—defining the terms of belonging to the "people" and the scope of their "domain." While subtle, this initial image suggests that the contours and coherence of Dakota people-hood itself depends on the "inclusive" and "extensive" dynamics of kinship networks. Indicating that "Dakota camp-circles were not haphazard assemblages of heterogeneous individuals" (25), Deloria further asserts that "the father-mother-child unit was not final and isolated": "it was only one of several others forming the larger family, the *tiyospaye* . . . This Dakota word is essential in describing tribal life. It denotes a group of families, bound together by blood and marriage ties, that lived side by side in the camp-circle" (40). The text's portrayal of kinship runs against the grain of the federal government's representation of native peoples as aggregations, or assemblages, of citizens whose belonging as subjects of the United States provides the foundation for administratively recognizable forms of native governance.

Camp circles are webs of relations around which Dakota sociality coalesces, as against the fetishization of either atomized personhood or the nuclear family. In fact, the specific terms of the latter have an enlarged field of reference, since "there are any number of men and women whom you also call father and mother"—"all the men whom your own father calls brother or cousin" and "the women whom your mother calls sister or cousin" (26). Deloria further notes the disjunction between that expanded conception of family and U.S. ideologies as instantiated through official record keeping, particularly in the education system. "If a child called 'Brother' someone entered on the roster as of an entirely different family, was he lying? It seemed so, because the intricacies of his kinship system had not yet been investigated" (116–117). The logic of conjugal homemaking appears not as an obvious feature of native life around which to develop a notion of tribal jurisdiction but as an imposition that results from a systemic failure to "investigate" the "intricacies" of indigenous peoplehood. There is no being Dakota without enmeshment in the "larger family" of a tiospaye; the tiospaye is a matrix of connections among relatives that follows "the rules imposed by kinship" (25), which cannot be reduced to an equivalency among individuals who all share the same status; and there is no Dakota "domain" over which governance could be exerted apart from the kinship relations that constitute tiospayes and link them to each other ("any strangers thrown together by circumstances are generally able to arrive at consistent terms for each other through some mutual relative" [27]).

As suggested previously, federal depictions of reorganization recycled the subjectivities of allotment in ways that made native governance appear as merely an instrumentality through which U.S. constitutional principles, federalist hierarchies, and ideologies of liberalism could be extended to native peoples in a noncoercive fulfillment of the responsibilities of benevolent guardianship. However, in displacing the series of privatizing presumptions on which that administrative vision of native politics depends, Deloria denaturalizes the process of reorganization, drawing attention to the ways it continues to fail to reflect native self-understandings and to impose a nuclear imaginary that fractures Dakota social formations. In *Speaking of Indians*, the idea of native governments passing laws for the "domestic relations" of their peoples becomes unintelligible, since there is no administration that operates as a distinct entity over and against the tiospaye. "Kinship held everybody in a fast net of interpersonal responsibility," and "that was practically all the government there was" (31–32).[68] The notion of "domestic relations" as a discrete topic requires the separation of the (normative) family unit from the unit/agent of governance, a split that Deloria refuses to acknowledge. She further observes that "everyone was literally in the public eye" (32), rejecting the idea of an isolated, intimate space or sphere of privacy that categorically is shielded from the awareness, assessment, and judgment of others—who, instead, are simultaneously one's fellow political subjects and relatives. In this way, the text suggests the irrelevance of *public* and *private* as ways of conceptualizing not only Dakota people (their interpersonal dynamics) but also the Dakotas *as a people* (their functioning as a polity).

Insistently returning to the ways bourgeois homemaking is alien to traditional placemaking and community formation, the text observes that administrative efforts to impose a conjugally centered spatiality have not succeeded in supplanting less isolating geographies of kinship. While "at length there came the time when individual allotments of land were made," in which Dakotas were separated into "father-mother-child units . . . often miles from their other relatives," even by the mid-twentieth century, more than forty years after allotment began on Teton reservations, "many Indians cannot yet feel complete with just their little family, their spouse and children" (92, 146). The process of detonating broader networks of kinship, shattering them into matrimonial-reproductive "units," has not altered or eradicated residual Dakota affective attachments structured around the model of the tiospaye. Deloria's use of the phrase "father-mother-child," conjoined as the terms are by hyphens rather than commas, suggests that the nuclear family functions as a distinct, freestanding entity within administrative and popular U.S. ideologies while also implying the ways it is ordered around a terrifyingly claustrophobic insularity.

Emphasizing the "little"-ness of the liberal "family" foregrounds the fact that the normative imagination of privatized intimacy within U.S. policy appears to many Dakotas, even by the 1940s, as a radical and uncomfortable diminishment of the scope of the emotional attachments established through

connections with one's "relatives" in traditional kinship dynamics and formations. Here we can see the ways that Deloria invokes sentimental familial
affection as a way of manifesting the ongoing experiential unnaturalness of
allotment and its legacy for those subjected to it, registering the persistence
of an older, alternative political economy as a structure of feeling. The terms,
categories, and strategies of differentiation by which reorganization seeks to
recognize native polities as such, then, appear in *Speaking of Indians* more as
fragmentation than acknowledgement, a reordering of kinship-inflected
lines of affiliation, forms of residency, and modes of governance in which
Dakotas "cannot yet feel complete." This affective disjunction also implicitly
serves as a rejoinder to the claim that the administrative regulations and
procedures designed to manage native "domestic relations" under allotment
can be understood under reorganization as merely aiding and giving formal
shape to existing but diffuse native desires.[69]

More than cutting across the privatizing distinction between the nuclear
"home" and the structures of band politics, Deloria uses the topos of kinship
to challenge the municipalization of Dakota politics, instead suggesting how
the various boundaries generated by federal policy continually are transected by processes of relation. She observes that "with relatives scattered
over the many camp-circles and communities, anyone could go visiting anywhere, and be at home" (38), adding that traditionally "any family for reasons valid to itself could depart at any time to visit relatives or sojourn for
longer or shorter periods in some other Dakota camp-circle" (40). Under
the regulations promulgated by the Secretary of the Interior in 1883 setting
up the Courts of Indian Offenses, such travel between reservations was
restricted. Administrators sought to deny ties among bands that crossed reservation lines in order to produce the reservation as a coherent bureaucratic
unit for the purposes of managing Indian affairs, and, as noted earlier, farm
agents on Teton reservations under Collier still had the authority to regulate
people's movement. By drawing attention to regular patterns of engagement
among relatives, the text challenges the legitimacy of "the imaginary lines of
demarcation" through which the United States maps Dakota space (86).
Kinship, then, marks not merely expansive formations of affection and habitation but a complex and shifting geopolitics of interdependence, alliance,
and belonging that is both inter-band and sub-band. In this set of dynamics,
bands and reservations do not function as insular or coordinating units, and
"home" is determined neither by a particular household nor by jurisdictional
locale, further intimating the ways that U.S. discourses draw on heterodomesticity as a way of normalizing its administrative mappings.[70]

More than critiquing the emergence and maintenance of the reservation
system, the text's depiction of the topology of kinship as fluid can be understood as a response to the way federal authorities used the figure of the tiospaye

to validate reorganization. As discussed earlier, the IRA was characterized as a repudiation of the violent, foolish, and exploitative policies of the past, a renunciation of federal imposition in favor of an acceptance of native traditions. In this vein, officials seized upon the tiospaye as a means of authenticating non-native political and economic projects, casting them as attempts to restore Sioux customs lost or displaced under allotment. This idea can be traced to H. Scudder Mekeel, who was hired to lead the BIA's applied anthropology team and who had done his doctoral fieldwork at Pine Ridge in the early 1930s. He suggested that the traditional mode of governance should serve as the basis for representation under the IRA constitutions, and the proposal was taken up by administrators, including Collier himself, who came to characterize such an approach as an acknowledgment of the "natural" dynamics of these peoples, drawing on "ancient Sioux communities, which even the allotment system has not been able to destroy."[71] The call for the use of the tiospaye as the ordering unit of Teton governance presented constitution drafting under the IRA as a process of restoring residual political formations to full visibility and legitimacy, positioning reorganization as a broad-based repudiation of "the allotment system" and as the vehicle through which U.S. policy would come to accept and even promote the preservation of native cultures.[72]

Adopted on some reservations and rejected on others (including Pine Ridge), this "community plan," as it was called, was opposed by many members of existing tribal councils as well as district councils for the reason that it displaced existing leaders and modes of leadership, including erasing the distinction between those chosen through electoral politics and those who gained positions due to their status as chiefs. In other words, the notion of using tiospayes as the basis for jurisdictional mapping and legislative representation actually effaced the complex structures that Sioux peoples had developed during the allotment period, their adaptation of older models of kinship-based governance to U.S. administrative frameworks and demands. While contradistinguishing tiospayes from the prior gridding of reservations into "districts," administrators and anthropologists who supported the community plan offered an account of tiospayes that utilized them as the basis for a kind of political districting basically indistinguishable from that of the United States, simulating tradition but constructing a version of the tiospaye that had little relation either to preallotment patterns of collectivity or to the constitutional councils that had emerged over the previous several decades which had been challenged by agents and which Teton peoples had fought to defend. Thus, even when federal officials include kinship formations as part of their administrative programs, seeking to signal a commitment to native notions of "community," such incorporations end up freezing a shifting matrix of belonging, subsistence, and care into the form of something like a municipality. In this vision of native governance, the tiospaye turns into a kind of geopolitical container at a scale between the allotment unit and the tribal council in ways that belie the dynamism within and among traditional kinship/residency units that Deloria illustrates.

Attempting to institutionalize the tiospaye gives the impression of recognizing tradition while not only evacuating it of its prior internal workings but dislodging it from the complex and shifting inter-band kinship networks that cut across it and in which it was enmeshed. Deloria particularly emphasizes the persistence of kinship geographies of affection, association, and interdependence and their ill-fit with the principles of U.S. liberalism.[73] Contrasting the American system of "get, get, get now" with a traditional Dakota ethos of "give, give, give to others," she observes, "today, the second system seems to be outmoded. In a world committed wholly to the other, it is out of place. It has to go. It goes reluctantly; indeed, it lingers and lingers still. It lingers because it is bound up with the kinship system, and that is still here. Kinship, as I have tried to show, was the whole of life in the past. It was what united the people" (120). The structures of Dakota politics on which the United States seeks to draw in legitimizing its own oversight of Indian affairs, then, are animated by a conception of interpersonal and trans-band relation that does not fit the economic program of reorganization, which relies on greater participation in the market organized around a maximization of wages/profit. Addressing the difficulties faced by younger Dakotas who seek to take part in the U.S. economy, Deloria notes, "It was not till they tried to do business that they were hopelessly blocked by the obligatory duties and kinship interdependence of the past that still persisted, hidden but strong" (131).[74] The text often portrays traditional kinship connections as a barrier to economic advancement, given the vast transformation of the Dakotas' social conditions wrought by U.S. policy, but in doing so, it also emphasizes the discrepancy between traditional ideals or social processes and the functioning of an imperially imposed political economy.[75] Inasmuch as the allotment program was predicated on the translation of native social formations into the terms of U.S. liberalism—private propertyholding by individual nuclear family units—the use of the tiospaye as an organizing figure in the "community plan" does not so much undo allotment as repackage it, less contesting its operative assumptions about the nature of residency, family, or governance than simulating traditional structures in ways that neither represent the actual functioning of the Dakota "kinship system" nor speak to the tensions generated by its "lingering" presence. The text, then, suggests that however one might understand the value of reorganization and whatever idiom it might use to express its structuring principles, it has little to do with prior modes of *peoplehood* and their residual influence on Dakota self-representations and social relations.

Rather than preserving or helping rejuvenate social formations that had been assaulted under allotment, officials' attempts to codify a version of custom as part of the legal apparatus of governance work to manage native tradition so as to make it appear compatible with U.S. policy objectives. These efforts are an extension of "decades of paternalism and protection" that have worked not only to deny the autonomy of native peoples but to hamper their ability to adapt to changed circumstances: "In the old days the Indians had dignity and pride. They still do . . . I am optimistic enough to think they would respond, especially if they are told to go ahead *in their own way*—that too is important—and if a chance is given them to do this without a kind of stifling oversight" (152–153). In addition to rejecting the "perpetual guardianship" that the United States exerts over native peoples (158), Deloria suggests that "protection" which seeks to define for native peoples what kinds of traditions should be maintained and how to do so can be nothing but "paternalism."

Such management of native culture fetishizes it, freezing it into a form that has little relationship to native self-understandings while constructing a framework for native identity that actually embodies U.S. imperatives— legitimizing the structure of "guardianship" by casting it as an embrace of indigenous ideals. The text explores this dynamic in an extended passage worth quoting in full:

> The Indian people—or any people—are a living plant. They must develop naturally, and, as they do, they drop off the lowest petals that have become dried up and useless and are hanging by a single fiber thread. Only the plant knows when to drop them in its development of ever better and fuller blood at the top. To insist and make it the laudable thing to keep up Indian customs, even when they are outgrown, or, on the other hand, to want results so fast that the happy use of Indians languages and the vestiges of customs, good or bad, are discouraged, wholesale, is to hurt the Indian plant seriously. (160–161)

For Deloria, the issue is less whether or not a particular practice or formation should be preserved than that the process of cultural retention, invention, and adaptation needs to be left in the hands of native peoples themselves, rather than the United States. Moreover, these moments implicitly condemn reorganization's wholesale replacement of existing governmental structures (like the constitutional councils discussed earlier), through which peoples sought to adapt "*in their own way*" to the circumstances created by U.S. intervention.[76]

In diagnosing the structural unevenness in Indian policy, its insistence on reifying certain (kinds of) customs as signs of authentic cultural difference while continuing to insert native peoples into U.S. political economy, Delo-ria's text contests the invocation of tradition as a means of validating an ongoing state-orchestrated transformation of native lifeways. Through its elaboration of preallotment Dakota sociality, it intimates the failure of offi-cial narratives of recognition to capture the internal workings of the tiospaye and the broader matrices of kinship in which it is embedded. Instead, the supposed autonomy signaled by tribes' control over their "domestic rela-tions" carries with it a series of assumptions about the nature of governance, including its separation from a distinct sphere that can be named "domes-tic." Deloria's account implies that these inbuilt presuppositions make the "father-mother-child unit" axiomatic even in the absence of a specific insis-tence on the naturalness of nuclearity, envisioning a "home" that is contra-distinguished from political institutions but that can be regulated by them.

This cleaving of family from politics facilitates the bureaucratic isolation of tiospayes from each other, helping depict them as categorically distinct units that can be linked to each other primarily through representative political assemblies. However, as Deloria's history indicates, such a vision fails to account for the ways the practices and principles of governance in the tiospayes themselves arise out of kinship relations, as well as the ways those bonds between members of different bands frustrate the treatment of the tiospaye as a de facto municipality—a local jurisdictional entity with a stable population over whom centralized authority is exerted. Illustrating the ways traditional Dakota modes of association, identification, and decision-making transect the distinctions animating U.S. liberalism (public/private, policy-making/familial intimacy, citizen/relative), *Speaking of Indians* inti-mates that while the imaginary of reorganization may simulate a concern for custom, it fundamentally depends on the ideology of heteroconjugality to provide its ordering mappings and forms of subjectivity.

KINSHIP AGAINST CULTURE

In *Indians of the Americas*, Collier argues that native peoples possess "what the world has lost," and that this "power for living" must be *recaptured* "lest it die" (7), further suggesting that "Indian societies must and can be discov-ered in their continuing existence, or regenerated, or set into being *de novo* and made use of" by serving "as an ethnic laboratory of universal meaning" (155, 159).[77] "Societies," he notes, "create a people's temperament, the world-view and the color and structure of personality among their members" (12), adding later that "this personality structure and bent of mind" is "*holistic—* the capacity to entertain complex wholes, and to maintain the complexities in a dynamic equilibrium" (163). Alluding to a wholeness broken by prior policy, this vision of native peoples understands indigenous sociality(/ies) in terms of "temperament" and "personality," threatening to reduce native identity(/ies) to the maintenance of a static ensemble of representative ideas and/or feelings. Joel Pfister has highlighted this tendency of Collier's to represent native identity in ways that facilitate its positioning as a vehicle for the edification of whites, observing that for Collier "what 'Indian' culture holds out to the larger culture . . . is social therapy" (196): "New Deal Natives would not be modernized so much as they would Indianize the modern" (208). In this way, reorganization involved forms of "government-powered Indianizing" in which a romanticizing fetishization of Indian "group"-ness was imposed on native peoples even while being narrated as having been derived from an effort to preserve their existing traditions (223).

As I have argued, Collier's ideas on the relation between native tradition and governance are predicated on a denunciation of allotment as repression (its effort "to crush Indian life"),[78] and from this perspective, eliminating previous injunctions against the performance of particular customs plays a crucial role in redressing the violence of prior policy. Quite early in his career as Commissioner, Collier repudiated the campaign to convert native peoples to Christianity, including repealing the previous ban on spiritual ceremonies and curtailing missionary activity on reservations. In a circular issued in January 1934, he asserts, "No interference with Indian religious life or ceremonial expression will hereafter be tolerated . . . The fullest constitutional liberty, in all matters affecting religion, conscience and culture, is insisted on for all Indians."[79] Official acceptance of native peoples' "liberty" with respect to their "religious life" serves as a refutation of the earlier program of attempting to eradicate native spiritual systems, but the "interference" Collier prohibits is measured against a set of "constitutional" principles that are taken as the a priori framework for Indian policy and native self-representation, disregarding existing native structures of governance (such as the Oglala Omniciye) and taking U.S. liberalism as the (hetero)normative core of what will constitute native politics. In this context, "religion, conscience, and culture" refer to discrete spheres of native activity and belief, the preservation of which indicates official U.S. appreciation of indigenous difference. These aspects of native social formations signify metonymically, signaling a "holistic" concern for "Indian"-ness and an attendant rolling back of the state suppression of *tradition*, but this supposed recognition circulates a conception of "culture" in which privatized heterodomesticity remains unquestioned.[80]

That reification of elements of native sociality, positioning them as stand-ins for tradition in toto, is less expressive of a failure to engage with anthropological notions of "culture" than an application of certain extant anthropological principles. Collier consulted with anthropologists (including Boas) both before and after the passage of the IRA, as well as creating an applied anthropology team of trained experts within the BIA,[81] and his description of the proper aims of Indian policy echoes the kind of formulations at play in the work of Boas and his students. In *The Culture Concept*, Michael A. Elliott observes that "by treating cultures as integrated wholes, the Boasian model . . . reinforces the distance among groups by insisting upon their ultimate differences and generating a search for the most authentic markers of these differences[,] . . . invit[ing] the observer to contemplate each culture as a system of internal connections rather than as a chapter in evolutionary history" (26).[82] Not only does the notion of chronicling and rejuvenating native traditions before they are extinct match the goals of what has been called "salvage" anthropology, an orientation present in Boasian conceptions of fieldwork, but the idea that indigenous social formations can be summed up through the citation of particular traits and beliefs—which express the essence of a people and can be extracted for the purpose of rethinking "modern" life—is a hallmark of anthropological scholarship in the 1930s and 1940s.

This trend can be seen in Ruth Benedict's *Patterns of Culture* (1934), her popular and influential account of intercultural difference and intracultural coherence.[83] In addition to referring to "primitive cultures" as "a laboratory in which we may study the diversity of human institutions" (17), her account presents cultures as differentiated unities in ways that can be seen as resonant with Collier's equation of social formation with "personality." She argues that "a culture, like an individual, is a more or less consistent pattern of thought and action" (46). This metaphoric individualization of collectivities can be seen in Collier's interest in the "kinds of personality-structures" generated by native cultures.[84] Benedict's portrayal of cultures as integrated totalities that can be typified by "ways of arriving at the values of existence" expands the Boasian predilection for emphasizing shared intellectual life (including spirituality and folklore) as the privileged sign of collectivity (78). While Benedict warns against "an [intellectual] operation that mutilates the subject" by reducing a culture to "some catchword characterization" (228), the presentation of a people as like an individual who can be psychologically profiled promotes a process whereby some traits come to stand for the collectivity. This process of typification/substitution produces the impression, in Pfister's terms, of *ethnodepth*—"'expressing' one's seemingly essential group identity, one's group soul" (237). Boasian strategies for representing "group identity," especially the form they took in the "culture and personality" approach prominent in the 1930s and 1940s, can be seen as providing a conceptual and discursive structure for Collier's notion of "culture," in which something like "religious life" appears as an emblematic stand-in for native collectivity and self-understanding(s). As Michaela di Leonardo suggests, "this legacy is directly connected to American anthropology's elision of political economy . . . [which reduces] human social reality to the narrow-compass notion of individual psychologies, *mentalities*, writ large" (20), part of a broader "unconcern with the phenomenon of state power" (78).

If Boas has been credited with developing (or at least helping promote and institutionalize) "the culture concept," Deloria's work can be read for the ways it deploys what might be termed "the kinship concept." Foregrounding the complex dynamics of Dakota family formation, and the ways they exceed the boundaries of a privatized household that can be contradistinguished from the field of governance, Deloria's work highlights dimensions of native experience that implicitly contest the forms of normalization/naturalization at play in reorganization's de facto vision of conjugal homemaking. Deloria's employment of the discourse of kinship can be seen as illustrating how the effect of "ethnodepth" comes at the expense of what might be called ethno-breadth—a sense of native collectivities as complex networks whose ordering patterns and operative principles cannot be abstracted from the dynamic relationships through which people engage with each other (which includes the problem of imposing a reified schema of social spheres, like "the domestic"). In this way, her writings, such as *Speaking of Indians* and her novel *Waterlily*, can be interpreted as refusing the metonymic narration of native peoplehood latent in Boasian anthropology and institutionalized in the Indian New Deal. Rather than simply transparently referring to specific dynamics of Dakota life or to a generic dimension of human experience, "kinship" has its own complex intellectual genealogy, appearing since the late nineteenth century primarily in (proto)anthropological accounts as a key part of producing a developmental hierarchy with bourgeois home-making at the apex and serving as an important part of the ideological architecture of allotment (as discussed in the Introduction and chapter 3). In fact, Boasian anthropology largely had left aside kinship for "culture" as an ordering paradigm at least in part due to the former's extensive and intimate association with a system of evolutionary ranking. By naming the social dynamics she addresses as "kinship," Deloria draws on the history of ethnology to contest the segmentation of Dakota social formations in Collier's Boas-inspired conception of culture; his approach divides up native life into discrete areas in which some are taken as more representative than others and in which each area is imagined to have its own "customs" but the definition of the area as such is a priori (i.e., "domestic relations").[85]

In particular, *Waterlily* productively (con)fuses the scholarly idiom of kinship with familial feeling, playing on the non-native fetishization of family to help make visible and to validate modes of social organization that are not shaped around a nuclear imaginary, highlighting their richness by showing them as saturated with sentiment and, therefore, in a sense embracing while also displacing allotment's structure of feeling. Scholarly readings of the novel, though, have tended to speak of "kinship" in denotative ways, treating it as neutrally referential rather than itself a concept with a long and difficult intellectual genealogy, of which Deloria likely would have been well aware given her anthropological training.[86] Deloria's use of the kinship concept in *Waterlily* emphasizes the presence of deep emotional bonds among members of the tiospaye as well as between members of different tiospayes, invoking a sentimental conception of family in order to make flexible Dakota social formations intelligible to non-native readers as more than the perverse/savage absence of bourgeois sensibilities. We also can see this strategy as taking up and refuting the longstanding representation of Indians as lacking proper sentimental affect, addressed in chapter 1, while linking such affect to native geopolitics—as opposed to making it a pedagogical tool for non-native publics (as discussed in chapters 2 and 5). Conversely, though, the text's employment of the discourse of kinship draws on that term's enmeshment in the history of ethnology, jettisoning the latter's evolutionary hierarchy while mobilizing its attention to social structure—as against the metonymic representation of tradition as religion or personality that seems to animate Collier's policy.[87] The vision of Dakota sociality that emerges, then, is both more affecting and extensive than in official accounts, portraying areas of Dakota life that primarily would be characterized as "domestic" by a non-native readership in ways that contest the insular logic of "domestic"-ity at play in reorganization's narration of native collectivity and politics.

The plot of the novel is organized around the quotidian experiences of a woman named Blue Bird and her daughter Waterlily, and the central events of their lives revolve around what largely could be characterized from an Anglo-American perspective as conventional familial dynamics—marriage, birth, and their complex relationships with their relatives, by both blood and matrimony. Early in the text, though, the narrator makes clear that this story cannot be apprehended through the categories of experience that accompany conjugal privacy. "Any family could maintain itself adequately as long as the father was a good hunter and the mother an industrious woman. But socially that was not enough; ideally it must be part of a larger family, constituted of related households, called a *tiyospaye*"; "all adults were responsible for the safety and happiness of their collective children" which produced in them "a feeling of security and self-assurance" (20). Even as Deloria disorients readers by indicating that the traditional social geography of Dakota life is not that of twentieth-century white America, she assures them that there are parallel kinds of emotions, such as a deep parental concern for children. At one point the narrator observes, "some people were marrying and some were dying and some were being born—all the natural and expectable things that happen wherever humans live together" (49). Circulating around a presumably natural cycle in which marriage and birth are signal moments, these shared feelings are not circumscribed as they are in bourgeois homemaking, instead expanding to encompass the entire tiospaye, which comes to resemble a nuclear unit in the intensity and intimacy of its affect.

At several points, the text illustrates that people living in tiospayes experience their own feelings of isolation and loss. At the beginning of the novel, Blue Bird and her grandmother are residing in the camp circle of a group who had found and adopted them after Blue Bird's parents had been killed in an attack and they could not find their way back to their relatives (although they later are reunited with their tiospaye after Blue Bird is abandoned by her first husband). Although she had married a man from this adoptive group, "Blue Bird had never been entirely happy either in her marriage or in her life in a camp circle that was not her own. It was not that the people were unkind . . . but she could not feel satisfied there. She never ceased to yearn for her own people" (8). Similarly, when Waterlily decides to marry a man who has offered horses to allow her family to complete the mourning ritual for her grandmother (Gloku, who is the mother of Rainbow—Blue Bird's second husband and Waterlily's adoptive father), she moves with him to his camp circle, and she comes to understand the situation of her uncle (married to Rainbow's sister Dream Woman), who "was like a perpetual visitor" and "could never quite relax as he might have at home" (163): "Life in the *tiyospaye* of Sacred Horse [Waterlily's husband] was, for Waterlily, like wearing ceremonial dress all the time" (176). These moments illustrate that the tiospaye is more than a neighborhood, instead appearing as an emotionally saturated space redolent with the sentimental associations of "home" (notably, in contrast to the kind of "ceremonial" formality that often functions as a metonymic stand-in for native "culture").

While highlighting the potential affective similarities between the tiospaye—and Dakota lifeways more generally (the cycle of marriage and birth)—and the bourgeois household, the novel portrays the more expansive field of devotion and care in the former as a sign of Dakota distinctiveness, a central feature at the core of tradition and communal identity. In describing Blue Bird's need to respect the importance of the relationship between Rainbow and his sisters, the text observes, "The intense loyalties between collaterals of opposite sexes were deep-seated, the result of lifelong training. They had been going on long before her time and would continue long after she was gone—as long as Dakotas remained Dakotas and their kinship sanctions endured. Everyone knew and accepted them and aimed to play his or her part within their framework" (60). Drawn from the anthropological idiom of kinship studies, the term "collaterals" (siblings and first cousins) positions the Dakotas as alien, occupying a social structure whose dynamics are presumably foreign to non-native readers, while the novel's emphasis on the emotional richness of familial interactions aims to incite reader empathy. Additionally, here "kinship" names the "framework" in which Dakotas live, an ensemble of shared practices and roles that serves as the basis for what it means to be Dakota and that is not abstractable as a worldview or a personality type. The novel orchestrates a complex play of reflection and refraction in which resemblance to Anglo-American ideals in some features does not imply symmetry and in which divergence does not mean the absence of the sentimental idiom privileged in dominant narratives of "home" and "family." In this way, kinship serves as a kind of translational matrix, articulating native tradition to non-native assumptions about the character of domesticity while distending the nuclear imaginary.

Although ultimately working to disjoint the equation of family with conjugality, the novel often is at pains to depict Dakota homemaking as a deeply heterogendered affair. The text seems to present marriage as if it were a necessary part of personal development (with regard to Waterlily's decision to wed, the narrator remarks, "after all, she must marry sometime" [153]),[88] and the arc of the story can be described in primarily matrimonial terms— Blue Bird's movement from her abusive first husband (Star Elk) to her model relationship with Rainbow and the difficulties of Waterlily's initial marriage as contrasted with her eventual union with her teenage crush (Lowanla, who turns out to be a cousin of Sacred Horse). In fact, inasmuch as the text can be described as a bildungsroman chronicling Waterlily's maturation, marriage is positioned as a vital, if sometimes fraught, part of that process. Moreover, Deloria consistently offers images of binarized gender, insisting that training in such forms of identification is a crucial aspect of Dakota child rearing. Blue Bird and then Waterlily continually receive advice on how to behave with feminine propriety, including not risking your "honor" by eloping with a man who just wants sex (13); sitting demurely rather than "cross[ing] your legs like men" (53); not flirting with boys, which is "contrary to all the rules of maidenly behavior" (112); letting men do the courting ("That is a man's part; a woman's is to be pursued") (136); and remaining a virgin until marriage ("your purity is without price") (136). Girls and women who fail to uphold these values are derided, such as Night Walker, whose extramarital sexuality is the topic of "snide" comments by others (137).[89] At one point, the narrator asserts:

> The tribe's concern was that its girls should become women and its boys men through normal and progressive steps without complications. And in the case of boys, this was a peculiarly delicate matter because of the belief that a

boy who was allowed to play girls' games and wear female dress was liable to come under a spell that would make him behave in a feminine manner all his life. (61)

Not only do the dynamics of Dakota gender in the novel appear to resemble dominant American conceptions of femininity in this period, especially in terms of sexual restraint and the effort to contain eroticism within marriage, but the preceding passage, with its fear of feminized boys, resonates quite powerfully with growing public concern among non-natives about the threat to the institution of the family and the safety of the nation posed by homosexual men, often conceptualized in terms of gender inversion.[90] As discussed in the previous chapter, and as will be addressed further later, the existence of the traditionally accepted social role of the winkte challenges Deloria's often rigidly dichotomous depiction of Dakota conceptions of sex/gender, but in seeming to efface this possibility in constructing a model of gendered maturation leading toward marriage, the novel brings the polymorphous affects of the tiospaye more in line with (hetero)normative assumptions about the nature of personhood, emphasizing the paradigmatic relation between sexual expression and procreation as well as the centrality of heteroconjugality to familial cohesion and social order.

While some of these dynamics in the text may be expressive of Deloria's own anxieties about never having married, attempting to forestall personal charges against her (especially in light of the fact that much of her work was sponsored by Christian organizations),[91] it also signals the workings of the bribe of straightness, which I began to address in my discussion of Zitkala-Ša. In utilizing the discourse of kinship partially as a way to draw on the feelings and forms of subjectivity associated with *family* for a white readership, the text also bears the burden of indicating the normality of the tiospaye. In this way, the novel's repeated invocation of notions of binarized gender and the centrality of marriage defer the charge of perversity/savagery. At the same time, though, that strategy dislocates native kinship systems from their prior anthropological placement within an evolutionary hierarchy culminating in bourgeois homemaking, gesturing toward newer ethnological approaches in which "kinship" (as descent) is foregrounded. The moves *Waterlily* makes to *straighten* Dakota sociality, then, work to facilitate non-native identification, but they also can be seen as taking part in a rehabilitation of kinship as an indispensable framework for analyzing native peoples, a perspective that markedly differs from the Collierian positioning of religion and ritual as emblematic of native "culture." Even while seeking to portray traditional social formations as normal/natural through appeal to the heterosexual imaginary, the novel highlights the matrix of familial relations as an indispensable feature of Dakota identity; in this way, it implicitly draws on extant anthropological models that eschew a Boasian emphasis on patterns of thought (largely adopted by Collier), recentering the aspects of social life usually collected under the rubric of "kinship."

In focusing on marriage, homemaking, child rearing, and interpersonal affect and intimacy, the text locates *the family* at the core of its account of prereservation life. Or rather, by emphasizing sentimental feeling, dimorphic gender difference, and matrimony, the novel evokes the idea of the family for Anglo-American readers, but while alluding to the heteronorm, Deloria insistently complicates her portrait of Dakota social dynamics, repeatedly returning to forms of association and alliance that do not fit into nuclear units. While earlier intimating that the destiny of all Dakota women is to marry, the novel at one point declares, "If her married life was obnoxious to her, she simply walked out of it without a word as to why . . . There was no economic need for her to endure in silence. She knew that her brothers and male cousins were ready to provide for her, and her own relatives to take her back into their midst. She did not have to hang on just to be supported by a husband" (179). Divorce appears as quite a simple and routine matter, one whose ease is due to the fact that conjugal pairs are not the basis of Dakota economy. Rather, the tiospaye with its extended web of relatives provides the structure for subsistence, a woman's sustained connection to male kin of her generation allowing her to leave her husband without risking destitution. Indicating that marriage is neither the paradigm for resource distribution nor a relationship that marks adult individuation from one's group of origin, this fleeting statement seems to qualify the novel's pervasive investment in romantic coupling, suggesting a discrepancy between that interest (as evidenced by the plot) and the structuring principles of the social milieu in which the story is set.

Additionally, the text features various forms of adoption which make clear that being a "relative" is not restricted to those with whom one has a blood connection or even to those within one's tiospaye.[92] As noted earlier, Blue Bird and her grandmother are incorporated into a camp circle not their own after their separation from their tiospaye ("the members of the camp circle adopted the newcomers as relatives" [11]). While readers are told that they never felt quite comfortable in this group, once they and Waterlily are reunited with their blood relatives, Waterlily develops a close relationship with Little Chief, Rainbow's son from his first marriage. After Rainbow and Blue Bird are married, the novel notes, "Waterlily was suddenly surrounded with so many new relatives . . . From the day when Little Chief [first] came to visit her, the two children had been as devoted as though they were brother and sister, and now they were really that and it was no different" (33). To be "really" "brother and sister" does not involve being related by blood (they are not presented as something like "step"-siblings), and Deloria further notes that their interaction "was no different" after than before the marriage that made them "really" siblings. Further, while not explicitly commenting on this dynamic, Rainbow's parents and sisters appear to be accepted as members of the tiospaye, and to see themselves as such, without qualification, which is notable given that they as a group are not connected by blood to the other members of the tiospaye.[93]

While indicating a certain elasticity to kinship, these adoptions could be characterized as in some ways similar to Euramerican "in-law" relationships and those that emerge from divorce and remarriage. Yet the novel also includes a kind of adoption/affiliation that cannot be assimilated to a conjugally based conception of family:

> A *kola* was someone special; his wishes and needs could not be ignored . . .
> "The best I have is for my fellow" was their code from the time they pledged
> eternal loyalty. . . .
>
> The demands on fellows were somewhat greater even than those on
> natural brothers, loyal and devoted as brothers were supposed to be. And
> automatically, like brothers, each fellow was son to the other's parents and
> father to his children. All other relatives were likewise shared . . . men in
> fellowhood must respect and venerate the other's wife like a sister. (98–99)

Kola relationships create kinship connections that are based neither on blood nor on marriage, instead emanating only from mutual affection. However, once pledged, fellowship functions as a familial bond, binding together not simply those who have taken a "solemn friendship pact" but their relatives as well (99). As the novel makes clear, this merger not only affects the fellows themselves, each one becoming a member of the family of the other, but the kin of one become related to that of the other.[94] For example, Rainbow's kola Palani comes to visit and invites Rainbow and his family to join Palani's tiospaye for the annual Sun Dance: "[W]hen they arrived at Palani's camp, the welcome accorded Rainbow's family was no different from that to lifelong relatives . . . The wives of the two brothers addressed each other as sisters, and all Palani's relatives also became appropriately related to Rainbow's family" (105). Additionally, when Waterlily leaves her tiospaye to live with Sacred Horse's family, as noted earlier, she feels isolated in the formality of her interactions with them, but she meets the relatives of Red Leaf, with whom her brother Ohiya had entered into fellowship and who treat her as their daughter, giving Waterlily the kind of easy comfort for which she yearns. More than simply illustrating the existence of possibilities for kin-making that exceed conjugality and parenthood, these kola bonds are central aspects of the novel's narrative: when attending the Sun Dance of Palani's tiospaye, Waterlily meets Lowanla, who will become her second husband; and Red Leaf's parents are a major component of the novel's discussion of her time with Sacred Horse. If the text's project is to offer something like a normative vision of prereservation Dakota life, its depiction of kola affiliations illustrates the importance of forms of care and intimacy that surpass the boundaries not only of romantic/reproductive relationships but of the tiospaye itself, using kinship to map patterns of intense and sustained affect that transect the central units through which reorganization envisions native identity and politics.

The dynamics I have been discussing, though, perhaps could be conceived more as description than intervention, an effort to provide a characterization of Dakota traditions that is absent from extant accounts rather than an attempt to respond critically to the structuring principles at play in post-IRA policy. However, in what seems to me impossible to construe as merely a coincidence, the novel addresses all the practices targeted by the code of Indian offenses in the 1880s—the Sun Dance, polygamy, the presence of medicine men, giving away property as part of mourning ritual, and traveling away from one's reservation—weaving its story in and through these elements of Dakota sociality.[95] As just discussed, the novel's representation of the Sun Dance comes in the context of Rainbow's relationship with his kola Palani, and while attending, Waterlily meets and develops a crush on Lowanla, her future husband. Additionally, during the ceremony itself, men who have vowed to give their bodies as offerings during the Sun Dance (either being suspended from the central pole until one's flesh tears or giving slices of flesh, both as a "promise . . . to the Great Spirit" [125]) are redeemed by their relatives—in one case a sister "ransom[ing] her brother" and in another two aunts volunteering to have their flesh cut to achieve the number of pieces promised (by Lowanla). In the latter case, others remark that "there was no precedent" for such action, but it is allowed because "it is admirable of sisters to honor a brother by being good to his child" (126–127). These aspects of the text's portrayal of the Sun Dance stage a connection between kinship and spirituality that Deloria suggests, in *Speaking of Indians*, is encoded within the Dakota language itself in that the words meaning "to address a relative" and "to pray" are in fact the same (28–29). When interpreted in light of the BIA's tendency under Collier to treat "religious freedom" as a metonym for native "culture," the novel's dramatization of the linkage between being a relative and praying brings the social dynamics denoted by kinship into the foreground as constitutive of Dakota subjectivities, further raising questions about the place of familial formations in the ideology of reorganization, specifically the ways they are segregated from other elements of native life that themselves tend to more regularly appear as signifiers of "tradition."

By embedding the various aspects of Dakota life that had been outlawed in a series of relationships that the text collates as kinship, Deloria suggests that the matrix of family that includes and exceeds romance (the persistent ties of tenderness, devotion, sharing, and responsibility that order tiospayes and create connections among them) serves as the structuring framework in which these diverse elements of Dakota culture operate. Put another way, the novel considers the kinds of relationships it chronicles (of couplehood, extended siblinghood, collective child rearing, adoption, kola fellowship, etc.) as constituting an integrated *kinship system* that itself provides the social infrastructure and normative parameters of Dakota tradition, and the rituals, practices, and statuses narrated as the substance of "culture" by Boasian anthropology and federal officials are portrayed as inextricably embedded in that system, which itself largely is ignored in those accounts or reduced to a set of "customs" constituted within an axiomatically privatized and maritally defined sphere. As discussed earlier, official commentary and regulations in the wake of the IRA's passage treat the Courts of Indian Offenses and the authorizing regulations not only as lawful but as expressive of the "customs and ethics of the tribe";[96] in tracing the intersection of the kinship system with the various acts outlawed by the United States, the novel offers a counterpoint against which to measure Collier's repeal of *some* of these provisions, highlighting the extent to which the interwoven social dynamics collected under the rubric of "kinship" are both crucial to Dakota collectivity and at odds with the concept of "domestic relations" as utilized in the discourses of reorganization.

In particular, the text's repeated references to polygamy, and its relative equanimity when doing so, suggest that the practice was a normal (if not necessarily routine) part of prereservation culture, bringing into relief the skewed picture of Dakota tradition institutionalized as the basis for recognition. Unlike the denunciation of plural marriage in official accounts of proper native homemaking both before and after the IRA, the novel offers absolutely no sense of outrage at its presence, or a suggestion that it is somehow morally tainted. Instead, it appears as a perfectly viable option in household formation. The first mention of polygamy in the text appears when her grandmother is considering Blue Bird's options. She thinks, "perhaps I should simply give the girl away in marriage now, to some kind and able householder, to be a co-wife," she herself having been a co-wife, but to her older sister rather than a woman to whom she was not related. The problem with this possibility for Blue Bird lies in the fact that she "had no sister in this camp circle," so any existing wife might come to resent her (12). Sisterhood and matrimony, then, do not appear as parts of distinct life stages, the intense bonds of one's childhood giving way to the intimacies of adulthood, instead potentially coexisting in the same relationship in ways that contest the privileging of romance over other emotional connections as the basis for delimiting "home." Furthermore, when Waterlily is being pursued by Sacred Horse, two of his father's three wives come to her village to present gifts to her, and the narrator observes that Sacred Horse's father "was able not only to take care of his three wives and their families, but also to maintain a large retinue of kinsmen besides" (149), later noting that "all the women were equally responsible for all the children . . . until an outsider was well acquainted, he could not tell which woman was the real mother of any child, except the nursing baby" (166). Emphasizing that these relationships produce a stable and loving environment in which everyone's material and emotional needs are met and parenting responsibilities are shared, Deloria refuses to pathologize them as perverse and/or barbaric, stretching the normative characteristics of allotment subjectivities to cover these plural unions. Allotment-era discourses present native sociality as lacking the affective fullness that supposedly only can be realized through bourgeois homemaking, and reorganization takes such assumptions as axiomatic in its narration of how native jurisdiction and political autonomy will be configured around a privatized marital domesticity. However, Waterlily's account of prereservation Dakota life suggests that polygamous households are as able to sustain proper familial feeling as any other, expanding the reference of *family* by situating it within broader matrices of *kinship* marked by the tiospaye and by sentimentally saturated relationships that transect the boundaries of the tiospaye. In this way, the text subtly draws attention to the ways federal policy divides up traditional geographies of affiliation and affect, implying that the selective circulation of figures of "custom" and "culture" under reorganization edits out the ongoing U.S. regulation of Dakota social formations.

In the previous chapter, I discussed the ways Zitkala-Ŝa embraced paganism but seemed to disavow polygamy in her stories, resituating the conjugal unit within broader kinship configurations but insisting on heteroromance as a frame to the exclusion of social roles and forms of eroticism that might signify as perverse to a non-native readership. By contrast, Waterlily not only presents polygamy as an uncontroversial element of Dakota tradition but in its mapping of kinship demonstrates how traditional formations made possible support for nonreproductive subjectivities, rendered aberrant within heteroconjugality. Thus, even as the text often deploys heteronormative assumptions (especially the repeated insistence on binarized gender roles and the unavoidability of marriage), it refuses to present them as the basis or limit of the *kinship system* it depicts. More than simply connecting "domestic" units, the tiospaye appears in the novel as an encompassing entity that has an existence greater than the sum of its households. The existence of this broader nexus of affection, interdependence, and support is what makes possible divorce, as noted earlier—a woman having the option of returning to her tiospaye of origin due to the fact that the matrix of relatives (by blood and otherwise) that comprises it are bound to support her. Similarly, the novel suggests that this kind of communal safety net made possible by kinship networks allows for members to make choices that do not lead toward marriage and reproduction. One of these options is becoming a "perpetual virgin." The novel observes that they "were a rarity, since it was the normal and accepted thing for women to marry" (139), but in having Leaping Fawn (Waterlily's cousin and Black Eagle's daughter) make the decision to become one, the text highlights the existence of this possibility, not just as an individual predilection but as a recognized kind of status. Although observing that "there was no set procedure" for how to declare one's desire to be a perpetual virgin, the text also notes that the "Virgin's Fire" is an available ceremony through which women of all ages can declare their chastity (139). If the event can serve as a way of dispelling rumors impugning a young woman's purity (which, Deloria suggests, would undercut her marriageability), it also can provide a means of publicly acknowledging and honoring a woman's intent never to marry. The ceremony is conducted by White Dawn, and "in her family group, which was large and influential, she was actually its central figure . . . , looked to for her wise judgments in all knotty family problems" (137). Discussing her importance within her family group in one sense works to portray White Dawn as *normal*, in the sense that she has not been cast out by her relatives and is seen by them as neither eccentric nor marginal, but in another sense, this description illustrates the ways that the composition of the family group makes possible White Dawn's status, creating a flexible configuration in which belonging is not measured against a nuclear standard that would position her as a spinster aunt rather than a "central figure."[97] After having declared her intent to remain a perpetual virgin, Leaping Fawn likewise assumes a place of honor in her family, serving as the ghostkeeper in the wake of the death of her grandmother Gloku (143).

In light of the fact that Deloria remained unmarried her entire life, one could read the inclusion of the status of perpetual virgin as a means of acknowledging the existence of a role for her within Dakota tradition. Scholars have noted the ways that Deloria sustained the kind of matrix of familial affections and responsibilities she addresses in her published work,[98] suggesting the continuing importance of the kinship system in structuring Dakota sociality and self-representation despite the privatizing imperatives of allotment and their repackaging under reorganization as a prerequisite for conceptualizing native political identity and autonomy. However, Woyaka is another potential analogue for Deloria in the novel, one who seems to push a bit further against ideologies of straightness. A "master" of "tribal lore," a keeper of the winter count, and a traveling educator, he bears the burden of preserving the people's past. As his grandfather tells him, "If you fail them, there might be nobody else to remind them of their tribal history" (51). His mission to preserve Dakota collectivity through remembrance and storytelling echoes the work of the novel itself, casting him as a figure for Deloria. This implicit identification would be notable in itself for its cross-sex nature and the potential opening up of gender identity it suggests, particularly in light of the novel's repeated emphasis on the presence among the Dakota of a binarized sex/gender system, but the connection at which the novel hints is even more intriguing when Woyaka is read in relation to the recognized presence of winktes in prereservation life.[99]

While never describing Woyaka as a winkte or depicting him in ways that fully conform to the social dynamics of that status, the novel does gesture in that direction. More than simply telling stories like any other elder, he seems to occupy a special role, as suggested both by his lifelong training for it and the fact that he is given an honored place in the camp circle when he arrives to visit. We do not hear of him engaging in traditional masculine pursuits like hunting or warfare, as we do with virtually all the other male characters, and in noting that he "was a strange man in certain respects," the text indicates that "he walked alone" and that "ordinary human comaraderie was not for him" (51), suggesting that he does not have a wife or children. Also, in a somewhat curious twist, the mention of "marrying" and "dying" as "the natural and expectable things that happen wherever humans live together" (49), which I discussed earlier, appears just before Woyaka is introduced, almost as if such an assurance of the ubiquity of marriage and the similarity of the Dakotas to non-natives in this respect were necessary as a kind of prophylactic against the potential taint of queerness that might cling to him for a non-native readership. In a letter to Ruth Benedict in July 1947 in which Deloria discusses the need for cuts in the manuscript of *Waterlily*, she expresses her intention to leave out "*Waterlily's* observing a *berdache*—in fact, all that winkte element."[100] Might Woyaka be the trace of those sections that were removed?

Rather than interpreting Woyaka as a closet winkte, or taking the resemblance between his role and the work of the novel as queering Deloria, the appearance of this suggestive figure and his implicit association with Deloria's act of authorship can be understood as an extension of the novel's exploration of both the ways the kinship system exceeds bourgeois nuclearity and the impossibility of separating something called "culture" from the networks of care and resource sharing that are signified under the sign of "kinship." In the previous chapter, I argued that Zitkala-Ša's "Soft-Hearted Sioux" suggests a disavowal of winkte identity in the story's alignment of heterogendered masculinity with the survival of Dakota traditions and community as against a feminizing missionary intrusion, but in contrast to that straight-ening of tradition, *Waterlily*'s flirtation with the figure of the winkte can be seen as avoiding outright charges of savage perversity while indicating the presence of accepted options other than marital manliness. Woyaka's knowl-edge comes from his grandfather's insistence on his learning the stories and the history, his travels are enabled by the willingness of various camp circles to help support him, and he refers to his listeners as "grandchildren" (50–51). In these ways, the "tribal lore" that he communicates—which from a Boasian-inspired perspective, such as Collier's, would be the essence of "culture"—appears inextricable from complex sets of familial relations that provide the infrastructure in which Dakota intellectual life is generated and circulated. Through the figure of Woyaka, Deloria further develops the novel's portrait of nonreproductive possibilities as readily available in Dakota tradition, suggesting the presence of social room for the winkte while not outright naming the role as such and perhaps signaling that Deloria can be understood as fulfilling a traditional role in the novel's act of ethnographic remembrance—rather than as adopting the anthropological perspective of outsiders or as nonnormative due to her professional work, as she likely would be seen within Euramerican ideologies of gender in the 1940s.[101]

In hinting at the winkte and explicitly addressing the recognition of per-petual virginity and the relative ease of divorce, *Waterlily* illustrates how the intra- and trans-tiospaye dynamics of kinship make possible choices and forms of subjectivity that cannot be captured within a conjugally centered framework. The matrix of affection and interdependence that provides the material context in which these options become accessible exceeds the boundaries of bourgeois homemaking, and it also cannot be captured within a metonymic notion of "culture" focused on "personality" and religious ritual. The novel presents the complex configurations characterized as "kin-ship" as the flexible yet binding force around which Dakota sociality coheres, indicating their centrality to any sense of Teton collective identity (political or otherwise). In doing so, the text is at pains to distinguish the system of kinship from a Euramerican vision of *family*, repudiating the insularity of the nuclear unit in favor of a series of overlapping and interpenetrating patterns of intimacy, responsibility, residency, and resource distribution that extend beyond marital couplehood and reproductive relations. Yet in highlighting the wider spheres and scope of feeling in Dakota tradition, Deloria also seeks to bridge the distance between Euramerican and native norms. Or, more precisely, she challenges institutionalized ideals of what is normative while presenting Dakota customs as *normal*, as sharing many of the features taken to be characteristic of civilized homemaking. Rather than simply working within the heterosexual imaginary, Deloria draws on some of its most prominent features, including the intensity of sentiment envisioned as typifying the "private" sphere and the self-evidence of heterogendered difference, in order to translate between Euramerican expectations and Dakota practices in ways that distend the idealized domesticity naturalized under both allotment and reorganization. Using these features of straightness to defer charges of sexual deviance and/or of barbaric brutality, the novel depicts native social cohesion as predicated on familial formations that cannot be reduced to isolated units based on marriage or blood, cannot be divided neatly into jurisdictional or municipal blocks, and in which processes of collective identification are not readily separable from networks of relatives (which themselves are not easily integrated into a liberal logic of political representation).

In *Patterns of Culture*, Ruth Benedict observes that psychological drives and types of behavior deemed pathological in one culture may be seen as benign or even honored in another. As evidence of this fact, and as proof of the methodological value of relativity in understanding concrete instances of cultural difference, she points to varying attitudes toward "homosexuality," suggesting that while "Western civilization tends to regard even a mild homosexual as an abnormal," many American Indian peoples have "the institution of the *berdache*" in which men "married other [non-berdache] men and lived with them" (262–263). Through this example, Benedict suggests that options for individual self-expression, for personality structures, may vary greatly across cultures, and while Collier's representation of native culture avoids what might be termed "sexuality" as a sign of Indian divergence from dominant Euramerican beliefs, instead opting for patterns and practices that can be characterized as spiritual/religious, he institutionalizes a version of Boasian relativity as a central feature of reorganization's project of recognition.[102] Contrasting itself with allotment's violent efforts to disaggregate peoples into propertied households, to *detribalize*, the Indian New Deal positioned its policy program as one of regeneration, as once again making possible the flourishing of indigenous forms of collectivity. To this end, official accounts of the IRA, before and after its passage, repeatedly cast it as a means of preserving Indian "customs," and in this vein, the political autonomy that the law ostensibly enables is imagined as expressive of suppressed native desires, providing institutional space to realize communal impulses long repressed by authoritarian federal mandates. The "self"-hood given vent in the federal promotion of Indian self-government, then, is depicted as being consistent with the kinds of "temperament" and worldview enshrined in/by tradition.

However, the kinds of collective identity articulated within official narratives of reorganization seem less to renounce many of the structuring principles of allotment than to reframe them as the predicates for governance itself, presenting bourgeois homemaking as at the core not simply of U.S.

initiatives but of native self-understandings. From one angle, the apparent differences between the discourses of allotment and of reorganization can be seen as "a multiplicitous push-pull movement within one overarching yet ever-developing hegemonic formation" whose ultimate aims was an "ever-inventive reproduction of workers and classes."[103] Yet the official depiction of native peoples under reorganization works not only to insert Indians into ever-expanding networks of capitalist production but to recast U.S. formulations and regulations as expressive of the self-evident structure of native governance. In particular, the notion of "domestic relations" serves as a way of demonstrating an acknowledgment of native authority over internal matters while simultaneously generating a structuring dialectic through which political subjectivity is contradistinguished from privatized familial intimacy. The "hegemonic formation" in which these policies participate, then, is specifically a heteronormative one, suggesting a "push-pull" between detribalization and recognition but one in which a nuclear imaginary helps create a shared framework through which to define the content and delimit the contours of political identity.

The focus in allotment discourses on producing a proper individuality that emerges into public space out of the affective cocoon of nuclearity appears to recede from the horizon of reorganization's aims, supplanted by a concern for the political and economic dimensions of native "community." However, when one considers the ways that "community" is mapped in official accounts of the goals of the IRA, it appears as an assemblage of maritally delineated homes over which political institutions will extend their jurisdiction, paralleling rather precisely the conceptual geography of U.S. liberalism that allotment sought to inculcate. While positing an "inherent sovereignty" as the basis for native authority, federal administrators depict native governments as *instrumentalities* through which the true beneficent principles of U.S. guardianship can be achieved. Rather than merely generating a contradiction, the potential tension between these seemingly antagonistic propositions is resolved by the assumption that the ideologically and institutionally engineered picture of "home" and "family" imposed as part of the United States' civilizing mission actually is indicative of the existing wishes and tendencies of native peoples themselves. The supposed obviousness of the dimensions of "domestic"-ity, in terms of both its internal composition and its differentiation from "politics," provides a discursive hinge through which to naturalize the legal structures and statuses through which that formation is sustained and made normative. Thus, the requirements of national citizenship, constitutional provisions, state law, and federalist hierarchy that serve as the grid of intelligibility for native governance under the IRA are not intrusions onto native autonomy but actually represent merely the self-evident preconditions of political life itself. The very disciplinary technologies created in the late nineteenth century to ensure compliance with the domesticating aims of federal policy (especially the Courts of Indian Offenses) appear under reorganization not as a vicious vestige of a superseded policy but as the architecture for the exercise of native sovereignty, a continuity that can be seen in the parallels between Collier's regulations and the law-and-order codes adopted by IRA governments.

Additionally, the framework adopted for acknowledging native peoples as polities through BIA-monitored constitution-making leaves aside the existing constitutions on many reservations, including those of the Teton Sioux. In contrast to reorganization's narrative of itself as rescuing tradition from institutional erasure, it actually worked to supersede native-driven processes of self-definition—new traditions—that had emerged as a result of participation in the treaty system. Positioning the IRA as if it were completely separate from the legacy of treaties allowed federal officials to disregard the forms of native governance that had developed in relation to the structures and history of treaty-making, as well as to supplant the normative understanding of native peoples as extraconstitutional entities that was part of the treaty system (at least as interpreted by native peoples). Moreover, many of those pre-IRA councils, such as the Oglala Omniciye, retained more of prereservation social dynamics than the reorganization councils—in particular the role of kinship (in the Teton case, the tiospaye) as a structuring force in native politics. Or put another way, interpellating native peoples within a statist conception of politics, ordered around a geopolitics of jurisdiction and nested governmental hierarchies, depended on the privatization of familial relations—displacing the tiospaye-centered councils as merely an artifact of the allotment-era past that was to be transcended in reorganization's liberation of native peoples from U.S. administrative tyranny.

Ella Deloria's work draws attention to this continued imposition of a nuclear norm and the attendant dislodging of the tiospaye from a substantive role in the new political economy promised by the IRA. Yet rather than pointing to distinct kinds of Dakota personality foreclosed by Euramerican culture, she instead foregrounds the complex formations of affection, alliance, and affiliation out of which Dakota individual and collective subjectivity emerges. Instead of emphasizing the abjection of "the berdache" as a kind of status lost by the imposition of "Western civilization," Deloria highlights the structuring dynamics of Dakota sociality, mapping out the ways they exceed the bounded spheres suggested by the ideal of the "father-mother-child unit." More specifically, the concept of *family* cannot simply refer to a romantic couple and their offspring but instead must be extended to include the entire tiospaye, given that it is composed of people who consider each other to be relatives and who engage with each other in ways that partake of the kind of emotionally rich and materially interdependent association thought to indicate the uniqueness of bourgeois homemaking. Expanding the domain of intimacy and affection associated with the conjugally defined household in this way reveals how the notion of "domestic relations" circulating within the discourse of reorganization depends on a broader liberal logic of social domains, in which there is a privatized place of care from which the possessive individual emerges as a public agent. Deloria's texts implicitly suggest that this understanding of citizenship predicated on sentimental subjectivity—a sort of personhood fashioned in the nuclear family so as to enable a particular kind of civic participation— simply does not fit traditional conceptions and patterns of collectivity, creating an ongoing tension between federally mandated frameworks and Dakota experience. Kinship in her work appears less as a rigidly delimited set of relationships contained within a specialized social arena than as a series of familial connections that cut across the boundaries of Euramerican categories and mappings, exceeding not only the reproductive unit but the tiospaye and even the reservation. Reciprocally, Deloria suggests that when the United States seeks to use native categories as part of its formulation of Indian affairs (such as making the tiospaye the basis for representation within IRA constitutions), those categories are decontextualized and reified in ways that not only bear little relationship to native social processes but actually undermine native efforts creatively to adapt to changed circumstances (like the existing reservation councils in which tiospayes did not function as municipal or electoral units).

In subtly contesting what can be understood as the heteronormative dimensions of reorganization—its institutionalization of notions of privacy, personhood, and perversity that are continuous with the ordering ideologies of allotment—does Deloria engage in what might be termed queer critique? While *Waterlily* suggests the limits of marriage, the possibility of polygamy, and the existence of nonreproductive statuses that were not pathologized, it also reaffirms for readers the centrality of heteroromance within tradition, pushing against the nuclear family norm but still in many ways seeking to expand normality to incorporate prereservation Dakota lifeways. Like Zitkala-Ša, Deloria to some extent accepts the bribe of straightness as the cost of challenging dominant ideologies of home and family, also coming at a critique of official narratives in the present through a depiction of the past. As in *Hope Leslie*, the representation of kinship serves as a way of reimagining what constitutes publicity in the creation and implementation of public policy, positioning nonromantic familial bonds as constitutive of collectivity. In *Speaking of Indians* and *Waterlily*, however, native peoples neither are a model for non-natives nor are disappearing; instead, her account of the tiospaye—and the dynamics of kinship more broadly—foregrounds the rightful autonomy of the Dakotas and the ways native sociality variably is effaced, mistranslated, fractured, and fetishized within institutionalized U.S. conceptions of native "culture" and "community." The texts examined in this chapter and the previous one, then, can be interpreted as interventions within state-orchestrated processes of subject production organized around, and naturalized through, the heterosexual imaginary, but they do not seek to generate or recover queer forms of subjectivity.

How do the intersections of residency, family formation, land tenure, racial identification, and sovereignty around which my discussion of straightness has turned thusfar continue to shape the contours of (counter) hegemonies at the end of the twentieth century and beginning of the twenty-first? If native peoples have held a prominent place in the emergence, con-solidation, and struggle over the ideal of conjugal homemaking as the norm for national identity and belonging, how does the history I have been tracing still animate current discourses of sexuality and native self-representation? The next two chapters will turn to efforts to address sexual and gender iden-tity in the context of the more familiar contemporary framework of hetero/ homo difference, considering the role depictions of native peoples and his-tories play in such projects.

5

FINDING "OUR" HISTORY

Gender, Sexuality, and the Space of Peoplehood in Stone Butch Blues *and* Mohawk Trail

It's time we took a leaf from the lessons Third Gender Brothers in other cultures have to teach us in how to reearn the respect and gratitude of our Hetero Communities for the *different people that we are*—as well as for the tales and gifts we bring to share. In other parts of the Earth, in the Third and Fourth Worlds, sedentary village cultures and quasi-civilized tribes . . . noticed that though most men seemed naturally inclined to be competitive, to be Warriors, Hunters, and Fathers, always there were those some who seemed to be *men not for killing and men not for War.*

If Warriors and Husbandmen were men of a First Gender, then these Differents would be men of a Third Gender—and so they are still perceived, *and loved and treasured*, by the largest tribe of Native Americans in the American Southwest today, the Diné, whom the whitemen call Navajo.

So it is now that I am proposing that we take a hand-up example from our potential allies in the Third and Fourth Worlds, whose cultures may well be overtaking, and even outnumbering, our Hetero Western so-called Free World sensibilities. I propose that we Gay Men *of all colors* prepare to present ourselves as the gentle non-competitive Third Gender men *of the Western World* with whole wardrobes and garages crammed with cultural and spiritual contributions to share.
—Harry Hay, "Remarks on Third Gender"

Recovery is the act of taking control over the forces that would destroy us. Recovery from alcohol and drug use—most definitely.

But another kind of recovery is taking place in our family. Recovery from the disease of homophobia. This disease has devastated my Indian family as surely as smallpox, alcohol, glue-sniffing, and tuberculosis have devastated our Nations.

On our separate, yet communal journeys, we have learned that a hegemonic gay and lesbian movement cannot encompass our complicated history—history that involves so much loss. Nor can a hegemonic gay and lesbian movement give us tools to heal our broken Nations. But our strength as a family not only gives tools, it helps *make* tools.

—Beth Brant, "Recovery and Transformation"

In the call for the first Radical Faerie gathering, Harry Hay, Don Kilhefner, Mitch Walker, and John Burnside propose the need for an "annual fairy-like gathering of the Rainbow Family Tribe" that would speak to the longings of "gay brothers [who] are feeling the need to come together[.]"[1] This proposal reflects Hay's lifelong commitment to trying to imagine forms of gay community that would challenge what he saw as the consumerist, exploitative, and objectifying dynamics of heterocentered society. In envisioning a kind of collectivity that could speak to this desire for distinctness, the choice of "tribe" marks native peoples as a crucial part of this attempt to envision an alternative trajectory for U.S. sexual minorities, one not shaped by the aspiration for assimilation into couple-centered privatization.[2] While in some sense replicating Catharine Maria Sedgwick's gesture discussed in chapter 2 ("my individual experience may perhaps benefit some one of all my tribe"),[3] what distinguishes this invocation is that it refers to an already existent category. If Sedgwick's statement indexes an inchoate longing for a kind of sociality in which her status as an unmarried woman would not position her as an outsider, the Radical Faerie call, as well as Hay's later comments quoted as epigraph, presumes the existence of an already constituted group of "Differents" who, at least in the "Western World," can be designated as "gay." The presence of sexual identity as a fully developed mode of classification indicates a vast historical gap between Sedgwick and Hay, shaped not simply by the ability of those in Hay's moment to provide a name for that which remains unspeakable in Sedgwick's but by a different structure of feeling. As I argued earlier, Sedgwick's queering of conjugal homemaking seeks to displace an emergent nuclear norm while suggesting that extended kinship connections (formed around affection and adoption as much as blood relation) can provide the basis for more capacious and democratic kinds of public life, whereas, Hay's writings emphasize a kind of collective self-realization for a minority defined in terms of its difference from the desires and gender dynamics of "heteros."[4]

What remains consistent, though, is that indigenous peoples provide an imaginative resource for such non-native refashionings. Although certainly part of the larger dynamic of "playing Indian," the kind of vision Hay offers more specifically points to the role of tropes of nativeness in settler political projects that seek to critique and displace the force of straightness. While this chapter will not focus on Hay, I want to dwell on him for a little longer as a way of laying out some of the concerns that will animate my discussion of the ways native "culture" comes to serve as a resource for counterhegemonic maneuvers by non-native members of sexual and gender minorities, and the ways such tactics obscure the ongoing role of heteronormativity in organizing and legitimizing imperial assaults on indigenous peoplehood. In "Remarks on Third Gender," Hay presents "gay men" as a "we" bound together by the fact that they share a gender that distinguishes them from the rest of the "Hetero Communities" to which they otherwise would belong, indicating an inherent basis for collectivity. In trying to name that difference in ways that locate it more precisely, he offers the concept of "third gender," which he presents as speaking to a transhistorical and transcultural kind of innate disposition among some subset of "men." The fact of its applicability across time and space is proven by the evidence from "other cultures"—"the Third and Fourth Worlds"—where such roles are acknowledged and accepted. However, while indicating that current Diné practices offer proof of the possibility of such positive recognition, he asserts that the lessons learned can be implemented by "Gay Men *of all colors*" representing "Third Gender men *of the Western World*," implicitly suggesting that "potential allies in the Third and Fourth Worlds" exist in some other space. What happens to the Diné here? Are they dematerialized entirely, their territorial presence utterly vacated? How does their continued existence as a distinct polity in "the Western World" fit into this framework?

The apparent incoherence of Hay's formulation makes sense if one focuses on the role that the discourse of culture performs in his mapping. As I argued in the previous chapter, twentieth-century U.S. government efforts to challenge the legacy of detribalization represented by allotment and the boarding school system relied on the claim that new policies (like those conducted under the aegis of the Indian Reorganization Act) were working to regenerate forms of indigenous "culture" and "community." However, the notions of native difference adopted by officials tended to cluster around ritual and religion in ways that largely were distinguished from the dynamics of governance itself, what would get to count as a viable institutional process or mode of social organization.[5] Liberal understandings of privacy, property, marriage, and homemaking—as well as the positioning of native governments as quasi-municipal *instrumentalities* of federal programs—tended to provide the infrastructure for official political recognition of native peoplehood.

From this perspective, Hay's despatialization of the Diné becomes legible as an extension of the culturalization of native peoples. He emphasizes that non-natives can learn from native people how to recognize the "cultural and spiritual contributions" of third gender men, because the cultural and spiritual are what native people do best. Put another way, native difference is construed as a special *cultural* ability to acknowledge and respect the *spiritual*. The Diné practices Hay is referencing are not understood here as contributing to the performance of a sovereignty distinct from that of the United States or as participating in a mode of collectivity at odds with the administrative parameters or imaginary of Indian policy.[6]

If "Third and Fourth World" peoples have a special ability to see and value gender difference, gay men can extrapolate such ideas for their own engagement with "Hetero Communities," since these principles are not enmeshed in sociopolitical formations whose logics might run counter to those ordering the settler state. Reciprocally, certain members of native peoples can be claimed as part of a sexual/gender minority "we" due to the fact that their "gifts" are seen as inborn and thus as having no inherent relationship to indigenous histories and political economies that might divide native "Third Gender Brothers" from their settler fellow feys.[7] In this way, as Scott Morgensen argues, the invocation of native precedent and the supposed continuity between a queer indigenous past and contemporary non-natives serves as a crucial aspect of forging and maintaining settler sexual modernity, members of non-native sexual minorities presenting themselves as inheritors of a tradition of nonstraightness in ways that help legitimize queerness by giving it a long, rich history while also *Americanizing* non-native queers as successors to queer Indian forebears.[8] Challenging heteronormativity in one sense by insisting on the legitimacy of homoerotic relationships and the need to validate other possibilities for self-expression than those of dimorphous gender, Hay reifies sexuality and gender by presenting nonhetero identity as continuous across all societies, thereby also casting "hetero" structures as themselves static and universal despite the vast differences in modes of kinship, marriage, household formation, governance, land tenure, and divisions of labor among the groups he references.[9] In doing so, he displaces the possibility of understanding heteronormativity as a particular kind of ideological and institutional matrix in which the nuclear family serves as the regulatory ideal through which racially and imperially dominated populations are disciplined in ways that seek to marginalize, pathologize, and/or dismantle their social formations.

Hay provides a fairly stark example of how the image of native peoples has been employed by non-native minorities to oppositional ends, but I want to suggest that this dynamic is less a matter of relative sophistication in conceptualizing sexual and gender identity than a de facto commitment to a politics whose counterhegemonic horizon is the settler state. Leslie Feinberg's *Stone Butch Blues* (1993) illustrates the limits of abstracting native *culture* as a model of how to recognize and appreciate queerness, showing how such abstraction fails to attend to the political economy of indigenous *peoplehood* (including the role of recognition for gender and sexual diversity within it). Feinberg offers a far more rich and complex mapping of the politics of identification, categorization, and privilege than Hay, examining the layered and fraught intersections of sexuality, gender, race, and class in butch/femme communities in Buffalo and New York City from the 1960s through the 1990s. The novel is acutely sensitive to the tense and even antagonistic relations among social movements, offering a finely textured account of the ways social positioning affects interpersonal intimacies and community formation. However, somewhat strikingly, Feinberg's perceptive and subtle detailing of how multiple kinds of identity operate simultaneously and interdependently to shape individual and collective experience is not extended to the text's native characters, who exist largely to validate the gender nonnormativity of Jess—the novel's white, Jewish, butch protagonist.[10] Divorced entirely from struggles for sovereignty and the specific challenges facing native peoples (in either urban or reservation spaces) in the latter half of the twentieth century, Indians appear as a pedagogical example. Feinberg produces a shared history for a queer "us" through the invocation of a genericized native past realized in the present through native characters whose cultural capacity to accept sexual/gender diversity is their most salient trait.

Although Feinberg does not utilize the term "tribe," Indians implicitly serve a similar function as in Hay's writings, enabling an image of collectivity presented as perfectly compatible with belonging to the settler state. Offering the labor union as a figure for how to organize resistance along multiple fronts in ways not predicated on mutual participation in a single identity group, the novel situates native people as a kind of inspiration for this vision of solidarity across difference, in which it is not merely tolerated but embraced. Even as Feinberg seeks to integrate the resistance to heteronormativity into a broader critique of the privatizing political economy of the contemporary United States, the text's activist vision remains embedded within an unreflexive commitment to participation in U.S. citizenship and the national public sphere, which, as in *Hope Leslie*, forecloses the issue of indigenous sovereignty and self-determination. In other words, native people teach non-natives how to come to terms with a transhistorical queerness within the scope of a multivalent social justice struggle that does not address the continuing role of heteronormativity as an invasive and regulatory force in U.S.-Indian affairs.[11]

The epigraph from Beth Brant—a self-defined Mohawk lesbian, feminist, and mother—helps highlight this absence. While underlining the violence of "homophobia," she frames it not as a danger to generic "gay and lesbian" subjects but as part of a larger assault on native "Nations." She contextualizes her comments within a project of "recovery" in which the aim is the continued survival of native peoples as such, as autonomous polities working to maintain themselves in the face of an ongoing "history that involves so much loss." The "hegemonic [non-native] gay and lesbian movement" reaches its limit in its inability to engage with the project of indigenous self-determination due to its formulation of aims in terms of settler-state belonging, which will not provide the "tools to heal . . . broken Nations." For her, the "our" and "us" refer to members of indigenous nations, and "homophobia" appears as a tactic within imperial programs of expropriation and exploitation, from which non-native gays and lesbians are not exempt. In a separate piece, she notes, "I have been hurt and ostracized by some Natives, men and women, who have made it clear that being a lesbian, or saying it out loud is not good for our community. I believe what they are really saying is—you embarrass me with your sexuality, therefore you embarrass our people, and *white* people will have even more ammunition to use against us."[12] Gesturing toward the dynamic that I have described in chapters 3 and 4 as the bribe of straightness, Brant suggests that the apparent extension of heterosexual privilege functions as part of a larger pattern of ongoing settler surveillance and management that works to render native modes of collectivity perverse and to delegitimize indigenous self-understandings. As against the gay/straight divide, she offers the notion of "family," which, while resembling the biologizing and privatizing rhetoric of bourgeois homemaking, more powerfully resonates in this context with kinship systems and their continuing role in shaping native sociospatiality.[13] Thus, Brant's creative work provides a counterpoint to a vision of queer solidarity in which Indians serve solely as a source of inspiration for articulating minoritarian sexual and gender identity in the United States rather than as participants in their own embattled nations.

UNITING THE "WE"

As against Hay's efforts to imagine a fairly totalizing "gay"-ness or "third-gender" status that can encompass nonnormative expressions of sexual and gender identity (at least among men), *Stone Butch Blues* makes a concerted effort to explore how the attempt to secure the boundaries of identity categories ends up excluding many people with whom productive solidarities could be built. The novel resists the tendency to define community formation and political advocacy in terms of a fundamental similarity among those linked together. Instead, it seeks to envision forms of alliance-in-difference in which variously situated kinds of social actors can see themselves as mutually implicated in systems that not only oppress all of them but pit them against each other in order to undermine the possibilities for collective organizing and transformation. In addition to troubling the borders of butchness, the text explores the ways that class and race play central roles in shaping the characters' experience of themselves and the social geography in which they move. In doing so, Feinberg refuses to understand heteronormativity as a simple distinction between heteros with privilege and queers without. In the "Afterword" to the tenth-anniversary edition, ze describes the writing of the novel "not as an expression of individual 'high' art but as a working-class organizer mimeographs a leaflet—a call to action," adding, "My life's work is about elevating collective organizing, not elevating individuals" (305–306).[14] In this vein, the novel repeatedly comes back to the labor union as a figure for how persons who do not occupy the same identity category, or whose vision of the contours of that identity differ significantly, can work together to change the structural conditions that deprive, degrade, and exploit all of them.

Yet in developing a working-class framework for forms of political organizing that extends beyond the workplace, Feinberg presents the main character—Jess—as learning how to participate in such networks from native people. That gesture casts native culture as a settler structure of feeling, a resource upon which non-natives can draw in creating more affectively rich and inclusive kinds of community. Put another way, displacing the existence of native polities as such, while also effacing the ongoing imperial efforts to regulate and restrict indigenous sovereignty, is crucial to the text's efforts to provide a more emotionally textured and expansive vision of what "union" can mean. Rather than faulting the novel for a lack of political awareness, I am suggesting that *Stone Butch Blues* is instructive in this vein precisely due to its commitments to consciousness-raising, tracking differences within and among marginalized groups, connecting fiction writing to politics, and building a larger and more sustainable movement for social justice. If Hay is somewhat of an easy target for a critique of the appropriation of Indians for a non-native queer politics, Feinberg's self-reflexivity, and hir lifelong work connecting LBGT issues to broader antiracist and socialist projects, makes the novel's portrayal of native peoples that much more surprising, suggesting the extent to which non-native opposition to heteronormativity draws on the image of native people in order to figure forms of collectivity that can resist state-sanctioned violence without actually contesting the terms of settler governance.

In contrast to a synecdochic vision of identity in which mutual belonging to a given category guarantees membership in a particular community, the novel instead understands community as itself both fluid and contested, involving variations on how individuals experience a specific identity in relation to other elements of their lives and struggle over what defines the community itself. Jess most often speaks of herself, and is described by others, as a "butch."[15] However, while that term is presented as having a somewhat obvious meaning at the outset, it comes under increasing pressure over the course of the novel, from within and without. In a conversation with Jess, Duffy, the chief shop steward for one of the factories at which Jess works who also becomes the character most associated with unionization, asks her whether two women in the plant are "lovers." When Jess reminds him that they are married to men, Duffy asks, "but aren't they butches?", to which Jess responds, "Well, they're he-shes, but they're not butches . . . I mean they look like Spencer Tracy and Montgomery Clift, but they really seem to love the guys they married." She adds, "it's not like they're getting off much easier by being married—they're still he-shes. They've gotta deal with the same shit butches do"; "they don't have a place to go like we do—I mean like the bars" (86–87). This scene suggests a continuity between "butch" and "he-she" as a form of gender expression but a discrepancy in terms of sexual object choice, desiring to be with another woman versus being attracted to men. However, rather than fully distinguishing the categories, Jess suggests that they have to "deal with the same shit," and later in the novel, in a speech before a "gay demonstration" in Greenwich Village, Jess describes herself as "a butch, a he-she" (296), implying a certain interchangeability between them. What most seems to distinguish the two is that butches "have a place to go," referring to the bars at which butches and femmes congregate.[16] While the dynamics of that space may be shaped around butch-femme sociality, and the erotics that characterize it, Jess represents it less as a place for persons of a particular sexual identity than as a site for community formation that provides solace and support for those present, and she regrets that the nonbutch he-shes do not seem to have a role to play in it, since their oppression correlates so closely to Jess's.

This moment is one of the many times the text marks the unnecessary exclusions that mark butch-femme community or by which butches are barred from other sites. If sexuality seems to provide a kind of organizing principle for butch-femme relations, it also serves as an animating force of conflict, both external and internal. When Jess's lover Theresa starts participating in "gay liberation and radical women's" groups at the university for which she works, she quickly finds that the other women see butches as "male chauvinist pigs" and femmes as "too feminine" and "sleeping with the enemy" (135–136).[17] In understanding butch-femme as simply a reproduction of heterosexuality, the campus women do not acknowledge the daily violence against butches for both their deviant gender and their homosexuality, nor do those at the university engage with the ways their own sexual and gender subjectivity is informed by their class privilege.[18] The text uses the term "lesbian" to refer to these women and their sense of themselves, rather than to indicate female homoeroticism per se (147–148, 214–215); thus, sexual identity and its associated modes of community formation (such as the lesbian dances on campus) remain transected by class difference. Yet the novel frames such separation not as a break within a properly united identity group but as a block to the creation of broader forms of oppositional solidarity. At one point, Jess quotes Theresa's critique of the campus women: "They're right about needing a revolution, but they're wrong to think they can do it without all of us" (214). While I will return a bit later to the novel's formulation of "us," here it indicates a more encompassing movement than that defined by any particular sexual/gender minority group's conception of its own boundaries.

Similarly, the novel explores the butch-femme pairing itself, suggesting its own definitional instability. Once Jess discovers that her friend Frankie, a longtime butch, is in a sexual relationship with another butch, she responds with horror and outrage, asking Frankie, "What makes you think you're still a butch" (207)? When Jess later contacts Frankie to reconcile, after Jess has begun a relationship with a male-bodied woman named Ruth, she admits, "what gets it for me is high femme . . . doesn't matter whether it's women or men—it's always high femme that pulls me by the waist and makes me sweat" (274). The novel indicates that the pressure to understand butchness as dependent on erotic attraction for femmes and to define that desire as for a female-bodied person emerged out of the particular milieu of the bar scene in which Frankie and Jess participated, which itself provided a sense of belonging denied to those whose matrix of gender and sexual experience did not mesh with its norms (such as the heterosexual he-shes). Through these examples, Feinberg indicates the value of community, as well as the kinds of repudiations it entails when conceptualized as congruent to a reified vision of personal identity.

In addition to suggesting that the notion of community must be expanded in ways that acknowledge more varied configurations of eroticism and gender expression, the novel explores the social topography of race. Feinberg utilizes Ed, an African American butch whom Jess knows from the bars, as a way of marking Jess's growing realization of her own white privilege, the official and unofficial kinds of segregation that shape urban space, and the existence of kinds of collectivity that cannot be encapsulated within—or subordinated to—sexual and gender identity. Fairly early in the novel, Jess and Ed discuss the East Side of Buffalo, which is the black side of town. In explaining her desire to go to clubs there, Ed observes, "I like being with my own people too" (54), and after Jess joins Ed for an evening on the East Side, they are stopped and assaulted by the police, during which one of the officers charges Jess with being a "fuckin' traitor" (57). Several years later, Jess hears of a fight at one of the bars between Ed and Grant, a white butch, over the war in Vietnam: "Grant said we ought to drop an A-bomb on Vietnam. She said no one would miss them. Ed told Grant she was a racist and said we should bring all the soldiers home. Ed said she felt like Muhammad Ali, that she didn't have any beef with the people over there" (125). As a result of Ed hitting Grant, who ends up with a concussion, the bartender (Meg) bans African Americans; in response, Jess intercedes, asserting in a meeting with Meg that "I wouldn't go to an all-white bar." In explaining to Jess the importance of intervening, Theresa argues, "Ed feels like she's in a war here at home . . . Cities are burning. There's troops in the streets" (125–128). These two incidents indicate not only the presence of racial difference among the butches and femmes but also the ways that butch-femme community in the bars on the West Side often depended on an unspoken white norm that when violated could lead to violence and racist exclusion, replicating in miniature the macrological patterns of racial partition and displacement that organize the geography of the city itself. More than working toward making predominantly white butch-femme community more inclusive for nonwhite individuals, the novel indicates that recognition of racial inequity alters one's understanding of how to map the position of butch-femme spaces within the nexus of multifaceted state policy and power. The text pushes toward a reconceptualization of such spaces—and thus the communities that form in and through them—as complexly implicated/enmeshed in structures of domination that do not appear as immediately related to sexuality and gender when viewed from a perspective based on reified identity categories.[19]

While articulating a more intersectional account of membership in an oppressed group, suggesting that to define personal identity along one axis both renders unmarked the forms of privilege one may possess and effaces the effect of other kinds of identity/oppression on how one experiences a given identity and its sociospatial contours, Feinberg further problematizes the notion that identity-based community itself can provide complete insulation against oppression. In the examples outlined here, the novel presents such community as tending to mask at best, or replicate at worst, other modes of oppression while potentially disabling cooperation among people who occupy varied identity positions. In an effort to envision forms of association, collaboration, and solidarity that work across while recognizing multiple kinds of social difference, the novel highlights the labor union as a model for politically aware and engaged community formation. The first example of this kind of collective organizing is when Jess is asked by Duffy to turn down the offer of a promotion in order for it to go to Leroy, an African American man who has been denied advancement due to the racism of the foreman; Jess responds, "Look, Duffy, I'm for the union . . . But butches can't even come to union meetings." When she tells the story to fellow butches at the factory, one of them explodes, "Fuck that shit. I don't want to be part of no union that doesn't want me." This comment leads Jess to underline the importance of unionization: "We can't just say 'fuck the union,' we're in it. The contract's up in October. What are we gonna do, go into the plant manager's office one at a time and negotiate? We don't have a chance. We've gotta make the guys see that they need us too" (83–84). Rather than suggesting that butches need to create their own distinct collective, Jess insists that they need to work within the structure of the union. The alternative would be a fracturing of opposition that leaves everyone vulnerable to manipulation by management. In fact, the effort to promote Jess over Leroy itself is such a manipulation, an effort to play oppressed groups off each other by exploiting existing tensions among them. If the white butches already are alienated from the union, they are less likely to protest when one of their own is advanced over a straight man of color, and if employees do not see themselves as aligned, the white butches are less likely to believe they have a stake in challenging forms of white supremacy that in this instance seem to work to their advantage. Moreover, the union serves as a vehicle not simply for trying to secure benefits to employees but for consciousness-raising among them, persuading people who occupy discrepant identity positions "that they need us too,"[20] and in doing so, it becomes a medium for a kind of coalition-building that, more than aggregating identity groups, works toward creating a durable sense of collectivity among them in the service of a movement for change that could better the circumstances of all of them.

This vision of nonidentitarian unity among apparently disparate persons and groups exceeds the workplace itself, providing the novel with its central trope of political mobilization.[21] When Jess's lover Theresa is trying to explain the significance of the women's movement to butches and femmes, she says to Jess, "I need the movement . . . Remember you once told me about a factory you worked where the guys didn't want the butches to come to union meetings . . . But you knew the union was a good thing . . . You tried to organize to get the butches into the union" (136), positioning the union as a frame through which to conceptualize other efforts to organize for social justice. After Jess speaks to a gay and lesbian rally at the end of the novel, she describes the experience to Duffy in these terms: "I wanted to tell them how it was in the plants, how when a contract's almost up management works overtime trying to divide everybody. I didn't know if they'd get what I meant if I said it took the whole membership to win the strike" (299). Here, the novel presents labor unions as a vital conceptual tool for generating connections among people who otherwise might see themselves as separated by forms of identification that, when used as the basis for community formation, can end up "divid[ing] everybody," ultimately reinforcing the authority of those already in power. Additionally, Jess indicates that this way of thinking, and the experience of unionization itself, may be alien to many of the listeners. More than simply describing existing political configurations, the trope of the union is aspirational, indexing concerns, strategies, and a kind of political imaginary that Feinberg represents as largely lacking from existing approaches to advocacy for sexual and gender minorities.

While making issues of class and poverty visible and central within these movements, the text's depiction of the union also seeks to endorse a kind of collectivity neither restricted to/by existing institutionalized identity categories (which themselves tend to deny internal variety and intersectionality) nor dependent on the production of a new kind of homogeneity, one predicated on the erasure of difference among participants. In talking about Frankie to Ruth, Jess's neighbor and lover, she notes, "I always wanted all of us who were different to be the same" (271). The novel implicitly juxtaposes this statement with Jess's speech at the rally, in which she asks, "I don't know what it would take to really change the world. But couldn't we get together and try to figure it out? Couldn't the *we* be bigger? Isn't there a way we could help fight each other's battles so that we're not always alone?" (296). The notion of the union appears pedagogical in promoting a shift from a vision of solidarity and struggle based on "same"-ness to one committed to a more capacious sense of community (mutual belonging to a "we") that does not demand fusion (the persistent sense of distinction in the phrase "each other's battles"). The "we" is forged through a deliberate extension of connection as opposed to a sense of always-already belonging to an "us" on the basis of shared being—which itself requires a disavowed policing of identity boundaries, as discussed earlier. Through the figure of the union, Feinberg aims to provide a way of imagining community and community formation that avoids the worst insulating and isolating tendencies of what might be termed identity politics while also retaining a sense of the positive power of identification (the camaraderie in the butch-femme bars or Ed's relation to her "people").

However, if "union" is to mean more than simply involvement in a particular organization for the purpose of fairly circumscribed goals, it needs to have an affective charge that can crystallize a feeling of unity—of belonging to a "we"—that is not merely instrumental, and the novel models and generates that sensation through its representation of native people. Although the text most consistently signals the recurring motif of the union through Duffy's various appearances, it earlier introduces the idea of profoundly felt solidarity among workers (both facilitated by the union and giving the union its force) through Jess's relation with native women in her first factory job. The size of the company is such that she is "the only he-she," but she is befriended by Muriel, "one of the older Native women who worked near [Jess] on the line."[22] Readers are told that "about half the women on the line were from the Six Nations. Most were Mohawk and Seneca." Despite the fact that Jess is non-native, she eventually is welcomed among them: "What we shared in common was that we worked cooperatively, day in and day out . . . We shared small bits of our culture, favorite foods, or revealed an embarrassing moment. It was just this potential for solidarity the foreman was always looking to sabotage."[23] "Solidarity" here entails more than simply acknowledging the fact of employment in the same place, instead involving the slow building of trust through a series of interactions not immediately related to the ostensible purpose that brings them together—in this case laboring on "the line." What matters in this process is less a structural analysis of relative positioning within a system of exploitation than a coming to understand and accept each other as part of a "cooperative," even if the participants do not initially share much outside the scope of that participation. The work of learning about and recognizing each other through engagements that exceed the immediate purpose for unionization is what makes solidarity powerful and dangerous, forging community out of what otherwise simply would be mutual presence in a specific space.

If Feinberg's aim here is to illustrate the cultural dynamics of working-class community formation on the job, so as to provide a more textured model for political organizing and action, why highlight the native women on the line? What is at stake for the novel in emphasizing Jess's relationship with these women in particular? What role does their nativeness play in the formulation of the concept of the union? The novel might be read simply as reflecting the actual composition of the workforce at a given factory in Buffalo, which seems quite plausible given the city's proximity to Seneca reservations and other Six Nations peoples and the various dislocations from Iroquois lands occurring just prior to and during the period covered by the novel (addressed further in the next section). Yet as with the figure of the union itself, the novel's portrayal of these women appears to be less descriptive than aspirational, presenting native practices as a kind of paradigm for how to give reach and affective substance to the union—to constitute a bigger "we." More than talking, gossiping, and exchanging stories, the native women perform "social songs" as part of beginning the day. The novel suggests that these are not simply popular tunes but also have specific traditional significance: "Sometimes one of the women would explain to us later what the song meant, or for which occasion or time of year it was sung." Jess begins to sing along, and the native women "smiled at each other with their eyes, and sang a little louder to allow me to raise my own voice a bit . . . It felt good to sing together." Soon afterward, Muriel invites Jess to a local powwow, to which she begins "to go regularly," including developing a crush on Muriel's daughter Yvonne, which "all the women noticed right away" and of which they appear to approve (or at least feel indifferent). Eventually, the women come to expect Jess to lead the song, refusing to sing if she does not, and when she finally does, "we all smiled at each other and sang with tears in our eyes." However, this development, which Jess (and, by extension, the novel) interprets as the women "honoring" her, results in her being let go just prior to being eligible to join the union: "I knew management had been watching the growing solidarity with great trepidation." This series of events and its positioning rather early within the arc of the plot creates a context for the notion of "solidarity" that saturates it in indigeneity. Or rather, the text borrows elements of native culture to provide a framework through which to delineate the kinds of bonding that can give emotional force to the idea of the union. The invocations of the latter throughout the novel allude back to this experience as a kind of originary moment, drawing on the vision of collectivity it provides to indicate the potential inherent within the union—its ability to produce a capacious "we" that can transect difference. The native women clearly are aware of and accept Jess's butchness and seem unfazed by its erotic dimensions as well (in their nonresponse to her attraction to Yvonne), and this apparent ability to embrace nonheteronormative gender and sexual identity marks native sociality as an ideal protoype for the kind of community Feinberg seeks to generate.

At the end of the chapter, after Jess is fired, Muriel says to her, "Now you learn to dance," suggesting a continuing relationship and Jess's ongoing involvement in native networks. However, Muriel is never heard from again, and, despite the fact that the events of the novel remain in Buffalo for the next 150 pages, Jess never again interacts with Six Nations women while living in the city, despite their historical presence in predominantly white butch-femme circles.[24] More than enacting another version of the trope of the vanishing Indian, the novel's construction of politically progressive collectivity relies on calling forth the tribal while hollowing it out, including erasing the persistent presence and political struggles of Six Nations peoples. As in Sedgwick's *Hope Leslie*, Indians educate non-natives in how to be more inclusive; in that novel, the issue is expanding family beyond the boundaries of the privatized, patriarchal, couple-centered home, whereas here the focus is on accepting persons who do not conform to the dictates of heterogender. Both, though, present indigeneity as a capacity for a certain kind of expansive feeling, an aptitude that Feinberg signals through the invitation of Jess to attend powwows and perform Haudenosaunee songs.

LOCATING THE NATIVE

While adoption is central to Sedgwick's text, *Stone Butch Blues* does not highlight native kinship systems, instead emphasizing the kinds of social activity that would signify as "culture" within the framework of Indian policy. As I argued in the previous chapter, the official discourses of reorganization indicated a commitment to recognizing aspects of native life that previously had been brutally repressed while at the same time naturalizing the heteronormative romance plot at the heart of allotment (as discussed in chapter 3)—treating the nuclear family form and the attendant split between the privatized familial household and politics as a self-evident frame through which to address the contours and character of tribal sovereignty. The disjunction between the intent to acknowledge and revitalize indigenous "traditions" and the superimposition of a liberal model of politics, property, and family was managed through the figure of "culture," which became a way of referring to religious rituals and other collective practices seen as separate from issues of family formation, homemaking, land tenure, and collective resource distribution. Feinberg's novel replicates the topology in which native *cultural* practices are divorced from mappings of kinship, occupancy, and governance. The text portrays the Six Nations women's response to Jess as a function of practices of inclusion that can embrace people with nonnormative identities, rather than interpreting such acceptance as enmeshed in a distinct (set of) indigenous social structure(s). Put another way, the native women can teach Jess a transferable feeling or sensation of *solidarity* through participation in singing and powwows only if such participation is not understood as bound up in the specificity of native collectivity and territoriality as peoples. While the Six Nations women have the space of the powwow that appears to be theirs (at least for the purposes of choosing to make it available to non-natives), these communities lack the spatiality associated with other marginalized groups in the novel, such as the East Side, where Ed can be among her "people," or the butch-femme bars on the West Side.[25] The novel explores neither the particular geography of urban native life nor its complex and shifting relations to extant Seneca reservations surrounding Buffalo or reservations farther away.

This relative despatialization of the communities to which the native women at the factory belong seems particularly striking given the numerous threats to Seneca, Tuscarora, and Mohawk sovereignty during the period in which the novel is set. The 1950s and 1960s were disastrous for Haudenosaunee reservations on land claimed by New York, witnessing not only a repudiation of their political autonomy but huge land losses for public works projects from which only non-natives benefited.[26] The largest and most publicized dislocation occurred due to the construction of the Kinzua Dam on the Allegany reservation. Dedicated on September 16, 1966, and ostensibly designed by the Army Corps of Engineers to protect Pittsburgh from flooding, the project led to the seizure of 9,000 acres of Seneca territory, approximately a third of the reservation, and from 1957 to 1964, more than 600 Senecas were displaced from their homes, virtually all of their land lying in the floodplain created by the dam. Asserting the authority to dispossess them for the supposed benefit of the general public required breaking the Treaty of Canandaigua (1794), which after enumerating the recognized lands of the Oneidas, Onondagas, Cayugas, and Senecas promised "never to claim the same, nor to disturb them, or any of the Six Nations, or their Indian friends residing thereon, and united with them, in the free use and enjoyment thereof."[27] Similar violations of the spirit of the treaty occurred at the Tuscarora and Akwesasne (St. Regis) reservations for the construction of a reservoir (560 acres) and expansion of the St. Lawrence Seaway (130 acres), respectively.[28]

These intrusions involved not simply the taking of native lands but the extension of legal authority over Haudenosaunee peoples through the expansion of federal plenary power and the federally sanctioned delegation of control over aspects of Indian affairs to the state of New York. That intent was made explicit in the congressional acts of 1948 and 1950 that transferred jurisdiction over criminal and civil matters to the state.[29] This campaign not only presaged but helped provide the policy framework for the larger movement toward the termination of native tribes in the 1950s and early 1960s. In this shift from the ideology of reorganization, the U.S. government sought to free Indians from federal "paternalism" by ending federal funding and fully bringing them under the legal authority of the states.[30] Rather than conceptualizing this change as an assault on sovereignty, officials presented it as liberating native peoples from the stifling superintendence of the BIA. As President Truman argued in a report to Congress in 1945, "The original purpose of the Indian Bureau was to help the Indian to become a citizen and it was intended as a service rather than as an administrative agency . . . [T]he present aim appears to be to keep the Indian an Indian and to make him satisfied with the limitations of a primitive form of existence." In a 1947 report, Truman embellished this point, observing, "Our basic purpose is to assist the Navajos—and other Indians—to become healthy, enlightened, and self-supporting citizens, able to enjoy the full fruits of our democracy and to contribute their share to the prosperity of our country."[31] Reiterating many of the central premises of allotment, such statements highlight the need for "the Indian" to cease to exist and for "the citizen" to take his place, understanding the achievement of the latter status as dependent on detribalization. Instead of seeking to give peoples greater political autonomy than they achieved under reorganization by scaling back the BIA's ability to set priorities as well as to veto and manage tribal initiatives, the government sought to "emancipate" native individuals from federal regulation by dismantling the entire trust structure. From 1948 to 1957, well over 3 million acres were removed from trust status, making them taxable and vulnerable to loss, especially given the persistently dire economic situation on reservations.[32]

In addition to the provision of funds for relocation of native people to cities, which I will address in the next section, this ideological (re)orientation was made manifest in a series of statutes passed by Congress in the mid-1950s. The two most prominent among them were House Concurrent Resolution 108 and Public Law 280, both adopted in 1953. The first indicated Congress's intent "to make the Indians . . . subject to the same laws . . . as are applicable to other citizens of the United States, and to end their status as wards," while also listing particular states and tribes that should be targeted for the transfer of federal funding and jurisdiction; the second actually transferred authority over criminal and civil matters to the states of California, Nebraska, Minnesota, Oregon, and Wisconsin, with a few tribes listed as exceptions.[33] When signing Public Law 280, President Eisenhower remarked, "its basic purpose represents still another step in granting equality to all Indians in the nation," framing the aims of termination as an extension of rights that would allow Indians to enter into the civilized modernity of citizenship—itself still imagined in the nuclear and privatizing terms discussed in the previous two chapters. While placing native peoples under state jurisdiction was not the same as terminating them, which entailed the end of all federal funding and no longer recognizing the tribe as a legal entity, 109 tribes were in fact terminated before the program officially was repudiated by President Nixon in 1970, affecting more than 1.3 million acres and 11,000 people.[34] Although not formally terminated, the Senecas and other Haudenosaunee peoples brought under the authority of New York State served as test subjects for the post-reorganization effort to roll back the (limited) gains for native sovereignty in the Indian New Deal. Their example also illustrates the ways the rhetoric of liberating Indians from imprisonment under BIA control dissimulated the commercial imperatives at play in seizing native lands, a project made easier by demoting peoples from treaty-recognized nations to communities whose status largely came under the purview of the state.

Stone Butch Blues remains silent on these developments, despite the symbolic importance of Haudenosaunee women in the novel. In doing so, it effaces the fact that the presence of the Seneca and Mohawk women in the factory can be traced to an ongoing history of state-sanctioned displacement, of which the seizures noted above simply were the most recent.[35] Moreover, the logic of termination disincentivized economic development on the reservations, since the uncertain legal status of the land worked against sustained investment by natives and non-natives. As Vine Deloria suggests, "many tribes have said that there is no incentive in building up their reservations if there is a chance they will be sold out unexpectedly in the near future" (136). Given the need to support oneself somehow, the absence of jobs on or immediately adjacent to reservations created an impetus for migration to cities, where the

kinds of factory jobs Feinberg addresses were available until the onset of dein-
dustrialization in the 1970s. The novel's portrayal of native women in Buffalo
as figures for a kind of generic union solidarity indexes the effects of termina-
tion-era policies that intensified dislocation from Haudenosaunee reservations while eliding these dynamics of settler intervention. In other words,
Feinberg's account of cultural bonds in the workplace leaves aside the complex
relations between these native women and their peoples, decontextualizing
them from contemporaneous struggles over sovereignty in ways that make
them more available as objects of identification for non-natives.

The text does register collective native resistance to settler policy in the
period, but in a rather distancing way. It notes Wounded Knee in passing
(141), the 1973 standoff on the Pine Ridge reservation between federal
officers and officials and an unpopular tribal council, on the one hand, and
opponents of the council and outside American Indian Movement (AIM)
activists, on the other, which became an emblem of the Red Power movement of the late 1960s and early 1970s. However, Feinberg remains silent
with respect to the well-publicized examples of Haudenosaunee conflict
with authorities that preceded Wounded Knee, such as the 1969 blockage of
the international bridge in the Akwesasne reservation to protest efforts to
charge Mohawks duties for moving within their own homeland, the 1971
effort by Onondagas and others to prevent the widening of Interstate 81
south of their reservation, and the sometimes armed resistance by Tuscaroras to developers on their reservation in the late 1950s. In fact, the latter has
been cited by native intellectuals and activists as a significant inspiration for
the growing militancy that provided the context for Wounded Knee. In
addition, Haudenosaunee participation was crucial to the pan-tribal organizations that helped galvanize the growing, and increasingly media visible,
opposition of native peoples to extant patterns of termination, neglect,
interference, exploitation, and dispossession in the 1960s.[36] What relevance
might these events have had for the Haudenosaunee women with whom Jess
bonds? Or perhaps more to the point, presenting these women as a way of
envisioning *union* absent any attention to the struggles by Haudenosaunee
peoples for self-determination helps create the impression of native practices as free-floating tools available to facilitate non-native processes of community formation—a culture that can be emulated in ways that enable the
construction of a bigger "we."[37]

If the novel's divorce of native practices from indigenous peoplehood
operates in the service of providing a structure of feeling that can animate
and expand the possibilities opened by the union, it also helps produce a
history for sexual and gender minorities that enables them to be addressed
as coherent collectivities reaching across time. Creating a historical presence
for gender minorities in particular appears to be one of the ways the text

challenges their marginalization, illustrating a relation between their erasure from history and their contemporary presentation as aberration and
abomination. In indicating the periods over which Jess's story stretches,
Feinberg mentions various events that received national publicity, including
the assassinations of John F. Kennedy and Malcolm X (23, 54), the rioting in
Newark and Detroit (105), and Wounded Knee (141). These passing references not only index for readers when the novel's events are occurring but
also underline the ways that the circumstances of Jess's life, the difficulties
she and other butches and femmes face, and the kinds of struggles against
oppression in which she is involved do not sync up with the well-rehearsed
symbols of national history, or even those of gay and lesbian history—such
as the Stonewall riots and the Anita Bryant campaign (131, 187).[38] Instead,
her life appears invisible within such narratives, not seen as valuable enough
to form part of the story of either the nation or the social movements seen as
relevant in transforming social consciousness in the United States in the
latter half of the twentieth century. At one point, Jess remarks, "I acknowledged that no matter who had been in the White House, it had always been
hard to be me" (224), suggesting the persistence of the conditions of oppression and exploitation that affect her, the distance of these concerns from the
dominant discourses of political life, and the stability and durability of her
sense of self despite the foreclosure of the possibility for nonpathologizing
public representation of her and people like her. Even as Feinberg challenges
efforts to police the borders of marginalized communities and explores the
complex intersections among race, gender, class, and sexuality, ze also seeks
to validate nonnormative gender identities as legitimate kinds of subject
positions, specifically by presenting them as having histories that have been
suppressed.

   While indicating the importance of recognizing that forgotten history as
part of an encompassing left politics, itself modeled on the figure of the
union, the text seems to require the elision of indigenous histories and
modes of collectivity so as to make native people and practices available as
a figure for the historicity of alternative forms of gendered identification.[39]
References to a native past are crucial to the novel's efforts to constitute a
minoritarian "we" that could serve as the subject for a counterhegemonic
history—a history that itself provides a visibility that licenses including the
minority as such in the broader "we" of union solidarity. When Jess is
beaten brutally in an attack in the subway and Ruth is caring for her, Ruth
observes, "I once read in an old drag magazine about a time, long, long ago,
when people like us were honored" (261); afterward, for Jess's birthday,
Ruth gives her a copy of Jonathan Ned Katz's Gay American History,
repeating the claim about "people like us" and noting a "whole section
about Native societies" (266). Jess takes up this formulation, indicating that

she has "been going to the library, looking up our history," finding that "we haven't always been hated" and tracing "the history of this ancient path we're walking" (271). The "we/us" here appears to refer to those whose gender identity does not fit the dimorphic model—in which there are only two options, they are understood as opposites, and gendered self-presentation and social roles are believed to be derived from inherent body types (of which there also are supposedly only two).[40] While practices with regard to alternatively gendered people clearly change ("native societies" differ from the contemporary United States), the "us" remains continuous across time (from "long, long ago" to the moment of Ruth's utterance), raising the question of what constitutes the "like"-ness the novel posits and what is at stake in that apparent identicality—that *identity*. Both members of native societies and non-natives such as Jess are imagined as sharing a commonality based on their expression and experience of gender, a kind of equivalence that seems easily to transect the indigenous/settler divide. In other words, Jess and the native people she sees as her forebears are on the same "path," bound together by an evident equivalence.[41] Thus, even as the novel seeks to complicate notions of gender and sexual identity, refusing the policing of categorical boundaries in ways discussed earlier, it naturalizes such identities as a primary aspect of personhood that can cross temporal, spatial, cultural, and political boundaries.

Indigenous practices of acceptance/honoring are seen as acting on a group whose identity as such is not in fact dependent on their participation in indigenous peoplehood, and the ostensible connection between native members of gender and/or sexual minorities and their non-native fellows makes those indigenous modes of inclusion, and associated forms of feeling, portable in democratizing social justice struggles by contemporary non-normatively gendered people. In this vein, the novel not only indicates that Ruth is connected to the Seneca people but also offers her experiences as a child as evidence for what it means to be part of the gender minoritarian "we." When caring for Jess after she is attacked, Ruth recalls, "When I was eight or nine my Uncle Dale tried to take me out with the men to prune the vines. But my mother said no. She and my aunt and my grandma took me to work with them. They already knew my nature" (261). Noting that her uncle used to take her to Bare Hill, "the birthplace of the Seneca nation," she remembers one day when a man approached them and said to her uncle, "Let the child be," which her uncle concludes "must have been one of the spirits of the Senecas who walk those hills," and afterward, he acquiesced to the idea that she "wasn't growing up to be a man" (262). Ruth's women relatives accept her gender identification seemingly without conflict or comment, other than to try to dissuade her uncle from forcing her to do men's work, and this unfraught acknowledgment appears as itself a function of traditional beliefs in light of the fact that her uncle is persuaded by "the spirits of the Senecas." Ruth's references to Jess as part of an "us" both before and after this anecdote position Ruth's interactions with her relatives as part of the shared "history" claimed by Jess as "our[s]," a history that can serve as a model to contemporary people and political movements about how to engage with members of a gender minoritarian "us." In this way, Seneca culture appears to provide a set of tools for affirming the existence and value of nonnormatively gendered persons in the United States, their cohesion as a group, and their proper acceptance by other communities within broader movements for social justice.[42]

Within this dynamic, however, what happens to the "we" of the "Seneca nation"? The text portrays Ruth's experiences as belonging to a "history" to which Jess, too, can lay claim, a history that provides a kind of background from which members of gender minorities can draw in arguing for the importance of greater visibility and acceptance. When Seneca social formations are framed as part of a shared heritage, though, what happens not only to contemporary Seneca territorial and political claims and self-representations but to the history of their existence as a distinct polity on which those claims rest? In Seneca conflict with the state of New York and the federal government in the 1950s through the 1970s, and Haudenosaunee struggles in this period more broadly, the assertion of indigenous self-determination often was bolstered by historical narratives focused on prior U.S. recognition of native sovereignty. Much of the Senecas' argument against the Kinzua Dam, as well as resistance to the flooding of reservation lands at Tuscarora and Akwesasne, turned on the citation of the Treaty of Canandaigua, as noted earlier. Through the invocation of this diplomatic pact, Haudenosaunee peoples sought to offer a particular account of the legal status of their lands as beyond state jurisdiction and subject to a more rigorous standard of protection than in ordinary federal law,[43] but in addition, the appeal to this treaty told a story of native collectivity, representing an indigenous "we" whose identity and claims as peoples precede that of the United States and are not dependent for their existence on the legal framework of the settler state—as indicated by the need in the early republic to negotiate a treaty with the Six Nations. Although U.S. courts did not accept this reasoning with respect to the Kinzua Dam and related cases, such historical reach proved decisive in the case of *Oneida Indian Nation v. County of Oneida* (1974). Prior to this U.S. Supreme Court decision, native nations on land claimed by New York had no avenue for bringing a case against the state for the illegal taking of land, since state law barred them from filing suit and the Eleventh Amendment of the U.S. Constitution prevented making one of the states a party in a federal case without its consent.[44] In order to get around this dilemma, the Oneidas filed suit in federal court for trespass damages against the counties of Oneida and Madison; the basis for this claim was that Oneida land nominally within those counties illegally had been taken by New York through state treaties that violated the federal Trade and Inter-course Act of 1793, which required a federal role (at least the presence of a commissioner) at all land cessions by native peoples. In what was to become a stunning precedent for native peoples, particularly on lands claimed by Maine, Massachusetts, Rhode Island, and Connecticut, the court found that federal courts did have jurisdiction over this kind of case and that such state "treaties" violated contemporaneous federal law and thus were illegitimate.[45] In these instances, memory of the 1790s provided a means of opposing efforts to cast Haudenosaunee peoples as merely dependent populations whose political status and spatiality rested purely on settler largesse, instead offering a counternarrative in which their existence as autonomous polities had been acknowledged by the United States and in which the casualization of their relationship with the United States resulted from an interested amnesia about actual precedent.

As in *Stone Butch Blues*, the Six Nations used history to make manifest longstanding oppressive and exploitative relationships that simply were nat-uralized as inevitable and self-evident in the present, but the latter history depends on distinguishing indigenous identity, whereas the novel's strategy is to make "native societies" the framework through which to make legible the continuity of a gender minoritarian "we." Thus, in the text, the content of native "nation"-ality appears to refer to a cultural predisposition toward acceptance of gender variation (learning from the "spirits of the Senecas"), which can serve as part of a pedagogy for non-natives, rather than to indi-cate the specificity of indigenous (geo)political formations. As the novel em-phasizes, in ways addressed earlier, people certainly belong to multiple identity categories, and the recognition of that intersectionality strengthens the possibilities for solidarity. However, the portrayal of Haudenosaunee people as themselves models of inclusivity makes indigeneity porous and portable in ways that work at cross-purposes to the aims and articulations of Haudenosaunee peoples in the period the novel chronicles, predicating sol-idarity between settlers and natives not on acknowledgment of the latter's sovereignty but on their availability for "union" with the former.

Issues of sovereignty are achingly proximate to the novel's depiction of Seneca people even while being continually obscured by its representational strategies. Invoking "the birthplace of the Seneca nation" (262), the novel locates Ruth's family on territory ceded by the Senecas in the late eighteenth century, vaguely gesturing toward a long history of displacement without addressing the existence and geopolitics of contemporary Seneca reserva-tions and governance. Additionally, in describing "Bare Hill," Ruth observes, "The government cut a road right through the burial grounds there" (262), which seems like a fairly generic trope of native dispossession, but the reference actually indexes and conflates two separate controversies relevant to New York State's recognition of Seneca sovereignty in the 1970s and 1980s. Whereas Bare Hill is a village just east of Canandaigua Lake, Boughton Hill is an area northwest of the lake, also known as Ganondagan, which had served as an important archaeological site due to its having been "the major Seneca village during the seventeenth century," opening as a state park in 1987. In 1971, excavators there came across grave sites and began removing bones and artifacts, a process protested by both the Seneca Nation and the Tonawanda Band.[46] During this period, Haudenosaunee peoples also were struggling with the state over efforts to expand two highways, Interstate 81 south of the Onondaga reservation and Route 17 on Allegany land, both of which generated active and well-publicized protest at different points in the early 1970s and mid-1980s.[47] Feinberg collapses these two sets of occurrences into each other, creating a composite that casts the violation of Seneca space as having occurred in an indeterminately located past rather than during the decades the novel chronicles while also reducing specific conflicts over jurisdiction and the legal scope of Seneca authority to a passing reference stripped of virtually all context. This moment is symptomatic of the ways the text both recognizes native collectivity for the purposes of suggesting it differs from dominant U.S. understandings of gender and evacuates it of contemporary political dimensionality and content.

This depiction of native peoplehood in terms of a kind of cultural essence also involves defining their identity in ways disconnected from native self-understandings. In particular, the novel offers a conception of Seneca identity that divorces it from still operative kinship systems. While by the mid-nineteenth century the Seneca Nation (composed of the Cattaraugus and Allegany reservations) had adopted an elective council distinct from traditional governance by chiefs and the Tonawanda reservation of Senecas had elected peacemakers chosen from among the chiefs, the clan system continued to serve as an important element of Seneca sociality and politics. In addition to the persistence of a traditional council at Tonawanda and its participation within the Iroquois League centered at Onondaga, Cattaraugus and Allegany continued to perform condolence ceremonies toward each other despite their formal separation from the League. Moreover, clan connections still shaped much of sociopolitical life in the Seneca Nation, which still defined membership through matrilineality. Moreover, with respect to the other Six Nations peoples on lands claimed by New York, there were struggles over governance at Akwesasne between traditional and state-organized councils, the Onondaga and Tuscarora nations retained traditional councils and participated in the Iroquois League, and clan mothers at Tuscarora were crucial to the opposition to the expansion of the reservoir there, suggesting that broader clan networks persist as a vital part of how Haudenosaunee collectivity and sovereignty are conceptualized.[48]

However, Feinberg's representation of Seneca identity does not engage with this prominent dynamic of Haudenosaunee history and politics. In the initial discussion of Ruth's identity as Seneca, the novel presents her mother, aunt, and grandmother as having recognized her gender before her uncle. Uncle Dale's acceptance is explained by reference to Seneca principles, so the reader is left to assume that Ruth's mother is also Seneca and that, given the continuing matrilineal orientation of the Senecas, Dale is her brother, taking up the responsibility for teaching and protection that would be his as the most closely related man of the child's clan. Readers later are told that Ruth's mother was one of the "summer people" who fell in love with her father and stayed among his relatives, which means that within a matrilineal framework Ruth is not Seneca. She says, "My heart's in these hills," echoing the feelings of her father and Dale, who "hear the hills calling them like lovers" (279), but while she may have grown up with Seneca relatives (including Dale, who clearly is her father's brother), she herself cannot belong to the Seneca Nation. The novel does not register this fact as an issue,[49] implying that she has inherited native identity through her father and that her mother has been de facto adopted, living among her husband's family and following their customs long after he is killed in a car accident. Ruth's status as Seneca, then, seems to depend on the intersection of two longstanding narratives: the vision of native culture as embracing outsiders, particularly white folks, in ways disconnected from indigenous geopolitics (discussed in chapter 2); and the possession of a racial Indianness that is distinct from actually existing native sociopolitical systems (as discussed in chapter 1). In this way, Ruth's character becomes a figure for a generic kind of nativeness that does not speak to acknowledged Seneca modes of peoplehood.

Additionally, in constructing Ruth's story, Feinberg rehearses a narrative of coming out in which the experience of alienation from one's birth family and homeplace is crucial.[50] Although the novel earlier indicates that Ruth's gender identity had been accepted by her family, she later states that she "escaped to save my life," adding, "My people aren't bad . . . I love them more since I left. They love me the best way they know how. I'm family. But it's hard, and I don't want anyone who's not family to see it" (278). The only sense the reader is given of why she needed to "escape" comes when she and Jess return to upstate New York, Ruth to visit with her family and Jess to address unresolved relationships in Buffalo. Ruth's relatives routinely refer to her as "Robbie," presumably her masculine name given at birth. At one point, her Aunt Hazel comments, "I don't know how you girls could live in that city with all them—," a statement that Ruth "cut[s] . . . off mid-sentence" (291), and Ruth's mother notes to Jess, "Folks may not understand her, and they may not always know what to say, but they know she's one of us" (292). These moments convey the sense that the primary difficulty Ruth faces among her relatives is her gender identity, which they do not necessarily "understand." Her relation to her "people" is as "family" who love her, but in order to express her sense of self, the novel suggests that she needs to leave them for the city, where she can find other people like herself with whom she can form community. While certainly not disputing the existence of homophobia and transphobia among native peoples, and that many LGBT and two-spirit natives are in fact alienated from their families and homeplaces due to their sexuality and/or gender expression,[51] I am suggesting that the novel's construction of Ruth's narrative potentially makes her story more familiar to non-native readers at the expense of exploring the possibility of ongoing commitments to Seneca sovereignty that are not displaced by individual movement away from Seneca land. Depicting Ruth as diasporic in this way could allow for greater engagement with issues of native nationality, but doing so would trouble the text's project of defining a minoritarian "we" by introducing a kind of difference that is less easily subsumed within the vision of "union" and that challenges the use of rhetorics of nativeness to coalesce and affectively enrich political projects and imaginaries centered on non-natives.

Feinberg consistently presents native people as accepting gender and sexual diversity in situations where they can be contrasted to non-native harassment, exploitation, and violence while presenting nonnormative gender/ sexual identification as primary when addressing individual self-representation. However, might there be an unexplored continuity between Ruth and the Haudenosaunee women of the factory? To what extent can Ruth's choices signify in terms of the ongoing displacement of (the) Seneca people in the mid-twentieth century? To what extent does the novel's formulation of Ruth's story foreclose these questions by repeatedly divorcing its discussion of native people from contemporary forms of native peoplehood? Native people in the novel help cohere the "we" of a minoritarian subjectivity by providing evidence of its continuity across time and a model/precedent for how that group can be included as part of a broader "we" in pursuit of social justice. In its ostensible ability to create unity across difference, native culture provides a way of envisioning solidarity as more than an instrumental means toward specific goals, instead presenting it as a capacious kind of community formation. Even as the novel suggests through the character of Ruth that belonging to the "we" of queer identity (figured in terms of gender, sexuality, both, or a complex mix) does not negate membership in the "we" of the Seneca Nation, the narration of the latter in the service of the former displaces the specific modalities of Seneca collectivity (including kinship), the distinctions between indigenous and settler political claims, and the connection between the "we" of native nationalities and the ongoing defense of tribal space and sovereignty. The novel articulates resistance to heteronormativity with struggles for racial and class justice but in ways that appear to demand a vision of intersectionality constituted from within a settler frame. The kind of solidarity *Stone Butch Blues* imagines seems to require a kind of selective memory in which native peoples have a history but one that exists in order to confirm a queer "we" whose complex and multivectored commitments do not include the defense of native peoplehood against contemporary threats, including the ongoing legacy of allotment and termination.

SOVEREIGNTY AND THE CITY

Feinberg works to forge a "we" for broad-based social change, based on the labor union and given greater cohesion and affective density as a community. Native peoples provide not only a model for a kind of community that can include sexual and gender minorities but a history that indicates the presence of queer people across time and culture, thereby qualifying them as minoritarian subjects who can be included as such in a more broadly formulated union/unity movement. While gesturing toward the existence of native land claims, the novel foregrounds the city as the space that matters—where queer subjectivities can flourish and a range of intersecting communities can come to realize the value of solidarity. Industry and urbanity intertwine in the text's political imaginary, however, in ways that bracket the territoriality of native nationality and circumscribe the scope of queer critique. The novel's efforts to envision a counterhegemonic coalition that could oppose multiple interwoven forms of oppression certainly exceeds a liberal call for greater property and privacy rights for (otherwise privileged) LGBT people, but it also depends on enfolding native people(s) into a primarily urban mass movement to resist racism, exploitation, and heteronormativity that does not acknowledge the specific ways those systems work together in an ongoing assault on indigenous land and peoplehood.

Looking to the work of Beth Brant, one sees an effort to indicate how native life in the city remains animated by a kind of sovereignty not registered as such within the discourses of the settler state. A lesbian Tyendinaga Mohawk of mixed parentage who grew up in Detroit, Brant explores how the experience of belonging to her people and of connection to her homeland persists despite distance from the reserve, a relationship felt and maintained most clearly through ongoing participation in kinship and clan networks.[52] This structure of feeling, illustrated in several of the stories in her collection *Mohawk Trail* (1985), registers dimensions and dynamics of peoplehood—embeddedness in a Mohawk "we"—that are not intelligible within either the framework of Indian policy (Canadian and U.S.) or the conception of native pedagogy/history Feinberg offers. The text develops ways of reimagining, in Reyna Ramirez's terms, Mohawk "cultural citizenship," shifting from a masculinist and statist notion of belonging predicated on being a resident subject within a state-determined jurisdictional space to a conception of networks of relation that "determine what constitutes authentic notions of culture, community, and identity" (125). Despite not being permanent occupants of legally recognized native landbases, indigenous persons in the city still participate in peoplehood, emphasizing their "strong rooted connection to tribe and homeland" and "extend[ing] the sense of territory" to encompass both urban and reservation sites as part of a more capacious vision of "Indian country."[53] Such a remapping of urbanity and indigeneity works against both the reification of the reservation/reserve as the only "authentic" place for native life, a perspective that elides the dislocating effects of structural underdevelopment, and the narration of migration to the city as freedom from reserves for individual families, which presents "melt[ing] them into the cities" as a method for the government of "terminating its trust responsibility."[54] In addition to drawing attention to the ways the settler state's ongoing management of reservation economies incentivizes diaspora, Brant's stories present native people(s) less as queer-friendly foils to dominant ideologies of gender and sexual normality than as themselves the subjects of forms of heteronormative regulation that work to dismember and erase indigeneity through the imposition of nuclear hetero-homemaking.[55] These texts link dominant ideologies of homemaking to the broader project of detribalization while illustrating how a continued commitment to Mohawk peoplehood pushes against the privatized isolation of the conjugal household.

The autobiographical story "Mohawk Trail" traces how Brant's extended familial relations provide an ongoing sense of connection to legally recognized Mohawk territory, which comes to infuse and remake the city as itself Mohawk space. It begins not with Brant's birth but with a place-based genealogy. Before introducing Brant's great-grandmother Eliza, the text observes, "There is a small body of water in Canada called the Bay of Quinte. Look for the three pine trees gnarled and entwined together. Woodland Indians, they call the people who live here. This is a reserve of Mohawks, the People of the Flint" (19). This initial reference to Tyendinaga, founded in the wake of the American Revolution by loyalist Mohawks, locates it as originary, or perhaps paradigmatic, as both the starting point and the frame for the lives of those about whom the story is written.[56] The persistent centrality of this space for the people and for the events yet to be addressed is signaled by the term "here" (as opposed to *there*), indicating that the narrative emerges from and continues to dwell within Tyendinaga rather than marking it as merely a spot to be left behind in the tale's movement or to be contrasted with the perspective from a different *here* at which the narrative will arrive and from which it principally speaks. The text's title further emphasizes this continuity by suggesting that the "trail" it will travel remains unambiguously "Mohawk," an identity linked to the reserve from the outset. However, the passage also describes Tyendinaga as "a reserve of Mohawks," and doing so subtly registers that while the Bay of Quinte will function as a home space—a point of reference for the characters and the text on which its imaginative geography is centered even when events are set elsewhere—it is not the exclusive location for Mohawk subjectivity or collectivity. *A* reserve implies both that there are other reserves and that Mohawk identity subsists wherever there are Mohawks present, creating a dialectical relationship in which territory over which Mohawks exert state-recognized sovereignty—reserves legally marked as such under Canadian and U.S. law—provide an anchor for dispersed spaces of residency elsewhere in that they remain linked as part of a larger formation with complex *trails* running among them. As James Clifford suggests, "there is an 'indigenous' specificity that eludes diaspora's emphasis on displacement, loss, and deferred desire for the homeland . . . The feeling that one has never left one's . . . ancestral home is strong, both as a lived reality and as a redemptive political myth" (212). By the time the text makes clear that the narrator is the descendant of women from this reserve, which happens within the first few paragraphs, it already has tied that lineage to Tyendinaga and an enduring sense of its "here"-ness for them. Bonds of kinship will signify as an index of belonging to a Mohawk "People"-hood that coheres in and around the reserves but exceeds them as well, "combin[ing] urban and rural life in a nationalistic continuum."[57]

In addition to connecting familial ties to a complex sense of place and political collectivity, the genealogy the text offers focuses less on lineal descent (or ascent from the narrator running backward in time) than on synchronous filiations within and across generations. While Brant discusses people who can be described as related to her by blood, she places the emphasis on their ongoing presence in each other's lives. Readers are told that Eliza's daughter Margaret married a man named Joseph, had nine children, and moved to Detroit, and Brant reveals the details of their lives, including her Uncle Doug's calls to them on Christmas and the careers of her aunts who had gone to college (19–20). These anecdotes bespeak ongoing proximity and emotional investment indicating not the divergence and distance from one's family of origin typical in dominant U.S. narratives of maturation (including in the coming-out structure of *Stone Butch Blues*) but a sustained connection among siblings who remain very much present to each other in quotidian ways. The fact that the story provides information on Brant's aunts and uncles before turning to her parents further illustrates that they cannot be relegated to a position as *extended* relatives—as merely ancillary to the nuclear ensemble that serves as the authentic basis for family. The text implicitly frames these bonds as aspects of peoplehood in its initial identification of Eliza as "a woman of the Turtle Clan," which given the matrilineal transmission of clan status would make Margaret one as well, and her husband is introduced as "of the Wolf Clan" (19). From the beginning, the characters are situated within Haudenosaunee kinship networks, which, as noted earlier in this chapter and more fully in chapter 1, provide the infrastructure for traditional governance and land tenure. The familial ties portrayed in the narrative gain meaning within this contextual frame, appearing as instantiations of clan dynamics even while occurring at a distance from Tyendinaga.[58]

Moreover, intergenerational conversation often tends back toward the reserve. While Brant's grandfather tried to teach her the Mohawk language until his death, a knowledge that attenuates in the absence of the density of speakers and regularity of usage the text implies would be available on the reserve, Brant's depiction of time with Margaret focuses on her persistent connection to Tyendinaga, observing that "she smelled like smoke and woods" and "ask[ing] her to tell me about the reserve" (21). Margaret's reminiscence dwells on her mother Eliza's "dreams of her family flying in the air, becoming seeds that sprouted on new ground" (21–22). Playing on the reproductive vision of sperm as the seed from which family grows, this image recasts Eliza as the locus of generative, matrilineal power while also recalling the earlier description of Tyendinaga as marked by "three pine trees" and Mohawks as "Woodland Indians" (19). Rather than indicating a conjugally centered unit, the figure of "family" references an expansive matrix shaped by clan membership that links the new space to the old, providing an essential continuity that enables the collective life of the reserve to grow and become rooted in the "ground" of the city.

The reasons provided for this movement gesture toward the ways settler policy shapes the political economy of the reserves, particularly how it creates conditions that propel migration away from legally acknowledged places of peoplehood and sovereignty. Margaret and Joseph decide to leave in order to secure "more opportunities" for their children (19), a phrase that seems to refer primarily to possibilities for formal schooling that will enable them to find jobs as professionals. Brant implies that the residents of the reserve did not have access to the kind of educational resources that would train them for high-waged work, also suggesting that such employment itself would be difficult to achieve in the vicinity of Tyendinaga. In subtly registering the diaspora created by the simultaneous stranglehold on native opportunities on reservation and government promotion of flight to the city, "Mohawk Trail" also indicates the failure of this strategy in breaking the bonds of peoplehood. Even as her father takes advantage of the greater possibilities for higher education afforded by presence in urban space, becoming a teacher who offers a class called "Indian History," "his dream was to teach on a reservation," a dream deferred by the "many debts from school" (21). Rather than being liberated from Mohawk identity by Euramerican training, he redirects the ends of education back toward the effort to sustain a distinct landbase, but this desire for return is frustrated by the very dynamics of state-orchestrated uneven development that created the conditions for migration in the first place.

The conditions on most reserves and reservations were shaped by decades of policy devoted more to containment and civilization than to developing a viable economy that would allow native peoples to function as distinct political entities while still participating in self-sustaining modes of production and trade with surrounding settler communities. In addition to cutting off peoples' primary forms of subsistence (in terms of hunting, traditional forms of agriculture, fishing, or existing exchange networks), Canada and the United States over the previous century had sought to diminish native landbases in favor of white occupancy, increasingly forcing indigenous people into the cash economy to provide for their basic necessities while structurally handicapping their efforts to provide for themselves. The migration of Brant's grandparents from Tyendinaga can be seen as resulting from these larger policy dynamics.[59] Originally founded in 1784 by loyalist Mohawks who left their settlement at Fort Hunter in order to remain aligned with the British and to evade U.S. reprisals for the war, the reserve slowly was whittled down over the next century from 14,000 square miles to only 17,000 acres. By the end of the nineteenth century, approximately 14 percent of the men were landless, the overall population having grown by a factor of ten since the founding (from about 100 to 1,000), and the arable land available for use had decreased by a factor of fifteen (about 92,000 to 6,000 acres). In addition to growing pressure to sell territory to satisfy settler demands once British immigration began in earnest after 1820, Mohawks on the reserve increasingly leased land to whites as a way of providing for themselves. To prevent warrior leaders from selling or claiming additional parcels, civil chiefs in 1835 instigated the state-sanctioned process of allotting the reserve in 200-acre units to each male head of a family, a decision that resembled similar strategies adopted while at Fort Hunter.

While seeking to forestall the wholesale loss or appropriation of reserve lands, the allotment did not solve the problem of extensive settler presence and a burgeoning timber industry, nor did it address how that presence disrupted subsistence and exchange patterns based on hunting as well as the ways population growth overwhelmed available resources on a shrinking landbase. To support themselves within a situation in which most reserve residents had fewer and fewer options short of simply leaving, an escalating number of families turned to leasing as a way of generating income, more than half of them by 1884. By the 1910s or 1920s, approximately when Brant's grandparents would have left for Detroit, at least one more generation had been born, intensifying the land shortage and further limiting the options for Mohawks trying to operate within an economy shaped by settler needs. While not necessarily actively providing funding for relocation to cities, the Canadian government continued to promote settler access to native resources and to constrain, if not outright prohibit, indigenous peoples' access to additional lands that could have ameliorated population crises on reserves.[60] Moreover, this artificial emergency created by inefficient, privatized, and corporate-friendly forms of land tenure was legitimized and animated by the claim that Indians were being introduced to civilization and eventually needed to be incorporated into it in order to become full citizens and participants in the march of progress. In fact, prior to 1961, a condition of enfranchisement as a Canadian citizen was the loss of one's legal status as an Indian, along with official membership in one's people (or "band")—a choice, however, available only to men. Although in Canada there was no allotment program per se, and thus no legal checkerboarding of non-native ownership on reserves, there was the same imperative toward detribalization and idealization of the nuclear family as the natural building block of social order (especially as enshrined in the Indian Act in ways discussed below).

In the context of termination, however, the United States did subsidize urbanization, replicating many of the broader forces that spurred indigenous diaspora in Canada while also providing direct federal funding for it. As noted earlier, the federal government shifted in the late 1940s into a policy philosophy that would come to be known as termination, prioritizing the end of federal funding to Indians, the transfer of jurisdiction over tribes and reservations to the states, and the eventual dismantling of tribes as legally recognized entities. Within this larger context, Commissioner of Indian Affairs Dillon S. Myer, who previously had overseen the internment of people of Japanese descent during World War II, created the Branch of Placement and Relocation in the BIA in 1951; its purpose was to facilitate Indian migration off-reservation to several targeted cities, including Chicago, Los Angeles, and Denver.[61] In order to address the impoverishment produced by the ongoing expropriation of native resources and exploitation of cheap native labor near reserves/reservations, the United States helped subsidize displacement, continuing the project of detribalization while repackaging it as an effort to liberate populations from an enforced dependency. The program involved providing relocates, usually men, with a one-way bus ticket to a city that had a field office and food and housing expenses for a month, either bringing (some of) his family—meaning wife and children—with him or with the idea that he could send for them once he was settled and gainfully employed. Later, under the Indian Vocational Training Act of 1957, centers were set up near reservations to provide skills necessary to be hired in selected kinds of jobs, although not necessarily ones that were prevalent near tribal homelands or in the cities to which they either would be sent or had the easiest access. These jobs usually had little possibility for advancement, and funding was not provided for Indians to get degrees beyond high school. With the addition of this component, the BIA was able to rename its efforts to produce migration off reservation from the "relocation program," which had gotten a significant amount of unfavorable coverage in mainstream media, to "employment assistance," recasting the incentivizing of diaspora within a terminationist agenda as the promotion of native welfare through upward mobility.

While from 1940 to 1960 more than 120,000 people left reservations for cities, only about 31,000 of them received federal assistance for the move, suggesting that the official relocation program cannot explain, or entirely be blamed for, the phenomenon.[62] However, the American Indian Policy Review Commission in its report in 1976 on the status of nonreservation Indians found not only that relocation was "used by the Government as a method of terminating its trust responsibility" (7), but that "Indian people in substantial numbers came to urban areas because of a lack of employment in addition to other social and economic problems existing on the reservation" (2). Thus, "for many Indians there was no other choice" than to leave the reservation, and "whether relocated by the BIA program or on their own, the emergence of migrated Indians in sizable numbers off the reservation is not a sign that they have chosen to be assimilated" (29). The cost of relocation from 1953 to 1960 came to almost $15 million, well over three times the amount allocated for credit to reservation projects under reorganization despite the claim that terminationist policies would decrease government spending on Indian affairs.[63] The privileging of relocation as a funding priority is symptomatic of a broader structural pattern of underdeveloping reservation economies, directing resources toward fracturing native communities, dispersing them as individual families into disparate urban settings (both within and among cities) that militated against maintaining tribal bonds, and almost entirely ceasing to extend services to them once they became generic citizens in urban space.

Since Tyendinaga falls under Canadian jurisdiction, Brant's family was not subject to the vicissitudes of U.S. termination policy, except inasmuch as there would not be federal resources available to native people in Detroit until the early 1970s, by which point Brant was in her early 30s.[64] While the nuclear imaginary that gave form to settler policy also provides the conceptual structure for envisioning relocation/urbanization, the very kinds of domestication privileged within that system appear in "Mohawk Trail" as sites of opposition to ideologies of privatization in which Mohawk sovereignty is maintained through memory. Brant observes, "After marrying white men, my aunts retired their jobs" (20), suggesting acquiescence to the kind of patriarchally led conjugality idealized in Indian policy as the aim of civilizing progress. Further, within a racializing frame in which Indianness is a quality passed in the blood (as addressed most extensively in chapter 1), the aunts' coupling with white men indicates an assimilationist trajectory in which nativeness will be diminished over the generations, dissolving into a sea of white majoritarian urbanity. However, rather than simply taking up normative roles as proper wives and mothers in the privatized household, her aunts "became secret artists, putting up huge amounts of quilts, needlework, and beadwork in the fruit cellars"; "when husbands and children slept," they would steal away to work on their creations, "By day the dutiful wife. By night, sewing and beading their souls into beauty that will be left behind after death, telling the stories of who these women were" (20–21). Basements become places that point back toward the reserve, or at least serve as generative spaces for kinds of practices that are envisioned as more prominent on the reserve and that contribute to the transmission of "stories" which embed the women's individual identities in a larger Mohawk collectivity—a native "we." Her aunts' preservation of aspects of Mohawk culture gains significance within the text's framing of them as "seeds" from Tyendinaga, implicitly representing their art as both linking them to the reserve and making a Mohawk place out of the city.

As opposed to Feinberg's portrayal of Haudenosaunee songs as a medium of inclusion and affirmation for non-natives, Brant's discussion of her aunts situates their activity within an expansive geography of peoplehood in which the constricted space of the basement—a figure for the limits of nuclear homemaking—appears as a single site in a chain that sustains Mohawk collectivity across the urban/reserve divide. Despite their apparent isolation, they each reenact traditions that link them to each other, to the generations of Mohawk women that preceded them, as well as to those women engaged in the same activities at Tyendinaga and other reserves in the present. Additionally, Brant's knowledge of these items and forms of artistic production suggest that she was a recipient of her aunts' stories. That awareness further positions her narrative—in its storytelling—as another version of the traditional work her aunts performed, one that draws on media more available to those in the city (access to the print public sphere) but that marks less an alienation from the reserve than a different kind of "trail" back to it. The text's remembering of Brant's aunts, then, functions as a way of marking the continued "here"-ness of Tyendinaga for Brant even though she remains in Detroit, "on new ground."

The text indicates, though, that all Margaret's children "married white," observing that Brant herself is "half-blood," with a Mohawk father and Anglo mother (19), and within a matrilineal kinship system, as with Ruth in *Stone Butch Blues*, having a non-Mohawk mother means not belonging to one of the clans and thus not being Mohawk. However, the narrative indicates that Brant's relatives clearly understand her to be Mohawk: her uncle asks her and her cousins at Christmas, "Were you good little Indians or bad little Indians" (19); her grandfather teaches her the Mohawk language; and her grandmother tells her tales of the reserve.[65] One difference between Ruth's (albeit imaginary) status and Brant's is the discrepant jurisdictional structures of Canadian and U.S. Indian policy. The latter provides for some flexibility in tribal determinations of membership, with the Senecas using matrilineality as the basis, whereas Canadian policy is predicated on a single statute—the Indian Act originally passed in 1868. Under the terms of an amendment added in 1876 and not rescinded until 1985, and thus still in force when Brant was born in 1941, non-native women who married native men gained status as band members for themselves and their children with those men, whereas native women who married non-native men lost status for themselves and their children.[66] Within this legal logic, Brant officially had status at Tyendinaga, but her aunts and their children did not. Although the story does not directly refer to the provisions or effects of the Indian Act, the dynamics the law entrenched provide a context that legally legitimizes Brant's identity as Mohawk and helps explain the circumstances that would prevent her aunts' return to Tyendinaga. Her father could dream of teaching on the reserve, but due to the gendered structures of Canadian Indian policy at the time, his sisters could not. Thus, patriarchal conjugality served as the official frame for sovereignty at the reserve and for displacement from it.

Rather than accepting state-orchestrated definitions of nativeness, though, Brant highlights women-centered self-understandings as the framework for Mohawk identity. She foregrounds clan belonging and the kinship ties it produces as the basis for the trail that connects her to the reserve, and in citing the clan system, she adopts nonstatist criteria as the grounds for identification as part of a Mohawk "we" and leaves open the possibility for adoption within it (such as by Margaret, who functions as a de facto clan mother for Brant's relatives).[67] As scholarship on various forms of queer diaspora has suggested, normative sexuality often serves as the condition for belonging to the new nation, which puts pressure on migrants to be respectable, while also influencing the terms of citizenship in the old nation, which seeks to be seen as respectable within the international system,[68] and Brant's refusal to define Mohawk identity in ways consistent with the settler policy at play on the reserve functions as opposition to the normalization of heter-opatriarchy in both the Indian Act and official modes of Mohawk nation-alism predicated on it. The story closes with Margaret's lesson/warning for Brant, "Don't forget who you are. Don't ever leave your family. They are what matters" (22). Unlike in the conventional coming-out structure in which identity and collectivity are achieved only through separation from one's rel-atives, the figure of "family" here speaks to the persistence of Mohawk self-representations and modes of sociality organized around kinship bonds that also tie one to a politicized sense of place. Although not addressing the legal discourse of sovereignty, the narrative emphasizes the ongoing connection to Tyendinaga and the ways the exigencies of economic distress and depri-vation that produce diaspora do not negate that relation, instead reconstitut-ing the city as a "new ground" of indigeneity in the perpetuation of those bonds.[69] In this way, the text details what can be described as a Mohawk structure of feeling that refuses a detribalizing nuclear imaginary which both produces and facilitates relocation, instead sustaining a "practical con-sciousness" of sovereignty in ways at odds with the "official consciousness" of Indian policy.[70]

"Mohawk Trail," however, does not address homosexuality per se and its significance in the context of the familial dynamics the story charts. In "A Simple Act," the final piece in the collection, Brant focuses on her intersec-tional experience as an urban native lesbian in ways that indicate the conti-nuities between homophobia and settler imperialism as parts of an encompassing heteronormative system.[71] The title phrase is used most di-rectly to describe the traditional fashioning of gourds into objects for house-hold use: "A simple act—requiring lifetimes to learn" (87). This reference frames the text as itself an effort to make usable Brant's own past, "carving and scooping" memory in ways that make it serviceable for "invent[ing] new from the old" (87–88). One of the central issues with which the story struggles is what is to be discarded or forgotten in this process, or more pre-cisely, what are the competing logics of value that shape possibilities for forging livable subjectivities.[72] Split into two stories of Brant's childhood, one of her desire for a neighbor girl and the other of a fire in her house, the text juxtaposes them so as to highlight the dynamics of isolation and con-demnation that haunt queer and Indian lives, tracing their potentially toxic influence on individual and collective self-understanding while also sug-gesting that an archaeology of abjection—"dredg[ing] for ghosts" (88)—can provide tools for an oppositional (re)visioning. Yet rather than sketching an analogy between native and sexual identities, Brant explores their complex enmeshment, such that one cannot serve simply as a somewhat hollowed-out figure for the other.

The first story in the text recalls Brant's relationship with Sandra, a Russian immigrant with whom she has her first sexual connection. From the outset, though, it contextualizes their closeness through an account of their alienation from those around them: "We had much in common. Our families were large and sloppy. We occupied places of honor due to our fair skin and hair. Assimilation separated us from our ancient and inherited places of home" (88). Their affection for each other emerges not out of a recognition of their mutual estrangement from dominant forms of gender and/or sexuality but out of the similarity in their diasporic distance from another place of "home." That fact produces quotidian emotional disturbances, registered in the depiction of their families as "large and sloppy" and the privileging of their "fair"-ness. Having failed to meet nuclear expectations, their households appear to them as excessive and undisciplined, threatening to rupture the privatized, insulated space of normative domesticity, and the explanation of this supposed unmanageability as a function of a racialized propensity toward disorder has been internalized as an idealization of lightness—symptomatic of the role "assimilation" plays in remapping psychic landscapes of value. The content and force of Brant and Sandra's increasing emotional attachment to each other remains inseparable from the multiple forms of dislocation they share: "We were girls from an undiscovered country. We were alien beings in families that were 'different.' Different among the different" (88). The growing intimacy and eroticism of their relationship signifies less as simply a deviation from their families than a compounding of patterns of "alien"-ation in which their understanding of the difference homoeroticism generates between them and their families emerges out of an existing awareness of the dangers of being "different" from a racialized, nuclear norm. The spatialization of this sensation ("an undiscovered country") recalls their position within diasporic geographies and indicates that their incipient desire is embedded within the experience of cultural and geopolitical displacement, drawing on a metaphor of discovery while inverting its usual valence by making non-native Detroit into the site of exploration.

While in some ways following a conventional narrative of queer maturation, the events that follow remain permeated by the stresses and stakes of "assimilation." As adolescents, they engage in erotic play, which the text suggests is central to Brant's emergent sense of herself and her body. "In the sixth and seventh grades our blood started to flow, our breasts turned into a reality of sweet flesh and waiting nipples. The place between our thighs filled with a wanting so tender, an intensity of heat from which our fingers emerged, shimmering with liquid energy, our bodies spent with the expression of our growing strength" (89). Orgasm generates both "energy" and a "growing strength," her sexual experiences with Sandra creating a powerful

kind of affirmation that can fortify her against the alienating effects of multilayered forms of *difference*.[73] When they are observed by a neighbor and he
tells their mothers, they are forbidden from seeing each other. The informant is described as "the boy next door" (89), suggestive not only of the
dominant ideology of heterosexual courtship as the proper trajectory of
individual growth but of a vision of all-American romance. This characterization condenses the relation between heteronormativity and belonging in
the space of the city, suggesting a double bind of surveillance in which the
girls are monitored for signs of development toward properly straight subjectivity while their families are judged for their ability to guide the girls in
this process as part of assessing their broader capability to integrate into
dominant patterns of sociality. In order to maintain the "morality of the
family," itself continually under suspicion by those "next door," both girls are
punished, the purpose of which was to "restor[e] us once again to our
rightful places" (89). These measures—"the belt marks, the silences, and the
shame" (89)—not only are calculated to reinsert them in their rightful position within a heterogendered model of desire but also to ward off the families' fears about already appearing out of place—the challenges to "morality"
posed by their excessive and "sloppy" performance of domesticity. As discussed in chapters 3 and 4, the bribe of straightness operates here as a possibility for (limited) acceptance of other kinds of familial and household
deviance if native people will disown explicit queerness, such as homoeroticism, and as a threat of further discipline should they not do so. The imperatives of compulsory heterosexuality operate with particular force on those
subjects whose presence already seems questionable and whose forms of
kinship and residency are viewed as signs of (racial) pathology.

The logic of heteroconjugal privatization that drives this abjection of
Brant's lesbianism also shapes the contours for normative memory. She says
of her relationship with Sandra, "our friendship was put away, locked up
inside our past" (89), making the past into a kind of carceral space in which
to enclose and detain that which is not fit for others to know. This depiction
resembles the image of the closet in which membership in a sexual minority
remains hidden, and in this vein, the aim of renarrating the past is to
reimagine it in ways that make possible the inventing of a space for sexual
identity out of the old silences and shame. However, the text also speaks of
native identity in similar terms. Brant observes, "In our house we spoke the
language of censure. Sentences stopped in the middle, The mixture of a
supposed-to-be-forgotten Mohawk, strangled with uneasy English" (91).
She then lists the various "secrets" she, her siblings, and her cousins inherited, including her uncle's alcohol-related death, her grandmother's trepidation at leaving the house due to verbal assaults by non-natives who call her
"dumb Indian" or "squaw," and her grandfather's early death from heart

disease traceable to "the poverty of food" available to him on the reserve as a child. The cumulative effect of these secrets is the feeling of being "shamed": "We didn't fit. We didn't belong" (92). Their experience as native people needed to be closed off, privatized, sealed unspoken into a personal and familial interiority. That process appears as an effort to render themselves generic, to downplay their difference from neighbors, schoolmates, and coworkers.

Unlike the hollowing-out of the gourds for use, this pursuit of belonging among non-natives threatens to empty them of a sense of peoplehood, which will be replaced by a self-destructive internalization of others' racist sentiments and perception of native people as lack—the absence of intelligence, culture, respectability. In *Our Elders Lived It*, a study of native life in an upper Great Lakes city she calls "Riverside," Deborah Davis Jackson observes that Indian parents' elliptical responses to their children's questions about both reservation life and examples of urban racism are the result of "trauma": "their parents' silences are transformed from absences into powerful presences . . . filled with a cacophony of competing messages—a mix of pride and shame, acceptance and rejection, whispering of something lost but not saying what it is" (113). Following on the discussion of the disciplining she and Sandra received for their attraction and intimacy, Brant's depiction of native shame resonates with the paradigm of the closet. In this way, it creates the potential for identification by non-native queers with the difficulties faced by diasporic Mohawks; articulates native experiences of homophobia to those of racism, refusing to see them as antagonistic or to interpret the former as irrelevant with respect to the latter; and suggests that these forms of oppression are not merely analogous but actually intertwined within an encompassing system that deploys multiple modes of pathologization.

Moreover, following the lead of queer analyses of shame, one can read Brant's experience of not "belong"-ing due to her Indianness as not simply a feeling to be excised or erased, to be supplanted by pride, for example. Rather, shame in the text appears as a trace of a felt nativeness that itself indexes kinds of belonging and identification which are intelligible only as racial deficit within settler (hetero)normativity.[74] From this perspective, the project of reworking the past involves not only combating the charge of perversity but reconnecting individual subjectivity to peoplehood in ways that provide a broader array of tools from which to "invent new" in the space of the city. Brant characterizes this process as "[b]alancing always, our life among the assimilators and our life of memory" (91), later adding, "Out of a past where amnesia was the expected. / Out of a past occupied with quiet. / Out of a past, I make truth for a future" (93). Through memory, the "secrets we held to ourselves," which had been "swallowed" (91), come to be understood not as innate to Indianness, an inherent emptiness filled with shame, but instead as parts of a larger history from which an alternative "truth" can be forged if one differently "carve[s] and scoop[s]" the past.

The text's portrayal of the fire in Brant's childhood household explores this respatialization of memory and its implications for challenging punishing and regulatory ideologies of privatization. She recalls:

> One night in August 1954, a fire in the basement.
> Things burned.
> Secret things.
> Indian things.
> Things the neighbors never saw.
> False Faces. Beaded necklaces. Old letters written in Mohawk. A turtle rattle.
> Corn husks.
> Secrets brought from home.
> Secrets protecting us in hostile places. (92)

The "secret"-ing of "Indian things" away from the judging eyes of non-natives replays the dynamics of the closet, including the neighbors' "anxious [desire] to not know" what was lost in the blaze—a settler version of the open secret in which sanctioned ignorance of the presence of homosexuality helps support compulsory heterosexuality through the presumption of straightness.[75] Here, though, there is the added connotation of being buried in the earth, as if interred. This image captures the essence of Colonel Richard Henry Pratt's injunction to "kill the Indian, save the man," the emphasis in official endorsements of allotment, relocation, and urbanization on the death of "Indian" identity as the condition for full membership in settler society.[76] However, like the discussion of the artistic work of Brant's aunts in "Mohawk Trail," the portrayal of the basement as a hidden space of tradition pushes against the notion of the familial household as an isolated unit, a space in which the "morality of the family" fits the contours of the neighbors' expectations. The "sloppy"-ness noted in the first part of "A Simple Act" is complemented in the second by an additional kind of excess. Breaching the boundaries of heteronormative domesticity, the things that burned reach back toward the reserve, marking it as "home," and by contrast, the city appears less as an emancipatory place than a "hostile" one.

Altering the prior association of "secrets" with shamed silence about the effects of heterosexism and racism, an internalized fear, loathing, and self-surveillance, the text recasts them as signs of an alternative spatiality. The isolating, pathologized interiority created by "being locked up inside our past" gives way to a new mapping: abject individual subjectivity is situated within broader networks of connection, which are sustained through the very beliefs/practices—the "secrets"—disavowed as deviant within the frame of normative nuclearity. While the loss of these items is devastating, Brant tracing the deaths of both her grandparents to their melancholy in the wake of the fire (92–93), the link to Tyendinaga and to peoplehood the "things" represented has not disappeared. If the fire serves as symbol of the larger assault on native identity and sovereignty ("Cultures gone up in flames"), Brant presents her recollection of it as a way of reconstructing not simply her individual past but her place within an expansive Mohawk geography— "filling the spaces where memory fails" (94). Her response to silence and shame is less to *come out* as native than to renarrate the networks in which she already is enmeshed. While her writing takes tradition out of the basement and puts it into circulation in the non-native public sphere, it involves not a declaration of suppressed identity that marks her as a member of a new collectivity but a working through of the trauma of dislocation from "home" and the force of "assimilation" condensed in the loss of artifacts in the fire.

Put another way, although the fire can be read as figuratively indicative of endangered Mohawk identity, it, and the emotional wounds it inflicted (particularly on Brant's grandparents), can be taken literally as evidence of how the privatization of indigeneity—its constriction as a set of cultural items contained within the individual household—makes peoplehood precarious precisely because it becomes objectified and cut off from a wider circulation that could make it less vulnerable to decimation. In this vein, the creation and publication of the story memorializes the specific grief from this event, and the ways it testifies to the dangers of Mohawk diaspora, while also positioning feelings and memory as a basis for (re)creating Mohawk networks, with the print public sphere serving as a vehicle for revitalizing and expanding on an already existing matrix of peoplehood. Within this frame, her relationship with Sandra can be reconceptualized: it is less merely a deviation from the "rightful place" of women as wives for "the boy[s] next door" than a powerful connection among women (a source of "strength") that, especially when considered in light of earlier stories in the collection like "Mohawk Trail," resonates with traditional matrilineality as against the ideal of patriarchal conjugality toward which Brant was forced. Her self-designation as "a woman lover" comes to appear as an extension of "the seemingly ordinary things that women do," such as carving gourds (90, 94), contextualizing her lesbianism within a commitment to a version of Mohawk sovereignty not structured by the terms or imperatives of settler policy and in which women's cultural work and desires are given priority.

Rather than calling for an affirmation of individual identity, "A Simple Act" situates Brant's sexuality within a struggle to make the city more like "home" and to challenge the heteronormative imperatives of "assimilation." They are shown to produce multivectored forms of shame that displace possibilities for other kinds of sociality not predicated on the heterogendered, privatized household. Resisting that model appears in Brant's work as a precondition for recognizing modes of native belonging in the city, and this critique of straightness also helps mark the ways that the state-sanctioned dispersal of native people from their landbases has failed to complete the process of detribalization, instead creating new and more expansive geographies of indigeneity. Reciprocally, she ties her sense of self, including her lesbianism and her work as a writer, to her participation in Mohawk peoplehood, "picking up trails I left so many lives ago" (94). In *Writing as Witness*, Brant argues, "homophobia is the eldest son of racism and one does not exist without the other. Our community suffers from both—externally and internally" (77). The parallelism between the two stories in "A Simple Act" indicates this sense of interdependence among forms of oppression and the need for forms of political consciousness and organizing that do not efface or minimize the one in the struggle against the other, predicating solidarity on simultaneous, integrated efforts to combat both as part of the broader project of strengthening native community(/ies).

Brant's texts trace affective dimensions of peoplehood—the silence of shame, the remembrance of the ongoing trauma of settlement, the sustaining matrix of kinship ties, the remaking of tradition and connection to a native landbase for everyday use in diaspora. In doing so, her stories implicitly refuse the gesture by which this indigenous archive of feelings is accessed by non-natives to thicken their own sense of collectivity or historicity.[77] That process is one of appropriation masquerading as alliance, and it requires the recasting of indigeneity as a version of Indianness—a porous and mobile (set of) figure(s) available for non-native use in legitimizing their counterhegemonic political projects. Critiquing *Stone Butch Blues* along these lines is useful not because the novel is overly simplistic, naive, or unreflexive in its imagining of struggle(s) for social justice. Instead, the text offers fearlessly intersectional and systemic modes of critique, refuses an easy symmetry between identity and community, and demonstrates an unyielding commitment to centering the experiences and organizing strategies of working-class and poor people. Its multifaceted richness is precisely what makes notable its enactment of what I have described as a settler structure of feeling—the ways the novel positions native people as an emotional resource for movements whose goals are neither defined by nor directed toward them. More than simply exoticizing Indians or straightforwardly recycling the narrative of them as vanishing/vanished, Feinberg presents still-existing indigenous beliefs, practices, and celebrations (like the powwow) as vital to hir ways of conceptualizing broad-based resistance to a heteronormative, racist, and exploitative social system, foregrounding the value of nativeness in (re)formulating a notion of *union*. Yet, as in reorganization, native *culture* and *community* are dissociated from indigenous self-representations.

If native nationality provides a canvas on which to sketch a history of the existence of gender and sexual minorities, providing a lesson about the importance of inclusion for contemporary movements, what happens to the contours and content of indigenous peoplehood? If the Senecas are seen as serving a pedagogical function for settlers, teaching them about accepting queerness, is there still a concern for the violation of treaties in the construction of the Kinzua Dam and the extension of state jurisdiction over Haudenosaunee peoples? Is there an awareness generated of the consequences of ideologies of termination and relocation for the particular peoples on whom Feinberg focuses? In "The Prose of Counter-Insurgency," Ranajit Guha notes that a certain kind of leftist history narrates the past of anticolonial opposition in India as the emergence of the nation such that "the rebel has no place in this history as the subject of rebellion" (71). Similarly, as suggested by Beth Brant's work, a kind of queer solidarity that cannot engage with indigenous collective subjectivities—on reservation, in the city, and in the complex relays among them—ends up recapitulating the terms of assimilation, normalizing settlement as the de facto frame for political analysis and, thereby, disabling discussion of the ongoing role of heteronormativity as a vital feature of settler imperialism.

6

Tradition and the Contemporary Queer

Sexuality, Nationality, and History in Drowning in Fire

On May 13, 2004, two Cherokee women, Kathy Reynolds and Dawn McKinley, sought and received a marriage license from the deputy court clerk of the Cherokee Nation. They were the first to take advantage of the fact that the Cherokee legal code defined marriage in gender-neutral terms. By May 14, the Chief Judge of the Cherokee Judicial Appeals Tribunal had ordered a thirty-day hold on the issuing of further licenses to same-sex couples, and three days later, in a unanimous vote, the Cherokee Tribal Council officially changed the legal code, closing the door to other gay and lesbian couples. In an effort to prevent a similar struggle in the Navajo Nation, the Navajo Council preemptively passed a law on April 22, 2005, defining marriage as the union of a man and a woman.[1] While clearly reflecting the trend in federal and state law of explicitly heterosexualizing the institution of marriage, a movement that was given powerful impetus by the Federal Defense of Marriage Act (1996) and that snowballed in the lead-up to the 2004 presidential election,[2] the Cherokee and Navajo governments justified their actions not as an attempt to bring the nations into alignment with emerging U.S. legal norms but instead as an effort to preserve tribal customs. The General Counsel for the Cherokee Nation indicated as part of his petitions to the court that "same sex marriages were not a part of Cherokee history or tradition" and that accepting the validity of Reynolds and McKinley's license "would fly in the face of the traditional definition and understanding of marriage of the Cherokee people." The sponsor of the Navajo bill, Larry Anderson, described the law's goal as "strengthen[ing] traditional Navajo values."[3]

Those who resisted the gendered constriction of marriage made parallel arguments. McKinley and Reynolds characterized the resistance to their marriage as "rooted in cultural and historic ignorance" of the actual dynamics "of a once brilliant culture that embraced freedom of choice for the individual in all aspects of his or her personal life," and Navajo President Joe Shirley Jr., over whose veto the law was passed, observed that "the legislation veiled a discriminatory aspect in the guise of family values, which goes against the Navajo teaching of non-discrimination and doing no psychological or physical harm."[4] Thus, tradition serves as the discursive terrain on which both proponents and opponents of same-sex marriage in tribal nations are moving, each side claiming to be the proper inheritor of the people's honored past and most cherished principles and each implicitly casting its position as a defense against the erosion produced by ongoing imperial intrusion.

The choice by some native governments to interpret queer couplings as an encroachment on their integrity as peoples raises the question of the degree to which sovereignty itself is becoming, or has become, intimately entwined with ideologies of straightness.[5] In *This Is Not a Peace Pipe*, Dale Turner notes, "We cannot hope to fully understand the meaning and content of Aboriginal rights without understanding first how colonialism has been woven into the normative political language that guides contemporary . . . legal and political practices" (30). Following this logic, the discussion of queer (im)possibilities within tribal law cannot be separated from analysis of the ways the United States' imperial control over the definition and management of political identity in Indian country shapes the options available to native governments and the stakes of their policy decisions. Turner further observes, "Phrases like 'traditional knowledge' and 'indigenous ways of knowing' have become commonplace . . . , yet we are not at all clear about what they mean *in relation to the legal and political discourses of the dominant culture*" (98). The citation of *tradition* can serve as a way of legitimizing governmental choices and strategies by rooting them in forms of authority separate from the framework of U.S. jurisdiction, but such an invocation does not itself make clear the complex *relation* between native modes of governance and official self-representation and the ideological and institutional structures of the settler state. If the Cherokee and Navajo national governments defend the outlawing of same-sex marriage as an imperative of tradition, in what ways might that depiction be overdetermined by the "normative political language" of the U.S. nation-state? In chapters 3 and 4, I explored the relation between straightness and sovereignty, more specifically how native peoples are subjected to the demand that they signify citizenship (whether to the United States or tribal nations) in terms of a heteronormative standard. Moreover, I have argued that a *bribe of straightness* functions as a way of calling for native intellectuals and communities to signify indigenous tradition in ways that make it appear less *queer*—that divorce it from what are taken to be forms of gender and sexual perversity. How might queer critique make more legible that dynamic, highlighting the ways straightness is "woven" into U.S. policy's production of political legiti-macy and thereby opening room for a broader genealogy of imperial efforts to constrain, regulate, and disavow native ways of being?

Craig Womack's novel *Drowning in Fire* (2001) takes up this question, exploring how an investigation of queer experience can open onto an accounting of the historic and ongoing imperial project of reorganizing Mus-cogee peoplehood.[6] Unlike many of the authors discussed earlier, the novel neither seeks to draw on native culture to construct a queer subjectivity nor attempts to contest detribalization while still privileging a version of romance that will make tradition palatable to Christian sensibilities. In my discussion of Zitkala-Ŝa and Ella Deloria, I described the latter strategy as a response to the bribe of straightness, native peoples gaining traction for nonnuclear ver-sions of home and family by disavowing nonheterogendered forms of desire and identity (like the winkte). Womack refuses that bribe, instead fore-grounding homoeroticism among the Creek people in the early and late twentieth century in ways that emphasize how identification with straight-ness is enmeshed in the continuing legacy of the civilization program and allotment. While not responding to the issue of same-sex marriage per se, given that it was published before the actions of the Cherokee Nation and the Navajo Nation and that the Creek Nation already had a similar statute,[7] the novel can be understood as reconfiguring the discourse of tradition by illu-minating how it has been reconceived and edited in response to the pressure to conform to U.S.-endorsed forms of sociality and subjectivity.[8]

If the rhetoric of "tradition" is a key part of contemporary governance within Indian nations, the novel's narration of intratribal homophobia as itself a result of the history of imperial intervention mounts a powerful counterhegemonic challenge, working toward not simply including LGBT, queer, and two-spirit-identified persons as part of their peoples but reimag-ining native nationalisms by tracking how compulsory heterosexuality helps naturalize the foreclosure of modes of collective identity not sanc-tioned by Indian law and policy. Like Beth Brant's work, discussed in the previous chapter, Womack's narrative seeks to contextualize homophobia within the project of tracking the ongoing violence of settlement and "heal[ing] our broken Nations."[9] However, while Brant focuses on her and her family's experience of dislocation and the *trails* connecting urban life back to legally recognized Mohawk land, Womack offers a greater historio-graphic sweep, tracking how contemporary forms of homophobia (from natives and non-natives alike) are embedded in patterns of settler-indigenous conflict over native peoples' autonomy that reach back to at least the allotment period. In his pathbreaking scholarly study, *Red on Red: Native American Literary Separatism*, Womack claims the term "queer" "because it acknowledges the importance of cultural differences and the usefulness of maintaining those differences rather than simply submitting to dominant-culture norms" (301). Put another way, by drawing into question the obviousness and ubiquity of straightness, Womack's queering of Creek tradition challenges other commonsensical notions of nationalism, developing a structure of feeling that highlights possibilities for social representation and self-representation—Creek differences—that have been targeted for eradication by U.S. ideologies.[10]

Drowning in Fire articulates the present and past to each other in ways that make clear that the text's aims extend far beyond the construction of Creek-specific forms of queer identity. Oscillating between the story of a burgeoning love affair between two Creek boys/men, Josh and Jimmy, in the 1970s and 1990s and the struggles for native independence surrounding Oklahoma statehood, ratified in 1907, the novel continually contextualizes queer desire not as a challenge to tribal belonging but as part of a long history of resistance to imperial efforts to destroy Creek peoplehood, tracking the relation between heteronormativity and the U.S. regulation of political legitimacy. The attempt to disavow or disown queerness, then, is thematized as an extension of the broader project of rendering invisible aspects of native culture and governance that do not fit U.S. national narratives, and reciprocally, those characters cast as most knowledgeable about Muscogee history and traditions are the ones most comfortable with the presence of homoeroticism in Creek communities.

In this way, the novel presents itself as a corrective to the macrological and micrological distortions produced by the ongoing legacy of imperial intervention. It offers a counterhistory that in refusing the unspeakability of Indian queerness, while showing the process through which it is made so, illustrates how the enforcement of sexual normality has been and continues to be inextricable from the broader program of inserting native peoples into, in Turner's phrase, "the normative political language" of the settler state. Yet, in positioning history as a form of opposition to the legacy of U.S. policy, *Drowning in Fire* differs from the uses of history in Catharine Sedgwick and Leslie Feinberg's work, discussed in chapters 2 and 5. They invoke a history of native presence as a way educating non-natives about unrealized possibilities for public imagination and mobilization, but they do so in ways that leave aside the self-determination of native peoples as peoples. By contrast, Womack foregrounds the relation between contesting sexual normalization and reconceptualizing and invigorating Creek sovereignty. As Womack suggests in *Red on Red*, "Extending the discussion of sovereignty beyond the legal realm to include the literary realm opens up the oral tradition to be read contemporarily by tribal nations so that definitions of sovereignty, which come from the oral tradition, might be used as a model for building nations in a way that revises, modifies, or rejects, rather than accepts as a model, the European and American nation" (60). By resituating figures of Christian theology—particularly water, snakes, and fire—within Creek oral tradition, the text destigmatizes homoeroticism, interrogates the assumptions about home and family undergirding Euramerican-style sovereignty, and traces the multidimensional force employed in extending that regime of national normality over native peoples. Rather than focusing on sites of policy-making, though, Womack explores how the ideologies of U.S. policy become part of everyday consciousness, examining the ways intersecting state-sanctioned visions of politics, property, privacy, and perversity have reordered and constrained Creeks' understanding of themselves. The novel's strategies for destabilizing—or queering—the seemingly obvious import of culturally freighted images work to open room for envisioning alternative models of sovereignty. In this way, it conveys the violence of U.S. intrusion, the transformative power of desire, and the ability of Creek storytelling to reimagine the scope and spaces of peoplehood in ways that promote self-determination.

WATER

Beth Brant suggests, "The exorcisms that the christian church has conducted over us have not worked."[11] The civilization, allotment, and Indian education programs, as discussed in previous chapters, illustrate how the U.S. government has sought to enforce Christian heteronuclearity as the structuring principle of social order, constructing and regulating zones of privacy in order to produce a social landscape denuded of forms of collectivity that could contest expansionism and capitalist development. *Drowning in Fire* historicizes the dissemination of such Christian ideology among the Creeks, presenting it as enmeshed in detribalizing U.S. policy initiatives. Through its central tropes, the novel explores the ways the conceptualization of homoeroticism as personal perversity and sin is an imperial inheritance that both enacts and effaces the broader assault on Creek peoplehood. By utilizing religiously charged Christian imagery while reframing it and rechanneling it, Womack recasts the personal experience of demonized queer desire as part of a shared legacy of attempted cultural erasure and geopolitical dismemberment.

More than offering a broad critique of the missionizing logic that underlies the effort to "civilize" native peoples, the text's central tropes allude to the ways Christian institutions directly have influenced and benefited from U.S. Indian policy. Starting with the creation of the Board of Indian Commissioners in 1869 under President Grant, which brought together representatives from different denominations in a largely advisory but sometimes supervisory body, the federal government committed itself to the explicit support of churches as part of its relation with native peoples. While the practice started under Grant of divvying up Indian agencies among Christian denominations and allowing them to choose agency personnel lasted only about five years, prominent U.S. officials continued to participate in Christian philanthropic organizations focused on the uplift of native peoples. In particular, the annual meetings of the "Friends of the Indian" at Lake Mohonk in the late nineteenth and early twentieth centuries largely defined the direction of Indian affairs in those years and was attended regularly by such leading federal figures as Commissioner of Indian Affairs Thomas J. Morgan and Senator Henry L. Dawes, who not only sponsored the General Allotment Act (1887) but served as the head of the commission created in 1893 to negotiate allotment agreements with the Creeks and the rest of the Five Tribes. While not having the direct backing of the state, nongovernmental associations like the "Friends" had a profound effect on the shape of policy-making by involving those with direct control over such matters in a cultural consensus about the need to make Indians more godly by organizing them as privatized nuclear family units (addressed at length in chapter 3). Moreover, the various congressional acts extending U.S. jurisdiction over and allotting Indian Territory removed Christian religious institutions from the purview of native governance, entrenching them in Indian communities. In addition to providing protection for Christian worship, making disruption of it a criminal offense, such laws gave fee simple title to churches for the grounds they occupied, making their tenure on (once) native lands permanent and eliminating the ability of indigenous peoples to remove missionaries or to exert any official control over the presence and influence of Christian institutions operating among them. Perhaps the most egregious collusion of church and state in Indian affairs occurred during the 1920s, in which various Secretaries of the Interior used the powers they held over "restricted" Indians (those deemed unable to handle their own affairs due to their excessive amounts of Indian "blood") to effect the deeding of fortunes from oil found on native land (particularly Muscogees') to church-run organizations, especially schools. In light of this pattern, the appearance of white Baptist discourse and congregations in the novel signals not simply cultural intervention among the Creeks but the legacy of a state-sanctioned, and at many points state-engineered, project of transforming native political economy to insert Indians into a more "civilized" model of morality while transferring native wealth and resources to institutions controlled by whites.[12]

Figures of water in the novel serve as vehicles for representing Josh's pent-up and pathologized erotic yearnings while resituating them within a deprivatizing vision of Creek history. Josh is a bookish teenager, not good at sports and called a "faggot" by his classmates. His friend Jimmy, on the other hand, is attractive and a star athlete. During a teenage sleepover at Jimmy's house with some other boys, in which the lack of sleeping bags results in Josh sharing Jimmy's bed, Jimmy embraces Josh, grasping his erection. In reflecting on this furtive sexual encounter, Josh connects it to Jimmy's rescue of him the previous year, when he almost drowned:

> I thought of that day at the lake, his arm falling away from my side once we'd
> landed on shore. I had drowned; Jimmy had saved me. He had come up out
> of the water with me in his arms, me gasping for air at first, then, him
> breathing into me on top of the raft . . . And now touching me in the middle
> of the night. He would have to wade back into the lake if he was going to
> escape the flames. The wages of sin. A kiss was drowning, a fire that took
> your breath away, sucking up oxygen, smoke that filled your lungs. He hadn't
> kissed me, but I wanted him to. (70–71)

Jimmy simultaneously brings salvation and temptation, the water serving as both the medium for and the escape from transgression, and similarly, the imagined kiss is both life (breath) and death (drowning).[13] These paradoxes turn on competing understandings of the attraction that animates/engulfs them. The reference to "flames" recalls the disciplining sermon of the preacher from Josh's parents' church, who proclaims, "Know ye not that neither liars, nor adulterers, nor fornicators, nor murderers, nor the effeminate shall inherit the kingdom of God" because "they give over the natural use of their bodies for that which is unseemly" and thus "their inheritance" is "the lake of fire" (63–64).

Tracing the ideology of damnation to a specific institutional site, the novel presents Josh's self-flagellation as a result of interpellation rather than an innate perversion. Indicating the racial makeup of that church and its implications for Josh's family, he observes, "My folks were afraid of their son's bad behavior getting back to the white Baptist church they attended, and they'd be kicked out" (59); "it was one of the very few white Baptist churches that allowed Indians who looked like us, like full-bloods" (63). The regulation of Josh's sexuality is depicted as part of an attempt to gain access to the privilege of whiteness, at least by association. What is palpable in the description of Josh's parents, however, is less their devotion than their anxiety. This worry extends far beyond what happens at church, reaching into virtually all aspects of life, and the attendant disciplining of oneself and one's immediate family serves as a displaced locus for the maintenance of racial hierarchy, portraying the dynamics of the latter as if it were a function of individuals' ability to conform their "behavior" to codes of respectability. As discussed in chapter 1, the racial logic of Indianness is attended by the attribution of deviance, as if an incapacity to obey proper patterns of affect and family formation were itself an inherent quality passed in the "blood." Abnormality provides the alibi for a system of racial disqualification.[14] Yet these strictures are less externally mandated than sought after. Josh's parents are "especially proud" to belong because in doing so they as "fullbloods" gain entry to a space of whiteness (63); they are "trying to get somewhere in the world by hanging out with the right kind of people" (106). Here we see the bribe of straightness at work, the promise of access into restricted forms of recognition and privilege contingent on proof of heterohomemaking. In the preacher's words marital romance is the exclusively "natural" expression of properly gendered desire, as against "unseemly" alternatives (63), but this self-evident, divinely ordained arrangement remains deeply fraught for Josh's parents, involving less easy accommodation than harried vigilance against the possibility that they will be found wanting.

The novel suggests, then, that the ideology of normality validates the ongoing white superintendence of native peoples while effacing the historical and political dynamics that enable the enforcement of bourgeois values in Indian country and that generate an identification with whiteness.[15] In this way, Womack explores how the rhetoric of normality does not so much replace that of civilization as provide a euphemizing way of translating the latter into a less apparently imperial and racializing medium. Since discourses of primitiveness and perversity are overlapping without being quite equivalent (as addressed in chapter 3), a person's possibility of entry into a privileged position within the heterosexual imaginary can be conditioned by his Indianness, continually reenacting the central premise of the ideology of the civilizing mission and allotment: to be native is to have improper forms of affect, home, and family.[16] The novel suggests that the discourse of sin takes part in the process of managing racial hierarchy, of determining which Indians will be allowed entry to and participation within whitecontrolled spaces.

Given this portrait of white congregations, the sexualized fantasies of immersion that punctuate turning-point moments in Josh and Jimmy's relationship take on added significance (97, 279), inhabiting the trope of baptism while scrambling its meaning by indicating emergence into a way of seeing/being in which queer desire is celebrated.[17] These scenes also help highlight the distinctions within Creek Christianity that the novel explores. Rather than presenting native identity and Christian belief as inherently antithetical, thereby potentially reinforcing the image of Muscogee culture as static, Womack repeatedly notes the presence of Indian Baptist churches, suggesting the possibility of forms of cultural change that are not shaped by identification with white-dominated institutions. Such congregations appear in all of the text's time frames: Josh's Aunt Lucy notes that her white father will not be part of one, and her quite traditionalist neighbor attends one (34, 221); Josh as a teenager observes that his grandparents are members (18); and as an adult Josh visits Jimmy and his family at the church grounds (255). These congregations are composed of Indians rather than whites, and we are told that the sermons are almost exclusively in Creek.[18] Josh and Jimmy's eroticized submerging, then, is indicative less of a break with Christianity per se than a reorientation of it in which it ceases to be constellated with, and to serve as a legitimizing discourse for, the institutional matrix of white power.

Rather than simply serving as a symbol of damnation, the figure of the lake in Josh's description of his teenage experiences signifies within two discrepant discursive formations. While offering readers the image of hell as a "lake of fire," the novel previously had described the artificial means by which many of the lakes in Creek country had been created. At the beginning of the text, Lucy, the sister of Josh's maternal grandmother, talks to him about federal water management in Creek territory. This discussion comes as a kind of epilogue to her recounting of the tale of the emergence of the people and how their lineage came to be the wolf clan: "[T]hey's no more wolfs today . . . I mean they aren't no clan by that name. They aren't no more actual wolfs either, to my way of knowing because when all the WPA was to put in big dams during the depression they drowned out all that wild country where wolfs and cougars and even bears lived in" (5). Josh's paternal grandfather, who along with Lucy serves as a figure for the persistence of the oral tradition and the importance of recounting the Creek past, also contributes to this representation of U.S. efforts to transform the landscape: "I used to farm right over yonder. Before the dam went in. Built it in '63, I think it was. Started gathering water in '64. Now, waters all over . . . Yep, had a house right over thataway. Your daddy was borned there. Now you can't get nowhere around here on the same roads you used to. All covered up" (19). These moments link water to the invasive force of U.S. policy, illuminating its attempt to suppress—to cover up—the memory of the people. The devastation and dislocation literally caused by the dams provide a metaphor for the broader aim of effacing Creek modes of belonging and placemaking.

In light of the profusion of references to Christian imagery and institutions in the text, the flooding caused by federal projects also calls to mind the biblical Flood, God's punishment for the world's lapse into sin. Here, though, the decimation is due not to divine retribution but to human (mis)judgment, subtly casting U.S. policy in Indian country as a profoundly violent and misguided attempt to play God. Moreover, the implicit juxtaposition of the "lake of fire" with the synthetic lakes created by environmental restructuring (such as the homophonic play of "damn" and "dam") suggests that the moral censure conveyed by reference to the former is no more "natural" than the latter. The novel intimates that the ideology of sin and hell simply may be a different, though related, version of the wave of destruction more graphically illustrated by federally produced flooding.

In this vein, Josh's eroticized dreams of drowning condense a broader clash between ways of conceptualizing and narrating Creek identity. Lucy's and Grandpa's stories help outline that struggle, illustrating not only how Indian policy materially reshapes Creek geography but how it seeks to reorder native self-understandings. At the end of a chapter devoted to her recounting of events in her childhood, Lucy describes a day trip from her nursing home with a friend: "We get closer to the dam, and I think about the giant concrete wall, how it holds back so much, and all the water that has covered up places where my daddy and mama use to live, now lying at the bottom of the lake. Water and memories, memories and water" (133). The government's exertion of control over Creek places is portrayed as analogous to the management of Creek memory, an effort to limit the possibilities of self-representation by covering over countervailing or disruptive collective histories. The novel positions itself as a kind of recovery, as an attempt to set flowing what has been *held back*. Josh's damned and dammed desires, then, resonate with a longer history of U.S. intervention. He describes his search for voice, for a depathologizing kind of self-naming, as "want[ing] words that moved like a wave, words that crashed against my dammed-up body, rising and spilling out, a great flood broken loose" (104), narrating his shamed silence as an extension of the other acts of enclosure and diversion perpetrated against the Creek people.

In linking Josh's process of self-discovery to the remembrance of a collective history that has been officially buried, the novel begins to develop a queer genealogy of Creek peoplehood. His queer yearnings become a synecdoche for suppressed aspects of Creek tradition, a process that occurs first in the depiction of his near drowning. Out on the raft on Lake Eufaula on a summer afternoon with Jimmy and other boys, Josh agrees to take part in a diving contest to see who can get a rock from the lake bottom. This choice both quiets the chorus of variations on "faggot" launched at him by the other boys and is designed to get his dive over with before Jimmy's turn: "[L]eading the contest would allow him to insist that Jimmy go right after him, bringing them even closer to each other's secrets, ready for Josh's messages" (16), which he imagines he can project into Jimmy's mind. The "secrets" that Josh believes he can transmit telepathically are precisely the feelings of attraction that the other boys mock. Later, he observes, "Someday I would step out of my secrets too, and leave them behind, and Jimmy would be the first person I spoke to" (54); in describing his history class only pages later, he adds, "There was the book and what everybody agreed happened, and then there were the secrets that no one talked about. Only a few people understood the secrets" (56). Together these moments tie the inexpressibility of Josh's desire to the elision of elements of the Creek past from official accounts, suggesting that the former functions as a subset of the latter.

In that same chapter, Josh recalls Grandpa's tale of the construction of Lake Eufaula. During the contest, Josh gets caught underwater; he "opened his eyes and saw the underwater city where he was tethered to the spokes of somebody's wagon wheel parked on the street in front of a building" (21). The story of the flooding of Grandpa's home and nearby lands by one of the federal dams in Creek territory appears in a break in the story of Josh's almost drowning, between his surfacing under the raft and getting his leg caught in fishing line. The history Grandpa offers, emerging as it does within the interstices of Josh's tale, reshapes Josh's perception of his surroundings, inflecting the meaning of his experience by transforming it from a scene of individual longing and trauma to one of collective suffering and displacement. Josh's fantasy of transmitting secret erotic messages becomes a vision of an entire city hidden beneath the water, linking his feelings of shame to a buried past whose traces remain legible to those who know where and how to look. The belief that his desire is perverse appears as like the lake itself, an unnatural formation whose givenness results from the attempted erasure of the violence through which it was imposed.

Through the image of the artificial lake, the text explores the institutionalized production of the "natural" and the effect of state ideologies and policies on quotidian Creek self-conception. Interweaving references to damnation with the destructive force of the dams, the text depicts the discourse of sin as the trace of a legacy of imperial intervention and dispossession. Womack casts the unblocking of Josh's desire as part of a process of reclaiming an occluded Creek past. The novel, then, portrays queerness as a window onto a communal inheritance in need of recovery, a position from which to rethink the contours and content of nationhood by emphasizing how it flows from shared ideals and memory rather than being formed out of the statutory parameters and "civilizing" program—the dammed-up container—of federal law.

SNAKES

The drowning chapter further is punctuated by Grandpa's tales of the tie-snake, a horned and hybrid creature that inhabits lakes and ponds, offering Josh and the reader a way of recasting the underwater world as a space of possibility, rather than simply of loss. When first describing the power of this magical figure, Grandpa observes, "white man never did catch this tie-snake" (19), portraying it and the places it inhabits as having escaped Euramerican regulation and thereby implicitly presenting the act of telling stories about it as a similar kind of evasion/retention. Indicating the potential for movement between worlds, the tie-snake, as we learn from Grandpa, was once a man but was metamorphosed into a new being because he consumed food made strange by its appearance in an unexpected place, and as the person-made-monster retreats, it creates a large body of water in its wake (24–26).[19] Lakes can be envisioned as the residue of astonishing acts of crossing between seemingly separate domains (land/water, human/snake) which defy static categories and systems of control. Josh's internalization of this idea is manifested in the fact that during his near drowning, when he looks at the fish line in which his leg is caught, he sees a "balled-up coil of snakes [that] had wrapped themselves around him" and that "moved in and out of each other, swaying in the lake bottom current and weaving between the wagon spokes." Furthermore, when Jimmy swims toward him, "Josh saw a snake with horns . . . The giant snake was trying to wrap itself around Josh" (22). If the novel portrays Jimmy as a paradoxical figure of temptation and salvation, here it also remakes him as a tie-snake, as part of a watery domain in which the erotic attachment that draws him and Josh together is an expression not of pathology but of a capacity for transformation, recognized and respected in Creek tradition.

In a discussion of the tie-snake in *Red on Red*, Womack argues, "anomalous beings can also be powerful; queerness has an important place" (244). The queerness toward which he gestures, and that emerges in the drowning scene in the novel, is less a matter of personal identity than semiotic disjunction, an opening of conventionalized social mappings to other cultural geographies that have been suppressed but not eliminated: "To exist as a nation, the community needs a perception of nationhood, that is stories . . . that help them imagine who they are as a people, how they came to be, and what cultural values they wish to preserve."[20] The stories of the oral tradition provide a way of reframing nationhood, queering the matrix of peoplehood by dislocating it from the "values" normalized by the United States, which, like Lake Eufaula, cover over the past while naturalizing that elision. Such storytelling, therefore, takes part in a process of counterhegemony, which can be described, in Gramsci's terms, "as a cultural battle to transform the popular 'mentality' " by playing on existing fissures within Creek self-understanding: "[T]he social group in question may indeed have its own conception of the world . . . ; a conception which manifests itself in action, but occasionally and in flashes . . . But this same group has, for reasons of submission and intellectual subordination, adopted a conception which is not its own but is borrowed from another group." From this perspective, Creeks can be thought of as having a "contradictory consciousness" in which Euramerican ideologies are at odds with indigenous philosophy—the contrast, for example, between the lake of fire and the tie-snake.[21] Here, counterhegemony has a different trajectory than in *Hope Leslie* or *Stone Butch Blues*, as discussed in chapters 2 and 5, in that it is directed toward reformulating Creek self-understandings and notions of Creek nationhood rather than articulated to reformulations of non-native publics through native pedagogy.

The tale of the king of the tie-snakes that closes the drowning chapter, and provides its title, positions sexuality as a site of contradiction/struggle in the revisioning of native nationhood. As Grandpa tells Josh, a chief sent his son with a message to the chief of another town. The boy loses the clay pot containing the message by tossing it into the water while skipping stones with friends, and when he dives in to retrieve it, he is seized by a tie-snake and brought to the throne of their king. After accomplishing several tasks set for him, the boy is sent back to the surface with the promise of aid for his father should he need it so long as the boy "don't tell him what you know." When the boy's town is attacked by enemies, he performs the required ritual, and the king appears and has the assailants subdued by snakes (29, 31). The story is about the failure to recognize the importance of political matters—the value of the father's message—but also the potential for unexpected alliances in time of crisis and the power of tradition and ritual as sources of renewal. Josh's response to the story, though, emphasizes the mystery at its heart and its resonance with his own life: "I burned to know the boy's secret, what he withheld from his father, what lay buried beneath the shadowy water" (31). The "secret" of the boy's knowledge, withheld from the reader as well, echoes Josh's "secret" longing for Jimmy. In the tale, an everyday occurrence, skipping stones, becomes suddenly invested with implications for the boy's people, transforming his and his father's sense of the physical and political landscape. Similarly, the text links this opening into unforeseen possibilities—the promise of tools for struggle with an invading foe—to Josh's desire, suggesting that beneath the privatizing shame lies the knowledge needed to protect the nation.

More than merely suggesting the possibility of accessing alternative modes of thought rooted in tradition, the novel uses the figure of the tie-snake to gesture toward specific historical dynamics of Muscogee politics and political consciousness. When spending time with Grandpa after Lucy's funeral, Josh remembers a story he was told about "Posey's hole": "It was haunted, the place where Alex Posey, the famous Creek poet, had drowned, taken under the waters, they said, by a tie-snake . . . due to Posey turning away from the Creek Nation after [Oklahoma] statehood and becoming involved in the selling of Creek allotments. The very river he loved so much had pulled him in, taken him under, the result of forgetting one's nation, giving in to white interests" (190). Like the earlier reference to the tie-snake's having escaped white capture/control, this anecdote positions the creature as the symbol and protector of Creek autonomy. It punishes native complicity in U.S. efforts to fragment Muscogee peoplehood, also indicating the continuing presence of collective "interests" that have been obscured through an institutionalized process of "forgetting." The dissemination of tie-snake tales, this one in particular, not only works to maintain a memory of Creek life, land tenure, and sovereignty before the concerted attempts at detribalization during the allotment era but also seeks to inculcate awareness of a history of opposition to such initiatives and the attendant struggles among Muscogees over the shape and future of the Creek Nation. The novel later characterizes this recurring double-sided pattern of conflict as "the spirit of resistance," suggesting less an isolated movement or set of pragmatic goals than an animating force of Creek identity and self-determination.

Yet more than indexing questions of governance, snake references are used throughout the novel to describe Jimmy, especially Josh's attraction to him. In his first appearance, he lifts himself onto the raft in Lake Eufaula "like a snake uncoiling" (11), and when as a teenager he takes Josh to a gay cruising spot, Josh notes, "I reached for his hand and let him coil his fingers tightly around mine" (101). Given the text's repetition of white Baptist condemnations of homosexuality as they circulate in Josh's consciousness, these serpentine images imply the presence of something satanic, casting Jimmy as a perverse influence leading Josh toward a fall from grace. In the latter half of the novel, though, this imagery becomes explicitly linked to the tie-snake. When as an adult Josh visits Lucy in the nursing home, where she is placed by Josh's parents due to her advanced Alzheimer's, she says, "Jimmy disappeared down a snake hole," inquiring of Josh, "Do you still miss him?" (171). Here she alludes to the story of the origin of the tie-snake while also renewing a supportive interest in Josh and Jimmy's relationship that she had shown in their youth. The link between tie-snake's potential for transformation and their desire for each other is made even more explicit once they are reunited as adults, just after Lucy's funeral. Accidentally running into each other at a party, they go back to Jimmy's place. While they are having sex, they notice "snakes everywhere," "snakes within snakes" (200), evoking the description of the tie-snake king's throne in Grandpa's story ("the platform was a heap of crawling snakes . . . Weaving in and out of each other" [29]). Jimmy cautions Josh, "The secret is, don't act like you're afraid. And then you won't be" (201), implicitly evoking the "secret" of the tie-snake kingdom kept by the chief's son in exchange for aid against his father's enemies. In rejecting heteronormative ideologies, associated with whiteness, Josh and Jimmy are portrayed as reclaiming a Creek perspective, a way of interpreting themselves more consistent with Muscogee ideals in which the "anomalous" is embraced as powerful and necessary. In applying the figure of the tie-snake to both opposition to allotment and the acceptance of queer eroticism, Womack positions the latter as an example of the broader "spirit of resistance" signaled by the former.

The novel further presents attitudes toward same-sex attraction as symptomatic of the degree to which one is infused by that spirit. The text illustrates this dynamic through Lucy's stories about Seborn and Tarbie. Remembering conversations between her mother and Dave, a Creek orphan legally put under the guardianship of her white father, Lucy recalls, "this one time I heard Dave telling her about a couple of men he seen over at the stomp dance. These two men live together back in the sand hills, away from everybody, without any women. Dave said, '. . . The young boys giggle when they see them two in camp, but the old ones always frown and tell them to show respect,'" a sentiment with which Lucy's mother agrees (35). The association of the men with "the old ones" and "the stomp dance" (which I will discuss at length in the next section) aligns them with traditional values. They are disclaimed by "the more 'progressive' citizens" of the Creek Nation "who'd accepted the ways of the whites, gone along with allotment of land" (222). The text correlates the phobic repudiation of the couple with an acceptance of alien ideals that literally fracture the Creek polity. Sexuality does not appear here as a stand-alone identity or issue, but attitudes toward it are depicted as indicative of a knowledge of and commitment to Muscogee principles as against fragmenting social divisions inserted into Creek life by whites. The "progressive" Creeks who identify with white institutions and policies seek to disown Seborn and Tarbie, but among "the conservatives, those guarding Creek land and traditions," they are "safe" (222).

Additionally, as members of the "conservative" community residing at Hickory Ground, the couple actively take part in the movement against allotment and Oklahoma statehood. Led by Chitto Harjo, this group is called the "Snakes," a translation of Chitto's name. Based on actual events, the novel's discussion of this group plays with the name given them by U.S. officials, folding it into the text's serpent tropology in ways that cast their opposition to federal intervention as an expression of a tie-snake ethos running through Creek history. By inserting a fictional same-sex couple into a documented struggle over Muscogee governance and land tenure, Womack presents the resistance to the heterosexual imaginary as continuous with the broader fight for self-determination. This connection parallels Ella Deloria's insistence, addressed in chapter 4, that Dakota decisions about their own collective future and social organization cannot be presumed to start from a self-evident acceptance of the "father-mother-child unit" as the atom of native sociality, but Womack offers a more explicit articulation of the relationship between refusing the obviousness of nuclearity and histories of direct political contestation. Using Seborn and Tarbie to connect Josh and Jimmy's changing understanding of themselves and their relation to their people to turn-of-the-century battles over political authority, the novel indicates that their fight for (self-) acceptance is part of a long genealogy of Creek efforts to contest imposed sociopolitical norms.

The Crazy Snake Uprising, as it has come to be called, began as a response to the Creek government's decision in 1900 to sign an allotment agreement with the United States. Originally, the Dawes Act authorizing the privatization of tribal lands had exempted Indian Territory, the lands occupied by tribes that had been removed to west of the Mississippi, but in 1893, Congress formed a committee, later known as the Dawes Commission, to assemble lists of the citizens of the "Five Civilized Tribes" and to make compacts with them that would enable the division of their lands and dissolution of their governments. While the Muscogee public largely repudiated this effort, including in at least two official referenda, the passage of the Curtis Act (1898) made allotment mandatory, giving the Secretary of the Interior the power to impose it absent the consent of the Five Tribes. In order to secure better terms, the Creek national government relented to negotiations, the agreement becoming official on March 1, 1901. Those Creeks who denied the legitimacy of the Curtis Act, earlier U.S. statutes constraining Creek jurisdiction, and the concessions by the constitutional Creek government gathered in increasing numbers at Hickory Ground, a movement that at its height included as many as 5,000 people, or about a third of the Creek Nation.[22] They formed their own government, refused to enroll as allottees or to be counted for the Dawes rolls, and sought to punish those who cooperated with the program of detribalization. As the novel observes, "Tarbie had been riding the countryside with the Lighthorsemen [Creek police force] looking for those who'd committed treason against the nation by signing up for allotments, leasing land to the 'stihuktis, or hiring whites as laborers." The text summarizes the Snake position as "[h]old on and salvage whatever was left. Don't give up anything else. Sell no more land. Uphold the Treaty of 1832, its promise of unbroken land tenure and Creek national government in Indian Territory into perpetuity" (224). Continuing direct opposition for almost a decade, the movement greatly was undermined in March 1909 due to the assault by local law enforcement officers on Harjo's home in which he was wounded and driven into exile, dying in the Choctaw Nation in 1911.[23]

The Crazy Snakes' fight against allotment and statehood was one in a long line of intratribal political conflicts over the shape and content of Creek sovereignty, reaching back to at least the early nineteenth century. One of the most notable features of Creek governance in the nineteenth and twentieth centuries is the routine eruption of significant challenges to U.S.-backed administrations by movements organized around town-based leadership that would emerge to contest the operation and legitimacy of Creek national institutions.

This process of a submerged political order suddenly dramatically appearing and changing the social landscape resonates with the tale of the tie-snake king and his "secret" knowledge, and Womack uses the trope of the tie-snake to theorize a particular Creek structure of feeling, investigating how non-"progressive" visions of Creek nationality are suppressed, the conditions of their survival, and the circumstances through which they become visible.[24] Although the novel emphasizes the Snakes' resistance to allotment and Oklahoma statehood, it also implicitly gestures toward the ways contention between the towns, or talwas, and the centralized national administration reaches back into the early nineteenth century.[25] In this period, the primary unit of Muscogee governance was the talwa. Each functioned as an independent entity but was composed of members of various matrilineal clans, creating a crosscutting pattern of connections that bound them together in a network of reciprocal responsibilities based on clan membership.[26] While towns periodically had gathered in councils prior to the late eighteenth century, often described as "national" events by scholars, the formation of a centralized government that asserted legislative authority over the towns and developed a coercive apparatus to enforce its decisions did not occur until after the American Revolution, when Benjamin Hawkins, the Indian agent for the southern states, helped organize a regular meeting composed of representatives from the towns which was led by a speaker and claimed the right to enact rules for Creek conduct, particularly to punish those who attacked whites and stole property. This effort to reconfigure Creek sociality was not merely an imposition from the outside, though, as the U.S.-backed project of consolidating political power and breaking up traditional town and clan dynamics gained support from an emergent Muscogee elite largely composed of the Euramerican-educated children of white traders who had lived in Creek communities and married Creek women.[27]

Thus, by the early nineteenth century, a distinct tension had emerged in Creek political life between two visions of nationality: one that conceived of the towns as under the jurisdiction of a unifying national government, itself largely committed to implementing bourgeois principles of ownership; and one that continued to see the towns as the fundamental site of political identification and the clans as the primary vehicle for maintaining social order.[28] That growing friction exploded in the Redstick War of 1813–1814.[29] A series of events ignited resentments that had been intensifying over the previous decade, particularly the encroachment of the national council on the purview of the talwas through land cessions and the adoption of a criminal code. Tecumseh, the Shawnee leader of an intertribal confederacy based in the western Great Lakes, entered into this volatile situation in 1811.[30] Traveling to the Creeks as part of his effort to gain support for a broad-based native alliance against U.S. encroachment, he helped galvanize Muscogee resistance to the authority arrogated by national leaders, who were perceived as complicitous with U.S. expansion into Creek country and intervention into intertribal affairs. This escalating conflict was brought to a head in 1812 and 1813 by the council-ordered murder of Creeks who had been responsible for killing both Americans and Creek police attempting to enforce anti-theft laws. Those who came to call themselves Redsticks retaliated against such "national" discipline, assaulting Tuckabatchee and Coweta (the sites of the council meetings), as well as settlements populated by the plantation-holding elite.[31] As part of the latter, an attack on Fort Mims in which Americans were killed brought the U.S. Army into the war, with the active support of some Creek leaders. The defeat of the Redsticks, and the death of approximately 800 of them, in March 1814 by forces under the command of Andrew Jackson at Tohopeka (otherwise known as Horseshoe Bend) ended active hostilities among the Creeks, although fighting continued farther south by those who had fled into Florida territory and joined Seminole communities.

Not only does the Crazy Snakes' repudiation of the actions of the Creek national government in the early twentieth century replay many of the issues at stake in the Redstick War, including the struggle over what constitutes legitimate political authority among the Muscogees, but the novel in several ways indexes the earlier conflict both explicitly and implicitly, allusively contextualizing turn-of-the-century events within a longstanding recursive clash between the clan/town matrix and elite managed modes of national sovereignty. The memory of Redstick opposition to elite displacement of existing social formations directly appears in the novel in the final chapter, in the mention of the tales of Bertha Bowleg, a neighbor from Lucy's youth: "She tells stories about the day her older brother traveled along the Tallapoosa River with his party of warriors from Upper Creek towns to fight against William McIntosh in the battle of Horseshoe Bend. Andrew Jackson made Creeks give up 25 million acres because of the treaty that come out of that lost war" (282–283). While Womack offers no further explanation of this ever-so-brief reference, it suggests a haunting, or perhaps more precisely a kind of surround. The very absence of elaboration presupposes that the hearer of both Bertha's and Lucy's stories will recognize the citation, and the fleeting mention of the Redstick War marks it as part of the assumed background against which the foregrounded events of the novel signify. In other words, it is positioned as a kind of not-quite-spoken Creek political/ historical common sense, the meaning of which inheres in a fight between the "Upper Creek towns" and the Anglo-educated elite (for which McIntosh serves as the icon) that is overdetermined by U.S. investments (Jackson's use of the war to validate the expropriation of millions of acres of Creek land). The repetition of this underlying dynamic can be seen in the depiction of the Snakes. During one of their councils, someone asserts, "We're the real Creek government . . . We wasn't give permission for the Okmulgee government to agree to disband and allot" (225) Later, while narrating the events surrounding Oklahoma statehood, Josh observes, "The Creek government hadn't always represented the full-blood point of view well, since the Creek progressives dominated the political leadership" (232). The battle to define what will count as Creek political "real"-ity fundamentally is shaped by a sustained "progressive" elision of "the full-blood point of view," a dynamic traceable back to the construction of a self-consciously "national" bureaucratic framework in the early nineteenth century.[32]

That conflict over the character of, and authority to define, Muscogee political identity also stretches forward into the late twentieth century, providing a backdrop for the early Josh and Jimmy chapters. The 1970s saw a resurgence of residual unresolved political tensions from the early 1900s. The agreement that Creek legislators ratified in 1901 assenting to allotment and the dissolution of the national government by 1906 was suspended by a federal law passed that year which mandated that "the tribal existence and present tribal governments of the Choctaw, Chickasaw, Cherokee, Creek, and Seminole Tribes or nations are hereby continued in full force and effect for all purposes authorized by law," with the provisos that all legislation passed by the national councils had to be approved by the President of the United States and that the Principal Chief of any of the Five Tribes could be removed by the President if he "shall refuse or neglect to perform the duties devolving upon him."[33] Despite the fact that federal law had left undisturbed most of the organizing structure of the Creek government under the 1867 constitution,[34] the Interior Department in 1907 usurped Creek elections and cited the 1906 U.S. statute as justification for making the office of Principal Chief a federal appointment in perpetuity, an illegal act continued until 1970. Moreover, the BIA simply disregarded the Creek council, behaving as if it had been abolished rather than explicitly maintained by Congress and thereby illustrating what one justice later called "an attitude which can only be characterized as bureaucratic imperialism."[35] Yet while the BIA in 1909 refused to allow elections for the council to proceed and thereafter more or less treated the Principal Chief as the exclusive representative of whatever Creek governmental authority it was willing to concede, the towns that same year formed what was called "the Creek Convention," continuing to meet more or less in the way they had previously; in 1944 that council ratified a new constitution formalizing the practices it had developed over the previous several decades.[36]

Two events in the early 1970s brought the battle over the relation between the Creek executive branch and the towns, and thus the challenge to the U.S. management of Muscogee governance, back to the foreground of Creek national law: the passage in 1970 of a federal law explicitly giving citizens of the Five Tribes the right popularly to elect their executives; and Principal Chief Claude Cox's effort in 1973 to draft and install a new Creek constitution. The latter threatened further to entrench and legitimize more fully the displacement of the talwas from the institutionalized matrix of Creek nationality, replacing them with a district-based system. Together, these events eventuated in a case that came before the U.S. district court in Washington, D.C., *Harjo v. Kleppe* (1976), in which the judge ruled that the BIA's practices with respect to the Creeks—particularly choosing Principal Chiefs and ignoring the Creek council—were patently illegal, further arguing that Cox's proposed constitution "alters the basic nature of the Creek Nation" by dislodging the towns from any substantive role in its political structure.[37] Although Judge Bryant ordered the creation of a commission to organize a series of referenda on aspects of Cox's proposal that were to eventuate in the submission of a constitution for approval by the federal government, the process was marked by a lack of BIA funding and oversight as well as stonewalling on the part of Cox, and it resulted in the passage in 1979 of a constitution weighted toward Cox's original proposal, including the adoption of a pattern of districting that superseded the talwas as the basis for representation.[38]

While not explicitly referenced in the novel, the legal struggle in the 1970s over the shape of Creek sovereignty is intimated in the timing of the chapters focused on Josh and Jimmy's youth, set in 1972, 1973, and 1978. Given the events discussed above, the choice to situate the boys' sexual coming-of-age in the years leading up to Cox's proposal of the new constitution and just prior to its adoption seems quite striking, but the novel remains silent on the public controversies surrounding Cox, his constitution, and the decision in *Harjo v. Kleppe*. How might this absence be explained? Or put another way, how does the novel draw on and reinterpret this history without directly chronicling it? At one point, as noted earlier, Josh observes, "There was the book, and what everybody agreed happened, and then there were the secrets that no one talked about" (56). In the text, the term "secrets" often designates residual formations that are not accepted as "political," not recognized as legitimate modes of sovereignty, and here the novel reaffirms its interest in processes of political organizing and association that exceed the normative structures of the United States and the U.S.-recognized Creek national government, such as its focus on the Snakes rather than on the Creek officials who negotiated with the Dawes Commission. Rather than highlighting the battle over the Creek constitution, especially given the ultimate legal loss by the towns, the novel rechannels the impressions surrounding that struggle to discussion of Josh's sexuality and self-understanding. Instead of the struggle in Creek politics that resulted in *Harjo v. Kleppe*, the novel emphasizes the "war" occurring in Josh's consciousness: "I hadn't thought that much about Grandpa's stories, or Lucy's, because the church stories were always at war against them . . . The church stories were a barrage in my head that never let up and blasted over my grandpa's and Lucy's voices" (105–106). Here, as elsewhere, Womack implicitly links the secrets of Creek history and politics to Josh's hidden desire, exploring the ways that the latter is implicated in the broader struggle over what stories or visions of Muscogee identity will shape the future of the nation.

The snake trope coalesces seemingly disparate experiences and struggles to show that they are expressive of persistent forms of national consciousness, providing a way of naming as political social dynamics that otherwise might not be considered such. As Raymond Williams suggests, what dominant frameworks "exclude may often be seen as the personal or the private, or as the natural or even the metaphysical . . . , since what the dominant has effectively seized is indeed the ruling definition of the social" (125). The tiesnake in particular becomes a way of characterizing a Creek structure of feeling that exceeds dominant political logics while simultaneously contesting U.S. efforts to exert metapolitical control over what will constitute viable modes of native sovereignty. Articulating and aligning itself with this genealogy of resistance, the novel extends the pattern to include Josh and Jimmy's opposition to others' attempts to portray them as perverse, snake figures often signaling the intensity of their desire. By linking their depathologizing vision of themselves to a renewed engagement with Creek political history (particularly the memory of the Crazy Snakes), Womack makes the native embrace of queerness part of a larger counterhegemonic critique of centralization and privatization, as instigated by the United States and institutionalized by some Creeks. Such ideologies have not only demonized same-sex desire but worked to displace traditional sociopolitical formations, like the talwas.

Instead of simply incorporating sexuality into a laundry list of issues that fall under the umbrella of self-determination, though, *Drowning* presents Josh and Jimmy as the bearers of Snake consciousness, inheriting it from Lucy.[39] Not coincidentally, the year in which Chitto Harjo dies is the one in which the novel's first chapter narrated by Lucy is set, implicitly presenting her as an inheritor of the spirit of the Snakes. That role is confirmed by her references to the ways U.S. policy enabled systemic theft of Creek lands by whites. She observes that Tulsa was "built upon land allotments of Muskokalkee peoples who was tricked by bankers and merchants, deliberately put into debt" (112), adding that many people she knew during her childhood had "already lost the family land 'cause the state and county found ways to steal it from us," including various forms of fraud: "[T]hey promised our families our allotments, then found ways to cheat us out of them, too, until forty years after statehood there wasn't hardly an Indian allotment in the country in the hands of the original family it was given to" (118–119). Allotment appears here as an elaborate con, not merely a violation of prior agreements but itself a kind of high-stakes shell game predicated on false appearances. Lured by the promise of security, Creeks are coaxed into financial arrangements that leave them poor and landless.[40] This process of temptation and deception illustrates the qualities attributed to the biblical snake far better than Josh and Jimmy's desire, subtly redirecting the discourse of sin away from homoeroticism and toward white expropriation as the figure of the snake is reclaimed for narrating a legacy of Muscogee anti-imperial critique and political organizing.

If Lucy is cast as an inheritor of Creek critical memory, Josh's storytelling shows him to be its latest keeper. He notes, "There was a lot of medicine in a person's brain, I figured, if he could collect his thoughts, consider the things he'd heard, make up stories to suit himself. Lucy told them, why couldn't I" (220)? We are told that Seborn had been called "history book" and that Lucy had been thought of "as a kind of local encyclopedia" due to her knowledge of "the history of families in Weleetka and Eufaula, all the way back to who settled where after Indian Removal in the 1830s" (220, 163), and since the story of Chitto Harjo and the Hickory Ground is actually told by Josh, that fact reveals him to be the most recent in this line. In the novel, the act of retaining and narrating the history of the Creek people is inextricable from "the spirit of resistance." Preserving the past, rendered "secret" by the institutionalized erasure of Muscogee traditions and the naturalization of Euramerican norms, works to keep alive the potential for kinds of collective identity submerged beneath U.S.-regulated bureaucracy.

The attempt by other Creeks to constrain and denigrate Josh and Jimmy's desire, then, appears as a kind of cultural amnesia, an inability or unwillingness to reckon with the enforced imperial restructuring of Creek life and an attendant tendency to treat imposed sociopolitical ideals—including the ideological structure of straightness—as given. Conversely, the refusal to be bound by such norms opens the possibility for accessing and rejuvenating residual political formations. During his story of the Snakes, Josh says of Seborn, "He was dreaming of taking back Indian land, land many claimed already was lost" (221), suggesting that extended historical consciousness can make thinkable options for Creek autonomy foreclosed as impossible in dominant discourse. Moreover, Womack presents Josh and Jimmy's relationship as a conduit to such an expanded awareness. Josh finishes his discussion of the Snakes by observing, "I was still here, Jimmy was still in Weleetka, and Creek land was still waiting for us to take it back" (247). Directly linking Josh's acceptance of his desire for Jimmy to his desire to reclaim Creek nationality, the passage implies that the one animates and makes imaginable the other.

The search for precedent for his relationship with Jimmy leads Josh into Lucy's stories, looking for a way of validating himself. As he notes late in the novel while visiting Jimmy at the grounds of his family's Indian Baptist congregation, "Surely this had happened before. Two men had sat next to each other, in church, or out under the arbor, who had once been lovers or still were" (257). Such investigation, though, also involves reframing the judgments others make of him. That reorientation opens onto an analysis of the lasting effects of the civilization and allotment programs on Muscogee self-conception, which further directs Josh toward an engagement with the history of Creek opposition to them. The novel crystallizes this process in a breathtaking moment in which the present and past merge. During his recounting of Chitto Harjo's movement, Josh says, "Me and Jimmy had gathered at Chitto's house . . . along with the other Snakes, because we had planned on going to the council grounds before all the trouble broke out" in 1909 (242). At that point, the story ceases to mention Seborn and Tarbie, indicating that in Josh's imagination he and Jimmy have taken their place. The two stories and time periods have become fused, and in seeing himself as one of the Snakes, Josh assumes the responsibility for helping realize Seborn's "dream."

The snake trope initially provides a conceptual hinge through which the novel recontextualizes Josh's queer desire from Christian sin to Creek tradition, not only neutralizing the stigma of the one in favor of the sense of transformation implicit in the other but opening up Josh and Jimmy's relationship to signify other kinds of potentiality as well. Following the logic of the story of the king of the tie-snakes, serpent figures in the text help signal social formations that lay hidden and that become visible in moments of crisis in ways that radically alter and remap the political landscape, with the Snakes appearing as the most prominent historical example of that pattern. Yet Womack also gestures both backward and forward from that point, suggesting a genealogy of periodic rupture in Creek politics in which elements of Muscogee social life seen as separate from the sphere of governance emerge into view. Through the snake trope, the novel illustrates not only how the oral tradition can serve as a vehicle for reconceptualizing Creek identity but how it offers a means of linking seemingly disparate struggles across time, expanding the meaning of politics and peoplehood by drawing attention to what has been submerged and made "secret." Thus, as a way of designating a particular kind of Creek historical and political consciousness, the figure of the tie-snake links the critique of the heteronorm to longstanding Muscogee efforts to contest the legitimacy of U.S.-imposed and U.S.-managed modes of sovereignty, associating Josh and Jimmy's questioning of Creek homophobia to a larger structure of feeling organized around the resistance to "progressive" forms of forgetting and the remembrance of an ongoing "spirit of resistance."

FIRE

The novel consistently portrays the present moment as inhabited by the unresolved conflicts and residual potentialities of the past, thereby suggesting the continuing possibility of "taking back" that which according to some "already was lost." This linkage, though, begs the question of precisely how what *was* impinges upon what *is*, as well as how social formations believed to be gone can reorder the present. In this final section, I will explore the ways the novel addresses these issues through its multivectored use of figures of fire. Womack employs this image in ways that present the nuclear family form as inextricably bound up in the legacy of allotment. Reciprocally, as against the atomizing imaginary of heterohomemaking, the text forges a connection between homoeroticism and a vision of Muscogee sociality organized around clans and towns, engaging in a queer traditionalist remapping of the Creek sociopolitical landscape.

At the center of this tropological reconfiguraiton of Creek collectivity lies the contrast between hell and the Green Corn ceremony. As discussed earlier, references to the "lake of fire" appear early and often in the novel, indicating the pervasive influence of white Baptist ideology on Josh's self-understanding and, by implication, on that of other Muscogees deeply identified with Eur-american-dominated institutions. Initially, Josh's feelings of desire are inseparable from the threat of damnation. In describing his first sexual encounter with Jimmy during the sleepover, he recalls, "I knew I was a freak, a grotesque, a rampant sinner, and as I lay in Jimmy's bed, his body against mine, I burned, I burned, I burned": "His fingertips slipped beneath the elastic band, and I felt a fire, a hot blue flame lapping and dancing over the surface of my skin when his hand grasped me, hard as a rock. I gasped and rolled over, afraid of the hot rising of my blood, afraid of the unknown, afraid of hellfire, afraid of what thrilled me" (64). Overwhelmed by waves of sensation, he only can understand his intuitive response as a *freakish* deformation that consigns him to perversion and perdition. While *thrilling*, the "unknown" is itself dangerous, a frightening falling away from the one true path. Such deviation is imagined as, like fire, destructive and consuming, a failing that irrevocably plunges one into sin.

By contrast, within the Green Corn ceremony, also known as the Busk, fire is a symbol of regeneration and the regular remaking of the world anew. Annually performed in midsummer, it is a four- to eight-day ritual that involves the rekindling of a sacred flame, a cycle of feasting and fasting, a series of dances, and the extinguishment and relighting of all the fires within a given town. As Joel Martin suggests, "To match its meaning . . . Europeans or Anglo-Americans would have had to combine Thanksgiving, New Year's festivities, Yom Kippur, Lent, and Mardi Gras" (34). Through this process, the people not only are cleansed but reborn, especially in light of the traditional association of fire with the Upper World, which includes the Maker of Break—the central power within Muscogee cosmology. From this perspective, fire is a force of creation as well as destruction, and the two are linked in an intimate dialectic the honoring of which lies at the center of Muscogee philosophy and temporality. While in some ways it has become smaller in scope, the Green Corn ceremony continues to be crucial to the socioreligious life of many Creek communities. Given this context, the figure of fire in the novel cannot help but allude to this celebration and the countervailing conception of collectivity it offers. Rather than suggesting a static and uncontestable norm from which individuals fall away, to be punished in an eternal burning, the Busk performs a regular rejuvenation of the community that reknits it through a shared negotiation of the relation between continuity and change, a this-world ritual conflagration in which acknowledging and embracing "the unknown" becomes a communal project.[41]

The significance of that annual event to the novel's historical and political imaginary, its role as a way of indexing core aspects of Creek peoplehood, is articulated most directly by Lucy in her discussion of both her memories of the past and her vision for the future. She notes, "I remembered Dave saying that his people purified everything by starting a new fire at the beginning of the year in July. They kept the fire sacred and rekindled it before eating the corn harvest. They done that at their Green Corn ceremony," and she adds, "Daddy never let us go to any Green Corn, but Mama had told me plenty about it" (47). Offering a description of the ceremony, this brief reference provides an alternative tenor for the text's fire metaphorics, situating them with a cyclical process of *purification* in which the people "rekindle" their relations with each other. More than merely a regularly occurring festival, the Green Corn has a "sacred" character, which is conveyed by the emphasis placed on it in the stories told by Dave and Lucy's mother. The opposition of Lucy's father to the ceremony also positions it as emblematizing aspects of Creek sovereignty under assault by whites, given that he appears in the novel as a synecdoche for U.S. intervention. In this way, the Busk functions in the novel literally as the climax of the Muscogee ritual calendar and a part of tradition targeted for elimination, as well as metonymically as a set of social principles embedded in the ceremony but extending broadly through Creek philosophy and social life.

The specifically political import of the Green Corn is indicated in Lucy's discussion of the legacy of allotment. She asserts:

They thought they could bring the Creek Nation down to its knees. But I'm an old woman and the Creek Nation is still here, and we still have our stomp dances, and I still see my grandkids, and even great-grandkids, there at the grounds dancing and sitting in the arbors. If you ask me, we won, even though we always got to keep on fighting. As long as we got this nation and those square grounds, we'll keep right on a-going, too. This is what I'm trying to learn my grandchildrens. (119)

While not addressing the ceremony explicitly, the mention of "dances" indicates the continuance of traditional religious celebrations and practices, of which the Busk is the most significant, among still-existing Creek towns. The symbolic regeneration of the people through the extinguishment and relighting of the central fire condenses the macrological preservation of Creek identity despite attempts to dismantle the nation, to *bring it down*, and the annual nature of the ceremony itself provides a metaphor for, as well as a concrete manifestation of, the effort "to keep on fighting" against those forces that would seek to end Creek history or to reorder Muscogee subjectivity.

Moreover, for Lucy, the performance of ritual, the "dancing," marks the survival of the sociospatial formations at the heart of Creek nationhood. One scholar has referred to the stomp grounds as "the vestiges of the old town squares."[42] Although the towns, or talwas, which had been central to Creek governance as autonomous decision-making bodies became more geographically diffuse and politically marginalized by the end of the nineteenth century, allotment-era U.S. and Creek national policy did not eliminate them, as indicated by their return to federal visibility in the 1970s in ways discussed earlier. The Green Corn ceremony had always been based in the towns, helping generate cohesion and legitimacy for them as sociopolitical units,[43] and in the wake of turn-of-the-century efforts to eviscerate Creek sovereignty, that ritual, now performed at the squares in the stomp grounds rather than at the center of administratively recognized towns, both represents and helps animate Muscogee collectivity and self-determination. Lucy's investment in the persistence of the "stomp dances," then, signals not just a concern for Creek spirituality, delineating its difference from Euramerican Christianity, but a desire to maintain the particular sociopolitical matrices that have sustained the Creek people in their struggle against imperial intervention. As with Ella Deloria's writing, and as against counterhegemonic appropriations of non-native struggles, *culture* here is situated within and indexes a political economy separate from that of the settler state. Green Corn imagery in the novel complements and extends the vision of Muscogee history and governance conveyed through the figure of the tie-snake, foregrounding sites and processes of identification that have defied U.S. management.

In light of the centrality of the Busk to the religio-political identity of the towns, I want to suggest that the text's references to the Green Corn and the survival of the stomp grounds represent what can be described as a talwa imaginary. The talwas' interwoven dynamics of kinship, spirituality, and governance provide a touchstone for the novel in developing its critique of U.S.-regulated modes of sovereignty and the "progressive" accession to them. As discussed previously, the text uses the tie-snake trope to sketch a genealogy of Creek opposition to imposed political structures and forms of social mapping, a "spirit of resistance" largely historically emerging out of town-based movements. In this vein, Womack employs the image of fire to explore the intricacies of Creek day-to-day struggles with the liberal ideologies circulated by white-dominated institutions, as well as to investigate the ethical and practical basis for alternatives to those ideologies—alternatives that grow out of traditional Creek philosophy and politics.

In describing Chitto Harjo's speech to a Senate committee hearing held in Indian Territory, Womack makes clear the centrality of the talwas to the oppositional collectivity of the Snakes. Harjo observes, "My seat at Hickory Grounds is determined by my clan. My clan is part of a town. My town is part of a fire. My fire is part of the red and white divisions of war and peace in our confederacy. My seat, my clan, my town, my fire, my nation" (240). The term "fire" here is a translation of the Muscogee word used to designate towns of the same moiety, of which there were two—red (war) and white (peace).[44] Each talwa itself also contained red and white chiefs, although the entire town belonged to only one moiety. Yet moieties also were crosscut by kinship ties among those belonging to different towns, and thus clan and fire formations helped bind together the talwas as part of a single confederacy even as they continued to function as autonomous units. In beginning his talk with this description of the traditional talwa-centered system of Creek governance, Harjo positions it as the legitimizing structure for his speech, as well as the necessary contextualizing framework through which to understand what he will say. Complementing (and in some sense amplifying) its Green Corn associations, the use of the term "fire" here with reference to Muscogee moieties suggests that the figures of "burning" sprinkled throughout the text are expressive in different ways of the recursive and pervasive confrontation between political paradigms displayed in the Senate committee hearing. These disparate moments, most of which have no apparent relation to what from a Euramerican perspective would be conceptualized as politics, together index how alternative understandings and practices of sovereignty persist despite the absence of official validation by either the United States or the native government recognized as legitimate by the United States—the fact that, as one of the Snakes puts it, "Nobody but us recognizes us" (226). For the novel, then, the Green Corn is both a synecdoche for the talwa system and a way of thinking about the continued survival and regular rejuvenation of that system in the face of the attempted dismantling and erasure of it.

Thus, what is at stake in the novel's employment of figures of fire, as with water and snakes, is who gets to define the terms of Muscogee nationhood and what will constitute political identity in that process. Further, the text implicitly asks, how does the struggle over sovereignty make "secret" certain knowledges, histories, and social formations, and how can sexuality be understood as intimately embedded in that dynamic and as a vehicle for reintegrating that which has been partitioned off as the merely private or the ostensibly unnatural? By shifting the association called forth by Josh's "burning" from hellfire to Green Corn, Womack recasts Josh's desire as expressive not of individual perversity/pathology but as an opening onto transformation, the "flame" of passion representing a localized instantiation of a cycle of collective rebirth. Josh's last name, Henneha, further indicates the novel's effort to link him to the towns and the Green Corn ceremony in particular, as this was the name for a set of town administrators among whom was one who served as a kind of town crier during the Busk.[45] While using the fire metaphor to displace heteronormative logics and to incorporate Josh's eroticism into the religio-political matrix of Muscogee tradition, the novel reciprocally suggests that the Busk becomes a lens through which Josh reinterprets his own experience. Like the tales of drowned towns and tie-snakes, the fire ritual provides a conceptual framework in which events and relationships take on alternative meanings to those disseminated by U.S. policy and white-dominated institutions. This kind of shift in perspective, the text intimates, can nurture an oppositional viewpoint, highlighting the limits and lacunae of entrenched political ideologies by emphasizing the disjunction between official discourse and quotidian forms of sociality and subjectivity.

The novel illustrates that process of working through what, in Gramscian terms noted earlier, can be described as "contradictory consciousness" in its depiction of Josh's unconscious. During his teenage years, he has a dream in which Green Corn imagery figures prominently. In it, Grandpa has handed him an ax to fell a tree, and while he is swinging, his father appears, taunting, "You swing that ax like a little four-year-old-girl." On his next strike, Josh realizes he has "cleaved asunder a black Bible," which then bursts into flames. He searches for words to communicate with his grandmother, who in the dream understands only Creek, and he then sees "two men standing in front of a fire, throwing something into the flames" as a crowd gathers about them, including Grandpa and Aunt Lucy: "One of the men says, 'Seborn, help the boy out . . . , ' and he motions for me to step within the circle." Josh responds by screaming biblical verses at the "he," who we can surmise is Tarbie due to the association with Seborn, but Josh notes, "The more I quote, the more muted my voice becomes until, at last, I wake up groaning, unable for several minutes to articulate words" (74–75).

The scene condenses the contrast between traditionalist and "progressive" ways of perceiving Josh and his relation to the Muscogee people. While his father engages in gender baiting, which is a form of sexuality baiting as well given the link the novel makes between condemnations of homoeroticism and *effeminacy*, Grandpa and Lucy are among those who seek to incorporate Josh into a shared ritual. This difference not only marks a discrepancy in attitudes among Creeks toward what might be termed queerness but also stages the problem for Josh of how to name himself, how to position himself and his "secret" desires within Creek community and culture. Identifying with and through the white Baptist congregation of his parents, as indicated by the quoting of scripture, yields only silence, a paralyzed absence of voice that generates isolation and pain ("groaning"). As an imposed, if routinized, presence, "the church stories" foreclose rather than enable individual self-articulation, and by implication collective self-determination. Conversely, fire imagery and its Green Corn associations suggest a continuity between personal experience and Muscogee history, as signified by the appearance of Seborn and Tarbie. In fact, Josh questions whether the dream actually is such, saying, "it feels as if I didn't dream it at all, and the vision lies at the deepest recesses of my memory" (73), suggesting a kind of communal subjectivity in which "memory" is transpersonal—stretching beyond the recollection of a given life.

The scene further juxtaposes the nuclear family with extended kin/clan connections and town belonging. In some sense pitting Josh's father against Aunt Lucy and Grandpa, as well as Seborn and Tarbie, the dream draws on the Busk imagery to devalue bourgeois homemaking in favor of the kind of extended familial networks around which both the towns and the grounds, the sites of the Green Corn, are organized. The text later indicates that Seborn and Tarbie's relationship was not central to their identities precisely because of the ways the political economy of matrilineal Creek kinship structures diminished the significance of reproductive coupling and individual households: "Naturally, both Seborn and Tarbie had family in their camp. They had women relatives who cooked and cleaned . . . while Tarbie and Seborn worked apart from them with the men." They "fit in" due to "the women with men," so "[t]hey didn't need wives" (221). The linkage between the Green Corn and kinship appears even tighter when one considers that the fire of the Green Corn ceremony is called poca, which means "grandfather."[46] Juxtaposing competing possibilities for Creek sociality, the scene sketches the ways contemporary debate over homosexuality rests on an existing fault line within Creek self-representation. The novel uses Josh's internal struggle to thematize how residual formations persist and adapt despite the dearth of official recognition while gesturing toward the particular political impositions with whose legacy Josh must negotiate, including the institutionalized ideal of heteronuclearity.

The lineage of that ideology is suggested by the resemblance between Josh's vision of the fire ceremony and one witnessed by Lucy in her youth. In it, four men, Seborn and Tarbie among them, stand around a fire performing a ritual near the cabin on the property adjoining Lucy's parents, which belongs to Dave's grandmother. Having followed the path from a nearby spring, Lucy observes them while hidden in a patch of reeds. Described by her as "stomp-dance kind of Indians," those assembled at the fire toss in several items belonging to Lucy's white father, including his razor strap and some of his hair, which had been collected by Dave after a haircut by Lucy's mother (44–45). The positioning of the logs around the fire in a square aligned with the four cardinal directions and the use of a turtle rattle indicate that the event is ceremonial, replicating in miniature features of the Green Corn. In the flames, Lucy sees a vision of a man rushing into a burning barn and dying as a result, a vision that replicates the circumstances of her father's death, which was occurring at the same time (46–50). As Lucy notes, "They had gathered to punish someone whose meanness had took more than one awful turn," "something about a relative of theirs being stolen might have been part of it" (46). Readers already know that Lucy's father is Dave's court-appointed guardian, that Dave recently had become wealthy due to oil reserves found on his allotment, and that he lived with his grandmother until Lucy's father intervened ("like Daddy said, them full-bloods ain't got enough sense to take care of their money when they get a heap of it, so they need white people to watch over them" [34]). The fire ritual, then, is designed to "punish" Lucy's father for his theft of Dave, which was part of an effort to expropriate the value of Creek land by proxy, since as guardian he gains access to Dave's property and oil income.[47]

The men gathered at the fire are Dave's uncles, Tarbie on his mother's side (accompanied by Seborn) and two from his father's side. They have failed in their attempts to use the legal system to fight Dave's categorization as an "orphan," a designation applied despite the presence of living relatives willing to care for him and one that enables him to be placed under white supervision, so they decide to try "their own ways of dealing with these kind of problems" (230–232). While Lucy does not fully recognize it at the time, and readers only retrospectively come to understand through revelations much later in the novel, the ceremony is a response to U.S. intervention in Creek clan structures, particularly the statutory definition of family in terms of a parent-child unit in ways that facilitate the broader program of allotment and detribalization. Only through such a construction of legally cognizable kinship can Dave be deemed an "orphan," the web of relations surrounding him ruled irrelevant in the state's adjudication of appropriate residency. As in Josh's dream, the nuclear family is set against a more expansive conception of kinship and associated forms of belonging, with the Busk-like fire marking kinds of Muscogee social networks made invisible in the institutionalization of a white Christian imaginary. The novel, therefore, presents more contemporary conflicts in Creek individual and collective consciousness around sexuality as the legacy of turn-of-the-century U.S. efforts to reorder native cultural and political formations.

In chapter 3, I explored the ways allotment-era policy sought to fracture indigenous social systems and to inculcate forms of heterohomemaking as a key part of the ideological and legal assault on the sovereignty of native peoples, and the guardian system toward which Womack gestures was a significant feature of this broader program, particularly in Indian Territory. The agreement signed with the Creek government in 1901 provided for allotments of 160 acres based on the model of the patriarchal nuclear family, but only 40 acres of each allotment was designated as a "homestead" and fully restricted from sale. The legal status of "restricted" Indian was created by the Burke Act (1906), which allowed the trust period in which native land was overseen by the federal government to be extended for up to twenty-five years at the discretion of the Secretary of the Interior on the basis of whether or not he found the allotment holder "competent and capable of managing his or her affairs."[48] The Five Civilized Tribes Closure Act (1908) embellished the general principle of restriction into an elaborate system of federal-state concurrence in which persons judged "incompetent" were put under the protection of a guardian appointed by the Oklahoma probate courts. The law restricted until 1931 the "homesteads" of "mixed-bloods" (those of one-half to three-quarters blood quantum) and the entire 160-acre allotment of "full-bloods"—allowing a counterdetermination to be made on a case-by-case basis by the Secretary of the Interior—while simultaneously lifting all restrictions on those with less than one-half blood quantum. This judgment of competency, as well as of native identity, based on relative transmission of racial Indianness clearly follows in the logic of Cooperian "gifts" discussed in chapter 1, although here allowing for a genealogically graduated spectrum of potential for bourgeois homemaking within a detribalizing program rather than the wholesale repudiation of Indian inheritance within the framework of removal. Virtually all the Indians who were "restricted" for the purposes of federal trust also were labeled "incompetent" for the purposes of state guardianship, and guardians of Indian estates charged fees as much as ten times the national average for white estates, as well as exerting control over leases which allowed guardians to reward friends and engage in elaborate kickback schemes.[49] The heterocalculus of blood quantum, as opposed to the more diffuse matrix of clan belonging, provided the framework for a system of racial management in which privatized resources were made available for white extraction.

If the fire ritual that Lucy witnesses serves as an indictment of the guardian system and its intertwined principles of nuclearity and racial superintendence, the novel further uses its depiction of Lucy's father to illustrate how the imperial project of restructuring Creek social life is enacted through the imposition of the bourgeois family form. In addition to seeking to sever Dave's connections to his kin, Lucy's father forbids her mother contact with hers. As Lucy observes, "Daddy didn't allow none of Mama's people over to the house" (50). In this way, he becomes an embodiment of the ideals of allotment; his claim to privacy performs a kind of territorialization that works to fragment peoplehood by forbidding prior modes of association. Rather than appearing merely as a personal predilection, his meanness not only is consistent with the terms of U.S. law but, the novel seems to suggest, is the fulfillment of its structuring logic. We are told that he, in fact, was part of the group responsible for the arrest and imprisonment of Chitto Harjo and the Snakes in 1901 (282), positioning him as an extension of the state. His domination of his home is made possible by policy while also serving as the expression of its in-built tendencies. The novel, therefore, casts his incestuous assaults on Lucy as the product of the institutionalized process of narrating isolation as care. The intimacy of heterohomemaking becomes the crucible for intrafamilial violence, which can be hidden behind the closed doors of the privatized household. Intercutting discussion of her father's abuse of her with references to the effects of allotment ("the dirty dog dealings of white folks") and the survival of the stomp grounds as the preeminent sign of the persistence of Creek nationality, Lucy situates his actions within the larger context of the U.S. assault on Creek identity (118–119).[50]

Womack actually presents Lucy's father as the devil, using that image to link the political economy of nuclearity to Christian fire. In Lucy's dreams, he appears as a shadowy figure she refers to as "Satan": "Satan is sitting on top of me, a-straddling my chest, burning me into a deep sleep . . . He wants to slip inside me. I fight him with everything I have"; his arm is "white," and his face is "a passing blur, blank and without form" (33–34). Allegorizing her father's sexual assault, Lucy's dream transposes it into the discourse of sin. Like Josh, Lucy's efforts to quote scripture as a weapon fail, waking "unable to scream" as her "supply of Bible" "dr[ies] up" (34). In portraying Lucy's father as the devil, the novel again suggests that allotment and its legacy are the true sin, while also implying that language and ideas taken from white-dominated institutions cannot of themselves provide an avenue to critical consciousness. Instead, the rhetoric of the Bible, which as I have been arguing works in the novel as a figure for state-sanctioned ideologies, yields only stifled silence.

The novel further explores how the discourse of sin is used to delimit and police the boundaries of an emergent social geography of straightness. When Lucy begins playing trumpet in jazz clubs, she is disowned by respectable families. She notes, "half of McIntosh County said any woman who'd lower herself to play the devil's music in a beer joint shouldn't be raising children a-tall. I was banned from speech in all the proper households," adding, "I could never see eye-to-eye with all their outstanding holiness and high-toned judgments" (120). Lucy's "devil"-ish excess — working in seedy places as well as doing work thought properly to belong to men — means that not only must she be barred from the "proper households" of others but that she should not create one of her own. Exiled from "progressive" notions of domestic bliss, she observes, "a good deal of the commotion was over the undeniable fact that I'd seen [the husbands'] ways when they got out from under their wives' aprons," including their dalliances with "dolled-up high-footin' gal[s]" and "beautiful colored boy[s]" (120). These failures to sustain marital monogamy suggest that the language of sin works less to discipline immortality than to regulate the public performance of privacy, ensuring that violations of fidelitous heterogendered matrimony will be represented as aberrations and individual "secrets" in ways that naturalize the ideal. Moreover, through the disdain shown toward Lucy for her cross-gendered behavior, the text illustrates that the condemnation of homosexuality is only one among a range of ways the heterosexual imaginary is secured in post-allotment forms of social mapping.

If Lucy's stories help frame Josh's by illuminating how an atomizing logic of heterohomemaking becomes normative, further indicating the vital role it plays in the imperial restructuring of Creek nationality, her stories also show the persistence of countervailing ways of imagining collectivity. In discussing her relations with her judgmental neighbors, she observes that she would give them food when they could not provide for themselves, "letting on like it was just something extra I didn't need, not like they was having hard times." This ethos of sharing is in marked contrast to their attitude toward her: "The ones that run me down as a juke-joint jezebel, I gave the most to in order to drive them close as I could to craziness and expose to the world the underlying nature of their holiness" (125). Lucy's generosity shows up the selfishness at play in "progressive" forms of "holiness." Further, in this giving, Lucy endorses a network of community interdependence and mutual support that reflects the spirit of the talwa, as opposed to the ostensibly self-sufficient household envisioned by the architects of allotment.

Offering a vision of Creek sociality in which the organizing principle is not the heterogendered marital unit at the heart of U.S. family and property law, Womack indicates that Lucy's inheritance is less wealth than profound anger: "The sins of the father passed down until the fourth generation they used to say in church, and I could feel the rage in me, sweeping me along in its current" (124). As indicated by her interactions with her neighbors, Lucy has accepted neither the narrative of the naturalness of the nuclear family nor the bourgeois political economy it helps legitimize, and her "rage" both indexes and animates that process of disavowal, opening her to potential associations and identifications foreclosed in her father's home (or by the kind of homemaking her father represents). Lucy's characterization of her response to her childhood as "my burning" and "white-hot hatred" implicitly presents the sociopolitical conflicts condensed in the fire imagery (hellfire v. Green Corn, allotment-aligned geographies v. the matrix of the towns) as matters of consciousness as well as conscience (124, 126).[51] Lucy's passionate hatred for her father leads her away from the isolated family life enforced by him and toward the stomp grounds, seeing in them a way of making a different future for her children and grandchildren by giving them tools "to keep on fighting" (119).

Thus, Lucy's "burning" resonates with, and becomes a prism through which to interpret, Josh's. While hers signals anger and his attraction, in both cases it puts them at odds with values taught them in their households and sends them in search of forms of community that can speak to their emotional needs, as well as enable them to speak about their experiences in a nonpathologizing way. As a figure of change, renewal, and sustained connection, the fire of the Green Corn provides a means of representing Lucy's and Josh's processes of self-(re)definition in a way that embeds it within the larger framework of Creek history and philosophy. Reciprocally, it suggests that the apparently personal turmoil which they each feel is generated by the endemic friction between the institutionalization of bourgeois ideals (overdetermined by U.S. imperatives) and the persistence of traditionalist conceptions of nationality.

Following the recursive logic structuring Green Corn ceremonialism, the past is never really past, instead persisting as potentiality in the present.[52] Or, put another way, what *is* does not unfold smoothly from what *was* but is punctuated by moments of fracture in which the present can be consumed and remade. In this way, contemporary queer experience replays in a reconstellated way the conflicts of the turn-of-the-century past; Josh and Jimmy both inherit the legacy of allotment and in a sense relive it. Their interactions with their families continually return to the ways struggles over sovereignty permeate daily life, suggesting that interlocking questions of governance, land tenure, and family formation seemingly settled in the years surrounding statehood remain open-ended. Through the depiction of Josh's parents, the novel illuminates how their perception of his sexuality as sickness and/or sin is embedded in the ongoing imperial project of breaking up native social networks into more tractable nuclear units, but conversely, the representation of Jimmy's family shows how such hegemonic assemblages remain vulnerable to forms of critical memory and lived practice that make available other conceptions of collectivity

While hardly appearing as a traditionalist, Jimmy's father is shown as engaged in an ongoing battle against allotment. When Jimmy's father is arrested for breaking a streetlight by throwing rocks at it, Jimmy defends his actions as a signal to the mayor who had been "buying up lakefront property and building houses in Eufaula." As Jimmy explains, his dad's "original family allotment used to be there until his brother sold the last twenty acres to the mayor. Dad says he's gonna tell the Baptist judge at the court the goddamned mayor oughta stay in goddamned Stidham" (84), and his father adds, "My brother got no right to sell that . . . Belongs in the family" (86). While expressing skepticism about the efficacy of such protest, the novel also uses it to highlight the absence of a legally viable redress for, or even a public forum to address, the continued expropriation of native land; more important, this misdirected act of aggression indicates the presence of sustained resentment against postallotment social geographies. Further, Jimmy's father appears to adopt what can be described as a talwa structure of feeling, as suggested by the gift he offers Jimmy late in the novel. After Josh and Jimmy's initial sexual encounter as adults, Jimmy defers intimacy because he is HIV-positive and is concerned about infecting Josh. Part of what allows them to work through this impasse is a photo given to Jimmy by his father, which Jimmy then presents "in a gold frame" to Josh. The picture is of a "young boy standing to the right of Lucy and Glen, leaning at a weird angle, goofing off like Charlie Chaplin." The boy is Jimmy's father, and Lucy had written on the back of the picture: "[T]heres alot of them used to sit in front of they houses like that and I guess us too that crazy boy come over and Lester took it" (277). In addition to strengthening the heretofore implicit connection between Jimmy's father's apparently bizarre forms of resistance and the kinds of oppositional memory and affect associated with Lucy and Grandpa ("Lester"),[53] the photo locates him within a community ethos of regular interaction that defies the "progressive" ideal of isolated privacy. Moreover, the fact that he gives Jimmy the photo after Jimmy has mentioned his recent run-in with Josh suggests that the picture also may function as a sign of acceptance of Josh and Jimmy's relationship. The recollection of townlike relations among households, which given Lucy's earlier comments also may have involved membership in the same stomp ground, becomes a vehicle of inclusion in the present, an opening onto a kind of belonging very much at odds with the anxious nuclear propriety performed by Josh's parents.

Additionally, Jimmy's mother belongs to the Indian Baptist Church, and like the stomp grounds, the church grounds are distinct spaces to which extended families belong and to which they come regularly as part of a ritual calendar.[54] The week after Josh and Jimmy are reunited, Josh goes to visit Jimmy at his family's home during the monthly camp service, and Josh notes, "One thing the stomp grounds and church grounds had in common was you went from camp to camp visiting and eating" (255). Moreover, the Baptist service links the participants' experiences to those of Creeks past, recalling continuity across time as well as coalescing a collective sense of ongoing struggle in the current moment. Josh further observes, "I didn't know what to make of this Creek Christian stuff. The white Christian stuff had nearly done me in, and I didn't know how much of an improvement I could expect from the red version" (255), but he reconsiders this comparison: "The songs, sung in Creek, were a stunning combination of Protestant cadences and Indian chant . . . I could feel my spirit drifting with the music toward the woods, along with those generations of Creek Christians who had come before, joining their voices— some of whom had sung Creek hymns along the trail during the forced march of Indian Removal in the 1830s" (258). Reaching back to the 1830s, this adoption of once-alien forms has itself become over time an embedded part of Creek life, one that can aid in remembering and resisting imperial dispossession and in promoting the survival and integrity of the people. The centrality of networks of kinship to the church grounds combined with the undercurrent of collective memory makes them appear as a version of the talwa spirit sustained by the stomp grounds. Illustrating once again the connection between present practices and the calling forth of the past, the portrayal of the Indian Baptist Church dissociates Christianity per se from the violence of U.S. policy, suggesting the ways the discourse of sin as it operates in Josh's consciousness is the result of a particular imperial process by which Christian figures have been made to surrogate for—and thus to naturalize—a postallotment political imaginary. Resituating these figures (the water of the flood, snakes, fire) within an alternative narrative, one embedded in the survival of the grounds— stomp or church—opens the possibility for reimagining Muscogee sociality and sovereignty.[55]

In the closing scene, the novel again reveals how everyday experience is suffused by a struggle over the past, present, and future of the Creek people. After returning home from a night at the local gay club, Josh and Jimmy begin dancing:

> . . . we are dancing and dancing and dancing and there is so much at stake and it makes all the difference in the world.
>
> So much difference that our dancing beckons others; they rise up out of the darkness to join us. We begin dancing for a nation of people, Mvskokvalke.

> *Loca.* Shell-shakers. Night dances under the arbors . . . *Shuguta shuguta*
> *shuguta*, women stepping toe to heel, the sound of shells shaking, the turtle
> voices. (294)

This final moment returns us to the Green Corn ceremony, as indicated by
the women's dance,[56] but the ritual emerges out of Josh and Jimmy's dancing,
the repetition of that term mirroring the rhythm of the shell shakers. Their
movement both recalls and calls forth the stomp grounds, which for Womack
as for Lucy seem to serve as the locus of Creek identity. The "nation," then, is
remade and rejuvenated through reestablishing kinds of association and
interdependence among the "people" that have no place in the "progressive"
ideal of bourgeois nuclearity. In this way, their dancing is animated by the
spirit of the Green Corn. The image is not marked as such, though, requiring
some prior sense of the Green Corn to recognize that is what is being
depicted. Like awareness of the Redstick War, discussed earlier, knowledge
of the stomp grounds seems to be part of what surrounds the novel's foregrounded stories, presenting the clan/town matrix—or the talwa imaginary,
as I have called it—as the organizing structure of Creek peoplehood and
casting queer experience as reinterpretable within and through that structure. Josh and Jimmy's intimate embrace breaks the continuity envisioned in
the sort of reproductive heterohomemaking desired by Josh's parents and in
some sense emblematized by Lucy's father, but that rupture also makes possible the regeneration of alternative affective connections, as represented by
the "others" who "rise up . . . to join [them]." The novel links their dancing to
that of the Green Corn while refusing to make the latter into merely a metaphoric vehicle for the former; instead, the former appears as an extension
of and avenue to the latter, their dancing pointing toward the sociality of the
stomp grounds.

Earlier in the novel, Josh describes his feelings of desire in the following
terms: "I carried with me a story ember, waiting for a chance to touch the
spark to tinder, to dance around the fire" (79). The trajectory of his "story" is
toward the Green Corn ceremony, thus portraying Josh's growing acceptance of his eroticism—and the interwoven historical, political, and spiritual
discoveries that accompany and enable his shift in self-perception—as part
of a cyclical process of communal remaking. The "story ember" in one sense
suggests a spark with which to start a new story, Josh's storytelling functioning *like* the Busk in providing the basis for a new narrative of himself
and the nation. But in another sense the phrase suggests that the story, Josh's
as well as the novel itself, is an ember with which to light an extratextual
flame, subtly alluding to the Muscogee oral tradition of talwas carrying
embers from their town fires during their removal to Indian Territory so as
to relight them in their new home.[57] From that perspective, the close of the

novel gestures toward the social infrastructure of the stomp grounds, which provides a depathologizing context for Josh and Jimmy; conversely, their story is cast as an "ember" through which to help regenerate the talwa imaginary in the midst of the ongoing legacy of U.S. intervention.

Whereas the native nations that have adopted banns on same-sex marriage have justified their actions through the invocation of "tradition," *Drowning in Fire* insists that the ideology of straightness is an imperial legacy that fractures Muscogee sociopolitical formations. Instead of marking the continuity of peoplehood, Creek heterohomemaking appears in the novel as an anxious performance that aligns one with the social vision of allotment as against the kinds of kinship connections and town-based political geography championed by the Snakes and coalesced in the Green Corn ceremony. Nonnormative sexuality and gender expression are linked to "queer" elements in Creek tradition, like the tie-snake; in this way, deviations from the heterosexual imaginary are used to indicate persistent fault lines in Creek self-representation and sovereignty, moments in daily life that when viewed through the prism of Creek philosophy make visible the continuing struggle over the shape and direction of Muscogee peoplehood. In this way, the novel offers a counterhegemonic reframing of tradition. Its project is less to recover customs imagined as lost or to create an analogy among forms of oppression than to take up persistent aspects of Creek collectivity (the practice of storytelling, the particular figures from those stories, the talwas, the Busk) and use them as a way of reconceptualizing the place of (homo)sexuality within Creek nationality, in the process resurveying the landscape of Creek history and politics.

Reciprocally, *Drowning in Fire* refuses to locate the contestation over Muscogee identity simply within the institutions deemed "political" in a postallotment context. The novel investigates how the efforts to discipline Josh and Jimmy's attraction depend on a privatizing conception of normality that reifies the nuclear household, displaces the towns and clans as sites of affection and association, affirms patriarchal authority, enforces gender binaries, and generates a profound identification with whiteness. These dynamics occur within a bourgeois social geography supported by the legal regulation of home and family. The text suggests that the ideology of straightness, as signaled by tropologies of sin, is an imperial imposition that undermines Muscogee sovereignty, aligning one with the social vision of allotment as against the talwa imaginary championed by the Snakes and coalesced in the Green Corn ceremony. Challenging the presumptive heterosexuality of tradition and the "progressive" vision of nationality, *Drowning in Fire* links support for the heteronorm to participation in the institutional and ideological apparatus of U.S. dominance. In so doing, it repudiates an imperial normality that has been and remains hostile to indigenous self-determination.

This project has occasioned numerous inquiries about how I would answer the question posed by the title: When did Indians become straight? From one angle, the question seems preposterous. If they were/are not straight, how did/do they survive? This line of thought, however, not only presumes a clear opposition between straight and queer, in which whatever is not one must be the other, but, following the auspicious example offered by Rick Santorum discussed in the Introduction, it assumes an inherent, common-sensical correlation between a particular social formation—the heteroconjugal nuclear family—and human reproduction itself. Yet suggesting that *straight* is something that native peoples might (be forced to) become opens the possibility that they may have been, and may still be, something else. A great deal of work within the history of sexuality and under the rubric of queer studies has shown how the sexual identities, categories of perversion, notions of desiring personhood, and understandings of intimacy and health available within the contemporary United States are the product of complex, interdependent, and shifting configurations in medical and psychiatric discourses, national and international law and policy, modes of production and exchange, and so forth. These studies refute the idea of an innate, unchangeable essence that one could call "sexuality," instead suggesting that the fusion of elements of social life and personal experience to each other within that concept is the product of multivectored system that can be termed *heteronormativity*.

More than shaping the terms of cultural intelligibility within the United States, though, that system helps (re)constitute the United States itself by coding indigenous social formations as other than governance. Or, more precisely, measuring indigenous polities against the standard of straightness (the ensemble held together by the institutionalized ideological force of the heterosexual imaginary) has provided, and continues to provide, a means of positioning a liberal framework, with its paradigmatic distinction between public and private spheres, as the self-evident model for governance—against which indigenous modes can be deemed partial, deviant, absent, and failed. Heteronormativity helps cohere and legitimize the settler state by casting indigenous nonidentity with respect to its jurisdictional logics as basically a series of category mistakes, perverse confusions of the familial and governmental that illustrate the fact that Indians must be trained how to have real home, family, and government. The concept of *kinship* can mark this translation. In this way, *kinship* becomes a means of indexing how indigenous peoples were interpellated into discourses of sexuality while also indicating that the reach of the latter in molding the contours of social life in the United States extends well beyond the marginalization of particular kinds of object choice and individual gender expression. Additionally, the presumption that conjugal domesticity is a basic feature of human existence allows native peoples to be understood as *Indians*, the products of a genealogical transmission of racial blood through reproductive pairing. From this perspective, facets of peoplehood at odds with U.S. legal precepts and mappings appear as racial idiosyncrasies rather than alternative forms of sovereignty. Or, since native identity is believed to inhere in the passage of blood through hetero-conception, indigeneity can be divorced from particular kinds of political collectivity: native polities can be treated as if they followed the same patterns of governance as all other polities (read, those normalized by the United States). To "become straight," then, involves a (set of) historical, legal, and geopolitical process(es) whereby native peoplehood is conceptualized and represented through an imposed comparative framework in which dominant settler ideals provide the standard.

In its historical scope, this study also aims to show that *straightness* does not simply precede engagement with indigenous peoples, existing as a preconstituted matrix into which they are inserted. Rather, it develops, at least partially, out of that engagement, the heteronormative assemblage of eroticism, marriage, childbearing and child rearing, homemaking and property-holding, and racial differentiation emerging in response to the continuing presence of native polities. The "Indian problem" operated at several levels: not only did peoples contest the particular policy aims and broader legal geography of the United States, but their forms of social organization often contrasted greatly with those that predominated in non-native communities, opening up possibilities for transformations in settler sociality that threatened to diffuse, if not disintegrate, the boundaries and political economy of the nation-state.[58] The official and popular push for control over indigenous lands and resources competed with the possibility of incorporation into existing indigenous networks. In this vein, the increasing emphasis within public discourse and policy on the nuclear household as the norm, and its circulation as a metonymic figure for the nation itself, can be seen as a response to the limits of hegemony. The growing inability of the U.S. government to gain consent from native peoples for its jurisdictional claims and economic objectives led to an attendant effort to envision the nation in ways that asserted and naturalized its coherence, portraying native modes of sociospatiality as a perverse/savage absence of the self-evident conditions for human health and welfare. The geopolitics of settler dominance and displacement increasingly were legitimized by transposing them into a biopolitical register focused on the (im)possibility of native belonging to the national family.

Conversely, for those non-natives who sought to challenge the terms of *straightness*, to imagine alternative possibilities beyond heteroconjugality and liberal political economy, native peoples provided a template, drawing on their status as a sign of aberrance in order to stage counterhegemonic opposition but still within an ideological frame that does not disturb (and, in fact, depends on) the geopolitics of settlement in which things native are always-already available for non-native use. If U.S. settler imperialism can be conceptualized as an imperative for native peoples to *become straight*, such a perspective emphatically does not mean that traditionally native peoples *were queer*. Rather, queer political projects that are launched by non-natives for non-natives, without a substantive engagement with the problematic of indigenous sovereignty, are as much a vector of settlement as those that are more clearly (hetero)normalizing. Thus, while offering a self-consciously queer critique, this study does not aim to produce or reveal queer native subjectivities, instead exploring the ways native intellectuals from various peoples, periods, and places have articulated versions of sovereignty that cut across the mappings and domains of U.S. liberal governance.

So when did Indians become straight? In some sense, they never have been, they always have been, and they never have ceased *becoming* so. These apparent contradictions have to do with the complex and shifting ways native polities have been inserted, erased, and translated within settler discourses. As one of the anonymous reviewers for this project put it, "the actual argument [of the book] suggests that the very concept of 'Indian' is already straight." To be *Indian* already is to be interpellated into a heteronormative framework in at least two overlapping senses: to be defined by reference to the procreative transmission of racial substance; and to be understood as possessing an innate inability to accommodate to the dynamics of sentimental domesticity—whether depicted as biological failing, evolutionary stage, or genericized capacity for affective expansiveness and communalism. Reciprocally, this special *Indian* disjunction from normative home and family allows for several seemingly disparate possibilities: the never-ending demand that they civilize, the ever-receding horizon of this imperative providing legitimacy for escalating intervention into the affairs of native peoples; the pronouncement of the need to help/fix native governance, since the absence of the natural stability of "domestic relations" must indicate a pathological failure of tribal governmental structures and policy; and/or the celebration of Indianness as a set of queer possibilities, somehow lost to non-native publics but reclaimable through prepolitical pedagogy. Putting native peoples into relation with straightness has been, and continues to be, one of the key settler technologies for producing and sustaining *Indianness* in all its facets, with "kinship" serving as the conceptual and ideological dumping ground/purgatory/detention center for kinds of sociospatiality—formations of sovereignty—that refuse that enforced relation.

Yet native intellectuals have employed and redirected the tropes of "kinship" in order to make visible their peoples' modes of governance, land tenure, and resource distribution, as well as the inapplicability to them of the liberal divide between homemaking and politics. Although, in foregrounding such efforts to contest the role of the heterosexual imaginary in projects of settlement, I also do not want to cordon off indigeneity into *kinship*, however construed, as its sphere of authenticity. Rather, my argument is a negative one in its emphasis on how settler discourses, official and oppositional, have worked to condition self-rule by native nations and to reinforce (explicitly and implicitly) the metapolitical authority of the U.S. state to determine what will constitute viable and legitimate forms of collectivity *within* its borders, enhancing its ability to normalize its jurisdictional geographies. To ask the question with which I began, then, is to suggest that the history of sexuality in the United States is deeply impoverished by not attending to how the United States is (re)produced as a settler state through discourses of sexuality and to acknowledge that programs of removal, detribalization, and multicultural recognition in Indian policy have relied, and continue to rely, on such discourses in crucial ways. Finally, to ask that question—when did Indians become straight—is to insist that heteronormativity functions as a key part of regulating native political self-representation and that queer analysis must grapple with the ways this ongoing history of *straightening* and *queering* powerfully shapes the possibilities for indigenous self-determination.

NOTES

INTRODUCTION

1. The Santorum broadcast was August 3, 2003. See http://www.foxnews.com/
story/0,2933,93646,00.html (accessed April 25, 2009); Deloria, *Speaking of Indians*, 24–25.

2. For examples, see Duggan, "The New Homonormativity"; Puar; and Warner, *The
Trouble*.

3. The phrase "compulsory heterosexuality" is borrowed from Adrienne Rich's essay
"Compulsory Heterosexuality and Lesbian Existence." My usage differs from that of Rich,
who uses the phrase to describe the historical and ongoing limitations in women's access
to resources outside of conjugal linkage with men, but her analysis ties sexuality to family
and household formation in ways that are significant in thinking about the intellectual
genealogy of the kind of analysis I am offering. On the complex relation between lesbian-
feminist writers and intellectuals (such as Rich) and queer theory, see Garber.

4. This formulation is inspired by Andrea Smith's similar move with respect to theorizing and organizing around sexual violence. See Smith, *Conquest*.

5. Michael Warner's introduction to the collection *Fear of a Queer Planet* usually is
cited as the first use of the term "heteronormativity."

6. On the imposition of the family ideal in early U.S. Indian policy, see Horsman;
and Perdue. For the impact of negative representations of native peoples' practices on
institutionalized U.S. sexual norms, especially in terms of promiscuity and polygamy, see
Adams, *Education for Extinction*; Cott, *Public Vows*; and Iversen, "A Debate."

7. For other scholarly work on the topic of gender diversity in Native American cultures, see Blackwood, "Sexuality and Gender"; Driskill, "Stolen"; Gilley; Grahn; Jacobs,
Thomas, and Lang; Lang; Medicine, "'Warrior Women'"; Miranda, "Extermination"; and
Williams, *Spirit and the Flesh*. For further discussion of the perils of applying Euramerican sexological categories cross-culturally, see Patton; Weston, *Long Slow Burn*, 147–175.

8. Such visibility, though, is an important project on its own given both the existence of heterosexism within native communities and the tendency to see native peoples as presumptively straight. See Brant, *Writing as Witness*; Driskill, "Stolen"; Gilley; Jacobs, Thomas, and Lang; Miranda, "Dildos"; Roscoe, *Living*; Womack, *Red on Red*, 271–303. In particular, I would like to thank Craig Womack for drawing my attention to this point; for an excellent account of our ongoing conversation, see Womack, "Suspicioning."

My analysis also owes a great debt to the critique of "heteropatriarchy" within native feminist scholarship. For examples, see Barker, "Gender"; Denetdale, "Chairmen"; Kauanui and Smith; Ramirez; Smith, *Conquest*. While foregrounding the experiences of indigenous women and the ways sexism has been abetted or actively sanctioned in contemporary native governance due to the effects of settler colonialism, this work has not focused on the specific ways in which U.S. policies have constructed and enforced a heteronormative framework in ways that displace and disavow extant indigenous alternatives.

9. While playfully invoking "straight"-ness, what I really am speaking about here is a system of heteronormativity, which is not equivalent to the privileging of heterosexual object choice, as I discuss later.

10. On the legal procedures for measuring native "blood quantum," see Cheyfitz, "(Post)Colonial"; Garroutte; Saunt, *Black, White, and Indian*; and Sturm.

11. While acknowledging Schneider's critique of the viability of kinship as an anthropological concept, more recent scholarship focused on "kinship" tends to do one of the following: add additional elements to the critique of the equation of kinship with a supposedly natural genealogical structure necessitated by reproduction (especially the role of gender, the household, and new reproductive technologies); conceptualize kinship as a form of knowledge production; or continue to insist that there is a core set of reproductive relations cross-culturally that can legitimize the comparison of social/cultural elaborations as "kinship." For examples, see Carsten; Collier and Yanagisako; Franklin and McKinnon; Harris, *Kinship*; Parkin; Strathern. These approaches, though, tend not to consider how the application of "kinship" takes part in translating peoples into the terms of a Euro-American political economy in ways that historically have served as a key vector of imperialism.

12. Notably, while the use of "kinship" as a central part of anthropological theory and practice far exceeds its initial usages, it was developed on the basis of observing and engaging with American Indians, in Lewis Henry Morgan's case the Senecas of the Tonawanda reservation. On Lewis Henry Morgan's ideas and influence, see Ben-Zvi; Bieder, Fortes; Kuper; Trautmann; and Weinbaum.

13. For others who have noted a similar limit in Schneider's critique, see Dolgin; Franklin and McKinnon; Peletz; Weston, *Long Slow Burn*, 58–61. For a fascinating discussion of the ways the rhetoric of kinship, and of familial "relations," emerged out of post-Enlightenment formulations of scientific knowledge in Europe, see Strathern. Her approach does treat kinship as a kind of translation, but less explicitly and in ways whose aims differ from mine.

14. As Jane Fishburne Collier and Sylvia Junko Yanagisako observe, "At the heart of kinship theory lies an analytic dichotomy between 'domestic' and 'political-jural' domains" which "assumes a 'domestic' sphere dedicated to sexuality and childrearing, associated primarily with women, and a 'public' sphere of legal rules and legitimate authority, associated primarily with men" (4).

15. See Boydston; Brown, *Domestic Individualism*; Chauncey, *Why Marriage*; Coontz; Cott, *Public Vows*; D'Emilio and Freedman; Dillon; Grossberg; and Merish.

16. In describing the effects of the doctrine of "Blood Is Thicker Than Water," Schneider suggests that biological closeness is taken as the standard against which to assess the strength of kinship bonds (165–177). Yet if biological resemblance/proximity actually were the implicit benchmark, the relationship between "genetrix and child and between a breeding couple" would not be the paradigmatic starting point for genealogical reckoning; siblings are more biologically alike than even parents and children, while reproductive partners are presumed to be biologically dissimilar. In other words, biological closeness is not the gradient, resemblance to the nuclear family is. On the ways the legal husband of the mother traditionally has been viewed in U.S. law as the "father" of the child, to the exclusion of the biological progenitor, see Dolgin. On siblings as a potential starting point for anthropological mappings of "kinship," see Peletz, 350. On the ways household formation serves as the unrecognized context for anthropology's attribution of enduring affect to genealogy, see Carsten, 31–56. Carsten also offers the astute observation, drawing on the work of Alexandra Ouroussouff, that "anthropological assumptions about Western individualism [and one could add "family"] derive from a tradition of philosophic liberalism, of which anthropology is itself part, rather than from an ethnography of Western people's lived experience in specific contexts" (97).

17. This sense of native polities as *not-quite* government can also be staged as *not-yet* government, as awaiting training in what real governance is. For an account of these dynamics as "colonial time," see Bruyneel.

18. On "nonidentity," see Adorno; Rifkin, *Manifesting*; Varadharajan.

19. Throughout the book, I do use phrases like "kinship system" or "kinship network" that can appear merely descriptive, as if "kinship" were commonsensically referential in the very ways, drawing on Schneider, I dispute. However, I employ those phrases in ways animated by the analysis presented here: indicating social formations that appear as "kinship" within an anthropologically inspired liberal framework but that function in ways at odds with the privatizing ideologies and geographies of settler policy.

20. See Rifkin, "Indigenizing Agamben."

21. See Murphy, "Sovereign." For examples of more complex renderings of contemporary "sovereignty," see Agamben; Nelson, *Finger*; Ong; and Sparke.

22. While U.S. Indian policy has shifted from periods of recognizing native polities in one form or another (treaties, the Indian Reorganization Act, the "era of self-determination" and "government-to-government" relations) and periods in which it sought to dismantle them (the assertion of conquest in the wake of the Revolutionary War, allotment, termination), both tendencies, I argue, are shaped by the assertion of a coherent settler "sovereignty" into

which native peoples are inserted. For discussion of the vacillation between these two modes, see Bruyneel; Pfister; and Wilkins, *American Indian Sovereignty*. For overviews of the history of federal Indian law, see Cheyfitz, "(Post)Colonial"; Deloria and Lytle; Getches, Wilkinson, and Williams; Prucha, *American Indian Treaties*.

23. A fuller version of this argument can be found in Alfred, *Peace, Power, Righteousness*. I also should note that Alfred is addressing settler-indigenous relations in Canada rather than the United States, but his observations also are applicable in the latter instance even if U.S. and Canadian policy frameworks are not equivalent. On Indian policy in Canada, see also Barker, "Gender"; Boldt; Howard-Bobiwash; Janovicek; Lawrence; Wotherspoon and Satzewich.

24. For recent efforts to address native peoples' performance of sovereignty as more multilayered and flexible, see Barker, *Sovereignty*; Biolosi, "Imagined Geographies"; Bruyneel; Cattelino.

25. For discussion of this dynamic with respect to other settler states, see Moreton-Robinson; Nelson; Niezen; and Povinelli, *Cunning*. For an extended discussion of this process in the antebellum United States, see Rifkin, *Manifesting*.

26. On the problems of settler administrations seeking to recognize indigenous difference, see Garroutte; Ivison, Patton, and Sanders; Niezen; Povinelli, *Cunning*; Simpson, "On Ethnographic"; and Smith, *Decolonizing*.

27. Dale Turner offers an example of this imbrication of native self-identification in state discourses in his discussion of Alfred's use of "nation" to name Mohawk political collectivity. He observes, "The Iroquois may view this form of recognition as empowering . . . but the discourse of nationhood remains very much a discourse of the state. The meaning of nationhood evolves out of the negotiated, ongoing political relationship" (110).

28. Denetdale, "Chairmen," 9.

29. Denetdale, "Carving," 293.

30. The term "heterogender" was coined by Chrys Ingraham to address the ways that contemporary Euramerican understandings of gender are inseparable from a conceptual and institutional investment in heterosexuality. See Ingraham.

31. "Two-Spirit" offers a pan-tribal way of designating the continuing presence of non-dimorphic gender systems among native peoples as well as providing an indigenous-centered alternative to the contemporary offshoots of Euro-American sexological categories (including "gay" and "transgender"). On identification as Two-Spirit, particularly as an alternative to the term "berdache," see Driskill, "Stolen"; Gilley; Jacobs, Thomas, and Lang.

32. In a similar vein, Beth Brant critiques the religion that emerged around the Seneca leader Handsome Lake in the early nineteenth century: "Handsome Lake introduced many christian-based concepts and 'ways' that he exhorted the People to follow. Among those messages were 'marriage' between men and women, the christian concept of adultery. . . , the disbanding of animal societies and the dances to honour these Totems, the ban against homosexuality, the confessing of witchcraft and the cessation of such practice,

the ban on women employing herbs and medicines for the purpose of abortion or birth control"; "I find nothing traditionally Onkwehonwe in this religion. Homophobia can thrive in the uneasy mixture of christian thought and Aboriginal belief. And it does" (*Writing as Witness*, 62–63).

33. For an incredibly astute and provocative discussion of how this negotiation works in the quotidian operation of the Hopi judicial system, see Richland.

34. Ferguson, 78.

35. On this process as "secondary marginalization," focused on the status of gays and lesbians in African American communities in the late twentieth century, see Cohen, *Boundaries of Blackness*.

36. In *The Cunning of Recognition*, Elizabeth Povinelli explores the relation between "recognition" of indigenous tradition by the multicultural, liberal settler state and its simultaneous construction of aspects of native sociality, particularly those deemed sexually perverse, as "repugnant culture." The bribe of straightness is a way of designating an aspect of this broader dialectic of indigenous abjection and a particular tactic through which certain native intellectuals (and governments) negotiate that tension.

37. On the work of "tolerance" in contemporary political discourse, particularly in the United States, see Brown, *Regulating*.

38. For a similar strategy, although pursued in different ways, see Bersani; Edelman; Halberstam, *In a Queer*.

39. The trope of intimacy generates the illusion of an "elsewhere" from political struggle, "a promised haven that distracts citizens from the unequal conditions of their political and economic lives . . . and shames them for any divergence between their lives and the intimate sphere that is alleged to be simple personhood" (553).

40. For an extended version of this argument, see Warner, *Trouble*.

41. Gramsci, 256.

42. Weston, however, does share the concern that the pursuit of entry into kinship may end up reaffirming normative patterns: "If gay people begin to pursue marriage, joint adoptions, and custody rights to the exclusion of seeking kinship status for some categories of friendship, it seems likely that gay families will develop in ways largely congruent with socio-economic and power relations in the larger society" (209).

43. In this vein, Freeman's reformulation of kinship shares much with Jose Muñoz's notion of "disidentification." See also Jakobsen, "Queer Is?."

44. For examples of approaches to queer kinship that highlight the constitutive role of state discourses and processes, see Brandzel; Eng; Luibhéid, *Entry Denied*; Luibhéid, "Sexuality"; and Somerville, "Queer *Loving*." However, they tend to treat "kinship" in ways reminiscent of Berlant and Warner, even if queers can gain some access by conforming to the ideal of nuclear conjugality. For discussion of diasporic queerness, see Cruz-Malavé and Manalansan; Cvetkovich; Gopinath; Manalansan, *Global Divas*; and Rodríguez.

45. She does address Claude Levi-Strauss's influence on Jacques Lacan, but she focuses on the former's universalization of the incest taboo rather than his relation to the history of ethnology.

46. See Morgensen, "Settler Homonationalism."

47. The phrase "queer of color critique" comes from Roderick Ferguson's *Aberrations in Black: Toward a Queer of Color Critique*, although not all scholars addressing these issues would describe their work in these terms.

48. On "racial formation," see Omi and Winant.

49. For useful accounts of the intersection of nineteenth-century sexological discourses and racial ideologies and imageries, see also Bederman; Duggan, *Sapphic Slashers*; Roscoe, *Changing Ones*; Somerville, *Queering*; and Stokes. For discussion of how Mormons ceased to be considered white due to their polygamous unions, see Bentley, "Marriage."

50. On the emergence of the notion of "the normal" and its implicit linkage to whiteness in the late nineteenth and early twentieth centuries, see Carter, *Heart*.

51. For similar kinds of formulations, see Brady; Muñoz; Puar; Rodríguez.

52. For a critique of queer of color formulations on this score, see Driskill, "Doubleweaving"; Smith, "Queer Theory."

53. For discussion of this dynamic in the antebellum period, see Rifkin, *Manifesting*.

54. See Denetdale, "Chairmen"; Justice, "Notes"; Smith, *Conquest*.

55. On the anthropological assumptions embedded in liberalism, see Chatterjee; Mehta; Povinelli, *Empire*.

56. For the notion of a racial grammar, see Silva; Stoler.

57. In "The Fourth Dimension," Nancy Bentley argues that African Americans can be understood as historically having been consigned to a state of "kinlessness" due to the ways they were racially barred from participating in normative forms of home and family. She suggests that this status itself was a function of "natal transmission" and that such relations of nonwhite inheritance were predicated on "a bare genealogy" (271). However, as a way of naming the "natural" centrality of hetero-reproduction to human sociality, the notion of "genealogy" itself is embedded within the emergent political economy of bourgeois homemaking. In other words, to define racial identity as "bare genealogy" is to say that the process of racialization occurs within, rather than outside of, the universalizing discourse of kinship Schneider charts.

Chrys Ingraham has used the notion of "heterogender" to mark the fact that "gender (under the patriarchal arrangements prevailing now) is inextricably bound up with heterosexuality" and the system of heteronormativity (204). Following Ingraham's lead, Katie Meacham, a student of mine in a class on the American Renaissance in a discussion of *Our Nig*, described the construction of racial privilege in the United States as the production of *heterowhiteness*, marking the ways that racial identity also is "bound up with heterosexuality."

58. For an elaboration of this point, see Weinbaum. However, she tends to suggest that all references to reproduction, that everything designated as kinship tout court, must be racializing, rather than suggesting that racial discourses frame human reproduction in particular ways.

CHAPTER 1

1. Jefferson, 61–62, 92–93; Foucault, 149.

2. For discussion of environmentalist explanations of Indian difference and its relation to eighteenth-century discourses of natural history and sympathy, see Carr; Sheehan; and Wallace, *Jefferson*. Jefferson is far less sanguine about the possibility that people of African descent can be civilized. See Jefferson, 137–143; Erkkila, 8–10; and Kazanjian, 89–138. In many ways, my analysis in this chapter is consonant with David Kazanjian's discussion of "racial governmentality": "imperial U.S. citizenship does not demand the assimilation of difference to a homogeneous national norm, but rather depends on the active production of a particular kind of difference—the calculable racial difference of a population" (123). However, rather than addressing the terms of inclusion for citizenship, I am focusing on the ways the creation of Indians as a population through discourses of "racial difference" works to occlude native modes of collectivity and self-representation in favor of liberal forms of governance. On this process, see Cheyfitz, "(Post)Colonial"; Garroutte; Kauanui; and Saunt, *Black, White, and Indian*.

3. For a reading of *Notes on the State of Virginia* as indicating the permeability of racial categories and the profusion of mixture among differently raced populations, see Erkkila, 37–61. In suggesting that the text "reveals the impossibility of eluding contact, mixture, and exchange across borders that are themselves fluid, contested, and subject to change" (38), Erkkila tends to cast the recognition of such malleability and flux as "radical" (52), but I am suggesting that such a reading takes race as an a priori framework for talking about native populations rather than asking what is at stake in understanding them as a racial group in the first place, even if the racial "border" between Indian and white is complicated, crossed, and contested.

4. For studies that tend toward such claims, see Burnham, *Captivity*; Doolen; Kazanjian; Konkle; and Scheckel.

5. I should note that Silva's argument heads in a very different direction from mine, instead tracing the ways European global understandings developed a racializing notion of *transparency* in which non-European peoples were understood as locked in their "cultural difference."

6. A similar effacement of the relation between what is taken for "intimacy" under colonial regimes and the existing sociopolitical formations of colonized peoples appears in Stoler's work on North America. See Stoler, "Tense."

7. My argument here runs counter to those that present the racialization of native peoples as necessarily contrary to the recognition of the *presence* of native governments. For example, in *Writing Indian Nations*, Maureen Konkle argues that depictions of Indian-white racial difference in the nineteenth century undercut the recognition of native autonomy and sovereignty in the treaty system by portraying native peoples as lacking the capacity for true self-governance: "[D]espite the historically prevailing view in U.S. society that Native governments are not really governments because Native peoples are essentially different from Europeans and their societies represent an earlier, primitive

moment in the history of mankind, the existence of treaties continues to counter that prevailing view" (8). Rather, I am suggesting that intermeshed discourses of race and sexuality helped provide a framework for what sorts of sociality would be recognized as governance, not so much denying the existence of native governments as only acknowledging versions of such that conform to an emergent liberal model.

8. See Namias, "Introduction," 4, 33–34; McWilliams, *Last*, 11.

9. See Hauptman, *Conspiracy*; Lopenzina; Taylor, *William Cooper's Town*; and Taylor, *Divided Ground*.

10. See Burnham, "'However Extravagant'"; Scheckel, 70–98; Tawil; and Wyss, "Captivity and Conversion." For an analysis that foregrounds Jemison's identity as Seneca, see Walsh. For literary critical discussion of Seneca self-representation in the nineteenth century, see Carlson, 39–65; Dennis; Ganter, "Red Jacket"; and Konkle, 224–287.

11. See Baym, "How Men and Women"; Erkkila, 13–20; Samuels, "Generation."

12. On "settler sexuality," see Morgensen, *Queer / Native / Settler*.

13. There is some disagreement over when Jemison was taken captive. The narrative says 1755, but later scholars have suggested that the eighteenth-century dates in the narrative are off by three years, putting her capture at 1758. See Namias, "Introduction," 13; Vail, 309–311. This last reference is to the 1918 edition of the *Narrative* edited by Charles Delamater Vail, which includes the appendix from the original 1824 edition, the chapters and notes added by other editors over the years, and Vail's own scholarship and commentary. Because Namias's edition is currently the one most widely circulated and it reprints the main part of the 1824 *Narrative*, I have chosen to use it as my baseline, but it contains neither the original appendix nor later editorial emendations and changes.

14. On Six Nations' adoption and clan structures, see Abler, "Seneca Moieties"; Bonvillian; Doxtator; Druke; Fenton (esp. 19–33, 214–223); Mann; Namias, "Introduction"; Parker, *History*, 28–31, 61–89; Rothenberg; Vaughn and Richter; Wallace, *Death and Rebirth*; and Walsh. The question of terminology in referring to the Iroquois Confederacy is a complicated one. Haudenosaunee is the name they use for themselves, which has been translated as "People of the Longhouse"—referring to the household structure in which members of a lineage (larger than the nuclear family) would reside. In the scholarly literature, "Iroquois League" is often used to refer to the ideal of the alliance and its operational principles as expressed in the story of its founding and the particular allocation of fifty leadership positions among the clans of the participating peoples, and "Iroquois Confederacy" is often used to refer to the shifting processes of governance and leadership as they actually functioned historically from the mid-seventeenth century onward, in relation to but not replicating the ideal of the League. See Abler, "Seneca Moieties"; Richter. Originally the Iroquois League was composed of five peoples, Mohawk, Seneca, Onondaga, Cayuga, and Oneida. With the entry of the Tuscaroras in the early eighteenth century, as a result of their displacement from their homes to the south due to war with Euramericans, the League went from being the Five Nations to the Six Nations. I tend to use the various terms interchangeably, but most often in this chapter I am discussing the Senecas in particular, which is reflected in my word choice.

15. Parallel cousins—the children of same-sex siblings—are considered siblings, and parallel aunts or uncles are considered mothers or fathers. For example, my mother's sister would be my mother, but my mother's brother would be my uncle, even though we would belong to the same clan. See the sources cited in the previous note.

16. Bonvillian, 57.

17. See Doxtator, 69–111; Foster, "Lost Women"; Mann, 115–182.

18. Namias suggests that Jemison was part of either the Turtle or the Heron clan ("Introduction," 25). However, her husband Hiokatoo is described in the text as the "cousin" of Farmer's Brother, specifically that they are the children of sisters, which would make them part of the same clan (129), and Farmer's Brother belonged to the Heron clan (Abler, *Cornplanter*, 118). Given the prohibitions on marriage between people of the same clan, I find it unlikely that Jemison would marry a fellow Heron, which would make her a member of the Turtle clan.

19. On the Treaty of Big Tree, see Abler, *Cornplanter*, 120–133; Densmore, 46–54; Ganter, *Collected Speeches*, 85–94; and Wilkinson, "Robert Morris."

20. See Fenton; Hauptman, *Conspiracy*; Taylor, *William Cooper's Town*; and Taylor, *Divided Ground*.

21. See Abler, *Cornplanter*, 120–121; Hauptman, *Conspiracy*, 1–23, 88–120; and Wilkinson, "Robert Morris."

22. See Densmore, 89–90; Hauptman, *Conspiracy*, 115, 148, 160.

23. On Jemison's voice in the text as "the narrator function," see Mielke, 79. She further describes Seaver as positioning "his authorship as a form of sentimental mediation that makes Jemison's heart visible to his audience in the private act of reading" (84).

24. For discussion of the relation between the text and captivity narratives, see Keitel; Walsh; Wyss, "Captivity and Conversion." Keitel's article, however, contains several factual errors about Jemison's tribal identification and that of her husbands. On the captivity narrative as a form from the seventeenth to the nineteenth centuries, see Burnham, *Captivity*; Castiglia, *Bound*; Ebersole; Namias, *White Captives*; and Strong, *Captive Selves*. I will address this genre in greater detail in chapter 2.

25. On the whole I agree with this caveat when reading as-told-to texts, and I have made a similar argument with respect to Black Hawk's narrative. See Rifkin, "Documenting Tradition." However, the difference between a text like Black Hawk's and one like Jemison's lies in the conditions of its production; whereas evidence suggests that the former was generated at the behest of the native speaker, the latter seems to depend entirely on Euramerican initiative. Even though such claims about the origins of the text cannot address why Jemison would agree to take part or capture the particular ways that she did, the issue of initial agency does seem to me quite important in thinking about the overall shape and aims of the resulting narrative, drawing attention, for example, to the pressures to validate a recent land cession that attach to Jemison's voice (in ways I will address at length later), which are not at play in Black Hawk's case (given that he was not a party to the 1832 treaty with the Sauks and officially was discredited as a spokesperson by that treaty).

26. On "property" as a particular kind of land tenure at odds with native practices, see Cheyfitz, *Poetics*. In *Sovereign Selves*, David Carlson discusses the shift in the legal status of the land engendered by Jemison's acquisition of citizenship (47), but he presents it as part of an effort by the United States to privilege individual over collective forms of identity rather than as a confrontation between different modes of collectivity—one organized around kinship networks and the other modeled on statehood. In this way, he sidesteps the role of racial discourse in normalizing the latter as the frame through which to approach native politics.

27. Susan Walsh suggests that the presence of Thomas Clute during the interviews that produced the *Narrative* indicates Jemison's "prudent insistence upon a lawyer's protection" (53), but the extent of his "protection" is quite questionable given that Clute's brother had sought control of Jemison's lands for six years and that Thomas had participated in the process of acquiring them for his brother and other agents of the Ogden Land Company.

28. The fact that she was naturalized is memorialized on her gravestone (Vail, 196). On the legal correlation of citizenship and whiteness in the antebellum period, see Haney López; Hartman; Kazanjian; and Takaki.

29. In addition to the formal consent of Seneca leaders, what distinguished the 1823 agreement from the lease and sale of 1817 was the presence of a federally appointed commissioner to oversee the proceedings, a requirement for purchases of native land specified in the Trade and Intercourse Acts regulating Indian affairs. See Prucha, *Documents*, 14–15, 17–21. The *Narrative* also skips past the fact that the anxiety over the 1817 agreement might have been generated, or at least exacerbated, by repeated Seneca refusals in the interim to sell their lands and to remove west, especially in 1819 and 1823. See Ganter, *Collected Speeches*, 198–219, 233–238; Ganter, "Red Jacket."

30. On these dates, see Ganter, *Collected Speeches*, 239–240; Namias, "Introduction," 3. In the appendix to the first edition of the *Narrative*, Seaver cites "assur[ance] by Capt. Horatio Jones" as evidence of the authenticity of a particular Seneca tradition, suggesting that Seaver and he were in active contact (Vail, 157), and as noted earlier, Jones in this period was functioning as an employee of the Ogden Land Company.

31. Burnham suggests that "Seaver uses the details of [Jemison's] life to dispossess her of her own story" and that this is part of a larger dynamic in U.S. Indian policy in which native peoples are recognized with voice/ownership so as to facilitate dispossession ("However Extravagant," 336). This argument, though, focuses on *Johnson v. McIntosh* (1823) rather than the specifics of Seneca struggles with the United States. In doing so, Burnham seems to me to miss the particular dynamics of race, voice, and representation at play in the text and the events surrounding it.

32. The piece from which I am quoting originally was published as "Can the Subaltern Speak?," from which I draw for the title of this section, but I am using the altered and extended version that appears as the chapter "History" in *A Critique of Postcolonial Reason*.

33. Seaver does acknowledge Seneca gender and kinship dynamics in the appendix, but in ways that segregate them from questions of governance. See Vail, 169–172, 175–176.

34. Hauptman, *Conspiracy*, 152.

35. On the 1826 "treaty" and its effects, see Densmore, 106–113; Ganter, *Collected Speeches*, 250–271; and Hauptman, *Conspiracy*, 153–161.

36. On this controversy, see Abler, "Seneca Moieties"; Carlson, 48–55; Hauptman, *Conspiracy*, 175–210; Society of Friends. The 1838 treaty was replaced by a supplemental treaty of 1842 in which the Senecas regained the Cattaraugus and Allegany reservations. The people of Tonawanda refused to sign the 1842 agreement, and eventually part of that reservation was restored to them through purchase in 1857.

37. The Senecas of the Allegany and Cattaraugus reservations did adopt majority rule and a republican form of government in 1848. See Cohen, *On the Drafting*, 8–9; Doxtator; O'Brien, *American Indian*, 97–109. My point, however, is not that such a choice runs against the grain of an innate Senecaness, but that the Senate's presumption in the late 1830s and early 1840s that majority rule is a self-evidently legitimate form of decision-making among the Senecas seems to depend on a conception of Seneca identity in which such identity has no relation to *kinds* of political process.

38. See Tawil. Scheckel suggests that the text situates Jemison's relation with her children as an ambivalent example of the power of bourgeois domesticity to domesticate Indians (85–90), but Tawil's argument that "the story of Jemison's family thus becomes an object lesson in the incommensurability of whiteness and Indianness defined as two essentially different forms of subjectivity" strikes me as better capturing the *Narrative*'s representation of Indian-white difference (107), although this interpretation addresses neither the historical shifts in articulations of race and family over prior decades nor the relation of such articulations to U.S.-native politics. On the ascendancy of insular senti-mental homemaking, including its dislocation of late-eighteenth-century models of civic-minded sympathy, see Burgett, *Sentimental*; Coontz; Cott, *Public Vows*; Dillon; Ellison; Merish; Stern; Weyler; and Zagarri, "Rights." I will address this shift more explicitly in the next section. On persistent forms of public masculine affect, see Hendler.

39. Thanks to Karen Kilcup for helping me clarify this point.

40. For an alternate reading of this passage as typifying the ways the text employs Euramerican domesticity to "familiarize difference," see Scheckel, 86–87. See also Tawil, 105.

41. See Dowd, *War under Heaven*; Fenton; Jennings, *Empire*; Mann; Parker, *History*; Schutt; and Wallace, *Death and Rebirth*, 111–134. These sources, though, do not necessarily agree on the character of the relationships among various peoples, particularly between Wyandots, the Haudenosaunee, and Haudenosaunee emigrants to the Ohio and western Great Lakes regions often referred to in historical documents and contemporary scholarship as "Mingos."

42. For extensive discussion of this process in a different regional context, see Brooks, *Captives and Cousins*.

43. See Povinelli, *Empire*.

44. This racial logic, which resembles that for African Americans in the period, shifts by the end of the nineteenth century to one in which the dilution of Indian *blood quantum* by mixture comes to serve as a way of supposedly liberating people from tribal belonging, creating the inverse of the one-drop rule for blackness. See note 2 above.

45. Kappler, vol. II, 1030.

46. For discussion of the role of fathers' clans among Haudenosaunee peoples, see Doxtator.

47. While not directly relevant to my analysis here, I wanted to note something about Thomas that has not been discussed in prior readings of the *Narrative*. In addition to charging his brother John with being a "witch," Thomas denounces his brother's polygamy, "consider[ing] it a violation of good and wholesome rules in society" (123–124). Together, these two suggest that Thomas likely was a follower of Handsome Lake, the Seneca prophet who began receiving visions in 1799 and whose influence spread very rapidly among the Senecas. One of his central tenets was the need to strengthen husband-wife relations, which included repudiating polygamy, and he also was known for making charges of witchcraft. Moreover, just prior to the emergence of Handsome Lake as a prophet, suspicion and charges of witchery had been gathering about Delawares living in Seneca villages on and near the Allegany reservation, suggesting perhaps that Thomas may be responding to a fear that he will be seen as a witch due to his having a Delaware father. Also, the *Narrative* notes that "on John's account he struck Hiokatoo" (124), but given that the text notes that Hiokatoo and Farmer's Brother were parallel cousins, or brothers in Seneca terms, Thomas's action may be related to the running power struggle between Handsome Lake and the leaders living at the Buffalo Creek reservation, including Farmer's Brother—some sources suggesting that Handsome Lake charged him with being a witch in the early years after first receiving his visions (Densmore, 59). On Handsome Lake's visions, his rise as a prophet, and charges of witchery before and after his ascent to prominence, see Wallace, *Death and Rebirth*. The discourse of witchery also was complexly intertwined with that of Seneca sovereignty in light of the trial of Tommy Jemmy in 1821, a Seneca man charged in New York state court with the murder of a Seneca woman for being a witch. He was found guilty but pardoned, and the next year, the state passed a law formally extending criminal jurisdiction over the Haudenosaunee "within" the state's borders. See Densmore, 95–97; Hauptman, *Conspiracy*, 115; Vail, 247.

48. There is also a brief reference to Cornplanter's death in the appendix Seaver created for the first edition (Vail, 179).

49. On the land grant, see Ganter, *Collected Speeches*, 31.

50. The *Narrative*'s discussion of Hiokatoo's wartime exploits and the murder of Jemison's sons Thomas and Jesse by her other son John add to its sensationalism.

51. An alternative reason based not on race but on kinship relations may be that her son Thomas was married to one of Allen's Seneca daughters (Vail, 201). The text does note that when Allen moved to the area "he soon became acquainted with my son Thomas" (109), but it says nothing of the marriages of Allen's children.

52. Walsh, however, describes these portraits as choices made by Jemison herself, a characterization that seems to me to overlook the problems of voice I discussed in the previous section.

53. On Cornplanter's life and public role, see Abler, *Cornplanter*; and Wallace, *Death and Rebirth*.

54. Mielke, 80.

55. Whether or not Cornplanter gained either the specific status of chief warrior or his more diffuse position as a "chief" as the result of it being passed to him through his clan is not clear, but the scholarly consensus seems to be that he did not inherit one of the fifty sachemships that composed the council of the Iroquois League, of which the Senecas held eight., Although, there also were two League "warrior" positions allocated to the Senecas in their role as "keeper of the western door" that were not counted in the tally of fifty (Abler, "Seneca Moieties," 462). A position among the official League sachems was occupied by his older brother Handsome Lake, which is itself not a name given to him but the translation of the name of the seat he held on the council.

56. In a petition to George Washington in December 1790, Cornplanter and two other chiefs observe, "When that great Country was given up, there were but few chiefs present. . . . And it is not the Six nations only, that reproach those Chiefs, with having given up that country"; they add, "we will not conceal from you, that the great God, and not m[a]n has preserved the Corn planter from his own nation: for they ask continually, where is the Land which our children and their children after them are to lie down on?" (Jemison and Schein, 239).

57. On the political situation of the Haudenosaunee in the wake of the American Revolution, the circumstances of treaties at Fort Stanwix (1784) and Fort Harmar (1789), the lead-up to the Treaty of Canandaigua (1794), Cornplanter's participation in settler-native negotiations in the 1780s and 1790s, and discussion of the annuities, onetime payments, and plots of land received by various Seneca leaders who participated in agreements with the federal government and the states, see Abler, *Cornplanter*, 58–134; Campisi and Starna; Densmore, 22–45; Fenton, 601–659; Ganter, *Collected Speeches*, 1–60; Jemison and Schein; Wallace, *Death and Rebirth*, 149–183; and Wilkinson, "Robert Morris," 274–278.

58. Campisi and Starna, 482. See Abler, *Cornplanter*, 110; and Fenton, 659.

59. See Dennis; Densmore; Ganter, *Collected Speeches*; Ganter, "Red Jacket"; and Konkle, 224–287. Some have suggested that Red Jacket was a "pine tree" chief, among those who were raised to positions of leadership due to their abilities rather than through lines of lineage. For a counterpoint that asserts that leadership among the Senecas was by lineage, see Abler, "Seneca Moieties."

60. Ganter, *Collected Speeches*, 142.

61. On the dynamics of the council leading to the Treaty of Big Tree, see Abler, *Cornplanter*, 123–132; Densmore, 50–54; Ganter, *Collected Speeches*, 85–94; Wilkinson, "Robert Morris."

62. Ganter, *Collected Speeches*, 93.

63. See Densmore, 34–35, 42; Ganter, *Collected Speeches*, xxvi, 20–21, 62, 99. Barbara Alice Mann suggests that Red Jacket was closely related to the holder of the title of Jigonsaseh ("Mother of the Nations"—the most prominent of the clan mothers who played a central role in the formation of the Iroquois League) and that "he was the *Jigonsaseh's* own Speaker" (168). On the Jigonsaseh, see Mann, 36–38, 134–174; Parker, *History*, 18–19.

64. "Timothy Pickering's answer to Red Jacket and Farmer's Brother" and "Speech of Seneca Billy for the women," Jennings, *Iroquois Indians*, reel 40.

65. Harris, "Life," 500–501; Ganter, *Collected Speeches*, 127. Parrish was adopted by Mohawks, but Jones was taken into the Seneca Wolf clan by Cornplanter's sister, making him Cornplanter's nephew. See Allen, "Personal Recollections"; Harris, "Life"; and "The Story of Captain Jasper Parrish."

66. See Densmore, 89–91; Ganter, *Collected Speeches*, 191–195, 222–224, 233–238, 243–245; Hemphill, vol. VII, 104, vol. VIII, 46. Parrish was subagent to the Haudenosaunee from 1803 to 1829, becoming virtual agent in 1818 with the retirement of Erastus Granger and the failure to appoint anyone to replace him. When Jones died, he left a landed estate valued at more than $100,000 (Harris, "Life," 514).

67. Ganter, *Collected Speeches*, 12, 30.

68. For discussion of the Condolence ceremony as a central feature of Haudenosaunee politics, see Fenton.

69. Ganter, *Collected Speeches*, 202. For other discussions of Red Jacket's mobilization of racial discourse, see Dennis; and Konkle, 232–238. Both suggest that he uses apparently racial tropes in the interest of securing Seneca sovereignty, but they do not focus on his position within the (geo)politics of Seneca kinship.

70. On the use of "tribe" for clan, see Allen, "Personal Recollections," 542; Densmore, 112; Ganter, *Collected Speeches*, 262; and Vail, 164, 169.

71. On Gardeau as largely inhabited by Jemison's children, see Hauptman, *Conspiracy*, 149; Seaver, 160. In a chapter added to the 1877 edition, William Clement Bryant notes, "It is not known how many descendants of the White Woman are now living, but they are sufficiently numerous to form a distinct clan of themselves" (Vail, 203). On the claims of Jemison's kin to land on the Genesee prior to the Revolutionary War, see Seaver, 86–89, 101–104; Vail, 368–369.

72. Harris, "Life," 484. On Big Tree, see Abler, *Cornplanter*, 78–81; Fenton, 650; Jemison and Schein, 235–248; and Wallace, *Death and Rebirth*, 166.

73. Vail notes that the last mention of Jemison's Seneca sisters is their presence at the birth of her first child (365).

74. Society of Friends, 121, 126, 133, 138; Vail, 201. However, given the uneven emergence of forms of patrilineality over the course of the nineteenth century, as suggested by Shongo's use of his father's last name, his leadership position might have come to him through his father's line, his paternal grandfather having been an important leader (Harris, "Life"; 390; Vail, 233). On the continuance of Seneca patterns of passing leadership positions through matrilineal lines into the 1830s and 1840s, see Abler, "Seneca Moieties." For the birth and death dates for Jemison's children, see Vail, 353–354.

75. Densmore, 123.

76. On the civilization program, see Horsman; Onuf; and Wallace, *Jefferson*. On Cherokee governance in the 1820s, see McLoughlin; Perdue; and Rifkin, "Representing."

77. My account differs from those that represent *Last of the Mohicans*, and *The Leatherstocking Tales* more broadly, as fundamentally challenging the legitimacy of displacing native peoples and the regime of propertyholding that validated white settlement. See Adams, *Guardian*; McWilliams, *Last*; and Rans. Such critical approaches tend to treat the discourse of Indian/white racial difference as itself obvious rather than an ideologically overdetermined way of representing the relation between native and settler geographies of occupancy and governance; therefore, they do not address how Cooper's racialism displaces forms of native political self-representation.

78. In *Intimacy America*, Peter Coviello suggests that the Jeffersonian republicanism of the late eighteenth century turned less on the possession of whiteness than on a notion of selfhood based on the holding of property, which indicated autonomy. Over the course of the early nineteenth century, the "specific kind of self-relation" demonstrated by propertyholding gave way to a form of racial self-possession that came to signal personal independence despite actual dependence on forms of wage labor and other sorts of economic contingency. Through identifying as white, becoming "fus[ed] into what we might call an *affect-nation*" (4), one could feel belonging with other whites in/as the nation but also could experience that belonging as an emotional bulwark against the mounting difficulty of securing a stable means of living (29–57). However, this argument overlooks the ways that forms of land tenure already were racialized in the late eighteenth century (with native territoriality represented as an expression of reproductively transmitted instincts) and the ways that connection of affect with racial identification emerged in tandem with changes in the political economy of household formation.

79. See Boydston; Coontz; D'Emilio and Freedman; Shamir; and Shammas.

80. See Banner; Calloway; Dowd, *War under Heaven*; Jones, *License*; and White, *Backcountry*.

81. On the importance of the Scottish Enlightenment to the imagining of home and family in the American colonies and early Republic, see Dillon; Ellison; Merish; and Zagarri, "Rights."

82. On the ways Jeffersonian agrarianism remains enmeshed in complex ways within a broadly mercantilist imaginary, in which the nation depends on international trade to provide manufactured goods, see McCoy; Onuf.

83. See also Cott, *Public Vows*; Fliegelman.

84. For a differently configured, but quite evocative, understanding of seriality as an emergent feature of white self-understanding in the backcountry, see White, *Backcountry*.

85. On Cora's complex status in the novel, see Baym, "How Men and Women"; McWilliams, *Last*, 73–74; and Rans, 123.

86. While the combat in *Last of the Mohicans* is for England during the Seven Years' War, Cooper assures readers in *The Prairie* that Heyward eventually fought quite ardently

on the side of the Americans during the Revolutionary War (112), and his grandson, who appears as a character in the later novel, serves in the U.S. military. For readings that suggest that the novel represents the Seven Years' War as meaningless bloodshed and thus challenges any triumphal narrative of the United States as successor to European claims on native lands, see McWilliams, *Last*, 26–28, 81–111; Rans, 102–130. This interpretation, though, underplays the importance of the narrative of Cora as an allegory of the need for national containment instead of imperial ambition.

87. On those early-twentieth-century developments, see Saunt, *Black, White, and Indian*; Thorne.

88. On Uncas's strangely "civilized" actions toward Cora and Alice, and the ways they prefigure the "vanishing" of his people, see Bergland, 83–96; McWilliams, *Last*, 55; and Romero, 35–51.

89. See Baym, "How Men and Women."

90. The emphasis on coupling and conjugal sentiment in *Last of the Mohicans* is at odds with the focus on the household, or perhaps more accurately the manorial estate, in *The Pioneers*. The shift in focus from a household which encompasses numerous kinds of relatives and nonrelated persons to the possibilities and dangers of marital union may suggest the ideological ascent of the nuclear family model over the course of the 1820s.

91. While many critics have interpreted Tamenund's rhetoric, especially at the very end of the novel, as signaling the vanishing of native peoples, John McWilliams observes that Tamenund states, "I have often seen the locust strip the leaves from the trees, but the season of blossoms has always come again" and "the time of the red-men has not yet come again" (*Last*, 305, 350), suggesting possibilities for future renewal rather than their disappearance entirely (McWilliams, *Last*, 106).

92. See also Caffrey.

93. In "Generation through Violence," Shirley Samuels rightly notes that the term "blood" gets used in the novel far more often to talk about the woundings that result from warfare than to address racial belonging. However, rather than seeing the former as eclipsing or displacing the latter, I would suggest that the struggle over territory that serves as the basis for warfare in the text is recast as a series of promptings in the blood, largely understanding geopolitics in terms of race.

94. McWilliams, *Last*, 17.

95. On this incredibly complex history, see Fenton; Goddard; Jennings, *Empire*; Jennings, "Pennsylvania"; Mann; Parker, *History*; Schutt; Wallace, *King*; and White, *Middle Ground*. These sources do not always agree, and I have assessed their claims against each other in providing this abbreviated synthesis.

96. On the tendency of Haudenosaunee leaders and spokespeople to refer to the Delaware as "women," particularly after 1742 in negotiations with Pennsylvania, see Jennings, "Pennsylvania"; Mann, 15–18; Schutt; and Shoemaker, 107–114.

97. The figure of Chingachgook likely was derived from a Mahican leader who served as a scout on the English side during the Seven Years' War (Frazier, 117–124). For other possible inspirations, including Hendrick Aupaumut, see Lopenzina, 1128.

98. See Schutt, 141–149.

99. For perhaps the best account of the kinship terms used by peoples for each other in the Northeast and Great Lakes regions, see Aupaumut, "Short Narration." I will discuss the text at length in the next chapter.

100. See Den Ouden. Given Cooper's reliance on Heckewelder's ways of framing native identity, the "Mohicans" are most closely tied to the Mahicans, since Heckewelder consistently describes the "Mohicans" as "Mahicanni" and observes that they tradition-ally resided on the Hudson River (xxvi, xli, 52). The conflation of Mohegans and Mahi-cans as "Mohicans" also may represent a blending for Cooper of the residents of Brotherton and New Stockbridge, respectively, resettled communities living on Oneida land since the mid-1780s. See Brooks, *Samson Occom*; Frazier; and Taylor, *Divided Ground*. For comparison of Brotherton and Cooperstown, see Lopenzina. For discussion of the founding of Cooperstown and its management by James Fenimore Cooper's father, see Taylor, *William Cooper's Town*.

101. On Teedyeschung's leadership, see Jennings, *Empire*; and Wallace, *King*. The most important hereditary leader among the eastern Delawares was Nutimus, but he did not have Teedyeschung's visibility.

102. On the rise of the figure of Tamenund, see Deloria, *Playing Indian*, 10–70.

103. If, as Geoffrey Rans has argued, *Last of the Mohicans* needs to be interpreted with an eye to the fact that its readers would understand the novel in the context of its prede-cessor, *The Pioneeers* (1823), the domestic imagery becomes even more forceful, given that Hawkeye and Chingachgook literally share a residence—the cabin—in the earlier novel. The homemaking of these two characters and Oliver Edwards in the *Pioneers* to some extent provides a prism through which to view the relationship among Hawkeye, Chingachgook, and Uncas in *Last of the Mohicans*.

104. A similar intimation occurs in both *The Pioneers* (Hawkeye says, "we have been brothers and more so than it means in the Indian tongue" [421]) and *The Prairie* (Hawk-eye observes of Chingachgook's death, "such as they who liv'd long together in friendship and kindness . . . should be permitted to give up life at such times, as when the death of one, leaves the other but little reason to wish to live" [250]). For the most famous analysis of homoeroticism in the novel, see Fiedler. For a discussion of problematic assumptions in Fiedler and more recent critics who have addressed interracial male bonding as a pro-gressive image, see Wiegman, "Fiedler." However, her account resolves nonwhiteness into blackness despite discussing *Last of the Mohicans* and *Moby-Dick*.

105. Various kinds of native adoption appear in both *The Pioneers* and *The Prairie*, the other Leatherstocking Tales produced in the 1820s. In the former, Oliver Edwards ini-tially is presented as being "descen[ded] from a Delaware chief" (143), leading readers to believe he is Chingachgook's biological son; later, the novel reveals that his grandfather, Major Effington, had been adopted into the Delawares by Chingachgook (441) (which as a man he actually could not do), yet the fact that Edwards is not *really* Indian in the sense of being mixed-blood means that he can take up the Effington estate supposedly held for them by Judge Temple and can marry Elizabeth Temple. See Cheyfitz, "Savage Law." In

The Prairie, the Pawnee leader Hard-Heart adopts Hawkeye as his father, but this process eventuates in the latter's burial among the Pawnees, suggesting Hawkeye's exceptionality among whites and the adoption's ultimate inconsequence for considering future native-settler relations.

106. My argument here differs from that of Laura Mielke's claim that Cooper's novels illustrate the failure of interracial sympathy to sustain a "middle ground" of Indian-white interaction (36–50). Instead, I am suggesting less that the text indicates the demise of some intercultural space than that it disavows native systems of kinship and political self-understanding. On the problems posed by the "middle ground" paradigm in recognizing widely shared native modes of diplomacy and landholding, see Rifkin, "Documenting Tradition."

CHAPTER 2

1. For comparisons of *Hope Leslie* to *Last of the Mohicans*, see Baym, "How Men and Women"; McWilliams, *New England's*, 78–80; Schweitzer, 165–168.

2. On sexology, see Bland and Doan; D'Emilio and Freedman; Ross.

3. These issues are powerfully present in Sedgwick's own life, given her choice not to marry and instead to live in her brothers' homes, her family's role in the displacement of the Mahicans from Stockbridge (where she was raised), and the marriages of members of her extended family to Indian men. See Frazier; Kelley, *Power*; Miles; and Weierman, 68–70.

4. Williams, *Marxism and Literature*, 130, 132. Sedgwick's text certainly is not the only one in which marriage and white-Indian interaction are combined. For discussion of the frontier romance, see Burnham, *Captivity*, 92–117; Castiglia, *Bound*, 106–136. These critics, though, have not focused on questions of kinship or on the possibility of authors' "queering" marriage. Moreover, *Hope Leslie* was the most popular of these texts and thus deserves special attention as an index of public debate/negotiation. See Bell, 213–214; Gossett and Bardes, 13, 28; and Stadler, 42.

5. Critics have tended to read the novel as a confrontation between the personal and the political operating in two simultaneous, yet somewhat conflicting, registers—the assertion of individual conscience in the face of immoral decisions made by officials and the racial disqualification of the Indian from participation in the democratized nation made possible by such ethical opposition. For readings that illustrate these patterns, see Fetterley; Gossett and Bardes; Karafilis; Maddox, *Removals*; Nelson, "Sympathy"; Schweitzer; Singley; Stadler; Tuthill; and Vásquez. These accounts largely assume that denying the rights of Indians as members of the U.S. nation-state is the primary violence enacted by the novel's vision of national regeneration, thereby offering a fairly limited interpretation of both the text's organizing metaphors and what is disavowed by them. To a greater or lesser extent, these formulations depend upon understanding native peoples as subjects of the United States rather than as separate, self-determining polities.

6. On "transtribal networks," see Rifkin, "Documenting Tradition."

7. On this potentially metonymic fusion, see Balibar; Brown, *Regulating*; Silva; Weinbaum.

8. On "intrasettler dialogue," see Trask, 25.

9. On Webster and the broader employment of the Puritan past in nineteenth-century imaginings, see Conforti, 181–186; McWilliams, *New England's*, 6–19.

10. For discussion of the importance of kinship in structuring political formations in European countries and Euro–settler states, especially as against efforts to cast such connection as an identifying trait of non-"western" peoples, see Carsten; Povinelli, *Empire*; and Stevens.

11. The generational/genealogical pattern present in Webster is not entirely absent in the novel. In the "Preface" the narrator refers to the "first settlers of New-England" as "our ancestors" and in the first chapter describes them as "our fathers" (5, 12). Later formulations of this relation, though, are more diffuse, noting what "the noble pilgrims lived and endured for us" while describing them as "an exiled and suffering people" and characterizing that amorphous "we" as "their posterity" (72–73, 144). A broader sense of historical antecedence displaces, or at least modifies, the literalism of bloodlines, and, as I will argue, the logic of lineal consanguinity structuring Webster's account is at odds with the lateral bonds and figures of siblinghood stressed in Sedgwick's narrative.

12. In the seventeenth century in England, marriage to a first cousin would not have been understood as incest, but it increasingly was considered such in the early-nineteenth-century United States. See Grossberg, 108–113.

13. On the parallel between the two Williams, see Castiglia, *Bound*, 167; Singley, 43.

14. On "affective individualism" as a formulation emerging out of Scottish Enlightenment notions of marriage and personhood, see Dillon, 123–160; Merish, 29–61; Zagarri, "Rights."

15. On the novel's portrait of Mrs. Fletcher and its implicit commentary on women's consignment to domesticity, see Castiglia, *Bound*, 160–161; Fetterley, 72; Gossett and Bardes, 21; Nelson, "Sympathy," 194; and Schweitzer, 184–185.

16. For different readings of the novel's setting that focus on its historical revisionism, see Burnham, *Captivity*, 105–111; Gould; Maddox, *Removals*, 89–95, 103–110; Nelson, "Sympathy," 193–199; and Singley, 42–44.

17. The synthesis I offer here is drawn from a wide range of sources, including Basch; Blumin; Boydston; Brown, *Domestic Individualism*; Burnham, *Captivity*; Coontz; Cott, *Bonds*; Cott, *Public Vows*; D'Emilio and Freedman; Dillon; Fliegelman; Freeman, *Wedding*; Godbeer; Grossberg; Lyons; Merish; Schweitzer; Shamir; Weyler; Zagarri, "Rights"; and Zagarri, "Morals."

18. Several recent studies have sought to rethink the relation between affect, interiority, domesticity, and family in the antebellum period. In *Family, Kinship, and Sympathy in Nineteenth-Century American Literature*, Cindy Weinstein argues that sympathy functions in ways that challenge the obviousness of biology as a basis for defining family, presenting this dynamic as a shift from an earlier formation. However, she presumes that

"family" necessarily was understood in biological terms prior to the early nineteenth century and overlooks the idea that the representations of shifting emotional configurations she examines might be an effect of the only emergent congruence of the single-family home, intimacy and affective intensity, and the nuclear family unit in the period she discusses. Similarly, Milette Shamir's *Inexpressible Privacy* offers a fascinating examination of how domestic space itself was gendered in ways that distinguished areas of gathering and entertainment, associated with women, from spaces of retreat/seclusion, associated with men, and she uses this distinction as a way of considering tensions within the notion of "privacy." However, she tends to treat selfhood in seclusion as a dehistoricized mode of being rather than itself a product of the emergence of nuclear homemaking she examines, extrapolating as universal a kind of subjectivity specific to a particular formation of kinship and residency. In *Interior States*, Christopher Castiglia explores the ways that social conflicts increasingly came to be represented as forms of internal emotional and psychological struggle, displacing the public sphere into, on the one hand, privatized selfhood and, on the other, a vision of uncontestable institutional consciousness. While offering a wonderful account of the displacements entailed by discourses of psychic interiority, his account tends to overlook the political economy of bourgeois household formation that provides the social infrastructure for the kinds of subjectivity he examines.

19. In an earlier exchange with Hope, Esther admonishes her, saying, "you do allow yourself too much liberty of thought and word: you certainly know that we owe implicit deference to our elders and ssuperiors;—we ought to be guided by their advice, and governed by their authority" (180). The description of Hope's actions as a pursuit of "liberty" and the stakes of her action as the "authority" of governance generate a similar set of associations as those described later.

20. For alternative readings of the novel's references to the English Civil War, see Fetterley, 76; Schweitzer, 167.

21. In her autobiography, written to her grandniece Alice in 1853, Sedgwick observes, "I can conceive of no truer image of the purity and happiness of the equal loves of Heaven than that which unites brothers and sisters," and her choice of residence reflects this sentiment, living most of her adult life in the households of her brothers Harry and Robert (Kelley, *Power*, 89). Judith Fetterley has suggested that the novel emphasizes brother-sister affection over parent-child (72, 83), and Chris Castiglia notes that "heterosexual romance is replaced in *Hope Leslie*, as it is in Sedgwick's autobiography, by sibling affection" (*Bound*, 171). On the ways Hope and Everell's relationship resembles Sedgwick's connection to her brothers, see Singley, 48.

22. While some critics have suggested that this parallel creates a mirroring effect, making the characters doppelgängers, such a reading depends on an atomizing logic that interprets affiliations between persons as signaling something about the individual identity of one or both characters rather than about the collectivity formed by their association. See Gossett and Bardes, 22; Singley, 42; Stadler, 42; and Vásquez, 173, 188. In "'My Sister! My sister!'" Judith Fetterley takes seriously Magawisca and Hope's potential

sisterhood, arguing that the former is cast as the true sister of the latter over and against her biological sister (Faith), but this connection is made in the context that both of them want to take on the social role/possibilities open to the brother (Everell), again making a relationship a figure for individual identity (80–81). Chris Castiglia argues that "Indians . . . and white women unite in their resistance to white, male control, forming a sympathetic and mutually supportive community" (*Bound*, 164–165), but this reading overlooks both the ways that white men (Everell, Digby, and Cradock) are incorporated into the familial network at the center of the novel and the import of representing "community" in terms of kinship, as an alternative to bourgeois homemaking and conjugal privatization.

23. Given the close association of "friendship" with siblinghood in the novel, Sedgwick may be drawing on an earlier set of meanings in which the term was used to refer to family members. See Cott, *Bonds*, 186. By contrast, Ivy Schweitzer offers a complex and layered interpretation of "friendship" in the novel as a revisioning of the classical and republican version of the concept in ways that acknowledge women's agency and bonds with each other, offering a particularly compelling juxtaposition of the novel with John Winthrop's mobilization of tropes of friendship in "Modell of Christian Charitie" (165–205). This reading, though, seems to me to efface the ways the text melds friendship with familial relation, rather than contradistinguishing them, and Schweitzer's argument tends to dichotomize friendship and family in ways that downplay references to nonnuclear understandings of kinship at play in the sources and scholarship she quotes. Also, while providing an incredibly rich intellectual history of Anglo-American discourses of friendship, Schweitzer overlooks the novel's repeated invocation of native feelings and social formations as a basis for settler rejuvenation. More broadly, her account depends far more on classical sources and early-modern reflections on them than on the archive of European-native contact and imperial governance.

24. See Dalke; Dillon, 118–139; Samuels, *Romances*; and Stern, 26–29. For a reading of nineteenth-century incest plots as suggesting the limits of linking sentiment to the family, see Hendler, 113–146.

25. While these incestuous intimations threaten to render depraved the novel's familial imaginary, the plot surrounding Philip Gardiner offers a counterweight around which to collect connotations of perversity. In addition to the obvious libertinage of his relationship with Rosa, his association with Thomas Morton is presented in decidedly sodomitical terms. In addition to describing Morton as "the man of pleasure," the novel has Morton attack Gardiner when the latter visits the former in his cell, throwing Gardiner to the ground and pinning him on his back in what seems like a quasi-rape scene (258–259). Gardiner's monarchist sentiments further link his sexual errancy to tyranny.

26. Several critics oddly describe Esther as being exiled despite the novel's explicit discussion of her reunion with Hope and Everell and the fact that the text concludes with discussion of her nonmarital happiness. See Fetterley, 79; Singley, 43; and Stadler, 52–53. Michelle Burnham interprets Esther's singleness as "upset[ting] the affective logic on which the historical romance relies" and thereby refusing "national union" along with

"marital union" (*Captivity*, 117). Such a reading, though, overlooks the ways the novel continually pushes against the insularity of conjugal homemaking as part of its vision of national union.

27. Although Sedgwick remained single her entire life, had no sustained relationships with men, and mentioned often in her journal and correspondence her powerful feelings for women, no one to my knowledge has sought to think about her as a protolesbian, which seems to me a surprising oversight.

28. Kelley, *Power*, 123. On the lives and cultural position of single women in the antebellum period, see Chambers-Schiller.

29. Exceptions to this point would be descriptions of polygamy and sodomy. While the technical term for a man with multiple wives is "polygyny," "polygamy" is used more frequently, so I have chosen to use the latter term.

30. On romantic primitivism, see also Deloria, *Playing Indian*; Povinelli, *Cunning*; Scheckel.

31. Prior to the attack by Magawisca's father, she and Everell are described by Mrs. Fletcher as "two young plants that have sprung up in close neighbourhood" (33), and in his attempt to dissuade Winthrop from orchestrating an engagement between his son and Esther, Mr. Fletcher characterizes the feelings between Everell and Hope as a "natural union" (152). Additionally, Magawisca uses the metaphor of "mingling with" a "stream" in discussing Faith's marriage to Oneco, an image she later repeats but this time with respect to Everell and Hope (188, 330).

32. In the "Preface," Sedgwick claims, "The Indians of North America are, perhaps, the only race of men of whom it may be said, that though conquered, they were never enslaved. They could not submit, and live" (6). In its baldest affirmation of native disappearance, the text later asserts, "it is not permitted to reasonable instructed man, to admire or regret tribes of human beings, who lived and died, leaving scarcely a more enduring memorial, than the forsaken nest that vanishes before one winter's storms" (83).

33. This event is based on the English massacre at Mystic village in 1637 that resulted in the death of anywhere from 400 to 700 Pequots, the vast majority of whom were noncombatants. On the events leading up to the assault and its aftermath, see Cave; Fickes; Karr; Salisbury. Mononotto is real, but Magawisca and Oneco are fictional. Mononotto's wife was captured but with two sons, and they were released within two years (Fickes, 70).

34. Several critics have interpreted Mononotto as another figure for patriarchal rule or for a monologic (as opposed to dialogic) cultural perspective. See Gould, 651; Maddox, *Removals*, 97–98, 106–107; Nelson, "Sympathy," 198; Tuthill, 100; and Vásquez, 182.

35. Adopting strangers as replacements for dead relatives likely was far less prevalent among Algonquian peoples in southern New England, like the Pequots, than among Iroquoian peoples, who engaged in what scholars have come to call "mourning wars." See Bragdon, 148–149; Demos; Haefeli and Sweeney; Strong, *Captive Selves*, 78–85; and Vaughn and Richter. While Algonquian practices came to resemble Iroquoian ones by the late seventeenth and early eighteenth centuries, Magawisca's implicit adoption of Everell can be understood as a projection of later developments onto earlier events as well

as a merger of different peoples into a generic Indian model, a process I will discuss further later.

36. On the captives, see Cave, 135–143. In *A Peep at the Pilgrims*, Harriet Cheney offers a novelistic version of these events, with which Sedgwick was familiar and to which she alludes in *Hope Leslie*. See Burnham, *Captivity*, 97–111.

37. Among the *OED* definitions for "obligation" are "the constraining power of a law, duty, contract, or (more generally) custom, habit, etc." and "a benefit or service for which gratitude is due; a kindness done or received."

38. Here I differ from Maureen Tuthill's reading of the novel as developing the "ethical groundwork to support Indian removal" (96). While the essay does an excellent job of tracking the largely critically unnoticed presence of conflict over land in the novel, Tuthill takes the absence of a critique of removal as "support" for it, rather than reading the former as the condition of the text's employment of native peoples as a tool in a struggle that requires silence on questions of sovereignty. My point is not that the novel resists removal but that reading it as necessarily either endorsing or opposing removal misses the ways it is engaged in a different kind of counterhegemonic project in another discursive register, one that itself forecloses discussion of native peoples as self-determining polities. On Sedgwick's personal opposition to the policy of Indian removal, see Weierman, 77.

39. Thanks to Karen Kilcup for helping me clarify this point.

40. On the dynamics and representation of English captivity in the seventeenth and eighteenth centuries, see Castiglia, *Bound*; Demos; Ebersole; Little; Namias, *White Captives*; Strong, *Captive Selves*; and Vaughn and Richter. My discussion of captivity discourse and the novel's allusions to Eunice Williams owes a great debt to Audra Simpson, whose paper delivered during the panel "Native Feminisms without Apology II" at the 2006 meeting of the American Studies Association raised crucial questions about the work performed by narratives of native adoption of whites in Euramerican cultural and political imaginaries. See Simpson, "Captivating Eunice."

41. On the captivity narrative's transition to romance, see Burnham, *Captivity*; Castiglia, *Bound*; and Ebersole. These studies tend to replicate the problem Povinelli describes, making Indian difference a metaphor for exploring the internal dynamics of liberalism in ways that tend to displace specific native histories, forms of collective identification, and political confrontations with the settler state, while using the contentless image of the Indian as counterhegemonic leverage within a Euramerican structure of feeling. For a similar critique, see Strong, *Captive Selves*, 9–13.

42. Williams, *Marxism and Literature*, 132.

43. On this trend, see Ebersole; Strong, *Captive Selves*.

44. Burnham, *Captivity*, 95.

45. See Bragdon, 140–181; Cave, 37–38, 64–68; O'Brien, *Dispossession*; Plane; and Salisbury, 39–48, 150–151.

46. Eunice was Sedgwick's second cousin twice removed. See Kelley, "Introduction"; Weierman, 66–69.

47. On the attack and the subsequent history, see Demos; Haefeli and Sweeney; Simpson, "Captivating Eunice"; and Williams, *Redeemed Captive*.

48. See Bell, 216–217; Burnham, *Captivity*, 110; Kelley, "Introduction," xxxviii; Weierman, 63–76. On the absence of Indian-white intermarriage in seventeenth-century New England, see Smits.

49. See 65, 74, 77, 89, 110, 188, 190.

50. Cave, 161.

51. See Cave, 157–161; Fickes; Karr. On the creation of Pequot reservations in Connecticut and their history during the eighteenth century, see Den Ouden.

52. Vaughn and Richter, 49. They also note that William Baker, a trader on the Connecticut, was reported to have "turned Indian" in Mohegan territory, but he was captured by Connecticut authorities and therefore could not be the captive who "dwelt" with the Pequots "for a long time" (Vaughn and Richer, 47; Smits, 15).

53. In "Domestic Frontier Romance, or, How the Sentimental Heroine Became White," Ezra F. Tawil argues that early-nineteenth-century narratives featuring captivity help produce the logic of blood racial difference. Tawil suggests that the races are distinguished in terms of their relation to the kinds of sentiment created in bourgeois home-making and through the naturalization of bonds among people of the same race. "By describing race in terms of kinship, domestic frontier fiction used one kind of classification to produce another," and "the 'whiteness' of the sentimental heroine" refers "to a special kind of subjectivity that was in turn the product of a particular kind of household" (101). Tawil adds that "'Indian blood,' according to Magawisca, is the repository of such qualities as strength, quickness, loyalty, courage, and virtue" (114). This reading, however, overlooks the novel's repeated insistence on the "love" that Magawisca and members of the Fletcher household feel for each other, and the associated dynamics of cross-"racial" kinship, as well as Magawisca's repeated reference to blood as a way of signifying her closeness to them.

54. I am less suggesting the danger of understanding Indians as *different* from Euramericans than highlighting the ways a fetishized/genericized version of that difference can disavow self-determination by foreclosing discussion of the metapolitical struggle over who has the authority to set the terms of legitimate governance, diplomacy, and land tenure. My reading, therefore, differs from both those who understand the positing of difference in the novel as an inherently racist/imperial maneuver and those who see difference as inherently destabilizing of the novel's imperial formulations. See Burnham, *Captivity*; Tuthill.

55. See Murphy, *Gathering*; Perdue; Rifkin, *Manifesting*; and Sleeper-Smith.

56. On the appearance of the Mahicans in the text, see Nelson, "Sympathy," 202; Tuthill, 105; Weierman, 68, 71–75.

57. Ephraim was Sedgwick's great-grandfather on her mother's side, making him Eunice Williams's first cousin once removed. See Kelley, "Introduction"; Weierman, 66–69.

58. Over the prior sixty years, the Mahicans had been displaced from their earlier role as trade middlemen in the region. Having maintained extensive relations of friendship

and exchange with surrounding and western peoples, they were very well positioned to take advantage of the Dutch fur trade in the early to mid-seventeenth century, but during the latter half of the century, they were pushed out by Mohawks eager to make themselves the mediators in existing commercial networks. On the history of the Mahicans and their dispossession, see Brooks, *Common Pot*, 21–50; Frazier; Miles; Taylor, "Captain Hendrick"; Wheeler; and Wyss, *Writing*, 81–122. For discussion of a very similar process of dispossession in one of the former "Praying Towns," see O'Brien, *Dispossession*. On Massachusetts laws with respect to Indians in the seventeenth and eighteenth centuries, see Kawashima.

59. In exploring the role of kinship in Mahican self-representation and native politics in the 1790s, I am not suggesting that kinship operated in identical ways for the various peoples I discuss. On differences among Algonquian peoples in southern New England, see Bragdon.

60. I would like to thank Lisa Brooks for very generously sharing her work on Aupaumut with me, as well as providing me with copies of his other narratives (from the collections of the Massachusetts Historical Society).

61. Scholars have described him in conflicting ways, as an accommodationist, an "intercultural broker," and the "prophet" of a different kind of "revivalist" movement than that led by the Shawnee Prophet (Tenskwatawa). See Gustafson, 257–264; Ronda and Ronda; Taylor, "Captain Hendrick"; and Wheeler. These accounts tend to envision him as an emblematic historical figure rather than focusing on the mapping of native geopolitics offered in his writings. Lisa Brooks avoids these problems, situating Aupaumut within an extended native space formed by longstanding modes of alliance and engagement. In *The Common Pot*, Brooks provides an extraordinarily detailed and exquisitely researched account of relations among Algonquian and Iroquoian peoples in western New England and into the Ohio valley, exploring how their complex, shifting, and enduring relations create forms of Native space whose ordering frameworks and logics differ greatly from those of Euro-American political structures. Within that larger project, my reading of Aupaumut seeks to pick up certain elements, amplify them, and focus attention in a different direction.

62. On the importance of kinship as a mode of engagement among peoples now, see Justice, "Go Away Water!". That essay explores the legacies of the very policies of division Hendrick Aupaumut addresses and to which his narrative serves as a response.

63. See Barnes; Cayton; Edmunds, 30–42; Hurt, *Indian Frontier*, 103–115; and White, *Middle Ground*, 413–468. Some have claimed that Aupaumut served as a counselor and translator for General Wayne in his campaign (Ronda and Ronda, 49; Taylor, "Captain Hendrick," 450). The basis for this assertion in particular documentary records or oral traditions, however, is unclear, especially given that Aupaumut is not listed as one of the eight translators in the Treaty of Greenville (Kappler, vol. II, 45). Additionally, participating in Wayne's campaign would be fairly difficult to reconcile with the evidence of Aupaumut's sustained diplomatic/kinship connections with the peoples of the Ohio region over the next twenty years. See Taylor, "Captain Hendrick"; Wheeler. However, Aupaumut

is listed as one of the translators for the Treaty of Fort Wayne in September 1809, which involved a number of the same peoples (Kappler, vol. II, 102), suggesting that some scholars may have confused the latter with the former.

64. *American State Papers: Indian Affairs*, vol. 1, 233.

65. After each speech, strings of wampum are given, suggesting that they are not incidental gifts but integral parts of the message itself. The connection between the transfer of wampum and longstanding relations of kinship among peoples is suggested in Aupaumut's indication of his need to bring his "bag of peace, in which there is ancient wampom," a reference clarified in his "History": "In this bag they keep all belts and strings which they received of their allies of different nations. The bag is, as it were, unmoveable; but it is always remain at Sachem's house, as hereditary with the office of a Sachem" (31). For discussion of Aupaumut's invocation of ritual and the significance of his bag of wampum, see Brooks, *Common Pot*, 139; Wyss, 110–112. On the relation in Aupaumut's narrative between oral tradition and various kinds of writing, including wampum, see Gustafson, 257–264. For an extended account of non-alphabetic writing, including the role of wampum in these negotiations, see Brooks, *Common Pot*.

66. In his history of the Mahican people, written around 1790, Aupaumut articulates this connection even more explicitly. After noting that "our forefathers . . . had allies, even in the remotest nations; and according to the ancient custom many of these nations made renewal of the covenants with us which their forefathers and ours had made," he tells the story of Mahican warfare and subsequent peacemaking with the Miami nation: "From that time [a] tract of land has been reserved for our nation to this day, and that covenant had been renewed at different times, and a number of our nation live on that land these several years past to this day" (Aupaumut, "History," 27). The presence of Mahicans on Miami land, perhaps living in Miami villages, is interpreted not as an attenuation of Mahican identity but as an expression and fortification of the "covenant" between peoples. For a discussion of social relations in the area Aupaumut visits during that period, see Tanner.

67. On efforts to acquire Oneida land in the period, see Hauptman, *Conspiracy*; Taylor, *Divided Ground*.

68. For complementary readings of this passage, see Brooks, *Common Pot*, 148; Wyss, *Writing*, 115. However, Wyss further argues that Aupaumut "challenges the basis of the current pan-Indian confederacy" by undermining its "racialized character," and in doing so, he "distances himself from other Natives" (114). This reading overlooks the role of kinship, rather than race, as the basis of union among peoples, and due to the emphasis on race, Wyss does not address the narrative's effort to call on the United States to be a good relative. In "Hendrick Aupaumut, Christian-Mahican Prophet," Rachel Wheeler argues that "Aupaumut's Christian-inflected vision extended the reach of native fictive kinship ties to forge fraternal bonds of mutual obligation between the citizens of a diverse American republic" (193), later suggesting that he "rejected a racialized division of humanity, insisting that good and evil people could be found among Indians and white[s]" (213). However, Wheeler ignores the ways that kinship as articulated in

Aupaumut's writings, at least during the 1790s, was not among "citizens" of the United States but among autonomous polities, particularly indigenous ones. Moreover, in the narrative, Aupaumut in speaking to a council of Shawnees and Delawares notes the importance of "contemplat[ing] the wellfare of our own colar" (91), a formulation he had used previously in conversation with U.S. officials (Taylor, "Captain Hendrick," 447). The distinction offered here, though, is not necessarily "racialized," instead suggesting the importance of continued solidarity among native peoples (already existing in the kinship bonds he describes) but doing so in the "color" idiom used by Euramericans.

69. The narrative offers numerous instances in which speakers from other nations use the phrase "Big Knifes" to refer to the United States, not simply to intruders who are U.S. citizens (Taylor, "Captain Hendrick," 444), illustrating Aupaumut's efforts to distinguish between the two while critiquing de facto U.S. support for such piecemeal invasion.

70. See Burnham, *Captivity*, 116–117; Tuthill, 99, 111.

71. Maureen Tuthill reads this exchange as evidencing, in Sedgwick's terms, Magawisca's "national pride" (Tuthill, 99).

72. In one of the first such moments, Nelema, in response to a seemingly innocent question about Everell by Mrs. Fletcher, gives vent to her rage: "I had sons too—and grandsons; but where are they? They trod the earth as lightly as that boy; but they have fallen like our forest trees, before the stroke of the English axe. Of all my race, there is not one, now, in whose veins my blood runs. Sometimes, when the spirits of the storm are howling about my wigwam, I hear the voices of my children crying for vengeance, and I could myself deal the death-blow" (37). Offering the first native account readers receive of the massacre of the Pequots and their allies, the speech sets the tone for later expressions of anti-English fury. Nelema's description of the murder of her family does not seem to point toward questions of collective identity and occupancy, instead entirely locating her desire for "vengeance" in her horror over the decimation of her descendants.

73. During her trial, Magawisca does offer what seems like an assertion of native political autonomy: "I am your prisoner, and ye may slay me, but I deny your right to judge me. My people have never passed under your yoke—not one of my race has ever acknowledged your authority" (286). However, I would read this moment less as an articulation of sovereignty than a demand akin to that of "no taxation without representation," especially given the ways the novel repeatedly suggests that the colonists have replicated the authoritarian forms of rule from which they supposedly fled. Additionally, the preceding statement is followed by reference to the virtual extermination of the Pequots ("my people are gone . . . to those shores that the bark of an enemy can never touch: think ye I fear to follow them?" [287]), transposing the issue of jurisdiction into that of mourning.

74. In the early seventeenth century, the Pequots, Narragansetts, and Mohegans were connected extensively through intermarriage at all levels. In the wake of the massacre of the Pequots, both the Narragansetts and the Mohegans signed a treaty in 1638 in which they agreed to submit disputes to the English for binding arbitration, and when Miantonomi (the Narragansett sachem referenced by Sedgwick) took part in an effort to kill

Uncas in retribution for the Mohegan murder of Narragansett tributaries, as well as in opposition to the Mohegan effort to woo groups formerly loyal to the Narragansetts, he was captured by Uncas, delivered to English authorities, and sentenced to death for violating the treaty. See Cave, 66–68, 146, 165–167; Oberg; Salisbury, 48, 150, 206–215, 226–234.

    75. Povinelli, *Cunning*, 58.

Chapter 3

    1. Morgan, *Ancient*, 512; *Reynolds v. U.S.*, 165–166.

    2. See Gordon.

    3. Note the similarity between this formulation and the statement by Rick Santorum with which I began the Introduction.

    4. See Cott, *Public Vows*; Bederman; D'Emilio and Freedman; Gordon; Hartman; Iversen, *Antipolygamy Controversy*; and Stanley.

    5. On the post-Reconstruction interest by reformers and former abolitionists in Indian affairs, see Adams, *Education for Extinction*; Hoxie; and Pfister.

    6. See Prucha, *American Indian Treaties*; Williams, *Linking Arms Together*. In *Frantic Panoramas*, Nancy Bentley characterizes this period as "the ruins of an absent diplomatic public" (175), and she offers a fascinating account of how Indian shows functioned as a kind of surrogation for the absence of formal diplomacy.

    7. Nancy Bentley offers a similar formulation in her discussion of the ways in which late-nineteenth-century opposition to Mormon polygamy "helped to give American nationalism the structure of a domestic novel" ("Marriage," 343).

    8. For background on Bonnin, see Bernardin; Davidson and Norris; Fisher; Heflin; Spack, "Dis/engagement." In the chapter, though, I will refer to her by using her chosen pseudonym. Several critics have misidentified her as Lakota, possibly because her pen name is from that language. See Smith, "A Second Tongue"; and Spack, "Re-visioning." Yankton is the Gallicized version of the name of one of the seven peoples of the Sioux, although "Sioux" itself is a misnomer—a French derivation of an Ojibwa insult for those tribes whose longstanding (ethnic?) alliance the term denotes. The Yanktons are often included in the term "Dakota," which also has been used to refer to all seven peoples—most notably by Ella Deloria. The terms "Dakota," "Nakota," and "Lakota" (the last of which usually refers to the westernmost Sioux people—the Tetons) often have been used to designate different groupings of the seven peoples, but these terms more properly refer to dialects of the language they all speak. For a good overview of available nomenclatures and their philologies, see DeMallie, "Sioux until 1850" and "Yankton and Yanktonai." I will use "Sioux" when referring to this collection of peoples or characteristics that apply to most of them, since it currently is the most common term among natives and non-natives.

    9. Scholars have disagreed about how to interpret Bonnin's political commitments, especially after she joins the Society of American Indians. For differing interpretations, see Maddox, *Citizen Indians*; Warrior, *Tribal Secrets*; and Welch.

10. As Patricia C. Albers asserts, kinship serves as the "primary idiom through which the Sioux and other Native Americans ordered their social relations of production, trade, war, ceremony, and recreation" ("Sioux," 254). My argument here with respect to heteronormativity borrows from Laura Wexler's similar move with respect to the "culture of sentiment." See Wexler.

11. Adams, *Education for Extinction*, 58–61.

12. Soon after introducing Indians to what had been an all-black school, Pratt received permission from Congress to open a school exclusively dedicated to Indian education in Carlisle, Pennsylvania, which would become the model for the twenty-four additional off-reservation Indian boarding schools opened across the country over the next twenty-five years. On Pratt and the history of Indian education more broadly, see Adams, *Education*; Hoxie; Littlefield; Lomawaima; Pfister; Pratt; Stefon; Trennert, "Educating Indian Girls"; and Trennert, "From Carlisle to Phoenix." The Annual Report of the Commissioner of Indian Affairs (ARCIA) is also an immensely rich source on the education program, containing the commissioner's comments on education as well as reports by superintendents of Indian education and from the various boarding schools. They were published annually by the Government Printing Office out of Washington, D.C.; rather than including them all in the bibliography, I simply cite them here by year and page number.

13. ARCIA, 1884, 186; ARCIA, 1888, xix. While the idea of acculturating native children to white bourgeois homemaking seemed to dominate the outing program as conducted in the east, out west the system often degenerated into simply a means of providing cheap Indian labor to the communities surrounding the boarding schools. See Adams, *Education*; Hoxie; Littlefield; and Trennert, "From Carlisle to Phoenix."

14. The experiment at Hampton and Carlisle was championed by eastern reform organizations, which in 1883 founded the Lake Mohonk Conference, an annual meeting at which the self-designated "Friends of the Indian" could gather to discuss the proper shape and direction of the civilization program—especially education. The most powerful figures in Indian policy, such as the various Commissioners of Indian Affairs and Senator Henry Dawes, were regular attendees.

15. On Morgan's background and influence, see Adams, *Education*, 61–64.

16. ARCIA, 1889, 93–114. Hereafter I will cite page numbers parenthetically.

17. For examples of fears expressed by those within the Indian education system of the threat of students giving into "licentiousness" (especially polygamy) when they return home, see ARCIA, 1884, 200; ARCIA, 1885, 220; and ARCIA, 1889, 335. In fact, legal marriage, as opposed to "marr[ying] in the Indian way," was a major criterion used by both Carlisle and Hampton to assess the success of former students. See Adams, *Education*, 287–288.

18. Morgan, "Rules for Indian Schools," ARCIA, 1890, cli. Quotations will be cited parenthetically by page number.

19. For discussion of how girls in the boarding schools resisted such superintendence, see Lomawaima. On students' forms of opposition more broadly, see Adams, *Education*; Pfister, 66–78.

20. On allotment, see Hoxie. As a result of the allotment program, native landholding declined from more than 138 million acres in 1881 to approximately 52 million acres in 1934 (Adams, *Education*, 344). Allottees were to receive citizenship at the end of the trust period, when their land passed into fee simple title. However, as of 1888, Indian women who married white men were granted citizenship and denied tribal status (Sullivan, 54).

21. For an edited text of the Dawes Act, see Prucha, *Documents*, 170–173.

22. Students at boarding schools annually were required to commemorate the passage of the Dawes Act—referred to as Indian Citizenship Day or Franchise Day. For Morgan's original order on this point, see ARCIA, 1890, clxvii–clxviii; for discussion of how the "holiday" was celebrated, see Adams, *Education*, 196–201.

23. For more on the process and importance of (re)naming in education and allotment, see Adams, *Education*, 108–111. For an alternative reading of official renaming as compatible with certain native traditions, see Pfister, 107–108.

24. These were published separately in consecutive issues of the *Atlantic Monthly* starting in January 1900. On Zitkala-Ša's autobiographical writing, see Bernardin; Enoch; Hannon; Maddox, *Citizen Indians*, 146–147; Okker; Velikova; and Wexler.

25. Bernardin, 229.

26. Quoted in Bernardin, 215–216.

27. When referring to her people, Zitkala-Ša uses the term "Dakota," and it is unclear whether she means all seven Sioux peoples, the groups to the east (excluding the Tetons), or the Yanktons specifically. My sense is that she is speaking from/about Yankton experience but that her comments are meant to apply broadly across tribal divisions. I therefore move back and forth between the terms "Yankton" and "Dakota," most often employing the latter given that it is the one she uses.

28. In fact, I would suggest that the stories are set less than a century prior to their publication. Susan Bernardin takes Zitkala-Ša's statement at face value, claiming that "The Trial Path" is "set in the precontact past" (216). However, the story prominently features horses as a routine part of Dakota life, and horses themselves were introduced onto the continent by Europeans and were not integrated into Dakota culture until the late eighteenth century. Moreover, the use of beads in "A Warrior's Daughter" suggests that it occurs no earlier than the nineteenth century. See Albers, "Symbiosis"; Deloria, *Speaking of Indians*; DeMallie, "Sioux until 1850"; and Hoover.

29. These stories also differ greatly from her later writing, particularly in *American Indian Magazine*, which tends to speak to current affairs in much more direct ways, often advocating for particular positions on given political issues. See Davidson and Norris. Part of what I am suggesting, though, is that we neither see her earlier work, especially the versions of traditional tales, as somehow apolitical in light of her later participation in national organizations and public commentary on current events nor read her later work and activism as the true expression of her politics in ways that make the earlier acts of storytelling simply a cover for an agenda that later becomes explicit. Instead, I think the more productive move is to consider the different kinds of cultural work performed by different genres and the sorts of commentary and critique enabled by them. For

discussion of Zitkala-Ša's work as part of a larger native intellectual formation in the early twentieth century, see Maddox, *Citizen Indians*.

30. On the prominence of kin-making intergenerationally and intragenerationally as mainstays of Sioux social life, see Deloria, *Speaking of Indians*; DeMallie, "Kinship and Biology"; and Walker, *Lakota Society*. As these sources note, blood relations could be distinguished terminologically from other kin but usually were not, especially when speaking to them.

31. As Ella Deloria notes, the Dakota words for "to address a relative" and "to pray" are the same (*Speaking of Indians*, 28–29).

32. See Heflin, "*I Remain*," 128–129.

33. Prior to the creation of the Yankton reservation, they were in possession of approximately 13 to 14 million acres in what is now the Dakotas. In 1858, a headman named Struck by the Ree (who two years earlier had been appointed principal chief of the Yanktons by General William S. Harney) led the party that negotiated a treaty selling more than 11 million acres to the United States and thereby creating the Yankton reservation. Condemned publicly by three of the seven bands that composed the Yankton people, this treaty was made for them without consulting them while they were out on their annual buffalo hunt. The terms of the treaty defined Yankton territory until the beginning of the allotment program in the 1880s. The Yanktons were the only Sioux tribe who never went to war against the United States: "Never having been at war with the Government they have never experienced that chastisement which has served to make the Santees and other branches of the great Sioux family submissive and easily governed" (ARCIA, 1887, 65). On Yankton history, see DeMallie, "Sioux until 1850" and "Yankton and Yanktonai"; Gibbon; Hoover; and Sansom-Flood. The agent during this period was J. F. Kinney.

34. She left for White's Manual Institute in 1884, returned in 1887, was on the reservation until 1891, and then went back to White's for another three years before attending Earlham College for two years. See Fisher, "Foreword." On White's, see Parker and Parker.

35. ARCIA, 1887, 58. By 1885 the agent had created his own ruling council of men appointed by him, described as the "board of advisors," but people on the reservation continued to look to and support traditional leaders (ARCIA, 1885, 59–60).

36. ARCIA, 1887, 56.

37. ARCIA, 1888, 65.

38. ARCIA, 1886, 100.

39. For examples, see ARCIA, 1884, 58; ARCIA, 1885, 58, 62; ARCIA, 1886, 94; ARCIA, 1887, 58; and ARCIA, 1888, 64.

40. ARCIA, 1887, 60. The giving away of wives likely refers to the fact that a man might sexually share his wife with close friends as a gesture of intimacy. However, if a woman objected, divorce was a very simple process, since the woman owned the tepee and virtually all the household goods; she simply could leave her husband's possessions outside her tepee or, if they were living with his kin, move back to her parents' band. See Deloria, *Speaking of Indians*; DeMallie "Male and Female"; and Walker, *Lakota Society*.

41. ARCIA, 1886, 99; ARCIA, 1885, 60.

42. ARCIA, 1887, 60; ARCIA, 1888, 65. In fact, as a prominent and frequent aspect of Yankton life, dances very well may have functioned as spaces for coordinating opposition to U.S. policy initiatives, suggesting an alternative motive for official condemnation of them. See ARCIA, 1887, 59. I also should note that the string of accusations leveled at "dances" usually appear in the context of the agent's admission of his failure to control them.

43. ARCIA, 1887, 53–54.

44. ARCIA, 1888, 65. Many, if not a majority, of the cases brought before the Indian court set up by the agent had to do with problems relating to illegal cohabitation and divorce. See ARCIA, 1886, 98; ARCIA, 1889, 174; ARCIA, 1890, 72–74.

45. Moreover, the agent repeatedly emphasizes that education is the vehicle through which the Yankton people will be elevated from their currently savage state. See ARCIA, 1887, 61. The reports include discussion of Yankton efforts to resist the removal of their children, to which the agent responded by withholding annuities, including rations.

46. See Albers, "Sioux Kinship"; Deloria, *Speaking of Indians*; DeMallie, "Kinship and Biology" and "Sioux until 1850"; Hoover; Medicine, *Learning to Be*; Standing Bear; and Walker, *Lakota Society*. More specifically, Yankton and other Sioux tribes tended to be divided into kinship units called tiospayes composed of a shifting number of blood and other relatives. A variable number of tiospayes, themselves linked by more distant kinship ties, would combine to form a camp circle with its own council, whose rule for the most part was by persuasion rather than coercion. In this way, belonging to the camp-circle as a geopolitical entity was defined by kinship. This formation will be addressed further in the next chapter.

47. This reading challenges Ruth Spack's contention that this story relies on "cultural and romantic language" instead of "political discourse" ("Re-visioning," 36).

48. While Tusee's choice to stay behind to rescue her captured lover is depicted as somewhat exceptional, the presence of women as part of the war party seems to be taken as fairly conventional: "Astride their ponies laden with food and deerskins, brave elderly women follow after their warriors"; "the war party of Indian men and their faithful women vanish beyond the southern skyline" (144). On Sioux women's participation in war, see Blackwood, "Sexuality and Gender"; Lang, *Men as Women*; and Medicine, "'Warrior Women.'"

49. For brief readings of the story that tend to focus on its gender dynamics, often in ways that underestimate the potential flexibility of gender identity among Sioux peoples, see Okker; Smith, "'A Second Tongue'"; Spack, "Re-visioning" and "Dis/engagement."

50. The reference to dances also recalls the attack on them led by the federal agent to the Yankton, discussed earlier. On Zitkala-Ša's opposition to the federal effort to ban native dancing, see Davidson and Norris, 235–238.

51. For discussion of "Why I Am a Pagan" and the changes made to it in its revision as "The Great Spirit" for *American Indian Stories*, see Velikova.

52. See Bentley, "Marriage"; Burgett, "On the Mormon Question"; Cott, *Public Vows*; Gordon; and Iversen, "A Debate." There is evidence that Zitkala-Ša was in fact a Mormon. See Davidson and Norris, xxviii–xxix; Hafen, "Zitkala Sa," 41.

53. See DeMallie, "Male and Female"; and Walker, *Lakota Society*.

54. This formulation draws on various scholarly accounts of the ways racialized populations seek to conform to a heteronormative ideal in order to signify as *national*—either in the sense of being full subjects of the nation-state or signifying as a nation-state within Euro-American-managed forms of international political economy. For examples, see Alexander; Gopinath; Luibhéid, *Entry Denied*; Puar; and Somerville, "Queer *Loving*."

55. See Hennessy.

56. See Roscoe, *Changing Ones*; Ross; and Somerville, *Queering*.

57. For discussion of the ways there may be multiple norms that can be played against each other within a system of "normativity," see Jakobsen, "Queer Is?".

58. See Gordon; Iversen, *Antipolygamy Controversy*.

59. Such a case was not possible until the passage of the Poland Act (1874), which took power over many cases away from Utah's probate judges, who largely were also Mormon bishops, gave the U.S. Marshal authority to select the pool of potential jurors, and allowed for polygamy convictions to be appealed to the U.S. Supreme Court (Gordon, 111–113).

60. A prior law sponsored by Edmunds, passed in 1882, criminalized "unlawful cohabitation," barred polygamists from jury service, and disenfranchised them. See *Davis v. Beason*; Gordon, 152–153.

61. For an extended discussion of this cross-hatching of "racialization" and "sexualization," see Burgett, "On the Mormon Question." However, like other commentators, Burgett overlooks the importance of native peoples to this debate, as well as to dynamics of racialization in the United States in the late nineteenth century.

62. While Indian tribes were found to be "domestic dependent nations" rather than "foreign nations" in *Cherokee Nation v. Georgia* (1831), the representation of their autonomy in internal matters still often was registered in political and judicial discourse through comparison to nations deemed "foreign." Native polygamy was not the subject of federal statute in this period, but the practice was outlawed in the 1883 regulations issued by the Secretary of the Interior, enforced by the Courts of Indian Offenses he created. See Hagan; *Opinions of the Solicitor*, 532–536; *Regulations of the Indian Office*. These developments are addressed further in chapter 4.

63. On the ways public opposition to polygamy emerges out of the "home mission" movement, and thus an engagement with native peoples, see Iversen, *Antipolygamy Controversy*.

64. See Harring, *Crow Dog's Case*; Wilkins, *American Indian Sovereignty*.

65. Gordon, 204.

66. On the significance and influence of Morgan's work, see Ben-Zvi; Bieder; Engels; Fortes; Kuper; Trautmann; and Weinbaum. Morgan is also an interesting figure for this study given his earlier work on the Iroquois Confederacy, the Senecas in particular, in the period just after that addressed in chapter 1. On Morgan's complex relationship with Ely S. Parker, a Seneca chief who served as his informant and who eventually became Commissioner of Indian Affairs under Ulysses S. Grant, see Deloria, *Playing Indian*, 71–94; Michaelson, 84–106; and Trautmann, 36–57.

67. See McClintock. This notion also resonates with Kevin Bruyneel's discussion of "colonial time."

68. While he does distinguish between "descriptive" and "classificatory" kinship terms, the latter representing "true" or blood relations, Morgan does not posit a categorical, a priori distinction between the "domestic" sphere and descent, or belonging to broader kinship groups (particularly clans), a difference that is read into Morgan's work by twentieth-century anthropologists. See Fortes; Trautmann.

In the mid-twentieth century, scholars began to use the term "descent" to refer to jural-political relations that were seen as predicated on birth/lineage but distinct from interpersonal affective bonds, reproduction, child care, and homemaking—themselves seen as a cross-culturally consistent core, an inevitable natural feature, of human reproduction itself. The extent to which "descent" could be included under the broader rubric of "kinship" or whether the latter term solely referred to social functions linked to (dominant Euro-notions of) domesticity (as opposed to "descent") was and continues to be a point of disagreement. See Harris, *Kinship*; Kuper; McKinnon; and Parkin.

69. However, Morgan does tend to refer to kinship systems as being passed through the "blood," but this formulation does not clearly suggest racial difference, particularly in light of the fact that the kind of blood remembrance he presents crosses the ethnological periods into which he divided human history and thereby serves as a vehicle for transmitting knowledge through time across conventional racial lines. On Morgan's use of a metaphorics of blood, see Bieder, 194–246. For discussion of Morgan's theory of inheritance, see Ben-Zvi. For readings of Morgan that equate blood with race, see Trautmann, 29, 138; Weinbaum, 106–144.

70. Gramsci, 377, 165, 195.

71. On ways of envisioning and articulating differences among populations of various kinds in the late nineteenth and early twentieth centuries, see Elliott; and Evans.

72. On the ways Mormon marriage in particular was cast as lacking in proper forms of conjugal affect, and as defective/barbaric on this basis, see Iversen, *Antipolygamy Controversy*.

73. On the traditional cultural role of the winkte, see Lang, *Men as Women*; Medicine, "'Warrior Women'"; Standing Bear, 92–93; Walker, *Lakota Society*; and Williams, *Spirit and the Flesh*. For discussion of winkte identity today and its uneasy relationship to gay/queer identification and its uneven acknowledgment on reservations, see the essays by Michael Red Earth and Doyle V. Robertson in Jacobs, Thomas, and Lang, 210–216, 228–235; and Gilley.

74. See Williams, *Spirit and the Flesh*.

75. For further theorization of the distinction, see Lang, *Men as Women*.

76. Unlike Roscoe's account, critical discussions of the links between race, gender, and sexuality in the nineteenth century largely have focused on comparative anatomy as the antecedent for sexology and have downplayed or overlooked entirely the role of ethnology. Scholarship has tended to associate the former with people of African descent, even while noting in passing that American Indians were subjects of anatomical study as well. Combined with the sidelining of ethnology, this emphasis has presented African

Americans and blackness as serving a more central role in the emergence of discourses of (homo)sexuality in the late-nineteenth-century United States than native peoples and Indianness, in many ways replicating the black/white paradigm within the history of sexuality. For examples, see Ross; Somerville, *Queering*; and Wiegman, *American Anatomies*. On the black/white paradigm and the ways it shapes accounts of race in the United States, see Perea. On the ways Lewis Henry Morgan's work may have facilitated the erasure of Indians as a distinct racial category and the emergence of the black/white binary in the twentieth century, see Ben-Zvi.

77. However, hermaphrodism could be understood less as a literal description of the body than as a metaphor for a distinct social role. In *Intermediate Types among Primitive Folk*, Edward Carpenter, one of the most well known of the homophile writers in turn-of-the-century Britain, asserts, "It is needless, of course, to say that these [descriptions of North American peoples in Euro-American accounts] were *not* [of] hermaphrodites in the strict sense of the term—*i.e.* human being uniting in one person the functions both of male and female. . . .But it is evident that they *were* intermediate types—in the sense of being men with much of the psychologic character of women or in some cases women with the mentality of men" (67–68).

78. On the dangers of seeing definitions/paradigms of sexuality as decisively supplanting each other, rather than as complexly and unevenly coexisting and interpenetrating, see Sedgwick, *Epistemology*.

79. In some homophile writings such as those of Edward Carpenter, who collaborated with Ellis, "homosexual temperament" is seen as making possible social evolution: "In various ways we can see the likelihood of this thesis, and the probability of the intermediate man or woman becoming a forward force in human evolution. . . . [N]ot wholly belonging to either of the two great progenitive branches of the human race, his nature would not find complete satisfaction in the activities of either branch, and he would necessarily create a new sphere of some kind for himself" (59). In this way, Carpenter retains the sense of a teleology of social development but does not present the acceptance of such "intermediate" persons in non-European cultures as itself evidence of their primitiveness.

80. For a fascinating account of same-sex eroticism among the Mormons, including the ways the renunciation of polygamy helped lead to a stricter regulation of all homosocial relations among them, see Quinn.

81. On white visions/fetishizations of native masculinity in the late nineteenth and early twentieth centuries, see Bederman; Deloria, *Playing Indian*. For a compelling discussion of how people who went through the Indian education system tactically sought to deploy white images of native peoples to their own ends, see Maddox, *Citizen Indians*; and Pfister, 97–132.

82. One could ask whether or not Zitkala-Ša actually would have been familiar with the winkte tradition, but given the amount of time she spent on-reservation in the 1880s and 1890s, and the agent's efforts to punish various kinds of deviancy in the same period, I would suggest that she would have been familiar with the various practices the agent sought to ban. Thanks to Andrea Smith for asking me to clarify this point.

CHAPTER 4

1. *Minutes of the Plains Congress*, 7–8, 29; Deloria, *Speaking of Indians*, 29.

2. For broad overviews of the IRA's passage and implementation, see Deloria and Lytle; Rusco, *Fateful Time*; Rusco, "Indian Reorganization Act"; and Taylor, *New Deal*.

3. Held on March 2–5, 1934, the Plains Congress was one of a number of such meetings with native peoples all over the country in order to explain to them the provisions of the Indian Reorganization Act, which was making its way through Congress at the time, get feedback on some of its provisions, and generate support for it, since each tribe/reservation eventually would have to vote on whether they would come under its terms. On Collier's efforts to generate native support for the act before its passage, see Biolosi, *Organizing*, 68–70; Deloria and Lytle, 101–121; and Rusco, *Fateful Time*, 212–217, 245–249.

4. The term "allotment" often is used to refer less to the General Allotment Act of 1887 than to the entire program surrounding and animated by it; similarly, I will use "reorganization" to refer to the ideological and practical projects surrounding the IRA.

5. There were significant differences between the version of the IRA drafted by Collier and the solicitors of the Interior Department (which was what Collier was talking about with native peoples at the Plains Congress) and the law that finally was passed by Congress. The two most important with respect to my argument are the changes in the land provisions and the removal of a provision creating a Court of Indian Affairs. The third section of the original prevented the Secretary of the Interior from issuing any further fee- patents, transferred to the chartered community the control of allotted lands upon the death of the allottee (the heir[s] receiving a certificate of proportional interest in tribal lands), and allowed the chartered community to exert a version of eminent domain over their territory in order to facilitate land consolidation programs for ranching, farming, and leasing. The final version did not end fee patenting (leading to the loss of thousands of more acres in the years following the law's passage), and it made all transfer of lands by allottees and their heirs voluntary, giving the "community" (as the legal tribal entity recognized by the bill was called) no authority to assert control over allotted land. The original bill also called for the creation of a Court of Indian Affairs, a district court–level judiciary, which would have had appellate jurisdiction over virtually all criminal and civil matters on-reservation (including those involving non-natives), but that section was excised in its entirety in the final draft. On these changes, see Deloria and Lytle; Rusco, *Fateful Time*; and Taylor, *New Deal*. The relationship I am suggesting between allotment and the IRA, however, does not depend solely on the version enacted by Congress but also speaks to Collier's original vision and his priorities in negotiating the shift from the latter to the former.

6. In *Individuality Incorporated*, Joel Pfister argues, "Despite the noncoercive intentions of the Indian Reorganization Act, it attempted to reorganize the tribes into what Collier, the community reformer, thought of as democratic and parliamentary bodies," but "Collier's classificatory emphasis on tribes overlooked the real day-to-day existence of working *communities*, especially the factor of clan autonomy" (203). The idea that

Collier's policy "overlooked" the gap between the official schemas for democratic governance and "day-to-day" forms of native sociality replicates the notion of a "clash" or contradiction between the IRA's aims and effects offered by Biolosi. Instead, I am suggesting
that the apparent lack of attention to the everyday dynamics of native life on-reservation
functions as a way of preserving, in Pfister's phrase, existing "machineries of subjectivity
management" that determine the acceptable shape of native sociopolitical organization
and articulations of sovereignty (230). In this way, I argue that more of the heteronormative structure subtending the allotment discourse of individualism is present in Collier's
modernist celebration of native communalism than Pfister suggests.

7. In an article in 1944, Collier himself noted, "The sharpest conflict and the most
disturbing conflict has occurred in the Sioux area and particularly at Pine Ridge" ("Collier Replies to Mekeel," 425).

8. Deloria uses the term "Dakota" as an inclusive reference to refer to all seven Sioux
peoples, and as she notes, her description of Dakota people(s) is most directly derived
from information about the Teton Sioux. Deloria was a Yankton Sioux who lived among
various Teton Sioux groups almost her entire life and wrote about them in light of her
anthropological training as a student and associate of Franz Boas. On Deloria's life, see
Deloria, "Introduction"; Gardner, "Speaking"; Medicine, *Learning to Be*, 269–288; and
Murray.

9. In challenging the universality of a distinction between public and private spheres
or the cross-cultural existence of a "domestic" sphere, I am drawing on a large body of
work by feminist anthropologists. For examples, see Albers and Medicine; Carsten;
Collier and Yanagisako; Strathern; Yanagisako and Delaney.

10. For this list of offenses, see *Regulations of the Indian Office*. The novel was written
over the course of the late 1930s and early 1940s but was not published until 1988, seven-
teen years after Deloria's death. See DeMallie, "Afterword"; Finn; Gardner, "Though It
Broke."

11. While generating a good deal of scholarly attention, reorganization has generated
utterly incommensurate understandings of its intent, operation, and long-term effects.
Although to some degree simply testifying to the ways intellectual debate works, particularly changes over time in analytical modes and emphases, this variety and the sharp
dichotomies that tend to characterize it also in many ways parallel the distribution of
native responses to the act at the time of its passage and during the reservation votes that
followed (whether to come under the IRA; if so, whether to adopt a constitution under
its terms; and if ratifying a constitution, whether to establish a business charter for the
purposes of receiving certain federal grants). Not only was there disagreement among
various segments of reservation populations over the value and efficacy of the new law,
but often members of the same group on a given reservation, who shared ideas about the
proper path their people should take, would adopt diametrically opposed positions on
the act. An attention to the ways reorganization both ended and incorporated allotment
can help explain this apparent paradox. For historical commentary on the IRA, see Daily;
Deloria and Lytle; Kelly, *Indian Affairs*; Pfister; Reinhardt, "Crude Replacement";

Robertson; Rusco, *Fateful Time*; Rusco, "Indian Reorganization Act"; Schwartz; Taylor, *New Deal*; and Washburn.

12. This claim runs against the grain of most of the assessments of John Collier and his vision for reorganization, which emphasize his interest in "community" organization and his disdain for individualist ways of thinking about how to address social issues. For examples, see Daily; Pfister; Rusco, *Fateful Time*; and Taylor, *New Deal*. While not denying that Collier most often frames his arguments in collective terms, I seek to indicate the ways the official conceptualization of communal identity surrounding the IRA relies on an ensemble of assumptions about the distinction between public and private spheres and the nature of political process and belonging that reinforces the heterosexualizing project of allotment as addressed in the previous chapter.

Critics of the IRA who sought to repeal it in the late 1930s and 1940s consistently presented it as endorsing a vision of native life at odds with the dominant possessive individualism of the United States. A 1939 report issued by the Senate Committee on Indian Affairs declares that "individual rights of inheritance, private ownership of property, and private enterprise are being discouraged and destroyed by reason of some provisions of the act itself," but this claim largely is a function of the committee's conclusion that the IRA "attempts to set up a state or a nation within a nation which is contrary to the intents and purposes of the American Republic" ("Repeal of the So-Called Wheeler-Howard Act," 3–4). In other words, the assessment of the law and Collier's program as anti-individualist derives from the assumption that any effort to preserve distinct native governments and polities was not simply communalist but communistic (see also Rosier, 1305–1307). The set of interlocking binaries that sustain this logic can be understood as continuing to shape assessments of reorganization.

13. *Minutes of the Plains Congress*, 5. Further citations from this source will be parenthetical.

14. This plan later is characterized by another official as a kind of sovereignty buffet: "This Bill, if it were passed just as it is, merely sets the self-government table. It puts out a table and puts all kinds of self-government dishes on from pie and roast beef down to a plate of soup" (110).

15. See 27, 33, 130.

16. For this understanding of "guardianship" as used by Collier and other officials with respect to the IRA, see Rusco, *Fateful Time*. At a number of points during the Plains Congress, Collier and others explain the damage wrought by land policies under allotment, particularly fee patenting and heirship fractioning.

17. This emphasis on protecting individual property rights could be explained as a response by Collier to the insistence on this point by Burton K. Wheeler, the chair of the Senate Committee on Indian Affairs and cosponsor of the IRA, during the Senate hearings that preceded the congresses (Rusco, *Fateful Time*, 242), but as I will suggest, Collier's depiction of property here seems consistent with other ideas about the scope of tribal governance and the nature of U.S. citizenship expressed by him in the Plains Congress and elsewhere.

18. Given the ways administrative judgments about "competency" often relied on assessments of blood quantum, the split between those who still possessed territory and those who did not often was characterized as one between "mixed-bloods" and "full-bloods," a dynamic and discourse that exacerbated existing conflicts on many reservations, including Pine Ridge. See Biolosi, *Organizing*; Deloria and Lytle; Macgregor; Robertson; Taylor, *New Deal*; and Thorne.

19. This claim seems particularly problematic in light of the fact that the courts already had recognized the authority of the federal government to maintain administrative authority over native persons and property even after they had fee simple title to their allotments and thus had become citizens (prior to the general extension of citizenship in 1924). See Wilkins, *American Indian Sovereignty*.

20. On the relation between family-making and property relations in eighteenth- and nineteenth-century Anglo-American ideologies, see Boydston; Brown, *Domestic Individualism*; Coontz; Cott, *Public Vows*; Dillon; D'Emilio and Freedman; Gordon; Grossberg; and Merish.

21. On the distinction between "property" and traditional native modes of occupancy, see Cheyfitz, *Poetics*.

22. In "The Birth of the Reservation," Thomas Biolosi suggests with respect to the process of allotment that "privatization of the means of production/subsistence creates fundamentally new subjects with radically new interests" (33), helping give rise to "the modern individual" among native peoples—in this case, the Lakotas. However, as in the discussion I offered of Joel Pfister in the previous chapter, Biolosi addresses privatization, individualization, and racialization through blood quantum without addressing the ways all these processes are part of a heteronormalization centered on the nuclear family as the axiomatic structure of social life.

23. Prucha, *Documents*, 171.

24. See 11, 39, 130. For various officials' use of this formulation elsewhere, or the synonymous description of native governments as "municipal," see Collier, "Genesis and Philosophy," 7; Rusco, *Fateful Time*, 237; Taylor, *New Deal*, 30; Wilkins, "Introduction," xxii.

25. At the time of reorganization, the agency actually was called the Office of Indian Affairs (OIA) rather than the Bureau of Indian Affairs (BIA), but I have chosen to use the latter because it is the more familiar acronym and the later name change did not indicate a fundamental change in the legal status or bureaucratic structure of the agency.

26. The agreement that enabled this act is often called the "Crook Treaty," since it was negotiated by General George Crook. Objections to the agreement included that it was based on the assent of three-quarters of the adult men belonging to all the relevant Sioux bands (a figure mandated by the 1868 Treaty of Fort Laramie), rather than three-quarters of the adult men in each band, and that the necessary consent was procured by bypassing the chiefs. On Teton history and politics in the middle to late nineteenth century, see Gibbon; Lazarus; Ostler; and Price.

27. On the tiospaye, see Albers, "Sioux Kinship"; Deloria, *Speaking of Indians*; DeMallie, "Kinship and Biology"; Medicine, *Learning to Be*; Standing Bear; and Walker, *Lakota Society*.

28. Robertson, 92.

29. Biolosi, *Organizing*, 45.

30. Biolosi, *Organizing*, 53.

31. On Teton politics prior to reorganization, in the late nineteenth century and early twentieth century, see Biolosi, *Organizing*; Clow, "Indian Reorganization Act"; Lazarus; Ostler; and Roberston. Both in the Plains Congress and elsewhere, those who described themselves as "full-bloods" expressed concern about the degree to which reorganization would mean the transfer of resources and power from them to "mixed-bloods." This hostility usually was expressed by people at the time, and has been analyzed by scholars, as a fear that land would be taken away from "restricted" Indians to give to those who had become landless after fee patenting, especially given that the criteria for restriction and fee patenting usually were articulated in terms of blood quantum. However, as Paul Robertson notes in his history of Pine Ridge, mixed-bloods were far less likely to be members of tiospayes and thus to be represented in the pre-IRA tiospaye-based councils (83–122), so the rhetoric of full-blood/mixed-blood difference also can be understood as in some ways an expression of tensions over the proper form of reservation governance, particularly the role that the tiospaye should play in it.

32. Elmer R. Rusco has argued that Collier, and virtually everyone in the government working in Indian affairs, operated under a "vacuum theory" of native politics, presuming that there were no surviving institutions of native governance on most reservations. See Rusco, *Fateful Time*.

33. Attendees' questions continually press on the official representation of the IRA as a radical and transformative break from existing policy. Members of the Rosebud delegation ask a question that will be repeated in various forms throughout the congress: "What is the meaning of the word Reservation? Does it include counties which were within the Reservation in 1889 but which are no longer in the Reservation" (44–45)? Querying the concept of the "reservation," participants seek to assess the degree to which Collier's claims signal a substantive reformation of the entrenched principles of Indian policy, which they apparently do not ("This bill would not correct a thing that took place in the past . . . only prevent that kind of thing from happening in the future" [128]). In a particularly perspicacious analysis of the role of the Plains Congress in the broader scope of federal policy-making, Jacob White Cow Killer of Pine Ridge observes, "Mr. Collier draws us a picture of the Bill. . . . After, I take back the provisions of the Bill to my people and present the good points to them and we accept it whole-heartedly and the Bill becomes a law in an entirely different form, I see that Mr. Collier will be criticized," adding, "when the Bill comes out in a law in entirely different form, I know that my people will call me a big liar" (97).

34. "Conditions on Sioux Reservations," 9. Further citations from this source will be parenthetical. The Pine Ridge constitution in place prior to the IRA and supplanted by it did make explicit reference to the Treaty of 1868 as a basis for Oglala self-representation and legal recognition (Cohen, *On the Drafting*, 7).

35. Similar sentiments are offered by speakers from Rosebud (11–12, 17–18).

36. Biolosi, *Organizing*, 151.

37. On the relation between efforts to organize around treaty claims and challenges to IRA governance, see also Biolosi, *Organizing*, 151–181; Clow, "Tribal Populations," 369–371; Lazarus, 163–164; Roberts, 39; *Survey of the Conditions of the Indians*, 21784–21794; and Taylor, *New Deal*, 145–146. In his contribution to a volume assessing the twenty-year record of reorganization, Collier presents the IRA as part of an effort to respect the history of treaty-making and its indication of a relationship among sovereigns. See Collier, "Genesis and Philosophy."

38. This opinion as well as the others quoted are collected in *Opinions of the Solicitor of the Department of the Interior Relating to Indian Affairs, 1917–1974*, vol. 1. Page numbers from this volume will be cited parenthetically. For discussion of these opinions, see Deloria and Lytle, 154–170; Rusco, "Indian Reorganization Act," 60–62; and Taylor, *New Deal*, 92–96. On Cohen, see Wilkins, "Introduction."

39. Kappler, *Indian Affairs*, vol. 5, 382.

40. Deloria and Lytle suggest that the opinion "worked steadily in one direction: buttressing the political powers of the tribe that had not been previously acknowledged by any organ, agency, or branch of the federal government" (159). However, the opinion makes explicit that its listing and explication of "inherent" powers comes directly from statutes and decisions; most of the opinion is dedicated to quoting from these sources.

41. The opinion offers an equally elliptical description of the conditions for valid intervention in native affairs: "The whole course of Congressional legislation with respect to the Indians has been based upon recognition of tribal autonomy, qualified only where the need for other types of governmental control has become clearly manifest" (454).

42. See 446, 454, 471, 475.

43. On the emergence of "domestic relations" as a legal concept in the late eighteenth and nineteenth centuries, see Cott, *Public Vows*; Gordon; and Grossberg.

44. The opinion, however, does note that the U.S. government has no legal authority—no congressional authorization—to outlaw polygamy among native peoples on their land (462). This point is qualified by the opinion's treatment of the regulations guiding the Court of Indian Offenses (which included the explicit outlawing of polygamy) as not only lawful but an expression of native desires, a maneuver I will address more fully later. Furthermore, in his regulations issued in 1935, Collier defines "adultery" as "hav[ing] sexual intercourse with another person, either of such person being married to a third person," thereby precluding the possibility of polygamy (*Law and Order Regulations*, 16).

45. For a reprint of the 1883 code, see *Regulations of the Indian Office*. By 1900, approximately two-thirds of the agencies had such courts. Each court was composed of three Indian justices, at first the top three officers of the Indian police force on the reservation but eventually becoming agent-appointed positions guided by concern that those who held them be "progressive" and of upstanding moral character. On the Courts, see Hagan; *Regulations of the Indian Office*; *Opinions of the Solicitor*, 532–536. Indian police forces were created in the late 1860s and 1870s (and given congressional recognition through funding in 1878) in order to provide a means for agents to maintain "law and

order" on reservation, as well as to provide an alternative to employing U.S. soldiers. See Hagan, 25–50. For discussion of coercive efforts by the BIA to document and control marriage and family relationships through departmental directives in the early part of the twentieth century, see Biolosi, "The Birth," 42–44.

46. On Collier's earlier opposition to the Courts, see Rusco, *Fateful Time*, 154, 167, 230. The attempt in the original version of the IRA to create a Court of Indian Affairs, which would have provided the possibility of appeal for all legal matters on-reservation, can be understood as an effort to eliminate the Courts. However, as Deloria and Lytle note, Collier offered virtually no resistance to the congressional excision of this section of the original bill during its progress through committee (131–132).

47. Biolosi, *Organizing*, 7–8; Hagan, 104–125.

48. The opinion here is quoting from a law review article by W. G. Rice Jr. entitled "The Position of the American Indian in the Law of the United States" (1934).

49. The case concerns defendants who were charged with violating a federal law prohibiting aiding in the escape of anyone convicted of a federal crime, or anyone being held in custody for trial on such charges. They were Umatillas who had sought to free a woman (simply referred to as "Minnie") imprisoned for having committed adultery in violation of BIA regulations; accepting the prosecutor's statement of facts, they contended that their actions did not fall under the statute since Minnie's adultery was not a "crime," in the sense that the prohibitions laid out in the regulations did not have the status or force of law. The federal district judge who tried the case rejected the defendants' claim, finding that "the United States, by virtue of its power and authority in the premises, has established a rule, which is, in effect, a law" (578–579); their attempt to free Minnie, therefore, fell within the terms of the federal statute.

50. This move is not entirely absent from *U.S. v. Clapox* either; the decision depicts "this Indian court and police" as "their first effort in the administration of justice" (579), marking administrative intervention as mere recognition through the use of the possessive "their."

51. Deloria and Lytle describe this line of argumentation as "mostly a fictional justification for vesting tribal courts with powers they had neither possessed nor exercised" (167), but such a reading seems to me to overlook the ways the argument works less to open room for a range of native formulations and formations than to normalize the "domestic"-ating aims of the Courts of Indian Offenses as an expression of native will.

52. At one point, the solicitor's opinion observes, "the regulation of the conduct of Indians upon the reservations in order to assure order and promote civilization is clearly within the purposes for which supervision over Indian affairs by the Secretary [of the Interior] and the Commissioner [of Indian affairs] was given" (535), and it further notes, "to date the set-up of the court has not been changed" (533).

53. *Law and Order Regulations*, 9. Further page numbers will be cited parenthetically. The regulations also state that "any matters that are not covered by traditional customs and usages of the tribe, or by applicable Federal laws and regulations, shall be decided by

the Court of Indian Offenses according to the laws of the State in which the matter in dispute may lie" (7), largely replicating the terms of the earlier regulations (see *Regulations of the Indian Office*, 104).

54. The Sioux reservations, for example, were divided into districts, each under its own "farm agent," a system that continued under reorganization. These administrators had discretion over large swaths of native life, including travel and the disbursement of funds from Individual Indian Money (IIM) accounts. See Biolosi, *Organizing*; Macgregor; Reinhardt, *Ruling Pine Ridge*, 42–76; and Robertson.

55. As specified in the law, reservations needed to choose to come under the IRA and then draft a constitution for which there would be a separate vote. Pine Ridge residents accepted the IRA on October 27, 1934, by a vote of 1,169 to 1,095 and ratified a constitution under the law on December 11, 1935, voting 1,348 to 1,041 (Biolosi, *Organizing*, 78, 98). While scholars have tended to reject the idea that people who objected to the IRA and the IRA constitutions showed their opposition by simply refusing to go to the polls, they have argued that the version of the IRA on which people thought they were voting was the one discussed in the various meetings with native peoples prior to the extensive changes made to the bill during the congressional committee process and that votes for constitutions may have had less to do with support for their particular provisions than with the fact that their adoption was understood as a necessary precursor to gaining access to the funds promised under the act.

56. The character of this change was described by the soon-to-be-ousted councilmen in the following terms: "[E]lderly illiterate gentlemen on this reservation are fighting desperately to revive their old . . . tribunal of chiefs" (Clow, "Indian Reorganization Act," 128). On the 1931 change in Pine Ridge governance, see Biolosi, *Organizing*, 53–59; Clow, "Indian Reorganization Act"; and Robertson, 167–171.

57. The Pine Ridge constitution of 1935 is reprinted in *Survey of the Conditions of the Indians in the United States*, pt. 37, 21732–21740.

58. Biolosi, *Organizing*, 85–86, 99. See also Taylor, *New Deal*, 96–98. Elmer Rusco has argued that the idea of a "model constitution" used by BIA officials when serving as technical advisers is a myth. See Rusco, "Indian Reorganization Act." His argument is targeted largely at Taylor's study, but he does not acknowledge Biolosi's argument on this score with respect to Pine Ridge and Rosebud, for which Biolosi offers persuasive evidence. See Biolosi, *Organizing*. Moreover, in his introduction to Felix S. Cohen's *On the Drafting of Tribal Constitutions*, a memorandum Cohen drafted in late 1934, David E. Wilkins makes reference to internal BIA documents that indicate the use of such a model; the model constitution that Cohen circulated in August 1935 lines up with the Pine Ridge constitution almost article for article, and the language of the former is in many places replicated exactly in the latter. See Cohen, *On the Drafting*, 173–177; Wilkins "Introduction."

The preamble of the Pine Ridge constitution notes that the Oglala Sioux Tribe will have "the power to exercise certain rights of home rule not inconsistent with Federal laws and our treaties" (21732), reiterating the premises articulated by officials in the Plains Congress and the Interior Department opinions while also leaving ambiguous the extent to which "Federal laws" meant those specifically appertaining to Indians or broader federal and constitutional principles (in light of native peoples' supposedly primary status as U.S. citizens). The latter is suggested by the provision for "Oaths of Office" that requires officials to promise to "support and defend the Constitution of the United States" (21739).

59. The code is reprinted in *Survey of the Conditions,* 21749–21766. On the regulation of marriage and sexual morality on Pine Ridge by the agent and through the Courts of Indian Offenses, see Biolosi, "Birth," 46 n. 31.

60. *Survey of the Conditions,* 21759, 21762, 21764, 21766.

61. According to Biolosi, the legal codes adopted at Pine Ridge and Rosebud were virtually identical (*Organizing,* 129). Additionally, while the preceding provisions were allowed to stand, laws passed by the Pine Ridge and Rosebud councils that were seen as interfering with residents' religious freedom were routinely overruled by administrators in the Indian affairs bureaucracy, suggesting that practices seen as "religion" were accorded more protection as signifying the kind of native culture whose rejuvenation the IRA was supposed to make possible. See Biolosi, *Organizing,* 126–150. This dynamic will be addressed more extensively in the section discussing Deloria's *Waterlily.*

62. Robertson, 173; *Survey of the Conditions of the Indians,* 21784–21794; Reinhardt, *Ruling Pine Ridge,* 61.

63. *Survey of the Conditions of the Indians,* 21788. In this statement, Short Horn and American Horse return insistently to the need to turn Oglala governance back over to full-bloods, as against the reorganization government, which they claim overwhelmingly is dominated by mixed-bloods. As noted earlier, though, the mixed-blood/full-blood split can be thought of less as an acceptance of blood quantum logics than as a way of talking about membership in tiospayes and the ways that U.S. policy created this conflict through reservation and allotment policy in the late nineteenth and early twentieth centuries. See Robertson.

64. The title of this section is a play on the collection *No More Separate Spheres!* edited by Cathy N. Davidson and Jessamyn Hatcher.

65. In using this term, I am playing on the feminist of color formulation of the concept of "intersectionality," which seeks to account for the ways multiple forms of identification operate simultaneously in complex and shifting ways. See Cohen, "Punks." Instead of thinking about how different kinds of identity work in and through each other, though, I am trying to address how the divisions and categories at play in dominant Anglo-American social mappings fail to capture modes of native sociality and self-representation. For a fascinating effort to rethink intersectionality as "assemblage," focusing less on the co-implication of existing categories of identity (race, class, gender, sexuality, etc.) than on the ways a range of disparate characteristics/dynamics are soldered together in forging new kinds of identification, see Puar.

66. Deloria not only was present during the period in which Pine Ridge residents were voting on the constitution, but she wrote Franz Boas about the views expressed by Oglala women in a separate council they had before the vote. In addition, Deloria served in 1938 as the translator for those opposing the IRA government in a petition they drafted

to the U.S. government. See the letters from Ella Deloria to Franz Boas on August 25, 1935, and February 12, 1938, in the Franz Boas Collection (hereafter FBC) at the American Philosophical Society in Philadelphia, PA. See also Gardner, "Speaking," 466; Hoefel, 191–192; Murray, "Ella Deloria," 117–118, 129. For a sense of Deloria's movement on and off Teton reservations in the 1930s, see her letters to Boas (FBC).

In "Walls and Bridges," Janet L. Finn suggests she will "situate Deloria's life and work in relation to key moments in federal Indian policy" (159). She notes that *Speaking of Indians* "talks back to the constricted images of family and household imposed by federal Indian policy" and that Deloria participated somewhat reluctantly in a federally funded assessment of Diné social dynamics, published as *The Navajo Indian Problem* in 1939 (170, 172). Additionally, Maria Eugenia Cotera notes that the episode in *Waterlily* where the title character encounters a bedraggled family detached from any particular village or band may be based on her observations about the effects "of assimilationist policies" on Rosebud and Pine Ridge reservations, particularly "the disintegration of the *tiospaye*" (58). These accounts allude to without significantly elaborating connections between the books Deloria authored and contemporaneous policy, and they do not explore the relationship between specific late-nineteenth-century initiatives and mid-twentieth-century programs.

67. Deloria also had extended correspondence and a complex professional connection with Ruth Benedict, who became her primary entrée into institutional anthropological and publishing circles after Boas's death. Their correspondence can be found in folders 28.3 and 28.4 of the Ruth Benedict Papers (hereafter RBP), courtesy of Vassar College (in Poughkeepsie, NY). See also Gardner, "Though It Broke"; Hoefel; and Murray.

68. Deloria notes the presence of councils, which she observes lacked coercive authority, and the existence of soldier societies that could use force to carry out leaders' orders "during migrations and communal buffalo hunts" (39).

69. The intervention that Deloria makes into reorganization's logic of heterohome-making can be seen more clearly when juxtaposed with that offered by Luther Standing Bear in *Land of the Spotted Eagle* (1933). While depicting the camp circle in ways that closely resemble *Speaking of Indians*, he presents a picture of Lakota life that makes it appear far more like the heterogendered nuclear family household, especially in the chapter "Home and Family": "The home was the center of Lakota society. . . . Here it was that offspring learned duty to parents, to lodge, to band, to tribe, and to self" (84). In this vision, "family" seems to occupy a separate, privileged space, resembling the topology of "domestic relations": "The integrity of the home was revered, and a man known as a good husband and a woman known as a good wife were honored members of society" (162). Further, although the text states outright that the bands were themselves composed of collections of relatives, tiospayes are introduced in the chapter "Civil Arrangements" as "the civil or governmental structure of Lakota society": "Each band was a social unit, under separate chieftainship, yet each band was an integral part of the nation" (120). The apparent shift in topics from one chapter to the next—"Home and Family" to "governmental" matters—simulates a kind of public/private split that can be

understood as legitimizing Lakota political and residential formations for a white audience by making them fit a familiar framework, even while repeatedly (perhaps tactically) marking the ways life in the tiospaye did not conform to the parameters of conjugal domesticity (such as the accepted presence of winktes [92–93], the existence of polygamy [116, 162], and the absence of pressure for people to marry if they did not wish to do so [153]).

70. On the continuing social role of tiospayes and their crossing of administrative boundaries, see Albers, "Sioux Kinship."

71. Biolosi, *Organizing*, 105.

72. On the appeal to tiospayes in the process of post-IRA constitution-making, see Biolosi, *Organizing*, 85–108; Collier, "Collier Replies to Mekeel"; Mekeel; Reinhardt, *Ruling Pine Ridge*, 80–91; and Taylor, *New Deal*, 89–91.

73. Deloria's familiarity with the community plan suggested by Mekeel may further be suggested by the fact that he served as a recommender for her (just as she was writing *Speaking of Indians*), suggesting that she was familiar with him and his work. See Deloria's applications for grants from the American Philosophical Society in 1943 and 1944 in folder 28.3, RBP; Murray, 139.

74. Here she may be referring, albeit obliquely, to the Red Shirt Table Cooperative, an initiative on Pine Ridge created by Superintendent William O. Roberts in which a particular "community" was chosen in which to establish a collective enterprise; imagined as a way of rejuvenating a traditional "neighborhood," in Roberts's terms, which had fallen into disarray and which supposedly lacked a coherent sense of leadership, the cooperative split into a gardening venture run by mixed-blood families and a livestock association operated by full-blood families, the former eventually being broken into privately held plots and the latter dissolving due to the need to help starving relatives living elsewhere rather than conserving stock for breeding. See Macgregor, 212; Reinhardt, *Ruling Pine Ridge*, 79–84; Roberts.

75. The text consistently presents U.S. intervention in the lives of native peoples as a violent imposition, at one point noting that the United States is pursuing "the liberation of all conquered people, except the one it itself had conquered!" (162), but it also repeatedly insists that even if brought through force and undesired by Dakota people the transformation of Dakota life due to imperialism is the context in which Dakota peoples must now operate, including finding ways of supporting themselves within a capitalist system. See Weaver, 112–113. In a letter on May 12, 1939, Deloria describes the apparatus of Indian policy as "a heartless monster of a machine, a Frankenstein, such an impersonal organ" (FBC).

The representation of tradition as a "block" may also be seen, at least partially, as due to the fact that the book was sponsored by the National Council of Churches, a white missionary organization. See Deloria, "Introduction"; Gardner, "Speaking," 465; letter of April 7, 1947, folder 28.4, RBP. For a fascinating discussion of her concerns about the pressure being exerted on her brother Vine to become a minister and her resistance to this idea, see the letter to Franz Boas August 21, 1928 (FBC).

Her letters to Ruth Benedict often comment on her anxieties about her audience and her capacity to speak about Dakota life intelligently. For example, in the letter of February 28, 1941, she declares, "my book [*Speaking of Indians?*] is going to be very simple and informal—like a letter. . . . And I won't even try to draw any conclusions myself. After all, a patient can't very well diagnose his own case" (folder 28.3, RBP), and in a letter dated February 13, 1947, she worries "that I am the glorified (?) native mouthpiece" (question mark in original, folder 28.4, RBP). Deloria also expressed concern that the longer, more academically ethnographic work on prereservation society that she was writing at the same time as her novel *Waterlily* would be seen as irrelevant when viewed against contemporary Dakota life. See the letters of January 1, 1944 (folder 28.3, RBP); April 26, July 6, and July 15, 1947, (folder 28.4, RBP).

76. For a similar reading of these moments, see Weaver, 112–114. For a contrasting contemporaneous study of Pine Ridge that fairly unrelentingly casts its residents as in a chaotic fall away from their traditional social structures, see Macgregor.

77. While *Indians of the Americas* was published soon after Collier left the BIA, the views expressed in the text seem consistent with his perspective as articulated in earlier publications both before and during his tenure as Commissioner of Indian Affairs. See Kelly, *Assault on Assimilation*; Rusco, *Fateful Time*; and Schwartz.

78. *Minutes of the Plains Congress*, 7.

79. Rusco, *Fateful Time*, 184. See also Biolosi, *Organizing*, 63–64; Daily, 60–79; and Deloria and Lytle, 62.

80. On the ways "religion" came to work as a signifier of Native difference in the early twentieth century, especially in the context of trying to gain legitimacy for Native practices under the first amendment, see Wenger.

81. On the role of anthropologists in shaping Collier's thinking and within the administration of the BIA in the 1930s, see Biolosi, *Organizing*, 85–108; Collier, "Collier Replies to Mekeel"; Collier, *Indians of the Americas*, 154–171; Collier, "Genesis and Philosophy"; Marden; Mekeel; Patterson, 71–102; Reinhardt, *Ruling Pine Ridge*, 77–105; Rusco, *Fateful Time*, 50–51, 189–190; and Taylor, *New Deal*.

82. On the emergence of what would be characterized as a Boasian notion of culture, its institutionalization through World War II, and the major intellectual features of Boasian anthropology, see Darnell, *Invisible Genealogies*; Darnell, *And Along Came Boas*; di Leonardo; Elliott; Evans; Handler; Hegeman; Hoefel; Krupat, 81–100; Kuper, 115–134; Patterson, *Social History*; Stocking, *Ethnographer's Magic* (chaps. 3 and 4); and Stocking, "Franz Boas."

83. This text is a particularly apt one to discuss in this context for several reasons. Not only was it published in the year of the IRA's passage, but Benedict was one of the supervisors for the joint BIA–University of Chicago research project into Indian personality, which generated five studies including Gordon Macgregor's account of the Dakotas, *Warriors without Weapons*. See RBP, folders 94.4 (Notes from the Chicago Seminar) and 94.7 (Field Guide to the Study of the Development of Inter-Personal Relations). Also, Benedict worked extensively with Deloria (especially after Boas's death in 1942) and

provided extensive and running commentary on *Waterlily* while Deloria was writing it. See RBP, folders 28.3 and 28.4. For discussion of the influence of Benedict's work in reflecting and extending discourses of "culture" in the 1930s, see di Leonardo, 184–190; Hegeman, 93–126.

84. Collier, *Indians of the Americas*, 10.

85. Moreover, Collier's assumptions about the meaning of family and "domestic"-ity may also be traced to developments within British social anthropology. In the first few decades of the twentieth century, the study of kinship, particularly in Great Britain, increasingly was moving toward a vision organized around a nuclear imaginary in which marital and parental imperatives are natural/universal and provide the basis/logic at the heart of other forms of kin-making and kin connection. Collier likely was exposed to this work through his interest in British and French forms of "indirect administration," in which such anthropological models were employed. On shifts in the study of kinship from the late nineteenth century to the mid-twentieth century, see Carsten; Collier and Yanagisako; Fortes; Harris, *Kinship*; Kuper; and Schneider, *Critique*. On Collier's praise of British and French colonial models, see Reinhardt, "Crude Replacement"; Rusco, *Fateful Time*, 160–162; Schwartz. In this vein, Deloria's representation of Dakota sociality in both *Speaking of Indians* and *Waterlily* can be understood as refusing the distinction made within social anthropology between "family" ("domestic" relations that follow from the facts of birth and true parentage) and "descent" (clan and lineage structures).

86. Critics largely have focused on the text's participation in Deloria's broader efforts to preserve traditional Dakota knowledges and transmit them to future generations, its emphasis on women and the importance of the various kinds of work that they perform (as opposed to the anthropological tendency to fetishize men's social roles), and its attempt to provide a more popularly accessible account than a conventional ethnography. See Cotera; DeMallie, "Afterword"; Finn; Gambrell; Gardner, "Though It Broke"; and Medicine, *Learning to Be*, 269–288. On Boasian experiments with fiction writing, see Krupat, 49–80.

87. In "All My Relatives Are Noble," Maria Eugenia Cotera argues that for Deloria, "'kinship' was not just an ethnographic concept—a relic of a time long past—it was a mode of tribal consciousness that could, indeed must, be translated into 'modern' environments" (57). On the ways responsibilities to relatives materially enabled Deloria's ethnographic work and took her away from it, see the letters in the FBC; Finn; Gardner, "Speaking"; Medicine, *Learning to Be*, 269–288; and Murray. *Waterlily* is a novelized version of an extended ethnography that Deloria worked on for many years. On the relationship between the two texts, see Gardner, "Though It Broke."

88. Given that the novel at this moment is talking about Waterlily's decision-making process, this particular line could be read as a reflection of Waterlily's thoughts rather than an authoritative pronouncement by the narrator.

89. One cannot help but think that this particular character's name is meant to connote prostitution, even though no such exchange is indicated in the text.

90. See Canaday; Chauncey, *Why Marriage?*. On the historical relation between Euro-American accounts of native gender systems and the emergence of the sexological discourse of inversion, see Roscoe, *Changing Ones*, 167–187.

91. Deloria's discussion of marriage is also fraught, in that not having been married she is not supposed to have knowledge of the intimate details of marital life. See Gambrell, 132–134; Gardner, "Speaking," 465. In a May 20, 1941, letter, she expresses the concern that addressing such matters would lead people in "Dakota country" to believe that she was only "posing as a virgin." She adds, "Here you have a practical demonstration of some of the cross-currents and underneath influences of Dakota thinking and life. It trips even anyone as apparently removed as I am, because I have a place among the people. And I *have to* keep it" (folder 28.4, RBP).

92. In "The American Indian Fiction Writers," Elizabeth Cook-Lynn has critiqued accounts of Sioux identity that present personal "feeling" as more important to belonging than blood connection, emphasizing blood as the basis for belonging to a tiospaye. While recognizing the danger of denying the role of what can be characterized as kinship to Sioux identity, I also think that, as Deloria suggests, kinship can be understood as having crucial non-blood dimensions without turning belonging into merely a declaration of individual predilection.

93. Rainbow is the brother of First Woman, who is the wife of Black Eagle, Blue Bird's cousin who is the "recognized head of our *tiyospaye*," and while Black Eagle initially had lived in First Woman's tiospaye, her parents and siblings decided to move with him back to his (22). Yet the novel never suggests that they do not feel part of the web of kinship that constitutes the tiospaye. In fact, as mentioned earlier, the husband of Dream Woman (who is Rainbow's sister) is described as feeling "like a perpetual visitor" (163), but she does not experience that sensation, implying that she, her parents, and her siblings feel at home and, thereby, suggesting that they have in some sense become family with the other people in Black Eagle's tiospaye despite not having a blood connection to them.

94. This account of "friendship" as interfamilial kinship can be contrasted to *Last of the Mohicans*' vision of isolated connection between Hawkeye and Chingachgook, discussed in chapter 1.

95. The Sun Dance, polygamy, and travel away from one's reservation have been addressed already or will be discussed later. Medicine people appear in the novel during the Sun Dance as well as during episodes in which Ohiya is encircled by a snake while in his cradle and Waterlily gets ill from eating too much pemmican (her recovery serving as the occasion for Rainbow holding a hunka ceremony in her honor, illustrating his parental devotion and affection for her) (68–73). In terms of giving away the property of the deceased, when Rainbow's mother, Gloku, dies, a large "redistribution" is held (159), and in order to make up for two horses that have been stolen but promised for the redistribution, Waterlily agrees to marry Sacred Horse, who offers to replace them as a kind of dowry.

96. *Opinions of the Solicitor*, 536.

97. This description of White Dawn can be contrasted with Catharine Maria Sedgwick's discussion of her feeling of being "unnatural" living in her brothers' households, discussed in chapter 2.

98. In particular, see the letters in FBC; Gardner, "Speaking"; and Medicine, *Learning to Be*, 269–288.

99. Such acceptance is noted in the accounts of both Benedict (262–264) and Standing Bear (92–93), which were published hovering around a decade before Deloria completed *Waterlily*.

100. See Gardner, "Though It Broke," 679–680; letter of July 6, 1947, folder 28.4, RBP. She also addresses what she described as "the berdaches" in her longer ethnographic work (letter of April 7, 1947, folder 28.4, RBP).

101. See di Leonardo.

102. In his discussions of Pueblo religion, Collier, in fact, was at pains to challenge the charges by non-natives that sexual debauchery was a key part of various rituals. See Collier, *Indians of the Americas*, 150–151; Daily, 36–59; and Kelly, *Assault on Assimilation*, 302–304. For a broader consideration of that controversy, see Wenger.

103. Pfister, 231–232.

CHAPTER 5

1. Hay, 239–240. For the epigraphs, see Hay, 295–296, 299; and Brant, *Writing as Witness*, 44–45. On the Radical Faeries, see Hennen; Morgensen, "Arrival at Home"; and Povinelli, *Empire*. I should note that I actively participate within faerie communities and have been to numerous Radical Faerie gatherings. My discussion of Hay, who is considered by many to be the "founder" of the faeries, is as an insider in several faerie communities who remains deeply troubled by the appropriation of native histories and cultural forms in those communities, and I certainly am not the only faerie critical of such dynamics within our communities.

2. On such participation in neoliberalism by sexual minorities, for which Lisa Duggan has coined the term "homonormativity," see Duggan, "New Homonormativity"; Manalansan, "Race, Violence"; and Puar. The Radical Faerie call is not the first use of "tribe" in this way (Nealon, 1–23), but it, among Hay's other writings, provides a useful starting place for beginning to think about the role that native peoples serve in contemporary articulations of nonnormative sexual and gender identity. See Morgensen, "Settler Homonationalism."

3. Kelley, *Power*, 123.

4. This impulse can be understood as part of the broader desire to cast sexual minorities as a kind of ethnic group or to consolidate the "ambient notion of the 'peoplehood' of lesbians and gay men" (Nealon, 7). See also Bravmann; Seidman. The scholarship on the complicated and uneven emergence of sexual identity categories in the twentieth century is vast. For examples, see Canaday; Chauncey, *Gay New York*; D'Emilio and

Freedman; Faderman; Ferguson; Floyd; Halberstam, *Female Masculinity*; Hennessy; Kennedy and Davis; Love; Nealon; and Stryker.

5. On this tendency within U.S. anthropology, see di Leonardo.

6. On the problems of using the concept of "third gender" as a way of naming non-European practices and identity formations, see Blackwood, "Reading Sexualities"; Towle and Morgan. On the role of heteropatriarchy in contemporary performances of Navajo nationalism, see Denetdale "Carving" and "Chairmen."

7. The language of "gifts" seems eerily to recall its role in Cooper's *Last of the Mohicans*, discussed in chapter 1. Here, though, rather than indicating "blood" distinction between Indians and whites, it marks a profound and innate difference between gays and heteros, a division that allows for imagined solidarity across the color line.

8. See Morgensen, *Queer / Native / Settler*.

9. As Morgensen also has argued, and very productively reminded me as part of our ongoing conversations, those same queer non-natives who from one perspective can be seen as appropriating indigeneity to legitimize settler presence also can, from another perspective, be understood as actively drawing attention to indigeneity and histories of settlement in ways that actually make possible the kinds of reflexive analysis Morgensen and I pursue. In other words, even as we critique folks like Hay, non-natives need to engage with the ways they are operating in a tradition with him. This kind of dynamic resonates with Kevin Floyd's recent efforts to rethink reification.

10. On Jess as transgender, see Prosser, 172–205. However, the character self-identifies as "butch" and a "he/she." On the emergence of the category of "transgender," see Currah; Denny; Feinberg, *Transgender Warriors*, ix–xiii; Stryker; Valentine; and Wilchins. On the complicated negotiations between butch, transgender, and transsexual identifications and communities, see Bergman; Halberstam, *Female Masculinity*, 141–174; Hale; and Rubin, "Of Catamites." Feinberg has described *Stone Butch Blues* as semiautobiographical, and at various points in hir life, ze has identified as "lesbian," "butch," and "transgender," not understanding these as necessarily mutually exclusive or existing in any kind of teleological relation to each other. See Feinberg, *Transgender Warriors*, ix–xiii, 98; Prosser, 177, 190–200.

11. This use of "queerness" as a catchall for participation in gender and sexual minority communities is subject to the critique that transgender issues often are subsumed within a gay- and lesbian-centered framework. See Jagose and Kulick; Minter; Namaste; Prosser; Stryker; and Valentine, 143–203. However, given the butch-femme focus of the novel itself and its clear borrowing of the strategy of earlier self-consciously "gay" writers, including its quotation of Jonathan Ned Katz's *Gay American History* as part of the basis for Jess's claim to closeness with native peoples, I am willing to risk this possibility in the interest of highlighting the stakes of settler appropriation of native peoples to validate identities that deviate from normative straightness. For Feinberg's own use of "queer" to link lgb struggles with transgender ones, see *Trans Liberation*, 95–105.

12. Brant, *Writing as Witness*, 76.

13. Brant often writes of the specific significance to her as a Mohawk of extended family and clan connections. On Haudenosaunee kinship systems and their translation into the racialized dynamics of settler conceptions of "family," see chapter 1.

14. When speaking about Feinberg, I use gender neutral pronouns (ze, hir, hirs, hirself), since that has been hir expressed preference. Earlier in hir life, ze did use the pronoun "she," but since has chosen to use neutral or masculine pronouns.

15. On referring to Jess using feminine pronouns, see Moses, 95 n. 14.

16. On the butch-femme bar scene in Buffalo in the late 1930s through the early 1960s, see Kennedy and Davis.

17. On Jess's relationship with Theresa, in particular the text's representation of "stone" butchness, see Cvetkovich, 73–79; Halberstam, *Female Masculinity*, 111–139.

18. On the differences between elite and working-class sexual minority communities in Buffalo, see Kennedy and Davis. On these distinctions in the novel, see Halberstam, *Female Masculinity*, 129–130; Moses. For examples of the critique of lesbian-feminism's tendency to reject roles and cross-gender identifications as simply reproducing domination, see Case; Halberstam, *Female Masculinity*, 111–139; Hart, 36–82; Moraga and Hollibaugh; Rubin, "Thinking Sex"; Stryker, 91–120. For a very compelling effort to reassert lesbian-feminist theory as both a forerunner and a corrective to queer theory, see Garber.

19. For an alternae reading of Jess's relation to Ed as enacting a troubling analogy, see Somerville, *Queering*, 172–175.

20. In this vein, the novel later revisits Duffy's call to choose Leroy over Jess, suggesting that accepting the binary logic of management did not serve the interests of union members either (101).

21. For discussion of the working-class ethos of the novel, see Moses. However, Moses addresses the novel's portrayal of the effects of poverty on gender and sexual minorities, and its intensification of surveillance and harassment by the police and other authorities, while devoting minimal attention to Feinberg's emphasis on labor unions as a model for broader forms of organizing and political collectivity.

22. Because the section discussing Muriel is only four pages (77–80), I will forgo specific page references for citations.

23. When addressing the novel's references to native people, most critics focus on its opening, in which Jess is described as being tended to by Diné women, and on the turquoise ring the women give her, which has an image of a dancing person that might be a woman or a man—the ring functioning as a figure for the complexity of Jess's gender identity. I have chosen to forgo discussion of these potentially more exoticizing parts of the text in order to address the role of images of nativeness in its formulation of the union concept and its representation of Haudenosaunee people, the native communities and reservations closest to Jess for the vast majority of the novel. For an interesting nonfictional inversion of Jess's story (a woman raised as a white Jew who finds out that she is actually Diné and was kidnapped at birth, rather than a Jewish woman in some sense desiring to be Diné), see Melanson; Strong, "To Forget."

24. See Kennedy and Davis, 16, 42, 116, 120, 396.

25. On the role of urban powwows in maintaining forms of tribal identification and as vehicles of native community formation in the city, see Ramirez, 59–65.

26. See Bilharz; Hauptman, *Iroquois Struggle*; Hauptman, *Formulating*; O'Brien, *American Indian*, 97–109; and Purcell.

27. Jemison and Schein, 297. For discussion of U.S.-Haudenosaunee relations in the 1780s and 1790s, see chapter 1.

28. The St. Lawrence project also resulted in the loss of 1,300 acres for the Mohawks of Caughnawaga (Hauptman, *Formulating*, 20). In the case of Akwesasne, the New York Court of Appeals found that state treaties and acts from the early to mid-nineteenth century had deprived the Mohawks of control over this land; in the case of the Tuscaroras, the U.S. Supreme Court held that the land in question was not technically a "reservation," since it had been purchased by the Tuscarora nation and was held in fee simple rather than in federal trust, thus leaving it open to federal eminent domain powers. See Hauptman, *Iroquois Struggle*, 146, 172–173.

29. See Hauptman, *Iroquois Struggle*, 45–64. For discussion of Haudenosaunee resistance to the unilateral extension of U.S. citizenship to American Indians in 1924, see Bruyneel, 97–121.

30. On the termination program, see Deloria, *Custer*; Fixico, *Termination*; Philp, *Termination*; Rosier; and Wilkinson, *Blood Struggle*.

31. Fixico, *Termination*, 18, 38.

32. Fixico, *Termination*, 175.

33. See Fixico, *Termination*, 91–133; Goldberg-Ambrose; Philp, *Termination*, 140–152; Prucha, *Documents*, 234–235.

34. Fixico, *Termination*, 112, 181; Prucha, *Documents*, 256–258.

35. By the mid-1980s, about 80 percent of native peoples in New York State lived in the cities of Buffalo, New York City, Niagara Falls, Rochester, and Syracuse (Hauptman, *Formulating*, 68).

36. See George-Kanentiio; Hauptman, *Iroquois Struggle*, 148–149, 205–229. For the continuing effort to treat Mohawk lands as on one side or other of the U.S.-Canadian border rather than as their own sovereign territories, see Simpson, "Subjects of Sovereignty."

37. In *Transgender Warriors*, Feinberg notes that learning about the presence of greater gender diversity among native peoples pushed hir "to act more forcefully in defense of the treaty, sovereignty, and self-determination rights of Native nations" (24). Although I do not question hir commitment to these issues, they appear only in this passing reference in *Transgender Warriors* and not at all in *Stone Butch Blues* despite the thematic importance of native peoples to that text.

38. See Prosser, 172–205.

39. On "left politics," see Cohen, "Punks."

40. For discussion of the limits of the dimorphic model, in terms of its historical/cultural specificity, the incoherence of attempts to define "male" and "female," and the model's failure to acknowledge the existence of a range of different kinds of bodies, see Butler, *Undoing Gender*; Greenberg; Roscoe, *Changing Ones*, 119–136; and Stryker, 1–29.

41. Feinberg's adoption of this strategy can be classed with other efforts to depict nondominant forms of gender expression within the U.S. context as part of a larger "third gender" that operates transhistorically and transculturally, such as those by Harry Hay discussed earlier. This project is even more pronounced in *Transgender Warriors* (esp. 21–29). As Evan B. Towle and Lynn M. Morgan argue in "Romancing the Transgender Native," in such crossings "'third gender' societies are accorded a primordial, foundational location in our thinking, as though they underlay or predated Western gender formulations," and "the 'third gender' concept lumps all nonnormative gender variations into one category, limiting our understandings of the range and diversity of gender ideologies and practices" (476–477). In the article, they extend this critique to *Transgender Warriors* (481–483, 487).

42. In the speeches by Feinberg collected in *Trans Liberation*, ze repeatedly asserts the importance of accepting each person in hir "own unique and hard-fought-for identity" (46), and in *Invisible Lives*, Viviane K. Namaste emphasizes the ways that representations (including scholarly) of transgender and transsexual people often seek to trace the origin of their sense of gendered identity rather than accepting the existence of people who identify in these ways and instead asking questions about their preferred self-representations and ability to access resources. On the devastating implications of a failure to recognize transgender and transsexual identities and needs within state-run agencies and institutions, see Spade. I should make clear that I am not in any way suggesting that transgender and transsexual persons and communities should not be affirmed as such and understood as collectivities for the purposes of organizing and advocating for laws, resources, and services that recognize their particular self-understandings. What I am arguing against is legitimizing such identification through narrating a history that undermines or ignores native identifications and peoplehood or that makes indigeneity into a vehicle of transgender empowerment in ways disconnected from the self-articulations and political goals of native people(s). See Morgensen, *Queer / Native / Settler*.

43. The Supreme Court found in *Lone Wolf v. Hitchcock* (1903) that Congress has the power to abrogate treaties if it explicitly indicates an intent to do so, and in 1958, the U.S. Court of Appeals found that Congress had done so with respect to the Treaty of Canandaigua by including a line item in 1957 in an appropriations bill allocating funds toward the Kinzua Dam (Hauptman, *Iroquois Struggle*, 85–104). An earlier effort to nullify the Treaty of Canandaigua in the U.S. Senate, as part of the inclusion of Six Nations reservations under state jurisdiction, had failed (Hauptman, *Iroquois Struggle*, 48–58).

44. The creation of the Indian Claims Commission in 1946 enabled the pursuit of such petitions, but a favorable judgment only could result in a monetary award equal to the value of the land at the time of taking, without interest or the possibility of restoring native sovereignty over the territory in question. On the Indian Claims Commission, see Fixico, *Termination*, 21–44; Philp, *Termination*, 16–33.

45. On this case, see Hauptman, *Iroquois Struggle*, 179–203; Shattuck. On the recent case *Sherrill v. Oneida*, which denied Oneida sovereignty over traditional lands which the

nation had purchased that had been illegally taken during the early Republic, see Bruyneel, 205–214; Rifkin, *Manifesting* ("Introduction").

46. Hauptman, *Formulating*, 65–67, 120.

47. Bilharz, 122–125; Hauptman, *Formulating*, 95–103.

48. As discussed in chapter 1, the first Treaty of Buffalo Creek (1838) ceded the reservations of Buffalo Creek, Cattaraugus, Tonawanda, and Allegany, but in the revision of that treaty in 1842, the Cattaraugus and Allegany reservations were restored. They together decided to adopt an elective republican government in 1848; the people of Tonawanda refused to join this effort, were able to purchase back part of their reservation in 1857, retained their traditional government, and remained part of the Iroquois League council centered at Onondaga (as opposed to the separate League council centered at the Six Nations reserve). The state imposed an elective council at Akwesasne in the late nineteenth century, and in 1862, the people of Tonawanda adopted a peacemakers' court elected from among existing chiefs, creating several elected administrative offices as well. The sources suggest that the continuance of the Longhouse religion of Handsome Lake tends to correlate with the retention of traditional clan structures (despite Handsome Lake's own emphasis on the importance of the nuclear family unit), so that the presence of the former may mark the latter even when there is no specific evidence of the latter's presence. For the above, see Bilharz, 80, 106, 119, 145–148, 155; Doxtator, 9, 34–35, 140, 277–325; Foster, 131; George-Kanentiio; Hauptman, *Conspiracy*, 191–212; Hauptman, *Iroquois Struggle*, 39–40, 52, 161, 166, 232; O'Brien, *American Indian*, 97–109; Shoemaker, "From Longhouse"; and Society of Friends.

49. I should be clear that I am not suggesting there is no way that someone without a Seneca mother could ever be understood as Seneca, but I am highlighting that the novel skips over the issue of matrilineality entirely.

50. On the importance of the "coming-out" story, and its racial, cultural, and spatial assumptions, see Bravmann; Ross; Weston, *Long Slow Burn*, 29–56.

51. On such dislocation, see Brant, *Writing as Witness*; Driskill, "Stolen"; Gilley; Jacobs, Thomas, and Lang; Roscoe, *Living the Spirit*.

52. "The word otara in Mohawk means land, clay or earth as well as clan and in asking an individual what clan they belong to (oh nisen'taroten'), one is literally asking[,] 'What is the outline or contour of your clay?'" (Doxtator, 6).

53. Ramirez, 12; Lobo, "Is Urban a Person," 93, 96.

54. American Indian Policy Review Commission, 7. On urban Indian life, see also Fixico, *Urban Indian*; Howard-Bobiwash; Jackson, *Our Elders*; Janovicek; Lawrence; Lobo, "Urban Clan Mothers"; Metcalf; and Straus and Valentino.

55. On native migrations as "diaspora," see Clifford; Ramirez.

56. On the history of Tyendinaga, see Doxtator; Hamori-Torok.

57. Deloria, *Custer*, 263. In *Writing as Witness*, Brant describes Tyendinaga as "home"; she notes that her family routinely would take trips to the reserve and that relatives from the reserve often would come stay with them in Detroit (110–111).

58. An elected council was adopted at Tyendinaga in 1874 to create a coordinated means of responding to repeated attempts by local whites to gain access to Mohawk timber and land, and as I will discuss further later, the passage of the Indian Act reshaped the official terms of belonging to the Tyendinaga reserve. However, these changes did not result in the erasure of the clans or their social influence. See Doxtator.

59. On the history and political economy of Tyendinaga in the nineteenth century, see Doxtator (esp. 161–216).

60. On Canadian policy, see Barker, "Gender"; Boldt; Emberley; Howard-Bobiwash; Janovicek; Lawrence; Shaw; Turner; and Wotherspoon and Satzewich.

61. On the relocation program, see American Indian Policy Review Commission, 23–45; Fixico, *Termination*, 134–157; Metcalf; and Philp, "Stride."

62. While acknowledging government complicity in the dislocation of people from reservations, some scholars have warned against understanding movement to the city only as a result of terminationist policies, a view that leaves aside some people's decision to embrace urban life or to see such movement in traditionalist terms. See Lobo, "Urban Clan Mothers"; Ramirez.

63. Philp, "Stride," 177, 188. See also Rosier, 1325.

64. See Danzinger.

65. In *Writing as Witness*, Brant notes that traditionally her father would have gone to live with her mother's family, but "since Mama was a white women . . . it was the natural course of things that the Brants would assimilate her and all offspring of the union" (109).

66. See Barker, "Gender"; Boldt (esp. 206–216); Janovicek; Lawrence; Shaw; and Simpson, "Captivating Eunice." On the effects of the Indian Act at Tyendinaga in the late nineteenth and early twentieth centuries, see Doxtator, 173–176, 190–194.

67. For development of the idea of unofficial clan mothers who provide safe haven to native people in urban areas, see Lobo, "Urban Clan Mothers."

68. See Cvetkovich, 118–155; Gopinath; Luibhéid, "Sexuality"; and Rodríguez.

69. On such "retribalization" in the city, see Straus and Valentino.

70. Williams, *Marxism and Literature*, 130.

71. For a reading of the story focused on its representation of the power of words, see Cullum.

72. The notion of livable subjectivities draws on Judith Butler's discussion of transgender identity in *Undoing Gender*.

73. In "Contemporary Two-Spirit Identity in the Fiction of Paula Gunn Allen and Beth Brant," Tara Prince-Hughes argues that Brant positions two-spirit characters as having a spiritual responsibility for continuing the traditions of their peoples, but Prince-Hughes often frames this idea as against a focus on sexuality/eroticism. However, Brant emphasizes sexual pleasure as itself an experience of the sacred. In *Writing as Witness*, she observes, "Sexuality, and the magic ability of our bodies to produce orgasm, was another way to please Creator and ensure all was well and in balance in our world" (55), arguing that part of the legacy of colonization is the demonization of the physical and a "hatred of sex" (56). For a more expansive effort to link ideas about (native) sexuality to processes of settler colonial-

ism, see Smith, *Conquest*. For discussion of the need to engage with native eroticism as part of challenging racist stereotypes and working toward a sense of wholeness and sovereignty for indigenous people(s), see Driskill, "Stolen"; Miranda, "Dildos"; Warrior, "Your Skin."

74. On reclaiming and exploring shame, see Cvetkovich; Love; Sedgwick and Frank; and Warner, *Trouble*.

75. On the "open secret," see Sedgwick, *Epistemology*. On the fire as the "erupt[ion]" of "suppressed secrets and imposed silence," see Cullum, 131–132.

76. On Pratt, see chapter 3.

77. On the notion of an "archive of feelings," see Cvetkovich.

CHAPTER 6

1. See Denetdale, "Carving"; Jacobi; Justice, "Notes"; Kannady.

2. On this pattern, see Chauncey, *Why Marriage?*.

3. Kannady, 370; Jacobi, 846. By contrast, the Coquille tribe passed a statute recognizing same-sex marriage in September 2008, http://www.indiancountrytoday.com/national/northwest/28287874.html (accessed December 6, 2009).

4. Kannady, 379; Jacobi, 847.

5. On the ways same-sex marriage actually might be a threat to native nations inasmuch as it could produce a backlash in which the United States further constricts their autonomy, see Fletcher.

6. I use "Muscogee" and "Creek" interchangeably. The official name of the nation is the "Muscogee (Creek) Nation," and while Muscogee is closer to the people's name for themselves, Creek is used very often colloquially and in official records. Also, Womack himself treats the two terms as synonyms. On this history of naming, see Martin, 6–13; Wickman, 10, 35–40.

Prior to the late eighteenth century, the Muscogees were more of a confederacy than a single people, tied together through kinship networks, division into two moieties (red and white), and bonds of alliance. On the nature and dynamics of this matrix, see Debo, 3–36; Ethridge; Green; Henry; Martin; Opler; Saunt, *New Order*; Wickman.

7. Kannady, 363.

8. In "Stolen from Our Bodies," Qwo-Li Driskill lays out a similar project of critique, describing the object as "making a journey to a Sovereign Erotic that mends our lives and communities" (51).

9. Brant, *Writing as Witness*, 45.

10. For an alternate reading of the "queerness" of tradition in the novel, through the prism of separatism, see Henry.

11. Brant, *Writing as Witness*, 44.

12. See Adams, *Education for Extinction*; Hoxie; Kappler, vol. I, 43, 47, 93, 736; Prucha, *American Indian Policy in Crisis*; and Thorne.

13. Jimmy "breathing into" Josh is particularly significant in light of the fact that the force of creation in Creek cosmology is known as the Maker of Breath, a figure also linked to fire and thus to the Green Corn ceremony (which I will discuss at length later). See Ethridge, 299; Grantham, 33, 81; Martin, 24–25; Swanton, 481–485.

14. For the emergence of a "race-evasive" and "power-evasive" ideology in which white power is coded as "normality," see Carter, *Heart*.

15. Conversely, through the portrayal of full-blood yearning for white acceptance, Womack denaturalizes Creek belonging as well, disaggregating culture and identification with native communities from degree of blood quantum and therefore subtly displacing a reproductively imagined and biologized vision of nationality, which one scholar has described as a recipe for "statistical extermination" (Garroutte, 57–58). The fact that Jimmy is of African descent and is often seen by non-Indians simply as black also functions as a critique of blood quantum logics of identity, especially in light of the ongoing, bitter disputes within the Five Tribes about whether or not black Indians deserve recognition as full citizens. On this struggle among the Creeks, see Saunt, *Black, White, and Indian*. For a reading of Jimmy's race, see Henry.

16. The continuity between Josh's parents' church and direct U.S. policy intervention is condensed in the fact that the church is located in Muskogee, the virtually all-white town that began as a train depot and became the premier site of allotment-era intervention as the base for the Indian agent of the Five Tribes, the federal circuit court, and the Dawes Commission. See Burton; Debo; and Saunt, *Black, White, and Indian*.

17. These moments also can be seen as turning the image of baptism toward the traditional Muscogee practice of ritual bathing, including during the Green Corn ceremony—the central event in the Creek spiritual calendar. See Debo, 298; Ethridge, 33; Swanton, 564, 567, 578, 588, 600. Also, several traditional tales tell of the flooding of the town of Coosa, especially important given that "Coosa" is said to be the previous name by which the Muscogees called themselves (Grantham, 207–209). The flooding of the towns due to U.S. damming, then, can be read from the perspective of the oral tradition as a repetition of a signal moment in Creek history/cosmology.

18. As John H. Moore notes, "the Mvskoke churches radically reorganized each 'church congregation' on the pre-existing pattern of the Etvlwa," the towns which were at the center of Creek life in ways I will address later in the chapter: "The church itself was called an Etvlwa, the pastor was selected from the leading clan and called Mekko [the traditional name for leading chiefs], and each church had from one to seven deacons selected from the lower-ranking clans and called Tvstvnvkke or some other traditional title" (168); "many of the Upper Creek tribal towns embraced the Baptist Church, since the Baptists were highly congregational rather than episcopal in their organization, and allowed the local churches to continue to speak their language, have their own native full-blood pastors, and be autonomous from one another, just as the traditional Etvlwas were" (175). On the presence of the Baptist church among the Creeks, see Debo, 118–119, 204, 297–298, 310–311; Fife; Hurt, "Creek"; Jackson, "Church"; Opler; Thorne; and Walker, "Tribal Towns."

19. In Womack's telling, the food is fish swimming in water trapped in a tree's branches. For other accounts of the origin of the tie-snake, see Gouge, 45–48; Grantham, 211–220; Swanton, 493. On the significance of tie-snake as a symbol of both the Lower World and crossing between worlds, see Grantham, 24–29; Justice, "Notes"; Martin, 25–26; and Swanton, 490–495.

20. Womack, *Red on Red*, 26.

21. Gramsci, 348, 327, 333.

22. Thorne, 31.

23. In March 1901, 253 of the Snakes, including Chitto Harjo, were indicted—more than 10 percent of the adult male Creek population—for "conspiracy to deprive unknown persons of their personal liberty" and "detaining them without lawful authority" (Harring, "Crazy Snake," 374–376). On the Crazy Snake Uprising, see Harring, "Crazy Snake"; Littlefield and Underhill; Morton, 189–194; and Opler, 47–51. Their demand for a return to the 1832 treaty, instead of the 1867 one made in the wake of the Civil War, is significant, in that the former contains a firmer promise to respect Creek sovereignty and gives less scope to U.S. intervention. As John H. Moore suggests in "The Mvskoke National Question in Oklahoma," according to the "Tribal Towns of the upper Creeks" "[t]here was only one treaty, they say, into which they freely entered, the treaty of 1832. As far as they are concerned, the other treaties, signed only by the mixed-blood elite never happened, and it is foolish to make any claims under those treaties" (174).

Over the course of the 1870s and early 1880s, Congress extended federal law over non-natives in Indian Territory, distributing judicial jurisdiction among three circuit court districts—western Arkansas, Kansas, and northern Texas. In 1874 the Union Agency was created to superintend the Five Tribes, and in the early 1880s, it was given a police force, whose ostensible purpose was to punish legal infractions by whites but which increasingly compromised the law enforcement mechanisms of the Five Tribes. In 1889, a federal court was created for Indian Territory, although still restricted to cases involving non-Indians. The next year its jurisdiction was extended to include conflicts between Indians of different nations, and the Unassigned Lands, the Creek territory ceded to the United States in 1866 originally for the purpose of relocating other native peoples, were incorporated as the territory of Oklahoma. The Cherokee outlet was added to that territory in 1893, the year in which the Dawes Commission was created. In 1895, an act was passed phasing out the jurisdiction of the Kansas and Texas courts in Indian Territory while breaking it up into three federal districts. In 1897, those courts were given full jurisdiction over all criminal and civil matters in Indian Territory, and virtually all legislation by the Five Tribes was made contingent on approval by the President of the United States. The Curtis Act, passed in 1898, abolished the courts of the Five Tribes in addition to mandating that they negotiate agreements with the Dawes Commission. On the assault in the 1880s and 1890s on the Creek government, and those of the Five Tribes more broadly, see Burton; Carter, "Snakes"; Debo; *Harjo v. Kleppe*; Harring, *Crow Dog's Case*, 57–99; Kappler, vol. I; Prucha, *American Indian Policy in Crisis*, 373–401; and Saunt, *Black, White, and Indian*.

24. While the novel regularly critiques "progressive" beliefs, presenting them as ultimately aligned with the social ideals promoted by allotment, it does not necessarily cast those implicitly or explicitly coded as progressives as supporters of U.S. rule. The "progressives" are not depicted as unanimously endorsing U.S. or white intervention into Creek affairs, but their acceptance of many of the operating assumptions of U.S. policy is represented as ultimately detrimental to the project of Muscokee self-determination, generating a disabling identification with white privilege and the structures of white-dominated institutions. The Creek government, however, did seek throughout the late nineteenth century to limit the number of whites who could claim citizenship in the nation even as it made provisions for those men who married Creek women and for laborers working on Creek lands. See Burton, 106–122, 171–201; Debo, 188, 244, 265, 363.

25. While the novel correlates the ideas endorsed by "progressives" with the logic of allotment, the investment of a significant minority of Creeks in ideas of private property, the nuclear family, and the marginalization (if not elimination) of town governance was not new in the late nineteenth century, dating back to the emergence of the elite in the late eighteenth century. See Green; Martin; Saunt, *New Order*; and Saunt, *Black, White, and Indian*. However, allotment can be seen in the novel as both a figure for the broader historical trajectory of Indian policy and a dramatic expansion of ideologies that had been present in U.S. governance for decades. The elements of the "progressive" vision of the nation, then, cannot be interpreted as the result of allotment-era policy, but such policy extends and intensifies them.

Although the National Council can be seen as a vehicle for the consolidation of elite authority in the late eighteenth and early nineteenth centuries, in the 1820s and early 1830s it increasingly became a resource for a town-based vision of Creek politics as the area known as the "Lower Towns," which had a much greater concentration of those Creeks literate in English and actively participating in the market economy, came under greater white pressure, their lands were ceded, and many of them relocated west of the Mississippi. These developments left the "Upper Towns" with a greater investment in and control of the Council. Those leaders associated with the Lower Towns, though, became ascendant in the Council again after removal to Indian Territory, especially in the wake of the Civil War. See Debo; Green; Harring, *Crow Dog's Case*, 73–81; and Saunt, *Black, White, and Indian*.

26. Moreover, the towns were divided into two moieties, red and white (the former associated most with war and the latter with peace), and every talwa also had an internal distinction between red and white headmen. These distinctions created bonds of affiliation among members of the same moiety, complementing the clans in generating a sense of solidarity and shared identity that did not contravene the autonomy of the talwas but transected them in ways that concretized lateral bonds of support and obligation. On Creek governance and sociality prior to 1800, see Ethridge; Green, 1–43; Martin, 17–84; O'Brien, *American Indian*, 20–23; Saunt, *New Order*, 11–37; and Wickman.

27. While they constituted only a small percentage of the overall Muskogee population, they gained increasing prominence in the 1780s and 1790s due to their growing wealth as middlemen in the fur trade and their role as translators and negotiators in

political engagements with whites. On late-eighteenth-century changes in Creek leadership and land tenure, particularly under the influence of Hawkins, see Debo, 37–71; Ethridge; Green, 36–43; Martin, 70–113; and Saunt, *New Order*, 67–185.

28. For discussion of the significance for native peoples of a shift from town- and clan-based governance to centralized bureaucracy, especially the relation of that change to the expanding institutional power of elites and the struggle over collective self-representation, see Rifkin, "Representing the Cherokee Nation."

29. On the Redstick War, see Debo, 75–83; Green, 40–43; Martin; and Saunt, *New Order*, 233–290. Apart from its political import, the Redstick War would be embedded in Creek memory due to the carnage it involved, resulting in the deaths of approximately 10 percent of the population (Saunt, *Black, White, and Red*, 20).

30. On the movement surrounding Tecumseh and his brother Tenskwatawa, see Dowd, *Spirited Resistance*; Edmunds; Hurt, *Indian Frontier*, 116–124; and White, *Middle Ground*, 503–517.

31. This self-designation both invoked a symbology connected to Tecumseh and played on the association of red sticks with the traditional forms of discipline among the Creeks. See Martin, 187; Saunt, *New Order*, 250.

32. The figure of the tie-snake itself is entwined in this history. In the lead-up to the Redstick War, after Tecumseh's visit to Creek country, a conjuror named Sam Isaacs gained prominence for his visions of a powerful tie-snake with which he claimed to be able to commune and thereby to gain knowledge of the future, and Isaacs also asserted a connection with Tecumseh and the Shawnee prophet, becoming "widely regarded as the Upper Muskogees' greatest shaman." Thus, his tie-snake-inspired prophecy provided part of the initial catalyzation for the uprising. However, after Isaacs, at the agent's and Council's behest, took part in the execution of Creeks thought responsible for the murder of white families on the Ohio, he was displaced from his position of authority among those opposed to the Council and was killed for his actions by the Redsticks. Additionally, in at least one of the versions of the tale of the king of the tie-snakes, the mission on which the boy is sent by his father is to get aid for those gathered in Tuckabatchee who have refused to join with the Redsticks and are awaiting an assault by them. When the tie-snake king reciprocates the boy's friendship by aiding him and his father against an attack by the town's enemies, those bound and detained by the king's serpent subjects are, in fact, the Redsticks. See Debo, 81–82; Grantham, 220–224; Martin, 124–128. The tie-snake's appearance in the novel, especially the story of the king, then, recalls the Redstick War, at least for readers familiar with the oral tradition and Creek history.

33. Kappler, vol. III, 181, 171.

34. The part of Creek governance most extensively altered by U.S. law was the judiciary, which had been abolished (along with all other tribal courts in Indian Territory) by the Curtis Act (1898); the previous year, U.S. federal judicial authority had been extended over all persons in Indian Territory, de facto displacing tribal jurisdiction in criminal and civil matters. See Kappler, vol. I, 88, 100.

35. *Harjo v. Kleppe*, 1130.

36. Although the council notified the BIA of the new constitution, the agency refused to recognize it because it did not fit the parameters specified under the Oklahoma Indian Welfare Act (1936), which largely extended the provisions of the Indian Reorganization Act to peoples in what had been Indian Territory. However, the Creek Convention was not seeking to form a government under the 1936 act but instead was acting in its capacity as a legislative body under the 1867 Creek constitution, which had been reaffirmed in the Five Tribes Act of 1906. Although the Principal Chief at that time agreed to abide by the terms of this new constitution, when John Davis took office in 1951 he repudiated the document and appointed his own "Creek Indian Council," whose role was advisory rather than legislative. In doing so, Davis was backed by the BIA, despite the fact that the agency had eventually recognized the Creek Convention, albeit unevenly, in the late 1940s. See *Harjo v. Kleppe*, 1137–1139; Moore, 164; O'Brien, *American Indian*, 131–132; Womack, *Red on Red*, 39. On the continuing centrality of the talwas and their invisibility within federal paradigms, see *Harjo v. Kleppe*; Holm; Hurt, "Creek"; Moore; and Opler.

37. *Harjo v. Kleppe*, 1144.

38. See Holm; Moore; O'Brien, *American Indian*, 133–134; Womack, *Red on Red*, 40. The Constitution of 1979 also changed the basis for membership in the Creek Nation, limiting it to "Muscogee (Creek) Indian[s] by blood" and thereby excluding descendants of the Creek freedman who had not been listed as having Indian "blood" on the Dawes rolls (Saunt, *Black, White, and Indian*, 214).

39. On this connection in the novel as an expression of a "sovereign erotic," see Driskill, "Stolen."

40. In the period from 1890 to 1940, the landholdings of the Five Tribes fell from 20 million acres to 1.8 million acres (Saunt, *Black, White, and Indian*, 160). By the late 1930s, the Muscogees had lost almost 3 million acres of land, remaining with only a single acre belonging to the tribe and 100,000 acres in individual allotments; eventually they bought back 5,000 acres of their lands (O'Brien, *American Indian*, 132).

41. On the Green Corn ceremony, traditionally and in contemporary life, see Grantham, 68–82; Hurt, "Creek," 10–12; Martin, 34–42; Opler; Swanton, 546–614; Walker, "Tribal Towns"; and Womack, *Red on Red*, 43–47.

42. Walker, "Tribal Towns," 56–57. See also Womack, *Red on Red*, 42–43.

43. Wickman, 94–95.

44. On Creek moieties as "fires," see also Debo, 6–7; Opler, 37; Walker, "Tribal Towns," 51; and Womack, *Red on Red*, 43.

45. See Debo, 13; Green, 8–10; O'Brien, *American Indian*, 22; Swanton; and Womack, *Red on Red*, 32, 45.

46. Hurt, "Creek," 12; Swanton, 484.

47. The novel here reflects the fact that many of those Creeks made wealthy as a result of oil reserves on their allotments had been associated with Chitto Harjo's movement. See Thorne, 14.

48. Kappler, vol. III, 182.

49. Thorne, 37–48. The citizenship rolls generated by the Dawes Commission contained blood quantum figures that were used as the basis for determinations about who was placed in various categories. For the theoretical, political, practical, and genealogical problems surrounding the Dawes rolls, see Garroutte; Saunt, *Black, White, and Indian.*

50. On the relation between sexual abuse by fathers and the heteronormative structure of nuclear family life, see Hart, 167–204; McKinnon, "American." Womack later makes clear that the depiction of Lucy's father is less about his whiteness per se than the institutionalized modes of homemaking that accompany the exertion of white power by having Lucy marry a white man, Glen (who treats her very well), as well as indicating that Lucy receives her first trumpet (which will become central to her self-expression as an adult) from her father's brother, who is as kind as her father is mean.

51. In the same vein, she observes, "That's the kind of thoughts that sometimes burns my mind" and notes the difficulty of getting rid of "the flames in my head" (35, 50).

52. Thanks to Bethany Schneider for consistently drawing my attention to Womack's nondevelopmentalist conception of time—the ways different periods "touch" in the text. For her take on Womack's self-representation, see Schneider, "Oklahobo."

53. In another of the fire scenes that punctuate the novel, Jimmy's father sets an AIM jacket ablaze atop a pile of garbage he is disposing of in his backyard. He acquired the jacket after beating up an AIM member who had been part of a group that had stolen a car and left him to be arrested for the theft in which he played no role and about which he knew nothing. Jimmy had been given the jacket by his father, who, in a conversation imagined by Josh, comments, "who needs an AIM jacket anyway? Those guys come around here mostly just to make trouble. They don't know anything about us. . . . They can't understand the way we think. We got enough problems of our own without worrying about manning an occupation off somewhere else" (68). This focus on the specificity of Creek issues occurs within the context of Jimmy's father's broader vision of accumulated local resistance: "If just one Indian dude, on every single reservation, synchronized their watches and struck a match all at the same time, we could burn down America" (65–66). In this way, Jimmy's father's "burn"-ing recalls Lucy's and Josh's, simultaneously refusing "progressive" ideals and invoking the regenerative potential of the Green Corn as a way of reimagining the political possibilities available in the present.

The mention of AIM signifies against the backdrop of Indian activism in 1973. As Josh notes, "this year, especially, it was in the air, the fear, the possibility, that good Oklahoma Indians who'd always minded their own business might take up with the uppity hell-raisers in South Dakota. White folks were waiting for an explosion in a state where poverty was quiet and hidden out behind the scrub oaks where no one could see it" (68–69). Alluding to the armed standoff with FBI agents at Wounded Knee on the Pine Ridge reservation, the passage suggests that white anxieties about native opposition are driven less by events in South Dakota than by the existing concerns of Indians in Oklahoma, which have gone unaddressed. The intimation of a possible "explosion" emanating from the "quiet and hidden" aspects of native life cannot help but implicitly reference the resurgence of the talwas in this period. Moreover, as scholars have noted, the conflict at Wounded Knee arose out of struggles over the authority and legitimacy of the U.S.-recognized tribal government that resonate with those occurring among the Creeks in the same period. See Holm; Reinhardt, *Ruling Pine Ridge*. See also chapter 4.

54. See Fife; Hurt, "Creek."

55. Although unsure of the degree to which closeted silence secures his and Jimmy's right to be present at the service, Josh wonders, "Surely this had happened before. Two men had sat next to each other . . . who had once been lovers or still were. . . . Of course, they didn't know about us; surely that would change things. Or did they" (257)? That question hangs over the novel's portrayal of the Indian Baptist Church, intimating that unlike Josh's parents and other "progressives" who affiliate with white Baptist churches, such congregants' attitudes might resemble those at the Hickory Ground with respect to Seborn and Tarbie: "[D]idn't have an explanation for it, never heard of such a thing in English and didn't have to explain it in Muskogee" (223).

56. See Debo, 293; Ethridge, 103; Swanton, 560, 574; Walker, "Tribal Towns," 6; Womack, *Red on Red*, 45.

57. See Debo, 106; Hurt, "Defining American Homelands," 26; Martin, 168; Moore, 173; and Swanton, 545.

58. Examples of such possible change include the emergence of métis communities, the incorporation of white captives into native communities, ongoing exchange with non-U.S. traders, and the adoption of "uncivilized" practices by whites (like Mormon polygamy). (I should note that by métis, I do not mean simply mixed-blood, but instead distinct communities that emerged through intermarriage while maintaining connections with kin belonging to particular native peoples. Thanks to Chris Andersen for his scrupulous analysis of the problematic ways this term gets deployed.) For discussion of these practices, see Rifkin, *Manifesting* (chaps. 2 and 3) and chapters 2 and 3 here.

WORKS CITED

Abler, Thomas S. "Seneca Moieties and Hereditary Chieftainships: The Early-Nineteenth-Century Political Organization of an Iroquois Nation." *Ethnohistory* 51.3 (2004): 459–488.

———. *Cornplanter: Chief Warrior of the Allegany Senecas*. Syracuse, N.Y.: Syracuse University Press, 2007.

Adams, Charles Hansford. *The Guardian of the Law: Authority and Identity in James Fenimore Cooper*. University Park: Pennsylvania State University Press, 1990.

Adams, David Wallace. *Education for Extinction: American Indians and the Boarding School Experience, 1875–1828*. Lawrence: University Press of Kansas, 1995.

Adorno, Theodor W. *Negative Dialectics* (1966). Trans. E. B. Ashton (1973). New York: Continuum, 1987.

Agamben, Giorgio. *Homo Sacer: Sovereign Power and Bare Life* (1995). Trans. Daniel Heller-Roazen. Stanford, Calif.: Stanford University Press, 1998.

Albers, Patricia C. "Sioux Kinship in a Colonial Setting." *Dialectical Anthropology* 6.3 (1982): 253–269.

———. "Symbiosis, Merger, and War: Contrasting Forms of Intertribal Relationship among Historic Plains Indians." In *The Political Economy of North American Indians*. Ed. John H. Moore. Norman: University of Oklahoma Press, 1993. 94–132.

Albers, Patricia, and Beatrice Medicine, eds. *The Hidden Half: Studies of Plains Indian Women*. New York: University Press of America, 1983.

Alexander, M. Jacqui. *Pedagogies of Crossing: Meditations on Feminism, Sexual Politics, Memory, and the Sacred*. Durham, N.C.: Duke University Press, 2005.

Alfred, Taiaiake. *Peace, Power, Righteousness: An Indigenous Manifesto*. Oxford: Oxford University Press, 1999.

———. "Sovereignty." In *Sovereignty Matters: Locations of Contestation and Possibility in Indigenous Strategies for Self-Determination*. Ed. Joanne Barker. Lincoln, NE: University of Nebraska Press, 2005. 33–50.

Allen, Orlando. "Personal Recollections of Captains Jones and Parrish, and of the Payment of Indian Annuities in Buffalo." In *The Garland Library of Narratives of North American Indian Captivities*. Vol. 105. Ed. Wilcomb E. Washburn. New York: Garland, 1976. 539–546.

American Indian Policy Review Commission (Task Force Eight). *Report on Urban and Rural Non-Reservation Indians: Final Report to the American Indian Policy Review Commission*. Washington, D.C.: U.S. Government Printing Office, 1976.

American State Papers: Indian Affairs. Vol. 1 (1832). Buffalo, NY: William S. Hein, 1998.

Aupaumut, Hendrick. "History of the Muh-he-con-nuk Indians." In *The Elders Wrote: An Anthology of Early Prose by North American Indians, 1768–1931*. Ed. Bernd Peyer. Berlin: Reimer, 1982. 25–33.

———. "A Short Narration of My Last Journey to the Western Country" (1792). In *Memoirs of the Historical Society of Pennsylvania*. Vol. 2, pt. 1. Philadelphia: M'Carty and Davis, 1827. 76–131.

Balibar, Etienne. "Is There a 'Neo-Racism'?" In *Race, Nation, Class: Ambiguous Identities*. Etienne Balibar and Immanuel Wallerstein (1988). Trans. Chris Turner. New York: Verso, 1991. 17–28.

Banner, Stuart. *How the Indians Lost Their Land: Law and Power on the Frontier*. Cambridge, Mass.: Harvard University Press, 2005.

Barker, Joanne. "Gender, Sovereignty, and the Discourse of Rights in Native Women's Activism." *Meridians: Feminism, Race, Transnationalism* 7.1 (2006): 127–161.

———, ed. *Sovereignty Matters: Locations of Contestation and Possibility in Indigenous Struggles for Self-Determination*. Lincoln: University of Nebraska Press, 2005.

Barnes, Celia. *Native American Power in the United States, 1783–1795*. Madison, N.J.: Farleigh Dickinson University Press, 2003.

Basch, Norma. "From the Bonds of Empire to the Bonds of Maternity." In *Devising Liberty: Preserving and Creating Freedom in the New American Republic*. Ed. David Thomas Konig. Stanford, Calif.: Stanford University Press, 1995. 217–242.

Baym, Nina. *American Women Writers and the Work of History, 1790–1860*. New Brunswick, N.J.: Rutgers University Press, 1995.

———. "How Men and Women Wrote Indian Stories." In *New Essays on* Last of the Mohicans. Ed. Daniel Peck. New York: Cambridge University Press, 1992. 67–86.

Bederman, Gail. *Manliness and Civilization: A Cultural History of Gender and Race in the United States, 1880–1917*. Chicago: University of Chicago Press, 1995.

Bell, Michael Davitt. "History and Romance Convention in Catharine Sedgwick's *Hope Leslie.*" *American Quarterly* 22.2 (1970): 213–221.

Benedict, Ruth. *Patterns of Culture* (1934). Boston: Houghton Mifflin, 2005.

Bentley, Nancy. "The Fourth Dimension: Kinlessness and African American Narrative." *Critical Inquiry* 35.1 (2009): 270–292.

———. "Marriage as Treason: Polygamy, Nation, and the Novel." In *The Futures of American Studies*. Ed. Donald Pease and Robyn Wiegman. Durham, N.C.: Duke University Press, 2002. 341–370.

————. *Frantic Panoramas: American Literature and Mass Culture, 1870–1920*. Philadelphia: University of Pennsylvania Press, 2009.

Ben-Zvi, Yael. "Where Did Red Go? Lewis Henry Morgan's Evolutionary Inheritance and U.S. Racial Imagination." *CR: The New Centennial Review* 7.2 (2007): 201–229.

Bergland, Renée L. *The National Uncanny: Indian Ghosts and American Subjects*. Hanover, N.J.: University Press of New England, 2000.

Bergman, S. Bear. *Butch Is a Noun*. San Francisco: Suspect Thought Press, 2006.

Berlant, Lauren, and Michael Warner. "Sex in Public." *Critical Inquiry* 24.2 (1998): 548–566.

Bernardin, Susan. "The Lessons of a Sentimental Education: Zitkala-Ša's Autobiographical Narratives." *Western American Literature* 32.3 (1997): 213–238.

Bersani, Leo. *Homos*. Cambridge, Mass.: Harvard University Press, 1995.

Bieder, Robert E. *Science Encounters the Indian, 1820–1880 : The Early Years of American Ethnology*. Norman: University of Oklahoma Press, 1986.

Bilharz, Joy Ann. *The Allegany Senecas and the Kinzua Dam: Forced Relocation through Two Generations*. Lincoln: University of Nebraska Press, 1998.

Biolosi, Thomas. "The Birth of the Reservation: Making the Modern Individual among the Lakota." *American Ethnologist* 22.1 (1995): 28–53.

————. "Imagined Geographies: Sovereignty, Indigenous Space, and American Indian Struggle." *American Ethnologist* 32.2 (2005): 239–259.

————. *Organizing the Lakota: The Political Economy of the New Deal on the Pine Ridge and Rosebud Reservations*. Tucson: University of Arizona Press, 1992.

Blackwood, Evelyn. "Reading Sexualities across Cultures: Anthropology and Theories of Sexuality." In *Out in Theory: The Emergence of Lesbian and Gay Anthropology*. Ed. Ellen Lewin and William L. Leap. Urbana: University of Illinois Press, 2002. 69–92.

————. "Sexuality and Gender in Certain Native American Tribes: The Case of Cross-Gender Females." *Signs* 10.1 (1984): 27–42.

Bland, Lucy, and Laura Doan, eds. *Sexology in Culture: Labeling Bodies and Desires*. Chicago: University of Chicago Press, 1998.

Blumin, Stuart M. *The Emergence of the Middle Class: Social Experience in the American City, 1760–1900*. New York: Cambridge University Press, 1989.

Boldt, Menno. *Surviving as Indians: The Challenge of Self-Government*. Toronto: University of Toronto Press, 1993.

Bonvillain, Nancy. "Iroquoian Women." In *Studies on Iroquoian Culture*. Ed. Nancy Bonvillain. Rindge, N.H.: Franklin Pierce College, 1980. 47–58.

Boydston, Jeanne. *Home and Work: Housework, Wages, and the Ideology of Labor in the Early Republic*. New York: Oxford University Press, 1990.

Brady, Mary Pat. *Extinct Lands, Temporal Geographies: Chicana Literature and the Urgency of Space*. Durham, N.C.: Duke University Press, 2002.

Bragdon, Kathleen J. *Native People of Southern New England, 1500–1650*. Norman: University of Oklahoma Press, 1996.

Brandzel, Amy. "Queering Citizenship? Same-Sex Marriage and the State." *GLQ* 11.2 (2005): 171–204.

Brant, Beth. *Mohawk Trail*. Ithaca, N.Y.: Firebrand Books, 1985.

———. *Writing as Witness: Essay and Talk*. Toronto: Women's Press, 1994.

Bravmann, Scott. *Queer Fictions of the Past: History, Culture, and Difference*. New York: Cambridge University Press, 1997.

Brooks, James F. *Captives and Cousins: Slavery, Kinship, and Community in the Southwest Borderlands*. Chapel Hill: University of North Carolina Press, 2002.

Brooks, Joanna, ed. *The Collected Writings of Samson Occom, Mohegan*. New York: Oxford University Press, 2006.

Brooks, Lisa. *The Common Pot: The Recovery of Native Space in the Northeast*. Minneapolis: University of Minnesota Press, 2008.

Brown, Gillian. *Domestic Individualism: Imagining Self in Nineteenth-Century America*. Berkeley: University of California Press, 1990.

Brown, Wendy. *Regulating Aversion: Tolerance in the Age of Identity and Empire*. Princeton, N.J.: Princeton University Press, 2006.

Bruyneel, Kevin. *The Third Space of Sovereignty: The Postcolonial Politics of U.S.- Indigenous Relations*. Minneapolis: University of Minnesota Press, 1997.

Burgett, Bruce. "On the Mormon Question: Race, Sex, and Polygamy in the 1850s and the 1990s." *American Quarterly* 57.1 (2005): 75–102.

———. *Sentimental Bodies: Sex, Gender, and Citizenship in the Early Republic*. Princeton, N.J.: Princeton University Press, 1998.

Burnham, Michelle. *Captivity and Sentiment: Cultural Exchange in American Literature, 1682–1861*. Hanover, N.H.: Dartmouth College, 1997.

———. "'However Extravagant the Pretension': Bivocalism and U.S. Nation- Building in *A Narrative of the Life of Mrs. Mary Jemison*." *Nineteenth-Century Contexts* 23 (2001): 325–347.

Burton, Jeffrey. *Indian Territory and the United States, 1866–1906*. Norman: University of Oklahoma Press, 1995.

Butler, Judith. *Antigone's Claim: Kinship Between Life and Death*. New York: Columbia University Press, 2000.

———. *Gender Trouble: Feminism and the Subversion of Identity*. New York: Routledge, 1990.

———. *Undoing Gender*. New York: Routledge, 2004.

Caffrey, Margaret M. "Complementary Power: Men and Women of the Lenni Lenape." *American Indian Quarterly* 24.1 (2000): 44–63.

Calloway, Colin G. *The Scratch of a Pen: 1763 and the Transformation of North America*. New York: Oxford University Press, 2006.

Campisi, Jack, and William A. Starna. "On the Road to Canandaigua: The Treaty of 1794." *American Indian Quarterly* 19.4 (1995): 467–490.

Canaday, Margot. *The Straight State: Sexuality and Citizenship in Twentieth-Century America*. Princeton, NJ: Princeton University Press, 2009.

Carlson, David J. *Sovereign Selves: American Indian Autobiography and the Law*. Urbana: University of Illinois Press, 2006.

Carpenter, Edward. *Intermediate Types among Primitive Folk* (1914). Kessinger.

Carr, Helen. *Inventing the American Primitive: Politics, Gender and the Representation of Native American Literary Traditions, 1789–1936.* New York: New York University Press, 1996.

Carsten, Janet. *After Kinship.* New York: Cambridge University Press, 2004.

Carter, Julian B. *The Heart of Whiteness: Normal Sexuality and Race in America, 1880–1940.* Durham, N.C.: Duke University Press, 2007.

Carter, Kent. "Snakes and Scribes: The Dawes Commission and the Enrollment of the Creeks." *Chronicles of Oklahoma* 75.4 (1997–1998): 384–413.

Case, Sue-Ellen. "Toward a Butch-Femme Aesthetic." In *The Lesbian and Gay Studies Reader.* Ed. Henry Abelove. New York: Routledge, 1993. 294–306.

Castiglia, Christopher. *Bound and Determined: Captivity, Culture-Crossing, and White Womanhood from Mary Rowlandson to Patty Hearst.* Chicago: University of Chicago Press, 1996.

———. *Interior States: Institutional Consciousness and the Inner Life of Democracy in the Antebellum United States.* Durham, N.C.: Duke University Press, 2008.

Cattelino, Jessica. *High Stakes: Florida Seminole Gaming and Sovereignty.* Durham, N.C.: Duke University Press, 2008.

Cave, Alfred A. *The Pequot War.* Amherst: University of Massachusetts Press, 1996.

Cayton, Andrew R. L. "'Noble Actors' upon 'the Theatre of Honour': Power and Civility in the Treaty of Greenville." In *Contact Points: American Frontiers from the Mohawk Valley to the Mississippi, 1750–1830.* Ed. Andrew R. L. Clayton and Fredrika J. Teute. Chapel Hill: University of North Carolina Press, 1998. 235–269.

Chambers-Schiller, Lee Virginia. *Liberty, A Better Husband: Single Women in America: The Generations of 1780–1840.* New Haven, Conn.: Yale University Press, 1984.

Chatterjee, Partha. *Nationalist Thought and the Colonial World: A Derivative Discourse?* London: Zed Books, 1986.

Chauncey, George. *Gay New York: Gender, Urban Culture, and the Making of the Gay Male World, 1890–1940.* New York: Basic Books, 1994.

———. *Why Marriage? The History Shaping Today's Debate Over Gay Equality.* 2nd ed. New York: Basic Books, 2005.

Cheyfitz, Eric. "The Navajo-Hopi Land Dispute: A Brief History." *interventions* 2:2 (2000): 248–275.

———. *The Poetics of Imperialism: Translation and Colonization from* The Tempest *to* Tarzan. Philadelphia: University of Pennsylvania Press, 1997.

———. "The (Post)Colonial Construction of Indian Country: U.S. American Indian Literatures and Federal Indian Law." In *The Columbia Guide to American Indian Literatures of the United States Since 1945.* Ed. Eric Cheyfitz. New York: Columbia University Press, 2006. 1–124.

———. "Savage Law: The Plot Against American Indians in *Johnson and Graham's Lessee v. M'Intosh* and *The Pioneers.*" In *Cultures of United States Imperialism.* Ed. Amy Kaplan and Donald E. Pease. Durham, N.C.: Duke University Press, 1993. 109–128.

Clifford, James. "Varieties of Indigenous Experience: Diasporas, Homelands, Sovereignties." In *Indigenous Experience Today*. Ed. Marisol de la Cadena and Orin Starn. Oxford: Berg, 2007. 197–223.

Clow, Richmond L. "The Indian Reorganization Act and the Loss of Tribal Sovereignty: Constitutions on the Rosebud and Pine Ridge Reservations." *Great Plains Quarterly* 7 (1987): 125–134.

———. "Tribal Populations in Transition: Sioux Reservations and Federal Policy, 1934–1965." *South Dakota History* 19.3 (1989): 362–391.

Cohen, Cathy J. *Boundaries of Blackness: AIDS and the Breakdown of Black Politics*. Chicago: University of Chicago Press, 1999.

———. "Punks, Bulldaggers, and Welfare Queens: The Radical Potential of Queer Politics?" *GLQ* 3.4 (1997): 437–465.

Cohen, Ed. *Talk on the Wilde Side: Toward a Genealogy of a Discourse on Male Sexualities*. New York: Routledge, 1993.

Cohen, Felix S. *On the Drafting of Tribal Constitutions*. Ed. and intro. David E. Wilkins. Norman: University of Oklahoma Press, 2006.

Collier, Jane Fishburne, and Sylvia Junko Yanagisako. *Gender and Kinship: Essays toward a Unified Analysis*. Stanford, Calif.: Stanford University Press, 1987.

Collier, John. "Collier Replies to Mekeel." *American Anthropologist* 46.3 (1944): 422–426.

———. "The Genesis and Philosophy of the Indian Reorganization Act." In *Indian Affairs and the Indian Reorganization Act: The Twenty Year Record*. Ed. William H. Kelly. Tucson: University of Arizona, 1954.

———. *Indians of the Americas* (1947). New York: Mentor and Plume Books.

"Conditions on Sioux Reservations." 76th Cong., 1st sess. Hearings before the House Committee on Indian Affairs.

Conforti, Joseph A. *Imagining New England: Explorations of Regional Identity from the Pilgrims to the Mid-Twentieth Century*. Chapel Hill: University of North Carolina Press, 2001.

Cook-Lynn, Elizabeth. "The American Indian Fiction Writers: Cosmopolitanism, Nationalism, the Third World, and First Nation Sovereignty." In *Why I Can't Read Wallace Stegner and Other Essays*. Madison: University of Wisconsin Press, 1996. 78–96.

Coontz, Stephanie. *The Social Origins of Private Life: A History of American Families 1600–1900*. New York: Verso, 1988.

Cooper, James Fenimore. *The Pioneers* (1823). New York: Penguin Books, 1988.

———. *The Last of the Mohicans* (1826). New York: Penguin Books, 1986.

———. *The Prairie* (1827). New York: Penguin Books, 1987.

Cotera, Maria Eugenia. "'All My Relatives Are Noble': Recovering the Feminine in Ella Cara Deloria's *Waterlily*." *American Indian Quarterly* 28.1–2 (2004): 52–72.

Cott, Nancy F. *The Bonds of Womanhood: "Woman's Sphere" in New England, 1780–1835*. New Haven, Conn.: Yale University Press, 1977.

———. *Public Vows: A History of Marriage and the Nation*. Cambridge, Mass.: Harvard University Press, 2000.

Coviello, Peter. *Intimacy America: Dreams of Affiliation in Antebellum Literature*. Minneapolis: University of Minnesota Press, 2005.

Cruz-Malavé, Arnaldo, and Martin F. Manalansan IV, eds. *Queer Globalizations: Citizenship and the Afterlife of Colonialism*. New York: New York University Press, 2002.

Cullum, Linda. "Survival's Song: Beth Brant and the Power of the Word." *MELUS* 24.3 (1999): 129–140.

Currah, Paisley. "Gender Pluralisms under the Transgender Umbrella." In *Transgender Rights*. Ed. Paisley Currah, Richard M. Juang, and Shannon Price Minter. Minneapolis: University of Minnesota Press, 2006. 3–31.

Cvetkovich, Ann. *An Archive of Feelings: Trauma, Sexuality, and Lesbian Public Cultures*. Durham, N.C.: Duke University Press, 2003.

Daily, David W. *Battle for the BIA: G. E. E. Lindquist and the Missionary Crusade Against John Collier*. Tucson: University of Arizona Press, 2004.

Dalke, Anne. "Original Vice: The Political Implications of Incest in the Early American Novel." *Early American Literature* 23 (1988): 189–201.

Danzinger, Edmund Jefferson, Jr. *Survival and Regeneration: Detroit's American Indian Community*. Detroit, Mich.: Wayne State University Press, 1991.

Darnell, Regna. *And Along Came Boas: Continuity and Revolution in Americanist Anthropology*. Philadelphia: John Benjamins, 1998.

———. *Invisible Genealogies: A History of Americanist Anthropology*. Lincoln: University of Nebraska Press, 2001.

Davidson, Cathy N., and Jessamyn Hatcher, eds. *No More Separate Spheres!* Durham, N.C.: Duke University Press, 2002.

Davidson, Cathy N., and Ada Norris. "Introduction." In *American Indian Stories, Legends, and Other Writings*. Zitkala-Ša. New York: Penguin Books, 2003.

Davis v. Beason. 133 U.S. 333 (1889).

Debo, Angie. *The Road to Disappearance: A History of the Creek Indians*. Norman: University of Oklahoma Press, 1941.

Deloria, Ella. *Speaking of Indians* (1944). Lincoln: University of Nebraska Press, 1998.

———. *Waterlily*. Lincoln: University of Nebraska Press, 1988.

Deloria, Philip J. *Playing Indian*. New Haven, Conn.: Yale University Press, 1998.

Deloria, Vine, Jr. *Custer Died for Your Sins: An Indian Manifesto* (1969). Norman: University of Oklahoma Press, 1988.

———. "Introduction." In *Speaking of Indians*. Ella Deloria. Lincoln: University of Nebraska Press, 1998. ix–xix.

Deloria, Vine, Jr. and Clifford M. Lytle. *The Nations Within: The Past and Future of American Indian Sovereignty*. Austin: University of Texas Press, 1984.

DeMallie, Raymond J. "Afterword." In *Waterlily*. Ella Cara Deloria. Lincoln: University of Nebraska Press, 1988. 233–244.

———. "Kinship and Biology in Sioux Culture." In *North American Indian Anthropology: Essays on Society and Culture*. Ed. Raymond J. DeMallie and Alfonso Ortiz. Norman: University of Oklahoma Press, 1994. 125–146.

———. "Male and Female in Traditional Lakota Culture." In *The Hidden Half: Studies of Plains Indian Women*. Ed. Patricia Albers and Beatrice Medicine. New York: University Press of America, 1983. 237–265.

———. "Sioux until 1850" and "Yankton and Yanktonai." In *Handbook of North American Indians*. Vol. 13.2, *Plains*. Ed. Raymond J. DeMallie. Washington, D.C.: Smithsonian Institution, 2001. 718–760, 777–793.

D'Emilio, John, and Estelle B. Freedman. *Intimate Matters: A History of Sexuality in America*. 2nd ed. Chicago: University of Chicago Press, 1997.

Demos, John. *The Unredeemed Captive: A Family Story from Early America*. New York: Vintage Books, 1994.

Denetdale, Jennifer Nez. "Carving Navajo National Boundaries: Patriotism, Tradition, and the Diné Marriage Act of 2005." *American Quarterly* 60.2 (2008): 289–294.

———. "Chairmen, Presidents, and Princesses: The Navajo Nation, Gender, and the Politics of Tradition." *Wicazo Sa Review* 21.1 (2006): 9–28.

Dennis, Matthew. "Red Jacket's Rhetoric: Postcolonial Persuasions on the Native Frontiers of the Early American Republic." In *American Indian Rhetorics of Survivance: Word Medicine, Word Magic*. Ed. Ernest Stromberg. Pittsburgh: University of Pittsburgh Press, 2006. 15–33.

Denny, Dallas. "Transgender Communities of the United States in the Late Twentieth Century." In *Transgender Rights*. Ed. Paisley Currah, Richard M. Juang, and Shannon Price Minter. Minneapolis: University of Minnesota Press, 2006. 171–191.

Den Ouden, Amy E. *Beyond Conquest: Native Peoples and the Struggle for History in New England*. Lincoln: University of Nebraska Press, 2005.

Densmore, Christopher. *Red Jacket: Iroquois Diplomat and Orator*. Syracuse, N.Y.: Syracuse University Press, 1999.

di Leonardo, Michaela. *Exotics at Home: Anthropologies, Others, American Modernity*. Chicago: University of Chicago Press, 1998.

Dillon, Elizabeth Maddock. *The Gender of Freedom: Fictions of Liberalism and the Literary Public Sphere*. Stanford, Calif.: Stanford University Press, 2004.

Dolgin, Janet L. "Family Law and the Facts of Family." In *Naturalizing Power: Essays in Feminist Cultural Analysis*. New York: Routledge, 1995. 47–68.

Doolen, Andy. *Fugitive Empire: Locating Early American Imperialism*. Minneapolis: University of Minnesota Press, 2005.

Dowd, Gregory Evans. *A Spirited Resistance: The North American Struggle for Unity, 1745–1815*. Baltimore: Johns Hopkins University Press, 1992.

———. *War Under Heaven: Pontiac, the Indian Nations, and the British Empire*. Baltimore: Johns Hopkins University Press, 2002.

Doxtator, Deborah. "What Happened to the Iroquois Clans? A Study of Clans in Three Nineteenth-Century Rotinonhysonni Communities." Ph.D. diss., University of Western Ontario, 1996.

Driskill, Qwo-Li. "Doubleweaving Two-Spirit Critiques: Building Alliances Between Native and Queer Studies." *GLQ* 16.1–2 (2010): 69–92.

———. "Stolen From Our Bodies: First Nations Two-Spirits/Queers and the Journey to a Sovereign Erotic." *Studies in American Indian Literature* 16.2 (2004): 50–64.

Druke, Mary A. "Linking Arms: The Structure of Iroquois Intertribal Diplomacy." In *Beyond the Covenant Chain: The Iroquois and Their Neighbors in Indian North America, 1600–1800.* Ed. Daniel K. Richter and James H. Merrell. Syracuse, N.Y.: Syracuse University Press, 1987. 29–39.

Duggan, Lisa. "The New Homonormativity: The Sexual Politics of Neoliberalism." In *Materializing Democracy: Toward a Revitalized Cultural Politics.* Ed. Russ Castronovo and Dana D. Nelson. Durham, N.C.: Duke University Press, 2002. 175–194.

———. *Sapphic Slashers: Sex, Violence, and American Modernity.* Durham, N.C.: Duke University Press, 2000.

Duggan, Lisa, and Nan D. Hunter. *Sex Wars: Sexual Dissent and Political Culture.* New York: Routledge, 1995.

Ebersole, Gary L. *Captured by Texts: Puritan to Postmodern Images of Indian Captivity.* Charlottesville: University of Virginia Press, 1995.

Edelman, Lee. *No Future: Queer Theory and the Death Drive.* Durham, N.C.: Duke University Press, 2004.

Edmunds, R. David. *Tecumseh and the Quest for Indian Leadership.* Boston: Little, Brown, 1984.

Elliott, Michael A. *The Culture Concept: Writing and Difference in the Age of Realism.* Minneapolis: University of Minnesota Press, 2002.

Ellis, Havelock. *Studies in the Psychology of Sex.* Vol. 2, *Sexual Inversion* (1927). Bibliobazaar, 2006.

Ellison, Julie. *Cato's Tears and the Making of Anglo-American Emotion.* Chicago: University of Chicago Press, 1999.

Emberley, Julia V. "The Bourgeois Family, Aboriginal Women, and Colonial Governance in Canada: A Study in Feminist Historical and Cultural Materialism." *Signs* 27.1 (2001): 59–85.

Eng, David. "Transnational Adoption and Queer Diasporas." *Social Text* 21.3 (2003): 1–37.

Engels, Frederick. *The Origin of the Family, Private Property, and the State* (1884). New York: International Publishers, 1971.

Enoch, Jessica. "Resisting the Script of Indian Education: Zitkala-Ša and the Carlisle Indian School." *College English* 65.2 (2002): 117–141.

Erkkila, Betsy. *Mixed Blood and Other Crosses: Rethinking American Literature from the Revolution to the Culture Wars.* Philadelphia: University of Pennsylvania Press, 2005.

Ethridge, Robbie. *Creek Country: The Creek Indians and Their World.* Chapel Hill: University of North Carolina Press, 2003.

Evans, Brad. *Before Cultures: The Ethnographic Imagination in American Literature, 1865–1920.* Chicago: University of Chicago Press, 2005.

Faderman, Lillian. *Odd Girls and Twilight Lovers: A History of Lesbian Life in Twentieth-Century America.* New York: Columbia University Press, 1991.

Feinberg, Leslie. *Stone Butch Blues* (1993). Los Angeles: Alyson Books, 2003.

———. *Transgender Warriors: Making History from Joan of Arc to Dennis Rodman*. Boston: Beacon Press, 1996.

———. *Trans Liberation: Beyond Pink or Blue*. Boston: Beacon Press, 1998.

Fenton, William N. *The Great Law of the Longhouse: A Political History of the Iroquois Confederacy*. Norman: University of Oklahoma Press, 1998.

Ferguson, Roderick A. *Aberrations in Black: Toward a Queer of Color Critique*. Minneapolis: University of Minnesota Press, 2004.

Fetterley, Judith. "'My Sister! My Sister!': The Rhetoric of Catharine Maria Sedgwick's *Hope Leslie*." In *No More Separate Spheres!* Ed. Cathy N. Davidson and Jessamyn Hatcher. Durham, N.C.: Duke University Press, 2002. 61–91

Fickes, Michael L. "'They Could Not Endure That Yoke': The Captivity of Pequot Women and Children after the War of 1637." *New England Quarterly* 73.1 (2000): 58–81.

Fiedler, Leslie A. *Love and Death in the American Novel*. New York: Stein and Day, 1966.

Fife, Sharon A. "Baptist Indian Church: Thlewarle Mekko Sapv Coko." *Chronicles of Oklahoma* 48.4 (1970–1971): 450–466.

Finn, Janet L. "Walls and Bridges: Cultural Mediation and the Legacy of Ella Deloria." *Frontiers* 21.3 (2000): 158–182.

Fisher, Dexter. "Foreword." In *American Indian Stories*. Zitkala-Ša. Lincoln: University of Nebraska Press, 1985.

Fixico, Donald L. *Termination and Relocation: Federal Indian Policy, 1945–1960*. Albuquerque: University of New Mexico Press, 1986.

———. *The Urban Indian Experience in America*. Albuquerque: University of New Mexico Press, 2000.

Fletcher, Matthew L. M. "Same-Sex Marriage, Indian Tribes, and the Constitution." *University of Miami Law Review* 61 (2006): 53–84.

Fliegelman, Jay. *Prodigals and Pilgrims: The American Revolution Against Patriarchal Authority, 1750–1800*. New York: Cambridge University Press, 1982.

Floyd, Kevin. *The Reification of Desire: Toward a Queer Marxism*. Minneapolis: University of Minnesota Press, 2009.

Fortes, Meyer. *Kinship and the Social order: The Legacy of Lewis Henry Morgan* (1969). New Brunswick: Aldine Transaction, 2006.

Foster, Martha Harroun. "Lost Women of the Matriarchy: Iroquois Women in the Historical Literature." *American Indian Culture and Research Journal* 19.3 (1995): 121–140.

Foucault, Michel. *The History of Sexuality, Vol. 1* (1976). Trans. Robert Hurley (1978). New York: Vintage Books, 1990.

Franklin, Sarah, and Susan McKinnon, eds. *Relative Values: Reconfiguring Kinship Studies*. Durham, N.C.: Duke University Press, 2001.

Frazier, Patrick. *The Mohicans of Stockbridge*. Lincoln: University of Nebraska Press, 1992.

Freeman, Elizabeth. "Packing History, Count(er)ing Generations." *New Literary History* 31 (2000): 727–744.

———. *The Wedding Complex: Forms of Belonging in Modern American Culture*. Durham, N.C.: Duke University Press, 2002.

Gambrell, Alice. *Women Intellectuals, Modernism, and Difference: Transatlantic Culture, 1919–1945*. New York: Cambridge University Press, 1997.

Ganter, Granville, ed. *The Collected Speeches of Sagoyewatha, or Red Jacket*. Syracuse, N.Y.: Syracuse University Press, 2006.

———. "Red Jacket and the Decolonization of Republican Virtue." *American Indian Quarterly* 31.4 (2007): 559–581.

Garber, Linda. *Identity Poetics: Race, Class, and the Lesbian-Feminist Roots of Queer Theory*. New York: Columbia University Press, 2001.

Gardner, Susan. "Speaking of Ella Deloria: Conversations with Joyzelle Gingway Godfrey, 1998–2000, Lower Brule Community College, South Dakota." *American Indian Quarterly* 24.3 (2000): 456–481.

———. "'Though It Broke My Heart to Cut Some Bits I Fancied': Ella Deloria's Original Design for *Waterlily*." *American Indian Quarterly* 27.3–4 (2003): 667–696.

Garroutte, Eva Marie. *Real Indians: Identity and the Survival of Native America*. Berkeley: University of California Press, 2003.

George-Kanentiio, Douglas M. *Iroquois on Fire: A Voice from the Mohawk Nation*. Lincoln: University of Nebraska Press, 2006.

Getches, David H., Charles F. Wilkinson, and Robert A. Williams Jr., eds. *Cases and Materials on Federal Indian Law*. St. Paul, Minn.: West Group, 1998.

Gibbon, Guy. *The Sioux: The Dakota and Lakota Nations*. Oxford: Blackwell, 2003.

Gilje, Paul A., ed. *Wages of Independence: Capitalism in the Early American Republic*. Madison, Wis.: Madison House, 1997.

Gilley, Brian Joseph. *Becoming Two-Spirit: Gay Identity and Social Acceptance in Indian Country*. Lincoln: University of Nebraska Press, 2006.

Godbeer, Richard. *Sexual Revolution in Early America*. Baltimore: Johns Hopkins University Press, 2002.

Goddard, Ives. "Delaware." In *Handbook of North American Indians*. Vol. 15, *Northeast*. Ed. Bruce G. Trigger. Washington, D.C.: Smithsonian Institution, 1978. 213–239.

Goldberg-Ambrose, Carole. *Planting Tail Feathers: Tribal Survival and Public Law 280*. Los Angeles: American Indian Studies Center, University of California, 1997.

Gopinath, Gayatri. *Impossible Desires: Queer Diasporas and South Asian Public Cultures*. Durham, N.C.: Duke University Press, 2005.

Gordon, Sarah Barringer. *The Mormon Question: Polygamy and Constitutional Conflict in Nineteenth-Century America*. Chapel Hill: University of North Carolina Press, 2002.

Gossett, Suzanne, and Barbara Ann Bardes. "Women and Political Power in the Republic: Two Early American Novels." *Legacy* 1–2 (Fall 1985): 13–30

Gouge, Earnest. *Totkv mocvse = New Fire: Creek Folktales*. Ed. and trans. Jack B. Martin, Margaret McKane Mauldin, and Juanita McGirt. Norman: University of Oklahoma Press, 2004.

Gould, Philip. "Catharine Maria Sedgwick's 'Recital' of the Pequot War." *American Literature* 66.4 (1994): 641–662.

Grahn, Judy. "Strange Country This: Lesbianism and North American Indian Tribes." *Journal of Homosexuality* 12.3–4 (1986): 43–57.

Gramsci, Antonio. *Selections from the Prison Notebooks*. Ed. and trans. Quintin Hoare and Geoffrey Nowell Smith. New York: International Publishers, 1971.

Grantham, Bill. *Creation Myths and Legends of the Creek Indians*. Gainesville: University Press of Florida, 2002.

Green, Michael D. *The Politics of Indian Removal: Creek Government and Society in Crisis*. Lincoln: University of Nebraska Press, 1982.

Greenberg, Julie A. "The Roads Less Traveled: The Problem with Binary Sex Categories." In *Transgender Rights*. Ed. Paisley Currah, Richard M. Juang, and Shannon Price Minter. Minneapolis: University of Minnesota Press, 2006. 51–73.

Grossberg, Michael. *Governing the Hearth: Law and the Family in Nineteenth-Century America*. Chapel Hill: University of North Carolina Press, 1985.

Guha, Ranajit. "The Prose of Counter-Insurgency." In *Selected Subaltern Studies*. Ed. Ranajit Guha and Gayatri Chakravorty Spivak. New York: Oxford University Press, 1988. 45–86.

Gustafson, Sandra M. *Eloquence Is Power: Oratory and Performance in Early America*. Chapel Hill: University of North Carolina Press, 2000.

Haefeli, Evan, and Kevin Sweeney. "Revisiting *The Redeemed Captive*: New Perspectives on the 1704 Attack on Deerfield." In *After King Philip's War: Presence and Persistence in Indian New England*. Ed. Colin G. Calloway. Hanover, N.H.: Dartmouth College, 1997. 29–71.

Hafen, P. Jane. "Zitkala-Ša: Sentimentality and Sovereignty." *Wicazo Sa Review* 12.2 (1997): 30–40.

Hagan, William T. *Indian Police and Judges: Experiments in Acculturation and Control*. New Haven, Conn.: Yale University Press, 1966.

Halberstam, Judith. *Female Masculinity*. Durham, N.C.: Duke University Press, 1998.

———. *In a Queer Time and Place: Transgender Bodies, Subcultural Lives*. New York: New York University Press, 2005.

Hale, C. Jacob. "Consuming the Living, Dis(re)membering the Dead in the Butch/FTM Borderlands." *GLQ* 4.2 (1998): 311–348.

Halperin, David M. *One Hundred Years of Homosexuality: And Other Essays on Greek Love*. New York: Routledge, 1990.

Hamori-Torok, Charles. "The Iroquois of Akwesasne (St. Regis), Mohawks of the Bay of Quinte (Tyendinaga), Onyota'a:ka (the Oneida of the Thames), and Wahta Mohawk (Gibson), 1750–1945." In *Aboriginal Ontario*. Ed. Edward S. Rogers and Donald B. Smith. Toronto: Dundurn Press, 1994. 258–272.

Handler, Richard. "Boasian Anthropology and the Critique of American Culture." *American Quarterly* 42.2 (1990): 252–273.

Haney López, Ian F. *White By Law: The Legal Construction of Race*. New York: New York University Press, 1996.

Hannon, Charles. "Zitkala-Sä and the Commercial Magazine Apparatus." In *"The Only Efficient Instrument": American Women Writers and the Periodical, 1837–1916*. Ed. Aleta Feinsod Cane and Susan Alves. Iowa City: University of Iowa Press, 2001. 179–229.

Harjo v. Kleppe. 420 F. Supp. 1110. 1976.

Harring, Sidney L. "Crazy Snake and the Creek Struggle for Sovereignty: The Native American Legal Culture and American Law." *American Journal of Legal History* 34.4 (1990): 365–380.

———. *Crow Dog's Case: American Indian Sovereignty, Tribal Law, and United States Law in the Nineteenth Century*. New York: Cambridge University Press, 1994.

Harris, C. C. *Kinship*. Minneapolis: University of Minnesota Press, 1990.

Harris, George H. "The Life of Horatio Jones." *Publications of the Buffalo Historical Society* 6 (1903): 383–514.

Hart, Lynda. *Between the Body and the Flesh: Performing Sadomasochism*. New York: Columbia University Press, 1998.

Hartman, Saidiya. *Scenes of Subjection: Terror, Slavery, and Self-Making in Nineteenth-Century America*. New York: Oxford University Press, 1997.

Hauptman, Laurence M. *Conspiracy of Interests: Iroquois Dispossession and the Rise of New York State*. Syracuse, N.Y.: Syracuse University Press, 1999.

———. *Formulating American Indian Policy in New York State, 1970–1986*. Albany: State University of New York Press, 1988.

———. *The Iroquois Struggle for Survival: World War II to Red Power*. Syracuse, N.Y.: Syracuse University Press, 1986.

Hay, Harry. *Radically Gay: Gay Liberation in the Words of Its Founders*. Ed. Will Roscoe. Boston: Beacon Press, 1996

Heckewelder, John. *History, Manners, and Customs of the Indian Nations Who Once Inhabited Pennsylvania and the Neighboring States* (1819). New York: Arno Press, 1971.

Heflin, Ruth J. *"I Remain Alive": The Sioux Literary Renaissance*. Syracuse, N.Y.: Syracuse University Press, 2000.

Hegeman, Susan. *Patterns for America: Modernism and the Concept of Culture*. Princeton, N.J.: Princeton University Press, 1999.

Hemphill, W. Edwin, ed. *The Papers of John C. Calhoun*. Vols. 7 and 8. Columbia: University of South Carolina Press, 1973–1975.

Hendler, Glenn. *Public Sentiments: Structures of Feeling in Nineteenth-Century American Literature*. Chapel Hill: University of North Carolina Press, 2001.

Hennen, Peter. "Fae Spirits and Gender Trouble: Resistance and Complicity among the Radical Faeries." *Journal of Contemporary Ethnography* 33.5 (2004): 499–533.

Hennessy, Rosemary. *Profit and Pleasure: Sexual Identities in Late Capitalism*. New York: Routledge, 2000.

Henry, Michelle. "Canonizing Craig Womack: Finding Native Literature's Place in Indian Country." *American Indian Quarterly* 28.1–2 (2004): 30–51.

Hoefel, Roseanne. "'Different by Degree': Ella Cara Deloria, Zora Neale Hurston, and Franz Boas Contend with Race and Ethnicity." *American Indian Quarterly* 25.2 (2001): 181–202.

Holm, Tom. "The Crisis in Tribal Government." In *American Indian Policy in the Twentieth Century*. Ed. Vine Deloria Jr. Norman: University of Oklahoma Press, 1985. 135–154.

Hoover, Herbert T., in collaboration with Leonard R. Bruguier. *The Yankton Sioux*. New York: Chelsea House, 1988.

Horsman, Reginald. *Expansion and American Indian Policy, 1783–1812*. East Lansing: Michigan State University Press, 1967.

Howard-Bobiwash, Heather. "Women's Class Strategies as Activism in Native Community Building in Toronto, 1950–1975." *American Indian Quarterly* 27.3–4 (2003): 566–582.

Hoxie, Frederick E. *A Final Promise: The Campaign to Assimilate the Indians, 1880–1920* (1984). Cambridge: Cambridge University Press, 1992.

Hurt, Douglas A. "The Creek (Muscogee) Homeland since 1907." *Southwestern Geographer* 5 (2001): 1–30.

———. "Defining American Homelands: A Creek Nation Example, 1828–1907." *Journal of Cultural Geography* 21.1 (2003): 19–43.

Hurt, R. Douglas. *The Indian Frontier, 1763–1846*. Albuquerque: University of New Mexico Press, 2002.

Ingraham, Chrys. "The Heterosexual Imaginary: Feminist Sociology and Theories of Gender." *Sociological Theory* 12.2 (1994): 203–219.

Iversen, Joan Smyth. *The Antipolygamy Controversy in U.S. Women's Movements, 1880–1925: A Debate on the American Home*. New York: Garland, 1997.

———. "A Debate on the American Home: The Antipolygamy Controversy, 1880–1890." In *American Sexual Politics: Sex, Gender, and Race since the Civil War*. Ed. John C. Fout and Maura Shaw Tantillo. Chicago: University of Chicago Press, 1990. 123–140.

Ivison, Duncan, Paul Patton, and Will Sanders, eds. *Political Theory and the Rights of Indigenous Peoples*. Cambridge: Cambridge University Press, 2000.

Jackson, Deborah Davis. *Our Elders Lived It: American Indian Identity in the City*. Dekalb: Northern Illinois University Press, 2002.

Jackson, Joe C. "Church School Education in the Creek Nation, 1898 to 1907." *Chronicles of Oklahoma* 46.3 (1968): 312–325.

Jacobi, Jeffrey S. "Two Spirits, Two Eras, Same Sex: For a Traditionalist Perspective on Native American Tribal Same-Sex Marriage Policy." *University of Michigan Journal of Law Reform* 39 (Summer 2006): 823–850.

Jacobs, Sue-Ellen, Wesley Thomas, and Sabine Lang. *Two-Spirit People: Native American Gender Identity, Sexuality, and Spirituality*. Urbana: University of Illinois Press, 1997.

Jagose, Annamarie, and Don Kulick, eds. "Thinking Sex/Thinking Gender." *GLQ* 10.2 (2004): 211–313.

Jaimes, M. Annette "American Indian Studies: Toward an Indigenous Model." *American Indian Culture and Research Journal* 11:3 (1987): 1–16.

Jakobsen, Janet R. "Can Homosexuals End Western Civilization as We Know It?" In *Queer Globalizations: Citizenship and the Afterlife of Colonialism*. Ed. Arnaldo Cruz-Malavé and Martin F. Manalansan IV. New York: New York University Press, 2002. 49–69.

———. "Queer Is? Queer Does? Normativity and the Problem of Resistance." *GLQ* 4.4 (1998): 511–536.

Janovicek, Nancy. "'Assisting Our Own': Urban Migration, Self-Governance, and Native Women's Organizing in Thunder Bay, Ontario, 1972–1989." *American Indian Quarterly* 27.3–4 (2003): 548–565.

Jefferson, Thomas. *Notes on the State of Virginia*. Chapel Hill: University of North Carolina Press, 1982.

Jemison, G. Peter, and Anna M. Schein, eds. *Treaty of Canandaigua 1794: 200 Years of Treaty Relations Between the Iroquois Confederacy and the United States*. Santa Fe: Clear Light, 2000.

Jennings, Francis. *Empire of Fortune: Crowns, Colonies, and Tribes in the Seven Years War in America*. New York: Norton, 1988.

——, ed. *Iroquois Indians: A Documentary History of the Diplomacy of the Six Nations and Their League*. Woodbridge, Conn.: Research Publications, 1984.

——. "Pennsylvania Indians and the Iroquois." In *Beyond the Covenant Chain: The Iroquois and Their Neighbors in Indian North America, 1600–1800*. Ed. Daniel K. Richter and James H. Merrell. Syracuse, N.Y.: Syracuse University Press, 1987. 75–91.

Jones, Dorothy V. *License for Empire: Colonialism by Treaty in Early America*. Chicago: University of Chicago Press, 1982.

Justice, Daniel Heath. "'Go Away, Water!': Kinship Criticism and the Decolonization Imperative." In *Reasoning Together*. Native Critics Collective. Norman: University of Oklahoma Press, 2008. 147–168.

——. "Notes Toward a Theory of Anomaly." *GLQ* 16.1–2 (2010): 207–242.

Kannady, Christopher L. "The State, Cherokee Nation, and Same-Sex Unions: In Re: Marriage License of McKinley and Reynolds." *American Indian Law Review* 29 (2004/2005): 363–381.

Kappler, Charles J. *Indian Affairs: Laws and Treaties*. 5 vols. Washington, D.C.: Government Printing Office, 1913.

Karafilis, Maria. "Catharine Maria Sedgwick's *Hope Leslie*: The Crisis Between Ethical Political Action and U.S. Literary Nationalism in the New Republic." *American Transcendental Quarterly* 12.4 (1998): 327–344.

Karr, Ronald Dale. "'Why Should You Be So Furious?': The Violence of the Pequot War." *Journal of American History* 85.3 (1998): 876–909.

Katz, Jonathan Ned. *The Invention of Heterosexuality*. New York: Dutton, 1995.

Kauanui, J. Kēhaulani. *Hawaiian Blood: Colonialism and the Politics of Sovereignty and Indigeneity*. Durham, N.C.: Duke University Press, 2008.

Kauanui, J. Kēhaulani, and Andrea Smith, eds. "Native Feminisms without Apology." *American Quarterly* 60.2 (2008): 241–316.

Kawashima, Yasuhide. *Puritan Justice and the Indian: White Man's Law in Massachusetts, 1630–1763*. Middleton, Conn.: Wesleyan University Press, 1986.

Kazanjian, David. *The Colonizing Trick: National Culture and Imperial Citizenship in Early America*. Minneapolis: University of Minnesota Press, 2003.

Keitel, Evelyne. "Captivity Narratives and the Powers of Horror: Eunice Williams and Mary Jemison, Captives Unredeemed." *1650–1850* 5 (2000): 275–297.

Kelley, Mary, ed. "Introduction." In *The Power of Her Sympathy: The Autobiography and Journal of Catharine Maria Sedgwick*. Boston: Massachusetts Historical Society, 1993.

———. *The Power of Her Sympathy: The Autobiography and Journal of Catharine Maria Sedgwick*. Boston: Massachusetts Historical Society, 1993.

Kelly, Lawrence C. *The Assault on Assimilation: John Collier and the Origins of Indian Policy Reform*. Albuquerque: University of New Mexico Press, 1983.

Kelly, William H., ed. *Indian Affairs and the Indian Reorganization Act: The Twenty Year Record*. Tucson: University of Arizona, 1954.

Kennedy, Elizabeth Lapovsky, and Madeline D. Davis. *Boots of Leather, Slippers of Gold: The History of a Lesbian Community*. New York: Penguin Books, 1994.

Kobogum v. Jackson Iron Company. 76 Mich. 498 (1889).

Konkle, Maureen. *Writing Indian Nations: Native Intellectuals and the Politics of Historiography, 1827–1863*. Chapel Hill: University of North Carolina Press, 2004.

Krupat, Arnold. *Ethnocriticism: Ethnography, History, Literature*. Berkeley: University of California Press, 1992.

Kuper, Adam. *The Reinvention of Primitive Society: Transformations of a Myth* (1988). London: Routledge, 1997.

Lang, Sabine. *Men as Women, Women as Men: Changing Gender in Native American Cultures*. Austin: University of Texas Press, 1998.

Late Corporation of Church of Jesus Christ, etc. v. U.S., 140 U.S. 665 (1890).

Law and Order Regulations Applying to All Indian Reservations Having Courts of Indian Offenses, and Containing Special Sections Relating to the Navajo Jurisdiction as Approved June 2, 1937. Washington, D.C.: Government Printing Office, 1937.

Lawrence, Bonita. *"Real" Indians and Others: Mixed-Blood Urban Native Peoples and Indigenous Nationhood*. Lincoln: University of Nebraska Press, 2004.

Lazarus, Edward. *Black Hills, White Justice: The Sioux Nation versus the United States, 1775 to the Present*. 2nd ed. Lincoln: University of Nebraska Press, 1999.

Leacock, Eleanor Burke. *Myths of Male Dominance: Collected Articles on Women Cross-Culturally*. New York: Monthly Review Press, 1981.

Lewis, Jan. "The Republican Wife: Virtue and Seduction in the Early Republic." *William and Mary Quarterly*, 3rd ser., 44.4 (1987): 689–721.

Little, Ann M. *Abraham in Arms: War and Gender in Colonial New England*. Philadelphia: University of Pennsylvania Press, 2007.

Littlefield, Alice. "Learning to Labor: Native American Education in the United States, 1880–1930." In *The Political Economy of North American Indians*. Ed. John H. Moore. Norman: University of Oklahoma Press, 1993. 43–59.

Littlefield, Daniel F., Jr., and Lonnie E. Underhill. "The 'Crazy Snake Uprising' of 1909: A Red, Black, or White Affair?" *Arizona and the West* 20.4 (1978): 307–324

Lobo, Susan. "Is Urban a Person or a Place? Characteristics of Urban Indian Country." *American Indian Culture and Research Journal* 22.4 (1998): 89–102.

———. "Urban Clan Mothers: Key Households in Cities." *American Indian Quarterly* 27.3–4 (2003): 505–522.

Lomawaima, K. Tsianina. "Domesticity in the Federal Indian Schools: The Power of Authority over Mind and Body." *American Ethnologist* 20.2 (1993): 227–240.

Lopenzina, Drew. "'The Whole Wilderness Shall Blossom as the Rose': Samson Occom, Joseph Johnson, and the Question of Native Settlement on Cooper's Frontier." *American Quarterly* 58.4 (2006): 1119–1145.

Love, Heather. *Feeling Backward: Loss and the Politics of Queer History*. Cambridge, Mass.: Harvard University Press, 2007.

Luibhéid, Eithne. *Entry Denied: Controlling Sexuality at the Border*. Minneapolis: University of Minnesota Press, 2002.

———. "Sexuality, Migration, and the Shifting Line between Legal and Illegal Status." *GLQ* 14.2–3 (2008): 289–315.

Lyons, Clare A. *Sex Among the Rabble: An Intimate History of Gender and Power in the Age of Revolution, Philadelphia, 1730–1830*. Chapel Hill: University of North Carolina Press, 2006.

Macgregor, Gordon. *Warriors without Weapons: A Study of the Society and Personality Development of the Pine Ridge Sioux*. Chicago: University of Chicago Press, 1946.

Maddox, Lucy. *Citizen Indians: Native American Intellectuals, Race, and Reform*. Ithaca, N.Y.: Cornell University Press, 2005.

———. *Removals: Nineteenth-Century American Literature and the Politics of Indian Affairs*. New York: Oxford University Press, 1991.

Manalansan, Martin F., IV. *Global Divas: Filipino Gay Men in the Diaspora*. Durham, N.C.: Duke University Press, 2003.

———. "Race, Violence, and Neoliberal Spatial Politics in the Global City." *Social Text* 84–85.3–4 (2005): 141–155.

Mann, Barbara Alice. *Iroquoian Women: The Gantowisas*. New York: Peter Lang, 2000.

Marden, David L. "Anthropologists and Federal Indian Policy Prior to 1940." *Indian Historian* 5 (Winter 1972): 19–26.

Martin, Joel W. *Sacred Revolt: The Muskogees' Struggle for a New World*. Boston: Beacon Press, 1991.

McClintock, Anne. *Imperial Leather: Race, Gender and Sexuality in the Colonial Contest*. New York: Routledge, 1995.

McCoy Drew R. *The Elusive Republic: Political Economy in Jeffersonian America*. Chapel Hill: University of North Carolina Press, 1980.

McKinnon, Susan. "American Kinship/ American Incest: Asymmetries in a Scientific Discourse." In *Naturalizing Power: Essays in Feminist Cultural Analysis*. New York: Routledge, 1995. 25–46.

———. "The Economies in Kinship and the Paternity of Culture: Origin Stories in Kinship Theory." In *Relative Values: Reconfiguring Kinship Studies*. Ed. Sarah Franklin and Susan McKinnon. Durham, N.C.: Duke University Press, 2001. 277–301.

McLoughlin, William G. *Cherokee Renascence in the New Republic*. Princeton, N.J.: Princeton University Press, 1986.

McWilliams, John. *The Last of the Mohicans: Civil Savagery and Savage Civility*. New York: Twayne, 1995.

———. *New England's Crises and Cultural Memory: Literature, Politics, History, Religion, 1620–1860*. New York: Cambridge University Press, 2004.

Medicine, Beatrice. *Learning to Be an Anthropologist and Remaining "Native."* Urbana: University of Illinois Press, 2001.

———. "'Warrior Women': Sex Role Alternatives for Plains Indian Women." In *The Hidden Half: Studies of Plains Indian Women*. Ed. Patricia Albers and Beatrice Medicine. New York: University Press of America, 1983. 267–280.

Mehta, Uday Singh. *Liberalism and Empire: A Study in Nineteenth-Century British Liberal Thought*. Chicago: University of Chicago Press, 1999.

Mekeel, Scudder. "An Appraisal of the Indian Reorganization Act." *American Anthropologist* 46.2 (1944): 209–217.

Melanson, Yvette, with Claire Safran. *Looking for Lost Bird: A Jewish Woman Discovers Her Navajo Roots*. New York: Avon Books, 1999.

Merish, Lori. *Sentimental Materialism: Gender, Commodity Culture, and Nineteenth-Century American Literature*. Durham, N.C.: Duke University Press, 2002.

Metcalf, Ann. "Navajo Women in the City: Lessons from a Quarter-Century of Relocation." *American Indian Quarterly* 6.1–2 (1982): 71–89.

Michaelson, Scott. *The Limits of Multiculturalism: Interrogating the Origins of American Anthropology*. Minneapolis: University of Minnesota Press, 1999.

Mielke, Laura L. *Moving Encounters: Sympathy and the Indian Question in Antebellum Literature*. Amherst: University of Massachusetts Press, 2008.

Miles, Lion G. "The Red Man Dispossessed: The Williams Family and the Alienation of Indian Land in Stockbridge, Massachusetts, 1736–1818." In *New England Encounters: Indians and Euroamericans, ca. 1600–1850*. Ed. Alden T. Vaughan. Boston: Northeastern University Press, 1999. 276–302.

Minter, Shannon Price. "Do Transsexuals Dream of Gay Rights? Getting Real about Transgender Inclusion." In *Transgender Rights*. Ed. Paisley Currah, Richard M. Juang, and Shannon Price Minter. Minneapolis: University of Minnesota Press, 2006. 141–170.

Minutes of the Plains Congress. Rapid City Indian School, Rapid City, South Dakota. March 2–5, 1934. Lawrence, Kans.: Haskell Institute, 1934.

Miranda, Deborah. "Dildos, Hummingbirds, and Driving Her Crazy." *Frontiers* 23.2 (2002): 135–149.

———. "Extermination of the *Joyas*: Gendercide in Spanish California." *GLQ* 16.1–2 (2010): 253–284.

Moore, John H. "The Mvskoke National Question in Oklahoma." *Science and Society* 52.2 (1988): 163–190.

Moraga, Cherríe, and Amber L. Hollibaugh. "What We're Rollin' around in Bed With." *My Dangerous Desires: A Queer Girl Dreaming Her Way Home*. Amber L. Hollibaugh. Durham, N.C.: Duke University Press, 2000. 62–84

Moreton-Robinson, Aileen, ed. *Sovereign Subjects: Indigenous Sovereignty Matters*. Crows Nest, NSW: Allen and Unwin, 1997.

Morgan, Lewis Henry. *Ancient Society* (1877). New York: Gordon Press, 1977.

Morgan, Thomas J. "Supplemental Report on Indian Education." In *Annual Report of the Commissioner of Indian Affairs to the Secretary of the Interior*. Washington, D.C.: The Office, 1990. 93–114.

Morgensen, Scott Lauria. "Arrival at Home: Radical Faerie Configurations of Sexuality and Place." *GLQ* 15.1 (2008): 67–96.

———. *Queer / Native / Settler : Colonial Desires, Queer Politics, and Indigenous Decolonization*. Minneapolis: University of Minnesota Press, 2010.

———. "Settler Homonationalism." *GLQ* 16.1–2 (2010): 105–131.

Morton, Ohland. "The Government of the Creek Indian." *Chronicles of Oklahoma* 8 (1930): 42–64, 189–225.

Moses, Cat. "Queering Class: Leslie Feinberg's *Stone Butch Blues*." *Studies in the Novel* 31.1 (1999): 74–97.

Muñoz, Jose Esteban. *Disidentifications: Queers of Color and the Performance of Politics*. Minneapolis: University of Minnesota Press, 1999.

Murphy, Alexander B. "The Sovereign State System as Political-Territorial Ideal: Historical and Contemporary Considerations." In *State Sovereignty as Social Construct*. Ed. Thomas J. and Cynthia Weber. Cambridge: Cambridge University Press, 1996. 81–120.

Murphy, Lucy Eldersveld. *A Gathering of Rivers: Indians, Métis, and Mining in the Western Great Lakes, 1737–1832*. Lincoln: University of Nebraska Press, 2000.

Murray, Janette K. "Ella Deloria: A Biographical Sketch and Literary Analysis." Ph.D. diss., University of North Dakota, 1974.

Namaste, Viviane K. *Invisible Lives: The Erasure of Transsexual and Transgendered People*. Chicago: University of Chicago Press, 2000.

Namias, June. "Introduction." In *A Narrative of the Life of Mrs. Mary Jemison*. Norman: University of Oklahoma Press, 1992. 3–45.

———. *White Captives: Gender and Ethnicity on the American Frontier*. Chapel Hill: University of North Carolina Press, 1993.

Nealon, Christopher. *Foundlings: Lesbian and Gay Historical Emotion before Stonewall*. Durham, N.C.: Duke University Press, 2001.

Nelson, Dana. "Sympathy as Strategy in Sedgwick's *Hope Leslie*." In *The Culture of Sentiment: Race, Gender, and Sentimentality in Nineteenth-Century America*. Ed. Shirley Samuels. New York: Oxford University Press, 1992. 191–202.

Nelson, Diane M. *A Finger in the Wound: Body Politics in Quincentennial Guatemala*. Berkeley: University of California Press, 1999.

Niezen, Ronald. *The Origins of Indigenism: Human Rights and the Politics of Identity*. Berkeley: University of California Press, 2003.

Oberg, Michael Leroy. "'We Are All the Sachems from East to West': A New Look at Miantonomi's Campaign of Resistance." *New England Quarterly* 77.3 (2004): 478–499.

O'Brien, Jean M. *Dispossession by Degrees: Indian Land and Identity in Natick, Massachusetts, 1650–1790*. New York: Cambridge University Press, 1997.

O'Brien, Sharon. *American Indian Tribal Governments*. Norman: University of Oklahoma Press, 1989.

Okker, Patricia. "Native American Literatures and the Canon: The Case of Zitkala-Ša." In *American Realism and the Canon*. Ed. Tom Quirk and Gary Scharnhorst. Newark: University of Delaware Press, 1994. 87–101.

Omi, Michael, and Howard Winant. *Racial Formation in the United States, from the 1960s to the 1990s*. New York: Routledge, 1994.

Ong, Aihwa. *Flexible Citizenship: The Cultural Logics of Transnationality*. Durham, N.C.: Duke University Press, 1999.

Onuf, Peter S. *Jefferson's Empire: The Language of American Nationhood*. Charlottesville: University Press of Virginia, 2000.

Opinions of the Solicitor of the Department of the Interior Relating to Indian Affairs 1917–1974. Vol. 1. Washington, D.C.: Government Printing Office, 1979.

Opler, Morris E. "Report of the History and Contemporary State of Aspects of Creek Social Organization." In *A Creek Source Book*. Ed. William C. Sturtevant. New York: Garland, 1987. 30–75.

Ostler, Jeffrey. *The Plains Sioux and U.S. Colonialism from Lewis and Clark to Wounded Knee*. New York: Cambridge University Press, 2004.

Owens, Robert M. "Jeffersonian Benevolence on the Ground: The Indian Land Cession Treaties of William Henry Harrison." *Journal of the Early Republic* 22 (Fall 2002): 405–435.

Parker, Arthur C. *The History of the Seneca Indians* (1926). Long Island, N.Y.: Ira J. Friedman, 1967.

Parker, John W., and Ruth Ann Parker. *Josiah White's Institute: The Interpretation and Implementation of His Vision*. Wabash, IN: White's Institute, 1983.

Parkin, Robert. *Kinship: An Introduction to the Basic Concepts*. Maden, Mass.: Blackwell, 1997.

Patterson, Thomas C. *A Social History of Anthropology in the United States*. New York: Berg, 2001.

Patton, Cindy. "Stealth Bombers of Desire: The Globalization of 'Alterity' in Emerging Democracies." In *Queer Globalizations: Citizenship and the Afterlife of Colonialism*. Ed. Arnaldo Cruz-Malavé and Martin F. Manalansan IV. New York: New York University Press, 2002. 195–218.

Perea, Juan F. "The Black/White Binary of Race," in *Critical Race Theory: The Cutting Edge*. Eds. Richard Delgado and Jean Stefancic. Philadelphia: Temple University Press, 2000. 344–353.

Peletz, Michael G. "Kinship Studies in Late Twentieth-Century Anthropology." *Annual Review of Anthropology* 24 (1995): 343–372.

Perdue, Theda. *Cherokee Women: Gender and Cultural Change, 1700–1835*. Lincoln: University of Nebraska Press, 1998.

Pfister, Joel. *Individuality Incorporated: Indians and the Multicultural Modern*. Durham, N.C.: Duke University Press, 2004.

Philp, Kenneth R. "Stride toward Freedom: The Relocation of Indians to Cities, 1952–1960." *Western Historical Quarterly* 16.2 (1985): 175–190.

————. *Termination Revisited: American Indians on the Trail to Self-Determination, 1933–1953*. Lincoln: University of Nebraska Press, 1999.

Pickering, Timothy, "Instructions to Captain Hendrick Aupaumut" (1792). In *American State Papers: Indian Affairs*. Vol. 1. Washington, D.C.: Gales and Seaton, 1832. 233.

Plane, Ann Marie. *Colonial Intimacies: Indian Marriage in Early New England*. Ithaca, N.Y.: Cornell University Press, 2000.

Povinelli, Elizabeth A. *The Cunning of Recognition: Indigenous Alterities and the Making of Australian Multiculturalism*. Durham, N.C.: Duke University Press, 2002.

————. *The Empire of Love: Toward a Theory of Intimacy, Genealogy, and Carnality*. Durham, N.C.: Duke University Press, 2006.

Pratt, Richard Henry. *Battlefield and Classroom: Four Decades with the American Indian, 1867–1904*. Ed. Robert M. Utley. New Haven, Conn.: Yale University Press, 1964.

Price, Catherine. "Lakotas and Euroamericans: Contrasted Concepts of 'Chieftainship' and Decision-Making Authority." *Ethnohistory* 41.3 (1994): 447–463.

Prince-Hughes, Tara. "Contemporary Two-Spirit Identity in the Fiction of Paula Gunn Allen and Beth Brant." *Studies in American Indian Literature* 10.4 (1998): 9–31.

Prosser, Jay. *Second Skins: The Body Narratives of Transsexuality*. New York: Columbia University Press, 1998.

Prucha, Francis Paul. *American Indian Policy in Crisis: Christian Reformers and the Indian, 1865–1900*. Norman: University of Oklahoma Press, 1976.

————. *American Indian Treaties: The History of a Political Anomaly*. Berkeley: University of California Press, 1994.

————, ed. *Documents of United States Indian Policy*. 3rd ed. Lincoln: University of Nebraska Press, 2000.

Puar, Jasbir K. *Terrorist Assemblages: Homonationalism in Queer Times*. Durham, N.C.: Duke University Press, 2007.

Purcell, Aaron D. "The Engineering of Forever: Arthur E. Morgan, the Seneca Indians, and the Kinzua Dam." *New York History* 78.3 (1997): 309–336.

Quinn, D. Michael. *Same-Sex Dynamics among Nineteenth-Century Americans: A Mormon Example*. Urbana: University of Illinois Press, 1996.

Ramirez, Reyna K. *Native Hubs: Culture, Community, and Belonging in Silicon Valley and Beyond*. Durham, N.C.: Duke University Press, 2007.

Rans, Geoffrey. *Cooper's Leather-Stocking Novels: A Secular Reading*. Chapel Hill: University of North Carolina Press, 1991.

Regulations of the Indian Office, Effective April 1, 1904. Washington, D.C.: Government Printing Office, 1904.

Reinhardt, Akim D. "A Crude Replacement: The Indian New Deal, Indirect Colonialism, and Pine Ridge Reservation." *Journal of Colonialism and Colonial History* 6.1 (2005).

————. *Ruling Pine Ridge: Oglala Lakota Politics from the IRA to Wounded Knee*. Lubbock: Texas Tech University Press, 2007.

"Repeal of the So-Called Wheeler-Howard Act." 76th Cong., 1st sess. S. Rep. 1047.

Reynolds v. U.S. 98 U.S. 145 (1879).

Rich, Adrienne. "Compulsory Heterosexuality and Lesbian Existence." In *Adrienne Rich's Poetry and Prose*. Ed. Barbara Charlesworth Gelpi and Albert Gelpi. New York: Norton, 1993. 203–224.

Richland, Justin. *Arguing with Tradition: The Language of Law in Hopi Tribal Court*. Chicago: University of Chicago Press, 2008.

Richter, Daniel K. "Ordeals of the Longhouse: The Five Nations in Early American History." In *Beyond the Covenant Chain: The Iroquois and Their Neighbors in Indian North America, 1600–1800*. Ed. Daniel K. Richter and James H. Merrell. Syracuse, N.Y.: Syracuse University Press, 1987. 11–27.

Rifkin, Mark. "Representing the Cherokee Nation: Subaltern Studies and Native American Sovereignty." *boundary 2* 32.3 (2005): 47–80.

———. "Documenting Tradition: Territoriality and Textuality in Black Hawk's Narrative." *American Literature* 80.4 (2008): 677–705.

———. "Indigenizing Agamben: Rethinking Sovereignty in Light of the 'Peculiar' Status of Native Peoples." *Cultural Critique* 72 (Fall 2009): 88–124.

———. *Manifesting America: The Imperial Construction of U.S. National Space*. New York: Oxford University Press, 2009.

Roberts, William O. "Successful Agriculture within the Reservation Framework." *Society for Applied Anthropology* 2.3 (1943): 37–44.

Robertson, Paul. *The Power of the Land: Identity, Ethnicity, and Class among the Oglala Lakota*. New York: Routledge, 2002.

Rodríguez, Juana María. *Queer Latinidad: Identity Practices, Discursive Spaces*. New York: New York University Press, 2003.

Romero, Lora. *Home Fronts: Domesticity and Its Critics in the Antebellum United States*. Durham, N.C.: Duke University Press, 1997.

Ronda, Jeanne, and James P. Ronda. "'As They Were Faithful': Chief Hendrick Aupaumut and the Struggle for Stockbridge Survival, 1757–1830." *American Indian Culture and Research Journal* 3.3 (1979): 43–55.

Roscoe, Will. *Changing Ones: Third and Fourth Genders in Native North America*. New York: St. Martin's Griffin, 1998.

———, ed. *Living the Spirit: A Gay American Indian Anthology*. New York: St. Martin's Press, 1988.

Rosier, Paul C. "'They Are Ancestral Homelands': Race, Place, and Politics in Cold War Native America, 1945–1961." *Journal of American History* 92.4 (2006): 1300–1326.

Ross, Marlon B. "Beyond the Closet as Raceless Paradigm." In *Black Queer Studies: A Critical Anthology*. Ed. E. Patrick Johnson and Mae G. Henderson. Durham, N.C.: Duke University Press, 2005. 161–189.

Rothenberg, Diane. "The Mothers of the Nation: Seneca Resistance to Quaker Intervention." In *Women and Colonization: Anthropological Perspectives*. Ed. Mona Etienne and Eleanor Leacock. New York: Praeger, 1980. 63–87.

Rubin, Gayle. "Of Catamites and Kings: Reflections on Butch, Gender, and Boundaries." In *The Persistent Desire: A Femme-Butch Reader*. Ed. Joan Nestle. Boston: Alyson, 1992. 466–482.

————. "Thinking Sex: Notes for a Radical Theory of the Politics of Sexuality." In *Pleasure and Danger: Exploring Female Sexuality*. Ed. Carole S. Vance. Boston: Routledge and Kegan Paul, 1984. 267–319.

Rusco, Elmer. *A Fateful Time: The Background and Legislative History of the Indian Reorganization Act*. Reno: University of Nevada Press, 2000.

————. "The Indian Reorganization Act and Indian Self-Government." In *American Indian Constitutional Reform and the Rebuilding of Native Nations*. Ed. Eric D. Lemont. Austin: University of Texas Press, 2006. 49–82.

Salisbury, Neal. *Manitou and Providence: Indians, Europeans, and the Making of New England, 1500–1643*. New York: Oxford University Press, 1982.

Samuels, Shirley. "Generation through Violence: Cooper and the Making of Americans." In *New Essays on* Last of the Mohicans. Ed. Daniel Peck. New York: Cambridge University Press, 1992. 87–114.

————. *Romances of the Republic: Women, the Family, and Violence in the Literature of the Early American Nation*. New York: Oxford University Press, 1996.

Sansom-Flood, Renée. *Lessons from Chouteau Creek: Yankton Memories of Dakota Territorial Intrigue*. Sioux Falls, SD: Center for Western Studies, 1986.

Saunt, Claudio. *Black, White, and Indian: Race and the Unmaking of an American Family*. New York: Oxford University Press, 2005.

————. *A New Order of Things: Property, Power, and the Transformation of the Creek Indians, 1733–1816*. New York: Cambridge University Press, 2003.

Scheckel, Susan. *The Insistence of the Indian: Race and Nationalism in Nineteenth-Century American Culture*. Princeton, N.J.: Princeton University Press, 1998.

Schneider, Bethany, "Oklahobo: Following Craig Womack's American Indian and Queer Studies." *SAQ* 106.2 (2007): 599–613.

Schneider, David M. *A Critique of the Study of Kinship*. Ann Arbor: University of Michigan Press, 1984.

Schutt, Amy C. *Peoples of the River Valleys: The Odyssey of the Delaware Indians*. Philadelphia: University of Pennsylvania Press, 2007.

Schwartz, E. A. "Red Atlantis Revisited: Community and Culture in the Writings of John Collier." *American Indian Quarterly* 18.4 (1994): 507–531.

Schweitzer, Ivy. *Perfecting Friendship: Politics and Affiliation in Early American Literature*. Chapel Hill, N.C.: University of North Carolina Press, 2006.

Seaver, James E. *A Narrative of the Life of Mrs. Mary Jemison* (1824). Ed. June Namias. Norman: University of Oklahoma Press, 1992.

Sedgwick, Catharine Maria. *Hope Leslie; or, Early Times in the Massachusetts* (1827). Ed. Mary Kelley. New Brunswick, N.J.: Rutgers University Press, 1987.

Sedgwick, Eve Kosofsky. *Epistemology of the Closet*. Berkeley: University of California Press, 1990.

Sedgwick, Eve Kosofsky, and Adam Frank. "Shame in the Cybernetic Fold: Reading Sylvan Tompkins." In *Shame and Its Sisters: A Sylvan Tompkins Reader*. Ed. Eve Kosofsky Sedgwick and Adam Frank. Durham, N.C.: Duke University Press, 1995. 1–28.

Seidman, Steven. "Identity and Politics in a 'Postmodern' Gay Culture: Some Historical and Conceptual Notes." In *Fear of a Queer Planet: Queer Politics and Social Theory*. Ed. Michael Warner. Minneapolis: University of Minnesota Press, 1993. 105–142.

Shamir, Milette. *Inexpressible Privacy: The Interior Life of Antebellum American Literature*. Philadelphia: University of Pennsylvania Press, 2006.

Shammas, Carole. *A History of Household Government in America*. Charlottesville: University of Virginia Press, 2002.

Shattuck, George C. *The Oneida Land Claims: A Legal History*. Syracuse, N.Y.: Syracuse University Press, 1991.

Shaw, Karena. "Creating/Negotiating Interstices: Indigenous Sovereignties." In *Sovereign Lives: Power in Global Politics*. Ed. Jenny Edkins, Véronique Pin-Fat, and Michael Shapiro. New York: Routledge, 2004. 165–187.

Sheehan, Bernard W. *Seeds of Extinction: Jeffersonian Philanthropy and the American Indian*. Chapel Hill: University of North Carolina Press, 1973.

Shoemaker, Nancy. "From Longhouse to Loghouse: Household Structure among the Senecas in 1900." *American Indian Quarterly* 15.3 (1991): 329–338.

———. *A Strange Likeness: Becoming Red and White in Eighteenth-Century North America*. New York: Oxford University Press, 2004.

Silva, Denise Ferreira da. *Toward a Global Idea of Race*. Minneapolis: University of Minnesota Press, 2007.

Simpson, Audra. "Captivating Eunice: Membership, Colonialism, and Gendered Citizenships of Grief." *Wicazo Sa Review* 24.2 (2009): 105–129.

———. "On Ethnographic Refusal: Indigeneity, 'Voice' and Colonial Citizenship." *Junctures* 9 (2007): 67–80.

———. "Subjects of Sovereignty: Indigeneity, the Revenue Rule, and Juridics of Failed Consent." *Law and Contemporary Problem* 71.3 (2008): 191–216.

———. "Paths Toward a Mohawk Nation: Narratives of Citizenship and Nationhood in Kahnawake." In *Political Theory and the Rights of Indigenous Peoples*. Ed. Duncan Ivison, Paul Patton, and Will Sanders. Cambridge: Cambridge University Press, 2000. 113–136.

Singley, Carol J. "Catharine Maria Sedgwick's *Hope Leslie*: Radical Frontier Romance." In *The (Other) American Traditions: Nineteenth-Century Women Writers*. Ed. Joyce W. Warren. New Brunswick, N.J.: Rutgers University Press, 1993. 39–53.

Sleeper-Smith, Susan. *Indian Women and French Men: Rethinking Cultural Encounter in the Western Great Lakes*. Amherst: University of Massachusetts Press, 2001.

Smith, Andrea. *Conquest: Sexual Violence and American Indian Genocide*. Cambridge, Mass.: South End Press, 2005.

———. "Queer Theory and Native Studies: The Heteronormativity of Settler Colonialism." *GLQ* 16.1–2 (2010): 41–68.

Smith, Jeanne. "'A Second Tongue': The Trickster's Voice in the Words of Zitkala-Ša." In *Tricksterism in Turn-of-the-Century American Literature: A Multicultural Perspective*. Ed. Elizabeth Ammons and Annette White-Parks. Hanover, N.H.: University Press of New England, 1994. 46–60.

Smith, Linda Tuhiwai. *Decolonizing Methodologies: Research and Indigenous Peoples.* New York: Zed Books, 1999.

Smits, David D. "'We Are Not to Grow Wild': Seventeenth-Century New England's Repudiation of Anglo-Indian Intermarriage." *American Indian Culture and Research Journal* 11.4 (1987): 1–32.

Society of Friends. *The Case of the Seneca Indians in the State of New York* [. . .]. Philadelphia: Merrihew and Thompson, 1840.

Somerville, Siobhan B. *Queering the Color Line: Race and the Invention of Homosexuality in American Culture.* Durham, N.C.: Duke University Press, 2000.

———. "Queer *Loving.*" *GLQ* 11.3 (2005): 335–370.

Spack, Ruth. "Dis/engagement: Zitkala-Ša's Letters to Carlos Montezuma, 1901–1902." *MELUS* 26.1 (2001): 173–204.

———. "Re-visioning Sioux Women: Zitkala-Ša's Revolutionary *American Indian Stories.*" *Legacy* 14.1 (1997): 25–42.

Spade, Dean. "Compliance Is Gendered: Struggling for Gender Self-Determination in a Hostile Economy." In *Transgender Rights.* Ed. Paisley Currah, Richard M. Juang, and Shannon Price Minter. Minneapolis: University of Minnesota Press, 2006. 217–241.

Sparke, Matthew. *In the Space of Theory: Postfoundational Geographies of the Nation-State.* Minneapolis: University of Minnesota Press, 2005.

Spivak, Gayatri Chakravorty. *A Critique of Postcolonial Reason: Toward a History of the Vanishing Present.* Cambridge, Mass.: Harvard University Press, 1999.

Stadler, Gustavus. "Magawisca's Body of Knowledge: Nation-Building in *Hope Leslie.*" *Yale Journal of Criticism* 12.1 (1999): 41–56.

Standing Bear, Luther. *Land of the Spotted Eagle* (1933). Lincoln: University of Nebraska Press, 2006.

Stanley, Amy Dru. *From Bondage to Contract: Wage Labor, Marriage, and the Market in the Age of Slave Emancipation.* New York: Cambridge University Press, 1998.

Stefon, Frederick J. "Richard Henry Pratt and His Indians." *Journal of Ethnic Studies* 15.2 (1987): 87–112.

Stern, Julia. *The Plight of Feeling: Sympathy and Dissent in the Early American Novel.* Chicago: University of Chicago Press, 1997.

Stevens, Jacqueline. *Reproducing the State.* Princeton, N.J.: Princeton University Press, 1999.

Stocking, George W., Jr. *The Ethnographer's Magic and Other Essays in the History of Anthropology.* Madison: University of Wisconsin Press, 1992.

———. "Franz Boas and the Culture Concept in Historical Perspective." In *Race, Culture and Evolution: Essays in the History of Anthropology.* New York: Free Press, 1968. 195–233, 344–349.

Stokes, Mason. *The Color of Sex: Whiteness, Heterosexuality, and the Fictions of White Supremacy.* Durham, N.C.: Duke University Press, 2001.

Stoler, Ann Laura. *Race and the Education of Desire: Foucault's History of Sexuality and the Colonial Order of Things.* Durham, N.C.: Duke University Press, 1995.

————. "Tense and Tender Ties: The Politics of Comparison in North American History and (Post) Colonial Studies." In *Haunted by Empire: Geographies of Intimacy in North American History*. Ed. Ann Laura Stoler. Durham, NC: Duke University Press, 2006. 23–67.

"The Story of Captain Jasper Parrish" (1903). In *The Garland Library of Narratives of North American Indian Captivities*. Vol. 105. Ed. Wilcomb E. Washburn. New York: Garland, 1976.

Strathern, Marilyn. *Kinship, Law and the Unexpected: Relatives Are Always a Surprise*. New York: Cambridge University Press, 2005.

Straus, Terry, and Debra Valentino. "Retribalization in Urban Indian Communities." *American Indian Culture and Research Journal* 22.4 (1998): 103–115.

Strong, Pauline Turner. *Captive Selves, Captivating Others: The Politics and Poetics of Colonial American Captivity Narratives*. Boulder, Colo.: Westview Press, 1999.

————. "To Forget Their Tongue, Their Name, and Their Whole Relation: Captivity, Extra-tribal Adoption, and the Indian Child Welfare Act." In *Relative Values: Reconfiguring Kinship Studies*. Ed. Sarah Franklin and Susan McKinnon. Durham, N.C.: Duke University Press, 2001. 468–493.

Sturm, Circe. *Blood Politics: Race, Culture, and Identity in the Cherokee Nation of Oklahoma*. Berkeley: University of California Press, 2002.

Stryker, Susan. *Transgender History*. Berkeley, Calif.: Seal Press, 2008.

Sullivan, Kathleen S. "Marriage and Federal Police Power." *Studies in American Political Development* 20 (Spring 2006): 45–56.

Survey of the Conditions of the Indians of the United States. Pt. 37. Washington, D.C.: Government Printing Office, 1940.

Swanton, John R. *Creek Religion and Medicine*. Lincoln: University of Nebraska Press, 2000.

Sweet, John Wood. *Bodies Politic: Negotiating Race in the American North, 1730–1830*. Baltimore: Johns Hopkins University Press, 2003.

Takaki, Ronald. *Iron Cages: Race and Culture in 19th-Century America*. New York: Oxford University Press, 1990.

Tanner, Helen Hornbeck. "The Glaize in 1792: A Composite Indian Community." *Ethnohistory* 25.1 (1978): 15–39.

Tawil, Ezra T. "Domestic Frontier Romance, or, How the Sentimental Heroine Became White." *NOVEL: A Forum on Fiction* 32.1 (1998): 99–124.

Taylor, Alan. "Captain Hendrick Aupaumut: The Dilemmas of an Intercultural Broker." *Ethnohistory* 43.3 (1996): 431–457.

————. *The Divided Ground: Indians, Settlers, and the Northern Borderland of the American Revolution*. New York: Vintage Books, 2007.

————. *William Cooper's Town: Power and Persuasion on the Frontier of the Early American Republic*. New York: Vintage Books, 1996.

Taylor, Graham D. *The New Deal and American Indian Tribalism: The Administration of the Indian Reorganization Act, 1934–45*. Lincoln: University of Nebraska Press, 1980.

Thorne, Tanis C. *The World's Richest Indian: The Scandal over Jackson Barnett's Oil Fortune*. New York: Oxford University Press, 2003.

Towle, Evan B., and Lynn M. Morgan. "Romancing the Transgender Native: Rethinking the Use of the 'Third Gender' Concept." *GLQ* 8.4 (2002): 469–497.

Trask, Haunani-Kay. *From a Native Daughter: Colonialism and Sovereignty in Hawai'i.* Honolulu: University of Hawai'i Press, 1999.

Trautmann, Thomas R. *Lewis Henry Morgan and the Invention of Kinship.* Berkeley: University of California Press, 1987.

Trennert, Robert A. "Educating Indian Girls at Nonreservation Boarding Schools, 1878–1920." In *Unequal Sisters: A Multicultural Reader in U.S. Women's History.* Ed. Ellen Carol DuBois and Vicki l. Ruiz. New York: Routledge, 1990. 224–237.

———. "From Carlisle to Phoenix: The Rise and Fall of the Indian Outing System, 1878–1930." *Pacific Historical Review* 52.3 (1983): 267–291.

Turner, Dale. *This Is Not a Peace Pipe: Towards a Critical Indigenous Philosophy.* Toronto: University of Toronto Press, 2006.

Tuthill, Maureen. "Land and the Narrative Site in Sedgwick's *Hope Leslie.*" *American Transcendental Quarterly* 19.2 (2005): 95–113.

United States v. Clapox. 35 F. 575 (1888).

Vail, Charles Delamater, ed. *A Narrative of the Life of Mary Jemison: The White Woman of the Genesee.* New York: American Scenic and Historic Preservation Society, 1918.

Valentine, David. *Imagining Transgender: An Ethnography of a Category.* Durham, N.C.: Duke University Press, 2007.

Varadharajan, Asha. *Exotic Parodies: Subjectivity in Adorno, Said, and Spivak.* Minneapolis: University of Minnesota Press, 1995.

Vásquez, Mark G. "'Your Sister Cannot Speak to You and Understand You as I Do': Native American Culture and Female Subjectivity in Lydia Maria Child and Catharine Maria Sedgwick." *American Transcendental Quarterly* 15.3 (2001): 173–190.

Vaughn, Alden T., and Daniel K. Richter. "Crossing the Cultural Divide: Indians and New Englanders, 1605–1763." *Proceedings of the American Antiquarian Society* 90 1 (1980): 23–99.

Velikova, Roumiana. "Troping in Zitkala-Ša's Autobiographical Writings, 1900–1921." *Arizona Quarterly* 56.1 (2000): 49–64.

Walker, Amelia Bell. "Tribal Towns, Stomp Grounds, and Land: Oklahoma Creeks after Removal." *Chicago Anthropology Exchange* 14.1–2 (1981): 50–69.

Walker, James R. *Lakota Society.* Ed. Raymond J. DeMallie. Lincoln: University of Nebraska Press, 1982.

Wallace, Anthony F. C. *The Death and Rebirth of the Seneca.* New York: Vintage Books, 1972.

———. *Jefferson and the Indians: The Tragic Fate of the First Americans.* Cambridge, Mass.: Harvard University Press, 1999.

———. *King of the Delawares: Teedyeschung, 1700–1763* (1949). Syracuse, New York: Syracuse University Press, 1990.

Walsh, Susan. "'With Them Was My Home': Native American Autobiography and *A Narrative of the Life of Mrs. Mary Jemison.*" *American Literature* 64.1 (1992): 49–70.

Warner, Michael. "Introduction." In *Fear of a Queer Planet: Queer Politics and Social Theory.* Minneapolis: University of Minnesota Press, 1993. vii–xxxi.

———. *The Trouble with Normal: Sex, Politics, and the Ethics of Queer Life*. New York: Free Press, 1999.

Warrior, Robert. *Tribal Secrets: Recovering American Indian Intellectual Traditions*. Minneapolis: University of Minnesota Press, 1995.

———. "Your Skin Is the Map: The Theoretical Challenge of Joy Harjo's Erotic Poetics." In *Reasoning Together*. The Native Critics Collective. Ed. Craig S. Womack, Daniel Heath Justice, and Christopher B. Teuton. Norman: University of Oklahoma Press, 2008. 340–352.

Washburn, Wilcomb E. "A Fifty-Year Perspective on the Indian Reorganization Act." *American Anthropologist* 86.2 (1984): 279–289.

Weaver, Jace. *That the People Might Live: Native American Literatures and Native American Community*. New York: Oxford University Press, 1997.

Weaver, Jace, Craig S. Womack, and Robert Warrior, eds. *American Indian Literary Nationalism*. Albuquerque: University of New Mexico Press, 2006.

Webster, Daniel. "Plymouth Oration." In *Speeches of Daniel Webster*. Ed. B. F. Tefft. New York: A. L. Burt, 1920. 63–118.

Weierman, Karen Woods. *One Nation, One Blood: Interracial Marriage in American Fiction, Scandal, and Law, 1820–1870*. Amherst: University of Massachusetts Press, 2005.

Weinbaum, Alys Eve. *Wayward Reproduction: Genealogies of Race and Nation in Transatlantic Modern Thought*. Durham, N.C.: Duke University Press, 2004.

Weinstein, Cindy. *Family, Kinship, and Sympathy in Nineteenth-Century American Literature*. New York: Cambridge University Press, 2004.

Welch, Deborah. "Gertrude Simmons Bonnin (Zitkala-Ša)." In *The New Warriors: Native American Leaders since 1900*. Ed. R. David Edmunds. Lincoln: University of Nebraska Press, 2001. 35–53.

Wenger, Tisa. *We Have a Religion: The 1920s Pueblo Indian Dance Controversy and American Religious Freedom*. Chapel Hill, NC: University of North Carolina Press, 2009.

Weston, Kath. *Families We Choose: Lesbians, Gays, Kinship*. New York: Columbia University Press, 1991.

———. *Long Slow Burn: Sexuality and Social Science*. New York: Routledge, 1998.

Wexler, Laura. "Tender Violence: Literary Eavesdropping, Domestic Fiction, and Educational Reform." In *The Culture of Sentiment: Race, Gender, and Sentimentality in Nineteenth-Century America*. Ed. Shirley Samuels. New York: Oxford University Press, 1992. 9–38.

Weyler, Karen. *Intricate Relations: Sexual and Economic Desire in American Fiction, 1789–1814*. Iowa City: University of Iowa Press, 2004.

Wheeler, Rachel. "Hendrick Aupaumut: Christian-Mahican Prophet." *Journal of the Early Republic* 25 (Summer 2005): 187–220.

White, Ed. *The Backcountry and the City: Colonization and Conflict in Early America*. Minneapolis: University of Minnesota Press, 2005.

White, Richard. *The Middle Ground: Indians, Empires, and Republics in the Great Lakes Region, 1650–1815*. Cambridge: Cambridge University Press, 1991.

Wickman, Patricia Riles. *The Tree That Bends: Discourse, Power, and the Survival of the Maskókî People*. Tuscaloosa: University of Alabama Press, 1999.

Wiegman, Robyn. *American Anatomies: Theorizing Race and Gender*. Durham, N.C.: Duke University Press, 1995.

———. "Fiedler and Sons." In *Race and the Subject of Masculinities*. Ed. Harry Stecopoulos and Michael Uebel. Durham, N.C.: Duke University Press, 1997. 45–68.

Wilchins, Riki Anne. *Read My Lips: Sexual Subversion and the End of Gender*. New York: Firebrand Books, 1997.

Wilkins, David E. *American Indian Sovereignty and the U.S. Supreme Court: The Masking of Justice*. Austin: University of Texas Press, 1997.

———. "Introduction." In *On the Drafting of Tribal Constitutions*. Felix S. Cohen. Ed. David E. Wilkins. Norman: University of Oklahoma Press, 2006. xi–xxxii.

Wilkins, David E., and K. Tsianina Lomawaima. *Uneven Ground: American Indian Sovereignty and Federal Law*. Norman: University of Oklahoma Press, 2001.

Wilkinson, Charles. *Blood Struggle: The Rise of Modern Indian Nations*. New York: Norton, 2005.

Wilkinson, Norman B. "Robert Morris and the Treaty of Big Tree." In *The Rape of Indian Lands*. Ed. Paul Wallace Gates. New York: Arno Press, 1979. 257–278.

Williams, John. *The Redeemed Captive Returning to Zion* (1707). Bedford, Mass.: Applewood Books.

Williams, Raymond. *Marxism and Literature*. Oxford: Oxford University Press, 1977.

Williams, Robert A. *Linking Arms Together: American Indian Treaty Visions of Law and Peace, 1600–1800*. New York: Oxford University Press, 1997.

Williams, Walter L. *The Spirit and the Flesh: Sexual Diversity in American Indian Culture*. Boston: Beacon Press, 1986.

Womack, Craig. *Drowning in Fire*. Tucson: University of Arizona Press, 2001.

———. *Red on Red: Native American Literary Separatism*. Minneapolis: University of Minnesota Press, 1999.

———. "Suspicioning: Imagining a Debate between Those Who Get Confused, and Those Who Don't, When They Read the Poems of Joy Harjo. Or What's an Old-Timey Gay Boy Like Me to Do?" *GLQ* 16.1–2 (2010): 133–155.

Wotherspoon, Terry, and Vic Satzewich. *First Nations: Race, Class, and Gender Relations*. Regina, Saskatchewan: Canadian Plains Research Center, 2000.

Wyss, Hilary E. "Captivity and Conversion: William Apess, Mary Jemison, and Narratives of Racial Identity." *American Indian Quarterly* 23.3–4 (1999): 63–82.

———. *Writing Indians: Literacy, Christianity, and Native Community in Early America*. Amherst: University of Massachusetts Press, 2000.

Yanagisako, Sylvia, and Carol Delaney, eds. *Naturalizing Power: Essays in Feminist Cultural Analysis*. New York: Routledge, 1995.

Zagarri, Rosemarie. "Morals, Manners, and the Republican Mother." *American Quarterly* 44.2 (1992): 192–215.

———. "The Rights of Man and Woman in Post-Revolutionary America." *William and Mary Quarterly*, 3rd ser., 55.2 (1998): 203–230.

Zitkala-Ša (Gertrude Simmons Bonnin). *American Indian Stories* (1921). Lincoln: University of Nebraska Press, 1985.

INDEX

Aberrations in Black (Ferguson), 33–35,
    322n.47
Adams, David Wallace, 150
adoption:
    after death of loved one, 51–52, 62,
        119–20, 122, 338n.35
    of Eunice Williams, 119–20
    by Iroquois, 51–52, 338n.35
    as metonym for indigenous
        sovereignty, 99
    by Pequots, 124, 340n.52
    See also Jemison, Mary
African Americans:
    and black nationalism, 35
    home and family formation, 33,
        322n.57
    one-drop rule, 328n.44
    post-Civil War, 146
    sexuality of, 33–34, 350n.76
    slavery, 146, 165
    See also people of color
AIM (American Indian Movement), 250
Akwesasne (St. Regis) reservation, 248,
    250, 253, 255, 369n.28, 371n.48
Albers, Patricia, 345n.10
Alfred, Taiaiake, 19–20, 21, 320n.27
Algonquian peoples:
    adoptions by, 338n.35
    alliances among, 89
    governance, 69, 123
    language, 87

See also Delawares;
    Mahicans; Miamis; Mohegans;
    Narragansetts; Pequots; Shawnees
Allegany reservation, 60, 247–48, 255,
    327n.36–37, 371n.48
Allen, Ebenezer, 66–67, 73, 328n.51
allotment program:
    citizenship under, 346n.20
    couched as benevolent liberation, 182
    detribalization as goal of, 40, 41, 158,
        181–82, 185, 195, 228, 235, 248,
        271, 305
    guardian system under, 305–6
    and Indian education program,
        152–53, 154
    in Indian Territory, 280, 290, 305–6
    inheritance under, 189
    land tenure under, 187–90
    as legacy for reorganization, 41,
        182–83, 185, 185–86, 187, 187–88,
        189, 189–90, 195, 199–200, 204,
        206–7, 228–29, 247, 353n.11
    as mandatory, 147, 290
    native governance persisting under,
        20, 35, 41
    native lands lost under, 346n.20
    native straightness as legacy of, 277
    and nuclear family norm, 16, 41,
        158–59, 168, 182, 183, 184,
        185, 187, 188, 195, 210, 229,
        247, 279, 305

411

as sexually aberrant, 32, 33–34
See also African Americans; native
   peoples
Pequots:
  figured in *Hope Leslie,* 100, 101, 110,
   118, 124, 138–39, 343n.72–73
  kidnappings/adoptions by, 124,
   340n.52
  kin-making among, 39, 343n.74
  massacred at Mystic village, 338n.33
  and Mohawks, 124
Pequot War of 1637, 100, 124
Pfister, Joel, 149–50, 213, 214, 352n.6,
  355n.22
Pickering, Timothy, 72, 130, 131
Pine Ridge reservation:
  and allotment, 193
  community plan of, 209
  constitution, 202, 359n.55, 359n.58,
   360n.66
  creation of Oglala Council, 193
  Deloria family at, 184, 205, 360n.66
  law-and-order regulations, 202–3,
   230, 360n.61
  1973 standoff, 250
  Red Shirt Table Cooperative, 362n.74
  and reorganization, 41, 183, 209,
   359n.55–56
  See also Wounded Knee incident
Pioneers, The (Cooper), 332n.90,
  333n.103–105
Plains Congress (1934):
  Collier's role in, 181, 185–92, 194–95,
   352n.5, 354n.16–17, 356n.33
  goals of, 352n.3
  native concerns, 191–92, 194, 356n.33
  rhetoric of, 190–91, 204
plural marriage. *See* Mormon plural
  marriage; polygamy
Pohquonnoppeet, 133
Poland Act (1874), 349n.59
Polly (Jemison's daughter), 76
polygamy:
  national outrage over, 165–66, 172
  Native American practice of, 7, 40,
   159, 160, 164, 166–67, 169, 172–73,
   184, 199, 201, 222, 223–24, 347n.40,
   357n.44
  outlawing in Mormons, 144, 165

outlawing in natives, 184, 199
use of term in text, 338n.29
U.S. Supreme court on, 165–68, 349n.59
See also American Indian Stories
  (Zitkala-Ša); Mormon plural
  marriage
Posey, Alex, 287
Potawatomies, 130
Povinelli, Elizabeth:
  The Cunning of Recognition, 120–21,
   190, 197, 321n.36
  The Empire of Love, 10–11, 12, 23, 63
  "Powers of Indian Tribes," 196–99, 200
Prairie, The (Cooper), 333n.104–105
Pratt, Richard Henry, 149, 271, 345n.12
Prince-Hughes, Tara, 372n.73
privatized domesticity:
  as dominant ideology of settler state,
   41, 77
  as natural expression of "family," 15, 25
  *See also Hope Leslie: Or, Early Times in
   the Massachusetts* (Sedgwick); nu-
   clear family (conjugal domesticity)
procreation. *See* reproduction
"Prose of Counter-Insurgency, The"
  (Guha), 137, 274
Public Law, 249, 280
Public Vows (Cott), 108
Puckonchehluh, 135–36
"Punks, Bulldaggers, and Welfare
  Queens" (Cohen), 6, 11
Puritans:
  in *Hope Leslie,* 105, 106, 107, 108,
   111–12, 117
  and Webster's speech, 104–5

queer:
  as binary opposite of straight, 32, 313
  as representative of cultural differences, 277–78
  as synonym for LBGT, 34
  See also gender diversity; queers; queer
   studies
queers:
  appropriating indigeneity as
   counterhegemonic support, 8,
   31–32, 238, 314–15, 367n.9, 370n.42
  challenging heterosexuality, 26–27,
   276–77

CPSIA information can be obtained
at www.ICGtesting.com
Printed in the USA
BVHW041704200323
660798BV00016B/229